Introducing
Social Stratification

INTRODUCING

Social

Stratification

The Causes & Consequences of Inequality

Kasturi DasGupta

LYNNE
RIENNER
PUBLISHERS

BOULDER
LONDON

Published in the United States of America in 2015 by
Lynne Rienner Publishers, Inc.
1800 30th Street, Boulder, Colorado 80301
www.rienner.com

and in the United Kingdom by
Lynne Rienner Publishers, Inc.
3 Henrietta Street, Covent Garden, London WC2E 8LU

Library of Congress Cataloging-in-Publication Data
DasGupta, Kasturi.
    Introducing social stratification : the causes and consequences
of inequality / Kasturi DasGupta.
        p. cm.
    Includes bibliographical references and index.
    ISBN 978-1-62637-183-5 (pb : alk. paper)
    1. Equality. 2. Social stratification. 3. Social status.
4. Social classes. I. Title.
    HM821.D378 2015
    305—dc23

                                          2014028352

British Cataloguing in Publication Data
A Cataloguing in Publication record for this book
is available from the British Library.

Printed and bound in the United States of America

 The paper used in this publication meets the requirements
of the American National Standard for Permanence of
Paper for Printed Library Materials Z39.48-1992.

5   4   3   2   1

*To all those who believe that alternative futures of
just and equitable societies are in fact possible*

Contents

Tables and Figures

Tables

Figures

Acknowledgments

THIS BOOK WOULD NOT HAVE BEEN POSSIBLE WITHOUT ANDREW Berzanskis and several others at Lynne Rienner Publishers. Andrew suggested, encouraged, and guided the project from the very beginning. Lesli Brooks Athanasoulis, senior project editor, and Jason Cook, copyeditor, gave critical suggestions to enhance and polish the content. Sally Glover buoyed my confidence. I can't thank them enough.

My colleagues Scott Bennett and Araceli Hernandez-Laroche gave important suggestions, both editorially and contextually. They, along with Cynthia Ninivaggi, were a constant source of inspiration.

I am grateful to the Georgian Court University library staff, especially Betty McBain, for their tireless help at every stage in the development of the book.

My husband, Anupam, made real sacrifices to see the process through. Joyee, my son, was my first editor. His thorough reading made for a better manuscript. My daughter Rupa helped with the design of the graphs. I am particularly thankful for her graphic rendition of the "median." My daughter Ria was a constant sounding board.

I owe this book to all of them.

—*Kasturi DasGupta*

1

Exploring Inequalities

THE UNITED STATES HAS ALWAYS BEEN AN UNEQUAL SOCIETY. THE degree of inequality has risen and fallen, but has always been a fact of life. The **Gilded Age**,* spanning the years immediately following **Reconstruction** and the early years of the twentieth century, was a time of glaring inequalities between the few rich and the majority teetering at the edge of economic uncertainty. Yet the country that emerged after World War II was a distinctly middle-class society. With ample jobs and decent wages, most Americans could look forward to a life of relative comfort and security. There were those who were desperately poor even then, but the image of a middle-class America obscured their lives.

Today, in the opening decades of the new millennium, the inequalities of a century ago seem to be returning with a renewed vengeance. Many are warning of a new Gilded Age in which the richest of the rich are pulling farther and farther away from the rest of society as never before.

Between 1977 and 2007, more than 60 percent of the nation's income went to the richest 1 percent of Americans. They earned it with their exorbitantly high salaries. But the most critical aspect of their extraordinary monetary rewards is the income they receive from their **capital**—specifically capital assets such as real estate, financial holdings, and investments—as rents, interests, and dividends.

More than anything, the widening gap, which is wider than it has ever been, is being created by this very fact. The money that the average person makes from salary or wages will never be able to garner the wealth that ownership of capital assets allows.

The majority of Americans have only their salaries to live on; they have very little if any income from capital assets. Even when an individual is

---

*Terms that appear in **bold** are defined in the Glossary, which begins on p. 387.

making a relatively high salary, it will never match what the richest 1 percent earn through returns to their capital assets.

There is much discussion of inequality these days, but most Americans have very little idea of its magnitude. Especially the distinct possibility that as the gap continues to widen and a future of ever more deepening and intensifying inequalities awaits us, we might in fact look back at the society today with the same nostalgia as we do for the glory days of relatively stabler economic times of the 1950s and 1960s.

Economists who are looking at the nature of inequality today are warning that these great income disparities are becoming entrenched and passed down from one generation to the next, creating "dynastic wealth." The problem today is not just the growing divide between the rich and the poor, but that these inequalities will be transferred across generations, continually widening the divide. Inherited wealth will play an ever-growing role in economic inequality in the coming decades.

And as capital assets and the wealth they generate become concentrated in the hands of fewer and fewer people, political power too becomes asymmetric, with democracy giving way to **oligarchy**, or the rule of a few. People with enormous wealth have enormous political influence to control political decisionmaking to protect mechanisms that benefit them. They also have enormous opportunities to control the media to their own advantage, to construct a dominant national **ideology** to influence public attitudes, and to control what people know and what they learn.

People with massive wealth can manipulate the messages and images that people see and hear. Through distraction and diversion, their primary objective is to obscure the reality of inequality in the United States today.

The 1 Percent and the 99 Percent

It was in the fall of 2011 that the economic divide in the United States between the richest citizens and the rest of society surfaced as never before in the public consciousness. The short-lived **Occupy Wall Street movement**, with its unique but increasingly popular narrative, made clear that the chasm between the richest 1 percent and the bottom 99 percent was at the heart of the troubles the country was facing—unemployment, foreclosures, and general insolvency.

The movement's primary intention was to draw attention to the way that big money from the top 1 percent and the most affluent in society influences government decisions, putting profits before people and the interests of the richest segments in society above the interests of the communities of the 99 percent. The Occupy movement wanted to show how private economic gain has replaced social welfare and well-being as the principal drivers of social policy initiatives, and how this has cumulatively engendered a process of deepening inequality.

As fleeting as it was, the movement was able to draw significant attention to insidious corporate insatiability, to the collusion and alliance between multinational corporations, giant banks, and the government as the real sources of the growing economic divide, and was somewhat successful in drawing the nation's attention to the problem of capitalism itself.

The United States has been portrayed as a country that is indisputably middle-class. The reigning mythology has often been one of **classlessness**. Any suggestion that the country is polarized between **haves and have-nots** is considered shocking and is typically rebuffed. Any talk of a class divide is dismissed impatiently as inflammatory "Marxism talk"[1] and akin to **class warfare**. Therefore, the foremost contribution of the Occupy movement has been to bring discussions of economic inequality, class, and the class divide out of the proverbial closet and into the mainstream.

The movement went so far as to suggest that class warfare in the United States is real and a top-down affair, waged by the rich against the middle class and poor. The movement pointed to the widening gulf between the rich and everyone else as being a consequence of policies and practices established through an intimate partnership between the corporate rich and their politician friends.

The Occupy movement, though fleeting and ephemeral, was successful in taking "class" out of the exclusive domain of social scientists and political activists, and placing it in the arena of public discourse as a subject worthy of serious investigation in averting the further downward spiraling of the economy and the nation.

And the movement seems to have unleashed a flood—because discussions on inequality seem to be everywhere. The media is awash with experts—economists, policy analysts, and journalists—trying to make sense of this conundrum. Even Pope Francis has joined the fray, saying that income inequality is "increasingly intolerable" and unfettered capitalism the "new tyranny." He has urged governments around the world to take an active role in the legitimate distribution of economic benefits by guaranteeing all citizens "dignified work, education and healthcare."[2]

Objectives of the Book

This book takes the bull by its horns. How does a system generate inequality? What are the processes that continue to widen the divide between the rich and the poor? What mechanisms ensure the longevity of persistent social inequalities? How does the economic divide of class intersect with exclusionary ideologies of **racism**, **sexism**, and **nativism** to create systems of chronic disadvantage and oppression? What structural processes obstruct attempts to fundamentally change inequitable systems? And if change is desired, how can it come about?

Sociologists have always interrogated the social phenomenon of **social inequality**. They have defined social inequality as the unequal distribution of income, wealth, opportunities, social status, prestige, and power—the resources people need in order to survive, thrive, and reach their full potential as human beings.

Social stratification is how different dimensions or sources of inequality—economic, political, and social—combine together to form complex structures of inequality of entire categories of people who are arranged hierarchically and have different degrees of access to desired resources (jobs, education) and rewards (good health, general well-being). Stratification is probably the most important subject in the entire discipline of sociology, since every aspect of our lives is profoundly affected by our position in society's system of social stratification.[3]

Structure of the Book

Part 1 of the book centers on the structures that generate, deepen, and perpetuate inequality. In Chapters 2 and 3, the objective is to describe how unequal American society is in terms of individual and group **socioeconomic status** variables. In order to do that, I start by looking at the degree of inequality and how that inequality affects a person's **life chances**.

In Chapter 2, the focus is primarily on the statistical evidence of inequality. I describe the degree of inequality in terms of quantitative parameters such as income, wealth, and the extent or degree of poverty. There is a massive quantity of mind-numbing data being continuously generated to substantiate these numbers, which I try to present as parsimoniously as possible. My hope is to convey the message without putting my readers to sleep.

In Chapter 3, in order to see how inequality shapes a person's life chances, I consider other socioeconomic status variables that have traditionally been used to gauge the divide in social well-being—quality of health and access to health care, homeownership and quality of housing, access to education and educational achievement, transportation, distribution of the tax burden, effectiveness of the social safety net, adequacy of retirement savings, the digital divide, and finally, income residential segregation and neighborhood quality.

Summary analysis of these attributes is presented in these first two chapters in order to highlight how socioeconomic status variables interconnect and overlap to determine the multifaceted ways in which individuals and communities experience the growing economic divide.

In Chapter 4 I examine the nature of the economic system we live in. When I ask my students to describe the nature of the system in which we live, they respond by saying that the United States is a democracy, that it is a free enterprise system based on a free market economy, and even that the United States is a **laissez-faire** society. The system they are referring to is **capitalism**, but that word eludes them, as it does most Americans.

Capitalism is characterized primarily by the private ownership of the means of production, with the principal objective of maximizing profit. It is a system that generates inequality in a natural, organic way, particularly under the conditions of **monopoly** control that are characteristic of capitalism today. Inequality is integral to capitalism and imperative for its continued expansion. In Chapter 4 the discussion focuses on the process through which economic inequality materializes and takes shape as an inevitable and inherent consequence of capitalism.

In Chapter 5 the discussion turns to how **globalization** and other contemporary transformations in the nature of capitalist enterprise have deepened inequality. This chapter starts from the premise that the single most definitive attribute of the economic downturn and the growing inequality has been the persistent job loss that the United States has experienced from 1975 to 2010.

Job loss in the **core** is characteristic of advanced capitalism when, in its quest to expand continuously, it must seek out global sources for labor, resources, and markets. In its search for the lowest cost of production, **corporate capitalism** has staked out the entire globe. This has far-reaching consequences for the domestic economy. As billions of very low-wage workers have been added to the global market, US workers have lost their economic edge.

Primarily during the years 1975–2010 we have witnessed structural changes, with the great bulk of employment moving from the industrial centers of the United States to other regions of the world, while US economic activity has moved from higher-wage sectors in manufacturing to lower-wage service jobs, ushering in a postindustrial economy with concurrent changes in the entire socioeconomic landscape.

The nature of economic activity has also drastically shifted from sectors that create wealth and jobs to those, such as **transnational financial speculation**, that create neither wealth nor jobs. These economic activities, however, bestow spectacular returns to a handful of well-placed individuals and financial institutions, further widening the income divide.

Mechanization has also narrowed job opportunities drastically. Design and installation of machines to do the jobs of humans has always been a way to reduce labor costs. Remember the **Luddites**, the early-nineteenth-century textile workers who protested against the growing use of machines for tasks formerly performed by skilled labor and broke the machines in desperation. The pressures of globalization, financial speculation, and mechanization have resulted in a flight of economic activity—both blue collar and white—to virtual spheres and foreign lands, and into the hands of speculators, machines, and robots. In communities across the United States, jobs that in the past were steppingstones to the middle class, to economic stability, and to realization of the American Dream, have departed the United States. And today this vacuum is deepening the economic divide at an ever-accelerating rate—devastating lives and neighborhoods in its wake.

The sources of equality or inequality are not mysterious. They reflect deliberate decisionmaking and conscious choices that government and corporations make regarding jobs, taxes, wages, executive pay, regulation or deregulation of corporate behavior, international trade treaties, immigration, cost of health care, cost of education, decisions of war and peace, decisions about whether to fortify or weaken the social safety net, and so forth.

The choices that the United States has made over time in these areas have generated an income gap of historic proportions. Since 2008 especially, structural inequality, in combination with economic recession and a mortgage crisis that has brought large segments of the country to its knees, has been regarded by many as fallout from weak-willed and inadequate government scrutiny of financial institutions and their activities.

In Chapter 6, therefore, the discussion centers on the interlinkages between government and the economy and how they impinge upon the distribution of income and wealth. Even though there have always been zealous proponents of **small government**, there is very little doubt that the government is in fact a strong presence in the economy. Through laws and policies, it has enormous influence on the distribution of resources in society.

Even though the economy, as a **reified entity**, obscures the real players, there is very little doubt that some players have more access to government decisionmaking than others and can successfully influence the contours of those decisions to their own advantage.

American sociology has been enriched by a history of incisive discourses on these themes. C. Wright Mills's concept of **power elite** and G. William Domhoff's concept of **ruling class** are forerunners to the observations and analysis of the Occupy movement. They point to the top 1 percent as being those who have a revolving-door relationship with the executive and legislative branches and therefore have exclusive access to the top echelons of power, unlike the common citizen.

In Chapter 7, I turn to how the US education system perpetuates inequality. There is a great divide in educational opportunities and educational outcomes in the United States. Public school education, which was envisioned as being the great equalizer, has fallen short of its promises.

The scholars I consult agree that children's educational outcomes do not depend simply on the schools, but also on the socioeconomic status of the families and the environments in which children live. Moreover, the educational outcomes often mirror the advantages or disadvantages that children's lives embody, perpetuating and reproducing their socioeconomic status.

Institutional discrimination in education pulls the rug out from under communities segregated by both race and class. Similarly, the skyrocketing cost of higher education, in combination with budget cuts in federal and state financial assistance, has made it increasingly difficult for young people in the US mainstream to receive a college education, which is increasingly touted as an imperative for success. For many scholars, this confirms their doubts regarding the actual ability of higher education to enable young people to transcend the barriers that socioeconomic class enforces.

There have always been those who have wanted to reform schools as a way to reform society. In Chapter 7, I consider the No Child Left Behind Act as one such attempt, keeping in mind that in every era, education reform has always been embedded in the ideologies and priorities of the reformers and their sponsors and has reflected their ideas of the purpose of education and schools for broader society.

In Part 1 of this book, therefore, I set the stage to demonstrate that all aspects of society work together to produce and regenerate the structures of inequality in a capitalist society. Inequality is a natural outcome of the process of capital accumulation, which is at the heart of a capitalist economy. The economic activities of a capitalist system reflect its primary motivation to maximize profit and continuously accelerate the speed and volume of capital accumulation. The government expedites this process with its policies, speeding up capital accumulation on the one hand and widening the income and wealth gap on the other. Capitalism therefore engenders inequality in the course of its normal operation.

In Part 2 of the book, the focus turns to the complex interlinkages between class and gender, race, and the practices of **othering**. When combined with race, gender, and the groups whom society constructs as "the other," class deepens and intensifies inequality. There are often disagreements on how exactly these categories intersect or how best to describe their intersectionalities, but there is broad agreement that these categories do combine in ways to magnify disadvantage.

I take the position in this book that class is the most salient category, since it is the common floor on which everyone's socioeconomic status primarily rests. Race and gender become conceptual categories through which the class divide is exacerbated and magnified. Since the approach of this book is to inquire into the structures that generate, reinforce, and thus perpetuate inequality, the analysis focuses on the motivations of the system to stack people a certain way in terms of class, race, and gender in order to achieve maximum gain for those who are positioned to profit the most from those arrangements. Chapter 8 explains this further.

In Chapter 9, I analyze the ways in which inequality intensifies when class and economic disadvantage combine with gender to make women's lives unmistakably difficult. In the United States, oppression of women prompted the development of three waves of social movements to address the subjugation of women and their status in society as second-class citizens.

The **first-wave women's movement** ended successfully with the passage of the Nineteenth Amendment to the US Constitution, which granted women the right to vote. However, almost forty years after the battles and victories of the **second-wave women's movement**, which gave women equal rights, women on average continue to earn less than men and are stretched to the limit as they try to work and raise families. And this gap persists even for men and women who have comparable work experience and education, such that for every dollar men make, women earn only 77 percent of it.

A large gender gap has always been present in the rates of poverty. In 2011, women had a poverty rate of 16.3 percent, compared to 13.6 percent among men.[4] At a time when almost half of marriages end in divorce, men's standard of living almost always improves following the breakup of a marriage, whereas women's plummets. The absence of affordable and quality day care, after-school care, paid family leave, affordable health care, and a higher minimum wage all combine to make many women's lives arduous.

Also in Chapter 9, I consider the 1996 Personal Responsibility and Work Opportunity Reconciliation Act, popularly known as President Bill Clinton's "Ending Welfare as We Know It" initiative, as a profound example of the intersection of class, gender, and race. This is an arena in which classism, sexism, and racism combine to entrap women, especially women of color, into a permanent state of disadvantage. The **third-wave women's movement** continues to address the complex oppression created by complex patterns of intersectionality.

In Chapter 10, I embark on a short historical journey to explain the complicated way in which race and racism, and class and capitalism, arose out of the same colonial dynamic. The objective is to further emphasize the class origins of both race and racism.

Today, the United States is nowhere near a **postracial** society. The election of an African American president and the visible gains of a black middle class have done little to change the lives of a third of African Americans—in the words of sociologist William Julius Wilson, the **truly disadvantaged**—who continue to live lives entrenched in deep poverty and disadvantage. With systematic losses in the kinds of jobs that sustained their lives in the past, today their sole connection to the global economy is through hyper-consumerism and drug abuse.

Affirmative action or **race- and gender-based preferential policies** that have been in place since 1965 have languished in the absence of real structural reform. The thinly veiled racism in the continuing controversies regarding President Barack Obama's American-ness reinforces black people's incredulity with the promises of the system and its claim to be colorblind. On June 25, 2013, when the US Supreme Court overturned a key provision of the 1965 Voting Rights Act that protected the rights of minority voters to cast their vote free of encumbrances, these doubts were reinforced. In the summer of 2014, police killed two unarmed black men, Eric Garner in New York and Michael Brown in Ferguson, Missouri. There was rioting and outrage at what was seen as unmistakable evidence of the interminable hold of racism in society and particularly in the criminal justice system.

In Chapter 11, I examine how the construction of "the other" facilitates the system of inequality. I argue that the **social constructions** of Native Americans as "savages," of African Americans as racially inferior, and of Latino immigrants as "illegals" have facilitated the processes of conquest, exploitation, and oppression that enabled the **accumulation of capital** as fundamental to the development of capitalism in the United States.

With Chapter 10 analyzing the confluence of race and class as it manifests in the lives of African Americans, the primary focus of Chapter 11 is on Native Americans and Latinos. The objective is to tie their experiences into the larger narrative on inequality and capitalism, mainly by bringing out the contradictions that are apparent, for example, in the role that Native Americans, together with their land and their resources, played in the development and growth of capitalism versus the reality of their continued disadvantage and destitution.

Similarly, there is nothing accidental in the construction of Latinos as "illegals." It is a deeply useful practice in its potential for generating profit. Illegality confines the immigrant into a space of unfathomable vulnerability, which sets in motion systems of exploitation and an entire culture of impunity. It is this vulnerability that makes Latino workers so targetable and fosters a schizophrenic national ideology that embraces them one minute and repulses them the next.

Caught in the middle, Latinos are not only exploited economically, but also victimized by immigration policies that divide families and steal their fundamental right to live without fear and with basic human dignity. Also in Chapter 11, I investigate the historical antecedents that have brought waves of immigrants from South America to the communities of the North.

So, is egregious inequality inevitable and immutable? Or are there ways in which the divide between the rich and everyone else can be bridged? Are there internal fuses or safeguards within capitalist socioeconomic systems that are able to hold the line? In Part 3 of the book, I deliberate on these questions and conclude that, in the United States, the various mechanisms for leveling the playing field have been systematically weakened.

In Chapter 12, I discuss labor unions as such a leveling device. Historically, labor unions played a critical role in promoting efforts for change in capitalist societies, by championing movements that advocated for social justice. In Europe, the United States, and elsewhere, fundamental social reforms were realized through the union movement. Unions spoke up and sided with the poor and the working and middle classes. They provided a countervailing power to the **hegemony** of the power elite. Strong unions were responsible for ending many of the most egregious workplace violations and also for urging the creation of programs that today make up the social safety net.

In the past several decades, however, the United States has seen a gradual eclipse of the union movement and a consequent undermining of its role in effecting social change. This decline has occurred as union membership has dwindled due to changes in the structure of the economy, the workplace, and work itself.

At the same time, a deliberate and persistent endeavor by anti-union forces in business and government, fed by an ideology rooted in the ideas of **conservatism** and **neoliberalism** has chipped away at the legal guarantees of the 1935 National Labor Relations Act, which gave workers the right to unionize and exercise collective bargaining to correct the power imbalances in the workplace.

As the power of US labor unions has dwindled, economic inequality has skyrocketed. The declining clout of the unions has left large segments of working people, in both the private and public sectors, powerless to deal with the continuous threat of joblessness, reshuffling and curtailing of their work schedules and work hours, and cuts in wages and benefits. Consequently, the gulf between them and the affluent has grown steadily and invariably.

In Chapter 13, I begin by recapping my major conclusions about the nature of inequality in the United States. Since the primary objective of this book is to examine the structures that generate, reinforce, and thus perpetuate inequality, my main argument originates from the premise that, in a capitalist society, inequality is created as part of the natural functioning of the system.

The need to accumulate more and more capital through ever-increasing profits has set in motion actions and decisions that have led to one of the biggest transfers of societal wealth in US history, as wealth has not trickled downstream to the majority but rather has surged upstream into the hands of the richest. Cutting the cost of labor to the barest minimum has been the most expedient choice for fattening the bottom line.

Therefore, the most definitive attribute of the economic downturn and growing inequality has been the persistent, ongoing loss of the kinds of jobs that in the past, particularly in the period following World War II, had enabled individuals to step into the middle class and also opened up avenues for social mobility.

In Chapter 13, I also explore ways in which the current state of affairs in the United States can be changed so every segment of society has a chance to realize among the most closely held fundamental beliefs in the ethos of this nation: that every individual is endowed with certain inalienable rights, among them are life, liberty, and the pursuit of happiness.

But as President Franklin Roosevelt stated, none of these rights can be realized in the absence of basic economic rights—those guaranteeing decent jobs, a living wage, affordable health care, decent housing, quality education, and security for the elderly, the sick, and the unemployed. If the capitalist system, as it stands today, has refused to ensure these basic economic rights and has violated the **social compact** as delineated in the Declaration of Independence, what options do people have?

If inequality is rooted in the choices that are made, as is argued in this book, then the most logical way to imagine alternatives to the status quo would be to make changes in those choices. But how to leverage power in society in a way so that policy choices reflect visions for a different future and reflect the collective will of the American people?

Of course, that would mean changing the contours of power—or at least balancing it with representation of those who have thus far remained invisible to those critical sectors of society where decisions with far-reaching consequences are made. In this last chapter, I consider the ways in which such change can be brought about and how to convince an increasingly cynical public that it can work.

First, I look to President Roosevelt and to Europe to develop a platform of social well-being that will inform the policies that are fundamental to delivering an "economics of shared prosperity," as delineated in Jacob Hacker and Nate Loewentheil's 2012 policy manual, "Prosperity Economics: Building an Economy for All."

Recognizing all along that power never cedes its position and privilege unless it has been forced to do so, we know that none of this will come to pass without a strong **collective social movement**, representing every segment of society, that makes it quite clear that the present situation is untenable, and that change is the existential imperative—the call of the hour.

We will not be able to build an alternative America, one that is just and egalitarian, unless visionary leaders, grassroots advocacy groups, civil rights organizations, unions, immigrant groups, minority groups (such as those based on sexual orientation), environmentalists, and the academic world join forces to demand such a future.

Notes

1. Rayfield, "Santorum."
2. Kaufman, "Pope Francis: 'Inequality Is the Root of Social Evil.'"
3. Robertson, *Sociology,* p. 254.
4. DeNavas-Walt, Proctor, and Smith, "Income, Poverty, and Health Insurance Coverage in the United States: 2011," p. 14.

Part 1
Structures of Inequality

2

Our Divided Society Today

THE DEGREE OF INEQUALITY THAT THE UNITED STATES FACES TODAY IS of historic proportions. All indices of welfare and well-being embody this undeniable reality. The chasm between the rich and the poor has reached a level comparable to one experienced in the late 1920s.

When the Berlin Wall fell in 1989, Francis Fukuyama confidently announced the **end of history** and the indisputable worldwide victory of capitalism.[1] But today, the deepening economic divide, not only in the United States but also in much of the Western industrialized world, is raising misgivings about the consequences of Fukuyama's claim in how it plays out in the lives of ordinary people.

The concept of an "end of history" is attributed to German philosopher G. W. F. Hegel and his intellectual progeny Karl Marx. For both Hegel and Marx, social evolution of the most fundamental structures of society was not open-ended; it did not go on indefinitely. It came to an end when the level of social evolution that was considered optimal was attained. For Marx, that would have been **communism**.

Francis Fukuyama reconceptualized the idea of an "end of history" to argue that with the defeat of the Soviet Union, it was the system of capitalism that actually attained worldwide victory to become the unparalleled, unquestioned, and universally preferred economic system of choice.

He maintained that the fall of the Berlin Wall marked the end of the ideological warfare that dominated the Cold War, and therefore marked the end of intellectual, geopolitical, military squabbling between two ideologies—capitalism and socialism—and the two nations that, more than any others, had embodied the two ideologies—the United States and the Soviet Union. So far as Fukuyama was concerned, history itself had become history.

When that claim was made, against the backdrop of the unraveling of the Soviet Union, was it assumed that people's lives, now freed of the "communist menace," would be significantly and qualitatively better? Since that most definitely has not happened, is this intensification of inequality "across a range of advanced industrial countries an underlying feature of late capitalist development," as Stephanie Moller and her colleagues ask?[2]

A recent report covering the thirty advanced industrial countries of the Organization for Economic Cooperation and Development (OECD) concluded that from the mid-1980s to the mid-2000s, the dominant pattern was one of increasing inequality. Along with the United States, inequality has risen precipitously in Finland, Germany, Italy, New Zealand, Norway, and Sweden.[3]

The indications that the system of capitalism itself is increasingly failing to deliver the means toward an adequate livelihood to large segments of society are apparent in two important facts. First, the most recent trends in inequality and its accompanying poverty, rather than being transient and temporary, are persistent and deepening. And second, unlike in previous recessions, the current decline in median income and subsequent rise in income inequality are largely attributed to declines in employment due to widespread **deindustrialization** and globalization rather than simply being the result of falling real earnings of the employed.[4]

The declines in employment have led to stagnant and falling incomes for large swaths of the population. For example, between 1970 and 2010, income going to wages and salaries fell by close to a trillion dollars.[5] The per capita median income, after adjusting for inflation, has remained virtually unchanged since 2000. And for the poor, incomes have actually declined. But at the same time, the top 1 percent of income earners have enjoyed unprecedented growth in their incomes. And the resulting chasm between the two groups—one experiencing stagnant or falling incomes and the other experiencing massive growth in their incomes—characterizes the structure of inequality in the United States today.

An often quoted paper written by Thomas Piketty and Emmanuel Saez examines income inequality in the United States in the years 1913–2002. It shows how the share of US national income going to the top of the income distribution had risen sharply during the early decades of the twentieth century. However, income concentration dropped dramatically following World Wars I and II, and then remained unchanged for the next few decades. Starting in 1975, income concentration at the top started to soar again, reaching pre–World War I levels by 2000.[6]

In 2012, the top 1 percent of income earners in the United States took home 22.5 percent of the total national income—almost a quarter of all income—their highest share since 1928.[7] Annie Lowrey, reporter for the *New York Times,* writes:

> The top 10 percent of earners took more than half of the country's total income
> in 2012, the highest level recorded since the government began collecting the

relevant data a century ago, according to an updated study by the prominent economists Emmanuel Saez and Thomas Piketty.

The figures underscore that even after the recession the country remains in a new Gilded Age, with income as concentrated as it was in the years that preceded the Depression of the 1930s, if not more so.

High stock prices, rising home values and surging corporate profits have buoyed the recovery-era incomes of the most affluent Americans, with the incomes of the rest still weighed down by high unemployment and stagnant wages for many blue- and white-collar workers.[8]

In 2013, the twenty-five highest-paid hedge fund managers made over $21 billion. This was twice as much as the combined salaries of all the kindergarten teachers in the United States. They made money betting on stocks in the airline, automobile, and housing-market industries, and in companies such as Wendy's and Cadbury. Meanwhile, President Barack Obama has been unable to secure financing for universal kindergarten education. Such over-the-top incomes have also been facilitated by what Nicholas Kristof refers to as the "egregious carried interest tax break"— whatever that means.[9]

The anger over inequality has invaded some corporate boardrooms. A report in the *New York Times* on April 18, 2012, talks about "a stinging rebuke" that Citigroup shareholders dealt when they "rebuffed" the bank's $15 million pay package for its chief executive officer (CEO). The report mentions that this was the first time the stock owners of a financial giant have "united in opposition to outsize compensation" for CEOs, which some even condemned as being "obscene."[10]

In this chapter and others, the objective is to crack the mystery as much as possible. What is causing this unprecedented divergence between the rich and the poor?

Inequality in the United States

The United States has been a deeply unequal society since its very inception. Large segments of the society have been mired in acute conditions of poverty and want for much of its history. The poor have also long been members of racial and ethnic minorities—Native Americans, blacks, Latinos—and their deprivation has been attributed to racial "deficiencies" or to the laws and customs underlying systems of discrimination that denied them equal access to resources and opportunities. The system of capitalism itself was seldom called to account.

The persistence of destitution and disadvantage among these groups even after the passage of civil rights laws in the 1960s simply reinforced racial stereotypes in the minds of many or pointed to the enduring legacies of racism and discrimination. Again, few pointed their fingers at capitalism.

When sociologist William Julius Wilson suggested that the tenacity with which destitution and poverty continued to haunt the "truly disadvantaged" should be seen in the light of class more than race, a firestorm from outraged social scientists rained down upon him. Wilson argued that, although rooted in historical discrimination, the persistence of deep pockets of poverty in the inner cities of the United States—often in more abject form than at the height of the **Jim Crow** era—could only be fully understood in light of structural changes in the economy.[11] He was referring to the shift from manufacturing to service jobs and the concomitant rise in levels of unemployment and underemployment in the inner city. In hindsight today, it seems that these minority communities were the proverbial canary in the coal mine.

What is happening in mainstream American society today—the unprecedented inequality that plagues the nation—is largely attributed to the flight of jobs from the territorial United States to the far reaches of the globe and the consequential depletion of income and wealth for large segments of the American people. Poverty and inequality are commonplace in the United States today, and this fact is an undeniable reality.

The economic distress is no longer invisible; it is no longer sequestered in the communities of blacks, Native Americans, and Hispanics. It has burst out into the open so clearly that its economic and class underpinnings can no longer be denied. So long as the faces of the poor were perceived as being primarily black or brown, they could be made invisible, their problems dismissed as being inconsequential to the larger society. But today, with so much of Middle America and white America suffering, the problem of inequality and poverty is the talk of the town and can no longer be ascribed simply to race.

With the publication of Charles Murray's book *Coming Apart,* attention is being focused on the white *underclass*—a term reserved until recently to characterize the pathologies of the inner-city African American community. Murray's primary focus is the breakdown of the traditional family values and the devastation wrought by drugs.[12] What he does not emphasize strongly enough is the hopelessness and despair that large segments of the white working class experience as they are systematically pushed out of the job market, creating an atmosphere in which drugs and disintegration of the family take root. Additionally, Anand Giridharadas writes that "a rising generation is often being reared by grandparents because parents are addicted, imprisoned, broke or all three."[13] So much of the poverty is darkened by loneliness, chaotic childhoods, and **anomie**.

As working-class whites fall off the economic ladder, class becomes the undeniable marker and the paramount delineator of the economic divide, eclipsing race and gender and becoming acknowledged as the "salient cleavage" distinctive of American society today.[14] A survey by the

MAKING CONNECTIONS
The White Underclass

Appalachia evokes two very iconic images of the United States, contradictory in many ways: the beauty of a bucolic country surrounded by the green Blue Mountains, and the poverty of the people who live there. When President Lyndon Johnson unveiled his war on poverty in 1964, "it was the squalor of the people in Appalachia [that] he had in mind," writes Trip Gabriel in a news report on the enduring poverty of rural America.[1]

McDowell County, in southern West Virginia, is the poorest region in a state that has symbolized entrenched, stubborn poverty for almost half a century. The programs that epitomized the war on poverty—Medicare, Medicaid, food stamps, free school lunches, and others—lifted tens of thousands out of poverty. But today the numbers of poor are again on the rise. In West Virginia in 2014, the poverty rate was 41 percent for families with children.

In 2014 the median annual household income for McDowell County was $22,000, the lowest in the state. The county also has the highest childhood obesity rate, and the highest teenage pregnancy rate, in the state. Prescription drug abuse is rampant, and the death rate from overdose in the county is more than eight times the national average. Consequently, West Virginia has the highest drug incarceration rates in the nation. And just like in West Virginia, drug abuse is widespread in much of rural America. Entire families are swept up in the scourge. And in the absence of parents, grandparents become entrusted with the responsibility of raising the children.

Academicians like Charles Murray attribute these problems to behaviors and pathologies that form a subculture that sociologist Oscar Lewis called a **culture of poverty**.[2] But culture is ultimately an adaptation. People develop behaviors and attitudes in response to the real circumstances of their lives. Cultural norms do not fall from thin air; they have deep socioeconomic roots.

As early as the nineteenth century, West Virginia's extraordinarily rich coal reserves brought mining companies to the state. Though the wealth seldom remained within the state, at least the mines offered good jobs—the only good jobs the people ever knew. But in the 1990s, when the great US steel industries in the Midwest and Pennsylvania started their steady decline, so did coal. West Virginia lost its major mines and the people their only employer. The poverty rate in the state, which had dropped to 24 percent in 1970, soared to 38 percent in 1990.

As of 2014 in McDowell County, only one in three residents have a job. There has been a steady exodus of people, but for those who have remained, drugs have become a way to escape the despondency that economic uncertainty brings. The only constructive activity that remains in the county is the building of prisons. But the well-paying jobs in corrections have gone to outsiders, since, as Trip Gabriel writes, the local people have not been able to pass the drug test.

And in the United States at large, as the federal government builds more prisons, the economy continues its downward spiral, and communities are devastated. Families break up, prescription drug abuse becomes pervasive, and rates of imprisonment skyrocket. At least the prisons will not go wanting.

Notes: 1. Gabriel, "50 Years Later, Hardship Hits Back," p. A1.
2. Murray, *Coming Apart;* Lewis, "The Culture of Poverty."

Pew Research Center, published in January 2012, even found that two thirds of Americans now believe that the conflict between the rich and the poor is the source of the greatest tension in American society—greater than that caused by the conflict between black and white or between immigrant and native-born.[15]

What Is Class?

The most important attribute of class is that it is an economic category derived from variables such as income and wealth. Therefore, in its most straightforward form, class is defined in terms of income and wealth: how much of that these individuals have places them in the upper class, the middle class, or among the poor. This is usually referred to as the **gradational determination of class**.

The **relational determination of class** emphasizes the fact that class is not just a category that someone occupies. Rather, class embodies a relationship between the proverbial haves and have-nots in terms of ownership (or lack of ownership) of the **means of production** or capital, a relationship that ultimately structures and reproduces inequality.[16] This is a significantly more critical determinant of class, much more so than categories of more or less income and wealth. Ownership of capital—land, factories, technology, restaurants, nursing homes, charter schools, retail businesses, and so forth—confers unique privileges on the owners, known as the capitalists, the **bourgeoisie**, or simply the haves. These privileges derive not just from the often lopsided share of earnings (profit) that accrue to the owners, but also, and more importantly, from the power of the owners to control capital in ways that deliver maximum returns.

Owners of the means of production can manage their sources of income to maximize their benefits in ways that others cannot. And very often, the economic destinies of others are impacted by those decisions. For example, the factory owner has the freedom to move their factory to a region where wages are low so that profits can be maximized. The capitalist has relative control over their own income; the worker (**proletariat**) who is hired does not.

This book makes use of both determinations of class. To describe the shape of income and wealth distribution in the United States, the gradational method is utilized. I take into account how much income and wealth accrue to each class—upper, upper-middle, middle, lower, and poor. Economists and statistical analysts at the US Census Bureau use the convention of referring to these classes as fifths, or **quintiles**. They refer to the class categories as the highest, fourth, middle, second, and the lowest fifths. In determining quintiles, the entire population of the United States is divided into five equal segments of 20 percent each along that gradational sequence, from the lowest (or poorest) fifth of earners to the highest (or richest) fifth. In this book, I use the gradational form for describing the class system in the United States.

The relational method is used as an analytical tool to answer the questions of why the distribution of income and wealth in the United States is the way it is, and why it has been so persistently and consistently skewed. Therefore, I use the relational form of class for the purpose of analyzing the class system of the United States. Looking at class as relational has profound significance in accounting for the maintenance and exacerbation of income and wealth inequalities.[17]

How Is Income Defined?

In its simplest definition, **income** is money in the pocket, in the checking account—liquid capital. It is what we are paid on a regular basis for the work we do—wages, salaries, and tips. It is also what we earn from the properties we own—rents, interest, and dividends.

The US Census Bureau defines money income as "income received on a regular basis before payments for personal income taxes, social security, union dues, Medicare deductions, etc." This does not include certain types of money received, such as capital gains. In its calculations of an individual's or household's income, the Census Bureau does not include **transfer payments**, such as "income from noncash benefits, such as food stamps, health benefits, subsidized housing, or goods produced and consumed on the farm."[18]

In their article on income inequality in the United States covering the period 1913–2002, economists Piketty and Saez, in clarifying what they measure as income, write:

> We use a gross income definition including all income items reported on tax returns and before all deductions: salaries and wages, small business and farm income, partnership and fiduciary income, dividends, interest, rents, royalties, and other small items reported as other income. Realized capital gains are not an annual flow of income (in general, capital gains are realized by individuals in a lumpy way) and form a very volatile component of income with large aggregate variations from year to year depending on stock price variations. Therefore, we focus mainly on series that exclude capital gains.[19]

Wealth

If income is the liquid asset that a household earns, **wealth** is its net worth—its fixed, marketable assets after debts have been subtracted. Real

MAKING CONNECTIONS

What Are Capital Gains?

Since neither of the definitions of income that we see here includes capital gains, we must be sure to understand what they are. This is important because, as we will see later, in comparison with what is considered income, a special reduced tax rate is reserved for capital gains. According to the tax code of the United States, the tax rate for income that people earn in wages and salaries—types of income that apply to the majority of Americans—is 35 percent. For capital gains, on the other hand, which only a minority of Americans are privileged to earn, the tax rate is only 15 percent. So, what exactly is a capital gain?

Capital gain is the gain or increase in the value of a capital asset investment or real estate investment relative to the value at the time of purchase. The gain is realized only if the asset or real estate is sold. A capital loss occurs when the value of a capital asset or investment decreases relative to its purchase price.

As we will see later, the kind of wealth that goes into large capital investments, which earn huge capital gains, accrues to a very small number of Americans, and these very few are the only people favorably located to enjoy a low tax rate compared to a majority of Americans, who are taxed on their salaries or incomes at a significantly higher rate. This is an important fact, since a sizable proportion of the income divide has been attributed to discriminatory tax rates.

Let us see how this affects our pocketbook. Imagine that you have been working as a receptionist since 1980, for thirty-five years. You earn $21,000 a year. Your income might have gone up a little each year, but given that the average salary that a receptionist made in 2013 was still hovering around $30,000 according to the Bureau of Labor Statistics,[1] I would not err in judgment by holding your salary to a constant of $21,000. It will make my calculations easier.

Also in 1980, your rich friend invested in Apple, purchasing 1,000 shares of stock at $20 per share when the company first went public. So she invested $20,000—nearly your entire income for that year.

In 2014, your friend decides to sell those 1,000 shares at a price of $520 per share. She earns $520,000—half a million dollars in capital gains. This year (and this year only because she wouldn't have to pay any taxes in the previous years since there was no activity, in this case selling, associated with the shares of stocks), she must pay a 15 percent tax rate on her capital gain of $500,000 ($520,000 minus the $20,000 initial investment), so she pays $75,000 in tax.

In contrast, you must pay 35 percent of your salary in taxes every year, as you have for the past thirty-five years. Your total income over this period is $735,000 ($21,000 × 35), so you pay $257,250 in tax—over a quarter million dollars.

Tax codes are very complex; here, I am simplifying. But this does not diminish the essence of the matter. One of the reasons why inequality has grown to the extent it has is attributed to this very fact. Individuals who own a lot of stocks and other assets are able to earn a lot more money and pay only a fraction of it in taxes compared to those whose only earning is their salary. Most Americans belong to the latter category.

Note: 1. Bureau of Labor Statistics, "Occupational Employment and Wages," May 2013.

estate, stocks, bonds, jewelry, valuable artwork, household goods, automobiles—these all add up to a person's or family's net worth after debts, such as home mortgage and credit card debt—have been subtracted.

The wealth that the rich own—real estate, capital assets, investments, and artworks—often generates rents, dividends, or capital gains. Whereas the wealth owned by the rest, in the form of consumer durables such as household goods or automobiles, has use value but seldom any exchange value, meaning that it does not generate a monetary return on a regular basis. By contrast, the wealth that the affluent own frequently generates recurring monetary returns.

Methods of Measuring Inequality

Two of the most common measures of income inequality are the **shares approach** and the **Gini index**. The shares approach considers how much of the national income is received by households or families, and the Gini index measures the degree of income concentration.[20]

In the shares approach, inequality is measured by calculating the share of aggregate income that is received by households or families—that is, how much of the total income generated from all reported economic activity in the nation is received by households or families. In the shares approach, households are ranked from poorest to richest on the basis of income and then divided into equal-sized populations groups, typically into quintiles, with each group representing 20 percent of the nation's total number of households. In 2011 the Census Bureau reported that the United States had just over 114 million households. *Inequality* is the term commonly used to describe an income distribution in which one or more quintiles account for less (or more) than 20 percent of aggregate income.[21] As Table 2.1 shows, the highest or richest quintile received more than 50 percent of the total national income in 2010 and 2011. Further, between those two years, the richest quintile's share of total income increased, whereas the share of every other income quintile fell.

The Gini index is the other measure used to gauge the degree of inequality, and is the more common measure of the two. It takes its name from Corrado Gini, an Italian statistician who developed the concept in his 1912 book, *Variability and Mutability.*

The Gini index compares the actual distribution of income in a society to a distribution of income that would be one of complete equality. The degree of inequality is expressed in terms of how much the actual distribution varies from the line of equality. It ranks the amount of inequality on a scale from 0 to 1. An index of 0 indicates perfect equality, with every person having an equal share of the national income and each quintile having

Table 2.1 Share of Aggregate Income Received by Each Quintile, 2010 and 2011

Quintile	2010		2011		Change, 2010–2011 (%)
	Income	Share (%)	Income	Share (%)	
Lowest	$11,341	3.3	$11,239	3.2	–0.9
Second	$29,432	8.5	$29,204	8.4	–0.8
Middle	$50,718	14.6	$49,842	14.3	–1.7
Fourth	$81,365	23.4	$80,080	23.0	–1.6
Highest	$174,734	50.3	$178,020	51.1	1.9

Source: Denavas-Walt, Proctor, and Smith, "Income, Poverty, and Health Insurance Coverage in the United States: 2011," table A-2, p. 38.

a 20 percent share. An index of 1 indicates perfect inequality, with one person having all the income—100 percent of a nation's total income—and the rest having none. Thus, higher Gini index values denote higher levels of inequality. The Gini index for the United States in 2011 was 0.477.

As Figure 2.1 shows, the Gini index of income concentration for the United States has been on the rise since 1968, indicating that the degree of inequality has increased and therefore resulted in the concentration of income in the hands of fewer and fewer individuals.

Table 2.2 compares the share of total income that went to each of the quintiles in 1968 and in 2011, showing that the lowest quintile's share remained almost unchanged over this period, hovering around 4 percent or less. The middle class, defined as the middle 60 percent of the households, saw their share shrink from 53.2 percent to 45.7 percent.

However, over the same period, the disproportionately large share that went to the highest quintile and the richest 5 percent of all US households rose steeply and relentlessly. The richest 20 percent's share of total household income rose from 42.6 percent to 51.1 percent, and the richest 5 percent's share rose from 16.3 percent to 22.3 percent.

These numbers give evidence that the high-income households are pulling farther and farther away not just from the lowest income quintiles, but also from the middle class (the middle 60 percent).[22] The Gini index of 0.477 for the United States in 2011 confirms this yawning divide between the richest Americans and everyone else.

Figure 2.2 further confirms this trend in the changing income distribution, from 1979 to 2007. According to the Congressional Budget Office, the income of the top 1 percent of earners increased during this period by an incredible 277 percent. The gains for all other groups paled by comparison. Even for the remaining 19 percent in the highest quintile, the income gain was only 65 percent. The middle 60 percent, the US middle class, saw a 38 percent rise in their incomes in the same period. For the bottom or poorest

Figure 2.1 The Increasing Concentration of Income Among US Households: Gini Index, 1968–2011

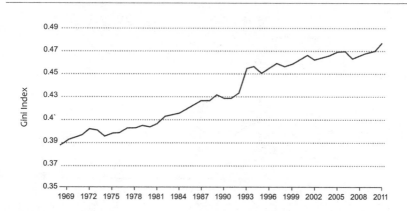

Source: US Census Bureau, "Income, Poverty, and Health Insurance Coverage in the United States: 2012," table A-2.

Table 2.2 Share of Aggregate Income Received by Each Quintile, 1968 and 2011 (percentages)

Quintile	1968 Share	2011 Share
Lowest	4.2	3.2
Second	11.1	8.4
Middle	17.6	14.3
Fourth	24.5	23.0
Highest	42.6	51.1
Richest 5 Percent	16.3	22.3

Source: Denavas-Walt, Proctor, and Smith, "Income, Poverty, and Health Insurance Coverage in the United States: 2011," table A-2, pp. 38, 42.

20 percent, in that period of more than twenty-five years, their income gain was only 18 percent.

We may also use **median household income** to ascertain the magnitude of inequality. The median is considered a better measure of the average income of a country than the mean. Comparing the median incomes over a period of time establishes the path of a nation's economic well-being or lack thereof. Since the median income carries a lot of weight in discussions of inequality, let us consider the definition used by the US Census Bureau.

Median household income includes the income of the head of household and of all other individuals, fifteen years of age and older, living in the household, whether they are related to the head of household or not. The median divides the income distribution into two equal parts, with half of the

Figure 2.2 Change in After-Tax Income, 1979–2007 (percent change in after-tax income since 1979)

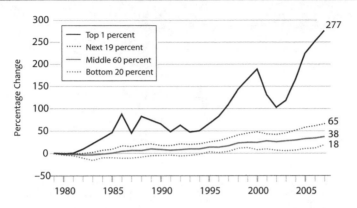

Source: Congressional Budget Office, "Trends in the Distribution of Household Income Between 1979 and 2007," p. 3.
Note: Percentage change adjusted for inflation.

cases falling below the median income and the other half rising above the median.[23] In 2011, the median annual household income of the United States was $50,054, which means that the number of households whose income was above this line was equal to the number of households whose income was below it. There are a few different estimates of median income in this book, which reflects yearly changes or different estimates by different sources. However, it seldom deviates very much from the median cited here, nor does it compromise the basic integrity and implication of those numbers.

The higher the median income, the more equitable—and less cramped— the distribution of income beneath that line. According to the US Census Bureau, in 2011 the American population numbered 311.6 million, and there were 114.2 million households, meaning an average of 2.72 individuals in each household. With a median household income of $50,054, there were thus 57 million households crowded beneath this line, and 57 million others spread out expansively above it.[24]

Figure 2.3 helps us visualize the cramped quarters for the 57 million households under the median income. If the median were higher, it would mean that these households and families could move up the income distribution and spread out somewhat more evenly. A median of $50,054 leaves the highest earners—the richest 1 percent of Americans, making over $250,000 annually—rather isolated at the top of the income distribution.

Furthermore, there has been an unmistakable downward trend in median family income. In 1999, the median income in the United States was at its peak, at $54,932. The decrease to $50,054 in 2011 represents a drop of 8.9 percent.[25] In comparing the median income of different racial

Figure 2.3 Median Annual Household Income Compared to Income Earned by the Richest 1 Percent, 2012

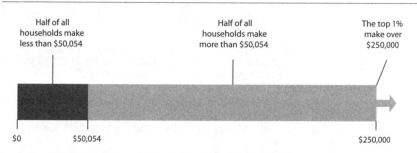

| Half of all households make less than $50,054 | Half of all households make more than $50,054 | The top 1% make over $250,000 |

$0 $50,054 $250,000

Source: US Census Bureau, "Current Population Report, 2012."

Figure 2.4 Median Annual Household Income by Race and Sex, 2011

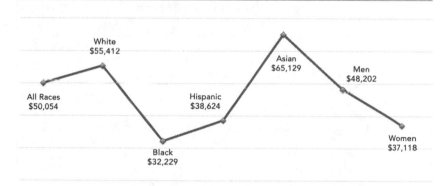

White $55,412

Asian $65,129

Men $48,202

All Races $50,054

Hispanic $38,624

Women $37,118

Black $32,229

Source: US Census Bureau, "Current Population Report, 2012."

groups and the income of men and women, we see in Figure 2.4 that in 2011, Asian households had the highest median income, at $65,129, with blacks and women making the lowest salaries, at $32,229 and $37,118 respectively. Deindustrialization and the "disappearance of work," as sociologist William Julius Wilson phrases it, have deprived blacks and Latinos of jobs that in earlier times were mainstays for many.

Continuing intransigence in implementing immigration reform has continued the economic subjugation of many Latinos. And for women, who are still in most cases the main care providers for their families, trying to balance work with family duties while earning unequal pay and also facing a continual absence of affordable day care, paid family leave, and affordable health care, can make for very difficult lives.

In Chapters 9 and 10 , the gender and racial dimensions of economic inequality are analyzed in greater detail. Here, suffice it to say that for many

MAKING CONNECTIONS
What Explains Asian American Success?

The perceived success of Asian Americans, especially at a time when the country is not doing so well, raises not just curiosity but also a certain degree of ire. *Asian American* is a broad term used to refer to at least twenty different ethnic groups who trace their roots to countries in the Pacific Rim, the Far East, and Southeast and South Asia. They represent a diversity of languages, cultures, histories, religions, and ways in which they came to the United States (some more recent than others) and took up life in their adopted land (some more contentious than others).

But despite their internal diversity, Asian Americans are distinctive when it comes to their educational and economic standing. As of 2010, 49 percent have at least a bachelor's degree if not higher, compared to 28 percent for the general US population; their median annual household income is $66,000, compared to $49,800 for the rest of the country. Among Indian Americans, 70 percent have at least a bachelor's degree, and a median annual household income of $88,000.[1]

Asian parents, like many immigrant parents, instill in their children strong values they brought with them from their native countries of education, hard work, and family, values which served them well as new immigrants. These values prepare the children well and help them attain university education and professions in highly skilled and well-paid jobs.

Asian American successes have led to the construction of the **model minority** stereotype. It emphasizes Asian American success as an example of a group that has overcome discrimination and has pulled themselves up by their own bootstraps. It attributes their success to hard work, academic excellence, economic success, submissiveness, and accommodation. They are held up as a "model" for other groups, which are seen as slackers. But like all stereotypes, there is an exaggeration of certain characteristics. Yes, there is ample evidence of Asian American attainment in education and material success, but that does not compensate for the continuing disadvantage of many others. The model-minority image becomes a convenient way to deny the assistance that many Asian Americans need and overlooks the institutional discrimination many face.

Each racial and ethnic group carries with it a historical legacy and contemporary experiences that affect how successful that group of people are in availing themselves of opportunities. It is in this context that the idea of the model minority needs to be interrogated. The stereotype assigns this group of people to a status that is used to appraise them in relation to other minorities. In this line of thinking, if other minorities have not been successful, it is because they have not shown the same perseverance as Asian Americans. The burden of failure is, for those other minorities, something they must bear alone. The scars of slavery, legal discrimination, and ongoing institutional discrimination are simply wiped off the slate.

Large-scale deindustrialization and the loss of low-skilled manufacturing jobs has destabilized the lives of many working-class blacks, whites, and Latinos. But at the same time, there is increased demand for more highly skilled and

(continues)

What Explains Asian American Success?

educated workers in science, technology, accounting, and management. Given this demand, coupled with a scarcity in the supply of highly skilled and educated workers, there have been substantial gains in the relative wages of this group. Therefore, opportunities have opened up in these areas for immigrant groups such as Indians, Chinese, Filipinos, Japanese, Koreans, and other Asians among others—those qualified in science, technology, engineering, and mathematics—to take up positions that would otherwise remain unfilled and which carry substantial monetary rewards.

Not all Asians in the United States fit this particular description, however. Some are recent immigrants. Some are undocumented and experience the marginalization suffered by any other group in their position. Many are employees in the service economy—both visibly and invisibly—making a minimum wage at the mercy of their employers in sweatshops, gas stations, convenience stores, and ethnic fast food joints. The success of their compatriots does not in any way diminish their disadvantage.

Note: 1. Pew Research Social and Demographic Trends, "The Rise of Asian Americans," http://www.pewsocialtrends.org/asianamericans-graphics/ (accessed October 21, 2014).

---

women, blacks, and Latinos, the barriers to overcoming poverty and economic disadvantage can often be insurmountable.

A Longitudinal Perspective

The media and airwaves are awash these days with evidence of the extent of the divide in wealth and income in the United States. This is a reality quite removed from the unprecedented prosperity enjoyed in the quarter of a century after the end of World War II. While it is undeniable that there was great inequality then, most men had jobs and most families were intact, even in the segregated, walled-off communities of people of color. Unemployment numbers were low, fluctuating closely around the 5 percent level that is considered a state of full employment.

The postwar economic boom lifted all boats, and the United States became mythologized as a country of unlimited opportunities where the dream of a middle-class life could indeed be attained. Even in the shadow of the Cold War and nuclear crisis, the country continued to provide the kinds of jobs that enabled individuals and families to step into the middle class, to be economically secure. All through the 1950s and 1960s, the United States was a strong middle-class country, with the upward mobility of future generations ensured.

However, evidence was always present that things were not quite as rosy as they seemed. In 1962, Michael Harrington published *The Other America,* in which he drew attention to the invisible world of the poor in the United States. He wrote of the "familiar America. Celebrated in speeches and advertised on television and the magazines. [And] the other America, those who live in the economic underworld of US life where though not impoverished in the same sense as those [in] poor nations where millions cling to hunger . . . [but those, nonetheless] maimed in body and spirit existing at levels beneath those necessary for human decency . . . fat with hunger [lessened] with cheap food, without adequate housing, education and medical care."[26]

That things were deteriorating for large groups of Americans was also evident in numbers published as early as 1992. In a front-page report on March 5, 1992, titled "Even Among the Well-Off, the Richest Get Richer," *New York Times* reporter Sylvia Nasar, referring to the most recent Congressional Budget Office data, wrote of the "recent evidence that the richest 1 percent of American families appears to have reaped most of the gains from the prosperity of the last decade and a half. An outsized 60% of the growth in after-tax income of all American families between 1977 and 1989—and an even heftier three-fourths of the gain in pre-tax income— went to the wealthiest 660,000 families."

She further wrote that in the course of just a dozen years—1977 to 1989—the average pre-tax income of families in the top 1 percent grew 77 percent, from $315,000 to $560,000. The typical US family "smack in the middle, or the median, of the income distribution—saw its income edge up only 4%. And the bottom 40% had actual declines in income." The pay of the average chief executive was 120 times greater than that of the average worker, compared to merely 35 times as much in the 1970s.[27]

On September 5, 1999, David Cay Johnston reported, also in the *New York Times,* that "the wealthiest 2.7 million have as much to spend as the poorest 100 million. A ratio which has more than doubled since 1977, when the top 1 percent had as much as the bottom 49 million." According to the Congressional Budget Office, in that same year, 1999, the top one-fifth of US households with the highest incomes earned half of all the income in the United States.[28]

Now I want to address what has become of those who occupy the top end of the economic continuum. Since the late 1970s, the income for the individuals who occupy the highest income category—referred to as the top 1 percent—has grown much faster than for anyone else in the income distribution. The two *New York Times* reports just referenced, from 1992 and 1999, signaled this trend even before it had dawned significantly in the public mind.

This massive increase in the incomes of the top 1 percent has become emblematic of the current state of inequality in the United States. The World Top Incomes Database, compiled by researchers at the Paris School of Economics and the University of California, Berkeley, found that in 2012 the **top 1 percent** of households had an average annual income of $1,264,065, which was 41 times more than what the average US household made, whose average annual income was $30,997. The **top 0.1 percent**, whose average annual household income was $6,373,782, made 206 times more than the average US household. The average annual household income for the **top 0.01 percent** in 2012 was $31 million.[29] The top 0.01 percent made 1000 times more than the average US household.

Therefore, it is the top 0.01 percent, within the top 1 percent category, who tower head-and-shoulders above not only the rest of society, but more incredibly also above those who are in the 99.9th to 99.99th percentile in the top 1 percent category. Analysis and evidence presented by Piketty and Saez also supports this stark picture of "divergence between the fortunes of the very wealthy and everyone else . . . (and) the extent to which the super rich got rich faster than the merely rich."[30]

Economists have taken to calling it **fractal inequality**, as writes Annie Lowrey in her report in the *New York Times,* in February 2014, on the enormous fortunes of the richest of the rich and on the inequality at the very top of the income distribution. There is a growing divergence between the fortunes of the 1 percent and those of the 0.1 percent (see Figure 2.5), or those

Figure 2.5 Inequality at the Top, 1970–2012

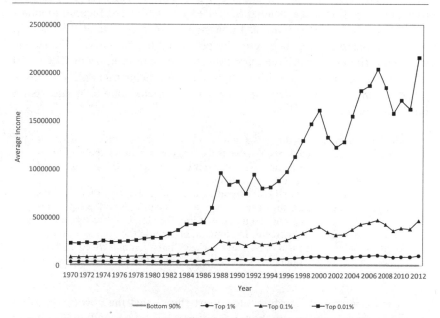

Source: F. Alvaredo, T. Atkinson, T. Piketty, and E. Saez, *The World Top Incomes Database,* topincomes.parisschoolofeconomics.eu/.

of the 0.01 percent or the 0.001 percent. "It is not just that the rich have pulled away from the average American," Lowrey writes, "it is that the richer you are, the more you have pulled away."[31]

In his singular work *Who Rules America?* G. William Domhoff notes: "It is important to realize that the lower half of that top 1 percent has far less than those in the top half; in fact, both wealth and income are super concentrated in the top 0.1 percent."[32] When we couple this observation with the information from Piketty and Saez that, in a country where there are around 114 million households, the top 0.01 percent comprises just 15,000 households, the significance of that "super concentration" becomes staggering.

This super-concentration of economic power, together with the consequent possibilities for influence-peddling in the workings of the government, becomes profoundly disturbing when we consider the primary thesis of this book: that the degree of inequality is not just the result of the workings of the dispassionate forces of the **invisible hand**, but is also the consequence of deliberate interference by those who are in a position to influence the workings of government and the economy and have a very passionate regard for the decisions that are made and how they are implemented. This point needs to be kept in mind continuously.

Unlike in previous times, the super-rich of today did not just inherit their riches. A bulk of those riches came from their astronomical salaries, benefits, and stock options. In the summer of 2012, the Economic Policy Institute published a report titled "CEO Pay and the Top 1%: How Executive Compensation and Financial Sector Pay Have Fueled Income Inequality." What the report's authors, Lawrence Mishel and Natalie Sabadish, write summarizes quite succinctly the point that the fortunes of the super-rich are attributable to a large extent on skyrocketing salaries of CEOs and those in the financial sector. Most significant, the Economic Policy Institute report unambiguously identifies the most critical source of the rising inequality in the United States:

> Growing income inequality has a number of sources, but a distinct aspect of rising inequality in the United States is the wage gap between the very highest earners—those in the upper 1.0 percent or even upper 0.1 percent—and other earners, including other high-wage earners.
> Driving this ever widening gap is the unequal growth in earnings enjoyed by those at the top. The average annual earnings of the top 1 percent of wage earners grew 156 percent from 1979 to 2007; for the top 0.1 percent they grew 362 percent. In contrast, earners in the 90th to 95th percentiles had wage growth of 34 percent, less than a tenth as much as those in the top 0.1 percent tier. Workers in the bottom 90 percent had the weakest wage growth, at 17 percent from 1979 to 2007.[33]

The Economic Policy Institute report shows that the upward distribution of household income to the top 1 percent has undoubtedly been driven by huge wage disparity. As a result, the total share of income received by the top 1 percent more than doubled between 1979 and 2007, widening the chasm between those at the top and the rest of Americans. In 2007, the average annual income of the top 1 percent of households was 42 times larger than the average income of a household in the bottom 90 percent. In 1979, it was 14 times larger. An even starker illustration of the growth in income inequality is that in 2007, the average income of a household in the top 0.1 percent was 220 times larger than the average income of a household in the bottom 90 percent, compared to 47 times larger in 1979.

Who are the top earners? In a study released in 2012 by Jon Bakija and his colleagues, a broad range of professions are represented in the top 1 percent and the top 0.01 percent. There are the "superstars"—entrepreneurs (3.6 percent of the primary taxpayers in the top 1 percent of the distribution of income [including capital gains] that are in each occupation); entertainers, actors, athletes, authors, and musicians (3.1 percent); doctors (4.4 percent); lawyers (6.2 percent); and a handful of star university scientists and professors (1.1 percent). Income growth has been high for all top-earning professionals. But according to Bakija and colleagues, "60 percent of the increase in income accruing to the top percentile of income distribution" in the period 1979–2005 went to chief executives, managers, supervisors, and financial services professionals.[34]

In the United States today, the average ratio of CEO pay to that of the worker is 331 to 1. In Britain the ratio is 24 to 1; in France, 15 to 1; and in Sweden, 13 to 1.[35] It has been said that the CEO of Wal-Mart, Michael Duke, makes as much during his lunch hour as his employees earn in a year. Let us look at the numbers.

The average hourly wage of a Wal-Mart sales associate is between $8.53 and $11.75. If the sales associate works full-time, which is 34 hours a week at Wal-Mart, this translates into an annual salary of approximately $15,081 to $20,774. Far below the $23,550 the federal government considers necessary to be above the poverty line for a family of four in 2013. Wal-Mart CEO Michael Duke made $35 million that year. His hourly salary was $16,826.[36] In 2011, Apple's Tim Cook received $378 million in salary, stock, and other benefits. This was 6,258 times the wage of an average Apple employee.[37] The foremost observation that can be made about the present state of economic inequality therefore arises from this spectacular increase in the incomes of the top 1 percent, and even more stunningly in the incomes of the top 0.01 percent—the latter of which comprises a mere 15,000 families.

According to economist Emmanuel Saez, from 2009 to 2012, as the economy came out of the Great Recession of 2007–2009, average real family income grew modestly, by 6 percent. The gains, however, were distributed very unevenly. The incomes for the top 1 percent grew 31.4 percent, while the incomes for the bottom 99 percent grew by only 0.4 percent. An incredible 95 percent of income gains were captured by the top 1 percent.[38]

Emmanuel Saez and his fellow economist Thomas Piketty, who have become much sought after for their groundbreaking analysis of income inequality and have even received the John Bates Clark Medal, an economic equivalent to the Nobel Prize, refer to the rising incomes of the topmost income earners as the return of the Gilded Age. This trend has also become known as the Great U-Turn, in that top incomes, after rising relatively modestly between the New Deal years and those following World War II and the 1970s, have risen steeply since then, reminiscent of the era of the "roaring" 1920s (see Figure 2.6).[39]

The primary impetus for this super-concentration of income at the top is coming from the returns on capital investments such as real estate, stocks, and bonds, and from the ownership of the tangible forms of means of production such as factories, technology, and retail businesses, capital being any asset that generates a monetary return.

As Figure 2.6 shows, the process through which income inequality, after leveling off in the immediate post–World War II era, started to evolve, beginning in the 1970s, toward a precipitous and inexorable concentration in the hands of the richest segments of society, as seen in the income data gathered by the Internal Revenue Service and tabulated by Piketty and Saez.

When we consider the wealth distribution in the United States, we realize that it is even more skewed than income. Almost 85 percent of the

Figure 2.6 The Great U-Turn and the New Gilded Age, 1917–2012

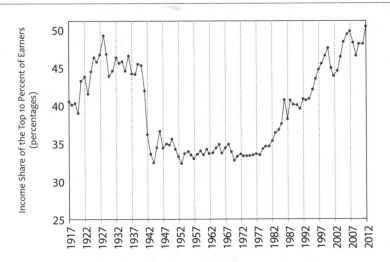

Source: Saez, "Striking It Richer: The Evolution of Top Incomes in the United States (Updated with 2012 Preliminary Estimates)," p. 8.

nation's net wealth is concentrated in the hands of the richest 20 percent, with the remaining 15 percent distributed among the bottom 80 percent, primarily wage and salary workers. Moreover, wealth inequality has increased sharply since 1980.

In *Who Rules America?* Domhoff explores the confluence of wealth, income, and power to answer the question he poses. Tables 2.3 and 2.4 and Figure 2.7, which illustrate the distribution of wealth in the United States, are borrowed from his treatise, in which he gives credit to New York University economist Edward Wolff for the latter's careful work in analyzing these data.

Table 2.3 Distribution of Net Worth in the United States, 1983–2010 (percentages)

Year	Top 1 Percent	Next 19 Percent	Bottom 80 Percent
1983	33.8	47.5	18.7
1989	37.4	46.2	16.5
1992	37.2	46.6	16.2
1995	38.5	45.4	16.1
1998	38.1	45.3	16.6
2001	33.4	51.0	15.6
2004	34.3	50.3	15.3
2007	34.6	50.5	15.0
2010	35.4	53.5	11.1

Source: Domhoff, "Wealth, Income, and Power."
Note: G. William Domhoff defines total net worth (assets) as the sum of: (1) the gross value of owner-occupied housing; (2) other real estate owned by the household; (3) cash and demand deposits; (4) time and savings deposits, certificates of deposit, and money market accounts; (5) government bonds, corporate bonds, foreign bonds, and other financial securities; (6) the cash surrender value of life insurance plans; (7) the cash surrender value of pension plans, including IRAs, Keogh, and 401(k) plans; (8) corporate stock and mutual funds; (9) net equity in unincorporated businesses; and (10) equity in trust funds.

Table 2.4 Distribution of Financial (Non-Home) Wealth in the United States, 1983–2010 (percentages)

Year	Top 1 Percent	Next 19 Percent	Bottom 80 Percent
1983	42.9	48.4	8.7
1989	46.9	46.5	6.6
1992	45.6	46.7	7.7
1995	47.2	45.9	7.0
1998	47.3	43.6	9.1
2001	39.7	51.5	8.7
2004	42.2	50.3	7.5
2007	42.7	50.3	7.0
2010	42.1	53.5	4.7

Source: Domhoff, "Wealth, Income, and Power."

Figure 2.7 Distribution of Net Worth and Financial Wealth in the United States, 2010

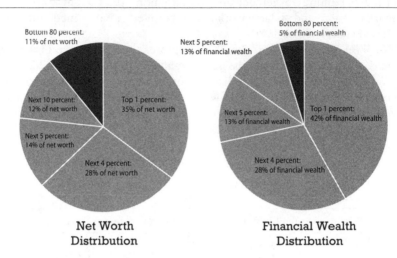

Net Worth
Distribution

Financial Wealth
Distribution

Source: Domhoff, "Wealth, Income, and Power."

The data we see here are staggering. As shown in Figure 2.7, the bottom 80 percent of Americans carry a net worth of only 11 percent of the total net worth in the United States, in comparison with the 35 percent carried by the top 1 percent. Even more shocking is the inequality in the ownership of financial wealth. The bottom 80 percent own barely 5 percent, whereas the top 1 percent own 42 percent. Thus almost half of all financial wealth is in the hands of the top 1 percent. What does this signify in terms of the power the top 1 percent wield over the lives of those whom they control through their ownership of income-producing financial assets and capital?

According to our earlier definition of class, a person's class is determined not just by their income or wealth but, more significantly, by their ownership or lack of ownership of the means of production or capital—the income-producing assets. Ownership of income-producing assets is fundamentally different, because it confers on the owners the privileges of controlling other people's lives. These are the assets that go into investments, which provide others with jobs and livelihoods, wages, and benefits.

By examining these numbers, Domhoff contends that, "in terms of types of financial wealth, the top one percent of households [have] 35% of all privately held stock, 64.4% of financial securities, and 62.4% of business equity. The top ten percent have 81% to 94% of stocks, bonds, trust funds, and business equity and almost 80% of non-home real estate. Since financial wealth is what counts as far as the control of income-producing assets, we can say that just 10% of the people own the United States of America."[40]

These numbers on income and wealth paint a picture of a grossly unequal society. It is a society made up of a small coterie of winners and a vast majority of those whose experience of the American Dream has been much less rewarding. As we look at this inequality from different perspectives, a clearer picture emerges of what it means to be an American in a nation venerated for being a land of opportunity and guaranteed upward mobility for those willing to work hard. Today, many of the people stuck in the middle face a future in which even basic economic security for their children seems uncertain, let alone the upward mobility taken for granted by past generations.

Inequality and Work

Economic security and the possibility of moving up the economic ladder— what sociologists refer to as **social mobility**—depend on the jobs that people have access to and how much they get paid for doing them. It is the work people do that determines their income and their life chances. Work is fundamental. And the reason people are falling off the economic ladder is simply because either they do not have jobs or their jobs do not pay adequately.

Jobs are created by individuals who own what Domhoff refers to as the income-producing assets—capital or the means of production. As much as we want to believe that in this free enterprise system anyone can start a business and be their own boss, the reality is that almost 90 percent of Americans must depend on someone else to give them a means of livelihood.

The number of small businesses in the United States has fallen over the years. So it is those at the top who own the lion's share of the financial resources, who create jobs on which people's livelihoods and well-being depend. And those at the top are not duty-bound to keep the well-being of the American people in mind when they make critical decisions regarding how they plan to invest their money.

Yet as the number of small, independent businesses keeps falling, as the government—the public sector—hires fewer people than it did in the 1960s and 1970s, and in the absence of New Deal–type job programs, Americans depend more and more on the private sector for their livelihoods.[41] And since 1980 the private sector is where the jobs have been lost, as financial capital roams the world to find the most profitable niches.

The concentration of income, together with the wide gap between the lowest and highest quintiles, needs to be seen in this context of a precipitous decline in jobs and wages among large segments of the population. According to the US Census Bureau

- In 2010, in the Midwestern states, joblessness in manufacturing and construction was the main reason for income decline and poverty, while in the Western states the decline came primarily from the collapse of the housing industry. In every region of the country, joblessness in general fueled the income decline.
- In 2010, about 48 million people aged eighteen to sixty-four did not work at all. In 2009, that number was 45 million.
- Between 2007 and 2010, the number of men working full-time, year-round, decreased by 6.6 million, and the number of women working full-time, year-round, decreased by 2.8 million.
- Between 2010 and 2011, changes in the share of aggregate household income by quintile indicated an increase in inequality, and a growing gap between the very top and the very bottom of the income ladder.[42]

As of January 2013, unemployment in the United States stood at 7.9 percent. But when those who have stopped looking for work, or who work part-time jobs when they want full-time jobs, are added in, the figure rises to 14.4 percent—a number that represents 22 million Americans.[43] The wealthy continue to benefit from booms in the stock market, even as unemployment continues to hold down the income of the great majority of wage earners, with "high unemployment depressing wage growth throughout the wage scale."[44]

How Many Are Poor?

The US Census Bureau placed the official poverty rate in 2010 at 15.1 percent, up from 14.3 percent in 2009. In 2010, 46.2 million people were living beneath the poverty line, up from 43.6 million in 2009. The total number of people living in poverty as of 2010 is the largest number in the fifty-two years for which poverty estimates have been published. The number has increased steadily since 2007.[45]

The Census Bureau's Report on Poverty

The following summarizes the main findings that the Census Bureau reported regarding the characteristics of poverty and the poor in the U.S in 2010.[46]

- Between 2007 and 2010, the poor became not just more numerous but also poorer, with 44.3 percent of them, or about 20.5 million, living in extreme poverty.

- Poverty has risen acutely among single mothers. More than 40 percent of the households headed by women now live below the poverty threshold—$22,050 for a family of four as of 2010. The rise is partly attributed, by many analysts, to the changes in the welfare system enacted by the 1996 Personal Responsibility and Work Opportunity Reconciliation Act, which ended "welfare as we know it" and made the system much more restrictive, requiring clients to work just as jobs were disappearing.
- Without food stamps, there would be 3.9 million more Americans living in poverty.
- Since January 2008, there has been a 64 percent rise in the number of people receiving food stamps. As of 2010, 45 million Americans receive food stamps—one in eight adults and one in four children—and there are 16.4 million children living in poverty, the highest number since 1962. The number of people receiving food stamps represents a 70 percent increase since 2007.
- In 2010, blacks experienced the highest poverty rate of any race, at 27 percent, up from 25 percent in 2009. The poverty rate for Hispanics was 26 percent, up from 25 percent, and for whites it was 9.9 percent, up from 9.4 percent.
- The poverty rate in suburbs, which have traditionally had the lowest rates of poverty in the country, experienced a sharp increase between 2001 and 2010, from 8 percent to 12 percent, much of it due to rising unemployment in the service, retail, and construction industries.
- The overall poverty numbers would be higher if President Barack Obama's stimulus bill did not provide cash benefits and tax credits.
- The main reason why so many are poor in the United States is because of joblessness. If the financial recession continues and jobs continue to be lost, then by 2015 there will be 10 million more individuals among the ranks of the poor.

The Official Poverty Measure

The numbers released by the Census Bureau reflect the use of the **official poverty measure** to determine how many in the United States are poor. This measure was developed in 1963 by Social Security Administration economist and statistician Mollie Orshansky, at a time when there was growing unease over the persistent poverty present in the midst of the affluence of the post–World War II period. In 1959, the poverty rate for the nation stood at 22 percent and the poverty rate for African Americans at a staggering 55 percent.

President Lyndon Johnson's war on poverty aimed at ameliorating the causes and symptoms of poverty by confronting it on many levels. In 1964 he signed the Economic Opportunity Act, which sought to address poverty at its very roots. Head Start, food stamps, Medicare/Medicaid, and the Fair Housing Act were the signature initiatives through which Johnson challenged the nation to raise a "Great Society" that would enable everyone, even the poor, to access the good life.

In 1970, the poverty rate dropped to 12 percent for all Americans and to 22 percent for African Americans. The Great Society proponents attributed the drop to the initiatives integral to the war on poverty, which were instrumental in encouraging economic growth and in moving people out of poverty.[47]

Two Ways of Looking at Poverty

In order to understand how poverty is measured, it is important to consider the two ways in which sociologists have described poverty—or to put it another way, the two dimensions of poverty: **absolute poverty** and **relative poverty**. A person is absolutely poor when deprived of the very basic means of survival—food, clothing, shelter. The stark images of hunger, disease, and despondency that one regularly comes across in the publicity material of the ever-mushrooming charities for Africans (outside the United States) are images of absolute, desperate poverty.

A person is relatively poor when their life does not measure up to the standards of living of their society—both real and assumed. If eating three meals daily is the convention of a society, a person who can afford to eat only once daily is considered to be relatively poor. If having a home, a decent place to live, is what everyone expects to have, then one is poor when he or she has a difficult time securing this. When having a car is considered the norm, not having one makes a person relatively poor. In the United States, most poverty is relative in nature.

Absolute, grinding poverty has been largely averted with the help of government programs such as the Supplemental Nutrition Assistance Program (SNAP), previously known as food stamps, and private charity. But among the relatively poor, there are still those who suffer hunger, whose children go to bed hungry on a daily basis. Their hunger is not abject like it is in the midst of a famine in the **third world**, but it is there snuffing out the human potential of many. In 2010, 48.8 million Americans, representing 16.1 percent of the US population, lived in food-insecure households, meaning they were hungry or faced food insecurity at some point during the year.[48]

In *Development as Freedom,* Nobel Laureate economist Amartya Sen compares African Americans with people from other countries, with respect to income and mortality rates, by focusing on the concepts of absolute and relative deprivation.[49] His analysis of the data shows that in the United States, blacks have a lower per capita income than whites. But at the same time, they are richer in terms of income than people in China, or Indians who reside in the southern state of Kerala.

But men in China or Kerala outlive African American men by many years, surviving to old age. Black men in New York City, San Francisco, St. Louis, and Washington, D.C., live fewer years than their counterparts in many third world countries. Even a Bangladeshi man, living in one of the poorest countries in the world, has a better chance of living beyond forty years of age than does a black man in inner-city America.

Sen concludes that African American men might be relatively deprived in terms of making less money than American whites. But African American men are absolutely deprived in comparison with low-income Indians, Chinese, and Bangladeshis, who live much longer than African Americans.

How Is the Poverty Line or Threshold Calculated?

When Orshansky developed the official poverty measure, she took into consideration both the absolute and relative dimensions of poverty. She calculated the price of a nutritionally minimum market basket of food—what individuals and families absolutely need to live for one year. She calculated this by looking at the relative price of a market basket of food purchased by fifty-eight types of American families, in order to determine a nutritional average. She then multiplied this by three, since, on average, food expenses in the United States consume one-third of a family's total income. The other two-thirds would allow for expenditures on other goods and services. This gave her the official poverty measure, and individuals and families who fell below this line or threshold were considered poor. In 1963, when the official poverty measure was first released, it was $3,128 for a family of four. In 2012, adjusted for inflation, it was $23,050.

This way of measuring poverty has been criticized as not reflecting the changing lifestyles and spending patterns of American families. As early as the spring of 1995, the National Academy of Sciences, in a report on a new approach to measuring poverty, identified several major weaknesses of the official poverty measure. The report indicated that among other weaknesses, the measure did not show how a family's disposable income increased with public benefit programs such as the federal earned income tax credit (EITC), food stamps, subsidized housing, and home energy assistance; or how a family's disposable income decreased when income taxes, Social Security payroll tax, child care, transportation for getting to work, health insurance premiums, and medical out-of-pocket (MOOP) costs were subtracted.[50]

In 2011, the Census Bureau took a major step in correcting the imperfections of the traditional poverty measure. At the urging of the Obama administration, the Census Bureau created the **supplemental poverty**

measure. The threshold for this measure of poverty in 2010 was $24,343 for a family of four, as opposed to the $22,113 threshold according to the official poverty measure. By this gauge, 49.1 million Americans, or 16 percent of the population, lived in poverty in November 2011, as opposed to 46.6 million according to the official poverty measure. Thus poverty rates were higher using the supplemental poverty measure compared with the official poverty measure.[51]

The Census Bureau continues to use the official poverty measure, however, in calculating the number of poor in the United States. Table 2.5 outlines a tabulation of what the supplemental poverty measure adds and subtracts to calculate the poverty threshold.

Social Inequality and Social Mobility

Is the United States still a land of opportunity? Is it possible for ordinary Americans to move up the proverbial ladder? Can parents still expect their children to have a better life compared to themselves? These questions are integral to our inquiry into **intergenerational social mobility**—or a child's chance of moving up the income distribution scale relative to his or her parents. There are two ways of looking at intergenerational mobility. It can be absolute or relative.

Absolute intergenerational mobility measures whether a person is making more money, living in a nicer house, enjoying more vacations, and so forth, than their parents did at the same age. This is referred to as the **income-based measure of social mobility**. In contrast, relative intergenerational mobility measures which rung of the income ladder a person lands on compared to their parents. If each rung on a ladder represents a different quintile or percentile, then which quintile or percentile does the son or

Table 2.5 What the Supplemental Poverty Measure Adds and Subtracts to Calculate the Poverty Threshold

Adds:	Subtracts:
Supplemental Nutrition Assistance Program (SNAP)	Taxes (plus credits such as the earned income tax credit [EITC])
National School Lunch Program	Expenses related to work
Supplementary Nutrition Program for Women, Infants, and Children (WIC)	Child-care expenses
Housing subsidies	Medical out-of-pocket (MOOP) expenses
Low-Income Home Energy Assistance Program (LIHEAP)	Child support paid

Source: Short, "The Research: Supplemental Poverty Measure: 2010."
Note: Supplemental poverty measure resources include money income from all sources.

daughter land on relative to their parents? This is referred to as the **rank-based measure of social mobility**.

Based on rank-based studies, intergenerational social mobility has remained unchanged, meaning that children remain in the same class they were born into. This is often referred to as the "sticky-top/sticky-bottom" phenomenon. Generation after generation, those at the top and those at the bottom remain at the top and bottom. It is a constant replaying of the **birth lottery**.[52]

Sociologist Charles Tilly attributes this fact of **durable inequality** to the options that people in the top income distribution have for **opportunity hoarding**. The tools needed to climb to the next rung of the ladder—higher education, high-paying jobs, access to a social network of people with influence, political clout—are all distorted in favor of the powerful.[53]

Inequality has increased because the incomes of the top 1 percent have skyrocketed. But for the bottom 99 percent, the children are still languishing at more or less the same income levels as those of their parents, because ultimately a "child's income depends more heavily on her parents' position in the income distribution today than in the past."[54] There is no getting around the influence of one's "birth lottery."

Conclusion

The numbers explored here present a disturbing picture of inequality in the United States today. The entire story hinges on the fundamental fact that individuals at the top of the income and wealth distribution have an unparalleled hold on the lives of other people—and not just lives of Americans, but also, due to economic globalization, the lives of people around the world. American and European dominance over the world is rooted in this essential fact. Access to vast financial assets gives individuals the power and resources to influence the political realm and the decisions made there.

The inequality that we see in the United States today is the fallout from all this. This inequality enmeshes the common man and common woman in a socioeconomic reality that determines their ability to life, liberty, and the pursuit of happiness. Yet they have very little control over this reality.

Notes

1. Fukuyama, "The End of History."
2. Moller, Alderson, and Nielsen, "Changing Patterns of Income Inequality," p. 1038.
3. Organization for Economic Cooperation and Development, "Growing Unequal?"

4. Moller, Alderson, and Nielsen, "Changing Patterns of Income Inequality," pp. 1048–1049.

5. Cassidy, "Forces of Divergence," p. 70.

6. Piketty and Saez, "Income Inequality in the United States," p. 5.

7. Lowrey, "Top 10% Took Home Half of U.S. Income," p. B4; Saez, "Striking It Richer."

8. Lowrey, "Top 10% Took Home Half of U.S. Income," p. B4.

9. Kristof, "It's Now the Canadian Dream," p. A29. See also Krugman, "Now That's Rich"; Stevenson, "Hedge Fund Moguls' Pay Has 1% Looking Up."

10. Silver-Greenberg and Schwartz, "Citigroup's Chief Rebuffed on Pay By Shareholders," p. A1.

11. Wilson, *The Truly Disadvantaged.*

12. Murray, *Coming Apart.*

13. Giridharadas, "The Immigrant Advantage," p. SR5.

14. Stille, "The Paradox of the New Elite," p. 1.

15. Tavernise, "Survey Finds Rising Strain Between Rich and Poor," p. A15.

16. I owe this very important clarification to one of my anonymous reviewers.

17. Ibid.

18. US Census Bureau, "About Income," http://www.census.gov/hhes/www/income/about/index.html (accessed April 23, 2012); Denavas-Walt, Proctor, and Smith, "Income, Poverty, and Health Insurance Coverage in the United States: 2010," p. 2. Piketty and Saez, "Income Inequality in the United States," p. 5.

19. Piketty and Saez, "Income Inequality in the United States," p. 5.

20. Denavas-Walt, Proctor, and Smith, "Income, Poverty, and Health Insurance Coverage in the United States: 2010," p. 10; Piketty and Saez, "Income Inequality in the United States," p. 5.

21. Levine, "The U.S. Income Distribution and Mobility."

22. Ibid., pp. 38, 42.

23. US Census Bureau, "State and County QuickFacts," http://quickfacts.census.gov/qfd/meta/long_INC110212.htm (accessed October 22, 2014).

24. Ibid.

25. Denavas-Walt, Proctor, and Smith, "Income, Poverty, and Health Insurance Coverage in the United States: 2011," p. 5.

26. Harrington, *The Other America,* pp. 1–2.

27. Nasar, "Even Among the Well-Off," p. A1.

28. Johnston, "The Gap Between Rich and Poor," p. A14.

29. Lowrey, "Even Among the Richest," p. F2.

30. Rattner, "The Rich Get Even Richer," p. A27.

31. Lowrey, "Even Among the Richest," p. F2.

32. Domhoff, "Wealth, Income, and Power."

33. Mishel and Sabadish, "CEO Pay and the Top 1%."

34. Bakija, Cole, and Heim, "Jobs and Income Growth of Top Earners," pp. 2, 34. See also Lowrey, "Even Among the Richest."

35. Hill, *Europe's Promise,* p. 99.

36. Nation Action, "Tell CEO Mike Duke"; Gomstyn, "Walmart CEO Pay."

37. Cassidy, "Forces of Divergence," p. 70.

38. Saez, "Striking It Richer," p. 6.

39. Saez, "Striking It Richer" (2009), p. 7.

40. Domhoff, "Wealth, Income, and Power."

41. Magdoff and Foster, "Class War and Labor's Declining Share," p. 1.

42. DeNavas-Walt, Proctor, and Smith, "Income, Poverty, and Health Insurance Coverage in the United States: 2010."

43. Ibid., p. 1.

44. Lowrey, "Income Flat in Recovery," p. B1.

45. DeNavas-Walt, Proctor, and Smith, "Income, Poverty, and Health Insurance Coverage in the United States: 2010," p. 14.

46. Ibid.

47. Germany, "War on Poverty."

48. Shepard, Setren, and Cooper, "Hunger in America."

49. Sen, *Development and Freedom,* pp. 21–24.

50. Short, "The Research: Supplemental Poverty Measure," p. 4.

51. Ibid., p. 5.

52. Chetty et al., "Is the United States Still a Land of Opportunity?" p. 1.

53. Tilly, *Durable Inequality;* Reeves, "The Glass Floor Problem."

54. Chetty et al., "Is the United States Still a Land of Opportunity?" p. 3.

3

How Inequality
Shapes Life Chances

THE POOR HAVE ALWAYS BEEN WITH US—SOMETIMES VISIBLY, BUT most often invisibly. In India, where I was born, poverty is present everywhere and is undeniable. The poor are as much a part of the social fabric as are the middle class and the affluent. Since residential segregation by class is not as severe in India as in the United States the poor can often be found sleeping on the pavement in front of the mansions of the super-rich.

In the United States, poverty is out of sight, giving credence to beliefs that in this ostensibly middle-class country, poverty is an exception and not the common experience of millions. Concealed in racially segregated communities, in rural America, in mining towns of the Appalachia, in Native American reservations, in the barrios of the migrant workers, poverty exists away from the public eye.

When the poor and homeless make their appearance on the urban streets, they simply reinforce the tenets of the dominant ideology, which posits that all success and failure is dependent on the individual. For example, it is superficially easy, but ultimately disingenuous, to attribute poverty to the substance abuse and mental illness that afflict so many of the poor rather than acknowledge the underlying, structural causes that lead to poverty in the first place. The true reality of being poor in the United States is therefore cloaked in ways that diminish its magnitude.

German sociologist Max Weber, in his book *The Protestant Ethic and the Spirit of Capitalism,* refers to the chances an individual has to attain a certain quality of life as being determined by the individual's access to critical resources such as food, shelter, education, employment, health care, and social capital. In this chapter, therefore, I consider the essential provisions and conditions that are critical in determining a person's quality of life. I examine the distribution and quality of these life-chance variables—housing, health, and education in particular—and how they affect the quality of communities where people live. I also consider the degree of accessibility to affordable transportation and mass transit and how this affects the economic prospects of a community. And how all of this cumulatively impacts the availability of support networks, or **social capital**.

Additionally for the poor—and increasingly for those in the middle class—teetering on the margins in these times of economic uncertainty, government income-transfer programs have become critical. These safety-net programs are in continuous danger of being dismantled as a result of rising deficits in federal and state budgets.

Poverty and inequality are felt in multiple dimensions in people's lived realities and life chances. Thus a true appreciation of what inequality and poverty entail requires not just an awareness of numbers, but an aggregate understanding of what the numbers mean in terms of what people have, what they don't, and how all of this all-encompassingly constructs the social context in which individuals and communities live.

Is your housing situation secure? Can you afford groceries? Do you feed your family with the cheapest fast food? Can you afford prescription medication?[1] Can you afford to shop at Whole Foods? Can you open your bedroom window and breathe clean air? If you must visit a social services department to update your personal information so you can continue to receive benefits, does the person working there intimidate you, embarrass you, and insult you? Are you disregarding the persistent pain in your back because you have no job, and therefore no health insurance? Do you lie awake at night worrying how you will be able to take care of your family when your unemployment check runs out after six months? Do you wake at dawn every morning to take public transportation to work, paying as much in the process of getting to your job as you make from your job?

There was a time when the middle class was a secure place to be. Most people hoped they would retire with a comfortable pension and watch their children reap the fruits of a thriving economy. Most people believed that things could and would only get better.

But where is that security today? Are you sure that your job as a systems engineer won't get outsourced to India? Or be given instead to five bright-eyed, tech-savvy immigrants from China—brought to the United States on a preferred visa arrangement, and grateful to work for one-fifth of your salary? What if your job is eliminated, so that a machine can do it at a fraction of the cost? If any of these scenarios comes true, how will you pay your mortgage? Your daughter's college tuition? How will you keep up with your car payments, let alone car repairs? Do you have sufficient savings to last until your unemployment insurance runs out? Where will you find another job? Will the provisions of the Affordable Care Act suffice to meet your health needs, especially if you have a chronic health problem that requires long-term medication? How will your son pay off his college debt if, after graduation, he can find only a minimum-wage job? What if your 401(k) savings are wiped out because your financial institution gambled with the money? There might seem to be no end to such worries given the reality of an unforgiving economy hanging over our heads like the sword of Damocles.

Homeownership and the Housing Crisis

In a country where the social construction of being an American is so tied up with homeownership, which "is indicative of both individual prosperity and good citizenship,"[2] the 2008 housing foreclosure crisis not only is emblematic of a deepening economic divide, but also can be seen as an impasse in the ideological underpinnings of an economic system that has been fabled as fair and rewarding of hard work and enterprise.

After peaking at 69 percent in the fourth quarter of 2004, homeownership rates in the United States for the fourth quarter of 2011 dropped to 66 percent. Also in 2011, 81 percent of those with a family income greater than or equal to the median income ($50,054) owned homes, compared to 51 percent of those earning less than the median family income. Much of this decline can be attributed to the unprecedented levels of mortgage default and foreclosure that epitomized the 2008 recession.[3]

The signs that a crisis in the housing market was brewing were evident in a report published by the US Department of Housing and Urban Development (HUD) in May 2005. The report discussed the 6–10 percent increase in house prices, more than twice the rate of inflation and far in excess of income increases for individuals and households. The report also noted that despite these price increases and stalled incomes, home sales incongruently remained strong, with the homeownership rate at a historical high of 69 percent. Given that the high prices of homes seemingly could not be explained by income growth, the report wondered "whether the prices [might] have been boosted by speculation to 'bubble' levels,"[4] and how the inflated prices might eventually impact household wealth, consumer spending, and borrowing.

What Created the Bubble and How Did It Burst?

The 1933 Glass-Steagall Act separated regular, everyday banks from investment banks in order to protect people's bank accounts from risky investments. The act was passed by Congress to rein in the ability of commercial banks to use depositors' money for speculative investment—reckless behavior that precipitated the stock market crash of 1929. The Glass-Steagall Act ensured that even as big banks pursued record profits, they would have to follow rules designed to protect consumers from financial ruin.

In 1999, however, Congress gave in to the increasing clamor for "deregulation" from the big banks and other financial giants and repealed the Glass-Steagall Act. Soon after, as the protections the act had offered to depositors and consumers were eliminated, the banks went back to their rash, risky, and often predatory ways.

By 2000, their actions had created an artificial economic bubble by driving up house prices to unprecedented levels and luring first-time home-owners, often minorities, by offering them high-risk mortgages at subprime rates. Contrary to conventional wisdom, subprime rates were higher than the interest rates of traditional mortgage loans and, furthermore, were designed to increase periodically after an interval of years. Often, the first-time home buyer either was unaware of this stipulation or did not fully comprehend its implications. Therefore, as the economy started to falter and people lost jobs and their incomes, they could not keep up with their mortgage payments, triggering the historic foreclosure crisis of 2008 and the economic meltdown that accompanied it.

It was a confluence of several conditions that caused the housing bubble to burst, starting in 2007:

- Home prices were increasing at record-high rates.
- High-cost, risky subprime loans constituted a large share of the mortgage market.
- Foreclosures among prime fixed-rate loans rose dramatically as the economy deteriorated in 2008 and into 2009.
- Delinquency and foreclosure rates accelerated among Alt-A loans, another fast-growing segment of the mortgage market.
- Banks and their agents made high profits at every stage of the loan approval process, leading to much of the surge in subprime lending.
- The flow of capital from lenders and investors pursuing high profits poured into ever-riskier loans, particularly after 2003. In a 2010 report to Congress on the root causes of foreclosures, authors Christopher Herbert and William Apgar write: "This flood of capital helped to spur rising home prices that masked the riskiness of the loans being made, and [led] to continued loosening of underwriting standards. When house price growth finally slowed in late 2006, the true nature of these risky loans was exposed and the 'house of cards' came tumbling down."[5]
- Unemployment, which was dramatically on the rise most prominently in the industrial states of the Midwest (Illinois, Indiana, Michigan, and Ohio), often precipitated homeowners' vulnerability by taking away their incomes.

What Are Subprime and Alt-A Loans?

A subprime loan is one that is offered to individuals who do not qualify for prime fixed-rate loans. Quite often, subprime borrowers are turned away from traditional lenders because of their low credit ratings, limited credit histories, or other factors that suggest they might default on debt repayment. Subprime loans tend to have a higher interest rate than the prime rate offered on traditional loans. The additional percentage points of interest often translate to tens of thousands of dollars' worth of additional interest payments over the life of a longer-term loan.[6]

Minorities are overrepresented in the subprime lending market. Even upper-income African American neighborhoods have more individuals carrying subprime loans compared to persons in low-income white neighborhoods. According to HUD reports, lenders target minority neighborhoods and steer borrowers toward loans they cannot afford.[7]

Alt-A(or Alternative-A) are loans made to borrowers who are unwilling or unable to provide full documentation on their mortgage application because they are self-employed with variable incomes or operating cash businesses. These loans also entail other features that may expose borrowers to large increases in loan payments over time. Alt-A loans are attractive to lenders because they carry higher interest rates compared to prime mortgages.[8]

The foreclosure crisis and the conditions that bred it have become the hallmarks of the economic downturn and deepening inequality that the United States continues to suffer. Many of the people who fell off the economic ladder were those who faced foreclosure of their homes, often precipitated by job loss and subsequent default on high-risk, high-cost subprime and Alt-A mortgages.

MAKING CONNECTIONS
Not Without a Fight

On May 2, 2012, New Jersey's Coalition to Save Our Homes sent out an urgent notice to all its fraternal organizations, labor unions, activists, and community groups. In the city of Orange, in Essex County, Susie Johnson, an eighty-year-old disabled grandmother, was facing illegal eviction from her home of many years. On May 10, the Essex County sheriff's office served Johnson the eviction papers, and all her worldly belongings were removed from her home and put to the curb. There was something terribly wrong, since Johnson had always paid her mortgage ontime to HomeSide Lending, the bank that serviced her loan.

What transpired in Johnson's case was a dizzying series of events that ultimately threatened her with imminent loss of her home through foreclosure. In August 2002, Washington Mutual acquired the mortgage portfolio of HomeSide Lending, and in March 2003, Johnson was notified that Washington Mutual would now be servicing her loan. Washington Mutual also notified Johnson that she was in default due to nonpayment of her mortgage since October 2002.

(continues)

Not Without a Fight

When Johnson denied missing any payments, the bank asked her to send in copies of receipts. She provided the bank with all her money order receipts and also sent the bank her payments for February and March 2003. In June 2003, Washington Mutual instituted foreclosure proceedings against Johnson, claiming delinquency back to January 2003. She made many attempts to reconcile the huge misunderstanding that was snowballing beyond her control. When all appeals failed, Johnson, at her wits' end, felt she had no recourse but to file for bankruptcy. It was now 2008.

In September 2008, Washington Mutual—the nation's largest savings and loan association—collapsed and was immediately acquired by JP Morgan Chase. In the spring of 2012, Johnson was informed by the Essex County sheriff's office that she would be evicted on May 12. When JP Morgan Chase was approached about the matter, the bank denied having any role in the impending eviction. It was difficult to single out who was driving the inexorable eviction process.

On the morning of May 10, 2012, after the Coalition to Save Our Homes had publicized the notice of the foreclosure and eviction against Johnson, thirty-five activists showed up in front of her house and laid themselves prone upon the street to stop the eviction. The coalition enlisted a pro bono lawyer to investigate Johnson's situation. The lawyer discovered that the original loan document was in the name of John Stolarenko, president of Eastwood Mortgage Bankers, who by this time had been tried and convicted of mortgage fraud. Because of the fraudulent nature of the original title, all later claims to it were invalid. JP Morgan Chase denied that it had ever serviced the loan or played any role in the eviction, claiming it had no paperwork on Johnson. Without the thirty-five brave souls who laid down their bodies on the street to stop the illegal eviction, who knows what might have become of Susie Johnson.

In investigating what happened to Johnson and others like her, the activists were able to obtain a glimpse into the murky, unscrupulous world of the banks and lenders who had caused the housing bubble through their unrealistic overvaluation of home prices every time new mortgages were negotiated, or were refinanced, or changed hands, as the banks merged. That is what happened to Johnson, who like most average Americans wasn't savvy enough to understand the small print or keep track of the complex and often fraudulent ways in which the mortgage business was being conducted—making them vulnerable even when playing by the rules.

Affordable Housing

In communities across the United States, there is also a crisis in securing affordable housing for renting. The emphasis on ownership, along with public policies that encourage homeownership—such as the home mortgage interest deduction from taxable income—weakens the rental market. Rental units dwindle as more and more units are converted into properties for sale. There is a scarcity of rental apartments and homes to begin with, and when one considers the question of affordability, the pool shrinks even smaller.

Affordable housing refers to rental housing units that are affordable for households with incomes under a specified limit. A unit is considered affordable when a household can rent it without spending more than 30 percent of its income on housing and utility costs. When there are more renter households than affordable rental housing units, serious crisis can ensue, often leading to homelessness. As more and more people experience job loss, foreclosure, and growing poverty—and market forces simultaneously drive rents higher—the shortage of affordable housing takes on critical proportions.

In 2010, according to the National Low Income Housing Coalition:[9]

- There were approximately 40 million renter households.
- The median income of households receiving HUD assistance was $10,200, or 17 percent of the median national income.
- Approximately 9.8 million HUD clients, or 72 percent of total HUD clients, had incomes that HUD classified as extremely low, defined as 30 percent of the median income for the county or metropolitan area in which one lives.
- For every 100 renter households classified as having an extremely low income, only 30 affordable housing units were available for rent.
- For every 100 renter households classified as having a very low income, defined as 31–50 percent of the median income for the county or metropolitan area, only 58 affordable housing units were available for rent.
- For every 100 renter households classified as having a low income, defined as 51–80 percent of the median income for the county or metropolitan area, 98 affordable housing units were available for rent.

Thus, in each of HUD's low-income categories, housing demand exceeds housing supply. This severe deficiency can be attributed to high rents, affordable units being occupied by higher-income renters, landlords not honoring rental assistance subsidies, and affordable units being in poor condition or far from jobs and transportation. Therefore, in circumstances of such insufficiency, a family wanting to avoid homelessness must secure a rental costing much more than what they can afford. As a consequence, almost three-fourths of households with extremely low income are left with less than 50 percent of their income to take care of all other costs after they have paid for rent and utilities.

In 2012 as in years past, "Out of Reach," the annual report of the National Low Income Housing Coalition, speaks to a fundamental truth:

A mismatch exists between the cost of living, the availability of rental assistance and the wages people earn day to day across the country.

With the number of low income renters on the rise, the argument for sustaining affordable housing assistance is timely.

- In 2012, a household must earn the equivalent of $37,960 in annual income to afford the national average two-bedroom Fair Market Rent of $949 per month.
- Assuming full-time, year-round employment, this translates into a national Housing Wage of $18.25 in 2012.
- This year the housing wage exceeds the average renter wage, $14.15, by over four dollars and is nearly three times the minimum wage.[10]

Much of why we have a housing crisis, therefore, is because working men and women do not make enough in salaries and wages to pay rent and utilities. Their wages are out of sync with the cost of housing and fair-market rent.

HUD's rental-housing assistance programs—privately owned subsidized housing, public housing, and housing-choice voucher programs (Section 8) that are administered through local public housing agencies and property owners—make housing affordable for 4.5 million low-income households. Still, as HUD's own findings indicate, in many communities around the country the supply of affordable units is grossly inadequate and many families go without assistance.

HUD's mission to provide "affordable rental homes in safe, mixed income communities that provide access to jobs, good schools, transportation, high quality services, and, most importantly, economic self-sufficiency"[11] underpins its rental-housing assistance programs and seems well-meaning and sincere. If the intentions asserted were in fact implemented to their fullest extent—with full revenue support—the housing situation in the United States would not be as dire.

However, in the face of unprecedented deficits in federal and state budgets, it is not surprising that deep cuts have been made in HUD's budget. There was an overall reduction of 9 percent in the 2012 budget, with much larger cuts to several affordable-housing and community development programs. The reduction in the 2012 budget came at a time when significant cuts over the preceding decade had already exposed low-income households to further-deteriorating living conditions and the threat of displacement from their homes. The cuts can also result in further loss of construction jobs, and increased risk of neighborhood blight as living conditions deteriorate and public housing renovation and development are abandoned.[12]

The Renter Eviction Crisis

Connie Pascale works for the Legal Services of New Jersey and has dedicated his life to advocating for the legal and civil rights of the poor. His battle has primarily been in the area of affordable-housing advocacy. Since

1985, he has argued that the problem of homelessness is rooted in the absence of affordable housing. It is Pascale who brought to my attention the work of sociologist Matthew Desmond, who studies poverty, housing, and eviction as formidable forces in the lives of the poor, particularly residents of segregated inner cities.

In introducing me to the work of Desmond, Pascale wrote:

> There are more than 170,000 eviction cases filed in NJ every year, while there are 1.06 million renter households. This means that nearly 1 in 6 tenants face eviction every year, and that only represents cases actually filed. The often tragic consequences for households and children—both personal and economic—are described in the article. (The worst form of discrimination against prospective tenants today is based solely upon their being named in an eviction action, whether they win the case or not.)
>
> This "eviction crisis" in NJ—which dwarfs the foreclosure crisis in terms of numbers of people affected—is largely ignored because it is primarily seen as a problem of low-income people and people of color. Just like eminent domain was no problem when it was called "urban renewal" and decimated poor minority neighborhoods. Eminent domain only became a "crisis" when the property of a middle-class white family was taken.[13]

Desmond's research shows just how common evictions are in the lives of poor people, particularly in lives of poor women. In Milwaukee, which the US Census Bureau lists as the nation's second most segregated city (Detroit being first), where Desmond has been conducting ethnographic research since 2008, he found that one in fourteen renting households are evicted every year.

This number does not include the numerous informal evictions that take place when landlords are unwilling to pay the legal fees and hourly charges for the eviction squads that accompany formal eviction processes. Those evicted end up in shelters or on the streets. Having a record of eviction makes it very difficult for individuals to find future rentals. The tremendous uncertainty that results affects both adults and children in grievous ways—poor performance in schools, depression, material hardship, and job loss. Desmond writes that eviction becomes

> not just a condition but also a cause of poverty. . . . If incarceration has become typical in the lives of men from impoverished black neighborhoods, eviction has become typical in the lives of women from these neighborhoods. Typical yet damaging, the consequences of eviction are many and severe: it often increases material hardship, decreases residential security, and brings about prolonged periods of homelessness, and can result in job loss, separation of families, and depression or even to suicide.[14]

Desmond attributes the high rates of eviction to the acute shortage of affordable housing, coupled with the almost 70 percent increase in median rents nationwide since 1997, adjusted for inflation. Neither the minimum wage nor welfare payments have kept up with this surge in rents.

MAKING CONNECTIONS

Tent Cities

Living today in the Tent City homeless encampment in Lakewood, New Jersey, are about 115 individuals—adult men and women who represent a segment of society besieged by problems, each intractable in its own way. These men and women are a microcosm of such populations throughout the country in places where economic issues combine with mental health problems and addiction problems to make finding solutions a Herculean task. They carry with them visible and invisible signs of physical and mental abuse, and often seek escape from the damage in drugs and alcohol. Considered either dangerous or eyesores, they are ostracized by the communities in which they find themselves.

These are people who have fallen through the cracks of a convoluted system of social services in which $6 million is spent every year to house people in motels. Yet Ocean County, where Tent City is located, has no homeless shelter nor any plan for permanent low-cost housing. In Tent City, Steven Brigham, a minister, has given each homeless dweller a tent in a clearing in the middle of a pine forest. Local do-gooders bring them food, water, and clothes. This is how they have survived since 2006. But this is not a solution.

The complex array of services these people require to be able to function in society, on their own, just do not exist in Ocean County. Their addictions and mental instabilities cloud their judgment and ostracize them from society at large. It is difficult to garner support to continue what Tent City does when individuals are seen as being responsible for their own predicament. Advocates implore that an assortment of services are needed to enable these homeless to survive with a modicum of dignity, regardless of whether or not they are ever able to become productive members of society.

If tent cities across the country are the only places where these individuals can stay, then the mental health services, drug and alcohol rehabilitation services, vocational and job-training services, and health-care services need to come to them. But there is deep resentment at giving the homeless handouts of what the rest of society must work for—though there is very little outrage at the millions of dollars wasted on nightly housing in pest-infested motel rooms, where drug abuse is rampant.

Tent City has saved millions of taxpayer dollars, as the kindness and compassion of the larger Ocean County community has enabled it to take care of hundreds of homeless men and women—evidence that, with a little imagination and support, these communities can become healthy and life-sustaining places where even deeply troubled souls can live with security and dignity. But this is a hard point to sell when the entire experiment is regarded as having no commercial value or outcome.

Homelessness

According to the National Alliance to End Homelessness, on any given night in 2011, more than 636,000 people experienced homelessness (sheltered or unsheltered) in the United States. HUD confirmed this number and further reported that approximately 1.6 million people experienced homelessness between October 1, 2009, and September 30, 2010. In 2011, a majority of the homeless were in emergency shelters or transitional-housing programs. But nearly four in ten were unsheltered—living on the streets or in cars, abandoned buildings, tents, or "places not intended for human inhabitation."[15] From 2009 to 2011, the number of the unsheltered homeless increased by 2 percent.

Individuals and families become homeless when they are unable to afford their rental or mortgage costs. Homelessness is primarily the consequence of economic factors compounded by the scarcity of affordable housing, as examined previously. Economic indicators that determine an individual or household's risk of becoming homeless include housing cost, unemployment, and foreclosure. On all of these indicators, conditions worsened between 2009 and 2011.

In January 2012 the National Alliance to End Homelessness released a report on the state of homelessness in the United States. The report examined national data released by HUD, the Departments of Health and Human Services, Justice, Labor, and Commerce, the US Census Bureau, and the private real estate research group RealtyTrac. The report made the following important observations:[16]

- Even as the total number of homeless declined between 2009 and 2011, the number of "severely housing cost burdened" households—those who spent more than 50 percent of their income on rent—increased by 6 percent between 2009 and 2010. Three-quarters of all poor renter households had severe housing cost burdens.
- In the same period, 2009–2011, unemployment rose by 4–10 percent across the country.
- In 2010, the fair-market rent for a one-bedroom unit was out of reach for individuals and families of the working poor, who, nationwide, were earning an average annual real income of $9,400.
- Increasing numbers of foreclosures jeopardized the housing situation for many during this period. Foreclosure activity increased 2 percent between 2009 and 2010. Nationally, one out of every forty-five housing units was in foreclosure in 2010.

Homelessness affects people of all ages, races, and ethnicities. But there are certain groups who are more susceptible to homelessness: people living in "doubled up" situations (staying with relatives, living in basements, or sleeping on couches, for example); people discharged from prison; people with substance abuse and mental health issues; young people who have aged out of foster care; and people without health insurance.[17]

Given the continuing scarcity in affordable housing, the constant threat of housing foreclosures, the enduring difficulty in finding employment, and the shrinking of government revenues to sustain the safety net, it is feared that homelessness will affect increasingly more individuals and families in the coming years.

Residential Segregation by Income

Residential segregation by income is one of the most unsettling consequences of the current inequality in the United States. As the country experiences more income inequality, rich and poor families are less likely to live in the same neighborhoods. Neighborhoods that are predominantly poor or are exclusively rich have surpassed in number those that are mixed-income.

In their pioneering research, Sean Reardon and Kendra Bischoff show how family income segregation grew significantly in almost all US metropolitan areas between 2000 and 2007.[18] In 1970, only 15 percent of families lived in neighborhoods that were classified as either affluent or poor. By 2007, 31 percent lived in such neighborhoods. The affluent live in exclusive neighborhoods segregated from the rest of the country much more so than the poor. Reardon and Bischoff's data show "a steady decline in the proportion of families living in middle-class neighborhoods from 1970 to 2007. In 1970, 65 percent of families lived in 'middle income' neighborhoods; by 2009 only 44 percent lived in such neighborhoods."[19]

Residential segregation by income takes place when there is a disparity between what the rich and the poor can afford to pay, primarily for housing. From here, the disparity snowballs into further and further inequality, leading to disparities in many other areas, such as schools, cultural and recreational resources, social services, parks and green spaces, environmental pollution, and the like, all of which ultimately determine the quality of life and social context in which individuals and families reside and, most critically, where their children are raised. "Income segregation creates disparities [that] limit opportunities of low income children for upward social and economic mobility and reinforces the reproduction of inequality, over time and across generations."[20]

Reardon and Bischoff also show that the income segregation among black and Hispanic families—among the rich and poor within these groups—grew very sharply from 2000 to 2007. By 2007, income segregation among black families, for example, was 60 percent greater than among white families. Their research also indicates, rather ironically, that "low-income black and Hispanic families are much more isolated from middle-class black and Hispanic families than are low-income white families from middle- and high-income white families."[21]

The primary reason for this is the emergence of a robust black middle class and the decrease in housing discrimination—both results of the civil rights victories of the 1960s. Sociologist William Julius Wilson describes this trend in his research on the concentration of poverty in the inner cities.

As late as the 1960s, inner cities, also known as urban ghettos, "featured a vertical integration of the urban black population" and "lower class, working class and middle class black families all lived more or less in the same communities (albeit in different neighborhoods), sent their children to the same schools, availed themselves of the same recreational facilities, and shopped at the same stores."[22] Today, black middle-class families no longer live in the ghettos and have moved into mainstream occupations, higher-income neighborhoods, and the suburbs. The inner cities of today "are populated almost exclusively by the most disadvantaged segments of the black urban community"—those that Wilson refers to as the "underclass."[23]

More and more, the newer patterns of residential segregation are attributable to income, class, and opportunity rather than just race and ethnicity. However, the racial segregation that African American and Hispanic communities have historically experienced has intensified their class disadvantage. This is most evident when we consider the fact that "residential segregation constitutes an important contributing cause of the current foreclosure crisis. The greater the degree of Hispanic and black segregation a metropolitan area exhibits, the higher the number and rate of foreclosures it experiences."[24]

Much of the increases in homeownership among black and Hispanic buyers during the 1990s can be attributed to subprime and risky mortgage lending. For example, as much as 43 percent of the increase in black homeownership in the 1990s was made possible by subprime lending. When the housing bubble burst starting in 2007, it was the minority communities who were disproportionately hurt and lost the most through the foreclosure of their homes. Therefore, racialized segregation intensified the consequences of the foreclosure crisis and other accompanying burdens, further deepening the inequalities and hardship that these historically disadvantaged communities have borne, often unevenly.

Gentrification is what pushes out the poor and middle-class residents from areas that had traditionally been their homes, when they become unable to compete with the money that young professionals, hired in the financial and technology sectors, bring with them. Consequently, economic disparity has ballooned in 94 of the 100 biggest US metropolitan areas since 1990, in cities such as Atlanta, Boston, Los Angeles, San Francisco, and Seattle. Million-dollar condos, gleaming new offices of tech firms, boutiques and high-end restaurants, exclusive transportation for the young professionals to and from offices—all of these draw "a well-heeled crowd" that increasingly pushes out middle- and low-income families.[25]

To stop residential segregation due to income disparity in the major metropolises, the exodus of low- and middle-class families to the suburbs must be stemmed. Academicians and politicians agree that cities must take steps to increase the minimum wage, support initiatives for affordable housing, improve schools, and expand public transportation. Unless these steps are taken, the hemorrhaging of low- and middle-class households to suburbs will continue and citics will become the exclusive domain of the very rich.

Health and a Healthy Environment

The well-being that good health confers is priceless. It is fundamental if success and happiness are to be enjoyed. More often than not, inequality of income and wealth finds expression in unequal experiences in health, illness, disease, and consequent well-being. Since our longevity is uncertain and unknown, each day of our lives is precious.

Yet most of the poor report a fewer average number of healthy days, which chips away at the most fundamental level of human contentment and well-being. The Centers for Disease Control and Prevention (CDC) releases a periodic report on health disparity and related inequalities. The latest report, published in January 2011, examined ongoing racial, ethnic, and economic disparities according to selected health indicators. For all indicators related to mortality (incidence or number of deaths in a population) and morbidity (incidence of ill health and disease in a population), those with lower incomes suffered the most.[26]

How Clean Is the Air Where You Live?

Where individuals live and how much money they make play a significant role in their quality of health. The poor in general, and particularly racial and ethnic minority groups, who are disproportionately concentrated in the lower echelons of income, are more likely to live in areas where they are exposed to considerably large doses of environmental pollutants. One of the most egregious cases of this lies in the eighty-five-mile stretch from New Orleans to Baton Rouge, Louisiana.

Home to a dense cluster of oil refineries and petrochemical plants, this area, which Greenpeace has labeled "polluters paradise," has an air quality rated as one of the worst in the nation for nitrogen oxides, particulate matter (a complex class of air pollutants), and sulfur dioxide.[27] Emboldened by lax environmental regulations, these refineries and plants pollute at a level that jeopardizes the health of the predominantly (50–64 percent)[28] African American communities who live here and who continue to carry with them the memories of servitude and indignity in the plantations that dotted these areas in the antebellum (pre–Civil War) South. Serious health problems, including cancer, respiratory irritation, nervous system problems, birth defects, and premature death,[29] haunt these communities, where 16–24 percent of residents live in poverty.[30]

In Church Rock, New Mexico, seven generations of the Navajo people have lived surrounded by arroyos and mesas. The uranium mines that once bordered their land have been closed for decades. But the radioactive dust, carried by the wind and runoff from rain, poses serious health threats, and today Church Rock's 300,000 inhabitants face the possibility of abandoning their ancient land. The Environmental Protection Agency, in trying to remove the waste and clean up more than 500 abandoned mines, has expressed utter shock at the extent of the uranium contamination. Yet the experience at Church Rock is only one example of the environmental crisis that many Native American communities are facing in the Southwest.[31]

Generally speaking, minority groups—whether racial, ethnic, or economic—are more likely to live in urban areas. These areas are disproportionately exposed to particulate matter and ground-level ozone created by vehicular traffic and industrial emissions, which the CDC associates with acute and chronic health outcomes such as lung cancer and exacerbation of respiratory and cardiovascular disease.[32]

On the other hand, those living in the suburbs of Maryland or northern Virginia, or in Stamford, Connecticut, or Minneapolis, Minnesota, have access to wide-open green spaces, farmers' markets, and bike paths in an environment of clean water and clean air, with no potential long-term health consequences from invisible pollutants.

At the People's Climate march in New York City in September 2014, one sign said "Class struggle is climate struggle." It captured the undeniable fact that as the effects of global warming increase, the poor will be the first to suffer. Devastating hurricanes such as Katrina left the poor, and primarily black poor, in New Orleans even more impoverished. The structural conditions such as residential segregation, the lack of transportation, and the lack of disposable resources made this population even more vulnerable and powerless to deal with the destruction that Katrina unleashed.

It is important to remember that as our environment becomes less hospitable due to climage change, it will be the poor who will be most affected.

Coronary Heart Disease, Stroke, Hypertension, Diabetes, and HIV

African Americans experience some of the highest rates of poverty in the country. In November 2011, according to the US Census Bureau, 27 percent of African American adults and 38 percent of African American children were living in poverty. It is instructive, therefore, that black men and women also had the highest rates of coronary heart disease in the United States. In the age group forty-five to seventy-four, black women had a 37.9 percent death rate from coronary heart disease, compared to 19.4 percent for white women; while black men had a 61.5 percent death rate, compared to 41.5 percent among white men.

Similarly, 39.0 percent of black women died of stroke before age seventy-five, compared to 17.3 percent of white women; while 60.0 percent of black men died of stroke before age seventy-five, compared to 31.1 percent of white men.[33] Blacks have a higher risk (42.0 percent) of hypertension and related complications than do whites (28.8 percent).[34]

Similarly, since the 1990s, the incidence of type 2 diabetes has been highest among adults in the minority racial and ethnic groups who experience the most socioeconomic disadvantage. And even as HIV infection rates continue to drop among white men, they continue to rise among racial and ethnic minorities and women. Between 2005 and 2008 the biggest increase in cases of newly HIV-infected individuals occurred among African Americans with a 46 percent increase, compared to a 16 percent increase among Native Americans and a 12 percent increase among Asians.[35]

Obesity

Many of the diseases cited here are related to the ballooning rate of obesity in the nation as a whole. Between 1976 and 2008, the rate of obesity in the United States increased from 15 to 34 percent. For black women in particular, at a rate of 51 percent in 2008, the prevalence of obesity is remarkably higher. Obesity rates are the likely result of an interaction of genetic, social, and cultural factors characterized by an abundance of cheap, easily available, high-calorie food, yet fewer shopping options for healthy foods, such as fresh fruits and vegetables, that are affordable.

It has often been noted that neighborhoods with large minority and economically destitute populations have fewer options when it comes to food shopping. This fact, combined with limited opportunities for physical activity, lower rates of breastfeeding, and cultural norms that provide little incentive for losing weight, creates a climate in which obesity and related health complications become overwhelming.[36]

Infant Mortality Rates

The infant mortality rate is the number of newborns per 1,000 live births who die before reaching their first birthday. Infant mortality rates are an important indicator of the health of a nation because they are associated with maternal health, quality of and access to medical care, socioeconomic conditions, and public health practices.

According to the Centers for Disease Control (CDC), in 2010 the US infant mortality rate was 6.1 infant deaths per 1,000 live births. A baby born in the United States, according to the CDC, is less likely to see its first birthday than one born in most European countries, Japan, Korea, and Australia. Further, the higher US mortality rates are due "entirely, or almost entirely, to high mortality among less advantaged groups."[37] High infant mortality rates reflect socioeconomic disadvantage, exacerbated by a combination of demographic and behavioral factors that this disadvantage engenders. For example, infant mortality rates are higher when infants are born to unmarried adolescent mothers in low-income categories who also have low educational levels and lack access to prenatal medical care.[38]

Mental Illness, Substance Abuse, and Poverty

For most Americans, it is the street person with all of his or her earthly belongings stacked on a shopping cart, or perhaps the person at the train or bus station who is dirty and unkempt, mentally unstable, and strung out on drugs or alcohol, who comes to epitomize the face of the poor. Of the chronically poor and homeless in the United States, 20 to 25 percent suffer from some form of severe mental illness.[39]

The vicious cycle created when mental illness, substance abuse, and poverty combine is almost impossible to break. Numerous studies have demonstrated the toxicity of this mix. Each of these three factors can be both a source and a consequence of the triad—each initiating a process that spirals out of control and commits the victim to a state of chronic destitution. The following list summarizes the different ways in which the lives of the mentally ill are impacted by different factors in society exacerbating the conditions of their impoverishment.

- People who live in poverty are often more susceptible to mental illness, because of the depression and hopelessness that ensue.
- Mental illness makes it difficult to obtain employment, carry out the responsibilities associated with paid work, and therefore retain a job.
- Mental illness makes it difficult for people to take care of themselves and makes them vulnerable to physical ailments.
- The mentally ill poor and homeless have higher health-care costs but no primary care, with the emergency room being their only site for receiving any health care at all.
- Mental illness makes it difficult for people to maintain stable relationships with family members, who are often the caretakers of the mentally ill.
- Half of the mentally ill homeless abuse alcohol and drugs, to which they often turn to relieve physical pain and mental anguish.
- The mentally ill homeless suffer compounded social stigma and isolation, pushing them deeper and deeper into impoverishment and deprivation.

The fact that almost a third of the homeless in the United States are seriously mentally ill can be traced back to the federal government of the

1980s, when neoconservative fiscal and social policies during and after the presidency of Ronald Reagan led to deinstitutionalization of the mentally ill, who flooded onto the streets instead.[40] Under the Reagan administration, care of the mentally ill was transferred to states and local governments, originally with guarantees of federal funding, but this funding shrank quickly with the administration's drastic cuts to social programs.

By 1985, the federal government covered just 11 percent of the budgets of mental health agencies.[41] Subsequently, as states faced increasing budget constraints, care for the mentally ill was outsourced to private providers who set their own rules, often with very little oversight.[42] As the critical services that the mentally ill needed dwindled at every level, more and more of them ended up on the streets. According to the National Alliance on Mental Illness, between 2009 and 2012, states cut a total of $4.35 billion in public mental health spending from their budgets.

Today, the homeless who are mentally ill and dependent on alcohol and other drugs are further cut off from state and federal safety nets, since they are required to be free of substance abuse before they can qualify for such aid. Ironically, this deprives them of the very social services, such as drug and alcohol rehabilitation, that would enable them to improve their lives.

MAKING CONNECTIONS

"Bad Decisions Don't Make You Poor; Being Poor Makes for Bad Decisions"

The poor have often been associated with bad behavior and bad choices, which are seen as the real causes of poverty rather than economic conditions, which in turn leads to the belief that the poor deserve their fate. Even though bad behavior is not the exclusive domain of the poor, they are less able than the middle class or the rich to hide it from the public. Government has often used the image of the "morally inferior poor"[1] to cut funding for food stamps, let unemployment benefits expire, and deny shelter to the homeless.

It is clear that economic conditions are what lead many poor people to bad behavior. For example, not having reliable transportation means that a person will have trouble keeping appointments; and lower levels of education and the stress of constantly juggling limited and uncertain resources might lead parents to become distracted.

Recently published studies suggest furthermore that the condition of being poor makes for bad decisions. The studies focus on a **causal relationship**, not merely a **correlational relationship**, between poverty and mental illness. For example, Anandi Mani and colleagues, in a study on low-income Americans and the global poor, found that "just contemplating a projected financial decision impacted performance on spatial and reasoning tests."[2]

(continues)

"Bad Decisions Don't Make You Poor; Being Poor Makes for Bad Decisions"

All of us are dependent on cognitive abilities, and these abilities have limits. Thus life for the poor becomes exceptionally challenging, given all they must manage: continually limited resources, severe budgetary constraints, the threat of losing a home, unpaid utility bills, contending with possible or real homelessness, having untreated illnesses, facing stern and often unsympathetic social service workers, and on top of all this, the pressures of parenting.

In such circumstances, there is constant "decision fatigue," stress, sleep loss, and the like, all of which impose a disproportionate "cognitive load which impedes cognitive capacity." Poverty creates certain mental processes "that undermine judgment and [lead] to poor decision making."[3]

Psychologist Kathleen Vehs, in another study, contends that the mental toll that poverty imposes is also responsible for depleting the ability for self-control and provoking unhealthy impulsive behaviors. Self-control, she writes, is possibly the "greatest human strength because it is involved in the ability to make choices."[4] Individuals who are in constant pain or are constantly required to make sacrifices deplete their self-control much faster than others who are not in constant pain or do not experience their lives as a series of "trade-offs." And the poor, who must constantly resist their urges and control their behavior to accord with their lack of resources, deplete their ability for impulse control much faster than others. "People become progressively worse . . . at self-control the more they have had to engage in self-control previously."[5]

Decisions requiring many trade-offs and constant battle with desires, which are common when people are poor, "render subsequent decisions prone to favoring impulsive, intuitive and often regrettable options."[6] There are myriad advantages to being affluent. The affluent can afford nicer things, and can afford to spend money in ways to make life more convenient. But as Matthew Yglesias writes, "the greatest convenience of all [is] the convenience that comes from not having to sweat the small stuff."[7] Constantly.

Notes: The title of this box comes from Matthew Yglesias's 2013 *Slate* article of the same name.
1. Egan, "Good Poor, Bad Poor," p. SR11.
2. Yglesias, "Bad Decisions Don't Make You Poor."
3. Quoted in Vehs, "The Poor's Poor Mental Power," p. 970.
4. Ibid.
5. Ibid.
6. Ibid.
7. Yglesias, "Bad Decisions Don't Make You Poor."

Insurance and Access to Health Care

According to the US Census Bureau, there were 48 million uninsured individuals in 2012, representing 15.4 percent of the total population.[43] Working full-time increases the likelihood of having insurance. The likelihood of being uninsured rises for individuals with low incomes, those who are part-time workers, and especially among the growing numbers who are unemployed.

Uninsured rates for the poor (those living at or below the federal poverty level) and the near poor (those living at less than three times above the federal poverty level—$66,000 for a family of four) were significantly higher compared to the uninsured rate for the nonpoor. Nearly half (47.9 percent) of uninsured adults were poor but still ineligible for Medicaid due to variances in Medicaid eligibility criteria from state to state.[44]

An estimated 11.4 million working-age adult Americans with chronic conditions do not have insurance and also have less access to medical care than their insured counterparts. This includes adults with cardiovascular disease, hypertension, and diabetes who have not visited a health professional and do not have a standard outpatient site for health care, such as through a primary care physician. These individuals are more likely to identify their standard site for care as an emergency department.

According to the CDC's estimates, "potentially preventable hospitalizations"—hospitalizations that having health insurance and coordinated primary care would have prevented—cost approximately $6 billion a year. In 2010 the savings from the 910,000 preventable hospitalizations would have more than offset program costs for investing in basic primary care.

The System of Privatized Health Care in the United States

Provisions to maintain good health—both physical and mental—are the hallmarks of a just society. Unlike the United States, most Western European nations and Canada have national health-care systems that make health care accessible and affordable to the majority of their citizens. In the United States, health care is predominantly a privatized system, with the primary motive being profit maximization, not provision of affordable and quality health care. There is very little incentive to keep the price of medical care, medical procedures, and medicines low and affordable.

It is eye-opening to compare the prices of some common medical procedures in the United States and its peer nations. For an angiogram, which costs $35 in Canada as of 2013, the average US price is $914. For a colonoscopy, which costs $655 in Switzerland, the average US price is $1,185. A hip replacement costs $7,731 in Spain and $40,364 in the United States, and an MRI scan costs $319 in the Netherlands and $1,121 in the United States. These high costs yield a $2.7 trillion annual health-care bill nationally for Americans.[45] But this colossal medical spending, numerous studies have shown, does not necessarily deliver better care to Americans. (See Chapter 13 for a further discussion.) Every time Americans go to their doctor, undergo tests and procedures, buy medications, or stay in a hospital, they pay much more, either from their own pockets or through their insurance plans, in comparison with their counterparts in Canada, France, the Netherlands, Spain, and Switzerland, to name just a few peer countries where health care is less expensive than in the United States.

In an August 2013 article in the *New York Times* titled "Doctors Who Profit from Radiation Prescribe It More," journalist Robert Pear reports on the findings by investigators from the Government Accountability Office that doctors often refer patients for radiation therapy and other lucrative treatments in which the doctors have a financial interest, such as owning the equipment and facilities or having financial ties to those who provide the treatment.[46]

For the uninsured, falling sick, even with a minor illness, puts them under a tremendous financial burden, and they risk losing everything they own. Without health insurance, individuals and families are teetering at the edge of bankruptcy every time sickness strikes. Everybody gets sick; no one can avoid it—it is our existential reality.

The poor, because they are often most at risk for illness, often also fall sick the most. Most European countries have recognized this and have put in place single-payer national health-care systems through which everyone is covered, regardless of whether they are rich or poor, resident or immigrant. Health care is recognized as a human right and European countries do not scrimp in providing it.

In the United States, most individuals and their families have private health insurance through their employers, or pay for insurance out of their own pockets. Health insurance is contingent upon a person's employment status and on terms that are determined by employers and insurance companies. Those who work part-time are in most instances not covered. Enrollment in a private insurance plan, such as Cobra, is prohibitively expensive.

As health-care costs have skyrocketed, coverage through employment has eroded and employees and their families are stuck with higher co-pays and deductibles. Without medical insurance, individuals and families risk devastating consequences in the event of catastrophic health emergencies, which often can lead to bankruptcy, indebtedness, and homelessness—an ever-accelerating spiral of despondency.

Patient Protection and the Affordable Care Act

On March 23, 2010, President Barack Obama signed the Patient Protection and Affordable Care Act, commonly known as the Affordable Care Act or more colloquially as Obamacare. It provides for comprehensive health insurance reform and puts in place steps that are urgently needed to ensure that more Americans receive health coverage.

It is the most historically significant overhaul of the US health-care system since the passage of Medicaid and Medicare in 1965. According to estimates by the Congressional Budget Office, by 2022 the Affordable Care Act will provide health insurance coverage for at least an additional 33 million Americans who would otherwise be uninsured. At the end of the first enrollment period, in April 2014, 8 million individuals had already signed up to buy insurance coverage through the government-run health-care marketplace.

As the name suggests, the health-care legislation has two features.[47] First, it has a patient bill of rights that includes a set of protections for individuals who buy insurance in the private health insurance market. Among these provisions are the following:

- Insurance companies are not allowed to discriminate based on pre-existing conditions.
- Young adults must be allowed coverage under a parent's health plan until they reach the age of twenty-six.
- Insurers cannot drop coverage arbitrarily, and individuals have the right to appeal if insurers deny payment or raise rates unreasonably.
- Insurance companies must cover expenses if an individual receives emergency care at a hospital or care facility outside the coverage network.
- Insurance companies must spend 80–85 percent of every premium dollar on medical care, as opposed to administrative costs and advertising.

Second, the Affordable Care Act seeks to expand health-care coverage, as follows:

- The health insurance marketplace is designed to make buying health-care coverage both easy and affordable. It allows individuals to compare health plans and enroll in one that meets their needs.
- Medicaid coverage will be expanded to cover families whose income is less than 133 percent of the federal poverty line ($31,322 for a family of four in 2013).
- For families whose income is between 133 percent and 400 percent of the federal poverty line ($31,322 to $94,200 for a family of four in 2013), they will receive tax credits on a sliding scale to help them pay for health insurance coverage.
- Insurance premiums are capped on the basis of ability to pay. Affordable coverage is defined as an insurance premium that is equal or less than 8 percent of a family's annual income.
- Small businesses that provide health insurance coverage for their employees will receive a 50 percent tax credit on their contribution.

Finally, the Affordable Care Act gives states the option of creating a so-called basic health plan, comprising the following:

- Provision of additional affordable coverage to families whose income is between 133 percent and 200 percent of the federal poverty line ($31,322 to $47,100 for a family of four in 2013) who have some Medicaid coverage.
- Provision of affordable coverage to properly documented immigrants.
- Provision for states to expand coverage beyond the federal minimum to children, low-income parents, caretaker relatives, pregnant women, and individuals with disabilities.

Although the two main objectives of the Affordable Care Act are to provide affordable health insurance for all US citizens and to reduce the cost of health care from its current annual level of $2.7 trillion, which amounts to $9,000 a year per man, woman, and child, the act falls short of offering a single-payer system of national health insurance and therefore fails to change, in any fundamental way, how health care is provided in the United States. But given the firestorm that has raged over the moderate provisions of this act, such a fundamental change might have instigated unprecedented opposition, an outcome that politicians go to great lengths to avoid.

But let us consider the single-payer model. As the name suggests, there would be a single payer—a national health-care insurance provider, not much different from Medicare, Medicaid, or federal compensation for veterans. Instead of premiums worth thousands of dollars being paid to private insurers, the premiums in a single-payer system would be embedded in a truly progressive income tax structure. Unfortunately, tax-shy Americans tend to abandon the single-payer ship the moment the talk turns to generating revenues through taxes. As a result, the common sense integral to the European model is drowned out by the clamor from market loyalists who would much rather preserve the present system of health care and its rich avenues for profit-making than opt for a system that would cover all Americans.

Education, Social Capital, and the Digital Divide

Education

Much of the discussion of disparities in education has traditionally focused on the racial divide. Recent studies, however, find that while the achievement gap between white and black students has narrowed over the past few decades, the gap between rich and poor students has grown.

Sociologist Sean Reardon's research shows that "the income achievement gap is now more than twice as large as the black-white achievement gap. In contrast to this, fifty years ago [in 1960] the black-white gap was one and a half to two times as large as the income gap."[48] This, according to Reardon, is not surprising, since in the 1960s the nation saw historically low levels of income inequality but high levels of racial inequality. And while racial inequality began to fall as desegregation, affirmative action, fair-housing laws, and changes in racial attitudes took hold, income inequality began to grow sharply in the 1970s and has accelerated ever since.

Another study, conducted by researchers from the University of Michigan, documents a dramatic 50 percent increase since the 1980s in the gap between college completion rates for rich and poor children. Taking into consideration the full impact of the current recession would most definitely "aggravate this trend."[49]

Similarly, data from the National Assessment of Educational Progress show that "more than 40 percent [of the] variation in average reading scores and 46 percent of the variation in average math scores across the states is associated with variation in child poverty rates." One reason for the growing achievement gap is the tremendous divide in the amount of resources that rich parents invest in their children compared to the resources that lower-income parents are able to invest. Affluent parents, in trying to prepare their children for admission to the most competitive colleges, provide them with advantages, such as private schooling, private tutors, and extracurricular involvement, that poorer parents, often single mothers who are "increasingly stretched for time and resources," are simply not able to afford.[50]

Researchers Sabino Kornrich and Frank Furstenberg have documented that "in 1972, Americans at the upper end of the income spectrum were spending five times as much per child as low income families. By 2007 that gap had grown to nine to one." The income gap leads to a per-child spending gap and an education gap that subsequently limit economic mobility.[51]

As early as 1966, the Coleman Report, widely regarded as the most important study of US education of the twentieth century, drew attention to the link between a family's socioeconomic status and their children's educational achievement.[52] The main intention of the Head Start program, an important piece of President Lyndon Johnson's war on poverty, was to weaken this link. But education reformers and public policies, such as No Child Left Behind, have focused on making schools better—by promoting high standards for students' test scores or by promoting the creation of charter schools—without taking into account the severe handicap faced by the children of the poor.

Research has repeatedly demonstrated how poor health and nutrition inhibit development and learning; how low-income children are at a disadvantage when they do not have access to high-quality early childhood educational programs; how parents, often single mothers, who are struggling with the consequences of economic marginalization and destitution, are simply unable to find the time to coach and support their children with their educational and extracurricular activities; how the uncertainties of everyday life among the poor disable learning outcomes; and how children in poor communities experience greater learning loss during summer vacation when their more privileged counterparts are enjoying enriching activities.

This reality is contrary to what Horace Mann, the father of public education in the United States, believed in. Mann, who established the nation's first public school in Lexington, Massachusetts, in 1839, thought that public schooling would be "the great equalizer of human conditions," the "balance wheel of the social machinery," and the "creator of wealth undreamed of." Poverty would most assuredly disappear as a broadening popular intelligence tapped new treasures of natural and material wealth. Along with abolishing poverty would go the rancorous discord between the "haves" and the "have-nots," which has characterized all of human history.[53]

The increasing education gap in the United States reflects the deeper divide in wealth and income between communities and a financing system that penalizes those with a lower base of property tax. Fewer resources mean that schools in poorer communities must forego art, music, and drama, not to mention advanced-placement classes and adequate libraries and science laboratories—all of which contribute to the development of an educationally well-rounded child.

Moreover, the insecurities and uncertainties that children face in poor and immigrant communities inhibit their ability to foster the habits and behaviors conducive to obtaining a good education. But these same habits and behaviors can be changed when the children of the poor are given the same support and opportunities that their middle-class peers enjoy. (In Chapter 7, which discusses how the education system perpetuates income inequality, we will return to these topics in more detail.)

Social Capital

Following the work of social scientists such as Pierre Bourdieu, James Coleman, and Robert Putnam, increasing attention is being paid to the concept of "social capital" as an important variable determining people's quality of life. Social capital comprises those forces in society that promote an individual's sense of belonging. It is based on feelings of social solidarity and social reciprocity among individuals and institutions.

Important components of social capital are the mutually understood social values, norms, moral obligations, and trust that undergird social networks and relationships among individuals and groups. Social capital is embedded in relationships in which people care for each other—offering support, advice, and help for no other reason than the natural sense that this is the right thing to do. In Sudhir Venkatesh's words, it is the "stay together gang."[54] People have social capital when they take care of each other's children, when they share responsibilities, when they connect one another to opportunities, when they give rides, when they offer a couch to sleep on, or a meal to share, or a chat on the porch.

Minority and immigrant communities can survive and thrive on social capital even when they are economically poor, and may have an advantage in their recognition that "people are all you have . . . [and] poverty is brightened only by community."[55] In contrast, communities are made poorer and lonelier when they do not have social capital. Even the material well-being of the affluent and the middle class cannot overcome the solitude and loneliness created by a lack of social capital. The anomie thus created can become the spawning ground for pathological behavior against self and society, with poverty of spirit routinely wreaking havoc on innocent bystanders.

The Digital Divide

In this age of information, when access to the Internet opens doors to numerous opportunities and resources, the inequalities between classes are intensified when the well-off have high-speed, broadband Internet access and the poor have either poor access or none at all. In November 2011, the Department of Commerce released a report titled "Exploring the Digital Nation" that analyzed broadband Internet adoption in the United States. The objective of the report was to provide information that "will inform efforts to close the gap and promote America's competitiveness in the global economy."[56]

The report found a strong correlation between broadband adoption and socioeconomic factors, such as income and education. Lower-income households, black and Latino households, people with less education, people with disabilities, and rural residents were less likely than their more affluent counterparts to have Internet service at home. For households with an annual income of less than $25,000, only 43 percent had broadband access in their homes, compared to 93 percent of households with incomes exceeding $100,000. Only 55 percent of black families and 57 percent of Latino families had Internet access at home, compared to 72 percent of white families.

This means that at a time when so much of life has moved online—information on and applications for social services; Internet classrooms and web-based higher education; information on job openings, online job applications, and even online job interviews through video conferencing; political activism and advocacy; and access to endless sources of information on just about everything—the stark racial, economic, and geographic digital divide leaves many behind in an "information darkness." Lacking the access and skills needed to succeed in today's information economy, those who live in the offline world become further isolated and unable to escape the already existing income inequality.

Transportation

Quality, affordable transportation is central for creating economic and social well-being for individuals and communities. Public transportation provides accessibility to employment opportunities and other services, breaking the social isolation and invisibility of socially disadvantaged groups. The ability of individuals, families, and communities to gain access to affordable transportation is critical if they are to have personal mobility and access to work, school, doctors, cultural activities, and shopping stores—particularly food stores.

The popular car culture of the United States, paralleled by a simultaneous absence of public transportation, puts the poor at an additional disadvantage. The poor use mass transit disproportionately because they are seldom able to afford the cost of buying or maintaining an automobile. But many without private automobiles do not have access to adequate public transportation because of insufficient route coverage, infrequency of services, prohibitive fares, or simply geographic isolation, with many of the poor living far from bus and subway stations. For the poor who live in suburban areas, which are customarily automobile-dependent, public transportation is not only inadequate but also unaffordable.

In the mid-twentieth century, before the automobile became affordable for the middle class, bus and rail public transportation was the dominant mode of travel. But after World War II, a vigorous urban renewal program changed the social dynamics of the cities. As Karen Brodkin writes:

> Federal programs brought private developers and public officials together to create downtown central business districts where there had formerly been a mix of manufacturing, commerce, and working-class neighborhoods. Manufacturing was scattered to the peripheries of the city, which were ringed and bisected by a national system of highways. . . . In Los Angeles, as in New York's Bronx, the postwar period saw massive freeway construction right through the heart of old working-class neighborhoods. In East Los Angeles and Santa Monica, Chicana/o and African American communities were divided in half or blasted to smithereens by the highways bringing Angelenos to the new white suburbs.[57]

As the affluent and the middle classes moved to the suburbs and increasingly commuted to work in their private automobiles, their ridership of the transit systems decreased. Consequently, the poor became the primary users of mass transit. And "having limited political influence and contributing to a dwindling share of operating revenues, these riders endured declining levels of service,"[58] often at prohibitive rates.

The high concentration of the poor in urban areas can be largely attributed to the accessibility of public transportation there. But the poor still lack access to jobs that are beyond the reach of public transportation, or that entail paying a transportation fare that is disproportionate to the wages and salaries individuals might be earning at those jobs, which increasingly involve providing a service. For example, a round-trip fare from New York or Philadelphia to a nursing home in Lakewood, New Jersey, might cost triple the amount that a health-care aide earns in an hour.

The inadequacy of public transportation in the United States today mirrors a deliberate policy choice to continue on a path that supports a car-centric, gas-dependent lifestyle. The US Congress regularly supports transportation bills that keep federal funding heavily tilted toward building more highways, and tilted away from building mass transit.[59] For large segments of the population, many of whom are disadvantaged, accessing opportunities for jobs, education, and services depends on the availability of reliable and affordable public transportation to all essential destinations. The absence of such transportation can be considered a violation of a basic human right, consigning the already destitute and poor to a status from which it becomes ever more challenging to recover.

MAKING CONNECTIONS
The Overlooked Importance of How People Get to Work

Jasmine is a thirty-seven-year-old African American woman who has been a resident at the Tent City homeless encampment in the Pine Barrens of Lakewood, New Jersey, for about ten months.

Jasmine is an articulate, intelligent woman with numerous licenses and certifications that allowed her to work as a florist, a hair stylist, a nurse's aide, and a home health-care aide. Paying not much more than minimum wage at most, none of the jobs alone paid her enough to support herself, so all her working life she held two or three jobs simultaneously. She had enough money to pay rent for a studio or one-bedroom apartment, but never enough to buy a car and maintain it.

Living in the suburbs of New Jersey—Keyport and Keansburg—she never had access to a transit bus line. Walking and taking cabs were her only ways of getting to work. Some days she said she walked for hours to get to work, whether that was a nursing home, hospital, grocery store, the garden department of a hardware store, or a private home. But she had a roof over her head—even if it was just to sleep beneath for a few hours late at night before waking up at dawn to trudge to work again.

(continues)

The Overlooked Importance of How People Get to Work

In 2006 she started "dropping things." Blood work showed that she was suffering from lupus. The disease was slowing her down and making it harder and harder for her to walk and take cabs and get to work ontime. Not having transportation, with the disease weakening her steadily, and with very little money left, she found a boardinghouse in Keansburg and a job at Home Depot, which was still an hour's walk away.

One day after she came back to the boardinghouse, tired and breathless, there was an altercation with one of the managers, who called her a "nigger." Jasmine called the police. She had stood up for her own dignity, but was evicted from the boardinghouse for being a troublemaker. She found shelter in the house of a cousin in Neptune, New Jersey, but she lost her job, because she was now living too far from Home Depot and commuting was impossible.

The little money she had was soon spent. She had no alternative but to move out of her cousin's house. Alongside other homeless, she started to live on an island near Union Beach, New Jersey, inside canvas covers, under a canopy of trees. On October 29, 2013, Hurricane Sandy hit and decimated the neighborhood in and around Union Beach. Whatever shelter the homeless had was now washed away. That is when she came to Tent City.

Jasmine hasn't seen a doctor in seven years. She feels her strength ebbing, and her blood pressure is erratic. In all this, there is one ray of positive news—she has state health coverage that allows her to see specialists. But without a car, she has no access to them unless a volunteer at Tent City drives her. She isn't hopeful about living much longer.

I asked Jasmine: If she could name one primary reason that led to her plight, what would it be? She said without hesitation that it was her bad decisions—that she was responsible for her predicaments. Not the fact that she had no transportation; not the fact that all her jobs paid so miserably that she had to work eighteen-hour days—when her health allowed; and not the fact that she had no respite even when her health was failing her.

She recalled that when she was in school, she had gone to New York to the United Nations and had for the first time seen homeless people on the streets. She couldn't believe that in a country as rich as the United States, there were people living on the streets. Today Jasmine still finds it hard to believe that she is one of them.

The Social Safety Net

In their broadest sense, the social welfare programs in the United States benefit a majority of Americans through Social Security, unemployment insurance, worker's compensation, tax deductions for interest on home mortgage payments, deferment of student loans, and the like, which are collectively referred to as transfer payments. And US citizens are regarded as being rightfully deserving of these services. But in the minds of many

Americans, who see welfare pejoratively, the poor are undeserving of such services. The US welfare system is wrought with such contradictions.

Social welfare comprises social services in the form of "means-tested" government benefits that enable the impoverished to maintain a minimum standard of living. It is a safety net that catches individuals and families, stopping them from becoming desperately and utterly destitute.

The programs in the US welfare system include cash assistance programs such as Temporary Aid to Needy Families (TANF); child support programs; energy or utility assistance; food assistance or food stamps in the form of the Supplemental Nutrition Assistance Program (SNAP) and the Supplementary Nutrition Program for Women, Infants, and Children (WIC); medical assistance in the form of Medicare and Medicaid; housing and rental subsidies; the earned income tax credit (EITC);[60] and vocational rehabilitation services.

No other government programs in the United States evoke as much controversy as do these welfare programs. There are some who see welfare as being woefully inadequate, an utterly imperfect system that is punitive in the way it discourages individuals from working, even as it chastises them for not working. These critics refer specifically to the 1996 welfare reform, known as the Personal Responsibility and Work Opportunity Reconciliation Act, which imposed work requirements, created new rules, and limited families to five years of access to welfare.

These critics maintain that when individuals who have been on TANF, SNAP, Medicaid, and rental assistance secure either full-time or part-time work that pays only a minimum wage, insufficient for even basic quality of life, they run the risk of losing an array of these benefits. They become worse off with a job than without one. Instead of having their incomes supplemented and enhanced by these programs, they lose them entirely. Or because they now have an income, however minimal, they can qualify only for reduced assistance. And so working at a job, instead of making their lives better, actually makes them poorer.

As the country faces job loss and as real wages stagnate or decline, means-tested welfare programs such as cash assistance, food stamps, and subsidies for child care and housing become critical to the survival of the working poor, particularly poor single mothers.[61] In contrast, most European countries recognize that the business cycle of a capitalist system can be capricious. People lose their jobs because of that. This awareness is fundamental to the European social welfare system, which is built to catch individuals and families when they lose jobs because of downward pressures of the economy.

The way welfare functions in the United States reflects the nation's ideological bias, in which personal responsibility, motivation, and ambition are central. This position holds that regardless of what the systemic and structural disadvantages may be, individuals and families should have the drive and determination to make it on their own. A majority of Americans subscribe to the notion of a small government whose role in mitigating individuals' and families' disadvantages should be minimal. This idea can be held, rather paradoxically, even by those who are receiving assistance, often leading to feelings of shame and unworthiness, which gives evidence to the power of this belief.[62]

Seen from this ideological perch, there is no incongruity in the fact that even as millions fall off the economic ladder as unemployment and poverty reach unprecedented highs, there are fewer poor people receiving government assistance today. According to a 2011 report by the Congressional Budget Office, "the share of benefits flowing to the least affluent households, the bottom fifth, has declined from 54 percent in 1979 to 36 percent in 2007."[63]

The contradictions between the ideological imperatives and the reality of the welfare program become even sharper when we consider the fact that, according to the Congressional Budget Office, even as the poor are receiving a smaller share of government benefits, spending on medical benefits, especially Medicare, will rise 60 percent over the next decade. But when the *New York Times* conducted a poll in which people were asked, "Which domestic program will probably increase the nation's deficit the most?" programs for the poor, such as Medicaid and food stamps, received the largest share of votes (27 percent).[64]

As the economy sputters and more and more middle-class Americans rely on government benefits such as the EITC (which as of 1975 enables families earning up to $49,317 annually to become eligible to receive a tax credit or refund), federally subsidized breakfast and lunch programs at schools, and Medicare coverage for their parents, many of them still support politicians who promise to cut government spending.[65] (In Chapter 13 the discussion centers on this very paradox—the phenomenon of individuals taking positions that are against their own interests.)

The role of government welfare programs in lessening poverty is given clear evidence in the US Census Bureau's November 2011 report on the supplementary poverty measure. The report shows that if the earned income tax credit were not included in the poverty measure, the rate of poverty would jump from 16 percent to 18 percent. For children, the poverty rate would jump from 18.2 percent to 22.4 percent. Similarly, if individuals and families did not receive food stamps, the overall poverty rate would rise from 16 percent to 17 percent and for children, from 18.2 percent to 21.2 percent. We see clear evidence of this in Figure 3.1, which shows that in 2012 the Supplemental Nutrition Assistance Program lifted 4 million people out of poverty.

Figure 3.1 Number of People Lifted Above Poverty by the Supplemental Nutrition Assistance Program, 1995–2012

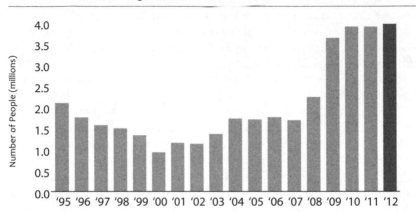

Source: Center on Budget and Policy Priorities, "Census Data Show Poverty and Inequality Remained High in 2012 and Median Income Was Stagnant, but Fewer Americans Were Uninsured."

When medical out-of-pocket costs are not subtracted from a family's income, the poverty rate for 2010 would be 12.7 percent rather than 16.0 percent.[66] Recent research has also shown how much worse the effects of unemployment and of the income declines due to the 2007–2009 recession would have been if they had not been offset by government welfare programs.[67]

Whose responsibility is it to ensure that individuals and families earn enough money to cover all their expenses—the basic bundle of goods and services, including food, clothing, shelter and utilities, health care, education, child care, transportation, compensation for sickness and injury, and some degree of leisure—so they can live with relative comfort, dignity, and security? The conventional wisdom has always been that all of this should be inextricably tied to work. The work people do for their employers should be compensated through payment of a reasonable wage, enrollment in health insurance, and provision of retirement pensions. There was once a kind of social compact—an agreement among the members of society—defining the rights and duties of both workers and employers, but that compact is fast disintegrating.

As jobs disappear, as wages stagnate or plummet, as employers eliminate most benefits, it is left to the government to step in. Looking at it from a different angle gives evidence that social welfare programs such as food stamps, government cash assistance, unemployment insurance, the earned income tax credit, school lunch programs, housing and utility subsidies, and the like, in fact subsidize employers who don't pay enough or deny benefits. Social welfare is more of a service to the employer—to the businesses and corporations—than it is a handout to individuals and families.

Let us look at the case of SNAP, popularly known as food stamps, and the two ways in which it benefits corporations such as Wal-Mart. Wal-Mart of course is famous for its low prices, and that is what has made it a retail giant. The motto that guides Wal-Mart is "everyday low costs equal everyday low prices." The low cost of producing things helps keep the prices of those things low.

Since, for any business, the cost of labor is the most expensive and recurring cost, one of the costs that Wal-Mart needs to keep in check is the price of labor. So more than anything, it is low wages that help make low prices possible. And if the wages Wal-Mart pays do not allow a family to meet their basic needs, such as putting food on the table, that family can turn to the federal government to make up the difference with food stamps.

As mentioned in Chapter 2, Wal-Mart pays its workers between $8.53 and $11.75 and hour. Let us assume $8.80 per hour for a full-time employee who works 34 hours a week, meaning an annual salary of approximately $17,000. This is a couple thousand dollars below the poverty threshold for a family of three, $19,530 in 2013. If a family of three made less than $25,400 that year, they qualified for food stamps. With food stamp money averaging $130 a month, this Wal-Mart employee goes shopping for food at the very place that offers the most food for that money—Wal-Mart itself, whose food shelves this employee may have stocked in the first place.

Of the total SNAP money that the federal government pays, 18 percent, or more than $13 billion, is taken in by Wal-Mart annually. And in this windfall, Wal-Mart is not alone. All big retailers and grocers make a great deal of money from SNAP, $76 billion total in 2013. Therefore, as the Ohio Grocers Association wrote in a letter to Congress when the debate about cutting SNAP was in full swing in 2014, "cutting SNAP doesn't just hurt the poor, it hurts businesses too!" Wal-Mart paid $1.9 million that year in lobbying Congress not to cut SNAP.[68]

Retirement is another economic uncertainty for many of America's poor. In the spring and summer of 2013, the PBS program *Frontline* aired an in-depth report on what Martin Smith, the Emmy-winning producer, director, and correspondent, called America's retirement crisis.[69] Much of the information presented here is drawn from that report.

In the 1970s, almost half of all American workers were covered by their employers with a guarantee of secure retirement. They were able to carry into retirement a large percentage of their salary and benefits, which along with what they were able to save ensured them of a comfortable life in their proverbial "golden years." The employers managed these retirement benefits, further easing any burden on the workers.

But in the 1990s the rules of the game began to change, with new accounting rules, market volatility, global competition, and the longevity of the general population cutting into the bottom line of employers. Consequently, employers started to shift the responsibility regarding management of retirement savings to the employees, and thus was born the mutual fund industry, which became the institution of choice for managing 401K and individual retirement accounts (IRAs).

These terms, "401(k)" and "IRA," though obscure at the outset, were suddenly on the minds and mouths of many employees, whether they understood anything about them or not. The average employee, who knew nothing about the intricacies of investing, was suddenly saddled with that responsibility, with their well-being in their retirement years wholly dependent on how well they would fare in choosing among myriad and complex investment options.

As of 2013, at least $10 trillion is invested in retirement funds, and companies compete to assume the lucrative role of financial service provider, giving merely "suitable" advice to an often ignorant public and making a handsome profit in turn. According to Teresa Ghilarducci, professor of economics at the New School in New York, most Americans know very little about the prices, quality, and dangers of the 401(k) or IRAs they invest in, and the financial planners involved in these products are able to protect themselves against regulations that would expose the real dangers and prices and are under no obligation to act in the best interests of their clients.[70]

For example, in their fine print, 401(k) plans hide more than they reveal about the fees that eat away at the final sum retirees will be able to collect. But when clients check their 401(k) statements, rarely are they able to identify the many fees hidden through obscure jargon. The fee that a mutual fund charges for managing the account, or pays a broker under the "revenue sharing" clause for helping the fund to acquire an account, together with many other such hidden fees, can compound over a lifetime to erode as much as two-thirds of a client's actual gains. Policy analyst and economist Robert Hiltonsmith calculated that, on average, a median-income, two-earner American family would pay a whopping $155,000 in fees over forty years of building a 401(k).[71]

At a time when retirement savings were reeling from the market collapse of spring 2000, and then again when the housing bubble burst beginning in 2007, the US labor department, which oversees the mutual fund industry, asked Congress to demand more transparency in the fee structures and hold the industry accountable by proposing a new fiduciary rule that would require financial advisers to put the interests of the clients they were advising before their own.

But every effort to rein in the mutual fund industry with government regulation failed. The formidable political power of the mutual fund industry and their persistent lobbying of lawmakers defeated any attempt to demand more transparency and responsibility from financial advisers toward their clients. Efforts at reform have fallen flat, fee structures are still invisible, and mutual funds are raking in phenomenal earnings by selling the most profitable products in total disregard of their fiduciary responsibility to do what is in the best interest of their clients and not just what is most "suitable" and most profitable for their own interests.

The country is facing total retirement chaos, with almost one-third of all Americans facing a future with no retirement savings, and at least half of Americans not being able to save at all because of salaries that barely keep them afloat today, together with the prospect of having to work for many more years than anticipated and still having an uncertain economic future. All the while, the financial advisers, planners, managers, and brokers of the mutual funds dole out billions of dollars in profits and bonuses, making money on the backs of people who work hard their entire lives to have some semblance of savings for their retirement years. For many Americans today, retirement has become a "bewildering and frightening challenge."[72]

Conclusion

Poverty is multifaceted and complex. As the gap between the rich and the poor widens and intensifies, inequality is felt in all aspects of life: where people live; what schools their children attend; how easy is it for them to obtain transportation—to work, to the doctor, to a cultural event; whether they must think twice before going to the doctor for a debilitating condition; who their neighbors are—a rich CEO, or a health-care aide working for minimum wage, or a laid-off machinist living on unemployment compensation; whether there are green spaces in their neighborhood; whether they stay up nights worrying about putting food on the table, or losing their home; what options they have if a new job means losing their food stamps or child-care assistance; how they will apply for a job whose application would take just minutes online when they cannot afford an Internet connection; and whether they have a community of friends, family, neighbors, and acquaintances to help them in times of need.

All these concerns and existential challenges are intricately connected to a person's economic position or class, which in turn is determined by their income and wealth and whether or not they own the means of production. It will depend on whether they make money from salaries and wages or from investment income, because that in turn will determine how much tax they will pay and also, more fundamentally, how much control they will have over their means of livelihood. Do they set the terms of their own lives, or does someone else?

Notes

1. See Klass, "Poverty's Lasting Ills," p. D4. If poverty is considered a disease that afflicts a person and society, what are its lasting ills? How does the experience

of poverty impact the health and development of children? And what steps have countries such as the United Kingdom taken to mitigate child poverty? Is there a lesson there for the United States?

2. Glaeser, "Rethinking the Federal Bias Toward Homeownership," pp. 5–37.

3. Callis and Kresin, "Social, Economic, and Housing Statistics Division."

4. Rodda and Goodman, "Recent House Price Trends and Homeownership Affordability," p. vii.

5. Herbert and Apgar Jr., "Report to Congress on the Root Causes of the Foreclosure Crisis."

6. US Department of Housing and Urban Development, "Subprime Lending," http://portal.hud.gov/hudportal/HUD?src=/program_offices/fair_housing_equal_opp/lending/subprime.

7. Ibid.

8. Sengupta, "Alt-A: The Forgotten Segment of the Mortgage Market," p. 56.

9. Bravve et al., "Out of Reach," p. 2.

10. Ibid., p. 5.

11. US Department of Housing and Urban Development (HUD), "An Overview of the HUD Budget," p. 1.

12. Fischer, "House Bill's Deep Cuts in Public Housing."

13. Connie Pascale, personal e-mail, February 26, 2014.

14. Desmond, "Eviction and the Reproduction of Urban Poverty."

15. HUD, "Fiscal Year 2013 Program," p. 1.

16. National Alliance to End Homelessness, "The State of Homelessness in America."

17. Ibid.

18. Reardon and Bischoff, "Income Inequality and Income Segregation."

19. Reardon and Bischoff, "Growth in the Residential Segregation of Families," p. 11.

20. Ibid., p. 5.

21. Ibid., p. 23.

22. Wilson, *The Truly Disadvantaged,* pp. 46–62.

23. Ibid.

24. Rugh and Massey, "Racial Segregation and the American Foreclosure Crisis," p. 644.

25. Lowrey, "Cities Advance Their Fight Against Rising Inequality."

26. Centers for Disease Control and Prevention, "CDC Health Disparities and Inequalities Report."

27. McQuaid, "Unwelcome Neighbors."

28. US Census Bureau, "State and County QuickFacts," http://quickfacts.census.gov/qfd/states/22/22093.html (St. James Parish) (accessed December 30, 2014); http://quickfacts.census.gov/qfd/states/22/2267250.html (St. Gabriel City) (accessed December 30, 2014).

29. National Academy of Public Administration, "Addressing Community Concerns."

30. US Census Bureau, "State and County QuickFacts," http://quickfacts.census.gov/qfd/states/22/22093.html (St. James Parish) (accessed December 30, 2014); http://quickfacts.census.gov/qfd/states/22/2267250.html (St. Gabriel City) (accessed December 30, 2014).

31. Frosh, "Nestled Amid Toxic Waste."

32. Raymond, Wheeler, and Brown, "Inadequate and Unhealthy Housing," pp. 21–27.

33. Keenan and Shaw, "Coronary Heart Disease and Stroke Deaths."

34. Keenan and Rosendorf, "Prevalence of Hypertension and Controlled Hypertension."

35. Hughes et al., "HIV Infection."

36. Freedman, "Obesity."

37. MacDorman et al., "International Comparisons of Infant Mortality," pp. 1–7; Ingraham, "Our Infant Mortality Rate Is a National Embarrassment."

38. MacDorman and Mathews, "Infant Deaths."

39. National Coalition for the Homeless, "Mental Illness and Homelessness."

40. Thomas, "Ronald Reagan and the Commitment of the Mentally Ill."

41. McClelland, "Schizophrenic Killer," p. 21.

42. Thomas, "Ronald Reagan and the Commitment of the Mentally Ill."

43. US Census Bureau, "Income, Poverty, and Health Insurance Coverage."

44. Moonsinghe, Zhu, and Truman, "Health Insurance Coverage," pp. 35–37.

45. Rosenthal, "The $2.7 Trillion Medical Bill," p. A1.

46. Pear, "Doctors Who Profit from Radiation," p. A12.

47. Klein, "11 Facts About the Affordable Care Act."

48. Reardon, "The Widening Academic Achievement Gap," p. 91.

49. Tavernise, "Poor Dropping Further Behind Rich in School," p. A1.

50. Ibid.

51. Ibid.

52. Coleman et al., *Equality of Educational Opportunity.*

53. Cremin, *The Republic and the School,* p. 8.

54. Venkatesh, *Gang Leader For a Day,* p. 247.

55. Giridharadas, "The Immigrant Advantage," p. SR5.

56. Crawford, "The New Digital Divide," p. 1.

57. Brodkin, "How Jews Became White Folks," p. 48.

58. Rose, "The Social Inequality of Public Transport."

59. Ibid.

60. The EITC is a credit for those who earn low to moderate incomes. It reduces taxes and can even mean receiving a refund, so working families can keep more of what they earn.

61. Collins and Mayer, *Both Hands Tied.*

62. Appelbaum and Gebeloff, "Even Critics of Safety Net Increasingly Depend on It."

63. Ibid.

64. Ibid.

65. Ibid.

66. Short, "The Research: Supplemental Poverty Measure."

67. Burkhauser and Larrimore, "How Changes in Employment, Earnings, and Public Transfers Make the First Two Years of the Great Recession (2007–2009) Different."

68. Clark, "Hungry for Savings."

69. Smith, "The Retirement Gamble."

70. Ibid.

71. Ibid.

72. Ibid.

4

The Nature of the Economic System

SOME DEGREE OF INEQUALITY IS INEVITABLE, BECAUSE HUMAN BEINGS have different abilities and skills. However, as much as writers such as Richard Herrnstein and Charles Murray have wanted to ascribe all differences to a divide primarily in intelligence and cognitive abilities, inequalities beyond a certain range are created by the structural characteristics of a social system.

In 1994, Herrnstein and Murray published a controversial book called *The Bell Curve: Intelligence and Class Structure in American Life,* and unleashed a torrent of outrage among fellow academicians and policymakers. It reopened centuries-old questions about the nature of human differences. Herrnstein and Murray asked whether the racial markers apparent to the naked eye might also harbor more fundamental differences in mental and moral endowments of different races.

As early as the seventeenth century, Joseph Arthur, Comte de Gobineau, had raised similar queries and had concluded that there indeed was a difference among racial lines, that the "yellow and black" races were intellectually and morally inferior to the whites, and that it was best to keep them at arm's length to avoid "dilution of pure stocks by inbreeding." Similarly, in the 1960s, Nobel Prize–winning physicist William Shockley and psychologist Arthur Jensen had pointed out that there was an immutable genetic link between race and intelligence that explained why blacks scored lower on IQ tests.[1]

All this supposedly "scientific" evidence added fodder to the prevailing racist attitudes that attributed the disadvantage that people of color suffered to their innate "inferiority." The argument being that no amount of social engineering in the form of progressive social policies could rectify what nature had destined.

Herrnstein and Murray joined this "distinguished legion" when they framed social class in the context of intelligence, arguing that the elite were also a "cognitive elite" distinguished by high scores on IQ tests and other measures of cognitive ability. The middle class were a "cognitive middle" stuck between the elite and the vast **underclass** of "dullards" lacking intellectual capacity to make their way up the social ladder. According to Herrnstein and Murray, intelligence determined who would be rich and who would be poor—not structural or sociological factors.

The most controversial aspect of the book was its dogged assertion that poverty, welfare dependency, illegitimacy, and crime all resulted from low intelligence. And since blacks scored significantly lower than whites on IQ tests and other such measures, they were the most likely to end up as welfare recipients and criminals.

In attributing IQ to genetics, Herrnstein and Murray turned a blind eye to the research that has consistently demonstrated the role of environmental factors and availability of educational resources in enhancing intellectual ability and cognitive skills. Those who are poor score lower on tests because they lack the resources that allow the affluent to surround their children with intellectually rich and creative experiences. (Chapter 7 considers this subject in more detail.) Herrnstein and Murray rejected the role of economic and structural factors in determining academic success and economic mobility. They argued that no amount of government assistance would enable the underclass to become middle class. It was all an exercise in futility.

Competing Explanations of Inequality

The Functionalist Explanation of Inequality

In most societies, how much individuals have in terms of income and wealth primarily depends on the work they do and the rewards (wages, salaries, social status) that the work generates. As proponents of **structural functionalism**, Kingsley Davis and Robert Moore argued persuasively that how much people earn depends on the work they do.[2] More specifically it depends on two factors: first, how important their work is—that is, how functionally unique it is, and how much the work of other people depends on it; and second, how much training and education is necessary to perform that work.

Therefore, the income difference that exists between a janitor and a professor at a university exists precisely because the professor's job is functionally unique (a physics professor can teach physics but not sociology, and vice versa); many others depend on it for their livelihood or otherwise (students, lab assistants, department secretaries, librarians, textbook publishers, writers, bookstores, etc.); and it requires learned skills and education. By contrast, as important as a janitor's job may be, it is not functionally unique to the same degree (a physics professor can perform a janitor's job, but not vice versa), nor does it require specialized skills and education—some practice and training with the work regimen and cleaning materials, of course, but not specialized education. Therefore, a certain degree of inequality can be attributed to the nature and the particular importance of the work, and to the training and education it requires. This explains why a physics professor makes more money than a janitor and, as Max Weber would also suggest, earns more social status.[3]

But this argument does not explain the scale of inequality, especially the scale of inequality in incomes that we are witnessing today. In other words, how much more does the physics professor or a chief executive officer of a company have to be paid to reflect these distinguishing features? For example, this argument does not explain why the CEO of a corporation in the United States makes between 380 and 475 times more, on average, than a worker for that corporation, when the ratio is much smaller in most European countries. As Table 4.1 shows, the CEO-to-worker pay ratio in the United States averaged out to 331 to 1 in 2013.[4]

For some companies the ratio is even larger. As noted in Chapter 2, the CEO-to-worker pay ratio for Apple is 6,258 to 1. In other words, it takes 6,258 Apple employees to match the total compensation that CEO Tim Cook receives ($378 million in 2011). According to an Economic Policy Institute report published in May 2012, "From 1978 to 2011, CEO compensation increased more than 725 percent, a rise substantially greater than stock market growth and the painfully slow 5.7 percent growth in worker compensation over the same period."[5] Is a CEO's job, together with the skills required to perform that job, so significantly unique that this person should be paid so much more than their employees? Why in the United States is the CEO's job considered more deserving of higher compensation compared to European or Japanese CEOs, for example? What has changed

Table 4.1 Average CEO-to-Worker Pay Ratio in the United States, 1983–2013

Year	CEO-to-Worker Pay Ratio
1983	46:1
1993	195:1
2003	301:1
2013	331:1[a]

Source: Executive Paywatch, "2013 CEO-to-Worker Pay Ratio," http://www.aflcio.org/Corporate-Watch/Paywatch-2014 (accessed October 16, 2014).

Note: a. Average CEO salary of $11.7 million compared to average worker salary of $35,239.

since the 1970s that has made the American CEO's work so much more important today?

In the mid-1970s, the American CEO was making, on average, 35 times more than the worker. By the end of the 1980s, executive pay was 120 times more than that of the worker, and in 2012 it was an average of 254 times more. According to the Economic Policy Institute report, much of the inequality in the United States can be directly attributed to this enormous gap between CEO pay and the wages of the average employee.

The Davis and Moore theory does very little to explain this gap. Similarly, Davis and Moore's way of understanding social inequality does not explain the current job trends that have resulted in such high rates of unemployment in the United States. For example, the Davis and Moore position cannot explain why important jobs of individuals at a software company— jobs that are functionally unique and require training and education—are lost, and the livelihoods of those individuals dismantled, when their company is outsourced to another country (such as India) where those same important jobs, requiring similar training and education, pay a much lower salary. There is no room in the Davis and Moore argument to account for decisions about jobs and salaries that are primarily based on the issue of cost and are only peripherally about qualifications and skills.

The degree of inequality, nationally and globally, and how inequality is generated, cannot be explained by Davis and Moore's quaint logic. The extent of inequality that we see in the United States today cannot be explained simply by referring to the functional uniqueness of a job and the education and training it requires. There are other, more fundamental forces at play here that determine the degree of inequality and the growing gap between rich and poor that we observe and experience.

The Conflict, Interactionist, and
Weberian Theories on Social Stratification

The conflict, interactionist, and Weberian theories on social stratification explain the social structures from which the rationale for inequality arises. They are descriptive theories describing the structural landscape in which social stratification is lodged. They describe the "what"—as in what characterizes the social stratification system of societies—instead of the "how"—as in how unequal distribution of resources, such as income and wealth, actually comes about. As we have seen, the structural functionalist position does answer the question of how inequalities of income and wealth come about.

The main tenet of structural functionalism that is at the basis of the Davis and Moore position argues that every aspect of society contributes to the maintenance of societal equilibrium—to its stability and order. According to this theory, society is characterized by **consensus**, because agreement is sought on how stability and order are to be realized, and on the cultural values and norms that support how income, wealth, status, and prestige are apportioned. It is society that decides which system of apportioning jobs and rewards is the best.

Conflict theory is the logical opposite of structural functionalism. The work of German sociologist Ralf Dahrendorf is the most representative of the conflict position, which argues, as the name implies, that society is rife with conflict. Conflict is ubiquitous, and conflict and dissension are integral to all structures in which some have authority over others. Individuals who have authority have the power to make decisions that others must obey. And that leads to conflict. Those who make decisions and those who must follow them are locked in a contentious relationship.

Dahrendorf refers to these relationships as "imperatively coordinated associations," meaning that authority is imperative and compulsory. Others must abide by these relationships. This dynamic automatically gives rise to conflict, out of which social stratification arises. There is very little consensus, if any, in the way that social stratification systems operate in the life of society.

Authority plays a significant role in Dahrendorf's view of social stratification, in terms of who makes decisions and who must obey them. The process of **institutionalization** ensures that certain positions in society are endowed with authority. Authority is inherent in such positions that people in certain classes occupy, and is not determined through the ownership of the means of production, as Marx and Engels would argue it should be.

Some classes are invested with authority and the power to control other people's lives, such as supervisors and managers. For those who occupy the class beneath these supervisors and managers, their lack of authority becomes the determining characteristic of their class position, as they are duty-bound to obey their supervisors and managers. Class is therefore determined by who does and who does not have authority. The differential distribution of authority between social classes is where class conflict arises.

Let us assume that a manager decides to withhold a pay raise for an employee. The employee will be upset with the decision. But if she or he asks for a raise, the manager can fire them and hire the next in line. The employee, if they do not want to lose their job, has no choice but to accept a stagnant wage. The authority of the manager trumps that of the worker. Thus the authority differential between the class of supervisors and managers, who have power, and the workers, who don't, becomes the paramount determinant of a society's system of social stratification.

The **interactionist theories** on social stratification are most associated with the works of Thorstein Veblen. In many ways, Veblen weds a macro- and micro-sociological approach in his analysis of class issues. On the one hand, he deals with macro-sociological structures such as business and industry, and in describing the dynamics between the two he adopts a position quite akin to that of the conflict sociologists. On the other hand, his most famous work deals with a micro-sociological study of the affluent and their lifestyle, one that is most definitely interactionist in its approach.

For Veblen the central problem in society is the tension between "business" and "industry." Business is made up of owners and "captains of industry," whose primary focus is maximizing profits by keeping prices high. In their effort to earn high profits, the business leaders limit production and supply, thus keeping prices high artificially. This obstructs the industrial system from operating at its fullest capacity in a way that would provide ample opportunities for employment and increase the general welfare and well-being of society.

Keenly interested in the radical causes of the first two decades of the twentieth century, Veblen was critical of capitalist institutions and culture. He argued that industry and "industrial arts" were created by the community of people over centuries. And the community was industry's rightful steward, since it was part of the **commons**, a common wealth of all people. But under capitalism, industry has come to be controlled by a few owners "through sabotage and salesmanship" for their own benefit.

With their misbegotten profits, the captains of industry carry on a lifestyle characterized by **conspicuous consumption** and **conspicuous leisure**. Conspicuous consumption is buying and surrounding oneself with material objects that are inordinately expensive and of little real value. Conspicuous leisure is the waste of time in nonproductive ways. The primary objective of such a lifestyle is to impress and influence others so that they end up emulating this way of life. In imitating the rich and their lifestyle, the entire society becomes wasteful—wasting time and money.

In many ways, Veblen's ideas are very relevant today when consumerism is at its pinnacle and people spend time, and money—which they often don't have—emulating the lifestyles of the rich and famous. And at the same time staying as far away from the lower classes as possible, making sure that the poor and homeless are "not in my backyard" (NIMBY).

The unequal distribution of wealth and income gives rise to divergent lifestyles, and society's attention turns to lifestyles. Yet the more critical questions about how those lifestyles came about become less important. Therefore, people view the homeless with disdain, seldom inquiring why people become homeless in the first place. At the same time, people admire the rich for their sensational ways of living, but seldom inquire what made their opulence possible. The admiration or contempt for the two lifestyles becomes a diversion concealing the actual dynamics that determine the parameters of how people live.

Max Weber described social stratification as having three dimensions—class, status, and power—and said that all people aspire to attain these things. Class is an economic category and depends on a person's income and professional credentials—whether doctor or blue-collar worker.

Status is about the prestige and honor attached to what people do. Supreme Court justices claim a lot of prestige and social status; used-car salesmen very little. Power is the ability that people have to control the circumstances of their lives. The machinist at a steel factory has less control over the circumstances of his life than does the person who owns the factory. The latter can hire and fire at will, promote and demote at will. The machinist, if part of a union, might have somewhat more control, but not enough to match the power of the owner. This is comparable to Dahrendorf's idea of the power of authority to get its own way.

What is interesting about Weber's analysis is that unlike Marx, who sees all three dimensions of social stratification flowing from class, Weber sees them as having independent realities. Class may or may not transfer into status—a prostitute may make a lot of money and belong to a higher economic class, but will draw no prestige or status. Mahatma Gandhi had no material wealth and so belonged to a lower class, but he made up for that with the status, prestige, and respect he commanded. We will return to Weber later in this chapter to discuss his analysis of capitalism.

Having reviewed some of the sociological perspectives on the structure and dynamics of the social stratification system in society, I am now ready to present the theoretical position that underpins my arguments in trying to explain income and wealth inequality.

Linking Social Systems and Inequality

In order to understand the extent of inequality that the United States experiences today, to understand why it is such a stubbornly enduring phenomenon, it is imperative that we understand how inequality is produced by the system that epitomizes this nation. The most widespread explanations of inequality talk about the loss of jobs and lack of technical preparedness of Americans in a world rendered "flat"[6] through globalization and technological innovations, changes in the structure of the economy, and skyrocketing salaries and bonuses on Wall Street, all of which are often attributed to greed, government complicity, and (depending on one's ideological position) the level of taxation of the rich—all of which really are symptoms and consequences of inequality rather than explanations of it. The explanation that I propose goes to the very root of what generates inequality: the system itself.

But what does it mean when we say that the system, or the society, or the economic system, or the social structure, generates inequality? We can use any of these concepts—society, economic system, or social structure— to express this idea without saying much at all.

But this is what is routinely done. We are in the habit of saying, "The system is just or unjust." "The economy is going up or down, creating jobs or wiping them out." Society, the economy, and the system are concepts that are constantly evoked as explanations, as if each of these entities, or **social facts** as Emile Durkheim would call them, had a life of its own and as a mechanism that somehow—and devoid of human intervention and agency—self-generates equality or inequality; employment or unemployment; poverty or prosperity; justice or injustice.

These are not, of course, by any token, self-generating mechanisms. But as sociologist George Ritzer writes, "The mind has the capacity to endow these structures with a separate and real existence; in sociological terms the mind has the capacity to reify these phenomena."[7] Reification occurs when "social structures that are created by people are endowed with a separate and real existence."[8] It is the process by which things that people create are seen as being natural and not controlled by human action—as being independent of human action. The economy, for example, is seen as working miraculously on its own without human intervention or human decisionmaking.

Many sociologists, such as Georg Lukacs, have described and analyzed this interesting phenomenon whereby human beings confront a self-made reality as being outside their control, whereby they are the "object" and not the "subject" of events. Max Weber and George Simmel considered reification as an almost inevitable fate of humankind, whereby humans become more and more powerless in the face of the objective reality that they themselves have created.

Karl Marx's analysis of the **fetishism of commodities** follows the same line of thinking. Humans create commodities, such as designer clothes, and then lose sight of the fact that it is they themselves who have given these commodities their form and value, instead kneeling down before their creations in supplication. The commodities take on a life of their own—with a power all their own, separate of human agency. And just like commodities, the economy, the state, society, and the market, too, are all "granted independent objective existence" separate of human agency. Simmel considered this "part of a universal tragedy." Max Weber similarly saw little escape from the inevitable reality of this **iron cage**. However, Marx saw this as "time bound," neither universal nor inevitable, and specific to the system of society called capitalism.[9]

As mentioned in Chapter 1, when I ask my students "What is the nature of the system we live in?" they respond by saying that the United States is a democracy, that it is a free enterprise system, that it is based on a free market economy. Some even say that the United States is a laissez-faire society. The system they are referring to is capitalism, but that word eludes them, as it does most Americans. Capitalism is fundamentally an economic system. It is an economic system that goes about resolving the three fundamental and interdependent economic problems all societies face in one way or another:

Any society, whether it consists of a totally collectivized communistic state, a tribe of South Sea Islanders, a capitalistic industrial nation, must somehow confront three fundamental and interdependent economic problems:

- *What* commodities shall be produced and in what quantities? That is, how much and which of alternative goods and services shall be produced?
- *How* shall goods be produced? That is, by whom and with what resources and in what technological manner are they to be produced?
- For *whom* shall goods be produced? That is, who is to get the benefit of the goods and services provided? Or to put the same thing in a different way, how is the total of the national product to be distributed among different individuals and families? A few rich and many poor? Or most people in modest comfort?[10]

Each economic system—capitalism, socialism, feudalism, slavery, hunting and gathering—confronts and resolves these three interdependent problems in distinct ways that give the economic system its unique character.

Each of these economic systems are a combination of **economic base and superstructure**. From the economic base a superstructure of political, legal, and cultural forms comes into being and nurtures and reinforces the economic arrangements and relationships. When the economic system of the United States was primarily determined by slavery, the entire political, legal, and cultural character of the nation was defined by that slavery. The political and legal decisions and the entire cultural complex—values, ideologies, customs, and mores—were erected to nurture and reinforce the system of slavery.

Similarly, the political and legal choices and the entire cultural edifice and consciousness of the present-day United States support and strengthen the capitalist economic system. Despite the desire of the true laissez-faire proponents to minimize and even eradicate the influence of government on the economy, in reality the entire enterprise of capitalism has always been inordinately impacted by the government—by all three branches, executive, legislative, and judicial. Similarly, the cultural ethos of the nation—its values, mores, ideologies, objectives, and priorities—also reflects the Weltanschauung, or worldview, of capitalism.

Adam Smith, Max Weber, and Capitalism

Adam Smith: The Wealth of Nations

Since Adam Smith and his book *The Wealth of Nations,* published in 1776, are evoked the most by the proponents of so-called free market capitalism to describe the logic and the mechanics of that system, it is appropriate to start our discussion of capitalism here.

Adam Smith envisioned a market populated by numerous buyers and sellers, each too small to influence the dynamics of the marketplace, whether the price of commodities, the wages of workers, the rate of profit, or some other factor. In his ideal of a competitive market, there were no large, business entities with monopoly powers. Monopolistic power and control were anathema to his idea of this system of perfect competition. In this system, each product—whether **commodity**, wage, profit, or rent—had its "natural price."

Smith describes "natural price" in the following terms: "When the price of any commodity is neither more nor less than what is sufficient to pay the rent of the land, the wages of the labour, and the profits of the stock employed in raising, preparing, and bringing it to the market, according to their natural rates, the commodity is then sold for what may be called its natural price. The commodity is then sold precisely for what it is worth, or for what it really costs the person who brings it to the market."[11]

The **market price** at which things are actually sold is not the same as the **natural price**. The market price "may either be above, or below, or exactly the same with its natural price." The market price is determined by the interplay of **supply**—"the quantity that is actually brought to the market"—and **demand**—"those who are willing to pay the natural price of the commodity, or the whole value of the rent, labour, and profit, which must be paid in order to bring it thither."[12]

If there is too much supply of a commodity (commodity A) and the market price is constantly below the natural price, then some of the entrepreneurs will shift their capital and stock to another commodity (commodity B) for which the returns are closer to the natural price. This will bring down the supply of commodity A, and the market price for it will once again reach a balance with its natural price. Too much investment now in commodity B will raise its supply and bring its market price below its natural price. As its price comes down, more people will flock to buy that product—so demand for that product rises. As the price of commodity B comes down, its producers will begin departing for more profitable pastures and products, supply will fall, and prices will once again rise to their natural level.

Adam Smith envisioned that this working of the "invisible hand" of the marketplace, by constantly urging the market price of all products and services to be at the level of their natural price, would produce outcomes for buyers and sellers, producers and consumers, entrepreneurs and workers, that would be fair and optimal for all.[13] In analyzing how the invisible hand would determine profit, Smith wrote of the producer that "the profit . . . is his **revenue**, the proper fund of his subsistence. . . . He advances to his workmen their wages, or their subsistence; so he advances to himself, in the same manner, his own subsistence, which is generally suitable to the profit which he may *reasonably* expect from the sale of his goods."[14] Smith believed that the expectation would be a reasonable one, close to the natural compensation that the perfectly competitive market would deliver.

Just as the market regulates both prices and quantities of goods according to public demand, so it also regulates the incomes, whether in the form of profits or wages, of those who combine forces to produce those goods. If profits in one line of business are markedly large, there will be a rush of other entrepreneurs into that field until surpluses thus created reduce the price and the profits and in turn push businesses out to other, more profitable areas. If wages are noticeably high in a particular kind of work, there will be a rush of individuals into this "favored occupation," until a surplus of workers pushes down those wages to the pay level of comparable jobs requiring a comparable degree of skill and training. In turn, this will push workers on to other professions where the wages are higher, until a surplus of workers there pushes the wages down. This cycle of ebbs and flows of capital and labor from one trade to another pushes profits and wages in one direction or another until the supply of each is best adjusted to the demand.[15]

This process assumes, as Adam Smith argues, "that all buyers and sellers are small, that there is no advertising or promotional cost or product differentiation, and that the attention of producers is on selling their goods at the best possible price, *rather than driving other producers out of the market to capture their market share*."[16] He was averse to any kind of monopoly power and believed that such power, "granted either to an individual or to a trading company [has] the same effect as a trade secret in trade or manufactures. The monopolists, by keeping the market constantly under stocked, by never fully supplying the effectual demand, sell their commodities much above the natural price, and raise their emoluments, whether they consist in wages or profits, greatly above the natural price." Further:

> The price of monopoly is upon every occasion the highest which can be got. The natural price, or the price of free competition, on the contrary, is the lowest. . . .
> The exclusive privileges of corporations, statutes of apprenticeship, and all those laws which restrain, in particular employments, the competition to a smaller number than might otherwise go into them, have the same tendency. They . . . keep up the market price of particular commodities above the natural price, and maintain both wages and profits of labour and the profits of the stock employed about them somewhat above their natural rate.[17]

In situations where there was "perfect liberty," the market price would always gravitate toward the natural price, thus ensuring the well-being of society.[18]

Adam Smith did not want the government to interfere with the self-regulating mechanism of the market, to which he attributed an almost omnipotent, self-determining character. He seemed to believe that it would be ludicrous to think that the government could somehow have power or control over a system that was not under the control or power of any particular individual or group. Here is what he wrote to describe the role of the government, which he refers to as the "sovereign":

> The sovereign is completely discharged from a duty, in the attempting to perform [said duty] he must always be exposed to innumerable delusions, and *for the proper performance of which no human wisdom or knowledge could ever be sufficient;* the duty of superintending the industry of private people, and of directing it towards the employments most suitable to the interest of society.
>
> According to the system of natural liberty, the sovereign has only three duties to attend to; three duties of great importance, indeed, but plain and intelligible to common understandings: first, the duty of protecting the society from the violence and invasion of other independent societies; secondly, the duty of protecting, as far as possible, every member of society from the injustice or oppression of every other member of it; and, thirdly, the duty of erecting and maintaining certain public works and certain public institutions, which it can never be for the interest of any individual, or small number of individuals, to erect and maintain; because the profit could never repay the expence to any individual or small number of individuals, though it may frequently do much more than repay it to a great society.[19]

In other words, even though Smith was opposed to government meddling with the operations of the market, he did not have qualms advocating for the sovereign's active role in ensuring social welfare for the greater society when private entrepreneurs would not be forthcoming to take up the charge, because those services—such as education, health care, building social infrastructure, public works, and basic research for discovery and invention—would not necessarily be profit-generating.

Thus the picture of so-called free market capitalism that emerges from Adam Smith's analysis in *The Wealth of Nations* is somewhat different from the system that his staunchest advocates exhort in his name.

Max Weber: The Protestant Ethic and the Spirit of Capitalism

Students of sociology encounter the topic of capitalism most often through Max Weber's theory of the **protestant ethic**, which encouraged the development of capitalism. In his book, *The Protestant Ethic and the Spirit of Capitalism,* Weber attributes the rise of capitalism in the West to a particular "spirit" most conducive to its development. That this "spirit" is fostered by Calvinism, an ascetic form of Protestantism, gives Weber's book its

MAKING CONNECTIONS
What Is Neoliberalism?

Those who advocate the ideology of neoliberalism evoke Adam Smith continuously to lend a certain authenticity to their ideas. But let us first consider the rather schizophrenic nature of the idea of **liberal** in the parlance of US politics and economics.

In politics, a liberal position is one presenting a set of ideas that are progressive and "left-wing." A liberal advocates for an active role for the government in supporting the disadvantaged and marginalized, as opposed to a "conservative" and "right-wing" position that argues for minimum government intervention in the lives of the average citizen.

Liberal politicians, however, are associated with social policies that are opposed by someone who is an economic liberal, or neoliberal. If liberal politicians want a more involved government, the economic liberal is one who wants just the opposite—a government completely out of people's lives and most importantly out of the market. Liberal politicians want government to regulate the market and control its excesses, whereas neoliberals want to liberalize the market by keeping government out of it as much as possible.

The most important tenet of neoliberalism is the emphasis on free markets—the idea that the market forces should be given primacy to determine the course of the economy and consequently people's lives. This implies that government should do nothing to regulate the market, should impose no burdens in terms of laws (such as a minimum wage), standards, and regulations to impede the free functioning of the market. Government should minimize its role by reducing or eliminating subsidies and transfer programs (welfare), and by privatizing state-run programs (such as Social Security).

This position does resemble, in spirit, the idea of the "invisible hand" and the laissez-faire society that Adam Smith espoused. But the similarity ends there, since the marketplace that Smith envisioned was characterized by perfect competition between numerous sellers; this was not the "imperfect" marketplace of today, over which a handful of corporations have monopoly control.

In the context of globalization, neoliberalism promotes lifting barriers to make trade between nations easier. Therefore it espouses the removal of tariffs and rules that can impede the free flow of capital, commodities, and raw materials (but most definitely not the free flow of people or labor) so that production systems can be made most profitable by locating the cheapest resources and labor.

The **Washington Consensus**, derived from the policies of the International Monetary Fund and World Bank and endorsed by the US government, is considered the "how-to" manual of neoliberalism. It emphasizes that poor nations must be integrated into the global capitalist system if they are to develop their economies. In order to facilitate that process, countries must open up their borders to direct foreign investment (multinational corporations) and foreign competition; governments must minimize expenditures on social programs (such as education and health care); state-owned enterprises (such as water supply) must be privatized; and the market must be freed to

(continues)

What Is Neoliberalism?

---

determine interest rates, wages, prices, and profits. The neoliberal prescription also champions broadening the tax base, deregulating the labor market, and discouraging and often outlawing collective bargaining.

The Washington Consensus encourages governments to adopt **structural adjustment policies**, or severe belt-tightening of their finances, as a precondition for borrowing money from international financial institutions to fund development programs. Neoliberalism is the ideology underpinning the development strategies that define present-day globalization.

---

name and purpose. The "spirit of capitalism" is based on the ethos of deferred gratification, hard work, and an avoidance of life's pleasures for the more worthy goal of earning money, increasing wealth, and attaining economic success without end, not because of personal greed but because it is a moral and ethical imperative and what God wants people to do.

Ben Franklin's famous Poor Richard maxims capture much of this "spirit": God gives all things to industry; plough deep while sluggards sleep and you shall have corn to sell and to keep; a stitch in time saves nine; procrastination is the thief of time; there are no gains without pains; not to oversee workmen is to leave them your purse open, and so forth—all preaching the virtues of industry, frugality, punctuality, diligence, and ultimately the idea that the habits that these behaviors form are imperative to the development of capitalism. Weber credited Protestantism, particularly Calvinism, as crucial to the rise of this "spirit." Weber probably would contend that the crisis in capitalism today is because of an eclipse of these values.

Capitalism rose in the West because the religion practiced there encouraged an "inner-worldly asceticism" that urged its followers not to renounce the world in order to seek salvation, but to work hard through self-denial for the sake of individual enterprise and the accumulation of wealth—and asserted that this was the real path to salvation. A world-denying asceticism or "otherworldly asceticism" that preaches the renunciation of all worldly matters for the realization of salvation, such as in Buddhism and Hinduism, was not conducive to development of the "spirit" that would create a system of capitalist enterprise and accumulation. But Protestantism provided a rationale that was fundamental in inspiring an "entrepreneurial motivation, key to the genesis of capitalism."[20]

Max Weber contends that the Protestant translation of the Bible

> expresses the value placed upon rational activity carried on according to the rational capitalistic principle, as the fulfillment of a God-given task. This . . . gave to the modern entrepreneur a fabulously clear conscience—and also [gave him] industrious workers; he gave to his employees as the wages of

their ascetic devotion to the calling and of co-operation in his ruthless exploitation of them through capitalism the proposal of eternal salvation. . . . [S]uch a powerful, unconsciously refined organization for the production of capitalistic individuals has never existed in any other church or religion.[21]

According to this rationale, employers and employees cooperate in capitalist enterprise to fulfill through their vocation a devotion to God. The employer's "ruthless exploitation" of his workers, and the workers' willing surrender to this exploitation, are inspired by the promise for each of eternal salvation. This provides the employer with a clear conscience in his exploitative ventures, and provides the worker faith that the misery he endures in his work might "pre-destine" his deliverance after death.

It was not, however, a conscious process. The Calvinists did not consciously seek to create a capitalist system; it was an unanticipated consequence of the Protestant ethic.[22] This idea that individuals create social structures that soon take on a life of their own and become reified entities over which people have no control is a running theme in much of Weber's sociology. Capitalism, **rationalization**, and the bureaucratic structures they spawn in corporations and government lead to impersonality, which ensures rationality and efficiency. Modern humans are increasingly cogs in a giant machine and can do little to influence these giants, which are cold and often insane and crush the human spirit—we are caught in an iron cage![23]

But Weber's analysis of capitalism is not really a "theory which is applicable in different times and places. It is a historical analysis of how a set of developments happened, in this case the 'spirit of capitalism' and the system it gave rise to in Western Europe."[24] It is an important analysis, but it does not help us much to understand how a capitalist system spawns inequality.

For a general theory of capitalism and how it is connected with our primary inquiry into the widening economic inequality in the United States, we now turn to Karl Marx.

Karl Marx and Capitalism

Invoking Karl Marx and his theories is not an easy matter, since his name, and the term **Marxism**, are wrought with so many misconceptions, misrepresentations, preconceptions, prejudices, and predilections. Mention of Marx often stirs up a heavy dose of mocking, ridicule, and even suspicion.

And because of the political lines invariably drawn, Marxism is dismissed as lacking scientific objectivity and balance. This is rather incongruous, since even a cursory perusal of Karl Marx's and Friedrich Engels's voluminous writings and complex logic, firmly embedded in history, economics, philosophy, and sociology, should dispel any questions regarding their exhaustive, thorough, and reasoned analysis.

They raise the ire of many because they question some of the integral principles of a system that most take for granted and hold above scrutiny or question. Until quite recently, Marxist social theory was consigned to the margins, out of reach of most sociology students. But Marx's notoriety has always preceded him. In the sociology classes I teach, most of my students have not heard of Max Weber, Auguste Comte, or Herbert Spencer. But they all know of Marx, or at least they think they do.

In his book *Marx's Concept of Man,* Erich Fromm writes:

> It is one of the peculiar ironies of history that there are no limits to the mis-understanding and distortion of theories, . . . there is no more drastic example of this phenomena than what has happened to the theory of Karl Marx in the last few decades. There is continuous reference to Marx and to Marxism in the press, in the speeches of politicians, in books and articles written by respectable social scientists and philosophers; yet with few exceptions, it seems that the politicians and newspapermen have never as much as glanced at a line written by Marx, and the social scientists are satisfied with a minimal knowledge of Marx. Apparently they feel safe in acting as experts in this field, since nobody with power and status in the social-research empire challenges their ignorant statements.[25]

To understand the system called capitalism, it is fundamental that we turn to Marx and his magnum opus *Das Kapital,* in which his "fundamental aim was to lay bare the laws of motion which govern the origins, the rise, the development, the decline and the disappearance of a given form of economic organization: the capitalist mode of production."[26] As Ernest Mandel writes in his introduction to the first volume of Marx's magnum opus: "What Marx's *Capital* explained was above all the ruthless and irresistible impulse to growth which characterizes production for private profit and the predominant use of profit for capital accumulation."[27]

In the current heyday of global capitalism, with its ever-growing polarization of the global society between a few very rich owners of capital and the great majority, trying to understand how the system exemplified by the capitalist mode of production itself might have generated this chasm leads us quite naturally to Marx and his analysis. Capitalism, which is characterized primarily by the private ownership of the means of production, with the principal objective to maximize profits, generates inequality in a natural and organic way. Inequality is integral to capitalism and imperative for its continued expansion. And the more unregulated and unfettered capitalism is, the more inequality it generates. In the rest of this chapter, therefore, following the logic offered by Marx, we examine how capitalism generates the processes that create a climate in which equality/inequality, poverty/prosperity, and equity/inequity are produced and tolerated.

In her concise and erudite book *The Origins of Capitalism,* Ellen Meiksins Wood writes:

Capitalism is a system in which goods and services, down to the most basic necessities of life, are produced for profitable exchange, where even human labor power is a commodity for sale in the market, and where, because all economic actors are dependent on the market, the requirements of competition and profit maximization are the fundamental rules of life. Because of those rules, it is a system uniquely driven to develop the forces of production and to improve the productivity of labor by technical means.

Above all, it is a system in which the bulk of society's work is done by propertyless laborers who are obliged to sell their labor power in exchange for a wage in order to gain access to the means of life. In the process of supplying the needs and wants of society, workers at the same time create profits for those who buy their labor power. In fact, the production of goods and services is subordinate to the production of capital and capitalist profit. The basic objective of the capitalist system, in other words, is the production and self-expansion of capital.[28]

It is in capital that the system of capitalism originates. Capital is the life force of capitalism, and the entire endeavor of capitalism is fueled by its infinite desire to accumulate more and more of it, to generate more and more capital.

What Is Capital?

So, what is capital? Is it money? Is it machines, factories, and technology? Is it the income-producing assets? Is it the means of production? Capital is all of this, and more. More than anything, capital is a process. Money in the pocket is not capital; money that is continuously invested and reinvested, either in corporations and firms or in speculative ventures where currencies and "futures" themselves are bought and sold to make a profit—money that continuously circulates, trying to augment its worth—is, technically speaking, capital in its true form. Its "boundless drive for enrichment, this passionate chase after value, makes the movement of capital . . . limitless."[29]

The aim of the capitalist is not to provide commodities or services to sustain "life and society."[30] It does not produce bread, shoes, clothes, video games, refrigerators, or cars because people need them, but because these products "make more and more money for the investor."[31] They are not produced and sold because of their "use value" per se, but because of the profit that can be made by their production and sale—that is, by their "exchange value." To the capitalist, therefore, the commodity is important only because it earns a profit—not because of any intrinsic value or lack thereof. The commodity—anything that can be bought and sold for profit—is a means to an end. And that end is an infinite craving for more and more profit, which leads to more and more capital accumulation.

Ernest Mandel, in describing what the capitalist mode of production is, also sketches its modus operandi:

> The capitalist mode of production is fundamentally determined by three conditions and three only: (1) the fact that the mass of producers are not owners of the means of production in the economic sense of the word, but have to sell their labor power to the owners; (2) the fact that these owners are organized into separate firms which compete with each other for the shares of the market on which the commodities are sold, for profitable fields of investment for *capital,* for sources of raw materials, etc.; (3) the fact that these same owners of the means of production (different firms, corporations) are, therefore, compelled to extort maximum surplus value from the producers, in order to accumulate more and more *capital.*[32]

The Structural Features of Capitalism

First and foremost, the workers do not own the machines, tools, technology, or resources that they work with as they go about producing goods and services and, in the process, earning their livelihood. The machinist at General Motors does not own the machines used to make the car; the sales clerk at Wal-Mart does not own the cash registers; the worker at McDonald's does not own the fryers, the grill, and the ovens; the systems analyst at IBM does not own the computer and the hard drive; the bank employee, financial analyst, or bond trader at JP Morgan Chase does not own the bonds, the software programs, or the money; the aide at a nursing home does not own any of the health-care tools.

Each of these groups of workers depend on the "means of production" to produce commodities in the form of goods (cars, hamburgers) or services (sales, banking, nursing)—but they do not own the means of production, nor do they own the product of their labor. Fewer and fewer people today are self-employed, so most have no choice other than selling their labor to the owners of these "means of production," or capitalists, in order to make a living.

Second, the owners of these various means of production are organized into separate firms that compete with each other for a share of the market. For example, General Motors competes with Ford, Toyota, and BMW; Wal-Mart with K-Mart and Costco; McDonald's with Burger King and Taco Bell; IBM with Microsoft and Apple; JP Morgan Chase with Goldman Sachs and Credit Suisse; and so on—each competing with the others to maximize the returns on their investment, in order to maximize their profits and become more competitive than the others. The objective is to become a monopoly—the sole seller of a product or service—by driving out all competition and capturing the entire market, thus paving the path to an endless cycle of capital accumulation.

Third, since the entire endeavor of capitalism is fueled by the "boundless" thirst to accumulate more and more capital, the exclusive enterprise of the system becomes the discovery of ways to extract maximum profit. The commodity, which is anything that can be bought and sold for profit, and can take the form of either goods (cars) or services (car mechanics), is what is produced to generate revenues or values that the capitalist desires to earn through ownership of the means of production—whether it is a car factory or an auto service station.

The Labor Theory of Value

But the owner alone cannot produce the commodity on the scale needed in order to earn revenue; workers are needed to do that. The owner may own all the factories and auto services, all the raw materials, but without workers, nothing will be accomplished. Workers are critical in the entire process of production.

All the machinery, technology, tools, and raw materials are ultimately "crystallized" in the product that the worker produces. Their work is ultimately the critical step that brings together all the other factors of production; it is the worker's final contribution that produces the commodity the capitalist then sells to earn profit. Without the worker, all the machinery, technology, tools, and raw materials will remain as nothing but a random assemblage.

The point is that no matter how many times materials and their components and machines are bought and sold, they do not create any new value. Whatever value they have when a capitalist buys them for use in production, the value afterward (minus natural depreciation) is the same. The value that earns the capitalist a profit is added solely by the activity of the worker. As Michael Parenti succinctly writes: "Of itself, capital cannot create anything; it is the thing that is created by labor."[33]

Let us suppose an entrepreneur sets up shop by investing $1,000 in machines and materials (constant capital). He wants to produce a particular widget. No matter how he configures and arranges the machines and materials, they will not produce any value on their own. So he hires a worker and pays him $100 (variable capital) to produce the widget. The worker uses the machine and raw materials to produce the widget, which the owner sells for $1,300. The cost of production for the owner was $1,100. The $200 surplus value was added to the product solely by the labor of the worker. This is true regardless of whether the commodity sold for profit is a product or a service.[34]

The worker produces what the capitalist needs to sell to make a profit, and the job performed provides the worker with the ability to pay for food, rent or mortgage, clothes, child-care costs, and the like. A majority of Americans must work for somebody else to earn their livelihoods. Data from the Federal Reserve indicate that the percentage of American households who own their own business continues to decline. More and more, the worker is dependent on someone else to provide a job and pay a wage or salary.

The cost of labor is the single most expensive item in the capitalist's costs of production. The machines, tools, cash registers, fryers, and so forth, are onetime purchases. These of course must be replaced and updated if the capitalist wants to remain competitive, but only periodically, not regularly. The raw materials, due to **economies of scale**, can be purchased cheaply and in bulk. But the cost of labor is cumulative. The wages and salaries must be paid on a regular basis—daily, weekly, or monthly. For the capitalist, minimizing the cost of labor is critical to maximizing profit.

Capitalism needs workers to produce, but profit cannot be maximized if workers are paid in terms equivalent to the total value that they produce. So in setting up and running a business, the labor cost is subject to the most scrutiny. And the constant tendency of capital is to force the cost of labor back toward zero.

Thus, slavery is the most efficient system for maximizing profit; the slave requires no payment, and only minimum upkeep for continued survival and labor. (Slave labor is discussed further in Chapter 10.) In the absence of slavery, driving down wages as much as possible and lengthening work hours are preferred ways to maintain a high rate of profit. But when a nation has minimum-wage provisions, or workers are vigilant and united in strong trade unions, corporations constantly shift their jobs to those countries where government scrutiny is minimal or absent and workers have little power to object to slavelike wages. Today, as globalization transforms the world into a single marketplace, and adds some 2 billion wage laborers to the available global work force through the opening up of China and the collapse of communism in Central and Eastern Europe,[35] capitalism, as the sole economic structure, pits workers in one country against those in another, in the process driving wages into the ground as profits soar limitlessly.

It is this last point—the rate of wages and salaries and the profits they help generate—that is the most critical to our analysis and understanding of income and wealth inequality in the United States and as more and more countries embrace capitalism as their model of economic development everywhere else. The capitalist system, in its quest to maximize profit and shift all wealth upward into the hands of those who own the means of production, innately produces inequality. This is not because of greed or malice; it is because the logic and pursuit of profit maximization are considered irrefutable and natural—and the capitalist mode of production is considered equally inexorable. The system is seen as being independent of human agency and reified, with individuals simply "actors on a stage" of a predetermined reality.

The Anatomy of Profit

In every society where there are rich and poor, where society is divided into classes, the wealth of the rich has its origins in the unpaid labor of society as a whole. The wealth of the slave master came from the unpaid labor of slaves; the wealth of the feudal lord from appropriating a portion of his subjects' harvest. In a capitalist society, the wealth of the capitalist comes from values extracted from what the worker produces over and above what the worker needs to produce to earn his or her own wage.

To better understand how to explain this, I visited my neighborhood McDonald's. It was a few hours past dinnertime, but the restaurant was still very busy, especially the drive-through. And the workers, between taking orders, flipping burgers, and attending the cash register, did not have a spare minute. The shift manager was personable and sociable, and I made the most of her sociability. "How many customers do you get each day?" I asked as I paid for my meal. "On average, including the drive-through, about a thousand; many more on weekends," she said.

I was taken aback. I had expected a much smaller number. But when I searched on the Internet for how many customers McDonald's serves in the United States, the number that came up was an average of 8 customers per minute—or almost 8,000 over the course of a day. For my small town, the number the young manager gave made sense. She checked the register, and the total number of customers so far this day was 888. They had sold $5,391.87 worth of their fast food between 6 A.M., when they started serving breakfast, and 10 P.M., when I bought my meal of a Big Mac, small fries, and small soft drink for $8.37.

This particular McDonald's had seven employees working at the time I visited. Considering that each worked an eight-hour shift, there would be fourteen workers in all for the sixteen hours between 6 A.M. and 10 P.M. A quick search on the Internet gave me the average hourly wages of workers at McDonald's:

- Shift manager: $9.58.
- In-store cashier: $7.79.
- Drive-through cashier: $7.84.
- Fry cook (two at my McDonald's): $8.46.
- Grill cook (two at my McDonald's): $7.79.

So, the average wage for the workers was $8.24 per hour, almost what I paid for my meal, $8.37. What I paid for my meal paid for one worker hour at my neighborhood McDonald's, but during that hour this McDonald's sold much more than one meal. For one employee working an eight-hour day, just eight customers like me would pay their entire wage for that day.

But collectively, the fourteen workers at this McDonald's served 888 customers. That comes to 63 customers per worker. So, how much more than what they earned for themselves did they earn for McDonald's in one day? Here lay the answer to my inquiry.

Below I outline what the workers at my neighborhood McDonald's made (on average) during that sixteen-hour period (6 A.M. to 10 P.M.), each working an eight-hour shift:

- Two shift managers, each working an eight-hour shift: $9.58 × 16 = $153.28.
- Two in-store cashiers, each working an eight-hour shift: $7.79 x 16 = $124.64.
- Two drive-through cashiers, each working an eight-hour shift: $7.84 × 16 = $125.44.
- Four fry cooks, each working an eight-hour day: $8.46 × 16(2) = $270.72.
- Four grill cooks, each working an eight-hour day: $7.79 × 16(2) = $249.28.

Thus, in that sixteen-hour period the workers collectively made $923.36. Given that they made and sold $5,391.87 worth of food during that period, total revenue per hour amounted to $336.99 ($5,391.87 ÷ 16)). Total wages per hour amounted to $57.71 ($923.36 ÷ 16).

Here are my conclusions:

- The fourteen fast food workers who work at my neighborhood McDonald's make a total of $57.71 an hour.
- In that hour, they make and sell $336.99 worth of food.
- Each hour they work, they collectively produce value worth $279.28 more than their wages ($336.99 minus $57.71).
- When they are producing $336.99 worth of value an hour, they really need to work just 10.27 minutes to earn the value of their total hourly wage of $57.71.
- This 10.27 is the **necessary labor time**—the time required for revenue to pay for their wage—calculated as the total hourly wage of the workers divided by the total hourly revenue they produce (57.71 ÷ 336.99 = 0.171 × 60 minutes = 10.27). Thus, in 10.27 minutes, the workers earn the value of what they produce; the rest of the time, they are not working for themselves. What they produce in the other 49.73 minutes does not belong to them; this is the **surplus value** that they produce. The profit of the workers' employer originates in this surplus value. Every hour they work, they make $279.28 worth of profit for the employer. But they cannot quit at the end of 10.27

minutes, because they have sold their labor to their employer at its hourly value. The value of that entire hour, therefore, belongs to the employer.[36]

At every step of the way, the machinists who made the fryers and ovens for McDonald's, the migrant worker who picked the lettuce and tomatoes, and the worker at the meat plant who processed and packaged the hamburger, all augmented the profit of the company with the value they produced for which they were not paid—the revenue over and above what was needed to earn their own wage. Thus, surplus value is the unpaid labor of workers that generates the profit that enables capital to accumulate limitlessly.

It is important to keep in mind that the value the worker creates is the most critical element. The owner can own all the machines, raw materials, and merchandise. But it is the McDonald's grill cook who makes the hamburger, the Nike worker who makes the shoe, the Wal-Mart cashier who rings up the purchase—without them, the capitalist cannot earn the value that generates profit and adds to accumulated capital.

Marx referred to this process of creating society's wealth as the **labor theory of value**. The worker is the most vital player, converting all the dead capital (machines, technology, raw materials) into real value. The worker's labor adds the value and creates the wealth—and the collective social labor of all workers creates the wealth of nations. That is why the worker is so critical in the entire cycle of how the wealth of nations is produced.

Yet when a vast part of this labor remains unpaid and unremunerated while the lion's share of the value produced is appropriated by the capitalist, it leads to the impoverishment of the worker and the enrichment of the employer—widening the gap between the rich and the poor in the larger society in a continuous cycle. This is the essence of the resulting exploitation, upon which rests the entire chain in the extraction of surplus value, and thereby profit. The use of the term *exploitation* here is not a moral injunction but simply a delineation of a process that leads to inequality, inequity, and injustice.

In a fast-breaking story in January 2012, it was reported that Apple makes $400,000 in profit per employee, per year—more than other large corporations such as Goldman Sachs, Exxon Mobil, and Google.[37] The fact that almost all of Apple's 70 million iPhones, 30 million iPads, and 59 million other products have been manufactured abroad means that most of Apple's workers are paid less than the minimum wage allowed in the United States; therefore, the surplus value they generate is colossal.

For example, in Foxconn City, China, 230,000 employees work twelve-hour days at a facility that makes iPhones, earning less than $17 a day. In June 2012, Apple announced that it had made $8.8 billion in profit in just the preceding three months—the same as Mongolia's entire economic output for all of 2011. How much surplus value did each worker generate to amass this sum? Every Apple employee produced $400,000 worth of revenue—surplus value—over and above what was needed to earn their own wage.[38]

In another news item about Apple in the *New York Times* in June 2012, reporter David Segal wrote about Jordon Golson, a worker at an Apple store in Salem, New Hampshire, and one of 30,000 service employees selling products in Apple stores. In a stretch of three months in 2011, Golson sold $750,000 worth of Apple products. He was earning $11.25 an hour, very much like most of Apple's service employees, who make $25,000 a year. As Segal wrote: "They work inside the world's fastest growing industry, for the most valuable company, run by one of the country's most richly compensated chief executives, Tim Cook. Last year, he received stock grants, which vest over a 10-year period that at today's share price would be worth more than $570 million."[39]

Let us see how much surplus value Golson created in those three months, which contributed toward producing some of Cook's spectacular compensation:

- Golson sold $750,000 worth of Apple products in three months, or 480 hours (12 weeks at 40 hours per week).
- He sold $1,562.50 worth of Apple products per hour ($750,000 ÷ 480).
- He earned $11.25 an hour, compared to the $1,562.50 he sold.
- In order to earn his wage of $11.25 an hour, when he is producing $1,562.50 an hour, Golson really needs to work just 26 seconds (11.25 ÷ 1,562.50 = 0.0072 × 3600 seconds = 25.92). This 26 seconds is the necessary labor time in which enough revenue is earned to pay for his wage.
- His unpaid labor for 7 hours, 59 minutes, 34 seconds per day, for 90 days, is the surplus value that he produced, which went into Apple's phenomenal profit.

All corporations and firms conduct their businesses through methods comparable to Apple's. Because of its phenomenal success, Apple has become the role model, with others busily emulating its business principles. For the capitalist, the objective is clear: maximize profit by scouring the world for the cheapest labor in order to extract the most surplus value.

In all class-based societies, the accumulated wealth of the richest comes from unpaid labor, or surplus labor. In slave societies it comes from the unpaid labor of slaves, and in capitalist societies from the unpaid labor of workers, the latter of whom are often paid spectacularly less than the value they produce. The capitalist reaps the profits of this accumulated surplus value, producing the endless cycle of capital accumulation, the raison d'être—the reason for being—of the capitalist mode of production.

Conclusion

Let us sum up the process through which profit is created, capital is accumulated, and society's wealth is concentrated in the hands of a few, to further clarify how capitalism creates inequality, and creates it organically, innately, and inevitably:

1. The workers must sell their labor to make a living; the great majority of us must depend on someone else to earn a livelihood.
2. The capitalist buys that labor through a wage or salary, which is the value paid for that labor.
3. The value of labor, however, is not the same as the value that labor produces. The value that labor produces is much more than the value the capitalist pays for labor.
4. The difference between the value of labor and the value that labor produces is surplus value.
5. Labor therefore can be divided into two components: one that produces the value equivalent to the worker's wage (necessary labor), and one that constitutes the surplus value for which the worker is not paid (surplus labor). It is this unpaid, surplus labor that produces surplus value.
6. The surplus value is created by the worker, and only the worker.
7. Finance capital, raw materials, and land used in the process of production do not create surplus value. It is the worker who assembles all this to create a product with use value (such as a car or an iPod) that will ultimately earn the revenue that will create the surplus value.
8. It is the new value created by the application of the worker's labor that must then be divided into wages to be paid to the worker, with the profit kept by the capitalist.
9. The higher the wage, the smaller the surplus value, and thus the smaller the profit. The lower the wage, the higher the surplus value and profit.
10. The sole objective of the capitalist is to maximize profit, and thus the capitalist's primary intent becomes to drive down wages.
11. Since the product of labor belongs to the capitalist, so does the surplus value.
12. The capitalist uses part of the surplus value to pay rent, interest, utility costs, taxes, and so forth. The part of surplus value retained by the capitalist is the profit.

13. What the capitalist does with surplus value (establish foundations, endowments, charities, philanthropies) is less important, for the purposes of this book, than the process through which that surplus value is extracted (constant lowering of wages, union busting, pitting high-wage workers at an automobile assembly plant in Detroit against their very low-wage counterparts in Mexico, etc.) and the consequences of that process—accumulation of wealth in the hands of a few and the widening of the gap between the rich and the poor. Much of the charitable activity (directed at the poor) that surplus value funds might not be necessary if the wages paid to workers truly reflected the wealth that workers create.

14. This process of extraction of surplus value is pursued in every sector of the capitalist economy, regardless of what is being produced, whether a good or a service, whether in a factory, hospital, nursing home, software firm, restaurant, landscaping industry, university, bank, or investment firm. Wherever the objective is to earn a profit, the underlying principle—that surplus value is generated by the worker—applies.

15. As wages are pushed lower, and profits skyrocket and wealth continues to flow upward—aided by the policies of a distinctively compliant "capitalist form of state power" (discussed further in Chapter 6) and abetted by the forces of globalization, mechanization, financialization, and the like—the chasm between the rich and the poor grows ever wider.

Thus there is nothing mysterious about why the gap between the rich and the poor has widened in the United States. It has followed a natural trajectory from the policies and practices of an economic system dedicated to the maximization of profit, to the exclusion of everything else. Economic inequality is an inevitable and inherent consequence of capitalism.

Michael Parenti writes: "Economic democracy means adequate food, housing and clothing for all; economic security at all age levels; good medical care regardless of ability to pay; free education to the highest level of one's ability; and the right to non-exploitative employment and a safe clean environment."[40] But capitalism is not in the business of providing economic democracy or "social justice." Not because it has failed to do so, but simply because it cannot do so if it must fulfill its existential purpose of maximizing profit and continuously accelerating the process of capital accumulation.

With the demise of the Soviet Union, the end of the Cold War, and the parting of the Iron Curtain, huge swaths of the world have opened up new realms for Western capitalism to exploit in its endless search for capital accumulation. The entire world has become a single marketplace as global capitalism "batters down all Chinese walls," roams the world looking for the cheapest labor and cheapest raw materials, and "compels all nations, on the pain of extinction, to adopt the bourgeois (capitalist) mode of production . . . and creates a world after its own image."[41]

As globalization opens up new vistas and new opportunities for corporations to maximize their returns, they leave behind the communities in the United States that were their mainstays for decades—Camden, Detroit, Chicago—rendering millions unemployed and tectering unsteadily at the cusp of this newest and deadliest economic reality, and thus pushing the economic divide even wider. Globalization has only amplified capitalism and its endless addiction to profit. Loyalty to one's own country and its people has evaporated in the face of this relentless search for ways to accumulate more and more capital. Globalization has combined with mechanization, corporate consolidation, and financialization to further deepen and intensify inequality. In its quest to expand continuously, capitalism must seek out global markets for labor, resources, markets, and consumers. But this has far-reaching economic consequences domestically.

Work that was done once by humans has been consigned to machines and robots, reducing the need for workers and increasing the profitability of corporations. In their rush to automate and computerize, millions of jobs on which people once depended have been lost. The jobs taking the place of those lost to globalization and mechanization are primarily service jobs that pay by the hour at the minimum wage, which is not enough to pull a family above the poverty level. We are therefore witnessing a profound structural change, from manufacturing to a service-based, postindustrial economy, with all the changes in jobs and wages that this entails.

The nature of economic activity has also drastically changed, from occupations that once created wealth, to occupations, such as transnational financial speculation, that create none—other than the spectacular returns they bring to well-placed individuals and financial institutions. The pressures of globalization and technological innovation have resulted in a flight of economic activity to the virtual spheres of Internet speculation and into the hands of machines and foreign lands. In communities across the United States, the absence of jobs that in the past were steppingstones to economic stability and to the middle class is deepening the economic divide.

Notes

1. Schmidt, "Trial May Focus on Race Genetics."
2. Davis and Moore, "Some Principles of Stratification."
3. Ibid.
4. AFL-CIO, "Executive Paywatch."
5. Mishel and Sabadish, "CEO Pay and the Top 1%," p. 2.
6. Friedman, *The World Is Flat.*

7. Ritzer and Goodman, *Sociological Theory*, pp. 55–56.

8. Ibid.

9. Ibid., p. 268.

10. Samuelson, *Economics*, pp. 17–18.

11. Smith, *An Inquiry into the Nature and Causes of the Wealth of Nations*, p. 55.

12. Ibid., p. 56.

13. Ibid., pp. 56–60.

14. Ibid., pp. 55–56 (emphasis added).

15. Heilbroner, "Commanding Heights."

16. Korten, "The Mythic Victory of Market Capitalism," p. 186 (emphasis added).

17. Smith, *An Inquiry into the Nature and Causes of the Wealth of Nations*, p. 61.

18. Ibid., p. 62.

19. Ibid., p. 651 (emphasis added).

20. Knapp, *One World, Many Worlds*, p. 91.

21. Weber, *The Protestant Ethic and the Spirit of Capitalism*, p. 30.

22. Ritzer and Goodman, *Sociological Theory*, p. 145.

23. Knapp, *One World, Many Worlds*, p. 80.

24. Ibid., p. 106.

25. Fromm, *Marx's Concept of Man*, p. 1.

26. Mandel, introduction to *Capital*, p. 12.

27. Ibid., p. 11.

28. Wood, *The Origin of Capitalism*, pp. 2–3.

29. Marx, *Capital*, pp. 253–254.

30. Parenti, *Land of Idols*, p. 73.

31. Ibid.

32. Mandel, introduction to *Capital*, pp. 81–82 (emphasis in original).

33. Parenti, *Land of Idols*, p. 75.

34. See discussion of Marxism at www.marxists.org.

35. Harvey, *Enigma of Capital*, p. 58.

36. Marx, *Capital*, p. 341.

37. Duhigg and Bradsher, "How US Lost Out on iPhone work," p. A1.

38. Ibid.

39. Segal, "Apple's Retail Army," p. A1.

40. Parenti, *Land of Idols*, p. 73.

41. Marx and Engels, *The Communist Manifesto*, pp. 39–40.

5

Globalization and Changing Economic Structures

EACH DAY AS PASSENGERS TRAVEL FROM WASHINGTON, D.C., TO NEW York, they see a sign on the Lower Trenton Bridge between Philadelphia, Pennsylvania, and Trenton, New Jersey, illuminated brightly at night, declaring proudly: "Trenton Makes, World Takes." It harkens back to a time when Trenton, like most of the United States, was a thriving manufacturing center. In 1911, when the sign was first installed, and in 1938, when a bigger and brighter sign replaced the original one, Trenton was a bustling manufacturing center for rubber, wire rope, steel, linoleum, ceramics, and cigars. Italian, Hungarian, and Jewish immigrants from Europe, and African American migrants from the US South, came to Trenton to work in the factories and take the first step to becoming middle-class Americans.

Today the factories are gone and all attempts to revitalize Trenton have been largely unsuccessful. Since Trenton is the capital of New Jersey, most individuals with jobs there are employed by the state. They work in the city, but do not call it home, escaping instead to the suburbs at the end of the workday. The white middle class has moved out, and today Trenton is primarily African American (52.0 percent in 2010) and Latino (33.7 percent), with an average per capita income of $17,400. Of its population, 24.5 percent live well below the federal poverty threshold of $23,201 for a family of four.[1]

The story is worse for neighboring Camden, New Jersey. Chris Hedges, in his recent article on the city in the newsmagazine *The Nation,* refers to it as the "City of Ruins." Camden, he writes, is the "poster child of postindustrial decay," with the drug trade being "one of the city's few thriving businesses." It was once "like America, an industrial giant. It was the destination for . . . immigrants, who in the middle of the last century, could find decent paying jobs that required little English or education."[2]

Here, too, the white middle class has moved out, and today 48.0 percent of Camden's 77,283 inhabitants are African American and 47 percent

113

are Latino. With an average per capita income of $12,807 and 36.1 percent of the population living below the poverty line,[3] Camden is regarded as the poorest metropolitan area in the United States. Hedges warns that Camden "stands as a warning of what huge pockets of the United States could turn into as we cement into place a permanent underclass of the unemployed, slash state and federal services in a desperate bid to cut massive deficits, watch cities and states go bankrupt and struggle to adjust to a neo-feudalism in which the working and middle class are decimated."[4]

Flint, Michigan, with a population of 101,558, has an average per capita income of $14,910, with 36.6 percent of its population living below the poverty line; 56.6 percent of the population is African American,[5] descendants of some 6 million blacks who left the South in the great exodus between 1915 and 1970, escaping segregation and the sharecropper life to fill the numerous manual jobs opening up in the industrial centers of the North.[6] Today, Flint, the birthplace of General Motors, is considered the most egregious example of deindustrialization. Birthplace also of Michael Moore, the city is featured in many of his movies, which document the breakdown of community that happens when jobs that anchor people's lives disappear.

A recent film titled *Detropia* documents the story of Detroit, a city with a population of 1.8 million in the 1950s that has since been decimated by deindustrialization, as automobile manufacturers began closing plants, and suburbanization, as new highways took people with money out of the city, leaving behind workers, primarily African American, amid "idle, rotting factories, with fantastic networks of chutes, pipes and stacks."[7] Detroit is populated by a constantly embattled middle class—such as those who faced the threat of losing their jobs at the city's American Axle company unless they agreed to a big pay cut. But the plant was shut down, the documentary informs, leaving the workers "stunned": "It's not just the lost money, they say; it's the humiliation, the sense that their work is worthless." The documentary is ultimately about the United States, "the impromptu graveyard of industrial ambition."[8]

As Monica Davey noted in a *New York Times* article in May 2014, today in Detroit there are 40,000 dilapidated buildings, hollowed-out remains of factories, and 114,000 parcels of vacant land. It will cost $850 million just to clean up the blight.[9] In the summer of 2013, the city of Detroit filed for bankruptcy, unable to pay its debt of at least $18 billion.[10] The loss of the industrial tax base was the leading culprit. Are other US cities facing a similar fate as they witness dissolution of their manufacturing base?

In 1950, 34 percent of Americans were employed in manufacturing.[11] Between 2000 and 2011, manufacturing employment fell by 5.6 million. By 2009, only 9 percent of the workforce was employed in direct manufacturing or production occupations—machinists, tire builders, metal workers, textile workers, engine assemblers, and the like.[12] Across the country, the steady drop in manufacturing jobs has become a source of serious concern, since this is associated with growing unemployment, rising income inequality, and a general breakdown of community—exactly what is happening in Trenton, Camden, and Flint.

There is a general consensus that the entire structure of the US economy has undergone a dramatic change. The country is no longer an industrial giant, with Americans today earning their livelihoods primarily in the service sector. The smokestacks are gone, and along with them the relatively higher salaries and benefits that the strong labor unions were able to negotiate for their members.

The bulk of the new jobs that are being added, that do not require college degrees, are primarily low-end service jobs—which pay the minimum wage. The largest increases in jobs have occurred in government and health care. But there is a mismatch between the levels of education that these latter jobs require—a few years of college, if not a college degree—and what those displaced from manufacturing jobs or otherwise unemployed can realistically offer.

Catherine Rampell, reporter for the *New York Times,* wrote in August 2012:

> While a majority of jobs lost during the downturn were in the middle range of wages, a majority of those added during the recovery have been low paying, according to a new report from the National Employment Law Project. Middle range wages in occupations such as construction, manufacturing and information, with median hourly wages of $13.84 to $21.13, accounted for 60 percent of the job losses from the beginning of 2008 to 2010. Lower wage occupations, with median hourly wages of $7.69 to $13.83, accounted for 21 percent of job losses during retraction. Since employment started expanding, they have accounted for 58 percent of all job growth. The occupations with the fastest growth were retail sales at a median wage of $10.97 an hour and food preparation workers at $9.04 an hour. Some of these lower paying jobs are being taken by people just entering the labor force, like recent high school and college graduates. Many though are being filled by older workers who lost more lucrative jobs and are just trying to scrape by.[13]

Across the country, job growth for the next decade is projected primarily in retail trade, health care, and food services. The average salary for these sectors, according to the US Bureau of Labor Statistics, was $30,000, in 2012, from a low of $18,720 for food service workers to a high of $67,930 for registered nurses.[14] Growth is also projected for a small base of high-end occupations, such as software developers, computer-systems analysts, and those in the biopharmaceutical industries. How many of the millions of laid-off American factory workers can realistically be retrained for the technical, mathematical, and problem-solving skills that the higher-paying jobs in the latter group require?

According to the Bureau of Labor Statistics, during the recession of 2007–2009 the US unemployment rate was higher than most other industrialized countries. The official unemployment rate for the entire nation in 2009 peaked at 10 percent.[15] By September 2014, the unemployment rate was close to half that, at 5.9 percent: 5.1 percent among whites and 11 percent among blacks. The government also reported that in September 2014 only 62.7 percent of the population was participating in the labor force. Where are the missing 56.8 percent of the working-age population? These are individuals who have stopped looking for work (2.2 million) and therefore are no longer included in the official unemployment figures, or who work part-time when they really need full-time work, or who work jobs that do not match their qualifications (7.1 million).[16] The economic crisis that the United States faces is primarily a crisis of jobs. The growing divide between the rich and the poor can be primarily attributed to the absence of decent-paying jobs for the large majority.

Stephanie Moller, Arthur Alderson, and François Nielsen, in their article "Changing Patterns of Income Inequality in US Counties," summarize the main arguments that much of the rest of this chapter will provide, and make the connection to rising inequality:

> Since the middle of the 20th century, employment in the secondary sector has declined in the United States and other industrial societies—a trend labeled *deindustrialization*—with corresponding expansion of the tertiary (service) sector. These labor force changes are sometimes interpreted as heralding the emergence of a postindustrial society. Deindustrialization was exacerbated by the 20th century globalization trend in which relatively low-skilled manufacturing jobs were "exported" abroad to developing economies offering inexpensive labor. The contributing role of deindustrialization in the inequality upswing was suspected early on. The rationale is that deindustrialization forces a shift of employment from the relatively high wage and egalitarian manufacturing sector to the more unequal tertiary sector, boosting the overall level of inequality.
>
> Inequality within the tertiary sector is relatively high because of the bifurcation of the sector into the very profitable, higher-wage producer services, including finance, insurance and real estate, on the one hand, and other, more labor-intensive, lower-wage services, including personal services, on the other hand. In addition, producer service industries are information- and knowledge-intensive; these industries have created more managerial and professional jobs than the remaining service industries, increasing income heterogeneity within this component of services.
>
> Differentiation within the service sector accounts for much of the association between post-industrialization and earnings inequality. We can predict the following associations between income inequality and the distribution of the resident labor force of a county among industry sectors. Controlling for other variables in the model, income inequality is expected to be (1) lower in

counties with higher employment in manufacturing, (2) higher in counties with higher employment in high-wage service industries, and (3) higher in counties with higher employment in low-wage service industries.[17]

Moller and her colleagues therefore provide a concise analysis to explain why, even as the economy has sputtered, leaving so many unemployed and leading to unprecedented levels of poverty, the profit margins of the richest 1 percent have reached unprecedented heights. There is a sense of bafflement here. For how can the incomes of the highest earners escalate even as more people lose their jobs? When the economy hits bottom, how can it be that everyone does not suffer equally?

According to a composite of numbers based on data from the New York State Comptroller's Office, the Federal Reserve, and the US Bureau of Labor Statistics, at the height of the Great Recession, between 2007 and 2009, as unemployment rose by 102 percent and home equity (market value of a house minus the mortgage balance, i.e., what is still owed on the house) fell by 35 percent, Wall Street profits soared by 720 percent.[18] But as discussed in previous chapters, there is nothing incongruent in this connection; in fact, the rise in profits has been facilitated by the rise in unemployment of US workers and the savings in labor cost that the unemployment made possible. Profits have risen and the financial rewards have become concentrated in the hands of a tiny elite because the shocks that the economy has experienced, due to such trends as globalization, mechanization, corporate consolidation, and financial speculation, have been borne by the working and middle classes.

According to Jacob Hacker and Paul Pierson, authors of *Winner-Take-All Politics,* the bottom half of the population, through lost jobs and lost income, has made possible unprecedented levels of income gain for the top earners. From roughly 9 percent in 1974, the income accruing to the top 1 percent has soared in recent years, to 23.5 percent in 2007 when corporate profit as a share of the economy reached a seventy-nine-year high, compared to the 24 percent in 1928, on the eve of the stock market crash.[19]

A *New York Times* survey inquiring into the occupations of the top 1 percent finds that the largest single group in the top 1 percent comprises those who list their occupation as manager—specifically of security companies, investment companies, and commodity brokerage firms. In his singular contribution to the study of inequality in the United States, G. William Domhoff does some "decompressing" of this group to see what types of wealth assets the 1 percent possess relative to the rest of Americans that enable them to participate in the economy so profitably.[20]

As Table 5.1 shows, the bottom 90 percent of Americans own a mere 12.2 percent of the kinds of assets (capital) that are able to earn a capital gain (such as interest, profit, and dividends). In contrast, the top 1 percent

Table 5.1 Wealth Distribution by Investment Asset, 2007

Asset	Top 1 Percent	Next 9 Percent	Bottom 90 Percent
Business equity	62.4	30.9	6.7
Financial securities	60.6	37.9	1.5
Trusts	38.9	40.5	20.6
Stocks and mutual funds	38.3	42.9	18.8
Nonhome real estate	28.3	48.6	23.1
Total investment assets	49.7	38.1	12.2

Source: Domhoff, "Wealth, Income, and Power."

own 49.7 percent of the same types of assets, which enables them to earn the lion's share of returns. The bottom 90 percent are unable to participate in this economy on their own terms because they do not have access to the right kinds of assets—the kinds of assets that create jobs. Since they do not own these types of investment assets, they must depend on those who do own them for their jobs and livelihoods. They are shut out completely from the processes that determine whether they will have jobs or not and whether they will have the power to bargain for wages, benefits, and other aspects of the work environment.

Ownership of capital confers on the owners the power to provide jobs or to take them away entirely. There is nothing to stop the owners from shutting down places of work, or firing those considered to be hindering their profit. And given that the foremost motive of the owners is to maximize profits (return on capital), all decisions about creating jobs or eliminating them are contingent on what will maximize returns. This is the sole and omnipresent goal—the sole rationale for investing.

Karl Marx regarded capitalism as a progressive force in history. It had broken down the barriers of feudal society and had established the industrial and technological capability for unlimited advancement. But capitalism carries within it the seeds of its own destruction, because of its inherent contradiction. It has the potential to provide everyone with the opportunity to live secure and comfortable lives, but private ownership and the private appropriation of profit, and the need to continuously maximize profit, continuously compromise this potential. Capitalism has made it possible for many Americans and also a fortunate few around the world to enjoy a standard of living of unprecedented wealth. But racked with and almost devoured by its internal contradiction, capitalism continually falls short of its promise.

The system of capitalism in which we live, work, study, and raise our families is guided solely by this overarching goal—an insatiable hunger for profit and capital accumulation. It is not about providing people with decent jobs that pay a decent wage so they can live with stability and dignity. It is not about providing goods and services that will enrich the lives of the entire nation. It is not about providing quality and affordable education, health care, child care, and elder care. It is not about creating sound communities where families can live without fear of guns and violence. It is not about ensuring that each individual has the opportunity to fulfill their human potential so they do not fall prey to the temptations of crime and drugs. It is not about protecting the environment so it can sustain life for generations to come. It is not at all about securing and ensuring a social compact. The focus is exclusively on profit.

"As a result of this," Jay Feldman, a retired corporate lawyer, wrote in the *New York Times* in August 2012, "we have witnessed corporate downsizings and outsourcing of jobs; restructuring of pension plans or their complete termination; reductions in health care benefits; and wage stagnation in spite of increased productivity. Domestic suppliers have been squeezed or, more often, replaced by cheap foreign sources. Customers seeking service are confronted with automated answering machines and foreign call centers. Environmental concerns are viewed as obstacles to profitability." But at the same time, "the senior managers of these enterprises have seen their compensation grow exponentially as a reward for their perceived contributions to the bottom line."[21]

The focus of this chapter is the complex dynamic that the desire for ever-higher levels of profit has instigated, and that extraordinary and unprecedented advances in technology have facilitated. A series of developments have reorganized, rearranged, and reconfigured the economic activities of the nation, continuously funneling money upward and concentrating wealth in the hands of fewer and fewer individuals.

What has the government done in the midst of this trend to protect the interests of the majority, their jobs, and their economic well-being? Nothing of any real significance. In fact, government policies themselves have played a critical role in permitting the changes that have diminished the economic prospects of the majority of the people of the nation compared to the affluence of the top corporate elite. Chapter 6 is devoted to deciphering how instrumental the government and its policies have been in facilitating the widening of the income divide. Here, we identify four particular processes that separately and in combination have resulted in the dramatic loss of jobs and the remarkable escalation in rates of profit:

- Mechanization, or the increasing use of machines to do the jobs that people once did.
- Globalization, or outsourcing of jobs to low-wage regions of the world.
- Corporate consolidation, through mergers, acquisitions, and leveraged buyouts, to reduce competition and produce massive layoffs.
- Financial speculation, which with its quick returns has become the choice pursuit of investors, instead of investment activities that produce real value and create jobs.

Mechanization and Restructuring of the Workplace

The loss of manufacturing jobs is the single most defining feature of the current state of the US economy. Sociologists have attributed this downturn to a phenomenon they identify as deindustrialization. They see the precipitous decline in manufacturing jobs as signaling the advent of a postindustrial society, occurring in the course of normal social evolution as breakthroughs in science and technology lead to innovations that enable manufacturing firms to install labor-saving devices, which reduce their need for workers as the labor productivity of each worker increases.

Therefore, the decline in the number of people employed in manufacturing is attributed to the rapid growth in labor productivity that has come about with the increased use of automation, mechanization, robotics, and other labor-saving technologies. Labor productivity in the United States has increased at a rate of 2.2 percent every year since 1947.[22] But increased labor productivity has led to higher levels of unemployment, since fewer workers are needed to produce the same amount of goods. So as workers become increasingly labor-productive, employers hire fewer workers, leading to an overall decline in the manufacturing sector's share of total national employment.[23]

It is in the nature of the capitalist marketplace that a corporate enterprise must constantly change, update, and improve its instruments of production and distribution if it is to remain competitive. Capitalists do not really have a choice if they are to stay competitive and keep profit margins high; they must constantly revolutionize production. In *The Communist Manifesto,* Karl Marx and Frederick Engels write: "The bourgeoisie cannot exist without constantly revolutionizing the instruments of production. . . . Constant revolutionizing of production, uninterrupted disturbance of all social conditions, everlasting uncertainty and agitation distinguish the bourgeois epoch from all earlier ones."[24]

Automated technology is becoming ubiquitous in every venue of economic activity—from manufacturing to retail to white-collar jobs—such that "workers are losing the race against the machine."[25] Technology, which John Maynard Keynes referred to as the "new disease of technological unemployment," has always displaced work and jobs.[26] But the pace of automation has accelerated recently, because of a combination of technologies including robotics, numerically controlled machines, computerized inventory control, voice recognition, and online commerce.[27]

We have all witnessed how automation has become a regular part of our lives. It is convenient and makes our lives easier. Capitalism is all about convenience, and convenience sells and fattens the bottom line, but at the expense of someone's livelihood. Labor-saving devices are desirable, but only in times of full employment, when individuals are not dependent on that labor for their livelihoods. If machines eliminate all jobs, how are the people who depend on those jobs supposed to make a living? What alternatives are there?

If there should ever come a time when there are enough jobs to employ every person who needs work, and when those jobs pay people enough to live comfortably, with dignity, and fulfill their potential, then there will be no problem relegating all the tedious, repetitive, mindless jobs to machines. But that time has not yet arrived.

A sure way to maximize profits is for manufacturing firms and corporations to adopt labor-saving devices. Machines are a onetime purchase requiring occasional maintenance and upgrades, but need not be paid a regular wage or provided with vacations and benefits. As Jeremy Rifkin writes, referring to the use of robots in car manufacturing:

> As the new generation of "smart" robots, armed with greater intelligence and flexibility, make their way to the market, automakers are far more likely to substitute them for workers, because robots are more cost effective. It is estimated that each robot replaces four jobs in the economy and, if in constant use twenty-four hours a day, will pay for itself in little more than a year. As more computerized operations are introduced into the manufacturing process, thousands of blue collar workers will become jobless.[28]

The range of service jobs that are continuously being lost to technology include:

- Banking, where ATMs are replacing human tellers.
- Customer service, which almost all businesses are replacing with computerized voice recognition.
- The office, where transformation from a paper-based environment to an entirely electronic environment is increasing the productivity of business and is good for the environment, but also is eliminating jobs for millions of clerical workers.
- Mail delivery, where technologies are reducing volume due to changes in how Americans communicate, move money, send packages, and buy goods. The US Postal Service is in danger of bankruptcy for this very reason, and millions of postal workers may lose their jobs as post offices are closed.
- Electronically automated shipping, which may result in a loss of tens of thousands of jobs in warehousing, shipping, and transportation.
- Wholesaling, where equipment retailers, as Rifkin writes, use "computerized monitoring and scanning equipment [to] dispatch shipping orders directly to manufacturers, bypassing wholesalers," and where

automated warehouses use "computer driven robots and remote controlled delivery vehicles [to] fill orders without the assistance of human
physical labor."[29]

- Retailing, where cashiers are being eliminated as self-scanning check-
  out allows consumers to complete their shopping at a faster pace.
- Access to technical help, where live support is being replaced by automated call centers facilitated by Internet technology, creating an economy that, as Nathan Newman puts it, is "centered on 'bits' and email
  in cyberspace."[30]
- Airports, where automated check-in counters are replacing airport
  personnel.

In each of these ways, labor costs are reduced, allowing for bigger returns
on capital. The unprecedented gains in profit margins and the subsequent
widening of the income divide have occurred because of the losses that the
working and middle classes have incurred due to innovations in technology.

Some sociologists look at declining jobs in manufacturing and the phenomenon of deindustrialization from a rather different perspective. It is
important to be familiar with this perspective, since it is so prevalent
throughout the entire discourse on postindustrialism. These sociologists
argue that as a society becomes more and more affluent, spending patterns
change and demand for services increases, leading to a fall in demand for
manufactured goods. Goods are durable and entail fewer purchases. A
household needs only a fixed number of appliances, which do not need to
be replaced continuously. However, services are needed continuously.

According to sociologists such as Daniel Bell, author of *Post Industrial
Society,* as a population becomes more and more affluent, its need for services increases proportionately—people more often go to restaurants, take
their clothes to be laundered, hire someone to mow their lawns, and go to
the gym. As consumers spend more of their disposable income on services,
the lowered demand for goods brings about a slowdown and then a decline
in manufacturing. From this perspective, deindustrialization is seen as a
natural progression as societies prosper.

This position is highly untenable, for two reasons. First, due to the
"new consumerism" that has taken hold in the United States, demand for
goods keeps increasing. As Juliet Schor discusses in her book *The Overspent American,* a sequel to her *The Overworked American,* this increased
consumerism is not so much about keeping up with the Joneses as it is
about emulating the preferences of the rich and the famous, whose lives,
congested with the latest trends in consuming, become the reference point
for so many Americans as they go about buying from an endless conveyer
belt of things—commodities, new ones every day, purchased with money
they often do not have.

MAKING CONNECTIONS
A Double Whammy: The Case of Textiles

Between 1990 and 2012, the US manufacturing sector lost 32.0 percent of its jobs, according to data published by the Bureau of Labor Statistics. This is a trend that has been experienced by every major manufacturing sector, but with the most dramatic job loss occurring in textiles and apparel manufacturing. The two sectors lost 76.5 percent of their jobs between 1990 and 2012. For every 100 jobs in textiles and apparel manufacturing in the United States in 1990, only 31 jobs in textiles and 15 jobs in apparel remained in 2012. In 1991, 56.2 percent of all clothing that Americans bought was US-made apparel, compared to a mere 2.5 percent in 2012.[1] In 1994, the North American Free Trade Agreement (NAFTA), which eliminated import duties on clothing manufactured in Mexico, provided strong incentive for US apparel makers to shift their factories to Mexico. The job loss in textiles began in earnest then. When China joined the World Trade Organization (WTO), it benefited from the latter's elimination of quotas regarding how much a country could export, which led the way to China's transformation into an "apparel powerhouse." Apparel and textile manufacturing relocated to China, and then to India and Bangladesh, wherever wages were even lower.

In a September 2013 report in the *New York Times,* Stephanie Clifford writes about the return of textile plants to towns in the United States like Gaffney, South Carolina, that were once strong centers of textile manufacturing until they lost out to the forces of globalization. This return of textile plants to the United States has been encouraged by consumer preference for US-made clothes and by textile plants seeking escape from prohibitive costs of transportation from outsourced factories in the third world. Parkdale Mills is the biggest buyer of raw cotton in the country and produces fabric for other US clothing companies. It reopened a plant in Gaffney called Carolina Cotton Woods in 2010. Labor costs in the United States today "aren't that much higher than overseas because [these plants] have turned to automation and are employing far fewer workers. . . . Machines have replaced humans at almost every point in the production process. Take Carolina Cotton Woods in Gaffney: The mill here produces 2.5 million pounds of yarn a week with about 140 workers. In 1980, that production level would have required more than 2000 people. . . . [P]oliticians' promises that American manufacturing means an abundance of jobs [are] complicated—yes, it means jobs, but nowhere near the scale there was before."[2]

Notes: 1. Clifford, "Textile Plants Humming, but Not with Workers," p. A1.
2. Ibid., p. A22.

People work harder and harder at jobs that do not pay much to begin with, often working two or three part-time, minimum wage jobs, just to have some money to spend on products to embellish themselves and their lives, just so they can feel good about themselves. As a consequence, personal debt in the United States is at an all-time high. Contrary to what was expected, postindustrialism has not meant a lesser need for goods. In fact, the rate at which people consume has made consumption their primary leisure activity and "consumer" their primary identity.

Second, there is a misconception regarding "durability" in this argument. According to Annie Leonard, author of *The Story of Stuff,* of all the things that people buy in the United States, only 1 percent are still being used six months after purchase. The rest has either been hauled off to the city dump or been stored away in overstuffed closets or rented storage boxes. This happens because "all goods are ultimately designed for the dump."[31]

The twin principles that guide US manufacturing—planned obsolescence and perceived obsolescence—ensure that things are designed to become obsolete quickly. Planned obsolescence is when products either are designed to break quickly or become useless within a short period of time so that consumers must buy the same product again and again.

Perceived obsolescence occurs when a product is perfectly functional but is "perceived" as being out-of-fashion or inappropriate and therefore useless. As Leonard documents, since World War II, television has been a primary source to drive consumer trends and fashions, goading people to buy more and more. Consumption is the fuel that keeps the "materials economy" of the capitalist system buzzing, and advertising is the tool that relentlessly stirs the desire to buy.[32]

Economist Victor Lebow summarized his hopes for the success of US capitalism in this famous quote: "Our enormously productive economy demands that we make consumption our way of life, that we convert the buying and use of goods into rituals, that we seek our spiritual satisfactions, our ego satisfactions, in consumption. We need things consumed, burned up, worn out, replaced, and discarded at an ever-accelerating pace."[33]

Given this background, it is hard to accept the argument that a decline in manufacturing jobs happens because people, as they become affluent, desire commodities less and turn to services instead. Demand for services has definitely increased, but this has not reduced consumers' desire for material goods. Thus, this argument, as an explanation for deindustrialization, seems rather weak. But in discrediting this argument, we reveal the critical role that consumption plays in the capitalist economic system.

Many of the problems that the United States has faced due to the downturn of the economy are worsened by the enormous consumer debt burden that Americans carry. It is a vicious cycle exacerbated by lost jobs and lost incomes. According to the Census Bureau, in 2011 69 percent of US households held some form of debt. The bureau defines debt as total money owed by households for credit cards, student debts, medical debts, and so forth. Median household debt has increased from $50,971 in 2000 to $70,000 in 2011.[34] According to the Federal Reserve, Americans carried a total of $13.3 trillion in total household debt in 2014, up from $11.5 trillion in 2011.[35] In 2009, the average credit card holder held 7.9 credit cards (1,245 billion cards divided by the 156 million people who hold them), and Americans on an average carried credit card debt of $4,000 per person.[36]

According to a report published by the Federal Reserve in June 2012, rising debt levels, in combination with declining incomes and the implosion of the housing market, have impacted the middle 60 percent of the population disproportionately. Therefore, as median income fell by almost 8 percent in 2010, and median net worth plunged by 40 percent in just three years, from $126,400 in 2007 to $77,300 in 2010, the economic well-being of the average American family slid back to its 1992 level.[37]

In this book, I argue that the dramatic loss of manufacturing jobs is not as much due to deindustrialization as it is a result of the restructuring of manufacturing with the aid of technology, which by increasing per-worker productivity has reduced the need for workers and even made them redundant. And as we will see, American workers in manufacturing have also lost out because the jobs that produce the commodities that people continue to buy—iPhones, iPads, and flat-screen televisions—simply no longer exist in the United States.

Globalization and the Income Divide

Not only has technological innovation rendered many workers redundant in manufacturing and service occupations in the United States, and thus led to their joblessness, but it has also facilitated the growth and expansion of market capitalism by opening up the world in ways previously unthinkable. Innovations in communication and international travel have opened up the world in unprecedented ways.

MAKING CONNECTIONS

When People Lose Their Jobs

Freehold, New Jersey, like many small towns of the US Northeast, was a manufacturing hub well into the 1970s. Nestle, 3M, Brockway Glass, Rug-mill, and Shirt Factories hired the local people and even some immigrants. There were businesses in Freehold that served the factories and the workers who were employed there in many different ways. There also were chicken farms, horse farms, and potato and corn farms. There was a train line that ran through Freehold, carrying passengers from New York and Trenton. From the stories that Jeanne and Charlie, the director and the treasurer of the food pantry Open Door, related, I could picture in my mind a bustling town with supermarkets and ice cream parlors that provided people with decent jobs and a comfortable life.

(continues)

When People Lose Their Jobs

Today, real estate is the only business in town. The farms have been sold to developers, who have built hundreds of homes. The downtown has seen some revival, as small restaurants run with immigrant labor draw an impressive crowd to Freehold on weekends. There is a sprinkling of bodegas that serve the Latino community, which makes up 42.9 percent of the town's population.[1] But the jobs that were the life force of the community aren't there anymore.

The absence of jobs has taken a toll on the lives of the people who live here, especially on the lives of the poor. One generation after another, they have carried the fallout that joblessness has created. When men don't have jobs, they don't form families. Without regular work schedules, they lose focus, motivation, and discipline. Alcohol, drugs, and promiscuity fill up their empty lives. Women are left to fend for themselves and their children. The women who first started coming to the social service offices and food pantries are now grandmothers carting in their daughters and granddaughters. Children are having children.

As I pulled into the Open Door parking lot one day, I watched a well-dressed woman and her teenage daughter loading bags of food into their rather decent-looking car as a volunteer came out with another bag. Jeanne, who has been the director of the food pantry for nearly two decades, told me: "These are the women who once used to donate to the pantry and served as volunteers here helping the poor; now they are on the other side of the counter themselves. Without the groceries they pick up at Open Door, they would have a difficult time putting food on their table."

People have been losing jobs and are in danger of losing their homes if they haven't lost them already. Many of the women have also been abandoned by their husbands and boyfriends, leaving them with no child support, and no resources at all. The numbers of these women have been rising exponentially.

Many of the women and families coming to Open Door these days are white; they probably had comfortable middle-class lives before their fortunes changed. I was surprised to hear even Jeanne had once been afraid that she herself would end up in the shoes of the women whom her food pantry serves. A few years earlier, her husband lost his job after working thirty years, and even with extended work experience he had a difficult time finding another job. Her job as director of the food pantry, which runs on a shoestring budget itself, was not at all adequate for them to continue the middle-class lifestyle they had built for themselves, little by little, in all those years. They had no health insurance for almost a year and a half.

When her husband eventually found a part-time job with Habitat for Humanity, it paid only a small percentage of what he had earned previously, but since it covered health insurance, they considered themselves lucky—especially because Jeanne was later diagnosed with breast cancer. She can only imagine the devastation that might have occurred if they'd had no health insurance. They also had saved up a little money during her husband's prior employment, their mortgage was paid up, and their children were grown and living on their own. They have a "safety net," Jeanne said, which most of her clients do not.

Note: 1. US Census Bureau, "State and County Quick Facts," http://quickfacts.census.gov/qfd/states/34/3425200.html (accessed December 31, 2014).

This has led to a dramatic surge in the world supply of labor. Since the early 1980s, the integration of the global labor markets has added billions of new workers. This fact in itself has put a tremendous downward pressure on the wages of not just American workers but also workers in every corner of the world. It is a basic economic principle that if there is a large supply of workers competing to work on a limited supply of capital (jobs), then wages will fall and the return on capital (profit) will increase. The more people there are in the labor pool from which capitalists can draw workers, the more steeply the capitalists can drive down wages.

Recent studies by noted economists have focused largely on economic globalization and emerging markets as explanations for deindustrialization, the ensuing rise in unemployment, and the consequent widening of the gulf between the rich and the poor. American workers today face competition from workers around the world who are paid much less money, making Americans "borderline-replaceable," according to David Leonhardt of the *New York Times,* which drives down wages precipitously.[38]

One of the most persuasive cases for this position has been made by Andrew Michael Spence, an American economist and Nobel Prize winner, and Sandile Hlatshwayo. In a 2011 paper titled "The Evolving Structure of the American Economy and the Employment Challenge," Spence and Hlatshwayo maintain that, with the liberalization of the world economy, as trade restrictions have been steadily removed, many manufacturing activities have been moving to emerging economies such as China and India. This trend is causing employment to fall throughout almost the entire US manufacturing sector.

So far, the jobs lost have been, for the most part, at the low end of the manufacturing chain—primarily labor-intensive, low-skilled jobs. But as the population in the emerging economies becomes more educated and technologically savvy, they will increasingly threaten the jobs at the higher end of the US manufacturing sector, creating job losses for both the more educated and the less educated. And due to developments in information technology, jobs that were formerly considered nontradable across borders—from radiology to accounting, insurance, and technical support—are also becoming tradable.

Most workers who permanently lost jobs in the mass layoffs involving outsourcing had been employed in manufacturing. Since the mid-1990s, this has been combined with Internet-facilitated outsourcing of service jobs that were previously deemed untradable across borders. The functions of a wide range of US knowledge workers in business services, medicine, accounting, computer programming, and telemarketing can now be done much more cheaply by workers residing in lower-wage countries.

As a result, the vast majority of new jobs that are being added to the US economy—almost 97 percent of them—are in those sectors where the jobs are nontradable across borders. These include service jobs in hospitals, schools, restaurants, construction, home health care, and day care, where wages are low, near the federal minimum; and low-paying government jobs, where the profit margin is low or nonexistent.[39] Even conservative icon Lou Dobbs, the anchor and managing editor of *Lou Dobbs Tonight,* spares no words as he lays the blame for "exporting America" fair and square in the lap of corporations, which in their relentless greed ship US jobs overseas for the sake of earning short-term profits.[40]

In the 1992 presidential campaign, independent candidate Ross Perot warned that if NAFTA went into effect, there would be a "giant sucking sound" of jobs going south to the cheap labor markets of Mexico. At that time, both of his opponents, George H. W. Bush and Bill Clinton, argued the contrary—that more jobs would be created in the United States due to NAFTA. But in fact, since 2000, multinationals have added as many jobs overseas as they have eliminated from the United States. According to Jason Breslow, between 2000 and 2008, US multinational corporations eliminated 2,500,000 jobs in the United States, but added almost the same number of jobs abroad.[41] In reality, none of the predicted job growth that NAFTA promised has materialized. According to an Economic Policy Institute report written by Robert Scott:

> As of 2010, US trade deficits with Mexico totaling $97.2 billion had displaced 682,900 US jobs. Of those jobs, 116,400 are likely economy-wide job losses because they were displaced between 2007 and 2010, when the US labor market was severely depressed.
>
> - Most of the jobs displaced by trade with Mexico as of 2010 were in manufacturing industries (415,000 jobs, 60.8 percent of the total jobs displaced).
> - Computer and electronic parts (150,300 jobs, 22 percent of the 682,900 displaced jobs) and motor vehicles and parts (108,000 jobs, 15.8 percent of the total) were the manufacturing industries hardest hit by growing bilateral trade deficits.
> - More jobs were created in Mexico (30,400) by the growth of net exports of autos and auto parts to the United States in 2010 than were created in the entire US auto industry in the same period.[42]

In total, at least 750,000 jobs have been lost as a direct result of NAFTA— four-fifths of them in manufacturing. And "when high-wage manufacturing jobs are replaced with service sector jobs that pay at least 23 percent less, the downward pressure on the wages of Americans is accelerated."[43]

As capital moves to the distant corners of the globe in search of more profitable investment opportunities, the consequent deindustrialization in the United States first eliminates manufacturing employment, and then jobs in other sectors of the economy. Retail stores, hair stylists, florists,

> ### MAKING CONNECTIONS
> #### No One Is Immune
>
> The outsourcing of jobs first started in manufacturing. Today no one is immune. Individuals working in professional "white-collar" capacities in telecommunications, investment, and technical support, and even lawyers and doctors, all can face imminent loss of their positions through outsourcing. This trend began as far back as the mid- and late 1990s, and shows no signs of abating. For example, in the summer of 2013, a renowned telecommunications company outsourced to India jobs that were connected with its production support team. About 25 percent of these employees were absorbed into the outsourced company in India. But for the other 75 percent, their jobs are lost forever. The company cited its need to cut costs across the board in order to be able to maintain its competitive edge. Almost 300 hundred men and women have lost their jobs in this fashion, their positions made permanently redundant.
>
> Similarly, senior technical support teams—individuals with advanced degrees and invaluable expertise who have served the companies for decades, are at the pinnacle of their careers, and are expecting comfortable retirement as a reward for years of payroll deductions—suddenly face unemployment as their jobs are either outsourced or absorbed by groups of immigrants, often from India and China, who have been brought to the United States under special visa provisions approved by Congress. The salary of a single senior employee can pay for several of these immigrant workers.
>
> Many of these senior employees are not yet sixty-five and therefore remain ineligible for Medicare. This fact is particularly important, since once they lose their jobs, they also lose their health-care benefits, leaving them vulnerable to catastrophic illness and bankruptcy. Such stories have become commonplace in communities across the country.

restaurants, movie theaters, bakeries, nurseries, and dry cleaners all see their clientele drop, and some might even close. Entire regions face an economic downturn as the primary manufacturing industries disappear. As the revenue-generating businesses fail, the municipalities face budget deficits, and, much like the city of Detroit, can run the risk of facing bankruptcy. In his book *The New Geography of Jobs*, Enrico Moretti calls this the multiplier effect.[44]

As wages decrease or stagnate, returns on capital increase, raising corporate profit. For many social researchers and observers, the evidence for the link between globalization and the widening economic inequality is undeniable. In his book *The Amoral Elephant: Globalization and the Struggle for Social Justice in the Twenty-First Century,* William Tabb writes that it is the most free market–oriented economies, such as the United States and United Kingdom, that "have experienced the most rapid increase in inequality during the recent period of accelerated globalization." Tabb refers to William Cline of the Institute for International Economics, who "finds that 39 percent of the increase in wage inequality over the last twenty years [since the 1990s] has been the result of international trade patterns." Therefore, "the process of capitalist globalization has inflicted its cost not only in the rest of the world, but on most Americans as well."[45]

Government policy has played a critical role in supporting global economic integration. Since the end of World War II, government restrictions on trade and capital flows have gradually declined, making it easier for companies to act as global players. But not until the ascent to power in the 1980s of Margaret Thatcher in the United Kingdom and Ronald Reagan in the United States did the free trade policies find committed advocates. In particular, the World Trade Organization, through rules developed to make it easier for companies to move production to low-wage countries with more business-friendly laws and regulations, has facilitated the inclusion of billions of additional workers in the global system. Further, trade agreements such as NAFTA, the Central American Free Trade Agreement (CAFTA), and the Free Trade Area of the Americas (FTAA) have provided an additional boost to economic integration between low-wage economies of Latin America, such as Mexico, and the high-wage economies of the United States and Canada.[46]

It is important to understand that although this lowering of trade barriers facilitated the unrestricted movement of capital, the workers, whenever they tried to move, faced militarized borders and uncompromising immigration laws, locking them into the stark economic realities of their own regions, making them defenseless in the face of the new challenges that global corporate capitalism has let loose, and giving them no choice but to settle for the jobs—paying slavelike wages—that the factories of the global corporations provide. Many opt to immigrate to the advanced industrialized countries in search of better lives, which then makes them vulnerable to an entirely new set of uncertain circumstances.

Maquiladoras, or assembly plants, dot the entire length of the US-Mexico border, from Tijuana, Mexico, to Brownsville, Texas. US companies such as General Motors, Ford, and General Electric have brought their operations to this 2,000-mile stretch, where there are about 3,000 maquiladora factories. The border in many ways epitomizes the real story behind globalization and its impact on the life and destiny of the worker—both American and Mexican. This is the story being played out in different regions of the world as globalization becomes the defining movement of our times.

Globalization is not a product nor a thing but a process. It is a process in which goods, capital, information, people, technology, money, communication, and culture move around globe, making national borders obsolete and leading to greater interconnectedness among people. It signals that we are all part of a steadily shrinking and increasingly interdependent world. Modern communication, transportation, and the Internet have all served to tie more and more countries and peoples together in increasingly complex ways.

Globalization is not an ephemeral phenomenon. It is a real thing, remolding the lives of everyone. Philosopher Peter Singer observes that today, "people living on opposite sides of the world are linked in ways previously unimaginable."[47] We now live in a virtually borderless world, a world that Benjamin Barber sees as "both coming together and falling apart"—as an ongoing dialectic of "Jihad vs. McWorld."[48] Not everyone experiences globalization the same way. It creates both winners and losers, but no one is left untouched.

Globalization has compressed buying and selling, producing and consuming, into a single marketplace. The great majority of the products Americans buy today are made elsewhere—the food we eat, the flowers that adorn our homes, the clothes we wear, the gadgets we play with. The entire world has become the supplier of the products and services that Americans desire. The prices have become so reasonable that almost everyone can afford them. The range of goods now available to the average consumer is unprecedented. The world has become one great mall, especially for those with disposable incomes. But as more and more of the things we buy are made elsewhere, jobs are lost when imports replace locally produced goods and services.

How Are Prices of Goods Kept Low?

The prices of goods are low because price does not reflect the actual cost that goes into the production and transportation of commodities. Much of this cost goes through a process called **externalization**, which means that the consumer is not paying for it, someone else is. Through their low wages, lack of health-care insurance and other benefits, and often hazardous working conditions, workers pay for every stage in the production and transportation of a commodity.

The environment too pays the price, when the costs of resource depletion and pollution are not factored in. The objective is not to burden consumers but to keep prices down and encourage them to buy more and more. This externalization of cost remains mostly invisible, unless a fire or a structural collapse in a clothing factory in Bangladesh, for example, kills hundreds of workers.

The consumer who, on the one hand, benefits from cheaper prices and a near infinite selection of products might therefore be the same person who stands to lose his livelihood when the company he works for takes his job elsewhere and hires someone else to produce the goods he once did. The part-time, minimum-wage job at a local convenience store that this person might be lucky enough to obtain, or the unemployment insurance and the little savings that he might be fortunate enough to have, leave him little choice but to shop only at Wal-Mart, with its cheap prices for products made almost entirely in China—the country to which his job might have been outsourced and where workers make penny wages and have no benefits. The irony is unmistakable. But this is exactly how the lives of American workers and their third world counterparts have become inextricably intertwined as globalization becomes the predominant social force of our times.

Corporate Consolidation

Through mergers, acquisitions, leveraged buyouts, and simply driving out the weaker players, the corporations of the global market constantly narrow the field of competition and concentrate economic power and decisionmaking in the hands of fewer and fewer monopolies. This process of consolidation sheds thousands of middle-class and blue-collar jobs, but adds millions of dollars to a corporation's profit margin, widening the income divide

---

MAKING CONNECTIONS
Women Working in Sweatshops

It is profoundly important to consider the collapse of the Rana Plaza building in Dhaka, Bangladesh, on April 24, 2013. Sweatshops belonging to many multinationals were housed in that sprawling but ill-constructed building. When it collapsed, over a thousand women were buried to death beneath the rubble, and thousands more were maimed for life. Entire families of mothers and daughters were killed, since the majority of the garment workers in countries such as Bangladesh are women. On November 24, 2012, about a hundred women died in a fire at another such building in Dhaka.[1]

Because the multinational corporations from Europe and the United States had outsourced much of the work of garment sewing to Bangladesh, this helped them distance themselves from the tragedy. Almost a year after the Rana Plaza collapsed, the injured and the families of the deceased had received no compensation from the multinationals. Much haggling is ongoing between the multinationals, the International Labour Organization (ILO), the government of Bangladesh, and the workers to determine who is responsible for paying the compensation and how much. In the meantime, the injured continue to suffer.

Note: 1. Bajaj, "Fatal Fire in Bangladesh"; Manik and Yardley, "Building Collapse in Bangladesh."

between workers and employers. Corporate consolidation means that there are fewer places for people to find work. As competition has diminished among the giant corporations, it has escalated among workers and small businesses, pitting the most powerless against each other for ever more limited opportunities, market share, and resources.

For Adam Smith, nothing could be more egregious, reinforcing his position that corporations are intrinsically "corrupting." Contrary to the position of his disciples, who constantly evoke his words to defend their actions, Smith not only was suspicious of corporate machinations, but also questioned their very necessity. As he wrote in *The Wealth of Nations:* "The pretence that corporations are necessary for the better government of trade, is without foundation." He also suspected that meetings and conversations of people in the same trade ended "in a conspiracy against the public, or in some contrivance to raise prices. [And] though law [read: government] cannot hinder people of the same trade from sometime assembling together, it ought to do nothing to facilitate such assemblies; much less render them necessary."[49]

Smith would be shocked to know that during the 1980s and 1990s in the United States, as leveraged buyouts, mergers, and acquisitions were happening at a maddening pace and millions of workers were losing their jobs, the government was barely interested in intervening in what it considered "merely another stage in the workings of the free market." Congressional leaders expressed grave concerns at what was happening, but took no initiative to stall the process. As Donald Bartlett and James Steele write, "the government rulebook encourages deal-making over creating jobs and rewards those who engineer new pieces of paper to be traded on Wall Street rather than those who engineer new products that can be manufactured and sold."[50]

Congress listened to experts from Wall Street and academics from famous business schools who referred to the layoffs of workers as "fat that needed to be eliminated." It mattered little that the "fat" they referred to were hardworking, loyal employees who in many cases had worked for these corporations for years, if not generations, nor that curbing the "fat" dismantled livelihoods, often destroying families and communities. The downturn in people's lives that came on the heels of those mergers, leveraged buyouts, and acquisitions weakened the position of American workers, rendering them powerless, especially as the now merged, consolidated corporations moved to exercise their monopoly power in the global marketplace, changing the economic landscape even more drastically.

Globalization has given a new twist to this process of corporate restructuring and consolidation, as retail giants scour the planet looking for cheaper and cheaper ways to produce goods and thereby endanger manufacturers, wholesalers, and their employees in the United States. David

Korten contends that "mass retailing superpowers—Wal-Mart, K-Mart, Toys 'R' Us, Home Depot, Target Stores, Costco—are some of the core firms in the retail world who favor suppliers who make things in low labor cost countries such as China or Bangladesh."[51] Corporations that are socially responsible and provide their workers with secure, well-paying jobs, pay their share of taxes, pay into their workers' retirement funds, and do their part to be environmentally responsible lose out in competition with those that are more than willing to move their factories and jobs to low-cost regions of the world where lax regulations abound.[52]

David Korten also refers to the practice in which established domestic companies with socially responsible business ethics are "raided" by other companies that regard them as being "inefficient," which leads to the latter being driven out of the market. He cites examples of "investment funds, such as The AmeriMax Maquiladora Fund, which specialize in the buying and selling of companies which have resisted moving their headquarters to low wage countries." Korten refers to the prospectus of this fund, which brazenly announces:

> The Fund will purchase established United States companies suitable for maquiladora acquisitions, wherein a part or all of the manufacturing operations will be relocated to Mexico to take advantage of the cost of labor. We anticipate that manufacturing companies that experience fully loaded, gross labor cost in the $7–$10 per hour range in the US may be able to utilize labor in a Mexican maquiladora at a fully loaded, gross labor cost of $1.15–$1.50 per hour. Though each situation may vary, it is estimated that this could translate into annual savings of $10,000–$17,000 per employee involved in the relocated manufacturing operations.[53]

As competitors are driven out of the market and corporate power becomes consolidated in the hands of fewer corporate giants, small businesses lose out, socially responsible entrepreneurs are defeated, neighborhood mom-and-pop shops can no longer compete, workers lose their livelihoods, and entire communities and regions lose their economic viability—and the gap between rich and poor continues to widen steadily.

When retail giant Wal-Mart moves into a neighborhood, it destroys more jobs than it adds. And the jobs that Wal-Mart does offer pay, on average, less than $10 an hour for the usual thirty-four-hour week, which is often not enough to pull an individual or family above the poverty threshold. And as Fred Goldstein has written:

> Not only does Wal-Mart pay low wages, it drives down wages throughout the retail industry. By using its leverage as the world's largest retailer, it pressures its suppliers to lower costs, increasing the exploitation of the supplier's own workers or by off-shoring to low wage countries. It is the biggest private employer in the world.

> Driving down wages at its 60,000 suppliers in the US and also in China, Singapore, Mexico, Indonesia, and Sri Lanka—Wal-Mart is Bangladesh's most important customer—the low prices which drive out competition in the US come from the wages that the workers in Bangladesh—most [of them] women, earn—$30 a month.[54]

Corporate consolidation, through which the economic power of certain corporations becomes more and more concentrated as their share of the market increases exponentially, drives up profit margins in unprecedented ways. At the same time, jobs are lost. Jobs that used to pay a living wage are replaced with those that pay much less. Thus the gap between rich and poor becomes even wider—all in the course of an economic system fulfilling its sole objective of profit maximization for a tiny elite who own and manage these monopolistic corporations.

Financial Speculation

Technological innovation and globalization of the world economic system have opened up another avenue of financial gain, one in which nothing concrete is ever created—no goods, no jobs, no services, nothing that can be considered as having added to a society's store of wealth—but one that yields enormous gains for the individuals who own the finance capital that allows them to participate.

With a few taps on a computer's keyboard, individuals from anywhere in the world can transfer enormous amounts of money as they speculate on currency futures, oil futures, and gas futures—anything that will yield them an instant profit. Trillions of dollars change hands each day in the international currency markets, much more than what is exchanged for buying and selling "concrete" goods and services in the same period. This is the world of global speculative finance, which has become the economic activity of choice for many.

For example, individuals buy and sell currencies to make money from fluctuations in the exchange rates. Complex financial instruments such as derivatives, which very few people understand, hide behind complex mathematical models that are used to make decisions based on a range of complex variables—variables that are not only about economic factors but also about geopolitical matters, innovations in science and technology, weather, and anything else that might be considered as having an impact on the exchange rates of currencies. The objective is to get in, make a quick profit, and get out, by engaging in any kind of speculative activity that will yield that quick profit.

But Nobel Laureate economist Joseph Stiglitz maintains that factories cannot be built, nor can jobs be created, with such quickly moving money.[55]

It is the World Bank and the International Monetary Fund—which emerged from the Bretton Woods conference convened in New Hampshire in 1944, to draw up plans for economic recovery in post–World War II Europe and to establish institutions and norms to avoid the economic debacles of the Great Depression—that created the global financial system that has facilitated this "money game."

Financial speculation is attractive because the return from it is so instantaneous. Some have likened it to gambling in a casino, where enormous risks are taken with the hope of instant gains. And just like gambling in a casino, financial speculation creates no real value yet brings huge returns to the lucky winners. The disproportionate returns further widen the gap between the few who benefit from this game and the great majority who do not.

In its report on the incomes of the top 1 percent of earners, the Economic Policy Institute states:

> The wages and compensation of executives, including CEOs, and of workers in finance reveal much about the rise in income inequality: The significant income growth at the very top of the income distribution over the last few decades was largely driven by households headed by someone who was either an executive or was employed in the financial sector. Executives, and workers in finance, accounted for 58 percent of the expansion of income for the top 1 percent and 67 percent of the increase in income for the top 0.1 percent from 1979 to 2005.[56]

Money invested in financial speculation takes funds away from other ways of investing that can grow a society's wealth. But traditional investment yields a profit in the long run, whereas the appeal of financial speculation is its high-speed, high-risk, high-return potential. Society as a whole loses out when real goods and services are not produced; real people are not hired to create real value and real wealth.

As Nobel Prize–winning economist Paul Krugman writes, "society is devoting an ever-growing share of its resources to financial wheeling and dealing, while getting little or nothing in return." He continues: "Finance has grown much faster than the economy as a whole. Specifically, the share of G.D.P. accruing to bankers, traders, and so on has doubled since 1980. . . . [T]here is clear correlation between the rise of modern finance and America's return to Gilded Age levels of inequality."[57]

The real irony is that financial gain goes to those who create "illusory wealth"—those who make the big money. Yet those members of society who are engaged in activities that create real value and real wealth make less and less money and are in constant danger of being entirely pushed out of the marketplace. (Recall the story of hedge fund investors and kindergarten teachers from Chapter 2.) Even though the value added by financial activity forms part of a nation's gross domestic product (GDP), its real contribution to a country's GDP is questionable and dubious.[58] Paul Krugman refers to Thomas Philippon, professor of finance at New York University, who argues that the bloated financial industry in the United States is actually wasting 2 percent of the GDP annually.[59]

What we therefore witness is the financialization of the US economy, whereby massive amounts of money are increasingly devoted to financial speculation, to what amounts to a no-growth casino economy. Returns on financial speculation are much faster and bigger than rises in salaries and wages. Much of the income divide is rooted in this basic fact.

Conclusion

Financial speculation, corporate consolidation, globalization, and mechanization form a complex web that leads to a polarization of society between winners and losers, widening the gap between the rich and the poor—not only in the United States but also worldwide. Each of these processes eliminates the jobs and livelihoods on which people must depend in order to survive. The problem of inequality is ultimately a problem of jobs, and of the difficulty of finding jobs in a marketplace where more and more are being eliminated. The economic system that defines the United States and, increasingly, the entire world—capitalism—is not really in the business of providing jobs. Its objective is to maximize profits.

It needs labor to produce goods—to transform dead capital into revenue-earning commodities and services. But laborers must be paid and provided benefits regularly, which cuts into the profit margin. Therefore, if capital can be accumulated without labor, or at least with the cheapest sort of labor, then that is what the capitalist will logically opt for. This is not about greed or malice. The systematic and deliberate manner in which capital goes about configuring ways to extract maximum profit cannot be attributed to something as arbitrary and capricious as human nature. It is built into the logic of the capitalist system and is the primary reason for its very existence.

In describing the rationale for work under capitalism, Michael Parenti writes: "What is unique about capitalism is the rational and systematic expropriation of labor for the sole purpose of capital accumulation. The ultimate purpose of work is not to perform services for consumers, nor sustain life and society, but to make more and more money for the investor. As Marx said, capital annexes living labor in order to make more capital."[60] And if any other option can be found to maximize profit and accumulate capital, then the system will opt for it.

When paying salaries, wages, and benefits gets in the way of maximizing profits, and when other means of making money, such as mechanization and financialization, are available, then jobs and people's livelihoods become expendable. That is exactly what we see happening, increasingly, as mechanization, globalization, corporate consolidation, and financial speculation devour the kinds of jobs that individuals, their families, and their communities depend on.

One reason why there is so much inequality in the world today is for the simple reason that people either do not have jobs, or have jobs that pay increasingly less and forego benefits. As a consequence, the wealth of nations is flowing upward, to those segments of the population who own capital and have the privilege of deciding how to use it. And when people's livelihoods and wages depend on the decisions of those privileged few, and those decisions are made to maximize return to the investor, the common men and women are left to struggle for their livelihoods.

Consider the position that sociologist Douglas Massey has taken on the matter of globalization and inequality. He maintains that the United States, compared to other industrialized countries, has always tolerated higher rates of inequality and has shied away from policies that would have leveled the playing field for everyone. Unlike its peer countries, the United States has allowed large segments of its people to remain poor without trying to rectify this poverty. As Massey writes:

> Although globalization may have produced rising pressures for inequality throughout the world, only in the United States have these pressures been allowed to be expressed so fully and the resulting inequality allowed to persist without redress. The United States is exceptional among developed nations for the amount of inequality it tolerates. The conundrum is why policies that benefit, at most, 20 per cent of the population have been allowed to move forward in a democratic republic where the rest of the 80 per cent have a regular opportunity to vote for alternative policies more in line with their material interests.

Massey suggests that one of the answers to this conundrum is "the rising role of money in American politics and the shift from a system of 'one person, one vote' to a new politics of 'one dollar, one vote.'"[61]

Notes

1. US Census Bureau, "State and Country QuickFacts," http://quickfacts.census .gov/qfd/states/34/3474000.html (Trenton, NJ) (accessed December 31, 2014).
2. Hedges, "City of Ruins," p. 1.
3. US Census Bureau, "State and Country QuickFacts," http://quickfacts.census .gov/qfd/states/34/3410000.html (Camden, NJ) (accessed December 31, 2014).
4. Hedges, "City of Ruins," p. 1.
5. US Census Bureau, "State and Country QuickFacts," http://quickfacts.census .gov/qfd/states/26/2629000.html (Flint, MI) (accessed December 31, 2014).

6. Wilkerson, *The Warmth of Other Suns.*

7. Denby, "Good Fights," p. 108.

8. Ibid.

9. Davey, "Detroit Urged to Tear Down 40,000 Buildings," p. A1.

10. Davey and Walsh, "Billions in Debt, Detroit Tumbles Into Insolvency," p. A1.

11. Kutscher, "Historical Trends," p. 6.

12. Tyson, "Why Manufacturing Still Matters."

13. Rampell, "Majority of Jobs Added in the Recovery Pay Low Wages," p. B1.

14. Bureau of Labor Statistics, "Occupational Employment Statistics, 2012."

15. Bureau of Labor Statistics, "The Recession of 2007–2009," p. 2.

16. Bureau of Labor Statistics, "Employment Situation Summary."

17. Moller, Alderson, and Nielsen, "Changing Patterns of Income Inequality," pp. 1048–1049.

18. Gilson and Perot, "It's the Inequality, Stupid."

19. Hacker and Pierson, *Winner-Take-All Politics,* p. 15.

20. Domhoff, "Wealth, Income, and Power."

21. Feldman, "Letters," p. SR2.

22. US Bureau of Labor Statistics, "Increasing Labor Productivity"; Associated Press, "Labor Productivity Rises 1.6%," p. B9.

23. Kollmeyer, "Explaining Deindustrialization."

24. Marx and Engels, *The Communist Manifesto,* p. 38.

25. See Steve Lohr, "More Jobs Predicted for Machines," p. B3.

26. Keynes, *Economic Possibilities for Our Grandchildren,* p. 3.

27. Lohr, "More Jobs Predicted for Machines," p. B3.

28. Rifkin, "New Technology and the End of Jobs," p. 114.

29. Ibid.

30. Newman, *Net Loss,* p. 2.

31. Leonard, *The Story of Stuff,* p. 161.

32. Ibid., pp. 155, 163.

33. Quoted in ibid., p. 160.

34. Vornovytskyy et al., "Household Debt in the U.S.: 2000 to 2011."

35. Federal Reserve, "Statistical Release," p. i.

36. US Census Bureau, "Statistical Abstract."

37. Bricker et al., "Changes in US Family Finances."

38. Leonhardt, "Globalization and the Income Slowdown."

39. Spence and Hlatshwayo, "The Evolving Structure of the American Economy."

40. Dobbs, *Exporting America,* p. 41.

41. Breslow, *Two American Families.*

42. Scott, "US-Mexico Trade and Job Displacement After NAFTA."

43. Dobbs, *Exporting America,* p. 73.

44. Moretti, *The New Geography of Jobs.*

45. Tabb, *The Amoral Elephant,* p. 163.

46. Ahearn, "Globalization, Worker Insecurity, and Policy Approaches."

47. Singer, *One World,* pp. 9–10.

48. Barber, *Jihad vs. McWorld.*

49. Smith, *An Inquiry into the Nature and Causes of the Wealth of Nations,* p. 128.

50. Bartlett and Steele, *America,* p. 25.

51. Korten, *When Corporations Rule the World,* p. 215.

52. Ibid., p. 197.
53. Ibid., pp. 203–204.
54. Goldstein, "Why Bosses Need Wal-Mart."
55. Stiglitz, *Making Globalization Work*, p. 34.
56. Mishel and Sabadish, "CEO Pay and the Top 1%."
57. Krugman, "Three Expensive Milliseconds," p. A23.
58. Turner, "Is Modern Finance a Productive Economic Activity?"
59. Krugman, "Three Expensive Milliseconds."
60. Parenti, *Land of Idols,* p. 73.
61. Massey, "Globalization and Inequality."

6

The Political Economy of Inequality

POLITICAL ECONOMY IS THE CONCEPT THAT HIGHLIGHTS THE ROLE OF government and government decisions in the economy. It illustrates how politics affects economics and vice versa, and how they together determine the most fundamental issues in society that impinge on the most vital aspects of all our lives. As much as Americans have been conditioned to believe that the economy is freestanding and that only the "invisible hand" of the impartial market forces determines its waxing and waning, there is very little doubt that the government is a strong presence and a strong player in the US economy.

Through laws and policies, the government has enormous influence on how the US economy functions and how essential resources are distributed in society. And even though the "political economy" as a reified entity obscures the real players, there is very little doubt that some players have more access to government decisionmaking than others and can successfully influence the contours of those decisions to their own advantage. The affluent have more influence by far on the government than the rest of the population, and have an inordinate sway over the decisions that are made. The rest of the country is affected by those decisions and is powerless to escape their fallout.

Economic Inequality and Democracy

It has always been a matter of reasoned conjecture that the voices of the poor and their advocates do not enter the halls of power. And if their voices are not heard, or are drowned out by the voices of the more powerful and dominant, then the needs and concerns of the poor are not addressed and little is done to change the conditions of their lives. In a democracy, the government is supposed to be the guardian of the entire multitude of citizens regardless of their station in life—whether race, class, or creed. But there is much deviation from this ideal as the power of money continuously trumps the concerns of common men and women.

In a number of recent US Supreme Court decisions, the inanimate but inordinately powerful voice of money has been equated to the real and sentient voice of the citizen. So much so that any restrictions on money to play a role in the political game are considered violations of money's "freedom of speech." Consequently, as money is allowed free reign, it distorts the balance of power, and democracy itself loses its veracity.

This is not just empty speculation. Political scientists and political sociologists have repeatedly shown how the wealthy have disproportionate power to influence the decisions and policies of the state, far more so than the average citizen. As early as 1913, in *An Economic Interpretation of the Constitution of the United States,* Charles Beard argued that the primary objective of the Constitution was to protect private property. The framers were predominantly members of the landed aristocracy, who represented the interests of plantation owners and rich merchants. But those who made up the majority of the population—small farmers, indentured servants, laborers, craftspeople, and slaves—counted for little when this foundational document of the republic was framed. Because political democracy without economic democracy is untenable, a system of social stratification characterized by grave economic inequalities that result in disproportionate affluence for a few always leads to a profound imbalance in political power.

Marxist analysis maintains that the class who owns the means of production also controls the state—the decisionmaking apparatus of society—and can use the state for its own benefit. As Marx and Friedrich Engels wrote in *The Communist Manifesto,* "the bourgeoisie has . . . since the establishment of modern industry and world market, conquered for itself, in the modern representative state, an exclusive political sway. The executive of the modern state is but a committee for managing the common affairs of the whole bourgeoisie."[1]

Martin Gilens and Benjamin Page conducted a multivariate analysis of a large dataset of diverse policy cases to objectively measure how much influence different sets of actors—average citizens, economic elites, and organized interest groups—have over public policy. In other words, who really rules? What is the political status of the broad base of US citizens—are they sovereign or semisovereign decisionmakers, or are they largely powerless? Gilens and Page discuss four theoretical traditions in the study of US politics that answer these questions in different ways:[2]

• **Majoritarian electoral democracy** theory argues that the policies of the US government are chiefly influenced by the collective will of average citizens. This is Abraham Lincoln's ideal of a government "of the people, by the people, for the people."

• **Economic elite domination** theory argues that US policymaking is dominated by individuals who have high levels of income and wealth. Sociologist G. William Domhoff offers strong evidence in defense of this theory when he shows how the economic elites—through lobbyists and campaign financing of politicians, through think tanks and foundations—dominate key decisions in US policymaking.[3]

• **Majoritarian pluralism** theory argues that citizens are represented in the diverse struggles between **interest groups**, which reflect the needs and interests of the populace. Also known as pluralist/populist democracy, this theoretical position holds that the needs of the average citizen are well served when interest groups engage each other on a diverse set of policy negotiations. Political sociologist Robert Dahl's study of politics in New Haven, Connecticut, is a classic study of majoritarian pluralism.[4]

• **Biased pluralism** theory focuses on what is characterized as the "upper-class accent" of the "universe of interest groups," which "tilt towards the wishes of corporations and business and professional association," in how they influence public policies. From this perspective powerful interest groups which represent businesses and major investors, "fund political parties in order to get policies that suit their economic interests. . . . Jacob Hacker and Paul Pierson's analysis of 'winner-take-all-politics,' which emphasizes the power of the finance industry, can be seen as a recent contribution to the literature of biased pluralism."[5]

Which theoretical understanding of US politics is correct? Gilens and Page, using a sophisticated statistical model to analyze data on the key variables that have influenced nearly 2,000 US government policy issues, have produced some striking findings. First and foremost, their data provide substantial support for theories of elite economic domination and biased pluralism, but not for theories of majoritarian electoral democracy or majoritarian pluralism.[6] In addition, Gilens and Page offer the following observations: "What do our findings say about democracy in America? Our findings indicate, the majority does *not* rule—at least not in the causal sense of actually determining policy outcomes. When a majority of citizens disagrees with economic elites and/or organized interests, they generally lose. Moreover, because of the strong status quo bias built into the US political system, even when fairly large majorities of Americans favor policy change, they generally do not get it."[7]

Gilens and Page also note: "When the preferences of economic elites and the stands of organized interest groups are controlled for, the preferences of the average American appear to have only miniscule, near-zero, statistically non-significant impact upon public-policy. . . . Furthermore, the preferences of economic elites have far more independent impact upon policy changes than the preferences of average citizens." When ordinary citizens "get the policies they favor, [it is] only because those policies happen also to be preferred by the economically elite citizens who wield the actual influence."[8]

Gilens and Page reject the argument that perhaps economic elites and interest-group leaders have more policy expertise than the average citizen, know what is best for the country as a whole, and therefore are working for the common good by transcending their own interest. But although these elites and leaders might know a lot about tax and regulatory policies, "how much do they know about the human impact of Social Security, food stamps, or unemployment insurance, none of which is likely to be crucial to their own well-being?"[9]

This study, published in 2014, bolsters the arguments that Gilens made in his 2012 book *Affluence and Influence: Economic Inequality and Political Power in America*. In the latter, Gilens demonstrated that policymakers bow to the preferences of the most affluent even when large segments of Americans—the middle class and the poor—have different positions on those policies. He pointed out that, whereas the well-off oppose proposals for government regulation, the poor and the middle class support such proposals. For example, in a 1985 survey, three-quarters of the poor and the middle class supported the requirement that employers should notify their workers a year in advance before closing down their place of work. But because the affluent opposed this idea in great numbers, policymakers in Washington, D.C., sided with them instead.

Similarly, extending unemployment benefits and raising the minimum wage were popular ideas with the general public, but because they were opposed by the affluent, Congress pushed back vehemently. Therefore, it is eye-opening that less than one-third of proposed social welfare policy changes that had 80 percent support from the public were eventually adopted. Gilens wonders how much of this might be related to the "fact that members of Congress and other influential policy makers all fall within the top decile of the income distribution themselves."[10]

This claim finds confirmation from a January 2013 report in the *New York Times* in which Jeremy Peters writes that many members of Congress "are so wealthy that their Congressional paychecks represent little more than a rounding error."[11] The base pay of members of Congress is $174,000. The 113th Congress, which was sworn into office in January 2013, is the richest ever, with a median net worth of $1,066,515 for each of its incoming members. This is about a million more than the net worth of average Americans. As another *New York Times* story adds:

> Largely insulated from the country's economic downturn since 2008, members of Congress—many of them among the "1 percenters" denounced by

Occupy Wall Street protesters—have gotten much richer even as most of the country has become much poorer in the last six years, according to an analysis by The New York Times based on data from the Center for Responsive Politics, a nonprofit research group.

Congress has never been a place for paupers. From plantation owners in the pre–Civil War era to industrialists in the early 1900s to ex-Wall Street financiers and Internet executives today, it has long been populated with the rich, including scions of families like the Guggenheims, Hearsts, Kennedys, and Rockefellers.

But rarely has the divide appeared so wide, or the public contrast so stark, between lawmakers and those they represent.[12]

Given this fact that the wealth gap between the lawmakers and their constituents has never been as wide as it is today, the question automatically arises: Can congressional leaders even relate to the economic challenges that so many of their constituents face? Moreover, since the economy, in its current state, serves congressional leaders and their patrons quite well, do they even have the political will to bring about changes in the status quo, if in so doing they must jeopardize the fortunes of their cohorts in the top 1 percent of income earners?

On the state of democracy in the United States, Gilens and Page conclude: "Americans do enjoy many features central to democratic governance, such as regular elections, freedom of speech and association, and a widespread (if still contested) franchise. But we believe that if policymaking is dominated by powerful business organizations and a small number of affluent Americans, then America's claims to be a democratic society are seriously threatened."[13]

As Michael Hardt and Antonio Negri write rather matter-of-factly: "The predominant contemporary form of sovereignty—if we still want to call it that—is completely embedded . . . not only by the rule of law but also equally by the rule of property. Said differently, the political is not an autonomous domain. . . . There is nothing extraordinary or exceptional about this form of power. We need to stop confusing politics with theology."[14]

What Hardt and Negri are saying is that the alliance between property and power needs to be exposed and changed, but that this political asymmetry is an inevitable corollary to the structures and processes of a capitalist system wherein "the power of property is concentrated in the hands of the few" and the majority need to sell their labor to maintain themselves, and wherein "the economic laws that structure social life . . . make hierarchies and subordinates seem natural and necessary."[15] And as Karl Marx wrote, "at its highest point the political constitution [in capitalist societies] is the constitution of private property."[16] In regard to the political economy of inequality, "what is central," Hardt and Negri write, is the recognition "that the concept of property and the defense of property remain the foundation of every modern political constitution. This is the sense in which the republic . . . is a republic of property."[17]

The inviolability or sacredness of property is a matter of the collective conscience. It is uncontestable and ingrained in the public mind. John Adams is believed to have said that as soon as private property and God become contested topics, the doom of the republic would be near. And the essence of the American Dream is the promise that sooner or later, every American, given the right mettle, can become a property owner. For those who don't yet own property, it is their lack of *mettle* that is to blame. The system is not culpable. The majority of Americans believe this, almost with a passion. And here we find a high correlation between how the elite and the masses think, which is not surprising given the elite's considerable influence in shaping public opinion. We will return to this last point in much detail in the Chapter 13.

The current system, defined by property, property rights, and the endless need to accumulate capital, is a given. The system functions to fortify itself dispassionately, organically—with little regard to issues of fairness and justice. The processes that constantly strengthen the hand of capital and property create the conditions that dispossess the majority of Americans.

The way property functions is largely invisible to the public eye. If the political economy of society can be envisaged as a stage, then most of the important dynamics—the processes that strengthen the hands of some while rendering others poor and powerless—are played out backstage. This is simply how the system works.

The Intersections of Wealth and Political Power

There are several ways in which wealth/property and political power mix that are ultimately harmful to the welfare of large segments of society. This continuous spillover, this influence-peddling, between money and power is continuously happening backstage—out of the public eye.

Unequal Democracy:
The Political Economy of the New Gilded Age

Political scientist Larry Bartels, in *Unequal Democracy: The Political Economy of the New Gilded Age,* presents meticulous evidence and a thorough analysis to illustrate that it is not just a matter of conjecture that political power cedes very little to the majority of the poor and the middle class in society. He provides a wealth of data to show how the promises of democracy and equal representation are continuously broken when those elected officials ignore the voices of the poor and the middle class.

Bartels acknowledges that he must tread into controversial and divisive territory when breaking the cardinal rule of partisan neutrality in scholarship.

But the data are much too compelling to ignore, showing incontrovertible evidence that the income gap increases during Republican presidencies and narrows during Democratic presidencies: "On average, the real incomes of middle-class families have grown twice as fast under Democrats as they have under Republicans, while the real incomes of working poor families have grown six times as fast under Democrats as they have under Republicans. . . . [A] great deal of economic inequality in the contemporary United States is specifically attributable to the policies and priorities of Republican presidents."[18]

Take the George W. Bush tax cuts of 2001 and 2003, for example, or the repeal of the estate tax in 2001. Or the eroding value of the minimum wage: in April 2014, a bill to raise the minimum wage from $7.25 to $10.10 was defeated in the Senate as Republicans and Democrats split cleanly along party lines, with Democrats supporting the measure and Republicans opposing it.

So, as the rules of the economic game are tweaked by those in power to favor one group of Americans over others, the entire edifice of democracy loses credibility, giving much weight to what Louis Brandeis, Supreme Court justice from 1916 to 1939, wrote: "We can have democracy in this country, or we can have great wealth concentrated in the hands of a few, but we cannot have both."[19]

The Politics of Rich and Poor: Wealth and Democracy

Two classic works by Kevin Phillips, *The Politics of Rich and Poor* and *Wealth and Democracy,* delve into this eternal tension between wealth and democracy. The former investigates the transformations that the United States experienced as a result of the policies put in place by the Ronald Reagan administration and how those policies and transformations favored the concentration of wealth in the hands of a small minority. In hindsight, these policies and that era can be seen as shaping the gross inequalities that the country would experience two decades later.

Wealth and Democracy is a tour-de-force, providing a rich analysis of how great fortunes in the United States have historically been amassed over time with the cooperation of the government. The steady slide of the country into a plutocracy at the approach of the third millennium was accomplished by "the determination and ability of wealth to reach beyond its own realm of money, and control politics and government as well." And so, continues Phillips, in the words of political scientist Samuel Huntington, "'money becomes evil not when it is used to buy goods but when it is used to buy power. . . . Economic inequalities become evil when they are translated into political inequalities.' Political inequalities, in turn, lead to more dangerous economic inequalities."[20]

Winner-Take-All Politics:
How Washington Made the Rich Richer

The subject of how much hold big money has on politics has found forceful expression in a book by political scientists Jacob Hacker and Paul Pierson, *Winner-Take-All Politics: How Washington Made the Rich Richer—and Turned Its Back on the Middle Class.* The book finds its context in the post-2008 aftermath of the great bailout of Wall Street by the federal government with billions of dollars of taxpayer money.

This was a time of great economic misfortune for the average American. Many lost jobs or lost their homes to foreclosure, yet on Wall Street, the big companies, investors, and executives were earning record profits. It is a story of two Americas, one that was reaping most of the economic rewards, and one whose fortunes and livelihoods were on a downward spiral.

Hacker and Pierson cite some numbers for the period 1979–2005 that are worth repeating:

> If the total income growth were a pie, the slice enjoyed by the roughly 300,000 people in the top tenth of 1 percent would be half as large as the slice enjoyed by the roughly 180 million in the bottom 60 percent.
> Little wonder that the share of Americans who see the United States as divided between "haves" and "have-nots" has risen sharply over the past two decades—although . . . the economic winners are more accurately portrayed as the "have-it-alls," so concentrated have the gains been at the very, very top.[21]

Confronted with this evidence of gross inequity, Hacker and Pierson are puzzled by some rather glaring problems: How can investors and hedge fund managers who are making billions of dollars pay less in taxes than their secretaries? And why have politicians slashed taxes on the rich even when their riches have skyrocketed?

The answers, they say, lie in the "profound changes in American democracy that have unfolded in our times. To uncover the path to winner-take-all requires seeing the transformation of American government over the last generation, a transformation that has fundamentally changed what government does, and for whom it does it. . . . But . . . our current crisis is merely the latest in a long struggle rooted in the interplay of American democracy and American capitalism."[22] Hacker and Pierson present considerable evidence showing that, "as resources flow toward the already most advantaged Americans, their ability to use those resources to shape policy increases. Rich Americans tend to support the economic policies from which they have so greatly benefited. This raises the disturbing prospect of a vicious cycle in which growing economic and political inequality are mutually reinforcing."[23] We will return to Hacker and Pierson later in this chapter when we consider specific government policies that have reshuffled the income-and-wealth deck in the United States.

Who the Elite Are and What
Political Sociologists Have to Say About Them

Who exactly are the affluent? Who are the elite? Who are the winners in this winner-take-all system? They are not just an amorphous category of random individuals who just accidentally happen to have enormous wealth. They are not winners in the sense of lottery winners, though in these days of reckless financial speculation, the distinction often becomes difficult to make.

Their winning fortunes and affluence are directly connected with their class position in a capitalist system that determines not just how much money they make but also their ownership of the means of production. For the top 1 percent of the richest individuals and households who make up the elite, it is the means of production that generate their profits, capital gains, and dividends, and gives them enormous power to control the lives of the workers. Let us revisit the words of G. William Domhoff, as quoted previously in Chapter 2: "In terms of types of financial wealth, the top one percent of households have 35% of all privately held stock, 64.4% of financial securities, and 62.4% of business equity. The top ten percent have 81% to 94% of stocks, bonds, trust funds, and business equity, and almost 80% of non-home real estate. Since financial wealth is what counts as far as the control of income-producing assets, we can say that just 10% of the people own the United States of America."[24]

Just like Domhoff, I situate the power of the affluent and the elite in terms of their class position in society. A class analysis does not just bemoan the widening gap between the rich and the poor; nor does it simply lament the injustice of so few having so much, and so many having so little. It also delves into the more fundamental questions about how the close association between government and those who own the income-producing assets—the means of production—influences and shapes the distribution of income and wealth in society. How does this alliance affect the decisions the government makes that shape the contours of the economy, the marketplace, and people's lives, and the government's response, or lack of response, to the needs of the poor and the indigent?

In his renowned 1956 book *The Power Elite,* C. Wright Mills contradicted the belief that US democracy was indeed a government "of the people, by the people, and for the people." At the time, the generally accepted idea was that power in American society was decentralized and no one group had control over it. Mills questioned the entire premise of this position and concluded just the opposite—that power in the United States was the purview of a "power elite." He defined the power elite as "those political, economic, and military circles which as an intricate set of overlapping cliques share decisions having national consequences. In so far as national events are decided, the power elite are those who decide them."[25]

Domhoff, in his comprehensive approach, explains who the power elite are and their rationale for exerting power over the government:

> The power elite is composed of members of the upper class who have taken on leadership roles in the corporate community and the policy network organizations. More formally, the power elite consists of those people who serve as directors or trustees in profit or nonprofit institutions controlled by the corporate community through stock ownership, financial support, or involvement on the board of directors . . . [and] who have an economic stake in preserving the governmental rules and regulations that maintain the current wealth and income distribution.[26]

How the Degree of Inequality Is Determined by Conscious Choice

The sources of equality or inequality are not mysterious. Even if we accept the basic premise that equality and inequality are the consequences of the impartial functioning of the marketplace, it is important to understand that the marketplace is not a freestanding, self-regulating, reified entity—it does not function in a political vacuum and it never did, other than in neoliberal mythology. Adam Smith's theoretical model of a perfectly competitive marketplace of numerous small buyers and sellers, each with perfect knowledge, and none powerful enough to influence the forces of the market, is in fact almost diametrically opposed to reality.

In this age of monopoly capitalism, the workings of the market reflect deliberate decisions and conscious choices by the US government and the nation's elected representatives regarding jobs, technology, taxes, wages, executive pay, regulation or deregulation of corporate behavior, international trade treaties, immigration, health care, education, decisions of war and peace, fortification or weakening of labor unions and the social safety net, and so forth. And each of these decisions affects corporate behavior, which in turn influences the life chances of the rest of the population, both in the United States and often in other countries as well.

The "choices" that the United States has made over time in these areas have generated an income gap of unprecedented proportions. Since 2008 especially, structural inequality, in combination with the recession and mortgage crisis, is regarded by many as being the consequence of deliberate decisionmaking in areas of financial deregulation, minimum wage, taxes, and trade treaties, and of the fallout from weak government scrutiny of financial institutions and their activities. As Larry Bartels contends in *Unequal Democracy,* politics profoundly shapes economics; economic inequality, therefore, is substantially a political phenomenon.

Most critical are policy decisions in the areas of financial deregulation, minimum wage, trade-treaty negotiation, and taxation and income transfer.

Deliberately instituted policies in these four vital areas have essentially remapped the distribution of income and wealth in the United States.

Financial Deregulation

Financial deregulation refers to rule changes that give financial institutions more freedom in how they do business, such as those determining how savings and loan (S&L) institutions, banks, and insurance companies should function. For example, in 1982 the Garn-St. Germain Depository Institutions Act was passed, which deregulated and loosened the caps on how much interest S&L institutions could pay to their depositors and also raised the limit, to $100,000, on deposits that the Federal Deposit Insurance Corporation (FDIC) would insure with taxpayer money. Consequently, a tidal wave of money was deposited into S&L accounts, with depositors hoping to receive high-interest returns with no risk of losing their money.

In the meantime, the S&Ls were becoming involved in increasingly risky and reckless business ventures. With mountains of cash from their depositors, they were investing in junk bonds, extravagant real estate, and holiday resorts that no one could afford. The S&L executives were taking huge salaries for themselves; even their secretaries were getting million-dollar paychecks. But the bottom soon fell out. The bad investments brought no returns; the deposit money had been squandered. By the time the dust settled in the 1990s, the federal government had paid $124 billion in taxpayer money to bail out the S&Ls. The S&L crisis created the greatest bank collapse since the Great Depression.

The decisions government makes in how the financial market is regulated or deregulated have lasting consequences in how resources end up being distributed in society. More recently, the Gramm-Leach-Biley Act of 1999, which repealed the Glass-Steagall Act of 1933, is seen as having a huge role in setting off the chain of events that led to the Great Recession of 2008, and in reshuffling the economic deck.

The stock market crash of 1929, the most devastating event in US economic history, which also set in motion the Great Depression, was seen to a large extent to be the result of the reckless behavior of big commercial banks that invested their depositors' money in risky, speculative ventures. In 1933, Congress passed the Glass-Steagall Act to separate commercial banks from investment banks in order to protect people's bank accounts from such irresponsible and out-of-control practices of the "powerful financial conglomerates."

The Gramm-Leach-Biley Act of 1999, which abolished the parameters that the Glass-Steagall Act of 1933 had instituted to restrain the activities of the big banks, is therefore considered "one of the biggest pieces of financial deregulation in recent decades."[27] Through this repeal, Congress made it possible for banks to once again combine their investment and commercial functions. The repeal was seen as a way to enable the banks to grow "larger and better and compete on the world stage." Treasury secretary Lawrence Summers, in responding to the repeal, said: "The historic legislation will enable American companies to compete in the world economy."[28]

In the view of many analysts and observers, however, the repeal of Glass-Steagall precipitated the financial meltdown that became emblematic of the economic downturn of 2008. The crisis on Wall Street, requiring a $700 billion federal bailout, was largely brought on by the huge banks, such as Citigroup and JP Morgan Chase, that were born when the repeal of Glass-Steagall meant that banks could now once again merge their commercial, investment, and insurance functions. Many of the risky and reckless activities of these financial giants, which created the artificial economic bubble and the unprecedented, unsustainable increase in housing prices that ensnared ordinary Americans and drove so many to total financial ruin, were facilitated by this repeal. (See the discussion of foreclosures in Chapter 3.)

The Gramm-Leach-Bliley Act is a complex piece of legislation whose true significance is difficult for the average American to fully understand or appreciate. And very much like most of the mechanisms that guide economic activity today, it is convoluted and impenetrable, its language loaded with esoteric terms such as "derivatives" and "credit-default swaps." Most people did not understand what had hit them, yet for a handful on Wall Street, the windfall from the repeal was unmatched.

When Glass-Steagall was revoked in 1999, it drew very few dissenters in Congress. It passed with overwhelming support from both Republicans and Democrats and was signed into law by President Bill Clinton. Only a handful in Congress opposed it. Leading the voice of dissenters was Senator Byron Dorgan, Democrat of North Dakota, who famously predicted: "I think we will look back in 10 years' time and say we should not have done this, but we did because we forgot the lessons of the past, and that which is true in the 1930s is true in 2010. We have now decided in the name of modernization to forget the lessons of the past, of safety and of soundness."[29]

During a speech in March 2008, then-senator Barack Obama echoed much of Senator Dorgan's sentiments when he said: "By the time the Glass-Steagall Act was repealed in 1999, the $300 million lobbying effort that drove deregulation was more about facilitating mergers than creating an efficient regulatory framework. Instead of establishing a 21st century regulatory framework, we simply dismantled the old one, 'thereby encouraging' a winner take all, anything goes environment that helped foster devastating dislocations in our economy."[30] A year later, Obama would preside over a nation swooning from the fallout of the repeal and would have to muster the resources of the nation to bail out the colossal financiers on Wall Street who had led the charge ten years earlier to repeal Glass-Steagall, and had found a Congress and president all too willing to comply.

The way in which Washington enriched a few at the expense of the many finds detailed analysis in Hacker and Pierson's *Winner-Take-All Politics,* and also in Gretchen Morgenson and Joshua Rosner's *Reckless Endangerment.* These books outline the close fraternity between the financial establishment and the political establishment; the ties between the CEOs of the financial conglomerates and their cronies in Washington; and the link between the financial analysts on Wall Street and their reincarnation as members of the president's cabinet—all part of a powerful dynamic that led to the near bankruptcy of the nation and the enrichment of a few, a highway robbery for which no one was ever held accountable.

In trying to attribute poverty and inequality to lapses in government policy, most have focused on what those policies have failed to deliver to the poor, instead of what the positions taken on policies deliver to the political elite. As Hacker and Pierson write, "The truth is that most people have missed the *visible* hand of government because they've been looking in the wrong place. They have talked about minimum wage, the Earned Income Tax Credit, Medicaid for vulnerable children and families—in short, programs that help those at the bottom. The real story, however, is what our national political elites have done for those at the top, both through their actions and through their deliberate failures to act."[31]

The Politics of the Minimum Wage

As discussed in Chapter 5, deindustrialization, automation, and globalization have led to a tremendous job loss in manufacturing. Since employment started expanding in 2010, 58 percent of the new jobs that are being added to the US economy are in sectors where the pay is very low and the minimum wage is often used for settling wage negotiations.

For low-wage workers, a low minimum wage diminishes their bargaining power, especially when many others are looking for work and support from the powerful labor unions of the past no longer exists. And when more and more people settle for minimum-wage jobs—because the alternatives are limited or because of lack of education and skills—the gap between their incomes and those at the higher end grows wider and wider.

Decisions about the minimum wage are within the purview of government, both federal and state. When government decides on a higher threshold for the minimum wage, it narrows the gap between the rich on the one hand and the middle class and the poor on the other. This is not rocket science: when people are paid a higher wage, it lowers the level of poverty they experience.

MAKING CONNECTIONS

"I'm Stuck: I'm Still in the Shelter"

Alpha Manzueta has lived in a New York City homeless shelter for three years with her two-and-a-half-year-old daughter. But if you saw her during the day, in her uniform directing traffic at Kennedy International Airport, you wouldn't be able to guess where she spends her nights.

In 2013, almost 28 percent of families living in shelters had a least one adult who worked, and 16 percent of single adults in shelters also had jobs. The work they did—as security guards, bank tellers, sales clerks, computer instructors, home health aides, and office support staff did not pay them enough to afford housing on their own.

Their plight shows the ever-widening gap between wages and rents. There are adults who work two jobs, as does Alpha, making $8 an hour in both, who are still unable to afford the exorbitant rents of apartments today. Some are homeless because they lost their jobs, their unemployment insurance ran out, and they could no longer afford their apartments.

The shortage of affordable places to live, together with long waiting lists for limited quantities of subsidized housing, explains why on any given night in New York, 50,000 people stay at homeless shelters. Individuals who shoulder responsibility in their day jobs must also obey curfews and follow the rules of the shelters—which they often find dehumanizing and insulting. But as homeless, they have little choice, and little hope that their lives will soon change.

In New York City, the gap between the rich and the poor continues to widen. In 2013, the average annual income for the lowest fifth of earners was $8,993, compared to $222,871 for the top fifth and $436,931 for the top 5 percent. The top figure is almost fifty times larger than the bottom figure. Almost a quarter of the New York City population live in food-insecure households and receive food stamps.[1]

Notes: The quotation that titles this box comes from Navarro, "In New York, Having a Job, or 2, Doesn't Mean Having a Home," p. A1.
1. Roberts, "Poverty Rate Up in City, and Income Gap is Wide," p. A24.

In Denmark, Burger King, McDonalds, Starbucks, and other multinational fast food chains pay their workers $20 an hour, wages which unions collectively bargained and won. When McDonalds first came to Denmark in the 1980s, it refused to accept the collectively bargained agreements and the workers participated in "raucous, union-led protests" for a year until McDonalds gave in. Danish workers earn two and a half times what their counterparts in the United States do. This does mean that the fast food chains aren't as profitable. One franchise owner acknowledged lower profits: "The company doesn't get as much profit, but the profit is shared a little differently. We don't want there to be a big difference between the richest and the poorest. . . . If that happens, we consider that we as a society have failed." In Denmark, fast food workers are guaranteed five weeks' paid vacation, paid parental leave, overtime pay, and a work schedule that they are given four weeks in advance.[32]

The story in New York City is slightly different. In November 2012, about 200 fast food workers in New York City walked off their jobs. Then, on August 29, 2013, the day after the fiftieth anniversary of the 1963 March on Washington, thousands of fast food workers walked off their jobs in sixty cities. They wanted everyone to know that it was impossible to survive in New York City, or anywhere else, on $7.25 an hour, the federal minimum wage. Those who walked off their jobs were but a tiny fraction of the millions who work in the fast food industry, which employs one in ten US workers.

They worked for highly profitable companies such as McDonald's, Taco Bell, Pizza Hut, KFC, and Wendy's. Jobs in the low-wage service industry, the fastest-growing job sector in the United States, are expected to grow even faster in the next decade. In the past, these jobs were mainly held by teenagers, who eventually moved on to better-paying careers. But today, a majority of fast food workers are adults, many of whom, in addition to supporting themselves, are also trying to raise families.

These are the jobs that symbolize the new US service economy of the early twenty-first century. In 1963, Bayard Rustin, one of the main organizers of the March on Washington, had called for a minimum wage that allowed people to "live with dignity." That call for dignity remains unanswered by those who have the power to make it happen.

According to Larry Bartels, "The dramatic rise and fall of the minimum wage over the past 70 years is one of the most remarkable aspects of the political economy of inequality."[33] The minimum wage covers the vast majority of the low-wage work force, and sets a minimum below which no worker will be allowed to fall. Bartels charts the history of the minimum wage from its birth in 1938 as a "major policy innovation" of the New Deal. The minimum wage increased steadily, from 25 cents per hour in 1938 (or about $3.60 in 2006 dollars) to $5.15 an hour in 1997. From 2007 to 2009, the wage then increased to its current rate of $7.25 an hour, as of 2014, in three increments. However, unlike Social Security benefits, the minimum wage has not been indexed to rise with inflation.[34] Therefore, the real value of the minimum wage has steadily declined.

As Douglass Massey writes:

> The golden age of the minimum wage was from 1948 to 1968, when in real terms it steadily rose from around $3.50 an hour to peak at $9.20 during the height of President Lyndon Johnson's Great Society. As inflation increased during the late 1960s and early 1970s, however, Congress declined to adjust the minimum wage and in real terms its value fell sharply, reaching $7.20 during the Nixon administration before stabilizing in the Ford and Carter

years. With the accession of Ronald Reagan to the presidency after 1980, the minimum wage resumed its race toward the bottom, reaching a value of just $5.40 in 1989. After fluctuating around $6.00 per hour during the Clinton years, the wage declined once again under President George W. Bush to end at $5.30 in 2005, the lowest level since Taft-Hartley passed in1949.[35]

Just since the increase to $7.25 an hour in July 2009, the minimum wage had lost 5 percent of its purchasing power to inflation as of 2012. If the minimum wage kept pace with inflation, it would have been around $10.38 an hour.[36] But even at $10.38, an adult working full-time or forty hours a week for fifty-two weeks ($21,590) would not make enough to lift their family above the poverty rate of $23,050 for a family of four, as of 2012.

Increasing the federal minimum wage is a commonsense policy to raise families out of poverty. The argument that raising the minimum wage will discourage employers from hiring new workers because they fear increases in their payroll expenses has often been used to oppose this policy. But the Economic Policy Institute contends that historical analyses of the minimum wage's impact on workers have never shown the large-scale job loss that conservative politicians have predicted.[37] And Larry Bartels writes: "Recent economic research suggests that the negative effects of minimum wage laws on employment are much less significant than has often been assumed, while declines in the real value of minimum wage have contributed substantially to increasing inequality in the bottom half of the income distribution."[38]

In January 2014, thirteen states—Arizona, Colorado, Connecticut, Florida, Missouri, Montana, New Jersey, New York, Ohio, Oregon, Rhode Island, Vermont, and Washington, raised their minimum wages. Between January and June 2014 twelve of these states (with the exception of New Jersey) added jobs at a faster pace (+0.99 percent) than the thirty-seven states that did not raise their minimum wage (+.68 percent.).[39] The experience of these states vindicates the position that has been taken by advocates of raising the minimum wage that a higher minimum wage does not discourage job growth.

Raising the minimum wage reduces the poverty rate. Many states in which laws require that wages keep pace with inflation have set their own minimum wages above the federal level. San Francisco, which sets its own minimum wage, will be the first to require companies to pay their workers more than $10 an hour. In at least nine other states, the minimum wage has been reset at anywhere from $7.64 to $9.04 an hour. These numbers still lag behind the minimum wages of other countries whose economic characteristics are comparable to those of the United States: Australia, $16.87 an hour as of 2014; France, $12.07; Ireland, $10.96; Canada, $10.20; and the United Kingdom, $10.46.

A minimum wage is just that—the floor below which no wages should fall. Trying to persuade Congress to index the minimum wage to inflation, so that it keeps up with the rising prices of consumer goods, has been a losing battle. And so it seems futile to even talk about a "living wage." Advocates for the poor and the middle class from across the country have said repeatedly that the current minimum wage does little to keep a family above poverty; neither does it pay for rents or mortgages so a family can also afford to stay sheltered.

Even the Republican candidate for president in 2012, Mitt Romney, has quite uncharacteristically and bravely voiced his support for raising the minimum wage. When Senate Republicans rejected a bill to increase the minimum wage to $10.10, Romney broke with his fellow conservatives to urge that they support the increase if they wanted to be seen as supporting good jobs with good pay for all Americans.

Bartels's research shows that in every public opinion survey conducted between 1960 and 2000, a majority of the public has favored raising the minimum wage. But over the same period, the real value of the minimum wage has declined significantly. In recent years, supporters for raising the minimum wage "have outnumbered the opponents by a margin of about four to one."[40]

But these voices don't seem to have penetrated the halls of Congress. Unlike the Wall Street financiers, who are given top billing in Washington, the voices of those who advocate for the poor get lost in the monied din. As Gilens, Bartels, Hacker, and Pierson have noted, Washington is not particularly responsive to the preferences of ordinary Americans. And there is a definite disconnect between public opinion and public policy.

Money, more than anything else, has hijacked the political discourse, so that politicians have invariably turned attention to those individuals and groups who have contributed to their campaign finances or to the causes they support. Calls for campaign finance reform have fallen on deaf ears.

In January 2010, the US Supreme Court's decision in the *Citizens United* case allowed corporations to spend unlimited amounts of money on campaign financing This ruling, more than anything, provides clear evidence of what I have been making in this chapter, which Matt Bai summarizes succinctly, "Citizens United unleashed a torrent of money from businesses and the multimillionaires who run them, and as a result we are now seeing the corporate takeover of American politics."[41] Some of the nation's largest and richest corporations, such as ExxonMobil and AT&T, have joined forces with rich corporate families such as the Koch brothers, under the banner of groups such as the American Legislative Exchange Council (ALEC), to amass millions of dollars for promoting legislative and congressional candidates who support positions that advance the interests of these corporations ahead of the interests of ordinary Americans.[42]

MAKING CONNECTIONS
Citizens United v. Federal Election Commission

In January 2010, in a five-to-four decision in the case *Citizens United v. Federal Election Commission,* the US Supreme Court granted corporations and unions the First Amendment right to spend freely in supporting candidates in elections, striking down any limits on independent campaign contributions. In endorsing this decision, the Court erased any distinction between human and nonhuman entities.

By granting a First Amendment guarantee of free speech to corporations, the Supreme Court essentially ruled that corporations were in fact human and therefore deserving of the same rights as any US citizen. And since corporations exercised free speech through their campaign contributions, placing any limits on this would go against the spirit of the First Amendment.

As expected, the decision opened the spending floodgates, with unprecedented amounts of money pouring into the coffers of Republican and Democratic candidates alike in the 2012 general elections. According to the Center for Public Integrity, a Washington, D.C.–based nonprofit organization that uses the tools of investigative journalism to "enhance democracy by revealing the abuses of power, corruption and betrayal of trust," close to a trillion dollars was spent in the ensuing electoral process, opening up even more avenues of corruption and influence-peddling in the political process.

This ultimately means that as long as money influences government decisions, the poor and the middle class will never get a fair chance to be heard in the halls of power or in the courts of justice, and their interests will never determine government policy. They will remain hostage to the vicissitudes of the "power elite." Policy choices that can mitigate the harsh realities of inequality and poverty will never gain political currency.

Jim Leach, who served as a member of the US House of Representatives from Iowa for thirty years, shows the capricious logic that the Supreme Court uses to determine who is human and who is not.[1] Leach argues that in the 1857 *Dred Scott* decision, the Court determined that black people were descendents of private property—slaves—and therefore could not claim to be human and thus forfeited their right to become US citizens. In the *Citizens United* decision, the Court defined a class of private property—corporations—as human.

Note: 1. Leach, "Citizens United."

That the preferences of the public do not get translated into public policy, compared to the preferences of the wealthy, is also a result of a precipitous decline in the countervailing power of unions. Recognizing the power of unions to advance the cause of the ordinary American, groups such as ALEC have inveighed against organized labor in no uncertain terms. They were instrumental to a large degree in orchestrating major defeats for unions in many states across the nation.[43]

In January 2013, union membership in the United States fell to a ninety-seven-year low of 11.3 percent of workers. Organized labor has been a strong advocate for the minimum wage and a guardian of worker rights. In Denmark, as in other European countries, unions have been successful in winning not just living wages but also a comprehensive safety net such as universal health care. Declining membership within its ranks means less power to counter those forces whose interest is primarily to make labor ineffective, if not completely superfluous. (In Chapter 12 we will return to discussion of the labor movement in greater detail, to place the growing inequality in the United States within the context of unions' declining power.)

MAKING CONNECTIONS

"The Poor Must Manage Their Money Better"

In the summer of 2013, fast food workers across the country walked off their jobs. From New York to Chicago, Detroit to Seattle, the workers wanted the nation to know that it was impossible to support themselves and their families on the wages they were making. Unlike in the past, when low-wage work in fast food and retail was done by the young, often teenagers, today it is adults who are turning to these jobs as the economy fails to create good-paying middle-class jobs.

This was confirmed by the US Labor Department in its August 2013 jobs report. The good news was that the unemployment rate had fallen to 7.4 percent, the lowest since December 2008. Almost 162,000 jobs had been added to the US economy. But the majority of these jobs were minimum-wage positions paying $7.25 an hour. Almost 60 percent of the new jobs were in the lowest third of the pay scale. Many individuals who lost their "good jobs" making $15 an hour or more have now found jobs in the fast food industry making minimum wage.

Yuki Noguchi, a National Public Radio reporter, interviewed some of these individuals for her August 2013 news report.[1] Morris Cornley, for example, had been a truck driver for almost two decades, making $17.45 an hour, before losing his job three years prior to being interviewed. At his current job at a fast food restaurant—Jimmy John's Sandwich Place, in Kansas City—he makes $7.35 an hour. Three generations of the Cornley family now work at fast food restaurants, but this is still not enough to put decent food on their own table. When the fast food workers across the nation walked off their jobs in the summer of 2013, demanding a $15-an-hour living wage, so did Mr. Cornley.

Noguchi also tells the story of Kareem Starks, who had to truncate his college education because he had no money and went to work for New York City's parks and recreation department, planting trees. He made $17 an hour and was certain that his work experience would help him find a job in the new "green economy." But in the two years since that job ended, he has been unable to land a new one, even after fifty to sixty interviews. Now he works at two minimum-wage jobs, one at McDonald's and the other at a security firm. Many of his colleagues, he tells Noguchi, are also those "who have slipped down the scale."

(continues)

"The Poor Must Manage Their Money Better"

In response to the publicity surrounding the working poor, Washington, D.C., passed a "living wage" bill requiring that large retailers pay their workers a minimum of $12.50 an hour. McDonald's came out with its own solution. It designed an absurdly unrealistic budget to help its workers manage their expenses.[2] The problem was not that the minimum wage was insufficient, company executives reasoned, but rather that the workers were not managing their finances properly.

What was most astounding about the McDonald's budget was its recommendation that employees get a second job. And the budget left out necessary expenses for food, child care, gasoline, and the like, and directed employees to set aside a mere $20 a month for health insurance. For single parents like Anthony Moore trying to raise two children on his $9/hour wage he makes at Burger King, this means foregoing doctors' visits, falling behind on rent and utility bill payments, and deciding whether to buy his children "food or clothes? If I made $20 an hour, I could actually live, instead of dreaming about living."[3]

Notes: 1. National Public Radio, "Quality vs. Quantity."
2. The McDonald's budget can be viewed in Philpott, "McDonald's to Employees."
3. Alderman and Greenhouse, "Serving Up Fries, for a Living Wage."

How Trade Treaties Are Negotiated

As discussed in Chapter 5, many Americans have lost their jobs due to the effects of globalization. And as people lose the jobs that had been their pathway to the middle class, they fall off the economic ladder. As corporations outsource their business to low-wage countries with lax regulations in order to maximize their profits, jobs are lost in the United States. Much of the income inequality of the past decade is rooted in this reality of jobs lost to outsourcing.

Trade liberalization is the cornerstone of globalization. The former amplifies the latter. Trade treaties are negotiated to open up borders by eliminating tariffs and export-import duties and by deregulating terms of investment, labor, and environmental protection statutes—a process that happens both in corporate offices and government offices, both domestically and abroad, away from the public eye, whether here or there. Since these trade treaties impact the lives of millions, it is important to consider how they are negotiated and agreed upon, to understand how the confluence of affluence and influence strengthens the hands of some and weakens the hands of others.

Are the elite organized along class lines? Do they coordinate their political activism around common issues of concern? Or are they autonomous actors who are unable to come together to sustain "unified class-oriented political action?"[44] In the field of political sociology, there is scholarship supporting both of these positions.

Some contend that the corporate rich, in their competition with each other, are incapable of forming a united front. This position is generally held by political sociologists who side with the tenets of majority pluralism and are critical of theories that emphasize the role of corporate power in the political process. But this position is unsustainable in light of the evidence presented so far that demonstrates how the corporate elite have a common class interest in influencing government policy in areas where all corporate players stand to gain.

The presence of corporate unity in influencing public policy has been repeatedly verified by sociologists who have documented corporate mobilization and corporate unity in how US trade policy is negotiated. These studies provide a "unique empirical context for exploring the political intersection of states and corporations."[45] They depict the "collective political agency" of multinational corporations, which "in concert with state actors initiate collective political action and shape the policy frameworks that undergird economic globalization and, in particular, multinational trade and investment."[46]

Michael Dreiling shows that the large corporations not only are the most important forces of economic globalization, but more importantly are immensely influential in "pressing states to initiate and ratify the very trade agreements and policy changes that facilitate the liberalization of global trade and investment." He also states: "Our robust test of corporate involvement in US trade politics allows us to contribute to a more empirically grounded understanding of the role of large corporations to advancing a neo liberal trade policy consensus in Washington, circa 1991–2005, and adds to sociological theories concerning the enduring political influence of large corporations."[47]

The case of the North American Free Trade Agreement, which eliminated barriers to trade between the United States, Canada, and Mexico, provides an excellent study of corporate unity and corporate activism in influencing US trade policy and liberalization of the global marketplace. There was widespread public opposition to NAFTA. But the fact that NAFTA was enacted despite this opposition shows the weakness of public opinion and labor unions in countering corporate power and swaying government decisionmaking to their own advantage. Given that so much of the widening of inequality in the United States came on the heels of trade liberalization and the subsequent flight of capital to regions with cheap labor, NAFTA can be seen as signaling a fundamental defeat for the American people and the process of democratic decisionmaking—and an unqualified victory for the corporate elite.

Michael Dreiling and Derek Darves trace the various tactics that corporate mobilization for NAFTA entailed. The authors move away from what are usually the most recognized forms of political behavior—political action committee (PAC) contributions and congressional testimony by corporate think tanks and spokespersons—in investigating the many different ways in which corporations influenced political decisions in the negotiating process for NAFTA.[48] They draw from economics, sociology, and political sociology to construct a theory of class cohesion among corporations and the degree of "embeddedness" of corporate actors in the political decision-making process. They start from the premise that the presence of **interlocking directorates** strengthens corporate unity. Interlocking directorates come about when corporate directors and members sit on the boards of, and have memberships in, multiple corporations. Simultaneously, they also "participate in prominent policy planning groups, and [have] common membership in ad hoc political alliances. This close cooperation reduces competition and enables the building of 'social cohesion of elites' and coordination in areas of 'corporate and policy planning.'"[49]

Dreiling and Darves position their examination of corporate activism in the NAFTA policymaking process in a historical context. They refer to the 1934 Reciprocal Trade Agreement Act (RTAA) as the most important piece of trade legislation ever passed by Congress, because it was successful in taking away the authority over matters of international commerce delegated to Congress by the US Constitution, and placing that authority in the hands of the president, away from the eyes of the public.

The delegation of trade policy authority to the president weakened the lobbying power of labor unions and other watchdogs, who generally keep the proceedings of Congress under their surveillance. As the RTAA increased executive autonomy over trade policy, it also created new opportunities for corporate political influence. Because the American public was not attentive to this seventy-five-year slow but critical transfer of decision-making authority on trade matters from the legislative to the executive branch, it was easy to conceal corporate involvement in the office of the nation's president. The public continued to believe that the "state actors were autonomous and rational in crafting trade policy."[50]

The primacy given to the executive branch played a critical role when NAFTA was negotiated. For example, Dreiling cites sources that confirm the role the Bill Clinton administration played in assisting the USA*NAFTA coalition to "successfully replace a Congressional majority opposed to NAFTA four months prior to the treaty vote with a relatively strong favorable majority by November of 1993."[51] The USA*NAFTA corporate coalition, which played an especially active role in campaigning for NAFTA, is a vivid example "lending support to a corporate unity, class cohesion account."[52] USA*NAFTA was an offshoot of the Business Roundtable, a national association of CEOs of the 200 largest transnational corporations. David Korten writes: "Whereas more inclusive business organizations such as the chambers of commerce and national associations of manufacturers include both large and small firms, . . . the members of the business roundtables are all large transnational corporations firmly aligned with the economic globalization agenda."[53] The Business Roundtable created a front organization, USA* NAFTA, with some 2,300 US corporations as members. The power the members of USA*NAFTA wielded is seen in their participation in the NAFTA negotiation process through representation on trade advisory committees responsible for shaping US trade policy as well as in their direct contact with President Clinton, who signed NAFTA into law on December 8, 1993.

The following accounts give evidence to their privileged position. As Dreiling observes, "Meeting directly with President Clinton for 'regular' briefings by White House officials, USA*NAFTA members of the Business Roundtable worked closely to select Lee Iacocca as the President's NAFTA Czar."[54] And further: "President Clinton and (Commerce Secretary) Mickey Kantor, with assistance from the corporate-sponsored USA*NAFTA" would identify corporations and business officials to pressure lawmakers who were opposed to NAFTA, in order to change their minds and "secure a reversal in their NAFTA-votes" and guarantee passage of the agreement.[55]

USA*NAFTA tried to build up public support with editorials, opinion pieces, news releases, and television commentaries. The corporate coalition retained highly prestigious public relations firms, law firms, and lobbyists to function as pressure groups. In total, an estimated $30–50 million was spent by proponents, making it one of the most expensive foreign policy campaigns in US history.[56]

According to David Korten, "nine of the USA*NAFTA state captains (Allied Signal, AT&T, General Electric, General Motors, Phelps Dodge, United Technologies, IBM, ITT, and TRW) were among the US corporations that had already shipped 180,000 jobs to Mexico during the twelve years prior to the passage of NAFTA."[57] Some had already been cited for violations of worker safety standards and environmental regulations.

As Michael Dreiling observes: "In this way, inter-corporate unity, and advocacy in trade policy in particular, can be viewed as a consequence of the institutional embeddedness of corporate executives in the policy formation process. These are not fragmented economic actors, but actors bound together in a social milieu best characterized by theorists of elite power structures and class domination."[58]

This rather dull account of the role corporate executives played in the negotiating process for NAFTA, ensuring its final victory, masks the grave fallout from NAFTA in real, human terms. NAFTA and other trade policies such as the General Agreement on Tariffs and Trade (GATT, which later morphed into the World Trade Organization), the Free Trade Area of the

Americas, the Central American Free Trade Agreement, and a slew of others, opened up the world and transformed it into a single marketplace wherein capital could find its best fit. With the primary objective of maximizing profits, capital nested wherever this could be guaranteed—through low-wage labor, cheap resources, and lax governmental regulations on workplace and environmental protection.

US workers lost out as their jobs were outsourced and their places of work shut down, thus destabilizing communities and livelihoods. More and more Americans shifted to service jobs that paid lower wages than what they were accustomed to. Inequality deepened so significantly that many social scientists designated the first two decades of the twenty-first century as a new Gilded Age. And labor unions, with falling membership and weakening power, could do very little to protect the public, to arrest the steady flow of wealth to the very top rungs of the income ladder, or to stop the unraveling of people's lives on the lower rungs—which NAFTA and such treaties were so adversely impacting.

In his second term, President Obama has made economic inequality one of his signature issues. He has issued executive orders to raise the minimum wage for federal contractors to $10.10 an hour, an almost 40 percent increase from the current federal minimum wage of $7.25 an hour as of 2009, and also to ensure that employees are paid fairly for overtime work. But at the same time, Obama is also calling for fast-track authority to speed up the passage of the Trans-Pacific Partnership (TPP), a twelve-nation free trade agreement among the United States and Latin American and Asian countries. The TPP, at its core, comprises the same "investor rights and privileges" agenda integral to NAFTA, which makes it extremely easy for firms to move their production to low-wage countries. If the TPP is implemented, more US jobs will be lost as US multinational corporations shift their factories overseas.

Tax Policies

How does the United States go about deciding what its tax structure will be? Who is to be taxed, and how much? Tax policies and transfer payments (discussed in Chapter 3) are ways that society redistributes income and tries to narrow the gap between the rich and poor.

Ideally, this is accomplished by instituting a combination of a progressive tax system, meaning that the more money one makes, the higher the tax rate on that person's income, and a system of progressive transfer payments (a social safety net), to ensure that no one will fall below a society's designated poverty line. The more progressive the tax system, the more generous the system of transfer income, and thus the less unequal a society is. But these matters generate tremendous disagreement and controversy among the competing political ideologies that influence lawmakers and citizens alike, determining their positions on taxation and social welfare.

Correction of gross inequalities of income and wealth is often attempted through establishment of equitable and redistributive tax conventions based on the strict principles of a progressive tax code, in which income from the highest earners is spread out to finance governmental programs such as mass transit and social welfare. Tax codes such as these, it is argued, not only narrow the gap between the richest and the rest, but also enable money to fund programs that benefit society as a whole.

The tax and transfer system that a society institutes redistributes the wealth and remedies glaring inequalities. By taxing those at the top and constructing a strong safety net to keep those who have experienced job loss or other adversity from falling into poverty, a society can bridge the deep disparity between the rich and the poor. Government has enormous power to shape the distribution of income by formulating a progressive code that taxes higher-income people at a higher tax rate, so that each citizen pays his or her fair share. And implementing a transfer system that provides people with the support they need when they are experiencing hard times helps them get back on their feet again.

In most advanced countries, tax and transfer policies have helped reduce the upsurge in economic inequality. But in the United States, as many researchers have noted, the government has adopted policies that have actually exacerbated the growth of inequality. On the one hand, tax rates for those at the top of the income distribution are currently at their lowest since the end of World War II, having fallen continuously since the 1980s. This has been accompanied by a parallel whittling down of the social welfare programs by making them not only more restrictive but also more punitive.

Emmanuel Saez and Thomas Piketty, in an article about income inequality and taxes, write that in the United States "the total share of pre-tax income accruing to the top 1% has more than doubled, from less than 10% in the 1970s to over 20% today [2013]. At the same time, top income tax rates on upper income earners have declined significantly since the 1970s. Top marginal income tax rates in the United States [were] above 70% in the 1970s, before the Reagan revolution drastically cut them by 40 percentage points within a decade. There is a strong correlation between the reductions in top tax rates and the increases in top 1% income shares. . . . [B]y contrast, France and Germany saw very little change in their top tax rates and their top 1% income shares during the same period."[59]

The argument that has often been provided to support the slashing of taxes on the very rich, as Saez and Piketty note, is that high tax rates may "discourage work effort and business creation. Lower tax rates would lead to more economic activity by the rich and hence more economic growth." But Saez and Piketty argue that "again data show that there is no correlation between cuts in top tax rates and average annual real GDP-per-capita growth." Increasing income concentration, encouraged to a large extent by low tax rates on the rich, has brought only mediocre economic growth (not enough to support further tax cuts), therefore, "the job of economists is to make a top tax rate of 80% thinkable again."[60] When government declines to follow a progressive tax structure, especially at a time when it is also facing large deficits and debts, the economic burden ultimately and invariably falls on the most vulnerable populations, which have already been made defenseless from the fallout of a market increasingly sculpted by global economic forces.

Sociologists Ho-fung Hung and Jaime Kucinskas, in their analysis of how globalization deepens inequality, assert that the "retrenchment of the redistributive and regulatory state, as evident in the unraveling welfare state in advanced capitalist countries, the collapse of state socialism in the East, and the retreat of the state-led development in the developing world, has incited a rise in within-nation inequality. With the demise of government's proactive efforts to redistribute income and protect the disadvantaged, the global free market force is unleashed, and ever increasing income disparities are permitted."[61] In other words, with a good redistributive mechanism in place, governments could have fortified their people's ability to face the challenges that globalization had unleashed. But in the absence of such policies, people were left defenseless.

Between 1979 and 2005 in the United States, according to the Congressional Budget Office, the inflation-adjusted average income of families in the middle of the income distribution rose 21 percent. In the same period, the average income of the very rich, the 0.01 percent of the income distribution, rose by 480 percent. In 2005 dollars, the average annual income of the very rich rose from $4.2 million to $24.3 million.[62]

Observing these numbers, Nobel Prize–winning economist and *New York Times* columnist Paul Krugman reinforces the contention that government policy is to blame for creating much of this disparity. Focusing on taxes, he writes that huge fortunes were created not just because of "big cuts in top income tax rates," but also because of the shift in taxation from *wealth* to *work*. "Tax rates on corporate profits, capital gains and dividends have all fallen, while the payroll tax—the main tax paid by most workers— has gone up." As a result, people with multimillion-dollar incomes derived from capital gains and dividends end up paying less taxes, as a percentage of their incomes, than do middle-class workers. He cites the nonpartisan Tax Policy Center, which estimates that a quarter of those making million-dollar incomes pay a 12.6 percent tax rate, "putting their tax burden below that of many middle-class workers."[63]

The recent surge in inequality in the United States has often been partially attributed to the tax cuts on both stock dividends (income for shareholders of corporations) and capital gains (income from trading assets) that President George W. Bush signed into law in 2003, just as the Iraq War was gathering steam. When Bush took office, the top tax rate on long-term capital gains was 20 percent. With the new law, the top rate on investment income dropped to 15 percent. Before this law went into effect, stock dividends were regarded as ordinary income, taxable at the 25–35 percent rate. With this new law, however, stock dividends were treated the same as capital gains and therefore were taxed at the much lower rate.

The top capital gains tax rate was 25 percent in the 1950s and the 1960s, and 35 percent in the 1970s. Today, it is 15 percent. Changes in the tax rate for capital gains have been the greatest contributor to the increases in income inequality since the 1990s.[64]

The tax code of the United States imposes two separate rates for individuals, one for wages and salaries (25–35 percent) and another for investment income (15 percent.) These are the federal taxes that most people refer to when any discussion on taxes comes up. This, however, does not include the many state and local taxes, such as sales taxes, that apply equally to everyone regardless of how rich or poor one is.

Though almost half of Americans own stocks and bonds, primarily in the form of 401(k) pension plans, the bulk of the financial assets of the nation are held by a very small minority. As G. William Domhoff notes: In terms of types of financial wealth, the top 1 percent of households have 35 percent of all privately held stock, 64.4 percent of financial securities, and 62.4 percent of business equity. The top 10 percent have 81 percent to 94 percent of stocks, bonds, trust funds, and business equity, and almost 80 percent of nonhome real estate.[65]

These are the assets that are taxed at the 15 percent rate. Because of the degree of concentration of these assets in the hands of the richest Americans, the large majority of taxpayers do not benefit from this low rate. In comparison, the top tax rate, of 25–35 percent, applies to the incomes that the majority of Americans make in the form of salaries and wages.

This is the reason why billionaires who live off investment income, like Warren Buffett, pay a lower tax rate than working-class people, whose income is from their wages and salaries. For 2011, according to Citizens for Tax Justice, an advocacy group that calls for a fair and sustainable tax system, when all taxes are taken into account, taxpayers in the top 1 percent paid only 29.0 percent of their income in local, state, and federal taxes, whereas taxpayers with an average income of $68,700 paid almost the same amount, 28.3 percent.[66]

Citizens for Tax Justice published another report in April 2012, just around the time when Americans were filing their tax returns for 2011, comparing two groups of taxpayers: those with incomes in the $60,000–65,000 range (the salary that Buffet's secretary is said to make), who have very little investment income and have an average effective tax rate of 21.3 percent; and those whose incomes exceed $10 million, who derive a majority of their income from investments and who consequently have an average effective tax rate of 15.3 percent. As shown in Table 6.1, the effective tax rate for the top 1 percent is not much higher than for the middle-class American.

Even though US corporations are taxed at a rate of 35 percent—one of the highest corporate tax rates in the world—many do not pay their fair share because of the numerous loopholes, subsidies, and avenues to avoid paying. Today "corporate tax loopholes are so out of control that most Americans can rightfully complain that they pay more federal income taxes than General Electric, Boeing, DuPont, Wells Fargo, Verizon . . . all put together."[67]

According to a special report published in November 2011 by Citizens for Tax Justice and the Institute on Taxation and Economic Policy, the 280 corporations in their study paid, on average, only half of the 35 percent tax rate and "many paid far less, including a number that paid nothing at all."[68]

Apple, the world's most profitable technology company, has been particularly adept at avoiding taxes. By spreading its operations to low-tax regions around the world, it decreased its global tax rate to 9.8 percent in 2012, on profits of $34.2 billion. Citing an example, the *New York Times* reported: "Apple's headquarters are in Cupertino, California. By putting an office at Reno, just 200 miles away, to collect and invest the company's profits, Apple sidesteps state income taxes on some of those gains. California's corporate tax rate is 8.84 percent. Nevada's? Zero."[69] The same *New York Times* article reports on dozens of other companies, including Cisco, Harley-Davidson, and Microsoft, that have also set up subsidiaries in Nevada that bypass taxes in other states. Hundreds of other corporations reap similar savings by locating their offices in Delaware. It is therefore not surprising that as corporate profits have continued to rise, effective corporate tax rates have fallen.

Table 6.1 Total Effective Tax Rates for Income Groups, 2011

Income Group	Total Effective Tax Rate (%)
Lowest 20 percent	17.4
Second 20 percent	21.2
Middle 20 percent	25.2
Fourth 20 percent	28.3
Next 10 percent	29.5
Next 5 percent	30.3
Next 4 percent	30.4
Top 1 percent	29.0

Source: Citizens for Tax Justice, "Buffett Rule Before the Senate."

States often maintain low corporate tax rates as a way to attract businesses. This is on top of the additional incentives that states offer to attract companies, which demand such incentives in return for the promise of job creation. As localities across the nation experience steep unemployment, billions of dollars in incentives are being awarded by mayors and governors to multinational corporations in their desperation to create jobs for their residents. "Incentives come in many forms: cash grants and loans; sales tax breaks; income tax credit and exemptions; free services; and property tax abatements. The income tax breaks add up to $18 billion and sales tax relief around $52 billion of the overall $80 billion in incentives."[70] States raised the money for these incentives by cutting public services and raising additional taxes totaling $156 billion.

The incentive money goes mainly to manufacturing companies, such as General Motors, but also to agriculture; the oil, gas, and mining industries; followed by Hollywood film businesses and technology companies such as Twitter and Facebook. The amount New York spends to entice Hollywood to film in the state each year "equals the cost of hiring 5,000 public school teachers."[71] But most of the time, the states and their residents end up on the losing end when the promised jobs do not materialize or the companies, after raking in their profits, leave on a whim. Adding insult to injury, slews of public services are then often cut, and taxes are raised to compensate for the revenue loss incurred when financial incentives were extended to companies with which the government leaders regularly hobnobbed.

As corporate taxes have declined, corporate profits have skyrocketed. As the rich are allowed to keep more and more of their income, the bulk of the tax burden falls on the middle class and incongruously on the poor, who can afford the taxes the least. Thus, the gap between the richest and the poorest grows wider and wider.

And here again we observe how government has changed the rules regarding taxes and stacked the benefits in favor of a very small group of the wealthiest. In his article on corporate mobilization and political power in the 1970s, Patrick Ackard refers to the "influence of a well-organized and unified business lobby representing all segments of capital to carry out a unified, class conscious policy offensive favoring greater reliance on market allocation of resources, a reduction of taxes and nondefense government expenditures [read: transfer payments], and a rollback of recently enacted regulations affecting industry."[72] Their dominance became a striking feature of policy struggles in the United States between 1974 and 1981, culminating in President Ronald Reagan's rise to power, the dismantling of the welfare state, and the whittling down of taxes for the very rich.

Kevin Phillips observes that "in a politics increasingly dominated by contributors and corporations, the middle three-fifths of the nation had little say in the actual re-sculpting of the tax code carried out between 1981 and 1990."[73] He puts the blame at the feet of both Republicans and Democrats, who were competing with each other to curry favor with the corporations and give away the most revenue. Corporations such as General Electric boasted that they had used provisions from the newest tax laws not only to "wipe out most of the company's tax liability but also to pick up $110 million in refunds from previous years."[74] The Economic Recovery Tax Act of 1981 instituted the biggest federal tax cut in history. The sum of corporate-claimed depreciation for 1982–1987 totaled an extraordinary $1.65 trillion.[75]

Alan Greenspan, who would later head the Federal Reserve, decided that while corporate and individual tax rates were falling for the top earners, payroll taxes on lower- and middle-class Americans had to be increased, prompting even *The Economist* of London to comment that the United States had the world's least-progressive tax structures.[76] The demise of progressive taxation of the richest has intensified income inequality in unprecedented ways. If the top tax rate had remained at its level of the 1970s, a very big chunk of today's growing gap between the super-rich and everyone else would disappear.[77]

Writing in 2008, Larry Bartels asserts:

> The most significant domestic policy initiative of the past decade has been a massive government-engineered transfer of additional wealth from the lower and middle classes to the rich in the form of substantial reductions in federal income taxes. Congress passed, and President Bush signed, two of the largest tax cuts in history in 2001 and 2003. One accounting put the total cost to the federal Treasury of those cuts from 2001 through 2003 at $4.6 trillion—more than twice the federal government's total annual budget at the time the measure was adopted.[78]

Hacker and Pierson make note of a subtler way in which the wealthy have been given much greater latitude: through diminished scrutiny and lax enforcement of tax laws. Rich people and corporations must report their complex earnings and capital gains, unlike most Americans, whose taxes get deducted from their paychecks. The rich have access to tax loopholes to skirt the tax laws that most Americans cannot avoid. Yet, even as the number of tax audits has increased for the poor taxpayers who claim the earned income tax credit, audits of high-income taxpayers and businesses have plummeted. Billions of dollars in tax revenues are lost as a result.[79]

In their book *Winner-Take-All Politics,* Hacker and Pierson introduce the concept of "drift" to indicate how government, through sheer inaction, can allow the status quo to continue, such as with tax loopholes that permit the rich to shovel millions into their already bloated treasuries. In making their case, Hacker and Pierson cite the practice of hedge fund managers treating their "extraordinary incomes as capital gains subject to only a 15 percent tax rate. In 2006, the top twenty-five hedge fund managers earned nearly $600 million on average, with the richest, James Simons, taking in

$1.7 billion."[80] The rule governing the tax on capital gains was made long before hedge funds became all the rage. Intense lobbying by the deep-pocketed beneficiaries and their supporters in Congress has stopped any efforts to correct this egregious loophole.

In the late spring of 2013, when blistering reports of Apple's avoidance of billions of dollars in taxes broke out in the media, the company's chief executive, Tim Cook, was summoned before the Senate's Permanent Committee on Investigations. The expectation was that the senators would conduct a serious investigation and the CEO would be "pummeled" and denounced for his company's tax avoidance tactics. Instead, as the *New York Times* reported, the hearing turned out to be more of a lovefest for Apple's products.[81]

Conclusion

Government plays a significant role in determining the rules that create and reinforce income and wealth inequalities in society. In the political economy of inequality, the winners and losers are determined not by the impartial dynamics of the marketplace, but by a government that is swayed by the influence of big money.

Notes

1. Marx and Engels, *The Communist Manifesto,* p. 37.
2. Gilens and Page, "Testing Theories of American Politics."
3. Domhoff, "Wealth, Income, and Power."
4. Gilens and Page, "Testing Theories of American Politics," p. 567.
5. Ibid.
6. Ibid., p. 564.
7. Ibid., p. 576.
8. Ibid., pp. 575, 576.
9. Ibid., pp. 576, 577.
10. Gilens, *Affluence and Influence,* p. 96.
11. Peters, "No Pay?" p. A13.
12. Lichtblau, "Economic Downturn Took a Detour at Capitol Hill," p. A1.
13. Gilens and Page, "Testing Theories of American Politics," p. 24.
14. Hardt and Negri, *Commonwealth,* p. 5.
15. Ibid., p. 7.
16. Ibid., p. 3.
17. Ibid., p. 15.
18. Bartels, *Unequal Democracy,* pp. 3–5.
19. Quoted in Gilens, *Affluence and Influence,* p. 1.
20. Phillips, *Wealth and Democracy,* p. xv.
21. Hacker and Pierson, *Winner-Take-All Politics,* p. 3.

22. Ibid., pp. 3–7.

23. Ibid.

24. Domhoff, "Wealth, Income, and Power."

25. Mills, *The Power Elite*, p. 18.

26. Domhoff, "Wealth, Income, and Power."

27. Leonhardt, "Washington's Invisible Hand," p. MM32.

28. Sanati, "10 Years Later, Looking at Repeal of Glass-Steagall."

29. Ibid.

30. Ibid.

31. Hacker and Pierson, *Winner-Take-All Politics*, p. 71 (emphasis in original).

32. Alderman and Greenhouse, "Serving Up Fries, for a Living Wage," pp. B1, B8.

33. Bartels, *Unequal Democracy*, p. 224.

34. Ibid., p. 225.

35. Massey, "Globalization and Inequality."

36. Markham, "The Real Value of the Minimum Wage."

37. Bernstein and Schmitt, *The Impact of the Minimum Wage*.

38. Bartels, *Unequal Democracy*, p. 226.

39. Wolcott, "2014 Job Creation Faster in States that Raised the Minimum Wage."

40. Bartels, *Unequal Democracy*, p. 226.

41. Bai, "How Did Political Money Get This Loud?" p. MM14.

42. Common Cause, "The American Legislative Executive Council."

43. Bartels, *Unequal Democracy*, p. 226; Hacker and Pierson, *Winner-Take-All Politics*, p. 56; and Kroll, "Meet the New Kochs."

44. Dreiling, "Class Embeddedness of Corporate Political Action."

45. Dreiling and Darves, "Corporate Unity in American Trade Policy," pp. 1514–1515.

46. Ibid., p. 1515.

47. Ibid.

48. Ibid., p. 1516.

49. Ibid., pp. 1514–1515.

50. Ibid., p. 1517.

51. Dreiling, "Class Embeddedness of Corporate Political Action," p. 24.

52. Drilling and Darves, "Corporate Unity in American Trade Policy," p. 1557.

53. Korten, *When Corporations Rule the World*, p. 146.

54. Dreiling, "Class Embeddedness of Corporate Political Action," p. 37.

55. Ibid., p. 38.

56. Ibid., p. 24.

57. Korten, *When Corporations Rule the World*, p. 147.

58. Dreiling, "Class Embeddedness of Corporate Political Action," p. 36.

59. Saez and Piketty, "Why the 1% Should Pay Tax at 80%."

60. Ibid.

61. Hung and Kucinskas, "Globalization and Global Inequality," p. 1482.

62. Krugman, "The Social Contract," p. A35.

63. Ibid.

64. Hungerford, *Taxes and the Economy*.

65. Domhoff, "Wealth, Income, and Power."

66. Citizens for Tax Justice, "Buffett Rule Before the Senate."

67. Ibid.

68. Citizens for Tax Justice and the Institute on Taxation and Economic Policy, "Corporate Tax Dodging in the Fifty States."

69. Duhigg and Kocieniewski, "How Apple Sidesteps Billions in Taxes," p. A1.
70. Story, "United States of Subsidies."
71. Ibid.
72. Ackard, "Corporate Mobilization and Political Power," p. 597.
73. Phillips, *Wealth and Democracy,* p. 220.
74. Ibid., p. 221.
75. Ibid.
76. Ibid., p. 222.
77. Hacker and Pierson, *Winner-Take-All Politics,* p. 49.
78. Bartels, *Unequal Democracy,* p. 162.
79. Hacker and Pierson, *Winner-Take-All Politics,* p. 50.
80. Ibid., p. 51.
81. Shear, "Torches and Pitchforks for I.R.S but Cheers for Apple," p. B1.

7

Education:
The Great Equalizer?

THERE IS A GREAT DIVIDE IN EDUCATIONAL OPPORTUNITIES AND EDU-
cational outcomes in the United States. Public education, envisioned to be
the "great equalizer," has continually fallen short of its promises. The
emphasis that it be community-driven in all aspects—from financing to
determination of the curriculum—combined with the reality that educational outcomes depend not simply on the schools but also on the environment in which the children live, has made for a system that reflects the par-
ticularities and idiosyncrasies of the community, perpetuating unique
advantages and disadvantages in the outcomes that the children ultimately
experience.

Institutional discrimination in education pulls the rug out from under
communities segregated by both race and class. And remedies such as affirmative action, with their promises to level the playing field, cannot be realized as long as deep-seated structural inequalities remain. Similarly, the
skyrocketing cost of higher education, in combination with federal and state
budget cuts in financial assistance, has made it extremely difficult for
young people who are fortunate enough to have graduated from the public
schools to receive a college education, which is increasingly touted as an
imperative for success.

This chapter draws from the works of educators, sociologists, economists, and historians in describing the nature and causes of these inequalities and recognizing how they perpetuate the structures of an oppressively
stratified society. These scholars converge on the position that inequalities
in educational opportunities and educational achievements are embedded in
the larger structural inequalities of society. Any attempts at reforming education will be superficial at best if they do not also seek to fix the deeper,
more fundamental economic inequalities. However, the experience with
repeated attempts at education reform in the United States has shown the

propensity to opt for shortcuts and easy fixes by introducing new pedagogies, new tests, new curricula, and new ways of organizing schools, and by reprimanding teachers, principals, and parents without adopting policies for comprehensive social reform.

In this era of global competition, the academic aptitude of a great majority of young people in the United States has fallen in comparison with their peers in other nations. But more significant, our failure to address education reform in the context of structural reform has ultimately led to a perpetuation and intensification of inequality in society, and to the creation of deep pockets of poverty in many parts of the country. The US education system has perpetuated poverty and inequality by failing to provide individuals with the necessary tools and capabilities to overcome disadvantage.

It is therefore important to consider the political economy of education reform—the motivation, priorities, and choices of the politicians and businesspeople who have guided the education policy of the nation. It is also important to recognize that the absence of political will to effect real reform in education follows the same trajectory as the absence of political will in effecting real change in other structural matters, such as ensuring that people have jobs, living wages, affordable housing, transportation, health care, safe neighborhoods, and a strong safety net.

In the 1980s and 1990s, Jonathan Kozol published a series of books that captured in shocking ways the "savage inequalities" in education and in every other aspect of material life that plague children's lives in the dark vestiges of urban America.[1] Nothing did more to raise the public's awareness of this collective tragedy than did Kozol's wrenching accounting of the lives of the poor from East St. Louis to the Bronx, from Chicago's South Side to the nation's capital. It is indeed ironic how little Camden, New Jersey, has changed since he first documented its anguish in 1991. These are the forgotten people. Roger Wilkins, son of civil rights leader Roy Wilkins, calls them America's "throwaway people."[2]

Academic Chances and Academic Success

In 2011, Greg Duncan and Richard Murnane edited a volume on rising inequality, schools, and children's life chances. It is a comprehensive look from the perspective of sociologists, economists, and experts in social and education policy

> to examine the toll that rising economic inequality is taking on education in the United States. Public education's preeminent commitment [is to equip] the children of the rich and poor alike with the capabilities they will need to compete in an increasingly knowledge-driven economy. But if the children of the well-off now systematically receive superior education to that of the

children of the disadvantaged, then rising inequality may perpetuate itself, and even accelerate in coming generations.[3]

The book looks at how unequal family resources, disadvantaged neighborhoods, insecure labor markets, and worsening school conditions of K–12 education are cumulatively undermining the core goal of public education to provide children with an equal chance at academic and economic success. Figure 7.1 shows this connection quite compellingly.

Families, neighborhoods, and local labor markets are all inordinately shaped by income inequality. Income inequality determines how much resources parents have at their disposal to spend on their children's education. It also determines where they live, and the extent to which they have access to libraries, quality child care, safe playgrounds, recreational facilities, and most importantly, good schools. Income inequality, therefore, determines how much children learn and the quality of children's educational attainment, both directly and indirectly.

In the period immediately after World War II, the United States was enjoying exceptional prosperity, and the connection between education and economic uplift was plainly evident. In 1975, almost three-quarters of teenagers were graduating from high school and a quarter of all young people were finishing college.[4] In the first half of the twentieth century, the numbers were much lower. The higher levels of education in the 1950s altered the social landscape as the United States became a middle-class nation. And even though there was significant inequality, rapid income growth among poorer Americans and the promise of intergenerational mobility made it less pernicious.

But by the 1980s, the story would be much different. The incomes of the wealthiest families were growing at a much faster rate than the incomes of everyone else, outpacing any gains made by the rest of the population. The fruits of economic growth were becoming concentrated in the hands of a very small percentage of families.

As we saw in previous chapters, the changes in the economy did not happen accidentally. There were powerful actors every step of the way, transforming the economy through deindustrialization, globalization, mech-

Figure 7.1 The Impacts of Income Inequality

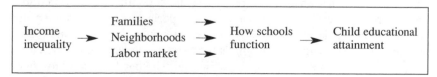

Source: Duncan and Murnane, *Whither Opportunity?* p. 8.

anization, and an increasing financialization of economic activities. Each of these changes meant that there were fewer employment opportunities for Americans, especially for those with relatively little formal education. The processes that create great wealth and great inequality are deliberate—they do not occur in a vacuum.

For young people who have been able to graduate from colleges and universities with specialized degrees, the economy has been extremely rewarding. But countless children, handicapped by the paltry incomes of their parents, unserved by inadequate and dysfunctional schools, and having to negotiate the violence-prone neighborhoods in which they live, have fallen behind precipitously in their educational attainment.

Sociologist Sean Reardon documents the startling growth in the chasm between the test scores of low-income children and those of their better-off peers, ongoing since at least 1943. His research provides resounding support for the question he poses for his inquiry: "As the income gap between high and low income families has widened, has the achievement gap between children in high and low income families also widened?"[5] He offers four explanations why there is such a strong "relationship between a family's position in the income distribution and their children's academic achievement [that] has grown substantially stronger during the last half century."[6] First, income inequality has grown since 1960; second, high-income families have more resources; third, they spend more resources on their children's education than do low-income families; and lastly, increasing residential segregation by income has led to greater differentiation in school quality and schooling opportunities between the rich and poor.[7] Reardon reminds us that this correlation has been well documented, beginning with James Coleman and his pathbreaking 1966 report on the role of equality in educational opportunity, in which he "famously highlighted the relationship between family socioeconomic status and student achievement."[8] An important sequel to this is that the income achievement gap today is now nearly twice as large as the black-white achievement gap from 1964: evidence that some progress has occurred in race relations, even as class and income inequalities remain deeply entrenched. Even though we have known of the income achievement gap, Reardon questions whether we are aware of the intricate ways in which this correlation actually comes about.

As the many studies that Duncan and Murnane include in their volume confirm, every circumstance of a child's life offers opportunities for success or barriers that ensure failure. The socioeconomic status of a child's family, the degree of stress that the child experiences while growing up, whether the child is surrounded by doting parents or parents facing imminent job loss, the quality of the child's food and health care, how much time the parents have to spend with the child and whether they can buy them books and send them to summer camp, music lessons, and SAT tutorials—

all of these factors add up and start influencing a child's academic aptitude even before he or she steps inside a school building.

From the standpoint of neuroscience, research shows that child development is to a large extent predicated on brain development. Though our understanding of how environment shapes brain development is still tentative, surely some of this is influenced by the socioeconomic context. Charles Nelson and Margaret Sheridan enumerate the numerous ways in which low parental socioeconomic status subjects the child to a higher probability of exposure to a variety of environmental influences that affect their brain development.[9] Low socioeconomic status along with poverty, unemployment, and other related circumstances are associated with chronic and traumatic stress, which can lead to health complications such as diabetes, heart disease, and hypertension and increased levels of morbidity and mortality—each directly resulting from the degree of access low–socioeconomic status families have to monetary resources, healthy food, grocery stores, and health care.

Individuals in low–socioeconomic status neighborhoods are more likely than those in more affluent neighborhoods to be living in unhealthy, rodent-infested homes, and are more likely to be exposed to high levels of air pollution and other factors resulting from unsafe neighborhoods, such as higher crime rates and higher rates of indiscriminate violence. Children in these neighborhoods are more likely to experience abuse and neglect and encounter individuals experiencing depressive disorders or addictions. All of these exposures associated with low socioeconomic status affect a child's developmental prospects even before she or he steps inside a kindergarten or an elementary school.

Parents supplement their children's learning in school through investments in early care and education programs; enrichment activities; purchase of books, toys, and computers; sports, music, and art lessons; travel, summer camps, extracurricular activities, after-school tutoring programs, and standardized-test preparatory classes; and ultimately through their financial support of college education. Parents' ability to make any of these investments is contingent upon their disposable income. As reported by Neeraj Kaushal, Katherine Magnuson, and Jane Waldfogel:

> Children from lower income families trail behind their economically advantaged counterparts because their parents have fewer resources to invest in them. Compared with more affluent parents, low income parents are less able to purchase items and environments for their children, including books and educational materials at home, high-quality child-care settings and schools, and safe neighborhoods. Economically disadvantaged parents may also have less time to invest in children, owing to the higher prevalence of single-parenthood, nonstandard work hours, and inflexible work schedules. It is the limited financial resources they have to spend on their children, particularly

during the early childhood years,that remains one of the central explanations for why poor children lag behind their peers.[10]

How much time parents spend with their children—to simply talk, play, read, or just hold them—plays a significant role in determining a child's academic success. Even on this count, there are deep social-class and racial disparities. Children from high-income families and those from predominantly white families spend much more time on nonroutine activities with adults—as much as 1,300 hours more, of which as much as 400 hours are spent on literacy activities—compared to their low-income or African American peers.

Sociologist and educator James Coleman uses the term "social capital" to refer to social interaction within families and considers its influence over children's academic development as being even more pertinent than parents' educational background.[11] The social interaction itself—for example, the conversations the adult has with the child—exposes the child to language structures and vocabulary that facilitate his or her cognitive development.[12] A working-class single mother with inflexible and uncertain time schedules, much more stressed out and burned out than her middle-class or upper-class counterpart, will be less able to give her child the time that she would like to give. And there is, of course, a very strong association between parental education and academic success in children, and this might be an even "more powerful predictor of student achievement than is family income."[13]

The single-parent household with the mother as the sole caregiver is a phenomenon most concentrated among the poorest segments of society. A single mother is stretched for money, resources, and time. She is highly likely to be young, with a low level of education. She does not have the disposable income to invest in anything other than the most basic needs to sustain her family; she lacks the time to interact in meaningful ways with her offspring. Her children do not have access to the parenting and material resources that can support educational success.

The absence of other adults, especially the biological father, tends to lead the children "to perform less well in school, have lower academic confidence, and attain fewer total years of education than children who live with both biological parents."[14] Scholars and policymakers fear that the changing structure of the American family, whereby more children are being raised by a single parent—most often the mother—"may both exacerbate existing inequalities and contribute to reproducing patterns of inequality across generations."[15] Moreover, children who have experienced family disruption do worse in school than those who have stable families with two parents.

As discussed in Chapter 3, residential segregation by income rose exponentially beginning in 1970. With rising income inequality, there has been an increasing segregation of families in terms of how much money they make. Rich, middle-class, and poor families do not live in the same neighborhoods. More significant, high-income families do not reside in the same areas as do the middle class, nor do they send their children to the same schools.[16] When race is also considered, segregation becomes even more acute, so much so that Camden, New Jersey, and Princeton, New Jersey, do not appear to belong to the same state or even the same country. The resources available to communities and the quality of the public schools mirror the economic disparities.

Consider also the fact that economic deprivation and residential segregation turn some neighborhoods into war zones filled with crime and random violence. For the children who live there—afraid, stressed, and traumatized—school becomes the least of their problems. Moreover, it becomes difficult for local schools in crime-ridden, violence-prone neighborhoods to attract and retain good teachers and administrators. Many adolescents give in to the lure of the street and soon either end up in prison or die violent deaths. The number of young people who die on the streets of urban America each year rivals the number of war casualties in Afghanistan. According to the US Department of Defense, there were a total of 2,210 fatalities in Afghanistan as of October 2014, for the entire period of the US military engagement in that country.[17] In 2013, the city of Chicago saw 2,185 shooting victims.[18] Children who have been traumatized growing up in such neighborhoods seldom improve academically, even when they are moved to low-poverty areas.[19]

In this increasingly multiracial/multiethnic society, residential segregation is no longer just limited to black-white segregation. In 2011, according

---

MAKING CONNECTIONS
School Funding

In the United States, $500 billion is spend each year to finance public education. All three levels of government—federal, state, and municipal—contribute toward educational funding. Almost half of the funding (44 percent) comes from the local governments. Most of the local funding is generated by property taxes. Wealthier, property-rich communities are better situated to collect higher property taxes. Poorer communities, on the other hand, have a lower property tax base and therefore yield lower property taxes. As a result, children who live in poor localities, who also have the highest need for an array of programs to support them, are locked into schools that have the "least resources, least qualified teachers and sub-standard facilities."[1]

Note: 1. New American Foundation, "Federal Education Budget Project."

to the US Census Bureau, 16.7 percent of the US population was Latino, compared to the 13.1 percent black population, yet these groups experience comparable rates of poverty, 25.4 percent for Latinos and 27.8 percent for blacks.[20] Increasingly, Latinos are concentrated in poor and volatile neighborhoods and, alongside their African American counterparts, attend schools where fewer and fewer of their classmates are white and middle class. According to a report published in September 2012 by the Civil Rights Project at the University of California, Los Angeles, "extreme segregation is becoming more common," as "the typical black or Latino student attends a school where almost two out of three classmates come from low income families. And schools with mostly minority and poor students were likely to have fewer resources, less assertive parent groups and less experienced teachers."[21]

The Roots of Educational Inequality

As disturbing as these facts are, they are undeniably the most persuasive in drawing our attention to what plagues our schools, our neighborhoods, and, most tragically, the families and children caught up in this terrible milieu. It is important to remind ourselves that unequal and failing schools, to which society commits so many of our young people, are natural byproducts of a capitalist economic system that creates inequality of income and wealth naturally and organically.

As we have seen, there is nothing mysterious about why the gulf between the rich and the poor has widened in the United States. It has followed a natural trajectory laid out by the policies and practices of a system dedicated to the maximization of profit to the exclusion of everything else. Economic inequality is an inevitable and inherent consequence of capitalism. Just as government decisions have played a significant role in determining the rules by which the economy operates and apportions income and wealth in society, we must be mindful of the same dynamic when examining disparities in academic achievement.

In *Ghetto Schooling: A Political Economy of Urban Educational Reform,* Jean Anyon documents the extent to which current urban educational failure is embedded in the past actions and decisions of powerful economic and political groups. Her focus in this book is Newark, New Jersey. She examines the historical political economy of the past century to illuminate how government policies at all levels—federal, state, and local—together with the practices of business, have devastated cities such as Newark, suffocating them economically and isolating them politically.

The same dynamic also formed and shaped the schools. For Anyon, to "discover why inner city schools have not improved, it is not enough to only examine present reform or educational practice. We need to understand how inner city schools have come to be what they are. For schools—like people—are products of their past, as well as of their present. It is a straightforward story of economic and political decisions and various actions and a demonstration of how they together affected the development of an American city and its schools."[22] Therefore, she is certain that fixing the educational system would require simultaneously fixing the problems of the city.

In 1976, Samuel Bowles and Herbert Gintis published a pathbreaking book, *Schooling in Capitalist America,* that addressed many of the questions raised here. In reintroducing their book twenty-five years later, the authors wrote the following, which resonated deeply with many readers:

> The project that eventually resulted in the publication of *Schooling in Capitalist America* (1976) began in 1968, stimulated by the then raging academic debates and social conflicts about the structure and purposes of education. We were then, and remain, hopeful that education can contribute to a more productive economy and a more equitable sharing of its benefits and burdens, as well as a society in which all are maximally free to pursue their own ends unimpeded by prejudice, lack of opportunity for learning, or material want. Our distress at how woefully the US educational system was then failing these objectives sparked our initial collaboration. Its continuing failure has prompted our recent return to the subject.[23]

Bowles and Gintis provide a clear-eyed analysis in which they combine Marxian analysis of capitalism with a John Dewey liberalism, rooted in an inherent faith that democratic and egalitarian reform movements can correct the egregious ills of inequality.[24] They regard capitalism as the primary obstacle to realizing the promise of a liberal education. When they consider the origins and evolution of the modern school system, they do not perceive it as a "gradual perfection of a democratic or pedagogical ideal." What they do see "is the product of a series of conflicts arising through the transformation of the social organization of work and the distribution of its rewards. In this process, the interests of the owners of the leading businesses tended to predominate."[25]

Bowles and Gintis agree that economic inequality is structural, a necessity of the capitalist economy, since it enables and makes possible the accumulation of capital in the hands of the wealthy, the bourgeoisie. The inequality that capitalism generates is passed on from one generation to the next, invalidating claims to the contrary that regard the US economic system to be one in which economic mobility across generations is a given.

Ideologically, education has been elevated to the status of being the unquestioned facilitator of social mobility. But Jean Anyon, like Bowles and Gintis, shows the futility of this argument. She refers to the fact that 70 percent of welfare recipients in 1999 had a high school diploma, up from 42 percent in 1979. The poor are much more educated now than they have been in the past, but they have still remained poor.[26] Similarly, she contends that even the "college degree is increasingly becoming less effective in guaranteeing middle class wages. The number of college graduates will continue to outpace occupations in which they will be able to make use of their degrees."[27]

A recent report in the *New York Times* said as much. More and more entry-level jobs, which pay little more than the minimum wage, are being filled entirely by college graduates—even jobs that do not require a college education. The report gave the examples of young people hired as mail couriers and receptionists making $37,000 a year and carrying student loan debts of $100,000.[28]

Between 1982 and 2007, college tuition and fees rose a whopping 439 percent, and since then have risen between 4 and 10 percent annually.[29] Other than for a precious few with hefty disposable incomes, college education today either is out of reach or comes at an outrageous price that straddles young people with a lifetime of debt—especially if the jobs they do get pay low wages, making it very difficult for them to move up the economic ladder or even maintain the socioeconomic status of their parents.

So, not only is upward mobility across generations now unlikely, but it has also been replaced by a strong likelihood of backward mobility as children are unable to attain the income level of their parents. For young people who don't have the resources to receive a college degree, or those who don't finish high school due to a confluence of factors, the future is even bleaker. Moreover, as inequality is transmitted from one generation to the next, it becomes chronically entrenched, widening the gulf between the opportunities of the rich and their children, and the opportunities of the poor and their children. Bowles and Gintis maintain that "schooling reproduces rather than ameliorates that inequality."[30] Intergenerational transmission of class status trumps any corrective that schooling can provide.

The education system reinforces inequality by failing to correct disparities and also by reproducing the **social relations of production**, on which capitalism is rooted through what Samuel Bowles and Herbert Gintis call the "correspondence principle." According to this principle, "the educational system fundamentally stratifies students according to their future positions in the workplace hierarchy. Schools do not just teach more or less; they teach different things to different people. In working class schools, students are rewarded for rote learning and following the rules, while in the schools of professional and managerial families, students are rewarded for creativity and independent thought."[31]

Schools reproduce a **reserve army of labor**—future workers that the system will need—and primes them with rewards and punishments for the hierarchies and authority structures that will be so much a part of their work lives. In the process, schools engender a kind of **alienation** among students that is similar to the alienation that workers experience in the capitalist economy. Such alienation can lead to organized, collective efforts to change the system—or to individual acts of aggression, hostility, and violence.

Bowles and Gintis's analysis is therefore **dialectical**, because they acknowledge the inherent contradiction of public education: the same system of education that re-creates inequalities can also inspire social movements to change those very systems. Even the worst schools teach their students to read and think. And through inspiration, students may come to demand their fair share. Just as Marx had determined that the capitalist system carries within it the seeds of its own destruction, it similarly follows from Bowles and Gintis's analysis that schools can create conditions for their own transformation, reform the entire system of inequality, and fulfill the true purpose of education in a democracy—thus validating the reformist ideas of John Dewey.

This glimmer of hope that can be found in Bowles and Gintis's analysis quickly vanishes when we face the fact that the alienation that children experience in crowded schools seldom finds expression in acts of collective political rebellion anymore. Instead, what we see more and more are private acts of aggression and hostility. Any collective action is usually confined to gangs and their turf wars.

Students are prepared by the schools to take up their position in the capitalist economy, wherein, if lucky, they will be paid the reasonable wages that the once-strong labor unions had bargained for them. Yet today, even this modest prospect is increasingly unlikely. As globalization and deindustrialization sap the economic vitality of cities, and as jobs requiring unskilled labor are increasingly shipped to other regions of the world, the question of what the United States should do with the young people who in previous times were absorbed by the manufacturing sector looms without any satisfactory resolution.

In her book *High Stakes Education,* Pauline Lipman quotes an author in the *Chicago Tribune* who asks the same question: "Where will they go, these poverty-level Chicagoans, mostly black, once invisible in the cities, but now inconvenient in the Global City?" The answer: "African-American and Latino students are under-represented in the 'college prep track' and over-represented in the 'military prep track' and the 'prison prep track.'"[32] Lipman documents their dwindling economic prospects, noting that "global economic expansion and the shift from manufacturing to a service, recreation, and consumption economy [have] led to a dramatic recomposition of the US labor force."[33] This recomposition has been accompanied by large variance between the salaries of those at the top of the income scale and the low wages, fewer health-care and retirement benefits, and overall job insecurity for those at the middle and bottom of the income scale. A large majority of those in the latter category are immigrants, people of color and women, who often are forced to work two or three part-time and temporary jobs. A large segment of the population, mainly African American and Latino/a youth, find little or no work, and become prime candidates for the "school-to-prison pipeline."[34]

As the opportunities for making a living in the legal economy evaporate, individuals turn to the illegal economy, either for the sake of survival or for the sake of escape. Whether it is black and Latino youth dealing drugs in the inner cities of America, or young white kids doped up with methamphetamine, losing their lives to drug overdose in communities across the nation, the groups must be seen, either directly or indirectly, as reeling from the fallout of lost manufacturing jobs, which once were certain sources of income for generations of families.

In the summer of 2013, Philadelphia announced that it would be closing twenty-three of its public schools. Thousands would be laid off in the process—teachers, principals, teacher aides, librarians, custodians, and guidance counselors. The city would instead invest $400 million in building a new prison complex.[35]

The No Child Left Behind Act

Parents who live in the shattered communities of urban America realize that there is something terribly wrong with the education system. They have continually implored their community leaders for real change in their public schools. Pauline Lipman looks at how policymakers have responded to those requests. She posits her inquiry of education policy and school reform in the context of neoliberalism—the "defining social paradigm" of our times. It is an ideology that guides the political economy of nations around the globe.

Lipman explains it like this: "Put simply, neoliberalism is an ensemble of economic and social policies, forms of governance, discourses and ideologies that promote individual self-interest, unrestricted flows of capital, deep reductions in the cost of labor, and sharp retrenchment of the public sphere."[36] The present forms of education policy and school reform have their underpinnings in these ideals of neoliberalism and neoliberal urbanism. And driving the policy is a "powerful coalition of interlocking business associations and government units that promote urban growth and development."[37]

When the No Child Left Behind Act of 2002 was first launched, Diane Ravitch was assistant education secretary under President George W. Bush. And in that capacity, she had heartily endorsed this education reform effort. But since then, in traveling around the country and listening to educators, she has become aware of the fundamental flaws of this act. In her book *The Death and Life of the Great American School System,* she traces the process by which the movement to reform the curriculum standards of public education in the United States was hijacked by the "testing" movement embodied by the No Child Left Behind Act. She traces the origins of the act to the Bush and Clinton administrations' advocacy of market reforms for the public sector, including deregulation and privatization.[38]

When George W. Bush became president, he brought with him the "high-stakes" testing and accountability model used in the Texas Achievement Assessment System of the 1990s. Both Republicans and Democrats embraced this "new era of school reform characterized as accountability, high stakes, testing, data driven decision making, choice, charter schools, privatization, deregulation, merit pay and competition among schools. Whatever could not be measured did not count."[39] Education reform was embedded in a language that business understood and appreciated.

David Hursh, in an article on the No Child Left Behind Act, refers to Texas's experiences with its achievement assessment system by drawing from research done by Linda McNeil for her book, *Contradictions of School Reform: Educational Costs of Standardized Testing.* McNeil had originally visited Houston schools to understand what was behind their success in educating low-income students. During the course of her research, the Texas Achievement Assessment System was implemented, and she observed that successful schools that had previously set high standards for their students now simply taught the more basic skills that would be required to pass the tests. "Rather than, for example, teaching students to write well, teachers taught students to write the five paragraph essay, with five sentences in each paragraph that would earn students passing grades on the standardized tests."[40]

Children from middle-class and upper-class families did better on the standardized tests. It was those from disadvantaged backgrounds who soon fell behind. And the urgency to raise test scores "by any means necessary" encouraged schools to "force weak students out of school before they [could] take the test."[41] The allure of the No Child Left Behind Act and the commodification of education can be better understood when we consider Ravitch's account of the manner in which earlier attempts at education reform were nipped in the bud. In the early 1990s, the US Department of Education endorsed an initiative to "develop voluntary national standards in history, English language arts, science, civics, economics, the arts, foreign languages, geography, and physical education. This was based on the belief that all children should have access to a broad education in arts and sciences."[42]

But even as this new initiative was being drafted, Lynne Cheney, who was the chairperson of the National Endowment for the Humanities, lambasted it for "left-wing bias." It created a firestorm among conservatives, prompting conservative radio personality Rush Limbaugh to urge that the standards should be "flushed down the toilet."[43] The vitriol convinced Congress and Bill Clinton, now president, to keep as far away from national standards as possible. Thus came the beginning of the decision to make educational standards a prerogative for the states.[44] Clinton's "Goals 2000" program gave states the money to write their own academic standards, pick their own tests—and decide the content of their school curriculum. Some states were better at determining content than others.

The No Child Left Behind Act incorporated two developments from the experiences of this period. The first was leaving it to the states to set their own educational goals and pick their own tests. Second, the controversy created over national standards convinced No Child Left Behind proponents of the wisdom of "retreating into the relative safety of standardized testing of basic skills."[45]

The No Child Left Behind Act is a reauthorization of the Elementary and Secondary Education Act of 1965. Its chief purpose, as the text of the law says, is to improve "the academic achievement of the disadvantaged." According to the law, this objective is to be fulfilled by "preparing, training, and recruiting high quality teachers and principals."[46] Under the act, each state must measure every public school student's progress in reading and math in each grade from three through eight, and at least once during grades ten through twelve. The purpose of this is to provide the crucial data needed to ascertain whether schools and teachers are doing their job.

The No Child Left Behind Act marks the first time that the federal government has intervened in the education system in such a major way. "Framing schooling in a language that business understands—regulation, accountability, quantification, quality assurance,"[47] the act enforces a "top down, punitive accountability and prescriptive standards, increased business involvement, and school leadership redefined as (corporate) managerialism."[48]

Diane Ravitch refers to the punitive aspects of No Child Left Behind Act, which "punishes" schools and teachers for the low test scores of their students. The disproportionate emphasis on test scores has led to cheating and other ways of "gaming the system." Instead of raising standards, "the strategy of measuring and punishing" has led to a lowering of standards as states "dumb down" their tests or change the way they score the tests to pad the numbers of students who "pass."[49]

Rachel Aviv documents the "shocking choices" school administrators and teachers in struggling school districts have made in order to avoid the closure of schools, often with the tacit approval of school superintendents. In some of the poorest school districts in the country, where schools are often the only place that children find adult supervision and protection from poverty and violence, cheating has become comparable to "an act of civil disobedience." Teachers in these schools wonder if the legislators who wrote the No Child Left Behind Act had ever even been near such schools where the main job of the teachers is to save the children from hunger, destitution, and violence.[50] According to a 2013 Government Accountability Office investigative report, instances of cheating by educators were found in forty states, including dozens of large cities such as Atlanta, Baltimore, Cincinnati, El Paso, Houston, Philadelphia, St. Louis, and Toledo, during the two years prior to publication of the report.[51] For teachers and school administrators, an unreasonable, unrelenting, and "toxic" No Child Left Behind culture of "high-stakes testing" and "meeting targets" at all costs, with total disregard for the real needs of students, has "created an atmosphere in which cheating . . . seem[s] like a reasonable option."[52]

Under the No Child Left Behind Act, each state creates its own tests. The quality of the tests varies according to the "competency and intentions of the state's educational bureaucracy. In New York, for example, the tests have been criticized for having poorly constructed, misleading and erroneous questions, or for using a grading scale that overstates or understates students' learning."[53] School districts and schools are paranoid about test scores because so much hinges on them. For example, if a school does not make "adequate yearly progress" for two consecutive years, it must be identified as "in need of improvement." As a consequence, students in these "in need of improvement" schools must be given the option of transferring to another public school, which in turn means that such schools could have their funding reduced or lose it entirely. Additional requirements are imposed for each successive year that a school fails to make adequate yearly progress. It must: provide students with supplemental services in the community, such as tutoring, after-school programs, remedial classes, or summer school; replace the school staff (read: teachers and principals); implement a new curriculum; and appoint an outside expert to advise the school, extend the school day or year, or reorganize the school internally. A school that fails for five consecutive years to make adequate yearly progress must either reopen as a charter school, replace all or most of the school staff who are relevant to the failure to make adequate yearly progress, or turn over its operations either to the state or to a private company with a demonstrated record of effectiveness.[54]

According to Ravitch, "The most toxic flaw in [the No Child Left Behind Act] was its legislative command that all students in every school must be proficient in reading and mathematics by 2014." If not, schools "will be closed, teachers will be fired, principals will lose their jobs, and some—perhaps many—public schools will be privatized."[55] The "remedies," such as tutoring, remedial classes, replacing the administration, and privatization, provide vast opportunities for private corporations to profit from public funding.[56]

It is ironic that although the No Child Left Behind Act is couched in the neoliberal vocabulary of "choice," it in fact provides schools, teachers, and students with very little choice in determining a curriculum that educates children instead of making them into test-taking machines. The only so-called choice that the act boasts of is the one parents are given to pull their children from "failing" schools and enroll them elsewhere. But as Ravitch shows persuasively, very few parents have taken advantage of this prerogative, choosing instead to keep their children in their own neighborhood schools.[57]

Parents want their neighborhood schools improved instead of shut down. This response is contrary to what political economist Albert Hirschman envisages as typical for Americans, whom the system encourages to prefer "flight rather than fight" when faced with adverse circumstances.[58] Flight is an economic response—exiting to a place that guarantees a better life—as opposed to fight, which is "a far more messy concept" and necessarily political, as people must "choose to exercise their voice."[59]

Report after report is also casting doubt over how much academic improvement the students who are transferred to charter schools actually make. As the editors of the *New York Times* have written: "Despite a growing number of studies showing that charter schools, financed with public money and operating in 40 states, are often worse than traditional schools, the state and local organizations that issue charters and oversee the schools are too hesitant to shut them down. A 2009 study from Stanford University's Center for Research on Educational Outcomes found that 37 percent of charter schools performed worse on student test measures than their traditional counterparts."[60]

When President Barack Obama took office and inherited Bush's No Child Left Behind Act, he and his secretary of education, Arne Duncan, renamed it "Race to the Top." The primary initiatives remained the same, with $4.3 billion set aside to "induce states to approve more charter schools and to rate teachers based on student performance."[61] But what is most disturbing is the way that the act makes it possible for large chunks of public funds to find their way into private pockets—often unscrupulously.[62]

David Harvey's concept of **accumulation by dispossession** comes to mind.[63] Harvey contends that since the 1970s, as capitalism has practiced a global neoliberal strategy, capital has grown not through real economic growth, whereby the tangible wealth of societies increases, but through dispossession, whereby public goods are taken away from societies and repossessed by private, corporate entities, thus expanding their purses.

This is exactly the point that David Hursh, Diane Ravitch, Pauline Lipman, and others make. The neoliberal ideology in which the No Child Left Behind Act is rooted turns schools and students into a contested terrain. By establishing policies and conditions that will invariably fall short of their objectives, it prepares private entities such as charter schools, tutoring companies, and testing services to seize every opportunity to access readily available public funds for the sole purpose of making a profit. This raises serious doubts about the true intentions of such punitive accountability—and of merit-based education and school reform. And as this ideology gains momentum, there is "no critical examination of the genesis of these policies, of whose interest they serve, of their social implications."[64]

Ravitch bemoans No Child Left Behind's complete disregard for the recommendations of a major report released in 1983 called *A Nation at Risk*. At the time of its release, there was the usual outcry from many progressives that the report did not seriously consider the handicaps that children experience from poverty and discrimination, and also endorsed a curriculum that did not give sufficient room to the voice and history of minorities. *A Nation at Risk* was published at a time when the United States was becoming aware of the shortcomings of its education system, with SAT scores falling and the nation's young people unable to measure up to the academic standards of other countries.[65] The report was an appeal for improving the quality of education across the board. It recommended "stronger high school graduation standards, more time for instruction and homework and higher standards for entry into the teaching profession and better salaries for teachers."[66]

In many ways, the report was a call for the United States to replicate what other countries with good education systems were doing routinely. It recommended that all high school students study the "basics": four years of English, three years each of math, science, and social studies, two years of a foreign language, and half a year of computer science. It also proposed that four-year colleges and universities raise their academic requirements.

Whereas the No Child Left Behind Act is a federal mandate—meaning that states that refuse to comply risk losing millions of dollars—the recommendations of the *Nation at Risk* report were optional. *A Nation at Risk* was rich in the educational content it proposed; the No Child Left Behind Act is not, requiring students to demonstrate measurable progress only in two areas—reading and math.

A Nation at Risk "said nothing about closing schools, privatization, state takeover of districts or other heavy handed forms of accountability."[67] With the No Child Left Behind Act, competition, charter schools, privatization, and test-based accountability are the primary tools of reform.

Children learn less when systems of testing and accountability lead to the narrowing and simplification of curriculum, because subjects that are not tested are eliminated, such as literature, history, and arts. Reflecting on this, Lipman asserts that this strategy "not only regulat[es] educational content and practice but defin[es] which knowledge, values, and behavior are considered legitimate."[68]

MAKING CONNECTIONS
The Case of Finland

One country that has caught the eye of everyone, other than policymakers, is Finland. Politicians would learn a thing or two if they paid attention, as Finnish schools have important advantages over those in the United States. For one, teaching is a respected and prestigious profession in Finland. The country's highly developed teacher preparation program is the centerpiece of its school reform strategy, and admission to elite teacher education programs is highly competitive.

In addition, Finland has a strong social welfare safety net; only 4 percent of children in Finland live in poverty compared to almost a quarter of the US population. In the United States, many children have no access to health care, but all Finnish children receive comprehensive health services free of charge. And higher education in Finland is free. The focus there is on cooperation, not competition—and on the development of the whole child, not just the attainment of high test scores.

There are four primary reasons why Finnish schools are regarded as among the best in the world, First, the Programme for International Student Assessment (PISA), which assesses the reading skills, mathematical literacy, and scientific literacy of fifteen-year-olds in the OECD countries, of which the United States is a member, finds Finland's schools to be among the highest-performing in the world. And this is accomplished without the test-taking regimen that young people in the United States are routinely subjected to.

Second, Finnish schools don't have testing, charter schools, vouchers, merit pay, competition, or evaluation of teachers on the basis of the test scores of their students. Third, there is equality of educational opportunity for all, as indicated by the fact that Finland has the least variation in school quality worldwide. And fourth, Finland has adopted many of the ideas of John Dewey, such as equality of educational opportunity, individualized instruction, and cooperative learning.

These strengths are combined with Finland's goal to address the academic, social, emotional, and physical needs of the child from a very early age. Children attend nine years of comprehensive schooling in a test-free environment in which they are encouraged to learn through the nurturing of their innate curiosity. Education is personalized, and nearly half of students receive specialized attention from trained professionals in the early years of schooling.

The Finnish curriculum requires the teaching of a vernacular language (either Finnish or Swedish), mathematics, foreign languages, history, geography, religion, ethics, physics, chemistry, biology, environmental science, and health. Creative arts such as music and drama are integrated with academic material to give students a wholesome experience that nurtures the entire person.

What the Finnish school system offers, together with the safety net that Finnish society provides, provides the Finnish child an exceptional start in life—and one that could easily be provided in the United States if the political will to do so were present.

Source: Ravitch, "Schools We Can Envy."

It is extraordinary how the No Child Left Behind Act succeeded in casting teachers, and particularly teachers' unions, as the most crucial factor in the success or failure of the student. "Little or no attention [was paid] to poverty, housing, unemployment, health needs, or other, social and economic problems. If students succeeded, it was the teacher who did it. If the students got low scores, it was the teacher's fault. Teachers were both the cause of low performance and the cure for low performance. The solution was to get rid of bad teachers and recruit new ones."[69]

Teachers and teachers' unions were singled out as the main barriers that needed to be removed if the students were to succeed. Conservatives, liberals, and even the nation's major newspapers chimed in and considered "a true reformer to be one who fought the teachers' unions and demanded merit pay based on student test scores. True reformers closed low performing schools and fired administrators and teachers. True reformers opposed teacher tenure."[70]

This demonization has even convinced large segments of the public that teachers are in fact the real stumbling block to the educational achievements of America's children. In community after community, even those with strong pro-union traditions, teachers are on the defensive as they face the possible denial of tenure protections or risk losing their jobs or having their paychecks frozen on the basis of student test results.[71]

In September 2012, 25,000 public school teachers in Chicago went on strike, riveting the nation's attention. The teachers were protesting "data driven education reform nationwide, which many perceived as being pushed by corporate interests and relying too heavily on standardized tests to measure student progress. Teachers spoke of rising class sizes, much needed social workers, a dearth of air-conditioned classrooms and slow to arrive reference books, and again and again, a sense of disrespect."[72]

It is much easier to blame teachers for students' failures than to address all the reasons that sociologists, demographers, economists, and educators recognize as actually responsible for the income-achievement gap—the gap in the educational attainment of children on the basis of the income and overall economic well-being of their parents. The complete failure of all federally mandated policies "to address poverty and racial inequality and decades of disinvestment in physical, economic, and social infrastructure in areas of the city where African-Americans and other people of color live"[73] is indeed staggering. It diverts the public's attention away from the real issues, such as poverty and lack of decent-paying jobs and health care, that need to be confronted if we are to truly improve educational outcomes in the United States and close the achievement gap.[74] "Non-school factors generate achievement gaps more so than do inequalities within and between schools themselves. Indeed, poor and working class students (and thus a disproportionate number of black students) achieve at lower levels regard-less of what occurs in school. The broader structure of social stratification produces class and racial disparities in learning, and school reforms cannot eliminate achievement gaps as long as that stratification is left intact."[75] But when such matters are not addressed, policies such as No Child Left Behind end up perpetuating and reinforcing the very injustice, inequality, and dis-advantages they claim to be fixing.

In September 2013, Jean Anyon, author of the previously mentioned book *Ghetto Schooling,* died. A *New York Times* obituary recognized her as a pioneer in exposing "the often inhospitable landscape where education, economics, race and class converge. She was among the first to assert that without accompanying social reforms like job creation, antipoverty initia-tives and urban renewal, the problems of education in urban, poor areas would never be surmounted. 'The structural basis for failure in inner-city schools is political, economic and cultural, and must be changed before meaningful school improvement projects can be successfully implemented,' she wrote in a 1995 article in the journal *Teachers College Record.* 'Edu-cational reforms cannot compensate for the ravages of society.'"[76] Let us consider some of Anyon's thoughts from another of her books, *Radical Possibilities:*

> How can a successfully reformed urban school benefit a low income student of color whose graduation will not lead to a job in which to make a living be-cause there are not enough jobs, and will not lead to the resources for college completion. New curriculum, standardized tests, or even nurturing, demo-cratic small schools do not create living wage jobs, and do not provide poor students with the funds and supports for enough further education to make a difference in their lives. Only government policy can mandate that jobs pro-vide decent wages; and adequate family income or public provision (such as the 1944 GI Bill that paid for the education of 8 million World War II veter-ans) are necessary to guarantee funds for college degrees to the millions of urban poor who want, and need, them.
>
> As a nation we have been counting on education to solve the problems of unemployment, joblessness, and poverty for many years. But education did not cause these problems, and education cannot solve them. An economic system that chases profits and casts people aside (especially people of color) is culpable.[77]

Social Inequalities and School Reform

Inequalities in education compromise every child's ability to fulfill his or her human potential, but nowhere else is this as egregiously felt as in those sectors of American society doubly marginalized by race and class. Though education reform has been aimed at all children, its primary target has always been the black child, who has always epitomized the historical and contemporary legacies of absolute disadvantage. (In Part 2 of this book, we will explore in more detail the challenges that arise when systems of inequality intersect across lines of class, race, gender, and immigrant status.)

William Reese relates the following in his book *America's Public Schools: From the Common School to "No Child Left Behind"*:

> After President Clinton met in 1996 with dozen of business leaders and politicians in yet another "educational summit" that promised to raise standards, a senior officer of the National School Boards Association asked: "What about children coming to school who aren't healthy, who are hungry, from crime-ridden neighborhoods, and who can't concentrate on learning because of all these other problems? How will standards fix those problems?" Schools cannot fix most of the problems they did not create, but, if historical precedent matters, that will not stop people from asking them to try.[78]

The question therefore arises: Why has it been so difficult to create a sincere and straightforward plan to reform education once and for all and transform it to fulfill its original purpose of being a channel for the realization of the common good? Simply put, because there is no political will to attempt something that does not benefit corporate America and its bottom line. As we saw in Chapter 6, on the political economy of inequality, those who make the big decisions that affect all our lives are unduly influenced by those who have the biggest purses and therefore the largest voice. And that is definitely not the voice of the single mother making minimum wage in two part-time jobs, living in inner-city America, and a paycheck away from homelessness.

But it was not always this way, at least not to this extent. There have been individuals and governments who offered solutions, though today their voices have become lost in the deafening clamor of corporate self-interest.

What Would George Counts, Horace Mann, and John Dewey Do?

In 1932, a well-known sociologist and educator named George Counts asked, "Dare the school build a new social order?" In a pamphlet bearing this title, Counts wrote:

> Like all simple and unsophisticated peoples we Americans have a sublime faith in education. Faced with any difficult problem of life we set our minds at rest sooner or later by the appeal to the school. We are convinced that education is the one unfailing remedy for every ill that man is subject, whether it be vice, crime, war, poverty, riches, injustice, racketeering, political corruption, race hatred, class conflict, or just plain original sin. We even speak

glibly and often about the general reconstruction of society through the school. We cling to the faith in spite of the fact that the very period in which our troubles have multiplied so rapidly has witnessed an unprecedented expansion of organized education. This would seem to suggest that our schools, instead of directing the course of change, are themselves driven by the very forces that are transforming the rest of the social order.[79]

But Counts was not discouraged. He believed in the power of schools to "indoctrinate students in the ethos of shared democratic commitments." In a society where "private gain-seeking is the dominant motif," schools and educators, Counts stressed, were uniquely able to mobilize Americans to join together in challenging social injustice and take the lead in social reconstruction. Counts urged democratic teachers to work at "building a new society . . . simultaneously both inside and outside school."[80] In the 1930s, Counts became a leading activist in the American Federation of Teachers. Daniel Perlstein writes that, as a unionist, Counts "continued to argue that teachers and teacher unions not limit themselves to questions of working conditions but rather be active agents in the democratization of US education."[81]

Education reformers have assumed the stature of heroes—readily recognizable figures such as Horace Mann and John Dewey, in particular. Yet in recounting their efforts at reform, what is often overlooked is how each constantly wrestled with the role of schools—a public good, in a society founded on the ideals of individualism. The idea of improving society—the public-civic sphere, becomes secondary given the constant drumbeat that schools must prepare students with marketable skills for the industrial economy, the private-corporate sphere.

Of course, it is much easier to design a curriculum to create a labor pool than it is to design one to realize the public good. How can schools ensure the fulfillment of the public good, whatever it is? And whose definition of public good should be the desired goal? As we have seen, the tension between public and private has continuously permeated the debates over schools and ideas for reforming them.

Nineteenth-century philosophers Ralph Waldo Emerson, Horace Mann, William Harris, and George Counts were more concerned with teaching the young how to live a good life than simply how to make a good living.[82] William Reese, in relating their philosophies, writes that they "believed that publicly funded, locally controlled schools open to all children . . . were carriers of common democratic values ensuring the survival of the Republic and stability of the social order. Education and public good were one and the same thing."[83] And "only through universal public education could children learn the wisdom of the past, learn mainstream majority values," while also being prepared for "the responsibilities of life in a free society."[84]

As Henry Giroux asserts: "Americans defined schooling as a public good and a fundamental right. Such a definition rightfully asserts the primacy of democratic values over corporate culture and commercial values. Schools are an important indicator of the well-being of a democratic society. They remind us of the civic values that must be passed on to young people. . . . Schooling is a site that offers students the opportunity to be involved in the deepest problems of society and to acquire the knowledge, skills, and ethical vocabulary necessary to participate in democratic public life."[85]

Consequently, the efforts of present-day reformers, who "no longer speak of public schools as part of some grand republican experiment"[86] and gauge success and failure primarily in the narrow language of economics and the market, seem to be, in the words of Larry Cuban and Dorothy Shipps, not simply less optimistic and less encompassing—but almost anemic.[87]

Education Reform as Social Reform: Federal Reconstruction, 1863–1877

The idea of public schools as vehicles for public good met its first test after Emancipation, when first the Union army, and then the federal government, found themselves entrusted with the responsibility of preparing the freedmen for "life in a free society" all across the Confederate Deep South. Ted Mitchell, in his recounting of this period, quotes W. E. B. Du Bois, who in emphasizing the former slaves' "personal agency" in education had remarked that "public education for all at public expense was, in the South, a Negro idea."[88] Mitchell continues:

> Reconstruction marks a decided turning point in the history of education, for it was the Reconstruction, and in particular the work of the Freedmen's Bureau, that brought the nation state into active agency in creating and maintaining educational programs. . . . [D]uring Reconstruction, the Yankee state confiscated lands and buildings for educational use, protected schools for former slaves by the force of arms, appointed an inspectorate for Southern schools, determined access and content in these schools, provided funds directly for the support of teachers, and, perhaps most telling of all, made readmission to the Union contingent upon Southern states adopting constitutional provisions establishing Northern-style common schools. In these critical ways, Reconstruction marked a new era in the relationship between the general government and the schools, one in which the schools became more directly than ever [an] instrument of state policy and state power.[89]

This would be the first time that the federal government would assume the task of education; for the first time, a federal office of education would be established. Free public schooling was provided to millions of black children and adults. Schools were given their pioneering opportunity to vindicate their public mandate—the monumental task of preparing the newly freed slaves to take their place as citizens of the United States.

Buoyed by this experience, many in the North supported a more aggressive role for the federal government in education. This experience convinced leaders and educators in the North that the federal government "must recognize the cause of general education as a part of its care." J. P. Wickersham, the president of the National Teacher's Association, told the audience at his presidential address in 1865: "The necessity now exists for the establishment of a department of public instruction in Washington."[90]

Mitchell writes that, "to Wickersham's mind, 'the start in this direction has been made by the establishment of the Freedmen's bureau.' [But only] when our youth all learn to read similar books, study similar lessons, submit to similar regulations in the schools, . . . shall [we] become one people, possessing an organic nationality, and the Republic will be safe for all time. The federal presence in education was institutionalized by the creation of the Office of Education in 1867."[91]

Mitchell also recalls an anecdote in which one superintendent of education wrote in 1868: "When parents come to me and ask for the establishment of schools, their plea is 'you know, sir we are citizens now and we want to learn our duty.'" And much of the material in the freedmen's texts did indeed focus on duty and liberty, and fielded questions concerning the nature of government.[92]

With the federal government as the sentinel, the South started preparing the former slaves in earnest for the kind of country that Emancipation and then the Thirteenth, Fourteenth, and Fifteenth Amendments to the US Constitution had pledged to create. Eric Foner, in his book *Reconstruction: America's Unfinished Revolution,* captures the excitement and promise of the short, fourteen-year period from 1863 to 1877. The Reconstruction, like Emancipation, "inspired blacks with a millennial sense of living at the dawn of a new era. Former slaves now stood on an equal footing with whites [in the words of one black speaker]; before them lay a 'field, too vast for contemplation.'"[93]

The accomplishments that Reconstruction enabled, short-lived as they were, remind us of the lost opportunity. The changes in the entire structure of society in the South and the public mandate of the schools went hand-in-hand. The progressive climate of those precious few years permeated every aspect of society and engendered unprecedented hope. Schools and their responsibility to educate for the public good were nurtured in an atmosphere where the public good was the priority in every other realm of society as well. There was no tension between these various agendas; they were in tandem—all working together to build the country a bright, democratic future in the true spirit of the Declaration of Independence. As Foner wistfully writes: "Reconstruction was one of the few times in American history that the South offered black men of talent and ambition not only the prospect of serving their race, but greater possibilities for personal advancement than existed in the North."[94]

With the ascendancy of Rutherford Hayes to the presidency in 1877, Reconstruction ended. Democrats who took control of state government in the South cut expenditures in every area of public welfare. The end of Reconstruction was particularly disastrous for public education. Some states completely dismantled the education systems so arduously built. Blacks suffered the most.

The racial gap in public expenditures that the end of Reconstruction brought about would steadily widen the gap in well-being between blacks and whites in every aspect of life. As Foner observes, it is impossible to determine the price blacks paid for the end of Reconstruction. In the words of W. E. B. Du Bois, "the slave went free; stood a brief moment in the sun; then moved back again toward slavery."[95]

Almost another century would pass before the rights of black citizens in the United States were again seriously addressed—first in 1954, when the Supreme Court, in *Brown v. Board of Education,* reversed *Plessy v. Ferguson* and its assertion of "separate but equal," and then with the passage of the Civil Rights Act of 1964 and affirmative action legislation in 1968. But the betrayal of the dream that Reconstruction had so persuasively and compellingly fostered would never again be reclaimed in the same way. The guarantee of a just, democratic, egalitarian society, with a system of education balancing the public good with the private will, continues to remain elusive.

The Servicemen's Readjustment Act

One other noteworthy instance in which the federal government intervened in a substantial way to improve people's lives was with the Servicemen's Readjustment Act of 1944, also known as the GI Bill of Rights. Earlier wars in the United States and other countries had taught a very important historical lesson: if returning veterans are not equipped with resources to readjust to civilian life in a satisfactory way, they can become a source of much unrest and turmoil.

The GI Bill was therefore put together to provide a comprehensive benefits package that included weekly remittance, money to buy a house, loans to start a business, comprehensive health insurance, and (the most popular provision) college tuition. Millions of veterans took advantage of the benefits. Colleges and universities were bursting at their seams as veterans started attending in droves.

The social and intellectual landscape of the country changed as graduating veterans filled the white-collar, middle-class jobs that the postwar period added in great numbers; moved into the suburban homes of the mushrooming Levittowns; and made countless scientific and technological innovations that have since transformed all our lives. The federal government spent a mere $14 billion on all those provisions, and the returns have been invaluable.

Of course, as Karen Brodkin has shown, the GI Bill, as wonderful as it was, was really affirmative action for the white GIs. African American GIs and women veterans never enjoyed the real benefits of the bill, as racism and sexism compromised their ability to become full beneficiaries.[96] But still, the GI Bill was government at its best. It gave the veterans peace of mind as Uncle Sam helped them get back on their feet and prepared them for a stable, prosperous, middle-class life.

If only every young person in the United States could be accorded the same while coming of age. If they could grow up with the knowledge that the country would help them to make a strong start as they make their way into adulthood, would we be in the same predicament today with education, economy, law and order, and the breakdown that we see in young people's lives everywhere?

Reconstruction and the GI Bill of Rights hinted at the capacity of the government to make radical changes and level the playing field in real terms, not solely in empty platitudes. They showed in a compelling way that the path to reforming an unequal system of education is to address the underlying structural inequities from which it arises.

Conclusion

The role that education has played in reinforcing structural inequalities should not be underestimated. Contrary to the belief in the power of education to enable individuals to climb up the social ladder, the social reality tells a different story. Children are handicapped by economic and social barriers even before they enter a classroom. Schools reflect the inadequacies of the neighborhoods in which they live.

Changes in schools and the academic achievements of students can only happen when the fundamental economic inequalities are addressed. School reform in the absence of fundamental economic and structural change is bound to fail. But most recent attempts to "improve" schools have been couched in the vocabulary and punitive logic of the market— their focus has been on measurement and accountability, primarily through a protocol of testing. But there are examples in US history when education reform was tied to fundamental changes in society. Though those attempts were short-lived, they provide an enduring vision of what is possible.

Notes

1. Kozol, *Savage Inequalities.*

2. Wilkins, *The Throwaway People.*

3. Duncan and Murnane, *Whither Opportunity?* p. xvii.

4. The federal government played a large role in making this possible, specifically through the 1944 GI Bill of Rights initiative, as discussed in greater detail later.

5. Reardon, "The Widening Academic Achievement Gap," p. 91.

6. Ibid., p.100.

7. Ibid.

8. Ibid., p. 92.

9. Nelson and Sheridan, "Lessons from Neuroscience Research," pp. 27–46.

10. Kaushal, Magnuson, and Waldfogel, "How Is Family Income Related to Investments in Children's Learning?" p. 188.

11. Coleman et al., *Equality of Educational Opportunity.*

12. Phillips, "Parenting, Time Use, and Disparities in Academic Outcomes."

13. Reardon, "The Widening Academic Achievement Gap," p. 109.

14. Sweeney, "Family Structure Instability," p. 229.

15. Ibid.

16. Reardon and Bischoff, "Income Inequality and Income Segregation."

17. US Department of Defense, "US Fatalities in Afghanistan."

18. *Chicago Tribune,* "Gun Fatalities in Chicago."

19. Burdick-Will, "Converging Evidence for Neighborhood Effects."

20. US Census Bureau, "Quick Facts," http://quickfacts.census.gov/qfd/index.html.

21. Motoko, "Segregation Prominent in Schools," p. A16.

22. Anyon, *Ghetto Schooling,* p. xv.

23. Bowles and Gintis, "Schooling in Capitalist America Revisited," p. 1.

24. Bowles and Gintis, "Schooling in Capitalist America Twenty-five Years Later," p. 344.

25. Bowles and Gintis, "Schooling in Capitalist America Revisited," p. 2.

26. Anyon, *Radical Possibilities,* p. 36.

27. Ibid.

28. Rampell, "It Takes a B.A. to Find a Job As a File Clerk," p. A1.

29. Bernstein, "The Hidden Costs of Higher Education," p. A19.

30. Bowles and Gintis, "Schooling in Capitalist America Twenty-five Years Later," p. 343.

31. McCrate, "Samuel Bowles and Herbert Gintis," p. 3.

32. Lipman, *High Stakes Education,* p. 1.

33. Ibid., p. 9.

34. Ibid.

35. Stroud, "Philadelphia Schools Closing."

36. Lipman, *The New Political Economy of Urban Education,* p. 6.

37. Lipman, "Making the Global City, Making Inequality," p. 383.

38. Ravitch, *The Death and Life of the Great American School System,* p. 9.

39. Ibid., p. 21.

40. Hursh, "Exacerbating Inequality," p. 301.

41. Ibid.

42. Ravitch, *The Death and Life of the Great American School System,* p. 16.

43. Ibid., p. 17.

44. Ibid., p. 19.

45. Ibid., p. 22.

46. US Department of Education, *Public Law 107–110.*

47. Lipman, "Making the Global City, Making Inequality," pp. 383, 394.

48. Ibid., pp. 46–47.

49. Inskeep, "Former 'No Child Left Behind' Advocate Turns Critic."

50. Aviv, "Wrong Answer."

51. Ibid., p. 62.

52. Ibid., p. 65.

53. Ibid.

54. US Department of Education, "Introduction: No Child Left Behind."

55. Ravitch, *The Death and Life of the Great American School System,* pp. 102–103.

56. Hursh, "Exacerbating Inequality" p. 297.

57. Ravitch, *The Death and Life of the Great American School System,* p. 100.

58. Quoted in Labaree, "No Exit," p. 114.

59. Ibid., p. 113.

60. *New York Times,* "Shuttering Bad Charter Schools," p. A24.

61. Russakoff, "Schooled," p. 58.

62. Ravitch, *The Death and Life of the Great American School System,* p. 101.

63. LeBaron, "Towards a Feminist Political Economy of Capitalism and Carcerality," p. 24.

64. Lipman, "Making the Global City, Making Inequality," p. 379.

65. Ravitch, "Schools We Can Envy," p. 25.

66. Ibid.

67. Ibid.

68. Lipman, "Making the Global City, Making Inequality," p. 382.

69. Ravitch, *The Death and Life of the Great American School System,* p. 182.

70. Ibid., p. 22.

71. Greenhouse, "In Standoff, Latest Sign of Unions Under Siege," p. A1.

72. Ibid., p. A14.

73. Lipman, *High Stakes Education,* p. 47.

74. Hursh, "Exacerbating Inequality," p. 305.

75. Condron, "Social Class."

76. Fox, "Jean Anyon Dies at 72," p. A22.

77. Anyon, *Radical Possibilities,* p. 3.

78. Reese, *America's Public Schools,* p. 332.

79. Counts, "Dare the School Build a New Social Order?"

80. Ibid.

81. Perlstein, "There Is No Escape from the Ogre of Indoctrination," pp. 51–58.

82. Reese, "Public Schools and the Elusive Search for the Public Good," p. 31.

83. Ibid., p. 2.

84. Ibid., p. 15.

85. Giroux, *Stealing Innocence,* pp. 83, 102.

86. Reese, "Public Schools and the Elusive Search for the Public Good," p. 30.

87. Cuban and Shipps, *Reconstructing the Common Good in Education,* p. 223.

88. Mitchell, "Turning Points," p. 39.

89. Ibid., p. 48.

90. Ibid.

91. Ibid.

92. Ibid., p. 43.
93. Foner, *Reconstruction,* p. 281.
94. Ibid., p. 286.
95. Ibid., p. 602.
96. Brodkin, "How Jews Became White," p. 100.

Part 2

Intersecting Systems of Inequality

8

Making Sense of
Intersecting Inequalities

OUR INQUIRY IN THIS AND THE NEXT THREE CHAPTERS TAKES US TO THE
ways in which being man or woman, being black, white, or Native American, or being an immigrant, whether documented or undocumented, enables
or impedes people's ability to secure employment and to make a decent living. The barriers that society creates to the realization of an individual's or
a group's basic human right to have access to food, clothing, shelter, health
care, and education—at the absolute minimum—become fraught with often
insurmountable challenges.

How society either facilitates or hinders the realization of these existential needs affects every other aspect of people's lives and the nature of
the communities in which they live. An examination of questions of self-
esteem and self-worth; alienation and anomie; self-discipline and work
ethic; family structure and welfare dependency; crime, violence, suicide,
addiction, and gang wars; objectification and hyper-consumerism; or xenophobia and nativism must therefore begin with an interrogation of the
sociostructural roots of material deprivation and how each racial, gender,
ethnic, and immigrant group experiences them.

In this inquiry, centered on income and wealth distribution and how
race, gender, and immigrant status deepen that divide, class is primary. It is
primary because, before anything else can happen, people must be able to
live, survive, and earn a living. And it is in the quest for gaining a living
and earning an income that the divide between rich and poor becomes
apparent and class inequality becomes evident.

Shaping Socioeconomic Status

Class is the common floor on which everyone's socioeconomic status prin-
cipally rests. Race and gender become conceptual categories through which

the class divide is exacerbated and magnified. In their combined manifestation, where the inequities of class, race, and gender are concurrently felt, the debate over whether one category is more oppressive than the others, or engenders a more salient form of oppression than the others, conceals a complex dialectic. It is important to make room for the unique historical legacies that each race and gender carries, and be mindful of the way those legacies shape their present-day reality. It is also critical that we acknowledge the distinctive ways in which we experience the disparagement and discrimination that our race or our gender provokes.

But beneath it all lies the paramount reality of jobs, wages, resources, outsourcing, downsizing, rents, mortgages, unions, schools, child care, health care, transportation, neighborhood safety, environmental pollution, and so on, which cumulatively create a basic and commonly felt experience of oppression irrespective of our unique historical and contemporary legacies that we attribute to race and gender.

When jobs are lost and people's economic fortunes plunge, everyone is affected, regardless of race and gender. But because of the unique legacies of each race and gender, the economic plunge is felt and experienced differently. In combination, each of these categories—class, race, and gender—yields a richer and more textured understanding of the structures of inequality and oppression.

When the mortgage crisis hit the country in 2008, people were losing their homes to foreclosure in every segment of society. But Jacob Rugh and Douglas Massey have shown that minority-dominant neighborhoods experienced disproportionate numbers of foreclosures. These neighborhoods are highly segregated, having experienced the legacy of redlining and institutional discrimination. They continue to be underserved by mainstream financial institutions. Those financial institutions that do exist—pawn shops, payday lenders, and check-cashing services—charge high fees and usurious rates of interest. Blacks and Hispanics, accustomed to such exploitation and unaware of alternatives, became easy targets for brokers marketing subprime loans.

Rugh and Massey's research found that "black borrowers who received loans in 2006 were three times more likely to receive a subprime than a prime loan; Hispanics twice as likely. . . . The tidal wave of foreclosures was concentrated in areas which only a few years earlier had been primary targets for the marketing of subprime loans. In the end, the housing boom and the immense profits it generated frequently came at the expense of poor minorities living in central cities and inner suburbs."[1]

All oppression is fundamentally rooted in class. Oppressions that are attributed to race and gender are also ultimately kindled by inequalities in income, wealth, and property. Class oppression is the ubiquitous oppression. Divisions and conflict stirred up by race, gender, and immigrant status intensify, justify, and facilitate class oppression. That is not to deny the egregiousness of racial and gendered oppression, but to show how they are not just independently oppressive; instead, they combine with class to form complex and paradoxical forms of disparity and unfairness.

Similarly, the point here is not to say that racial and gendered oppression are lesser forms of injustice than class inequality—not at all—but to emphasize that class inequality, when combined with distortions that racism and sexism engender, intensifies the exploitation and oppression of the racial and gender groups who are deemed inferior, and singles them out for brutal forms of abuse and subjugation. History stands witness to this.

Considering Intersecting Categories

There are often disagreements on how exactly these categories intersect or how best to describe their intersectionalities, even when sociologists are certain that, in their combined reality, class, race, and gender deepen and intensify inequality. But does one status precede the others, set the stage for the others, or act as a precondition for the others?

This inquiry becomes complicated when scholars take positions claiming the primacy of one status over the others. Those who see oppression from the lens of gender have considered that to be primary. Others have considered race to be the nucleus of all oppression. Those who have made the case for the predominance of class have often misjudged the severity of oppression based on the socially constructed categories of race and gender.

Feminist sociologist Patricia Hill Collins talks about a "matrix of domination" that interlocking systems of race, class, and gender generates.[2] Similarly, others have remarked that race, class, and gender cannot be "teased out and torn apart" and seen as separate entities. They must be understood as a combined reality in order to explain social outcomes.

Postmodernism considers these categories and others, such as age, ability, sexuality, religion, nationality, and first world–third world status, all to be key markers of identity and fundamental to how life plays out distinctly for each group. In doing so, it dismisses any effort at finding a common source of inequality and oppression, or a common ground on which to organize movements for social change.

Since the approach this book takes is to inquire into the structures that generate, reinforce, and thus perpetuate inequality, the analysis here focuses on the motivations of the system to stack people a certain way in terms of class, race, and gender in order to achieve maximum gain for those who are positioned to profit the most from those arrangements. The question here: Who ultimately stands to gain?

Further, the focus here is on material gain. How do gender and race determine how income and wealth are distributed in society? And more fundamentally, who in society has the power to influence the rules and laws that determine the ways in which individuals who belong to particular categories of gender and race participate in the economy and society?

The rules of this engagement are not absolute. They can change to accommodate transformations in the structures of society and sometimes in response to social movements that demand change in one form or another. But what is vitally important to bear in mind is that those who control the means of producing the material wealth of society, and who have the power to influence decisionmaking at every level in the political-economic sphere, will never (yes, never) negotiate the rules of engagement in ways that fundamentally compromise their ability, in any manner, to maximize their material gain.

As long as systems of inequality remain, the political economy of society will determine people's access to jobs, livelihoods, income, and other such material opportunities in the context of maximizing gain and maximizing profit for the affluent. Gender and race become strategic classifications in this equation. They can be configured, in one way or another, to always ensure maximum gain for those at the top, with disadvantage and oppression intensifying as one falls down the social ladder, ultimately conferring absolute deprivation to those at the absolute bottom in society's interlocking hierarchy of class, race, gender, and immigrant status.

In fact, the composite of disadvantage that gender and race places upon the poorest diminishes as one moves up the ladder of socioeconomic class. Race and gender are most burdensome when a person is poor, where class status—income and wealth—does not confer the protection it does to those in higher classes. As a person climbs up the economic ladder, race and gender become less and less fundamental in the determination of their status in society, to the extent that when a woman or person of color is fortunate enough to rise to the top of political or corporate power, their economic status, to a very large extent, trumps their gender and race status. This is true no matter how much they might advocate for their race or gender, no matter how much they are emulated as a role model—so much so that when a woman or person of color is at the apex of their career, their actions and decisions can often become indistinguishable from those of their male or white counterparts.

When Barack Obama became the first African American president, there was almost a collective sigh of relief from all those constituencies of people who for decades had felt left out. With his election, there was a certain faith that now the needs of the poor and especially those of the people of color would finally be addressed. But that promise has by now been wholly broken, as President Obama has embraced both policies and policy advisers who are indistinguishable from those his predecessors solicited. According to his critics, President Obama has surrounded himself with individuals like Lawrence Summers, Timothy Geithner, Rahm Emanuel,

Mary Schapiro, and others who have moved in and out of the revolving door between corporate America and top administrative positions.

These are individuals whose policies caused the economic meltdown of 2008. President Obama put in place a package of so-called bailouts that used taxpayer money to salvage their own economic fortunes, often at the expense of the fortunes of the country at large. Perhaps even more disheartening, President Obama's policies on immigration have resulted in almost 2 million deportations during his tenure—deportations that have broken up families, including separating young children from their parents.

Similarly, the leaders in many South Asian countries, where women have often been presidents and prime ministers, have failed, in the same vein, to deliver on the promises made to the members of their own racial or gender group. As individuals move up the social ladder, class and class interests often eclipse race and gender interests and the loyalties therein.[3]

Insights from US History

Class, both by itself and then interlinked with race, has always been the primary source of inequality in the United States. Class—an economic category—is always the fundamental division in any society. But awareness of this fact is politically subversive, since it erases all other divisions among people based on race, gender, religion, immigration status, nationality, or sexual orientation, or at least makes those divisions secondary.

Whether you are poor and struggling to put food on the table, or a middle-class factory worker worrying that your job is going to be outsourced, or a rich capitalist figuring out the best way to cut costs and maximize profit—it matters little whether you are white or black, man or woman, Catholic or Protestant, gay or straight, immigrant or citizen. The fundamental division depends on an individual's economic standing—because as mentioned earlier, before anything else can happen, people must be able to earn a livelihood so they can survive and hopefully even thrive.

But in all class-based societies, race, religion, gender, or any other **descriptive category** is socially constructed in opportunistic ways to obscure people's awareness of this existential truth, this most salient divide originating in class. The historical record shows that, again and again, categories that signify our natural diversity as human beings are contrived to conceal the categories that the economic system creates. In many ways, this argument is at the heart of this book, and we will return to it later in much more detail.

To put this argument about the salience of class into a larger historical context and consider how race and then slavery became categorical in breaking up alliances that class organically fostered, let us reflect on

---

MAKING CONNECTIONS

The Story of C. P. Ellis as Told to Studs Terkel

Studs Terkel was a US author who captured the lives of ordinary citizens in his oral histories. He interviewed C. P. Ellis, who was a Klansman and president of the Durham, North Carolina, chapter of the Ku Klux Klan. Ellis, in his conversations with Terkel, talks poignantly of his reasons for why people like him hated blacks and why he became a Klansman.[1]

A majority of Klansmen are low-income whites—marginalized, shut out of any meaningful role in society. Joining the Klan gives them a sense of belonging, the feeling that they are part of something. Their economic deprivation fills them with bitterness and the need to find someone to blame for their predicament. As Ellis tells Terkel, "I didn't know who to blame. I began to blame it on black people. I had to hate somebody. Hatin' America is hard to do because you can't see it to hate it. You gotta have somethin' to look at to hate."

What is remarkable about Ellis is that he sees how the powerful people, living respectable lives, manipulated those like him to think and feel this way. He tells Terkel, "most of them are merchants or maybe an attorney, an insurance agent, people like that. As long as they kept low-income whites and low-income blacks fightin', they're gonna maintain control. People are being used by those in control, those who have all the wealth. . . . [They] simply don't want those who don't have it to have any part of it. Black and white. When it comes to money, the green, the other colors make no difference."

Ellis left the Klan and went on to become a labor organizer, a profession that forced him to meet and work with Jews, blacks, and Catholics, all the people he had despised in his Klansman days. He says tenderly: "I found out they're people just like me. They cried, they cussed, they prayed, they had desires. Just like myself. Thank God, I got to the point where I can look beyond labels."

Ellis was still in the Klan when Martin Luther King Jr. was assassinated. He recalled how all the Klansmen threw a party, "really rejoicin' cause that son of a bitch was dead. . . . [S]ince I changed, I've set down and listened to the tapes of Martin Luther King. I listen to it and tears come to my eyes 'cause I know what he's saying now. I know what's happening."

Note: Terkel, "C. P. Ellis."

---

colonial America at a time when slavery had still not become legally and firmly codified into the social structure. Ronald Takaki, in his history of multicultural America, argues that race was "discovered" as a way to split the class alliances that **Bacon's Rebellion** had kindled, to the chagrin of the colonial aristocracy.[4]

Bacon's Rebellion, considered by historians the largest rebellion of its kind prior to the American Revolution, refers to the uprising in 1675–1676 that burst into colonial Virginia when Nathaniel Bacon, a landowner and member of the Virginia council (also referred to as the governor's council, which was made up of Virginia's wealthiest and most prominent men), organized a militia by arming both white indentured servants and black slaves. His initial targets were the Native Americans in Virginia. He felt that raiding Native American villages would be a good way for this "giddy multitude" to blow off steam—wear off their anger and discontent against the white colonial elite.

White indentured servants—mostly poor immigrants from England, Ireland, and Germany—had been lured to the American colonies with the promise of land. But they soon realized that the landed aristocracy of colonial Virginia were unwilling to part with any portion of their land and were solely interested in their status as laborers and servants. The futility of their dream of landownership and economic solvency fed their growing frustration.

The racial distinction between white indentured servants and blacks had not yet been legally codified; both white indentured servants and black slaves occupied a common socioeconomic space that was defined by their class oppression and "un-free-ness." Legal distinctions between black slaves and white indentured servants did not appear until the 1660s.[5]

Historian Kenneth Stampp observed that "Negro and white servants of the seventeenth century seemed to be remarkably unconcerned about their visible physical differences. They toiled together in the fields, fraternized during leisure hours, and, in and out of wedlock, collaborated in siring a numerous progeny."[6] There was simmering anger and a constant desire to escape. There were ample instances of whites and blacks running away together, only to be captured and returned to abuse and exploitation. Bacon brought these two groups together and, as Takaki writes, "unleashed a radical class boundlessness that threatened the very foundation of [the colonial] order in Virginia . . . [making real] the specter of class revolution."[7]

It matters little that Bacon's rationale for the rebellion was really to get back at the governor of Virginia, William Berkeley, for personal grievances, by fomenting unrest. Berkeley declared Bacon a rebel and charged him with treason. Bacon stormed into Jamestown and burned the city to the ground. Bacon and the rebels were soon defeated, but not before demonstrating the power of class. Bacon's Rebellion demonstrated to the colonial aristocracy the danger of poor whites and poor blacks uniting to challenge authority. And this realization hastened the "turn to slavery," to deliberately and urgently institutionalizing laws that drew unambiguous racial distinctions between black and white workers. Blacks remained slaves with an unequivocal status of inferiority, whereas all whites were elevated to a status of racial superiority regardless of class.

By ensuring ways to privilege the white worker as blacks sank deeper and deeper into slavery, class oppression of the poor whites was appeased by instilling in them a feeling of racial supremacy. W. E. B. Du Bois regards the low wages that the white worker received as being compensated in part by the wages of whiteness, a "public and psychological wage." In clarifying what Du Bois meant, David Roediger writes about "the idea that the pleasures of whiteness functions as a 'wage' for white workers. That is, status and privileges conferred by race could be used to make up for alienating and exploitative relationships. . . . [R]ace feeling and the benefits conferred by whiteness made white workers forget their practically identical interests with the black poor and accept stunted lives for themselves and for those more oppressed than themselves."[8]

Harold Baron conveys the idea that "the badge of whiteness permitted even the lowly to use prejudice, violence, and local political influence to push blacks [further] down."[9] And for blacks, slavery meant unspeakable and unimaginable oppression that, through intimidation, violence, and physical pain, created a despondency that extinguished for centuries any hope of an alliance with the oppressing race.

Ever since, race and racism have been convenient ways to distract the nation from its more pressing problems. It has always been easier to talk of inequality as being rooted in race than in class. If all oppression is believed to be based in race, or gender, or religion, then changing the system requires nothing more than introspection and a change of heart: be tolerant, don't be prejudiced, don't discriminate against people because of their color or gender.

However, recognition of oppression as being class-based requires serious consideration and critique of the structural underpinnings of society, in which gross inequalities of income and wealth can only be bridged through deliberate redistribution of income and wealth. If we understand that income and wealth are finite—that there is only so much to go around— then making things fair, just, and equal would mean rearranging how income and wealth are distributed. This is a zero-sum distribution: if someone has more, then someone else has less. There is no getting around this fact. As Bell Hooks writes: "Class matters. Race and gender can be used as screens to deflect attention away from the harsh realities class politics exposes."[10] It is impossible to talk about ending any other kind of injustice—racial, gender, immigrant—without talking about class.

Noted historian Jacqueline Jones, in her book *A Dreadful Deceit: The Myth of Race from the Colonial Era to Obama's America,* makes a strong case that the country's racial problems have little to do with racism and everything to do with economic exploitation. She argues that race and racism have constantly been used to mask the actual power struggles for control of other people's labor—that racial ideologies, with their power to detract, distract, and intimidate, "are like mob violence, disenfranchisement and discriminatory laws—merely tactics used to secure material advantages."[11] Therefore, hostility among the white working-class toward blacks is rooted primarily in economic competition. Furthermore, Jones bolsters Takaki's argument that race served as a useful tool to drive a wedge between poor whites and poor blacks in a united front against white elites. And today the subordination of blacks is so total and deeply entrenched in the economic structure that racial myths are no longer needed. "Vulnerable blacks can be defrauded, imprisoned, disenfranchised and left to die in floodwaters without appeals to race."[12]

Conclusion

In this chapter, my objective was to explain why I consider class to be the most salient distinction in society. I argue that race and gender oppressions intensify class disadvantage. Economic inequality is the first line of attack—the absence of jobs, low wages, unequal educational resources, and homelessness affect people regardless of color or gender. But groups that carry with them the experience of historical inequality due to their race or gender feel oppressions that originate in economic class in a much more formidable way. Recognizing the commonality of class is subversive because it unifies people on the basis of a commonly felt oppression.

Class and economics are primary. In the next three chapters I discuss the inequalities that women, blacks, Native Americans, and Latinos experience, and explore their oppression through the lens of class. As I evaluate the steps that the United States has taken to make amends for past discrimination and oppression, I hope to demonstrate how the omission of class from the civil rights movement of the 1960s, for example, has resulted in an incomplete victory, one that would ultimately erode the opportunities promised and leave women and people of color still mired in class disadvantage.

Notes

1. Rugh and Massey, "Racial Segregation and the American Foreclosure Crisis," p. 634.
2. Collins, "Toward a New Vision."
3. Personal interview with Ariana A. DasGupta, acting assistant dean and program coordinator, Douglass Residential College, Rutgers University, New Brunswick, N.J., November 26, 2013.
4. Takaki, *A Different Mirror.*
5. Wilson, *Racism,* p. 50.
6. Stampp, *The Peculiar Institution,* pp. 21–22.
7. Takaki, *A Different Mirror,* pp. 64–65.
8. Roediger, *The Wages of Whiteness,* p. 13.
9. Baron, "The Demand for Black Labor," p. 516.
10. Hooks, *Where We Stand,* p. 7.
11. Quoted in Shelby, "It's the Economy," p. 19.
12. Ibid.

9

Gender

THE WINTER OF 2013–2014 IN THE UNITED STATES WAS UNUSUALLY cold, with record-low temperatures is some places, such as Chattanooga, Tennessee. It meant expensive heating bills for low-wage workers with salaries already stretched to the limit. The Episcopal Metropolitan Ministries, according to its website, is "Chattanooga's financial emergency room," dedicated to preventing homelessness by helping individuals with basic needs such as rent, utility payments, and food. All across the country, organizations such as these have become mainstays in efforts to prevent homelessness in their communities. Most of the people who seek help from the Episcopal Metropolitan Ministries have low-wage jobs (like most people in Chattanooga), working at poultry plants, fast food restaurants, and discount stores, and don't make enough money to pay their heating bills and feed their families. A majority of them are women, many of whom work as housekeepers.[1]

It was not always this way. Chattanooga was once a manufacturing town, with apparel factories, textile mills, and metal foundries. The jobs available didn't necessarily require a high school degree, but nonetheless were steppingstones into the middle class for many. Since the 1980s, the factories and foundries in Chattanooga, and around the country, began shutting their doors and moving elsewhere for the sake of cutting costs. Today, low-paying service-sector jobs fill the void created by the absence of manufacturing jobs, and the residents of Chattanooga lack the education and technical skills needed for higher-paying jobs in information and technology sectors.

As the economy continues to lose manufacturing jobs, and as many jobs—both in manufacturing and retail—become automated, both men's and women's employment choices become limited. The problem of inequality is ultimately a problem of jobs—both their insufficient number and their

217

low pay—which leads to continuing economic disadvantage, particularly for women.

With so many people in low-wage jobs in Chattanooga, the city has a high poverty rate. Compared to 15 percent for the nation as a whole, 27 percent of the city's residents are poor. Two-thirds of the city's poor households are headed by women, especially women of color. Erika McCurdy is one of them, an African American single mother of two. She was among those who sought help from the Metropolitan Ministries during the winter of 2013–2014 to pay her utility bill, which skyrocketed when temperatures hit the deep freeze. She has worked as a nurse's aide at an assisted-living facility for fifteen years, and in 2014 was still making only $9 an hour. There were many weeks when she couldn't make ends meet, especially the weeks when only twenty hours of work was available. Erika is certain that she couldn't live without the assistance she receives from Metropolitan and also from her relatives and friends. Even if she worked full-time, she would make only $19,530 a year, right at the poverty threshold for a family of three.

In 2012, of the 10 million low-income working families with children in the United States, 39 percent were headed by working mothers. The numbers are much higher for African Americans (65 percent) and Latinos (45 percent).[2] When it comes to low-income working mothers, two of the most critical factors that explain their lower earnings are the kinds of jobs they do and the fact that, on average, women continue to earn less than their male counterparts, even in jobs where the majority of the workers are women.

Since 2000, and especially since the economic recession of 2007–2009, the fastest-growing jobs have been in the low-wage service and retail sectors. These are jobs that typically pay the minimum wage, employ primarily women, do not lead to careers, and offer minimal benefits such as health care, child care, vacation, sick leave, family leave, or pension plans. Some of these women earn such low pay because they work in part-time positions. But even when women work full-time in the service and retail sectors—at least thirty-five hours a week—they remain poor. And for the higher-paying, middle-class jobs that have been added since the Great Recession, the majority of working mothers lack the education and technical skills to access them.

Two-thirds of minimum-wage women workers in the United States today are health aides, cashiers, maids and housekeepers, personal-care aides, administrative assistants, cooks, child-care workers, fast food workers, elementary school teachers, home health aides, medical assistants, retail sales workers, librarians, office and administrative support workers, secretaries, receptionists, customer service representatives, waitresses, maids, janitors, hairdressers, and cosmetologists. As Table 9.1 shows, there is a large income differential between men and women in occupations that

Table 9.1 Median Weekly Earnings of Full-Time Workers by Occupation and Sex, 2012

	Men		Women	
Occupation	Number of Workers (thousands)	Median Weekly Earnings ($)	Number of Workers (thousands)	Median Weekly Earnings ($)
Management, professional and related	19,926	1,328	21,059	951
Human resource workers	158	1,249	401	944
Accountants and auditors	585	1,350	886	996
Professional and related	10,804	1,267	13,189	928
Community and social service	714	869	1,177	820
Social workers	134	856	535	845
Education, training, and library	1,766	1,133	4,687	858
Elementary and middle-school teachers	464	1,128	1,971	921
Other teachers and instructors	151	917	220	729
Librarians	24	n/a	120	960
Health care practitioners and related	1,471	1,245	4,320	980
Registered nurses	230	1,189	1,946	1,086
Health care support	290	529	2,060	477
Nursing and home health aides	173	508	1,285	445
Waiters and waitresses	322	456	569	396
Fast food workers	57	406	109	368
Maids and housekeepers	123	425	668	395
Personal care and related	603	569	1,637	428
Hairdressers and cosmetologists	22	n/a	272	468
Child-care workers	31	n/a	395	386
Personal-care aides	99	465	450	412
Sales	9,202	768	13,914	610
Cashiers	407	400	941	368
Office administrative support	3,774	700	9,909	629
Bookkeepers	102	740	755	652
Customer service representatives	502	684	1,033	585
Receptionists	73	604	758	524
Secretaries and administrative assistants	105	803	2,146	665

Sources: US Census, *Household Income 2012;* US Bureau of Labor Statistics, *Median Weekly Earnings of Full-time and Wage and Salary Workers by Detailed Occupation and Sex.*

are predominantly serviced by women. This gives evidence to the incongruent reality that men still get paid more than women when they enter occupations predominantly held by women.

In 2012, the median annual personal income in the United States was $51,371. For the occupations shown in the table, yearly median incomes for women ranged from $19,136 (for fast food workers and cashiers) to $56,472 (for registered nurses); for men, the range was $20,800 (for fast food workers and cashiers) to $69,056 for management positions (including chief executives and financial managers), which most likely swelled the high end of this range, since these positions are predominantly held by men. For both men and women, the real median household income for 2012 was 3.53 percent lower than the median household income of $53,252 in 1999, when incomes peaked.[3]

That women's incomes for most occupations in the United States are near or often below the poverty threshold explains the following for 2012:

- The poverty rates for women remained at historically high levels in 2012.
- 14.5 percent of women were poor, compared to 11 percent of men.
- The poverty rate for black women was 25.1 percent, for Hispanic women 24.8 percent, and for Native American women 34.4 percent.[4]
- Families headed by women had a poverty rate of 40.9 percent, compared to 22.6 percent for families headed by men.
- For families headed by white women the poverty rate was 33.1 percent, for families headed by black women it was 46.7 percent, for families headed by Hispanic women it was 48.6 percent, and for families headed by Native American women it was 56.9 percent.
- More than half of all poor children (56.1 percent) lived in families headed by women.
- Nearly 13.2 percent of single women with children worked full time year round in 2012.[5]

These facts about women's poverty prompted Diane Pearce to coin the term "feminization of poverty." She meant to emphasize the fact that, around the world, the majority of the poor are women. And if a woman is poor, so are her children.[6]

Why Are Women Poor?

Women's continuing economic disadvantages and persistent poverty can be largely attributed to the following:

- Women are poor because they are paid less, and because they are segregated into occupations that have low salaries and wages.
- Women spend a disproportionate amount of time, compared to men, as their families' primary caregivers—a role for which labor is unpaid.
- Pregnancy and childrearing interrupt a woman's work history and affect her income and advancement potential.
- Domestic violence can affect a woman's life, both personally and professionally, in profound ways that can often lead to poverty and homelessness.
- A woman who is a single parent bears the inequitable cost of raising her children.

- Following divorce, a man's standard of living often improves, whereas a woman's plummets.
- The absence of affordable and quality day care, after-school care, paid family leave, and health care, together with a low minimum wage, relegates many women to lives of arduous poverty.

Nor should we lose sight of the consequences of the continuing **sexual objectification** of women, which diminishes their true worth and prevents them from realizing their full human potential. Relatedly, women continue to face discrimination and sexual harassment at work, which can lead to a hostile work environment and job loss.

Generally, women are poor for the same systemic reasons that men are poor. But given the special burdens that women carry compared to men, their inequality and resulting disadvantage are intensified. By the same token, provisions that would improve women's economic circumstances—job growth; a higher minimum wage; a comprehensive benefit package with coverage for health care, family care, family leave, vacation, retirement care, and quality child care; flexible work hours; better transportation; a stronger safety net—would enhance men's work lives too. In the absence of these provisions, both men's and women's lives are unnecessarily harsh—but women's lives more so than men's.

The changes needed to improve the lives of both men and women require deliberate and fundamental action on how corporations open up work opportunities and determine salary and benefit packages for their employees, and how government discerns its role in building strong safety nets and social infrastructures as a floor below which no one is allowed to fall. If these changes are not made, then inequality and the consequences that accompany it—as the natural fallout from capitalism, an economic system in which the primary objective is profit maximization—will continue.

As Martha Gimenez writes: "As long as capitalism rules, men and women will remain oppressed since their ability to satisfy their needs will remain subordinate to the changing needs of capital accumulation, [and] the most women can expect under capitalist conditions, is a stratification profile that mirrors that of men." She also offers Karl Marx's argument that government will do what is necessary to "abolish distinctions that act as barriers to political participation by all citizens, [but will] not abolish the social relations that are the basis for those distinctions."[7] Therefore, the Civil Rights Act of 1964, the Voting Rights Act of 1965, and affirmative action were relatively easy to legislate to ensure equal participation in the political arena. But government will do nothing about the fundamental premises that brought about the distinctions between blacks and whites, men and women, rich and poor in the first place.

These economic disparities that are fostered by capitalist social relations or relations of production lead to the "exclusion of a growing proportion of the property-less population, male or female, from access to the minimum conditions necessary for their reproductions."[8] This means that those who do not own the means of production lack access to jobs that pay sufficiently to maintain not only themselves but also future generations of workers. Changing this will require upending society. Legislating civil rights is much easier than legislating fundamental economic rights.

MAKING CONNECTIONS
The Heterosexual Advantage

Sexism and **heterosexism** are two sides of the same coin. The structures of **patriarchy** that lead to discrimination and entrenched prejudice against women are the same ones that create homophobia and bias against gay men and lesbians. Gay men are regarded as being weak, for they are seen as being too much like women; and lesbians, in flouting traditional ideas of womanhood, are seen as threatening the entire edifice of patriarchy. In either case, the chauvinism is rooted in sexism, and in fixed notions about men and women and their roles in society.

When individuals are derided and mocked for being or even suspected as being gay or lesbian, the intention is to belittle and ridicule a sexual orientation that is not heterosexual. And often, the victims of that scorn make the choice to oppress themselves—become invisible—by hiding their sexual orientation. This creates a burden for gays and lesbians that heterosexual people can seldom fathom. Even though statutory obstacles to marriage and child adoption for gays and lesbians are being slowly dismantled, deep homophobia and resentment still persist in many parts of society.

Every time a child or a young person commits suicide because of unbearable mocking and teasing, or even physical assault—often by complete strangers—for being or suspected of being homosexual, the pervasiveness of homophobia becomes evident. This oppression and violence against gays and lesbians is intended to enforce "proper" gender roles and thereby preserve patriarchy and its underpinning in compulsory heterosexuality. The primary oppression that gays and lesbians suffer is often their compulsory invisibility—often institutionalized through injunctions such as the US military's former policy, Don't Ask, Don't Tell.

Much is known about the "witch-hunt" persecution of communists and civil rights workers conducted by the Federal Bureau of Investigation under the leadership of J. Edgar Hoover. But very little attention is paid to Hoover's equally obsessive efforts to persecute gays and lesbians in the government and academia.[1] When President Dwight Eisenhower took office, he issued Executive Order 10450 authorizing investigations to determine the "suitability" of federal employees. Sexual "perversion" was one such area of inquiry. Astronomer Franklin Kameny, who went on to become a noteworthy leader in the gay rights movement, was fired in 1957 due to "unsuitability."

(continues)

The Heterosexual Advantage

And just as the landmark Civil Rights Act banning discrimination on the basis of race, religion, sex, or national origin was being signed in 1964, gays were being barred from federal positions in the name of morality. Memos were being written by officials at the Civil Service Commission advocating the firing of "suspected" gays. White House aide Walter Jenkins, one of President Lyndon Johnson's most trusted advisers, lost his job because he was suspected of being a homosexual a month before these memos were written.

In 1975, facing lawsuits and protests, the US government finally rescinded this policy. But even today, though it is unlawful for the federal government to fire employees due to their sexual orientation, there are no such safeguards in the private sector.[2] In corporate America, the invisibility that lesbian, gay, bisexual, and transgender (LGBT) people experience is often referred to as the "pink ceiling." LGBT employees are expected to keep their sexual orientation hidden so as not to offend customers. Claire Miller writes that "here discrimination is camouflaged as a 'business strategy'—we are tolerant but our customers are not—[which] is seen as an acceptable justification."[3]

A report published in 2014 by the Deloitte consulting firm and New York University "found that 83 percent of gay, lesbian and bi-sexual people hide aspects of their identity at work, often because they say their bosses expect them to."[4] There are very few openly gay executives at the nation's thousand biggest companies. The same insular culture that historically kept women and people of color out of the ranks of company executives also keeps LGBT people out today.

In the fall of 2014, Apple CEO Tim Cook revealed that he was gay and became the first CEO of a major corporation to do so. His disclosure was welcome, but must be seen in the context of overlapping realities of oppressions: the ones he himself felt from having to conform to mandatory norms of heterosexuality, and those that he caused to numerous others by the decisions he made as the Apple CEO.

Notes: 1. Apuzzo, "Uncovered Papers," pp. A13, A19.
2. Ibid.
3. Miller, "Where Are the Gay Chief Executives?" p. SR4.
4. Ibid.

Poor Women and the State

The Clinton administration's welfare reform was ostensibly meant to help poor women escape poverty. But since it was predicated on stereotypical notions about the women—instead of valid structural processes—welfare reform evolved into an arena where racism, classism, and sexism have combined to entrap women, especially women of color, into a permanent state of disadvantage.

Notions that prompted the reform alleged that welfare had become a way of life for women, that they had no desire to work, and that they had additional children simply to increase their benefits. These conceptions came together to create what Rebekah Smith refers to as "the inflammatory stereotype of the black welfare queen."[9] Smith refers to "social science research [that] has consistently concluded that this is not true. The median benefit increase for a new child—$71 per month—is barely enough to cover the monthly cost of diapers, formula and clothing. [Anyone] who thinks that women go through nine months of pregnancy, the pain of childbirth and 18 years of rearing a child [for this measly amount] . . . must be a man."[10]

In the Netherlands, where the notion of welfare is entirely different compared to the United States, families with children, regardless of whether they are rich, middle class, or poor, receive payments of $665, four times a year, to assist them with the costs of raising a child. In the United States, in contrast, the word *welfare* provokes images of "the lazy, black welfare mother who breeds children at the expense of the taxpayers in order to increase the amount of her welfare check."[11]

What is missing from this so-called rationalization is any acknowledgment of the role played by structural inequalities in making men and women poor, which include the following:[12]

- Lack of jobs that pay a living wage.
- Lack of quality and affordable day care.
- Absence of fathers, with or without jobs.
- Government's half-hearted initiative in enforcing child support.
- Lack of adequate and dependable transportation systems.
- Penalization of women who work through premature elimination of their welfare benefits.

President Bill Clinton's 1996 Welfare Reform, Personal Responsibility, and Work Opportunity Reconciliation Act, which promised to "end welfare as a way of life," should be seen in the light of the neoliberal policies fashionable among policymakers at that time. Such policies are rooted in the ideology that the market is primary and should drive all economic policies as well as social, educational, and political decisions. The neoliberal position considers government to be a facilitator of this ideology and holds that the government must reduce its own role in economic and social reform as much as possible.

The 1996 welfare reform reversed the path pioneered under President Franklin Roosevelt and continued by President Lyndon Johnson, whereby the two presidents established programs and policies in which the government actively engaged in poverty reduction. Aid to Dependent Children (ADC) was created as part of President Roosevelt's New Deal program, in the Social Security Act of 1935, and was renamed Aid to Families with Dependent Children (AFDC) during John Kennedy's presidency. It was designed to provide cash assistance to poor families—primarily mothers and their children. And in 1964, President Johnson signed the Equal Opportunity Act, which was part of his national war on poverty initiative. Through this act, the federal government adopted a set of policies and programs such as Medicare, Medicaid, a higher minimum wage, food stamps, Head Start, housing assistance, and cost-of-living increases for Social Security—which, along with AFDC, would be instrumental in reducing poverty from 22.4 percent in 1964 to 11.1 percent in 1973.

President Clinton's antipoverty initiative came in 1996 in the form of the Personal Responsibility and Work Opportunity Reconciliation Act. It was directed primarily at mothers and their dependent children, and ended AFDC and replaced it with a new program called Temporary Assistance for Needy Families (TANF), a joint federal-state cash assistance program for low-income families with children. Gene Falk of the Congressional Research Service describes the Clinton welfare reform initiative as one that emphasizes participation in the labor force as a primary strategy for reducing dependence of single mothers and their children on public assistance.[13] The policy requires recipients to find work, thus increasing exponentially the numbers of individuals vying for low-wage work in an already saturated labor market.

The simple law of economics tells us that as the supply of workers increases, their bargaining power in the workplace to demand better wages, better work hours, and a better work environment decreases. In a labor market where many are looking for work, the workers always have the weaker hand, especially if they have little skill, education, or experience to offer.

The work requirement is the cornerstone of the new welfare policy—its objective is to compel the adult recipients of TANF assistance to acquire work within two years of enrolling in the program. Maria Cancian and Daniel Meyer, in their analysis of "work after welfare," write that the emphasis on work has been accompanied by the fervent belief in the minds of proponents of this policy that "any job is superior to welfare and that women should begin working, even in jobs with low wages, because their work experience will eventually lead them to success."[14]

Cancian and Meyer assert that when women have limited education and job skills, a work-first policy, instead of one that emphasizes education and skill development, limits women to jobs that have limited prospects for providing either sufficient income or advancement opportunities. Moreover, when jobs are scarce to begin with, few women who have limited education and skills can be expected to secure what might be considered good jobs. Not surprisingly, Cancian and Meyer find that the median hourly wage for TANF recipients who leave the program is only $6.73, even five years after leaving. Less than 5 percent worked full-time, full-year, during the first five years after leaving welfare.[15]

Regardless, to stress the consequences of noncompliance with the work requirement, Congress passed a mandatory time limit. Recipients can receive cash assistance under TANF for a maximum of five years. This includes child-care assistance and transitional Medicaid, but also requires the recipient to identify the biological fathers of her children, an indication of the belief integral to the Personal Responsibility and Work Opportunity Reconciliation Act that "marriage is the foundation of a successful society" and provides the best antidote to poverty.

In the funding specifications for TANF, there is a category titled "healthy marriage/responsible fatherhood grant."[16] In this context, poor people's intimate relations and marriage status, as Anna Igra contends, "are not a private matter; they have become an integral part of the welfare system itself."[17] Therefore, being poor means that your life choices are open to public scrutiny.

Since many details of implementing TANF have been moved to the state level, states have been given the option of imposing further sanctions to either remove or restrict the benefits that TANF families receive.[18] Consequently, many states have adopted "family caps" as part of their implementation of welfare reform. The objective of these caps is to restrict "the amount of a family's welfare grant at a level correlated to the number of children in the family at the time the family began receiving assistance." Family caps are premised on the view that poor women, stereotypically the "lazy, black welfare mother who breeds children at the taxpayer's expense, intentionally get[s] pregnant in order to increase their benefits," even though the social science data do not support this position.[19]

The 1996 welfare reform law also established a lifetime ban on eligibility for TANF and food stamps for those convicted of a drug-related felony. Individual states had the option of establishing "individual responsibility plans," which required participation in a substance abuse treatment program and included a provision to sanction families for failure to comply.[20]

Gwendolyn Mink has argued persuasively that "the Personal Responsibility Act removes poor single mothers from the welfare state to the police state. . . . In this welfare police state, poor single mothers must purchase their families' short term survival by sacrificing basic rights . . . but only if they reveal their most intimate relations. The law treats them and the public perceives them as breeders rather than mothers, as dependents rather than workers—in short as people sorely in need of discipline, control and reform."[21]

The median monthly TANF benefit in the United States as of 2012 was $427 for a family of three (a parent and two children), ranging from $170 in Mississippi to $770 in New York and $923 in Alaska.[22] But the vast majority of TANF families remain poor even with the benefit. And if families have another source of income, they receive an even smaller benefit, and yet can still be financially sanctioned if they fail to meet the program's work requirement. It is a real dilemma. Furthermore, according to the Center on Budget and Policy Priorities, in 2012 cash benefits for the nation's poorest continued to erode as inflation diminished their purchasing power.[23]

Today, nearly two decades after the 1996 welfare reform, almost half of the US work force is female. But although the incomes of a vast majority of single mothers with children have increased, these women continue to live in poverty. Most jobs that women find do not pay enough to support a family or even pull them above the poverty line. The retail, housekeeping, health aide, and other hospitality jobs that women have entered in vast numbers are low-paying, part-time jobs. These are also jobs in which "the employer has lots of flexibility to hire, fire, cut your hours, re-arrange your schedule," whereas workers have no such flexibility.[24]

Moreover, these jobs typically offer minimum wage for the temporary or low-skilled work they require, and do not include health insurance or other benefits. It is also important to keep in mind that securing a job and having an income often means that the women will lose their eligibility for critically needed TANF benefits such as rental assistance, Medicaid, food stamps, and child care, thus jeopardizing the health and well-being of their children and much more. Karen Seccombe, Delores James, and Kimberly Battle Walters have shown in their research that it is clear that "without continued assistance with health insurance, child-care, transportation, food stamps, and subsidized housing, working becomes not only prohibitive but sometimes downright dangerous."[25] Instead of continuing these benefits until the women could afford to pay for them on their own, until they had stable jobs and better incomes—in other words, supplementing their income until they were truly self-sufficient—eliminating these benefits altogether put these women right back where they started from.

It is a paradox that is built into the welfare system. Once individuals start working, even if the job pays just at or slightly above the poverty level, they run the risk of losing their benefits. In their research, Seccombe, James, and Walters capture the frustration that many of the women they interviewed felt. As one interviewee said: "I got off the system, got a job at Hardee's. I was honest and told them I had a job. They took my assistance away, raised my rent, took away Medicaid."[26] This research was grounded in the real-world experience of women, black and white—desperately wanting to work, but realizing that employment was reducing their already meager standard of living and placing their children at risk.

Welfare Reform and Its Impact on Poor Women and Children

The policy choices that directed the 1996 welfare reform made the lives of poor women and their children more difficult and arduous. It did not lessen the conditions of their material disadvantage. A very different set of choices, devoted to the idea of helping poor women become self-sufficient, would have yielded more positive results.

First, the requirement that women find work would have been a laudable goal if individuals were provided the skills and education necessary to obtain jobs that paid more than the absolute minimum. Second, the work requirement may indeed have encouraged individuals to break the cycle of dependency if they had been assured that their small incomes would be shored up by benefits such as rental assistance, Medicaid, child-care support, and transportation subsidies. But in the absence of both these stipulations, "ending welfare as we know it" (as President Clinton characterized the reform) made poor women's and children's lives worse.

For many women, working was a positive experience. It made them proud and had definite psychological benefits. It made them feel good about themselves and enabled them to send positive messages to their children. They wanted to work, and the decision to return to welfare was an unpleasant one—one made out of desperation, not calculation.[27]

Quite contrary to the stereotypes that have often been associated with poor women, especially poor black women, the women wanted to work; they did not want to return to welfare. But the 1996 welfare reform, with its punitive stance, impacted the lives of poor women and their children by combining with the adversities that already existed in their socioeconomic context, exacerbating their hardships and often forcing them to return to welfare just to survive.

It is critically important that we consider the different areas in which the 1996 welfare reform had a vast impact on the lives of women and their children:

- The requirement that they find work has to be assessed in the context of an overall job crisis for large segments of the US population. But because of particularly severe shortages of jobs in poor neighborhoods, women often had to commute long distances. This created problems, since child-care providers were not always available for women leaving early and returning late.
- One-fifth to one-third of TANF leavers return to welfare within one year. For the women returning to TANF, this was not a strategic, premeditated, or calculated move.
- Since leaving TANF, 25–33 percent of families experienced food insecurity.[28]
- They experienced a severe lack of affordable child care. This is a critically important point when we consider that many women live in areas of high poverty concentration and high crime. Going to work was often contingent upon finding affordable child care to ensure that their children were safe.

- The challenges for going to work were exacerbated by the fact that transportation is a major barrier to women getting and keeping jobs. Most women cannot afford to buy an automobile or pay for its upkeep. Public transportation is often expensive and unreliable, with limited hours of service and limited routes.
- It mostly means getting up early, getting children to child care, navigating a complicated public transportation system, not having enough time to prepare food or rest—the system primes itself for failure.
- Women wanted to work but were compelled to quit because working would mean a reduction or loss of welfare benefits—health insurance, child care, transportation, food stamps, and subsidized housing—all of which would lower their standard of living and jeopardize their children's health. Women were frustrated that the "system actually discourages them from working by raising their rent, eliminating Medicaid and cutting off needed social services before these women have a chance to establish themselves."[29]
- Health problems were a constant challenge for the women—asthma, depression, back pain, high blood pressure; their children were sick more often than children from the upper classes, and the mothers were afraid of being in a situation where they did not have health care.
- Children pay a high price for welfare reform when mothers, pushed into low-wage work, "spend less time with their pre-school children, talk with their children less, suffer twice the rate of clinical depression . . . and cut meals to make ends meet."[30]
- Even when jobs offered medical insurance, premiums and co-payments needed to be paid, which the women couldn't afford.
- Some states offer transitional Medicaid coverage and child-care services, but many participants were either unaware of or confused by the rules. Caseworkers, who are crucial in aiding women to make the transition, were often abusive, neglectful, humiliating, and stereotyping in how they treated the women and deliberately withheld critical information.
- The welfare reforms led to dramatic caseload reductions, as had been the objective. From a historic peak of 5.1 million families receiving cash assistance in March 1994, 1.9 million families were receiving TANF assistance in December 2010.[31] Even with the 2007–2009 economic downturn, the caseload between 2007 and 2010 rose only 16 percent.[32]
- But as a consequence of the reform, the safety net itself has weakened considerably. Poverty crept up to an unprecedented level and in 2011, 15 percent of the total population was poor, or 42 million people.

Poor women's lives are more difficult today, nearly two decades since the 1996 welfare reform went into effect. Between 1970 and 2001 the incarceration rate of women of color increased by 2,800 percent. Women are incarcerated for nonviolent "survival crimes" driven by poverty and abuse of alcohol and drugs, such as sex work, drug couriering, fraud, and embezzlement.

Women offenders are typically undereducated, low-skilled with intermittent work experience, and survivors of physical and sexual abuse, with many physical and mental problems. Almost two-thirds of women offenders are reported as never having held a job that paid more than $6.50 an hour.[33] "The speed at which women are entering boardrooms is not half as fast as that of women entering prisons for crimes of poverty."[34]

Welfare reform did not change marriage rates, since the reason why marriage rates were falling off in the first place has not changed. As William Julius Wilson has explained, men who have no jobs are not marriageable men; women are unlikely to marry them and form families. "Male joblessness is the single most important factor underlying the rise in unwed mothers among poor black women. Yet, this factor has received scant attention in recent discussions."[35]

For most people in Europe, the term *welfare* conjures up a broad picture that includes schools, parks, police, health care, child care, elder care, fire protection, and such. In the United States, *welfare* in its narrowest interpretation brings to mind the racialized image of a never-married young woman with her children, a stereotype that has undoubtedly contributed to growing sentiments in the public opposition to welfare.

The 1996 welfare reform in the United States shows how poor black women have been used to create a racialized stereotype as "sexually irresponsible welfare queens," living the high life by taking advantage of the system, and who were undeserving of government assistance and needed to be reformed. This image infected the public's view of the poor who depend on welfare and in turn impacted public policy.[36]

Scholars, in trying to make sense of the continuing racial oppression at a time of "color-blindness," have also evoked these very themes to explain what Eduardo Bonilla-Silva calls "color-coded inequality." People of color are poor because in today's climate of "color-blindness" they are "otherized softly." This color-blind, laissez-faire racism based on elements of traditional liberalism "blames blacks themselves for their poorer relative economic standing, seeing it as the function of perceived cultural inferiority."[37]

This position states that even though they are human like "you and me," blacks and Latinos just don't work hard enough; they just don't have the work ethic and are themselves responsible for their poor economic standing. Traditional forms of racism based on notions of biological inferiority are rearticulated in terms of cultural inferiority, which are now claimed to be fundamental in determining the persistent socioeconomic deprivations in the lives of the black poor, especially poor black women.

The stereotyped image of the welfare recipient as someone who is to blame for his or her situation gives society a convenient scapegoat to focus on instead of deeper, more complicated root causes of poverty. It allows the discussion about complex matters such as poverty and inequality to be attributed to the capriciousness of human nature, instead of the structures and processes of society that ultimately lead to concentration of wealth and generate its natural corollary—deep inequality and poverty.

In the fall of 2013, a large national survey was commissioned by the Center for American Progress, the American Association of Retired Persons, and the news journal *The Atlantic* to determine Americans' attitudes toward family and the economy. The results of the survey show that single mothers and low-income women were more likely to report that the economy simply does not work for people like them.[38] They said that even when they made all the right choices in life, they could not get ahead, because the economy does not work for economically vulnerable women. And women of color, in particular, felt that the stakes in life were overwhelmingly stacked against them.

When they were asked what government could do to improve the economic security of workers and families, their responses were not surprising, as shown in Table 9.2.

"Two Nations" of Women

In the United States there are "two nations" of women. One is made up of the women for whom poverty and disadvantage is the existential reality. In many ways their lives mirror the lives of men who occupy the same socioeconomic spheres. Absence of steady, decent-paying jobs is the fundamental crisis that both face. Men without jobs are made redundant by society—but women, because they are often mothers and primary caregivers, have to find ways to keep their loved ones afloat and therefore have to stay engaged in the struggle to make ends meet. Less than one-third of single mothers receive state-mandated child support from the fathers of their children in any given year, primarily because the men do not have jobs or are incarcerated. And women, as we have seen, toil on with low-paying jobs, lack of affordable and quality child care, absence of sick leave, and dozens of other handicaps. Their children often inherit their economic disadvantage, with poverty and want becoming a way of life.

The other nation is made up of women who are the fortunate beneficiaries of the civil rights victories of the 1960s. These victories opened doors to higher education and professions with benefits and prestige that had previously been closed to women. Race (white) and class (middle and upper-middle) combined to place these women in social settings that conferred

Table 9.2 Support for Government Policies to Help Workers and Families, 2013 (percentage of respondents who strongly favored a policy)

	White Women	African American Women	Latina Women
Ensure that women earn equal pay for equal work, in order to raise wages for working women and families	79	82	81
Protect pregnant women and new mothers so they cannot be fired or demoted when they become pregnant or take maternity leave	69	72	68
Expand access to high-quality, affordable child care for working families	58	79	50
Establish paid leave for workers who provide care for elderly parents or disabled children	54	71	59
Increase the minimum wage to establish a mandatory national living wage of $10 per hour, or $42,000 for a dual-income family of four, and automatically increase the minimum wage to rise with inflation	50	81	54
Increase the number of single mothers who attend college by providing them with financial assistance and child care	46	66	55
Consolidate the federal government's social welfare programs—such as food stamps, rental assistance, job training, and disability assistance—into a single debit-card account for needy individuals, thereby streamlining the application process and saving money by eliminating bureaucracy	29	40	35

Source: Center for American Progress, "A New Force for America's Families," table 3.

upon them educational and professional advantages that being black or poor could not. In many ways their success has been spectacular, but disadvantages intrinsic to social constructions of gender and the ones associated with sexism have often challenged them as they seek continued professional success.

It is important to consider the fact that the success of professional women has also been made possible by the women whom they hire to clean their homes, take care of their children, and generally fill in as caretakers and caregivers. These are the women who live on the edge due to low wages, missing benefits, and other work-related uncertainties. Many of these women are immigrants—both documented and undocumented. In the United States as of 2012, there were 800,000 low-income, female-headed working families who belonged to this latter category.[39]

Barbara Ehrenreich and Arlie Hochschild juxtapose these two categories of women—the successful and their "help"—as embodying the same gender-role dynamics as between men and women.[40] The success of the professional woman is made possible by the role that the housecleaner/

babysitter/caregiver provides. And the work of the latter takes place behind closed doors, away from public scrutiny, providing an atmosphere for possible violation of basic human rights, over and above the insufficient wages and long work hours.

Women's Inequality and Pay Inequity

Since the second-wave women's movement and the passage of the major civil rights laws, there have been many areas of real, tangible gain. Women now make up almost half the work force—49 percent. More women than men have college degrees—36 percent compared to 28 percent for men. Even though only a handful of women sit on the corporate and university boards and congressional committees, the gains, though slow, have been undeniable.[41] The appointment of Janet Yellen as the first woman to head the Federal Reserve, and the choice of Mary Teresa Barra to be the CEO of General Motors, seem to have broken down the last vestiges of men's monopoly of critically important institutional leadership positions. These are historic victories for women.

Title IX of the Educational Amendments of 1972 prohibited sex discrimination in educational institutions. In its interpretation of the amendment, the American Civil Liberties Union maintained that "while most famous for its requirement that schools provide girls with equal athletic opportunities, the law applies to all educational programs that receive federal funding, and to all aspects of a school's educational system."[42]

Hillary Clinton was the third female secretary of state. Four women have now sat on the Supreme Court—Sandra Day O'Connor, Ruth Bader Ginsberg, Sonia Sotomayor, and Elena Kagan. Nancy Pelosi has served as House Minority Leader and as the sixtieth Speaker of the House. Women and people of color now sit on corporate boards and in the offices of mayors, governors, university presidents, and attorneys general. The breakthroughs that women and people of color have made are indeed phenomenal.

And even though they still are awaiting ratification of the Equal Rights Amendment, mandating equal pay for comparable work, almost 60 percent of all women in the United States were in the labor force at the dawn of the new millennium. In 2010, according to the Bureau of Labor Statistics, "13 percent of architects and engineers and 32 percent of physicians and surgeons were women, . . . 60 percent of accountants and auditors and 82 percent of elementary and middle school teachers were women . . . [and] women accounted for the majority of all workers in the financial activities industry and in education and health services."[43]

It is very encouraging that women are present in the labor force in such large numbers. Although for many this has not necessarily translated into a more secure and satisfactory life, there are those who have experienced tremendous professional success and have risen to ranks of leadership in their places of work, which couldn't have been imagined in decades past.

This fact, however, pales when we consider that more than five decades after President John Kennedy signed the Equal Pay Act in 1963, women's earnings on the average continue to be lower than men's. By the end of 2012, women who worked full-time had a median weekly earning of $692. Men who worked full-time had a median weekly earning of $875. The median weekly earning of African American women was $594.[44] According to the US Census Bureau, women who worked full-time in 2012 earned, on average, only 77 cents for every dollar men earned. African American women earned only 64 cents and Latinas only 54 cents for every dollar earned by white men.[45]

The issue of pay equity became headline news when the circumstances surrounding the firing of *New York Times* executive editor Jill Abramson by the top management were brought to light in May 2014. She was the first woman ever to occupy that top position. Abramson had just recently discovered that her pay and pension benefits as executive editor and before that as managing editor were considerably less than those of the male colleagues she had replaced. This made plain that no woman, regardless of how high and coveted a professional position she might be in, can ever be fully certain that she is being compensated equitably. When she confronted the top management about her pay situation, she was characterized as being "pushy."

There have been many explanations of this persistent, unchanging wage gap. The continuing sexism and sex discrimination that women experience, their interrupted work histories, and their uncompensated **reproductive work**[46] in the family, combined with the lack of paid family leave, lack of quality and affordable day care, low minimum wage, and part-time instead of full-time work—guarantee the varying degrees of inequality that working women experience. For most women in the work force, these might be logical explanations, however unfair.

But in accounting for the pay inequity experienced by the "top brass" of women holding the highest professional positions, like the one Abramson occupied, these explanations fall far short and may even seem disingenuous. Many women and feminists wonder what the fact that someone of Abramson's stature can't get equal pay for equal work means for women in much less stellar positions. The media has been abuzz, full of speculation regarding the circumstances of her firing, all of which raises very important questions regarding stereotypes of women and how this impinges on their real roles and challenges in leadership positions.

The Equal Pay Act was signed into law in 1963 with the expectation that it would end gender-based pay discrimination. But with very limited enforcement tools to ensure its implementation, the law has been unable to achieve its promise of closing the wage gap. In the meantime, even though women's participation in the labor force has grown by leaps and bounds, pay equity has been somewhat of a mirage.

In 1998 in a landmark case, Lilly Ledbetter sued the Goodyear Tire and Rubber Company for paying her significantly less than her male counterparts. When the lawsuit eventually reached the Supreme Court, her claim was denied on a statute-of-limitations technicality—too much time had elapsed for her claim to remain legitimate. But her case struck a chord with thousands of women who had similar experiences. Consequently, in 2009—at a time when the US Congress had a Democratic majority in both the Senate and the House of Representatives, the Ledbetter Fair Pay Restoration Act was passed and President Barack Obama signed it enthusiastically. This act gave women the right to sue their employees for wage discrimination. But it still did not give women the tools to fight against the wage gap itself.

It is against this background that Barbara Mikulski, Democratic senator from Maryland, introduced the Paycheck Fairness Act in the Senate in April 2014. The hope was that it would finally succeed in securing equal pay for equal work for all Americans. The bill would amend and update the Equal Pay Act of 1963 by giving workers stronger enforcement tools and remedies to help close, once and for all, the pay gap between men and women.

The Paycheck Fairness Act would prohibit employer retaliation against employees who share their salary information with each other. This would eliminate the "culture of silence" that keeps women in the dark about pay discrimination. It would also require the Department of Labor to collect wage data from employers, broken down by race and gender, and require employers to demonstrate that wage differentials between men and women in the same jobs are for reasons other than gender.

The Senate Republicans, however, blocked a vote to open a debate on the Paycheck Fairness Act, killing the measure for the foreseeable future. In blocking this measure, the Republicans argued that women are paid less than men because women choose professions that are low-paying—choosing social work instead of medicine or law, for example. This argument is fundamentally incorrect, because the issue of pay equity does not concern pay differentials of different jobs but the fact that men and women are paid differently in the same jobs.

For example, Harvard University labor economist Claudia Goldin has found that women doctors and surgeons earn 71 percent of men's salaries, women who are financial specialists make 66 percent of what men in the same occupation earn, and women who are lawyers and judges make 82 percent of what men earn.[47] The primary variable that explains this wage differential among men and women in the same professions, according to

Goldin's study, is workplace flexibility. In professions where long hours, face time at the office, and being available at all hours are valued, wage gaps seem to be the highest. Employers pay people who spend long hours at the office disproportionately more than those who do not.

Women who are still expected to shoulder a disproportionate amount of responsibility with family and child care are the ones who cannot stay longer at the office, or be on call all the time, and subsequently lose out on the pay. According to Goldin's analysis, when men start placing more value on these responsibilities—as they gradually are—there will be more pay-equity. But until that happens, women will continue to make less money than men.

The defeat of the Paycheck Fairness Act, along with the defeat for the equal-pay movement in general, took place in the same political environment in which the Equal Rights Amendment has remained moribund, being defeated every time that it has been introduced in the US Congress since 1972.

Alice Paul was a women's rights activist whose final push of the suffragist campaign led to the passage of the Nineteenth Amendment in 1920, which gave women the right to vote after a protracted struggle of seventy-five years. In 1923 she penned the Equal Rights Amendment, in which she wrote, in simple but forceful language, that "Equality of Rights under the law shall not be denied or abridged by the United States or any State on account of sex." Yet almost a century later, the country still has not passed the amendment.

MAKING CONNECTIONS
The Three Waves of the Women's Movement

There have been three waves of women's movement for empowerment in the United States. The first wave was successful in giving them a political voice through enfranchisement. In the second wave, women, along with African Americans, fought to make fundamental changes in society to claim equal rights and opportunities. In the third and ongoing wave, the objective is to make changes in ways that will make the United States, and eventually the world, a better place for everyone, not just women.

The women's suffrage movement was a struggle that lasted almost seventy-five years and culminated in the passage of the Nineteenth Amendment in 1920, which gave women the right. Stalwarts of the suffrage movement, such as Elizabeth Cady Stanton and Susan B. Anthony, questioned what kind of a republic the United States was when women had been denied the vote for almost 130 years.

(continues)

The Three Waves of the Women's Movement

Abolitionists and suffragists worked together even though race and gender sometimes made for uncomfortable alliances, especially when the Fifteenth Amendment gave black men the right to vote ahead of white women. The final push of the movement came when a small but determined group of women, led by Alice Paul, picketed the White House from January 1917 to June 1919, lambasting President Woodrow Wilson for denying women their rightful voice.

The real story of the suffrage movement is too big to be told here. But the sacrifice and determination that the women displayed in those long years of struggle are discredited when women today don't exercise the right to vote, most often simply because of apathy.

When Betty Friedan wrote her book *The Feminine Mystique* in 1963, she touched a nerve in the hearts and minds of white middle-class women and started, almost singlehandedly, the second wave of the women's movement. In the days after World War II, the country was in the midst of unprecedented economic well-being; many had climbed into the middle class and women were surrounded by gadgets to simplify their housework. The general attitude was: What more could women want? But in fact, women had never been unhappier. They were expected to be good wives and mothers when they wanted to be much more.

Their unhappiness found voice in Friedan's book, which talked about this mystique of why women, surrounded by so much affluence and comfort, were so miserable. It raised fundamental issues about women's sexual objectification, as exemplified by the parade of women in beauty pageants. Reproductive rights were a major focus, and the Supreme Court's decision in *Roe v. Wade* in 1973, legalizing abortion, was one of the second-wave's enduring and continuously contested victories. Major civil rights legislation was passed in the mid-1960s that tore down the walls that had kept women from realizing their full potential. And today, women are where they are, in terms of professional and educational success, because of the achievements of the second wave.

The third wave has expanded the movement to address the continuing challenges faced by women of color, immigrant women, and poor women. It focuses attention on the fallout from colonialism and the new problems that are being created as corporate globalization engenders new forms of oppression, often subsumed under the term *neocolonialism*. And it is here that race, class, gender, and immigration status combine to give real substance to the complex world we live in. The battles that the third wave engages in unify those segments of society who, due to classism, racism, sexism, militarism, colonialism, and neocolonialism, share a common past and a common future.

And as global warming and environmental destruction take their toll, the third wave has also incorporated an ecofeminist dimension. Ecofeminists argue that an important connection exists between the treatment of women, people of color, and the poor, and treatment of the environment, which sustains all life. Ecofeminists argue that a critical relationship exists between social justice and environmental justice. And today, environmental justice is the floor upon which all other struggles must rest.

Conclusion

If the United States isn't ready to pass the Equal Rights Amendment, or isn't serious about implementing the Equal Pay Act, then it should come as little surprise that women who are in top positions in their professions are also constantly having to contest judgments of their "styles" of management and leadership, judgments that are still primarily rooted in stereotypical notions about gender roles.

Soraya Chemaly, in blogging for the magazine *Ms.,* captures women's sentiments when she says that the "abrupt firing of Jill Abramson was like watching a ripple of **misogyny** move through the air in slow motion."[48] Chemaly believes that Abramson is paying the price for "our very gendered ideas about power and leadership [whereby] women who transcend their **gender socialization** and exhibit confident authority are inevitably penalized." Abramson is "countercultural" in terms of the stereotypes most associated with women. Contrary to these constructions, she is "experienced, powerful, strong-willed, assertive, decisive, and display[s] leadership qualities which are quite contrary to the embedded notions of gendered behavior."

But society takes one look at these no-nonsense women and girls and portrays them as "unnatural." They become described as "brusque, pushy, and aggressive with body language, speech patterns which exude ambition and confidence . . . [indicating that] lack of deference in women is so unattractive!"

Women such as these, who defy the accepted standards of dress and language—both verbal and body language—because they see these as speaking not of "femaleness" but of "powerlessness," are seen as outcasts in our gender-framed cultural schema. Many believe, especially women, that this is why Abramson was fired. She occupied "paper-thin ranks of women in leadership." She was a role model and, as Chemaly writes, "did more to level the gender playing field at the *New York Times* than anyone before her."

If journalist, essayist, and playwright Nora Ephron were still alive, she might have said that the firing of Jill Abramson is a personal attack on all women. It feels personal to women because it is personal. Just as the continued sitting of Clarence Thomas on the Supreme Court is an affront to all women, not just Anita Hill.[49]

Women feel sexism in multilayered and complex ways—not much different than how race and color are experienced. For both "nations" of women—the professionals and the working poor—sexism and gender-framed cultural schemas are experienced in both the public sphere and the private, in both material ways and also in their political and psychological manifestations. All of which combine to perpetuate the incongruous marginalization of women.

Notes

1. Greenhouse, "The Walls Close In."
2. Povich, Roberts, and Mather, "Low-Income Working Mothers and State Policy."
3. US Census, *Household Income 2012;* US Bureau of Labor Statistics, "Median Weekly Earnings of Full-time Wage and Salary Workers by Detailed Occupation and Sex."
4. National Women's Law Center, "National Snapshot: Poverty Among Women and Families."
5. Ibid.
6. Pearce, *The Feminization of Poverty,* p. 28.
7. Gimenez, "Capitalism and the Oppression of Women," p. 29.
8. Ibid., p. 22.
9. Smith, "Family Caps in Welfare Reform," p. 163.
10. Ibid., pp. 157–158.
11. Ibid., p. 163.
12. Seccombe, James, and Walters, "'They Think You Ain't Much of Nothing.'"
13. Falk, "The Temporary Assistance for Needy Families (TANF) Block Grant," p. 1.
14. Cancian and Meyer, "Work After Welfare," p. 69.
15. Ibid., p. 84.
16. Falk, "Temporary Assistance for Needy Families (TANF) Block Grant," p. 4–5.
17. Igra, "Marriage as Welfare," p. 608.
18. Lindhorst and Mancoske, "The Social and Economic Impact of Sanctions and Time Limits."
19. Smith, "Family Caps in Welfare Reform," p. 151.
20. Falk, "Temporary Assistance for Needy Families (TANF) Block Grant," p. 3.
21. Mink, *Welfare's End,* p. 133.
22. Falk, "Temporary Assistance for Needy Families (TANF) Block Grant," pp. 12–13.
23. Finch and Schott, "The Value of TANF Cash Benefits" p. 1.
24. Pollitt, "The Poor," p. 10.
25. Seccombe, James, and Walters, "'They Think You Ain't Much of Nothing,'" p. 859.
26. Ibid.
27. Anderson, Halter, and Gryzlak, "Difficulties After Leaving TANF."
28. Lindhorst and Mancoske, "The Social and Economic Impact of Sanctions and Time Limits."
29. Seccombe, James, and Walters, "'They Think You Ain't Much of Nothing,'" p. 859.
30. Conniff, "The Right Welfare Reform," p. 5.
31. Falk, "The Temporary Assistance for Needy Families (TANF) Block Grant," pp. 8–9.
32. Ibid.
33. Alfred and Chlup, "Neoliberalism, Illiteracy, and Poverty," pp. 241–243.
34. Penny, "What's the Point of Smashing the Glass Ceiling?" p. 18.
35. Wilson, *The Truly Disadvantaged,* p. 73.
36. Clawson and Trice, "Poverty As We Know It."
37. Bonilla-Silva, *Racism Without Racists,* p. 7.

38. Center for American Progress, "A New Force for America's Families."

39. Povich, Roberts, and Mather, "Low-Income Working Mothers and State Policy."

40. Ehrenreich and Hochschild, "Global Women in the New Economy."

41. Luscombe, "Confidence Women."

42. American Civil Liberties Union, *Title IX: Gender Equity in Education.*

43. US Department of Labor, "Women in the Labor Force."

44. US Bureau of Labor Statistics, "Usual Weekly Earnings of Wage and Salary Workers."

45. White House Council on Women and Girls, "Keeping America's Women Moving Forward."

46. The term *reproductive work* entails the work that is performed predominantly by women within the family to maintain and nurture current and future generations of workers. This work is not considered labor because it is unpaid.

47. Miller, "Pay Gap Is Because of Gender, Not Jobs," p. B3.

48. Chemaly, "Women Don't Fear Power, Power Fears Women."

49. Goldstein, "Nora Ephron and Why Women Take Jill Abramson's Firing Personally."

10

Race

JON JETER, A *WASHINGTON POST* BUREAU CHIEF FOR SOUTH AFRICA, wrote in October 2013 that "for every dollar in assets owned by whites in the United States, blacks own less than a nickel, a racial divide that is wider than South Africa's at any point during the apartheid era."[1] In doing so, he exposed the reality of a stark divide between the wealth of white Americans and that of black Americans.

The Survey of Income and Program Participation, undertaken by the US Census Bureau, is considered the most comprehensive source of data on household wealth in the United States by race and ethnicity. The Pew Research Center analyzed these data on the net worth of households in 2009. The results showed that the median wealth of white households was twenty times that of black households and eighteen times that of Hispanic households. Specifically, the median net worth of white households was $113,149, compared to $5,677 for black households and $6,325 for Hispanic households.[2] Since the government began publishing such data in 1984, these ratios have never before been so lopsided.

As discussed in Chapter 3, the bursting of the housing market bubble in 2006, and the Great Recession that followed from late 2007 to 2009, took a heavier toll on the wealth and assets of minorities than on the wealth and assets of whites. Hispanic households lost 66 percent of their net worth and black households lost 53 percent, while white households lost 16 percent.[3] According to data gathered by the Survey of Consumer Finances, conducted every three years by the Board of Governors of the Federal Reserve System, whereas whites collectively held 88.4 percent of the nation's wealth in 2010—blacks collectively held 2.7 percent and Hispanics 4.0 percent.[4]

These numbers embody a terrible paradox that becomes apparent when we put them in the context of the historical forces that generated the wealth of the United States in the first place. It is critical to recognize that a terrible reality of oppression, conquest, disadvantage, and destitution—both historical and contemporary—hides behind these numbers. This **racialization** of economic disadvantage happened over the course of centuries. Thus, any serious analysis of the racial/class divide must begin by tracking the historical forces that spawned and undergirded, presaged and preordained the degree and intensity of inequality that we perceive between black and white Americans today. We must begin by considering the underlying intersectionality between race and class.

The Complex Dynamics of Race and Class

There is nothing simple about the interconnection between race and class. Race originates in class but then takes on a life of its own. Class has an objective reality, race a subjective and ideological one. Race originates in class, but cannot be reduced to class. Yet it is impossible to gauge the dynamic that race and class concurrently create without first grasping the interplay between the two.

In order to understand the complex intersectionality of race and class, it is paramount to recognize that, in many ways, the same process of capitalist accumulation that created class also created race. This is not to discount or underestimate the political, legal, cultural, and psychological embellishments that evolved to exaggerate and amplify racial categories. Neither is it to trivialize the profound, complicated role race plays in how people experience their lives.

However, for the purposes of our inquiry into the origins of inequality between different racial groups, it is critical to emphasize the fact that race proved to be a useful and enduring tool to expedite the process of appropriation and exploitation essential for capitalist accumulation. And from this underlying motivation emerged laws, customs, political ideas, social practices, and ideologies that shaped and reinforced race-based oppressive structures.

Colonization and colonial conquest marginalized large swaths of humanity, whether they were the indigenous in the Americas, Africa, or Asia. And the racialization of these groups was a corollary to their expropriation and dispossession. Michael Omi and Howard Winant describe racialization as the process by which racial meaning is extended to a previously racially unclassified social entity—such as a group, a relationship, or a social practice.[5] This occurs when culturally diverse groups such as the Navaho, the Hopi, the Cherokee, and the Iroquois are all classified as "Native American" (or "Indian"), or when different tribal groups such as the Ibo, the Yoruba, the Fulani, and the Hausa are all forced into the category "black." This also occurs when the relationship between slave master and slave, contrary to its practice in antiquity, is delineated in racial terms.

The logic that guided this process was integral to the European exploration of the "new worlds" and the Europeans' "discovery of races" as they encountered different members of the human family. Omi and Winant explain how these encounters challenged the Europeans' existing notions of the origin and evolution of human beings. The Europeans doubted that people so different from them could even be human, defined as having a "soul." Through new theories of "polygenesis," it was argued that these other peoples had emerged out of different evolutionary processes and therefore were not human in the way that the Europeans were human. The discovery and conquest of the "new worlds" cemented in the minds of the Europeans their own superior status by virtue of their race, their "whiteness."

The indigenous of the Americas were socially constructed in terms of their "racial markers"—skin color, facial configuration or phenotype, and hair texture. To the Europeans, comparing all these features with their own familiar "norm" revealed the indigenous peoples' intrinsic inferiority, intellectual incapacity, and decadent moral character. Similarly, the tribal and atavistic religions and cultures in the Americas struck the Europeans as "savagery" and "born of the devil." The fact that the indigenous were not Christian was considered further proof of their decadence and inferiority.

The communal ownership of resources and property that most indigenous peoples practiced was looked upon as "uncivilized" and wasteful. It was considered no different than how animals lived. In the eyes of the Europeans, the indigenous wasted time and did not work hard, did not apply themselves, did not utilize the land and its resources to the fullest capacity—meaning they did not "exploit" those resources as, supposedly, God intended.

All of this was a sure indication that the native peoples of the Americas did not deserve the opulence that nature had bestowed upon them. And since the native peoples were squandering this natural bounty, it was "moral and ethical" for the Europeans to honor nature and God's generosity by taking that bounty—by force, violence, and genocide if necessary—and putting it to good use.

Racialization, which was fundamentally rooted in this interpretation of human diversity, was therefore the process in which "different" was also defined as deficient, inferior, and undeserving. As Omi and Winant contend, this presumed deficiency became the foremost argument and justification for conquest, the wholesale "expropriation of property, the denial of political rights, the introduction of slavery and other forms of coercive labor, as well as outright extermination."[6] Each of these practices was fundamental to the process that enabled the European colonizers to transfer enormous wealth—natural resources, minerals, slave labor—to their own coffers. This is the wealth that became foundational in spurring the industrial revolution and the development of capitalism in Europe and North America.

To grasp this dynamic of a common etiology, or cause, of racial formation and appropriation for all colonized peoples—and its intricate correlation with the process of **primitive capital accumulation**—let us begin by sampling of some of the episodes in the historical experience of nations since European colonialism extended its firm hold over much of the world. It is fundamental to recognize that the impoverishment of black Americans and the destitution of third world countries are part and parcel of this same web. The "color line" that W. E. B. Du Bois predicted would be the "problem of the twentieth century" embraces this dual reality—black and white, third world and first world.

Most of us are familiar with the genocide against the Native Americans (the main subject of Chapter 11) and the Atlantic slave trade, which generated untold riches for European "conquistadors" and slave-trading nations, such as Britain, France, the Netherlands, Portugal, Spain, and the United States. Adam Hochschild tells the story of the Belgian conquest of the Congo, a legacy from which much of central Africa still hasn't recovered. In his book *King Leopold's Ghost: A Story of Greed, Terror, and Heroism in Colonial Africa,* he begins by relating the experiences of Edmund Morel, a British journalist who had been hired by a Liverpool shipping company to oversee the loading and unloading of ships that were traveling back and forth between Europe and the Congo in central Africa.[7]

At the port of Antwerp, Belgium, in either 1897 or 1898, Morel sees ships from the Congo "arriving filled to the hatch covers with ivory and rubber." But when the ships are steaming back to Congo, they mostly carry "army officers, firearms and ammunitions. There is no trade going on here," Morel realizes. "Little or nothing is being exchanged for the rubber and ivory. . . . [R]iches were streaming to Europe with almost no goods being sent back to Africa to pay for them."[8] He quickly recognizes the telltale signs of slave labor. This "discovery" led Morel to a lifelong campaign to bring to light atrocities associated with the almost "genocidal plundering" of the Congo by King Leopold and Belgian colonialism at large, which might have taken as many as 10 million lives.

Today, the wholesale looting of the country now known as the Democratic Republic of Congo (DRC) continues. A corrupt, incompetent government stands by as people continue to die by the millions in civil wars fueled by rival groups trying to control the rich trade in diamonds, gold, uranium, copper, and new wonder minerals such as columbo-tantalite or coltan that are needed to produce cellular phones, computers, jet engines, missiles, and ships. Along with "blood diamonds," now there is "blood coltan," alluding to the tremendous human cost that the DRC pays as profits are wrung from the extraction and trade of the mineral. The story of the DRC and the transfer of wealth that shocked Morel had started centuries earlier and was repeated on every continent of the Southern Hemisphere—from Asia to South America—that came face to face with European colonialism.

Uruguayan writer Eduardo Galeano refers to this "five centuries of pillage" as an unending process of bloodletting from the "open veins of Latin America." The gold, silver, and sugar of the colonies built European capital—and impoverished Latin America.[9] Particularly poignant is the story of Potosi, Bolivia. The Cerro Rico—or "rich hill"—produced so much silver for the Spaniards that it was said they could have built a silver bridge from Potosi, across the Atlantic, to the "door of the royal palace" in Seville, Spain. This was silver that fed into European banks and stimulated the growth of industries, factories, and markets—the mainstays of the burgeoning capitalist business enterprise on that continent.

The "rich hill" is said to have "devoured" at least 8 million indigenous Latin Americans in the three centuries after the rich vein of silver was discovered in 1545. The Spaniards bored 5,000 tunnels into the hill and forced the indigenous Latin Americans into the cold, airless mines of the Andes. The resulting amount of silver shipped to Europe over the next century and a half was three times Europe's total reserves, as estimated by noted economic historian Earl Jefferson Hamilton.[10] Galeano, along with economists Paul Baran, Andre Gunder Frank, and many others, maintain that this silver not only stimulated European economic development, "but one may say made it possible."[11] By contrast, Potosi today is a poor town in one of the hemisphere's poorest countries.

In India, on the other side of the world, chroniclers of the Mughal Empire, which ruled India at the time when the British East India Company made its appearance, estimated that 100,000 million pounds sterling was being drained out of the country every year. The British were taking cotton from India to the spinning jennies and power looms in England and then shipping the assembled cloth back to India to be sold at a price with which the fine muslin cloth woven by the Indians could not compete.[12]

Until the 1750s, before the British arrived, India was the main producer of fine muslin textiles, which earned India an export surplus. By the early 1800s, British colonialism had reversed the process by demolishing the Indian textile industry. Between 1820 and 1840, 12,000 textile markets controlled and operated by peasants and entrepreneurs were closed down as Britain monopolized them. A supplier of cloth and muslin no longer, India became an exporter of raw materials such as cotton and indigo. The capital gleaned from the Indian market and its raw materials helped finance England's industrial revolution. At the beginning of the colonial experience, the subcontinent was richer than the British crown. At the end of the colonial period, it was measurably poorer.

Trinidad-born historian and philosopher C. L. R. James considers the Atlantic slave trade and the enslavement of Africans in America to be the most epic event in the history of colonialism, one that transformed the economic and sociopolitical landscape of two continents.[13] In the three centuries of the European slave trade, from roughly 1550 to 1850, no one knows exactly how many Africans were taken from their native land to labor first in the mines and then the plantations of the Americas. Conservative estimates put the number at 15 million. Others have said that it could be 50 million or even higher. Countless numbers of Africans died during the merciless transatlantic voyage, in slave raids, and in wars, while others died simply waiting either to be shipped or sold.

It was the capital gained from the slave trade and slavery that "fertilized" the industrial revolution in Europe and later in North America. The slave trade and slavery were fundamental for the development of capitalism in both regions. Karl Marx considered slavery in the Americas to be fundamental for the development of capitalism not only in the New World, but in Europe as well. As early as 1847, he made the following observation: "Direct slavery is just as much the pivot of bourgeois industry as machinery, credits, etc. Without slavery you have no cotton; without cotton you have no modern industry. It is slavery that has given colonies their value; it is colonies that have created world trade, and it is world trade that is the pre-condition of large scale industry. Thus, slavery is an economic category of the greatest importance."[14]

German economist Ernest Mandel made a rough estimate of the value of the gold and silver taken from Latin America just up to 1660, the capital extracted solely by France from the slave trade, the profits from slave labor in the British Antilles, and the British looting of India. Eduardo Galeano, in reporting Mandel's estimate, writes: "The total exceeds the capital invested in all European industrial enterprises operated by steam in about 1800. This enormous mass of capital . . . created a favorable climate for investment in Europe, stimulated the 'spirit of enterprise' [or Max Weber's 'spirit of capitalism'], and directly financed the establishment of manufacturers, which in turn gave a strong thrust to the Industrial Revolution."[15]

Large-scale accumulation of capital was a prerequisite for the emergence of capitalism in Europe. The colonial expansion of Europe, facilitated by beliefs about the natural inferiority of the new races "discovered" in the colonized lands, yielded a process that Marx called "the primitive accumulation of capital," which he described as follows in the context of colonial plunder:

> The discovery of gold and silver in America, the extirpation, enslavement, and entombment in the mines of the aboriginal population, the beginning of the conquest and looting of the East Indies, the turning of Africa into a warren for the hunting of black skins, signalized the rosy dawn of the era of capitalist production. These idyllic proceedings are the chief momenta of primitive accumulation. This phase of the accumulation process was accomplished not only by domestic exploitation, but also by the looting of traditional stores

of non-European peoples and the fostering of a new system of slavery to exploit their labor.[16]

There are clear historical processes that create the wealth of certain nations and the poverty of others—the enormous affluence of some groups and the grinding deprivation of others. The wealth and poverty that we see in the United States today have these historical antecedents. In order to understand present-day inequality, we must visit the forces that created it. This is especially true when we consider the linkages between class and race—or, in other words, when we try to explain why poverty and economic inequality are so entrenched and stubborn in African American and Native American communities. This is particularly ironic since it was the labor of the enslaved African Americans, working on plantations carved out of land seized from the Native Americans, that created the seed capital for the industrialization and economic development of the United States, making it into a global powerhouse.

Slavery and Capitalism

There was a profound irony in relegating entire groups of humanity to a system of confinement and servitude in mines and plantations of the New World to feed an economic system—capitalism—based on the ideas of free markets and wage labor. These ideas aside, in the creation of capital it mattered little if the labor producing it was free or enslaved—especially since the enslaved labor of the plantations of the US South produced a surplus value unsurpassed by what the farms of the North, working with wage labor, produced.

Kenneth Stampp considers "black slavery in the South [to be] the most productive and profitable mode of production."[17] Blacks performed tasks that white labor considered too backbreaking and dangerous. Blacks had no say in the matter. They worked all year long, clearing and preparing land for cotton, sugar, or tobacco. They planted and harvested—including doing all other ancillary work connected with the production and preparation of crops and food, such as constructing and repairing buildings and tools. The list of all the work the slaves did for the maintenance of the slave masters, their families, and their property is indeed endless. Slaves had very little time to call their own. But in the little time they had for themselves, they grew their own food, stitched their own clothes, and took care of their quarters. For the plantation owners, there was very little, if any, maintenance cost for the slaves.

Carter Wilson has compiled data calculated by economists to quantify the enhanced degree of profitability that enslaved labor produced compared to free or wage labor. On the average, the numbers demonstrate that income grew 30 percent faster in Southern plantations worked by slaves compared to the farms in the North employing wage labor. Similarly, Southern plantations were 40 percent more cost-efficient than Northern farms.[18]

Slave labor was captive labor, which in itself provided many benefits. The slave could find no legal protection for transgressions against his or her human rights. Wilson writes: "The amount of work a master could extract from a slave was limited only by the life of a slave. . . . [C]learly, planters were able to extract a higher level of work output from slaves than they could from free laborers."[19]

Historians increasingly agree that the inestimable riches that slave labor garnered for Southern planters were critically important for the economic development of the entire nation. Regardless of how violent and bloody the Civil War was and how it threatened the unity of the nation, this does not distract from the fundamental logic of this position, which sees the economic destinies of the South and the North as inextricably bound in the institution and fruits of slavery—indelibly entrenched in a violent, racist ideology.

The development of capitalism is rooted in significant and intricate ways in this **peculiar institution** and the vast riches that the slave labor embedded in it produced. Sven Beckert and Seth Rockman, in their book *Slavery's Capitalism: A New History of American Economic Development,* maintain that slavery and capitalism were deeply entangled with one another as the United States grew into an economic power in the nineteenth century. As Rockman writes in one of his papers:

> By connecting the stories of New York financiers, Virginia slavers, Connecticut shipbuilders, and Alabama land speculators, historians have made slavery central to the history of capitalism. In an age of industry predicated on the transformation of slave-grown cotton into textiles, the plantation and the factory must necessarily be discussed together rather than separately. In the blur of commodities and capital that flowed between regions, it becomes harder to locate the boundary between a capitalist North and a slave South.[20]

Rockman compares the significance of cotton to the industrial economy of the nineteenth century to oil's importance in the twentieth and twenty-first centuries. The United States was the Saudi Arabia of cotton. Cotton was the most valuable thing that the United States produced, and it became the country's most important export commodity. Between 1816 and 1820, cotton constituted 39 percent of the total value of exports, whereas from 1836 to 1840 it constituted 63 percent of the total value.[21] Cotton, therefore, connected the Southern plantation economy to the Northern banking industry, New England textile factories, and the economy of Great Britain.

The money brought by the export of cotton led to the proliferation of some of the largest banks, investment houses, and insurance and shipping companies. Income from the export of cotton provided the lifeblood for a variety of such enterprises, which became fundamental to the industrial revolution of the United States and the development of the country as a capitalist nation. Some of the most revered and renowned universities in the United States—Brown, Harvard, Yale, Princeton, Rutgers, and many more—"were soaked in the sweat, tears and often blood" of slaves and Native Americans. Craig S. Wilder documents how the "founding, financing and development of higher education in the colonies were thoroughly intertwined with the economic and social forces that transformed West and Central Africa through the slave trade and the devastated indigenous nations of the Americas. The academy was a beneficiary and defender of these processes."[22]

Over 80 percent of the raw cotton that was fed into Great Britain's textile mills came from the US South. The textiles produced in the factories in Manchester, Lancashire, and other mill towns accounted for almost half of all British exports. (And it was this factory-produced cheap cloth that flooded the markets in India, and drove the indigenous craftspeople to destitution and bankruptcy.) The economy of Great Britain therefore relied in potent ways on the cotton produced by slave labor in the plantations of the US South.

Cotton also fed the industrial revolution in textiles in the United States. For instance, 67 percent of the cotton produced in 1860 was consumed by the textile factories in New England alone. Historian Ronald Bailey writes that as the Civil War loomed ahead, "New England's economy, so fundamentally [dependent] upon the textile industry, was inextricably intertwined to the labor of black people working as slaves in the US South."[23] Massachusetts senator Charles Sumner, an avowed abolitionist, "decried 'the unholy alliance of the lords of the lash and the lords of the loom'—a damning acknowledgement of the impossibility of New England's industrial revolution without access to slave-grown cotton."[24]

Cotton produced by slaves—commodified, chattel human beings—was the most critical and indispensable element in the emergence of financial institutions, technologies, and industries in the United States, undergirding the country's takeoff as an economic powerhouse and a modern capitalist nation. Cotton, sugar, tobacco, and rum were the new luxury items that colonialism and conquest produced. They grew on land that was seized from the indigenous peoples who had lived there for generations. It was produced with the labor of human beings who had been bought, sold, and owned as property. Racialization had rendered them inferior beings, which vastly facilitated their subjugation and transformation into commodity and chattel.

Thus it is an incontrovertible fact that much of the wealth of the United States came from the surplus value created by the labor of enslaved blacks—commodified human beings who were critical to the emergence of modern capitalism and indispensable for the country's commercial ascent.[25] One can only speculate what trajectory America's economic destiny would have taken in the absence of cotton and slavery. Racial categories were contrived to facilitate appropriation and oppression for the sake of economic gain. The primary goal was to dehumanize entire groups of people to justify their treatment as property, for the economic benefit of those who had the ability to make these determinations due to their political and economic power. In the United States and elsewhere, racial indignity abetted the wholesale oppression of black people for the sake of economic gain.

Frantz Fanon was able to capture the tortured and damaged spirit and psyche that racism created. He was a black man, a humanist, and a radical psychiatrist who was born in Martinique. He dedicated his life to serving as a witness to the liberation struggles in Algeria against French colonialism and documenting the indignity of the colonial experience in books that are read all over the world.

In the United States, we see the same penetrating exposition on the thorny and compelling relationship between race and self in the writings of W. E. B. Du Bois. He famously wrote: "It is a peculiar sensation, this double-consciousness, this sense of always looking at one's self through the eyes of others, of measuring one's soul by the tape of a world that looks on in amused contempt and pity. One ever feels his two-ness—an American, a Negro: two souls, two thoughts, two unreconciled strivings: two warring ideals in one dark body, whose dogged strength alone keeps it from being torn asunder."[26]

Even though Fanon recognized the economic aspects of colonial plunder in facilitating capitalist accumulation, he experienced race personally and insisted that at its most basic level, "it was [ultimately] a question of one race dominating another."[27] How can one separate the violent injunction of race, which questions one's fundamental humanity, from the indignity of class oppression, which denies one the opportunity to survive as a human being? As Fanon wrote:

> This world divided into compartments, this world cut into two is inhabited by two different species. . . . The governing race is first and foremost those who come from elsewhere, those who are unlike the original inhabitants, "the others." The settler's town is a strongly built town, all made of stone and steel. It is a brightly lit town. . . . [T]he native town is a hungry town, starved of bread, of meat, of shoes, of coal, of light. The native town is a town on its knees, a town wallowing in the mire. It is a town of niggers.[28]

To break the stranglehold of what Fanon called the "geography of hunger" and begin the process of "self-liberation," it is imperative to demystify race and racism by talking of its scheming, opportunistic, and violent past to unmask it for what it really is: a sinister vehicle to divide and conquer, so some can benefit as others "wallow in the mire."

The Present-Day Landscape of Race and Class

The most enduring legacy of historical racism in the United States today is the fact that, generally speaking, blacks and whites continue to occupy spaces in which they seldom encounter each other. As of 2009, 62 percent of all blacks in the United States continue to live in highly segregated metropolitan areas—a reality that has remained unchanged despite all efforts to change it.[29]

Each community, black or white, "provides a distinct social environment" and continues to be characterized by the privileges or the disadvantages that they have historically borne. Lauren Kirvo, Ruth Peterson, and Danielle Kuhl observe: "Indeed, whites live almost exclusively in highly advantaged neighborhoods, while blacks and Latinos reside in highly disadvantaged local communities. This combination of segregation and ethnoracial differentials in the social and economic conditions provides the basic structural context within which people of different races and ethnicities live and social problems play out."[30]

The ghetto, euphemistically called the "inner city," has historical antecedents. Racism of the past created the ghetto. During the Great Migration, between 1915 and 1970, more than 6 million blacks moved out of the South to cities across the Northeast, Midwest, and West. They were intent on escaping the Jim Crow racism of the South and the violence perpetrated by the Klan and other white supremacist groups. The brief period of hope and progress that Reconstruction (1865–1877) delivered had been quickly extinguished by conservative forces in the South, with help from white terrorism. Joe Feagin and Clairece Booher-Feagin describe how white terrorists killed, maimed, and raped thousands and "gradually destroyed the often progressive southern governments."[31] Furthermore, the Supreme Court, in its decision in *Plessy v. Ferguson* (1896), upheld racial segregation and legitimized its practice in every segment of society by arguing that white racist attitudes were natural and that no legislation could eradicate such attitudes.

From 1880 to 1924, almost 23 million European immigrants had come to the industrial North, and they had formed the majority of the mining and manufacturing workers. But nativist, anti-immigration forces prevailed upon Congress to pass the National Origins Act (1924), which nearly halted immigration from Europe and Asia entirely. African Americans stepped in to fill the void left by the decline in immigration. Violence and segregation pushed them out of the South, and entry-level jobs opening up in the flourishing factories pulled them to the North, inspiring the Great Migration, as black people moved to what many saw as the "promised land," with the hopes of being embraced by the "warmth of other suns," to borrow Isabel Wilkerson's evocative phrase.[32]

They might have escaped the brutal racism of the South, but they were still subject to **restrictive covenants** and segregationist customs practiced in the Northern cities, which were often enforced through violence, compelling the new migrants to settle in separate, walled-off neighborhoods. Race riots, burnings, and bombings in the urban North took the place of lynchings in the Southern countryside. The Chicago riots of 1919, which shut the city down for thirteen days, were some of the worst the country had seen. New York City, Detroit, St. Louis, and towns in New Jersey saw occasional rioting well into the 1960s. Segregation suffocated African Americans at all levels of society—in housing, schools, public facilities, public transportation, parks, swimming pools, public events, restaurants, lunch counters, hotels, and hospitals.

Despite the difficulties faced by these African American migrants in their new communities, more black men and women now had jobs compared to in the 1980s or later, even though most of the jobs were the "least desirable, lowest paying and the most unstable."[33] It is a terrible irony of fate that from the perspective of today, we can actually be wistful for those earlier times when it comes to the matter of jobs.

In his narration in the documentary "Throwaway People," Roger Wilkins talks about the Washington, D.C., neighborhood called Shaw, which drew many migrant families from the South. They came to low-skilled jobs that still paid enough for a man to support his family. They lived in the ghetto, but there was stability.[34] During those early years of blacks' first migration to the urban North, 72 percent of black families with children under age eighteen were male-headed. Most women who headed families were widows.[35]

The ghetto community was vertically integrated by class, so that rich, poor, and middle-class black families lived in the same segregated neighborhoods. They attended the same churches; their children went to the same schools; people patronized the same local businesses and banks—most of which were locally owned. Children saw individuals who were unemployed, families with absent fathers, and people involved in crime. But they also saw many people who were regularly going to work and returning to their families at the end of the day, and recognized that most of their neighbors were not involved in criminal activity. The neighborhood provided role models and work and family norms for young people to emulate.

Between 1910 and 1940, more and more African Americans found jobs in industries such as steel, railroads, and meatpacking. Most jobs open to blacks were unskilled and often dangerous, and the hiring of blacks instigated walkouts and protest from white workers, who were accustomed to working in all-white plants. Ford Motor Company was one of the first automotive manufacturers to hire blacks extensively, often for skilled positions. But prior to World War II, other major companies refused to hire blacks for anything but menial jobs. However, in the booming defense industries that came on the heels of the war, both African Americans and women found decent-paying jobs in shipyards and aircraft factories. By 1950, blacks were increasingly finding jobs in chemical, rubber, and metal factories. By the end of the 1970s, almost half of all African Americans were working as operators, fabricators, transporters, and laborers.

Compared to the rest of the country, these were still desperately poor communities, and were regularly subjected to the abuses and insults of racism that had led to their creation in the first place, but there was a certain stability in people's lives.

The Complex Dynamics of the Inner City

It is difficult to separate the complex dynamics that created the inner city as we see it today, with its myriad problems of crime, violence, incarceration,

---

MAKING CONNECTIONS
What About Reparations?

Slavery and the wealth wrung from the blood, sweat, and tears of black people hoisted the United States to a position of unprecedented prosperity and power in the pantheon of nations. But what did blacks get in return for their unmitigated sacrifice? Ta-Nehisi Coates, in his 2014 article "The Case for Reparations" in *The Atlantic,* quotes the editors from the *Chicago Tribune,* who wrote in 1891: "they have been taught Christian civilization, and to speak the noble English language instead of some African gibberish. The account is square with the ex-slaves." Coates quotes a similar sentiment expressed in 1906 by a John Pendleton Kennedy, author of *Swallow Barn,* who wrote that "no people have ever passed from barbarism to civilization" as rapidly as the blacks, with slavery as the midwife, the conduit. What more, he asked, could blacks want?

After centuries of slavery and unspeakable oppression, instead of recompense, the vile racism of these messages found expression in the decades of brazen discrimination, segregation, predation, violence, terrorism, police brutality, and incarceration that black people have routinely lived through. And today, though the conditions of their lives are better than they were fifty years ago at the end of the 1950s and early 1960s, blacks continue to live markedly different lives than whites. They are poorer. Even middle-class blacks have significantly less wealth than their white counterparts. Black poverty is distinctly different. Coates refers to President Lyndon Johnson's historic civil rights speech, in which Johnson described black poverty as being "obstinately different . . . [a] consequence of ancient brutality, past injustice, and present prejudice." It is a stubborn impoverishment that continues to corrode both materially and spiritually.

(continues)

What About Reparations?

And even when African Americans have struggled against the odds and tried to attain a certain degree of dignity in their lives, they have been pushed down through predation, intimidation, and fraud. If homeownership is the ultimate proof of economic success, blacks' attempts at it have often been foiled by real estate brokers, lenders, and banks, who have made millions through unscrupulous practices. The discriminatory policies of the Federal Housing Administration and the redlining practiced by the lending agencies simply facilitated this chicanery.

There have been openings—few and far between—that history accorded to bring about restitution and uplift in the lives of black people. But each time, the promise has been reneged. The dream of Reconstruction died when federal troops were withdrawn. Similarly, the New Deal and the GI Bill fell short when an atmosphere rife with racism and structural handicaps left blacks empty-handed. Coates's article is filled with an intense moral outrage at the utter injustice that continues to be meted out to African Americans by a country built on their backs.

In 1989, Congressman John Conyers Jr. introduced a bill in Congress (House Resolution 40) with the aspiration to have this august assembly study the enduring trauma of slavery and consider reparation proposals for African Americans. But since then, with the passage of time, the case for reparations has weakened, even though the passage of time has done little to ameliorate the grievous injury wrought upon African Americans through slavery and decades of discrimination and violence. And even if reparations are considered, how can money alone suffice? What amount will capture "the multi-century plunder of black people," as Coates asks? Can the country ever fully repay African Americans?

Perhaps reparations require a final and honest accounting and purging of the "collective soul" sullied through centuries of crimes against the collective humanity of black people. As Coates writes poignantly: "What I'm talking about is more than recompense for past injustices—more than a handout, a payoff, hush money, or a reluctant bribe. What I'm talking about is a national reckoning that would lead to spiritual renewal. Reparations would mean a revolution of the American consciousness."

unemployment, substance abuse, substandard schools, female-headed families, absent fathers, and, above all, as Kenneth Clark calls it, the tremendous "burden of despair."[36]

Two reasons, however, stand out persuasively as providing some rationale on the instability and volatility of the inner city. First, structural changes in the economy caused the disappearance of industrial jobs on which large segments of the African American work force depended, leading to the crumbling of the inner-city communities. Therefore, it would be accurate to assert that the breakdown in the ghetto community is primarily rooted in the destabilization of its economic foundation. Second, the exodus of middle-class and upper-class blacks from the inner city, following the passage of the major civil rights legislation, unhinged the lives of those left behind in ways no one could have predicted.

Somewhere around the 1970s, fundamental changes started occurring in the economy. Nationally, service jobs started steadily replacing the factory jobs on which working-class blacks depended. In time, technology, globalization, and increasing financialization of economic activity meant that inner-city residents had fewer and fewer of the kinds of jobs that in earlier years had been their steppingstones to a certain degree of economic solvency.

Since black men were highly concentrated in manufacturing, economic globalization and the subsequent shift of manufacturing jobs offshore meant that black workers were affected more adversely than white and Hispanic workers. Manufacturing jobs that were unionized had higher salaries and carried benefits such as health insurance, vacations, and sick leave. The nonunionized service jobs paid minimum wage and provided no benefits.

As factories closed and people's disposable incomes fell precipitously, retail and service jobs started to leave the cities too. Supermarkets, banks, department stores, doctors' offices, restaurants, and movie halls started moving to the suburbs in record numbers—leaving behind liquor stores, small laundries, pawn shops, currency exchanges, quick loan services, and a few fast food restaurants.

Without transportation, inner-city residents had very little chance to reach the jobs that were moving farther and farther away. The new jobs that were being added in metropolitan areas, separated, perhaps, by a bus or subway ride, required skills in computers, information technology, accounting, and financial services—skills the inner-city residents did not have and therefore were unable to benefit from. A "serious mismatch" became apparent in the education distribution that poor minorities had and the changing educational requirements of the transforming economy.[37]

Even public policies joined this process of what Loïc Wacquant calls the "devalorization and desertification" of the ghetto. Federal, state, and city governments refused to "throw money into a black hole" even as they denounced the urban schools to be decrepit.[38] As this process of abandonment has become institutionalized, "it is no exaggeration," writes Wacquant, "to say that, in broad swathes of the historic Black Belt, the regular wage-labour economy has been superseded by the irregular and illegal street economy as the primary source of employment and income."[39] Or as sociologist William Julius Wilson writes, "as the prospects for employment diminish, other alternatives such as welfare and the underground economy are not only increasingly relied on, they come to be seen as a way of life."[40]

In a recent study, Marc Levine of the University of Wisconsin–Milwaukee looks at the rates of employment of black males in the nation's largest metropolitan areas in 2010 as compared to the figures in 1970. In all instances, there was a precipitous drop in the number of black men ages sixteen to sixty-four who had jobs. In 1970, 73.4 percent of Milwaukee black men had jobs; by 2010 the number dropped to 44.7 percent. In Detroit, only 43 percent of all eligible black men had jobs in 2010, compared to 72 percent in 1970. In Chicago, where 72 percent had jobs in 1970, only 48 percent did in 2010.[41]

In city after city, Levine documents the crisis that black men are facing in securing gainful employment and concludes that "over the past four decades, the job market for working-age African American males has essentially collapsed in cities across the country. By 2010, in five of the nation's largest metropolitan areas, fewer than half of working-age black males held jobs, compared to 85 percent forty years ago. . . . Many innercity neighborhoods across the US continued to experience the social and economic distress that occurs, to borrow William Julius Wilson's evocative expression, when work disappears."[42] Since 1970, white men have also experienced job loss, but according to Levine the job loss for whites has not been nearly as steep as for blacks.

The continued presence of racial bias and negative attitudes toward urban black men also becomes a stumbling block as they seek employment.[43] Poor black men's social isolation, their "lack of sustained interaction with individuals and institutions that represent mainstream society," also means that they have limited or no access to informal job networks.[44]

Beginning in the 1970s, successive generations of blacks started falling off the economic ladder. Their communities started disintegrating; fewer and fewer adults were forming families; children were being born to mothers who were children themselves; schools were becoming dysfunctional; neighborhoods were becoming contested territories for gangs and drug dealers; random gun violence was threatening the lives of the residents of these communities; and more and more young black men were facing incarceration, without any hope that life would be different once they "did time" and returned to society.

In the absence of opportunities in the legitimate capitalist economy, an "outlaw capitalism" took root in the inner city. Sudhir Venkatesh, who coined this term, writes that much economic activity in the poorest parts of America's inner cities began taking the form of drug dealing, extortion, gambling, prostitution, selling stolen property, and many other such schemes controlled largely by street gangs. Very much like mainstream capitalism, this outlaw capitalism created its own winners and losers. Gang leaders netted small fortunes, but for "the rest of the community, the payout of this outlaw economy—drug addiction and public violence—was considerably less appealing."[45]

Taking note of the ever-present danger of violence, Wacquant notes poignantly: "The atmosphere of dull tension that pervades the hyper-ghetto [had become] similar to [the ubiquitous violence and unpredictability] that stamp daily life in a country ravaged by civil war."[46] As the notoriety of these inner cities spread, so did their social isolation, deepening their segregation from the rest of the country.

Communities Segregated by Intense Poverty

As segregation became entrenched, so did pockets of concentrated poverty. According to the US Census Bureau, between 2006 and 2010, blacks had the smallest proportion of the US population, just 36 percent, living in the census tract with the lowest poverty rate. In comparison, 67 percent of whites and 71 percent of Asians lived in the census tract with the lowest poverty rate. Almost half of all African Americans, 47 percent, lived in the census tract with the highest poverty rate.[47]

In 1987, William Julius Wilson tracked the process by which poverty became more and more concentrated in the nation's fifty largest cities. In city after city, even as the total population fell, the number of individuals who were poor increased. In the five largest major cities—New York, Chicago, Los Angeles, Philadelphia, and Detroit—total population fell by 9 percent between 1970 and 1980, yet the population living in poverty increased by 22 percent.[48] Moreover, the population living in areas of extreme poverty—places where the poverty rate was 40 percent—grew by a staggering 161 percent. Wilson attributed this to the "profound social transformation" that inner-city neighborhoods had undergone, not only in terms of the "increasing rates of social dislocation—crime, joblessness, out-of-wedlock births, female headed families and welfare dependency, but also in the changing economic class structure of the ghetto neighborhoods."[49]

These neighborhoods, which in earlier years had featured vertical integration of lower-, working-, and middle-class professional families, were entering a time when middle-class black families, followed by increasing numbers of stable working-class families, were leaving the inner-city neighborhoods. The civil rights victories of the mid-1960s had cleared the way for these families to move into better neighborhoods with better schools and work toward assimilating into mainstream American society.

Their exodus eroded the local institutions, churches, and schools—and removed the role models who could reinforce the values of education, work, and family.[50] The inner city became home to the poorest of the poor, now bereft of the "social buffer" that might have been able to "deflect the full impact of the kind of prolonged and increasing joblessness that plagued inner city neighborhoods."[51]

The increasing joblessness and the steady out-migration of the middle- and working-class families have created a ripple effect, "resulting in an exponential increase in social dislocation," crime, female-headed families, welfare dependency, out-of-wedlock births, and the like. Even today,

Wilson's 1987 analysis of the tangled web of problems in the inner-city communities of African Americans remains compelling.

In *Stuck in Place: Urban Neighborhoods and the End of Progress Towards Racial Equality,* author Richard Sharkey writes that as of 2012–2013, "over 70 percent of African Americans who live in today's poorest, most racially segregated neighborhoods are from the same families that lived in the ghettos of the 1970s. The American ghetto appears to be inherited."[52]

The Tentative Black Middle Class

Mary Pattillo-McCoy took exception to Wilson's central thesis—about the exodus of the middle class to supposedly greener pastures—in her book, *Black Picket Fences: Privilege and Peril Among the Black Middle Class,* in which she argues that the black middle class could not go very far from the ghetto they tried to leave. In three years of research in Groveland, a black middle-class neighborhood on Chicago's South Side, she found a community that continues to face the reality of racial segregation to the same extent as the black poor.

The middle-class African Americans, very much like their poorer brethren in the deep inner city, and unlike most white middle-class families, "must contend with crime, dilapidated housing, and social disorder in the deteriorating poor neighborhoods which continue to grow in their direction."[53] The inequality between the black middle class and the white is ultimately rooted in their phenomenal wealth disparity; the black middle class is really the black lower-middle class.

In Groveland, the one black doctor and the few African American lawyers are not representative of the black middle class, most of whom hold sales and clerical jobs that pay much less than the professional and managerial jobs that their white counterparts hold. The black middle-class neighborhoods, such as Groveland, far from being enclaves of social mobility and success, are "in constant jeopardy" because of their unique composition and location.[54] But even as the black poor fall off the economic ladder entirely and the black middle class try desperately to hang on to its lowest rungs, a hyper-consumerism runs rampant in Groveland as well as in the ghetto, integrating the lives of the residents with global capitalism in a cynical way.

Television is often the only sustained connection that links the inner city and the enclaves of the black middle class to mainstream American society. Television comes bearing messages of the near mythical power of material objects, such as "Nike Air Jordan basketball shoes, Georgetown jogging suits, Girbaud Jeans, fourteen carat gold necklaces, Karl Kani leather jackets, and Tommy Hilfiger boxer shorts,"[55] to instantly grant social status, confidence, and self-esteem and denote gang affiliation. Black youth have become conspicuous consumers, and multinational corporations have been quick to take notice. Not only have the corporations marketed these commodities using clever tactics, but they have gone a step further and commodified black youth culture in order to sell it back to an eager global consumer market.

As Bakari Kitwana writes: "Today, more and more Black youth are turning to rap music, music videos, designer clothing, popular Black films, and television programs, for values and identity. One can find faces, bodies, attitudes, and language of Black youth attached to slick advertisements that sell what have become global products, whether it's Coca Cola and Pepsi, Reebok and Nike sneakers. Working diligently behind the scene and toward the bottom line are the multinational corporations that produce, distribute and shape these images."[56] In quoting philosopher Cornel West, Kitwana writes: "The irony in our present moment is that just as young black men are murdered, maimed and imprisoned in record numbers, their styles have become disproportionately influential in shaping popular culture."[57]

The Mixed Legacy of Civil Rights and Economic "Progress"

The terrible dislocation that is perceptible in the ghetto community today paradoxically started at the same time when "the most sweeping antidiscrimination programs were enacted and implemented."[58] The women's movement and the civil rights movement revolutionized people's consciousness. There was awareness and an acknowledgment of racial and gendered discrimination and how it relegated people to second-class status. Important legislative initiatives were adopted to redress historical practices of discrimination and injustice that had denied people their rightful opportunities.

In 1954, the Supreme Court's decision in *Brown v. Board of Education* started tearing down some of those historical barriers. It overturned the "separate but equal" doctrine embodied in the 1896 *Plessy v. Ferguson* decision, and the Court argued that the idea of singling people out for unequal treatment was inherently unconstitutional. This paved the path for the groundbreaking initiatives that the country would see in the mid-1960s.

The Civil Rights Act of 1964 made it illegal to discriminate on the basis of sex and race. The walls had started to come down. But did blacks have the skills and education to go out and compete on an equal footing with others who had never been discriminated against? The Civil Rights Act was akin to a second emancipation, but what could that freedom be worth without a real chance to succeed?

As President Johnson said forcefully when he gave the commencement address at Howard University in June 1965:

> But freedom is not enough. You do not wipe away the scars of centuries by saying: Now you are free to go where you want, and do as you desire, and choose the leaders you please. You do not take a person who, for years, has been hobbled by chains and liberate him, bring him up to the starting line of a race and then say, "You are free to compete with all the others," and still justly believe that you have been completely fair. Thus, it is not enough just to open the gates of opportunity. All our citizens must have the ability to walk through those gates. . . . [W]e seek not just freedom but opportunity. We seek not just legal equity but human ability, not just equality as a right and a theory but equality as a fact and equality as a result.[59]

True to his sentiment, President Johnson authorized the practice of affirmative action through an executive order in 1965, requiring employers to "recruit and advance qualified minorities, women, persons with disabilities . . . and incorporate these procedures into the company's written personnel policies."[60] The entire objective of affirmative action was to make civil rights a true reality in the lives of minorities. It was a policy to level the playing field by giving women and people of color an extra hand through preferential hiring and preferential admissions to universities so the realization of a fair and just society could be accelerated.

For universities, this was nothing new; they had always used preferences in the admission process, preferring children of alumni, athletes, and students from particular geographic regions to balance out the student body. With affirmative action they were being asked to take into consideration the race of a student and the burden of history it epitomized.

The legislative victories of the women's movement and the civil rights movement and the changes they brought to the national consciousness altered the landscape of the country in fundamental ways. Doors of opportunity opened up for women and people of color. The country we see today is heir to the historic breakthroughs of that era.

On January 20, 2009, Barack Obama assumed the presidency of the United States. More than 2 million people stood witness as he took the oath of office to become the forty-fourth president and the first black man to occupy the White House. It was one of the proudest moments in the nation's history, proof that the country had risen above the acrimony of race and had regarded a person "not by the color of his skin, but by the content of his character," as slain civil rights leader Martin Luther King Jr. had so hoped. The frosty chill of that January morning did little to cool the enthusiasm of those gathered or the collective optimism of a nation that maybe, even amid a recession and two wars, the country had finally turned a corner.

There is little doubt that women's lives and the lives of people of color have dramatically changed and that the country is a different place than what it was forty-five years ago in the late 1960s. But only half the battle has been won. Even as significant strides are made, deep pockets of deprivation and want still remain. Large segments of people in communities of color, and women on the lower rungs of the class system, have in many ways been left behind.

Generally speaking, white middle-class women and black middle-class men and women have been successful in securing the openings that the Civil Rights Act and affirmative action made possible. Their class, social networks, education, and communities positioned them in favorable ways to benefit from these new opportunities. But since the major civil rights victories of the mid-1960s, the benefits have not trickled down to the rest. Not only are the lives of men and women who have been left behind unchanged, but in many ways their lives are more difficult.

This is the direct consequence of not extending the dialogue about civil rights to one about basic economic rights; any serious discussion about class was left off the table. Ever since, it has been easier to talk about racism and sexism—about tolerance and fighting bigotry—than to draw attention to the economic underpinnings of discrimination and inequality.

The former called forth a change in consciousness, how people behaved with those of other races, and what language they used in public spaces; the latter entails serious discussions of the socioeconomic structures in which racial and gendered inequality are rooted. One called for a change of heart; the other calls for a fundamental change in the structures of wealth and income distribution. One called for political correctness; the other requires a political will to make critical choices in correcting the fundamental structural flaws of society. And therein lies the crux of the matter.

Following the Civil Rights Act of 1964, President Johnson promoted the idea of the Great Society by passing laws that waged a war on poverty (food stamps), guaranteed health care to Americans over sixty-five and the poor (Medicare and Medicaid), and made it possible for four- and five-year-olds from disadvantaged families to start school (Head Start). This was a fitting time to begin an even more comprehensive economic rights agenda. The Poor People's Campaign hoped to do just that.

In November 1967, Martin Luther King Jr. and other leaders of the Southern Christian Leadership Conference began planning a campaign that gave the organization a new direction. As King explained: "We are going to take this movement and we are going to reach out to the poor people in all directions in this country . . . into the Southwest after the Indians, into the west after the Chicanos, into Appalachia after the poor whites, and into the ghettos after Negroes and Puerto Ricans. And we are going to bring them together and enlarge this campaign into something bigger than just a civil rights movement for Negroes."[61]

The new movement, which would become known as the Poor People's Campaign, took King across the nation. As he met with Latinos, Native Americans, and the white poor, he emphasized that the focus of the new movement needed to be on "class issues, on the gulf between the haves and the have-nots."[62] He testified before Congress and underscored the urgent need for jobs, job training, and education if the promises of the Civil Rights Act were to be realized. He had a strong supporter and advocate in Robert Kennedy, the presidential hopeful.

In early April of 1968, King traveled to Memphis, Tennessee, to join a sanitation workers' strike that Richard Kahlenberg describes as "a miniature version of the multiracial class based coalition he was seeking to put together nationally. On this trip, on April 4th, he was assassinated."[63] The cities of the nation went up in flames, as did the hopes for configuring a class-based coalition and redirecting the civil rights movement into one demanding economic rights for the nation's disadvantaged regardless of race.

In his landmark book *The Remedy: Class, Race, and Affirmative Action,* Kahlenberg refers to King and Robert Kennedy as two very different people who were drawn together by their common belief that "class inequality was the central obstacle to justice in the post–civil rights era."[64] After the assassination of King, Kennedy picked up the mantle of continuing the struggle for economic justice for all. Kahlenberg writes that Kennedy "was increasingly convinced, as King had been, that the racial lens through which liberals addressed social inequality was insufficient. It was pointless, he said, to talk about the real problem in America being black and white; it was really rich and poor, which was a much more complex subject."[65]

With his presidential primary picking up speed, Kennedy traveled the country with the message of reaching out "toward those who still suffer within our country, whether they be white or whether they be black."[66] The enthusiasm with which Kennedy was embraced by blacks and whites alike made it seem that his message was getting through to the voters. Kennedy recognized that after the passage of the Civil Rights Act of 1964 and affirmative action in 1965, the country was at a crossroads and that now was a ripe moment to take the critical turn toward addressing the issues of class and economic inequality, to truly fulfill the guarantees of those other initiatives and to continue the social experiment to usher in a nation more equitable and just for all.

But two months after King's assassination, moments after declaring victory in the California presidential primary, Robert Kennedy was shot dead in Los Angeles. "The Poor People's Campaign . . . closed its tents . . . its goals unmet, its promise withered," writes Kahlenberg.[67] With the defeat of the Poor People's Campaign, with the untimely death of its two major proponents, the subject of class as an organizational principle and policy initiative retreated into the shadows. It would not reenter the public consciousness until it was brought back fleetingly by the Occupy Wall Street movement, on the heels of the Great Recession of 2008. Any reference to class and the need to address the major divisions that it has endangered still remains elusive.

This is not to argue at all that race is not pertinent or that the United States somehow became postracial after the passage of the civil rights legislation, or even after the election of its first black president. There is an absolute need to continue vigilance on matters of race. Yet perhaps race continues to be an incendiary issue because the historical moment when the country could have been put on a different trajectory was lost as the Great Society programs fell short of their promise and the Poor People's Campaign disintegrated and took with it any hopes for class alliances between blacks and whites.

The problems that economic deprivation visits upon blacks, Native Americans, and poor women today must be considered in the light of that failure and the tragic, untimely loss of two visionary leaders.

Black Men, the Prison Pipeline, and the Political Economy of Incarceration

Much of my sociological understanding of the fate of black America centers on my readings of the work of eminent African American men and women, sociologists, and scholars. And among the men whose writing I have read—Cornel West, William Julius Wilson, and Henry Louis Gates, to name the most prominent—all speak of experiences in which they have encountered fear, discomfort, inattention, and even hostility from whites when they happened to share an elevator, tried to hail a cab in New York City, or just tried to enter their own place of residence.

The perception that society has of the danger posed by black men is one that the media depict, one that news of crime and violence in the inner city confirms, and one that is deeply rooted in racist stereotypes, holdovers from the past. The cold facts about black men, crime, violence, and incarceration do little to assuage these fears. Since the 1980s, the rate of incarceration in the United States has exploded. Today, the United States has the biggest incarcerated population in the world. As of 2013, in nearly 4,600 prisons across the country, the incarcerated population in the United States numbers about 2.3 million, of whom African Americans constitute nearly 1 million. Latinos and African Americans together make up 58 percent of the total prison population, even though they constitute only a quarter of the total US population.[68] News reports of drug and gang violence, such as drive-by shootings, give credence to these statistics and validate the stereotypes that people hold.

MAKING CONNECTIONS
Where Affirmative Action Went Wrong

In the minds of its architects, affirmative action was never meant to be a permanent fixture, but a temporary cure to correct the effects of historical discrimination (slavery and de jure, or legal, discrimination), contemporary discrimination (de facto, or real-life discrimination, which is illegal but still ongoing), and institutional discrimination (inferior schools, segregated neighborhoods, low-paying jobs, and poverty). Its policies were provisional and were to be phased out when real gains in employment and education became apparent in successive generations.

But for that to occur, society would have to commit to fundamental social reforms. Segregated neighborhoods would have to be dismantled; schools would have to improve; people would need the assurance that jobs would be available; they would have to be paid wages that allowed them to live with dignity; there would need to be job-training programs, vocational education programs, quality health care, child care, ways for people to buy homes and start businesses, and so on.

In January 1944, in his State of the Union address, President Franklin Roosevelt had spelled out the same provisions in what he had called his Second Bill of Rights—a bill of economic rights. Fundamental structural and institutional changes would have to be implemented so individuals could build their social capital and participate in society as true equals. And since real social, educational, and economic reforms were not race-specific programs, they had the potential to bolster and fortify every citizen and every community.

Affirmative action became a permanent fixture because these structural changes in schools, jobs, and neighborhoods did not happen. The continued absence of such reforms has often condemned minorities, the poor, and their communities to living lives of abject deprivation. For adults and their children growing up in these communities, still segregated more than five decades after the major civil rights laws were passed, affirmative action holds out very little hope. For the large majority of minorities and poor, affirmative action is not a solution to the problems they face.[1]

Therefore, educational opportunities and employment positions almost always go to those in the minority who are the most favorably positioned to benefit from "preferences" due to family background, family resources, and educational preparedness. The vast majority of those designated for "preferential" treatment have not been able to claim advantages, because economic and racial oppression has left them with few of the critical resources necessary to compete effectively.

The real beneficiaries have been those among the disadvantaged who are relatively privileged. In the United States, this has created what many social scientists refer to as the "two nations of Black America": a growing black middle class, who are the fortunate beneficiaries of affirmative action, and the rest, those largely bypassed by these policies and locked into ever-deepening cycles of poverty and disadvantage.[2]

Notes: 1. Wilson, *The Truly Disadvantaged,* p. 112.
2. DasGupta, "A Checkered Legacy."

The New Jim Crow

In place of a serious public policy to deal with what is happening in the inner cities—such as an infusion of funds to bolster the schools, investment in public work projects for unemployed individuals, provision of loans to small businesses, job training, job placement, quality child-care programs for young mothers, steps to tighten the social safety net, construction of affordable housing, investment in infrastructure, and the like—the United States has instead spent over $1 trillion in its three-decade war on drugs.[69] The response to these myriad problems has often just been to build more prisons.

Michelle Alexander has written a groundbreaking book in which she argues that the "racial caste system" has not ended in the United States and in fact functions very effectively under the mask of the war on drugs, denying African Americans, especially black men, the opportunities and resources needed to climb out of poverty and disadvantage. She argues persuasively that contrary to what is generally assumed, the war on drugs and the mass incarceration that followed came not in response to any crisis caused by crack cocaine in the inner-city neighborhoods:

> President Ronald Reagan officially announced the current drug war in 1982, before crack became an issue in the media or a crisis in poor black neighborhoods. A few years after the drug war was declared, crack began to spread rapidly in the poor black neighborhoods of Los Angeles and later emerged in cities across the country. . . . Conspiracy theorists surely must be forgiven for their bold accusations of genocide, in light of the devastation wrought by crack cocaine and the drug war, and the odd coincidence that an illegal drug crisis suddenly appeared in the black community after—not before—a drug war had been declared.[70]

Alexander shows that through the targeting and mass incarceration of black men, the war on drugs has decimated communities of color. In the process, the US criminal justice system has

> emerged as a stunningly comprehensive and well-designed system of racialized control that functions in a manner strikingly similar to Jim Crow. Once [the incarcerated] are released, they are often denied the right to vote, excluded from juries, and relegated to a racially segregated and subordinate existence.
>
> Through a web of laws, regulations and informal rules, all of which are powerfully reinforced by social stigma, they are confined to the margins of mainstream society and denied access to the mainstream economy. They are legally denied the right to obtain employment, housing and public benefits—much as African Americans were once forced into a segregated, second-class citizenship in the Jim Crow era.[71]

Alexander argues that, because of incarceration, a huge percentage of African Americans are not even free to move up the economic ladder. It is not just a matter of lacking opportunity, or attending poor schools, or being plagued by poverty; the current system of control permanently locks them out of the mainstream society and economy. Earlier systems of control, such as slavery and Jim Crow, were designed to exploit and control black labor for the benefit of the system.

Today, large segments of the African American population are considered unnecessary to the functioning of the new global economy and therefore disposable. The factories that needed their cheap labor have shut down; African Americans don't have the skills that the new jobs in computers and information technology require; the service jobs mushrooming in the suburbs are far away from where they live. So, what does a society do with surplus black labor? Is a criminal justice policy that creates a guaranteed "pipeline" between the inner city and prison a substitute for an inner-city employment policy, or an effective labor market policy?[72]

Prisons are big business. If for some reason prisons were closed and the country returned to pre–drug war incarceration rates, this would devastate the many rural communities who have become dependent on prisons for jobs and economic growth; far in excess of a million people would lose their jobs. Prisons are deeply embedded in private-sector investment. Alexander points out that "rich and powerful people, including former Vice President Dick Cheney, have invested millions in prisons. They are deeply interested in expanding the market—increasing the supply of prisoners—not eliminating the pool of people who can be held captive for a profit."[73]

There are many other companies that profit from this system of mass incarceration. These include phone companies, gun manufacturers, and the private health-care providers that the state hires, at exorbitant rates, to provide health care in the prisons; corporations that hire prison labor; and everybody else who benefits from each new prison that is built—politicians, bankers, realtors, lawyers—a long list indeed. "All of these corporate and political interests have a stake in expansion—not elimination—of the system of mass incarceration."[74]

Politics, Policy, and Criminal Justice

In 1972, America's prisons held approximately 350,000 people. In 2012, the prison population had risen to more than 2 million.[75] The United States comprises only 5 percent of the world's total population, but accounts for 25 percent of the world's prison population. The United States locks up more of its citizens than any other country in the world. According to data gathered by the Pew Research Center, one out of every thirty-one adult Americans, including those on probation and parole, was involved in one way or the other with the criminal justice system as of 2009.[76]

The racial and class dimensions of incarceration are staggering given that most individuals under the supervision of the US correctional system come from poor and minority communities. They made up 60 percent of the US prison population in 2014. By some estimates, one in three black men will serve time in prison at some point in their lives. In 2009, 62 percent of black children aged seventeen or younger were growing up in a household where a parent was in prison.[77] The disastrous fallout from these numbers for the families and communities of the incarcerated is profoundly disturbing.

The prevalent belief is that the high rates of incarceration are reflective of the war on drugs. But paradoxically, the rates of imprisonment have increased as crime rates have fallen. While crime rates fell by 45 percent between 1990 and 2012, incarceration rates increased by 222 percent between 1980 and 2012.[78] What has driven the increase in the size of the prison population is not crime but government policy.

Genevieve LeBaron and Adrienne Roberts draw attention to how class-based and racialized patterns of criminalization and incarceration "have emerged as the preferred public response to the problems created by poverty."[79] In the New Deal and Great Society approaches, the government managed economic marginality with policies that provided social assistance and welfare. In contrast, for the neoliberal social and economic policies of the present era, incarceration and criminalization have become the preferred methods.

LeBaron and Roberts cite studies by sociologist Loïc Wacquant and social geographist Ruth Gilmore that have demonstrated a positive correlation between levels of unemployment and rates of imprisonment—as unemployment increased, so did the numbers of people imprisoned. However, research conducted by Katherine Beckett and Bruce Western demonstrates "a negative correlation between welfare spending and rates of incarceration," so as welfare spending goes up rates of incarceration drop. LeBaron and Roberts present Wacquant's argument that "the trend towards mass imprisonment in the United States is directly related to the shift away from the welfare management of poverty."[80] Therefore as the government spent less and less money on social services and financial assistance for the poor, the rate of incarceration accelerated.

The United States spends more money on incarceration than it does on food stamps. As *New York Times* reporter Eduardo Porter writes: "The United States spent about $80 billion on its system of jails and prisons in 2010—about $260 for every resident in the nation. By contrast, its budget for food stamps was $227 per person."[81] More money is spent on corrections than on education, social services, health services, family services, vocational education, and other key government programs meant to support the poor as they struggle to put their lives in order.

A majority of those behind bars are not being held for violent offenses, but for a range of transgressions that are simply disorderly or antisocial in nature. In the absence of regular jobs, many of these offenses can be seen simply as attempts to secure livelihoods outside the formal marketplace through drug dealing, prostitution, and petty crime. Incarceration has become the solution no matter how minor the infraction. Sociologist Bruce Western maintains that "prison became a last resort for a whole variety of social failures whether caused by problems with mental health, drug abuse or unemployment."[82]

Other scholars see the same patterns. In their book *Why Are So Many Americans in Prison?* Steven Raphael and Michael Stoll contend that "increasing concentration of income at the top follows the incarceration rate almost perfectly."[83] Sociologist Devah Pager similarly argues that as the distance between the rich and poor continues to widen, the easier it becomes to impose these punitive policies.[84]

Harsh sentencing policies instituted at both the federal level and the state level since 1975 are primarily responsible for the explosion in the number of people incarcerated. Deliberate policy decisions such as mandatory sentencing, long sentences, "three-strikes" laws to punish repeat offenders, intensified criminalization of drug-related activity, and punishing crack cocaine offenses a hundred times more harshly than those related to powder cocaine have all led to this unprecedented surge in the prison population, disproportionately affecting African Americans.

Beginning in the mid-1980s, the US government started outsourcing the business of incarceration. In 1984, the first such contract went to the Correctional Corporation of America (CCA). Heavily subsidized by taxpayer money, the private prison industry moved into communities increasingly abandoned by the globalized economy. In many rural communities, the private prison has become the sole employer.

As incarceration rates have skyrocketed, there is increasing need for prison space. Facing budget shortfalls, both the federal government and state governments have handed over the task of management and housing of the incarcerated to private companies, because outsourcing of prison management and construction of private prisons are considered cheaper options and save taxpayer money. But studies by the Government Accountability Office, the National Institute of Justice, and the University of Utah find little or no evidence of tax savings.[85] At a time when policies of neoliberalism advocate shrinking the size and scope of government by either outsourcing or privatizing what was once exclusively a service connected with the government, this trend toward more and more privatization of functions connected with the incarcerated is not surprising. Private prison companies contract with federal and state governments to either take over management of a government-run facility or to build private prisons to house the incarcerated. They charge the government a daily rate that covers their operating costs and also assures them a profit.

There are more private prison contracts at present than ever before. According to a report published by the Justice Policy Institute in 2011, there has been a substantial growth in the number of incarcerated individuals held in private facilities since 2000, enabling the private prison companies to earn record revenues. Two companies own and operate the majority of for-profit private prisons in the United States: the aforementioned CCA, and the GEO Group. According to the report,[86] as the revenues of private prison companies have grown, so has their political clout. They have used their money to build political power and influence the US Congress and state legislatures to promote policies that lead to higher rates of incarceration—including immigrant detention (discussed further in Chapter 11).

The Justice Policy Institute report documents the three strategies that the private prison companies have used to influence state and federal policy: direct campaign contributions, lobbying, and building relationships and networks:

• *Direct campaign contributions.* Between 2000 and 2011, the CCA and GEO Group political action committees contributed nearly $10 million to candidates and political parties in state and federal elections.

• *Lobbying.* Between 2000 and 2011, private prison companies spent over $21 million lobbying Congress alone. But their lobbying also extends to state legislatures. Lobbying firms and individual lobbyists are employed to advocate for their business interests. According to the Justice Policy Institute report, "since they make money from putting people behind bars, their lobbying efforts engage in an aggressive political strategy to influence criminal justice policies in ways that lead to more people in prison."

• *Building relationships and networks.* The report also shows how private prison companies have benefited from their close relationships with elected officials. It gives examples of cases across the country where former employees in the industry are appointed to key state and federal positions. In Ohio, for example, a former CCA employee and close acquaintance of Governor John Kasich was appointed to head the Ohio Department of Rehabilitation and Correction. And Kasich, soon after assuming the governorship, proposed the privatization of five Ohio prisons.

As millions of manufacturing jobs disappear due to the impact of globalization, and as government's role changes from providing protective and welfare services to help people manage their economic plight to instead incarcerating people on a massive scale, the very fact that the private prison industry stands to gain from this arrangement is unpalatable. The political influence of the private prison industry can never be matched by that of the poor or their advocates.

It is their marginality that makes the poor expendable. And in an economic environment with limited opportunities for unskilled labor, the poor become increasingly superfluous and inconsequential. As an advocate for the poor said in the documentary "Throwaway People": "all the cotton has been picked, all the shoes have been shined, all the factories have been outsourced—what do you do with excess labor at this moment in time?" Most often the answer has been to build more prisons![87]

In the US Congress and state legislatures, any advocacy for a comprehensive package of social policies to help individuals get back on their feet again essentially falls on deaf ears. Voices that advocate for commonsense initiatives—such as opportunities to complete education that might have been interrupted for one reason or the other, vocational training, skill training, retraining, apprenticeships, low-interest loans to start small businesses, unemployment insurance, income support for families, child care for low-income single mothers, rental assistance, transportation, drug and alcohol rehabilitation, health care (including mental health), and the like—get lost in the constant drumbeat that exaggerates the need to balance budgets, eliminate waste, and keep government out of people's lives. But none of these concerns seem to stop the increasing funneling of taxpayer money to building prisons and subsidizing private ones.

As I have continuously argued, a certain degree of inequality is natural. But the egregious inequality that we see in the United States today is a consequence of deliberate policy choices made by a society in which the lives of the rich and the poor continue to diverge. And the poor, considered expendable, are left farther and farther behind.

Conclusion

So we have come full circle. The United States is a capitalist society. Profit is its holy grail. Anything can be turned into a commodity if it can secure economic gain for those who are favorably placed to benefit from it. And that is what the system of mass incarceration ultimately delivers.

Capitalist development has occurred from the moment the first black slave was brought to the Americas and through the brutal exploitation of blacks as workers, consumers, and commodities. The commodified labor of black people generated the capital that became foundational in the development of capitalism and US economic might.

Manning Marable maintains that "America's 'democratic' government and 'free enterprise' system are structured deliberately and specifically to maximize Black oppression. Blacks have never been equal partners in the American Social Contract, because the system exists not to develop, but to under-develop Black people."[88] Malcolm X was doubtful that racism could exist without capitalism or a similar form of economic oppression, and vice versa.[89] Similarly, W. E. B. Du Bois believed that "capitalism and racism were inextricably tied together. . . . And that one could not struggle decisively against racism and remain a proponent of capitalism . . . [and that] the road toward democracy and antiracist society must also lead toward socialism"[90] But Du Bois was hopeful and reasoned that "it is only a question of time when white working men and black working men will see their common cause against the aggressions of exploiting capitalists."[91]

The intricate connection between racism and capitalism is seeping into the public consciousness too, as was evidenced on August 24, 2013, by the signs people carried at the commemoration of the fiftieth anniversary of the 1963 March on Washington. One sign declared: "Racism and Capitalism— Preying on the People."

It is true that large groups of blacks in the United States have made their way into the middle and upper-middle classes. They are the fortunate beneficiaries of the civil rights and women's rights movements of the 1960s. But for a significant segment of the African American population, poverty and destitution remain the persistent reality.

Rooted in the ideology of neoliberalism, government has seen its role, anchored in the primary objective of profit maximization, as one of facilitating the values and priorities of the marketplace. Instead of the focus being on job creation, job training, skill development, real educational reform, and other efforts to increase the human capital of African Americans and the poor, the objective has been to release them into the market. In an environment of job scarcity, the poor, with little education and a lack of skills, have fallen deeper into economic insecurity.

Instead of addressing these issues, the government's primary strategy has been to control the fallout from the conditions that constant poverty and destitution have naturally spawned—poverty-induced crime and drug abuse resulting in a record number of individuals incarcerated by the criminal justice system in its increasingly privatized prison-industrial complex.

Antipoverty measures have focused on welfare, and welfare reform, to alter the behavior of the poor, particularly poor women of color, instead of on altering the structures of economic inequality—wealth concentration, unfair tax codes, crumbling schools, and, most significant, the shortage of jobs—that have fostered that behavior.

Notes

1. Jeter, "Worse Than Apartheid"; Kristof, "When Whites Just Don't Get It."
2. Kochhar et al., "Wealth Gap Rises to Record Highs Between Whites, Blacks and Hispanics."
3. Ibid.
4. Bruenig, "The Racial Wealth Gap."
5. Omi and Winant, "Racial Formation."
6. Ibid., p. 13.

7. Hochschild, *King Leopold's Ghost.*

8. Ibid., p. 2.

9. Galeano, *Open Veins of Latin America.*

10. Ibid., p. 23.

11. Ibid.; and Neuman, "For Miners, Increasing Risk on a Mountain at the Heart of Bolivia's Identity," p. A9.

12. Misra, "Who Were the Sepoys of 1857?"

13. James, "The Atlantic Slave Trade and Slavery."

14. Quoted in ibid., p. 216.

15. Galeano, *Open Veins of Latin America,* p. 28.

16. Quoted in Baron, "The Demand for Black Labor," p. 512.

17. Stampp, *The Peculiar Institution,* p. 85.

18. Wilson, *Racism,* p. 71.

19. Ibid., p. 72.

20. Rockman, "The Future of Civil War Era Studies."

21. Takaki, *A Different Mirror,* pp. 81–82.

22. Wilder, *Ebony and Ivy,* pp. 1–2.

23. Quoted in Gates, "Why Was Cotton 'King'?".

24. Quoted in Beckert and Rockman, "Partners in Iniquity."

25. Beckert and Rockman, "How Slavery Led to Modern Capitalism."

26. Du Bois, *The Souls of Black Folks,* p. 9.

27. Hansen, *A Frantz Fanon Study Guide,* p. 8.

28. Fanon, *The Wretched of the Earth,* pp. 39–40.

29. Kirvo et al., "Segregation, Racial Structure, and Neighborhood Violent Crime," p. 1766.

30. Ibid.

31. Feagin and Booher-Feagin, *Racial and Ethnic Relations,* p. 179.

32. Wilkerson, *The Warmth of Other Suns.*

33. Wilson, *Racism,* p. 124.

34. Goodman, "How a Grim Black Area Got That Way."

35. Wilson, *The Truly Disadvantaged,* pp. 30–32, 65.

36. Ibid., p. 4.

37. Ibid., p. 41.

38. Wacquant, *Urban Outcasts,* p. 222.

39. Ibid., p. 223.

40. Wilson, *The Truly Disadvantaged,* p. 57.

41. Levine, "Race and Male Employment in the Wake of the Great Recession," p. 14.

42. Ibid., p. 2.

43. Pager, Western, and Bonikowski, "Discrimination in a Low-Wage Labor Market."

44. Wilson, *More Than Just Race,* pp. 73–74.

45. Venkatesh, *Gang Leader for a Day,* pp. 37–38.

46. Wacquant, *Urban Outcasts,* p. 223.

47. US Census Bureau, "Areas with Concentrated Poverty."

48. Wilson, *The Truly Disadvantaged,* p. 46.

49. Ibid., p. 49.

50. Parry, "The Neighborhood Effect."

51. Wilson, *The Truly Disadvantaged,* p. 56.

52. Sharkey, *Stuck in Place,* p. 9.

53. Pattillo-McCoy, *Black Picket Fences,* p. 6.

54. Ibid., p. 28.

55. Ibid., p. 146.

56. Kitwana, *The Hip Hop Generation*, p. 9.

57. Ibid., p. 10.

58. Wilson, *The Truly Disadvantaged*, p. 30.

59. Johnson, "To Fulfill These Rights."

60. US Department of Labor, "Hiring: Affirmative Action."

61. Quoted in Kahlenberg, *The Remedy*, p. xxvii.

62. Ibid.

63. Ibid., p. xxviii.

64. Ibid., p. xxvii.

65. Ibid., p. xxix.

66. Ibid., p. xviii.

67. Ibid., p. xxx.

68. National Association for the Advancement of Colored People, "Criminal Justice Fact Sheet."

69. Franklin, "Former Cops Agree."

70. Alexander, *The New Jim Crow,* pp. 5–6.

71. Ibid., p. 4.

72. Levine, "Race and Male Employment in the Wake of the Great Recession," p. 39.

73. Alexander, *The New Jim Crow,* p. 281.

74. Ibid., pp. 219–220.

75. Ibid., p. 8; The Sentencing Project, "Trends in U.S. Corrections," p. 2.

76. Pew Research on States, "State of Recidivism," p. 1.

77. Badger, "The Meteoric, Costly and Unprecedented Rise of Incarceration in America."

78. Pazzanese, "Punitive Damages."

79. LeBaron and Roberts, "Toward a Feminist Political Economy of Capitalism and Carcerality," p. 26.

80. Ibid., p. 27.

81. Porter, "In the U.S., Punishment Comes Before the Crimes," p. B1.

82. Quoted in ibid., p. B9.

83. Ibid.

84. Ibid.

85. Justice Policy Institute, "Gaming the System," p. 32.

86. Ibid, pp. 3, 4, 15.

87. Wilkins, "Throwaway People."

88. Marable, *How Capitalism Underdeveloped Black America*, p. 2.

89. Marable, *Malcolm X*, p. 343.

90. Marable, *How Capitalism Underdeveloped Black America*, pp. 15, 18.

91. Du Bois, quoted in ibid., p. 23.

11

Nativism, Citizenship, and Colonialism

PINE RIDGE, SOUTH DAKOTA, IS HOME TO THE OGLALA LAKOTA TRIBE and is part of the Great Sioux Reservation established under the Fort Laramie Treaty of 1868. Ensconced in one of the most breathtaking vistas of the country, the Pine Ridge Reservation is also the poorest of the Native American reservations in the United States, with a poverty rate that rivals that of the third world. Nicholas Kristof writes that in terms of inequality, the Native Americans at Pine Ridge represent "the bottom of the national heap."[1]

The US Census Bureau reports that in the 2007–2011 period, 14,059 individuals lived in Shannon County, South Dakota, which is home to the Pine Ridge, Rosebud, Cheyenne River, and Crow Creek Reservations. Native Americans made up 92.4 percent of the population, and whites 5.4 percent. The per capita annual income for the county was $7,887, compared with $27,915 for the entire nation; the median annual income was $25,228, compared to $64,293 for the country as a whole; 53.5 percent of Shannon County's population were living below the federal poverty threshold, compared to 14.3 percent for all Americans; 53.1 percent of the population were unemployed, compared to a national unemployment rate of 8.7 percent. The mean value of housing units in the county, which 51 percent of the reservation population occupied, was $16,800, compared to the South Dakota average of $127,000.[2]

As appalling as these numbers are, there are others that portray a picture of even deeper destitution. For example, according to the American Indian Humanitarian Foundation, 97 percent of the population at the Pine Ridge Reservation were living below the federal poverty line. The US Census Bureau placed the median annual household income at Pine Ridge at $20,568 in 2010. The unemployment rate vacillated between 85 and 95 percent. The Department of Interior reported an unemployment rate among the Oglala Lakota at Pine Ridge of 89 percent in 2005.

The infant mortality rate at Pine Ridge is the highest in the nation, perhaps 300 percent above the national average. At least 60 percent of the homes on the reservation are without electricity, running water, and adequate heating. Life expectancy for an Oglala Sioux man is forty-eight years; for a woman it is fifty-two. More than half the reservation's adults battle one or more of the following: alcoholism, diabetes, heart disease, cancer, tuberculosis, malnutrition, or hypothermia—the national statistics for all of which pale in comparison. The teenage suicide rate at Pine Ridge is 150 percent higher than the national average for this age group.

These numbers, at first glance, may seem improbable. Could the poverty rate really be 85–95 percent? Could the infant mortality rate and the teenage suicide rate really be so astronomically high? But repeated searches of websites maintained by some of the Native American tribes produce the same grim data. On the whole, these numbers bear witness to the profound devastation that history has wrought in the lives of the residents of Pine Ridge and in the lives of all indigenous peoples of the Americas.

The Census Bureau reports that there are 5.2 million Native Americans and Alaskan Natives as of 2010. They constitute a mere 1.7 percent of the total US population, and belong to 566 federally recognized tribes. There are 324 federally recognized native reservations, in which 22 percent of the total population of Native Americans and Alaskan Natives live. Between 2000 and 2010, the total US population grew by 9.7 percent, from 281.4 million to 308.7 million. In comparison, the Native American/Alaskan Native population grew 27.0 percent, from 4.1 million to 5.2 million. Most of the increase for the latter has been attributed to the increasing size of the mixed-race category, as 44 percent of the Native American/Alaskan Native individuals report belonging to more than one race.[3]

There has always been disagreement regarding the pre-Columbian population in the Americas. The numbers have fluctuated, from ethnologist James Mooney's estimate of 1.5 million in North America, to anthropologist Alfred Kroeber's estimate of 8.4 million in all of the Americas, to anthropologist Henry Dobyns's estimate of as many as 122 million in North America.[4] The numbers seem to fluctuate according to the political and ideological position that anthropologists and historians have taken. Those who argue that the arrival of the Europeans did not have much effect on the indigenous peoples usually cite the smaller numbers.

But historical demographers agree that within a handful of generations after first contact with Europeans, 90 to 99 percent of the total pre-Columbian population of all indigenous peoples throughout the Americas was decimated.[5] The magnitude of this near extinction is hard to grasp. As David Stannard writes, "on the average, for every 20 natives alive at the moment of contact only 1 stood in their place when the bloodbath was over."[6] Through a deliberate policy of genocide, exposure to disease, expulsion, and forced assimilation over the course of five centuries, the indigenous peoples of the Americas have become the most marginalized and disadvantaged minorities in the country.

This history is of course well known. The objective here is to frame that history in the context of the development of US capitalism, especially by focusing on the social construction of the Native American, which facilitated that process. Scholars such as Ronald Takaki have argued that the social construction of the indigenous as "savages" lent support to the entire notion that they were undeserving of the bounty—fertile lands, verdant forests, and the gold, silver, and other resources—that nature had bequeathed to them. And therefore it was easily justifiable and acceptable to exterminate them and clear the land for speculation and capitalist enterprise.

Natives, Slaves, and Capitalism

In December 1890, just ten days before the massacre at Wounded Knee in Pine Ridge, South Dakota, which would kill hundreds—two-thirds of them women and children—L. Frank Baum, who would later write *The Wizard of Oz,* wrote in the *Aberdeen Saturday Pioneer:* "The Whites, by law of conquest, by justice of civilization, are the masters of the American continent. . . . [I]n order to protect our civilization, wipe these untamed and untamable creatures from the face of the earth."[7] Similar calls for extermination had been repeated in other newspapers along the American frontier, to which an endless flow of white settlers journeyed and arrived as squatters on Native American lands. In March 1863, the editor of the *Rocky Mountain News* wrote: "They are a dissolute, vagabondish, brutal and ungrateful race, and ought to be wiped from the face of the earth."[8]

In the winter of the next year, November 1864, the Sand Creek massacre in eastern Colorado would brutally crush the unarmed villages of the Cheyenne and the Arapaho peoples—and again, two-thirds of those killed were women and children. Years later, during his presidency in 1901–1909, Theodore Roosevelt would comment that the Sand Creek massacre was "as righteous and beneficial a deed as ever took place on the frontier."[9]

Governor Frederick Pitkin of Colorado, speaking of the need to remove the Ute people, exposed the real motives underlying those provocations. He had the backing of miners and ranchers who coveted the vast Ute holdings in western Colorado. "My idea is that, unless removed by the government, they must necessarily be exterminated. The state would be willing to settle the Indian trouble at its own expense. The advantages that would accrue from the throwing open of 12,000,000 acres of land to miners and settlers would more than compensate all the expenses incurred."[10] Consequently, by the end of 1882, the Ute were driven out of their ancestral lands and forced onto the reservations in Utah.

Such stories of forced removals and massacres inundate the history of the conquest of the Americas and the devastation and tragedy that it brought upon the indigenous peoples of the land. The underlying theme remains the same—the lust for land, gold, and resources and the supposed savagery of the original inhabitants who had undeservedly been bestowed this bounty. The English colonizers of North America, as sociologist Ronald Takaki reminds us, "possessed tremendous power to define the places and people they were conquering. As they made their way westward, they developed an ideology of 'savagery.'"[11] The social construction of the Native Americans as "ignorant heathens" and "diabolical savages" occurred in the "economic context of competition for land."[12]

The most important signifier of "civilization" in the English mind was private property. Native American land tenureship involved communal ownership, and there was no legitimacy for this in the English mind. Property and constant efforts for its expansion were existential obligations. It was a vocation that God, the English believed, intended for man to pursue. Only under conditions of private ownership, they were certain, would individuals have the motivation and drive to work hard, accumulate wealth, and prosper. Only under systems of private property were land and resources properly utilized; only when individuals took full control of the land, and worked it to the fullest to obtain its resources, were they truly appreciating what God had bequeathed to them.

Native Americans were considered heathens and savages because, in their communal ownership and nomadic ways, they took no control of the resources around them. "Indians were sinfully squandering America's resources." They were irresponsible, lazy, no better than "foxes and wild beasts."[13] They were incapable of civilization and therefore totally undeserving of the great natural wealth that surrounded them.

In 1616, epidemics ravaged the Native American villages of New England, decimating the populations of the tribes. For the English colonists, this was a literal godsend, and they interpreted these tragedies as divinely ordained opportunities to clear the land so they could take possession of it. John Winthrop, a leading personality among the Puritan founders of New England, "declared that the decimation of Indians by smallpox manifested a Puritan destiny: God was *making room* for the colonists and 'hath hereby cleared our title to this place.'"[14] Disease, massacre, and forced removal cleared more and more land for mining, ranching, lumbering, and then railroading, prompting President Theodore Roosevelt to write in 1889, in *The Winning of the West:* "The settler, the pioneer have at bottom had justice on their side; this great continent could not have been kept as nothing but a game reserve for squalid savages."[15]

Andrew Jackson was the architect of the removal of the Native Americans. His own fortunes were tied up with their fate. When he was elected president in 1828, he orchestrated the treaties that dispossessed the Native Americans of the East Coast of their ancestral lands—lands that rapidly came under the possession of white settlers and their cotton plantations. Jackson approached his destruction of the Native Americans and the appropriation of their lands in a philosophical vein. "What good man," he asked, "would prefer a country covered with forests and ranged by a few thousand savages to our extensive Republic, studded with cities, towns, and prosperous farms . . . fitted with all the blessings of liberty, civilization and religion?"[16]

The colonization of North America, the expropriation of the land and resources that once were under the purview of the Native Americans, and the tremendous economic windfall of that endeavor helped fuel the industrial revolution in England and the United States. The land cleared would be cultivated for tobacco, rice, sugar, and cotton.

This violent appropriation of Native American land was thus followed closely by a parallel rise in the number of Africans who were being violently enslaved to transform those lands into profitable plantations. Between 1820 and 1850, the number of slaves in just one Southern state—Alabama—swelled from 42,000 to 343,000. There were similar increases in the numbers of slaves in all the cotton-producing states.[17] Land and slaves provided the capital needed for the development of a nascent capitalist industrial system both in the New World and in Europe.

Douglass North, in his economic history of the United States from 1790 to 1860, the period in which the nation evolved into a major industrial economy, "second only to Britain in manufacturing," maps out the role of cotton in bringing about this transformation. It was cotton that created the capital that made possible the industrialization of the Northeast. As he writes:

> It was cotton which was the most important influence in the growth of the market size and the consequent expansion of the economy. . . . [I]t was cotton that initiated the concomitant expansion in income, in the size of the domestic markets, and creation of the social overhead investment. Cotton also accounted for the accelerated pace of westward migration as well as for the movement of people out of self-sufficiency into the market economy. Without cotton the development in the size of the market would have been a much [more] lengthy process. . . . In short, cotton was the most important proximate cause of expansion . . . cotton was indeed king.[18]

England's textile manufacturing depended on the cotton exported from the United States. As England's textile mills grew, so did the cotton exports and the need of the United States to expand into new lands and bring them under "cotton acreage." North writes that the availability of "virgin lands" in Louisiana, Alabama, Mississippi, Arkansas, and Florida meant that any increase in the price of cotton "was sufficient to cause fields in which corn and other grains were already growing to be plowed up and replanted in cotton."[19] But in his otherwise thorough account, North neglects to mention that the so-called virgin lands were already occupied, and that those occupants had to be removed and their corn plowed under, to make room for cotton. To white Americans, there was only one way to treat land: as Patricia Limerick puts it, to "divide it, distribute it, register it."[20] Native Americans did not treat their land this way and therefore, in the minds of white Americans, had forfeited all claims to it. From this point of view, then, North's omission of the indigenous occupancy of the land is quite logical.

In sum, cotton provided the crucial stimulus for the market revolution in the United States. Cotton exports provided the raw materials for the textile manufacturers in Lancashire and Manchester, the cradle of the industrial revolution in England. The profits from these cotton exports also provided the capital for the burgeoning industries in the US North. Cotton was grown on lands seized from the Native Americans and harvested by slaves. With each Native American tribe that was forced from the lands, there was a concomitant increase in the number of slaves acquired.

Slavery and the dispossession of the Native Americans are interwoven realities. Not much research has been done to explore this interlinkage. Alexandra Harmon, Colleen O'Neill, and Paul Rosier, in their research into the role of Native Americans in the development of capitalism, contend that very little research has been undertaken regarding "interwoven economic histories of the United States and the Native American."[21] The trajectory of the development of US capitalism and the necessity of land and resources to early US economic development can be better understood by considering the role of Native Americans.[22]

The land that was seized from the Native Americans also yielded gold, silver, coal, oil, water, bauxite, uranium, and other resources fundamental to the growth of US capitalism. As Harmon and her colleagues note: "The biggest structural change in early American history was the wresting away of native land and its transformation from communal property into capitalist private property."[23] The Dawes Act of 1887 was instrumental in this transformation.

From 100 Percent to 1 Percent: The Total Dispossession of the Native Americans

As the nineteenth century came to a close and with the Native American population decimated, the question the country faced was what to do with the remaining Native Americans, notwithstanding that General William Sherman, "if not for the civilian interference, . . . would have got rid of all American Indians."[24] Thomas Jefferson had hoped to "save the Indians": "But in order to survive the Indian must adopt the culture of the white man. They must no longer live so boundlessly; instead they must enclose their farms as private property and learn arithmetic so they would be able to keep accounts of their production."[25] But even as Jefferson expressed an interest in the survival of Native Americans, his main concern was to make more and more land available to the white settlers.

In 1887, the Dawes Act allotted each Native American family 160 acres of land and made them landowners—owners of private property—and US citizens. This would destroy the old system of communal property and the "communistic nature of tribalism"[26] and thus convert Native Americans to the habits of "civilized" human beings, as it was assumed that their status as landowners would motivate their individual self-interest. The breakup of the reservations would also yield "surplus land" that would be sold off to whites. Living side by side with their white neighbors, the Native Americans could be further coached in the "ways of civilization."

In one year alone, 1891—four years after the passage of the Dawes Act—Native Americans would lose one-seventh of all of their land, 117 million acres in all. In 1902, the transfer of lands from Native Americans to whites was hastened when Congress passed a new law requiring that all allotted land, upon the death of the owners, be sold at public auctions by the heirs. If the heirs were unable to purchase their own family lands, they would lose what had been their family property.

A government official remarked: "Under the present system every Indian's land comes into the market after his death, so that it will be but a few years at most before all Indians' land will have passed into the possession of the settlers." In referencing this remark, Ronald Takaki observes that by 1933, "almost half of the Indians living on reservations that had been subject to the allotment were landless. By then, the Indians had lost about 60 percent of the 138,000,000 acre land base they had owned at the time of the Dawes Act. Allotment had transformed Indians into a landless people."[27]

In 1934, President Franklin Roosevelt, on the advice of John Collier, offered Native Americans a "New Deal." A critic of individualism, Collier saw that allotment was destroying the Native American communal way of life. The goal of government policy, Collier believed, should be to maintain the culture of Native Americans on their communally owned land. On June 18, 1934, President Roosevelt signed the Indian Reorganization Act. It abolished the allotment program and reestablished reservations; tribes became sovereign and self-governing entities.[28]

Navigating a Changed Landscape

Native Americans were not hapless in the face of the misfortune that pervaded their lives after their encounter with the Europeans. It is true that they were unable to withstand this onslaught. But this defeat does not invalidate the fact, contrary to the prevailing view, as Harmon, O'Neill, and Rosier write, that the Native Americans were "dynamic economic actors. The Cherokee prior to their removal in the 1830s were similar in economic terms to their white neighbors. Some earned their livings in market activities . . . and the improvements they had made on their land increased white demands for removal."[29]

When land was seized from the Native Americans, it also came with "capital improvements" such as "trails, tracks, cleared farm fields and established crops, such as corn."[30] Savvy traders in deerskin, the Native Americans saw the growing European presence as a market for food and handicrafts. For the whites, Native Americans were economic competition.

The defeat of the Native Americans needs to be understood not only in terms of their loss of land, but also as the undermining of their entrepreneurship and material aspirations, as Europeans and then Americans "stymied many Indian attempts to participate in mining, ranching, farming, and the other principal enterprises of capitalism in the nineteenth-century American West."[31] Growing federal intrusion in the reservations "hampered Indian attempts to create a tribal oil industry"; as well, many Native Americans had hoped to "turn the demand for gold to their advantage, either by staking claims to gold bearing streams or by working for wages in the mines," but the rush of individuals "soon devastated indigenous communities, caus[ing] environmental degradation and anti-Indian violence."[32]

During the Cold War, uranium extracted by Native American workers from Native American lands was critical in facilitating the strong position of the United States in the global economy. Uranium provided new opportunities for paid employment—most Native Americans were ordinary miners, but there were Navajos who owned mining permits and served as mine managers. Wages were low and working conditions were dangerous, and many Native American workers died of cancers from uranium exposure. Today, Native Americans of the US Southwest continue to live in the midst of contamination from uranium mining, water pollution, water scarcity, strip mining, atomic testing, and nuclear waste. These communities face some of the worst exposure to environmental contaminants in the United States.

Wage labor is critically important to capitalism, but the role of Native Americans in wage labor has rarely been acknowledged. From the beginning of the colonial exposure, Native Americans seized the opportunity "to earn any material rewards they could for their labor and services—toiling as domestic servants, building railroad tracks, herding cattle in commercial ranches, working in gold, copper and uranium mines—in virtually every job category known to Americans."[33]

Native American lands, crops, and "capital improvements"; gold, silver, copper, uranium, and timber from Native American lands; and Native American wage labor built the foundation on which US capitalism would grow. It is not possible to explain the development of US capitalism without examining the process of expropriation of the continent's valuable resources from the indigenous peoples of the land.

The majority of natural resources in the United States are situated on reservation lands—60 percent of uranium, 33 percent of low-sulphur coal, 25 percent of oil, and 15 percent of all natural gases, along with vast resources of gold, copper, bauxite, and timber.[34] Every effort was made to "prove" that Native Americans were undeserving of the land and resources, since they, supposedly, had no entrepreneurial drive and were squandering the wealth.

Economic historians, to the contrary, are focusing attention on the Native American as a savvy and sophisticated economic player—one who seized the opportunities that the coming of the white man brought. Native Americans were not inert bystanders in the face of the devastation that colonial conquest brought. They tried to take advantage of the economic opportunities that opened as a result of that exposure. They were not the passive "savages"—whether "noble" or "demonic"—that history has stereotyped them to be.

Today, US society is somewhat bemused and incredulous at the recent embrace of capitalism by various Native American tribes, evident in the popularity and success of the gaming/casino industry. But it should not surprise an astute student of US history, which gives ample evidence of the enterprise and initiative of the Native Americans. This aspect of the Native American has been lost in the face of the more overwhelming and heartrending evidence of their ultimate defeat and destruction—the loss of resources, the loss of power to control whatever remained, and eventually the decimation of their numbers as immigrants flooded into the United States. Today, the descendants of these teeming millions of indigenous peoples, who five centuries ago populated the lands that would become the United States, constitute an infinitesimal 1.7 percent of the total US population. A third of them are "corralled" in reservations, living marginalized lives of utter poverty and destitution.

The development of the casino industry must be seen in the context of the absence of any economic revitalization and development of the Native American reservations in recent memory. Badly conceived plans of the Commerce Department's Economic Development Administration in the 1970s resulted in millions spent to build vacation resorts and industrial parks on the reservations. But by 1980, only 5 percent of the small factories in the industrial parks were being used. In the 1980s, the Reagan administration's slashing of many of the federal programs that provided jobs for Native Americans on the reservations increased their unemployment. Among the Navajo, for example, unemployment soared to 72 percent in 1982, up from 38 percent the previous year. Similarly, the unemployment rate at the Pine Ridge Reservation increased from 56 percent in 1981 to 72 percent the following year.[35]

In early 2013, the "sequester debate"—the contentious wrangling over the federal budget between Republican members of Congress and President Barack Obama—became big news. A *New York Times* editorial in March 2013 reported that the budget cuts, "which have shown remarkable indifference to life sustaining government services, [would] impose cuts of 5 percent across the Indian Health Service, the modestly financed agency within the United States Department of Health and Human Services that provides basic health care to two million American Indians and native Alaskans." The editorial continues:

> It is underfinanced for its mission and cannot tolerate more deprivation. Here lies a little-noticed example of moral abdication. The biggest federal health and safety-net programs—Social Security, Medicaid, the Children's Health Insurance Program, the Supplemental Nutrition Assistance Program, Supplemental Social Security, the veteran's compensation and health benefits are all exempt from sequestration. But the Indian Health Service (health care provider for some of the poorest and sickest Americans, living in some of the most remote and medically underserved parts of the country) is not.[36]

Another *New York Times* editorial, in July 2013, reported on budget cuts in education, health, and safety affecting the welfare and well-being of all Native Americans, from the Oglala Sioux of South Dakota to the Navajo of Arizona. When asked how these cuts would affect the lives of these tribes, Richard Zephier, executive director of the Oglala Sioux, said: "More people sick, fewer people educated, fewer people getting general assistance; more domestic violence, more alcoholism."[37] Reneging on solemn treaty obligations to a Native American tribe is an old story, said the editorial, and the actions of lawmakers today are no exception.

This forced removal, forced assimilation, land allotment, and land reorganization, along with the mismanagement and corruption of the Bureau of Indian Affairs and continued neglect by the federal government and state governments, have made the reservations the poorest places in the United States. High rates of poverty, unemployment, violence, substance abuse, disease, and infant mortality, along with a life expectancy that is lower than the national average, high rates of suicide, inadequate and substandard housing, a high school dropout rate that is double the national average, and more, continue to plague the lives of Native Americans stuck in remote, desolate, barren outskirts of the country.

In this desolation, the only bright light is the casino/gaming industry. In 1988, Congress passed the Indian Gaming Regulatory Act. It requires that all proceeds from gaming activities be used to promote the economic development and welfare of the tribes. Tribal leaders and the Native American community did not come to gaming as a way of life easily. There was much soul-searching, caution, and skepticism about how such an enterprise would affect the quality of life for tribal members and how it would reflect on their spiritual belief systems. But in the absence of any other options, gaming became an attractive alternative.

In his account of the Native American gaming industry, James Schaap writes:

> As of 2008, 233 Indian tribes, including two Alaska Native villages, operated 411 casinos, bingo halls, and pull-tab operations in 28 states creating some 636,000 jobs. . . . Indian gaming revenues topped $26.7 billion. Tribal gaming has done what no other antipoverty program has been able to accomplish in reversing the cycle of displacement and impoverishment of Native Americans: tribal gaming has been hailed as the "new buffalo" for Indians [and] credited with wresting once destitute reservations from the grip of poverty, unemployment, and welfare dependency.[38]

Native American tribes have invested their gambling revenues in schools, roads, nursing homes, law enforcement, and businesses. They have also invested in various ventures in order to diversify "the existing mix of business enterprises," as a result of which "92 percent of the gaming tribes have experienced major growth in new employment opportunities."[39] The social and economic results have been invaluable. For example, the Foxwoods Casino Resort in Connecticut, owned by the Mashantucket Pequot, is the world's largest casino and has become an economic powerhouse, enriching the surrounding community, the state, and the fortunes of the tribe, and garnering the Mashantucket Pequot significant political clout in the process.

Even the successful casinos, though, have been plagued by suspicions of mismanagement, corruption, ties to organized crime, and the presence of profit-seeking foreign speculators. It cannot be denied that much of the celebrated increase in the numbers of mixed-race Native Americans that the US Census Bureau has reported is due to the increasing number of Americans who, motivated by the economic opportunities that the Native American gaming industry has opened, desire to become official members of Native American tribes in order to benefit legitimately from the success of this industry.

The Native American nations that have established the most successful gaming facilities on their reservations have also shown caution as they consider the membership applications of those who hope to join, subjecting them to intense scrutiny and circumspection. This has caused discord and controversy, as tribes have tried to zealously guard the process for limiting their numbers.

Since 2000, the practice of disenrollment, through which current members of a tribe who are alleged not to have legitimate proof of their membership are asked to leave the tribe, has become a contentious issue among at least thirty tribes in seventeen states, as Native Americans who lose membership face an uncertain future. They risk losing their monthly allowance paid from casino profits. Additionally they can also lose housing allowances, college scholarships, and their children's access to tribal schools. In California, some 2,500 Native Americans have been disenrolled by two dozen tribes since 2000 due to insufficient evidence of legitimate ancestry.[40]

Tribal councils, which have the final authority in decisions regarding enrollment and disenrollment, are also responsible for setting the rules that determine legitimate tribal ancestry. As hundreds are disenrolled from the tribes, there have been accusations of arbitrary decisionmaking by the tribal councils, which are accountable to no one, whether the Bureau of Indian Affairs, the federal government, or state governments. And as disenrollment increases, the benefits from casino revenues that accrue to the remaining members increase. Both victims of disenrollment and sympathetic observers bemoan that Native Americans are facing another campaign of "depopulation" today, except that this time it is the Native Americans themselves who are responsible.[41]

Not all tribes have been fortunate in the gaming business. Very little revenue is generated by small casinos located in hard-to-reach places. The success of casinos depends almost exclusively on their location. Those near urban and easily accessible areas have been much more successful than those in remote areas, which is where most of the tribes have always lived. The success of the casinos, therefore, does not counteract the need for different initiatives, both governmental and nongovernmental, to help ameliorate the chronic problems that so many Native Americans continue to face on their reservations. It was their land, resources, and labor, wrested from them with unspeakable violence and inhumanity, that built the floor on which US capitalism took root and flourished. But the process also created the conditions that perpetuate their destitution and disadvantage. Not only have investments not been made to bring about critical structural changes on reservations, such as better schools, job opportunities, and development of local businesses, other than casinos for the fortunate few, but social programs as well, which so many depend on, are continuously eroding. The plight of Native Americans seldom makes it in the news. They are the other "throwaway people," inconsequential to the existential reality of the nation.

Socially constructing Native Americans as "savages" to assuage the Christian notion of a "soul" was used to justify the breaking of treaties, the reneging of promises, the massacre of entire tribes, and the forceful removal of others from their ancestral lands—all so that the "Jeffersonian version of John Winthrop's 'city upon a hill' could be realized."[42] But it matters little whether the stereotype of the Native American as a "savage" was a deliberate construction of purposeful and premeditated design and ideology. What matters is that, couched in the jargon of "civilization" and "manifest destiny," the construction of this stereotype successfully realized its objectives—the decimation and impoverishment of the indigenous—committing them to the seemingly endless "savage" existence in which they continue to languish, five centuries after first contact.

A Nation of Immigrants?

With the indigenous vanquished, it was now left to the white Anglo-Saxon Protestant, the undisputed master of the New World, to define and shape this land's future destiny. In time it would become iconic as a "melting pot," a land of immigrants, and hailed as a crucible into which came peoples from all corners of the world, to be melted and molded into "American"; hence the motto *e pluribus unum*—"out of many, one."

But as historian John Hope Franklin has reminded us, it has always been easier for some to blend in than for others.[43] Some have always stood apart, and it has always been their burden to prove their American-ness, to prove that they belong. Each wave of immigrants came at a particular juncture in the development of the capitalist economic system, and their experience in the United States was molded by that fundamental reality. Regardless of the language in which it was couched—racism, national security, or xenophobia—the conflict and hostility the new immigrants faced was always economic in substance; it was about competition and control over land, resources, jobs, wages, privileges, and power.

Africans came involuntarily, enslaved as property. Plantation capitalism needed their labor to till the land. The Native Americans had turned out to be unsuitable for the rigorous labor that a plantation economy demanded. The white indentured servants from England, Germany, and Ireland, who made up 75 percent of the population of the colonies, experienced the same economic oppression as the Africans, with one significant difference: at the end of their period of indenture they would become free.

In the 1660s, Virginia started to institutionalize slavery, characterizing the Africans as property and requiring their service to their owners for the duration of their lives. Blacks were relegated to a "racially subordinate and stigmatized status, one below all whites regardless of their class."[44] The "racialization" of the class oppression of blacks served to pit them against the white laborers. For example, when poor whites were being recruited "for the struggle for liberty" during the American Revolution, they were promised "a bounty of three hundred acres of land and a slave—a healthy, sound Negro between ten and thirty years of age."[45]

In analyzing these historical currents, Ronald Takaki documents the fears about "class tensions and conflicts" that occupied the colonial landed gentry and how strategically important it was to ensure that white laborers would never consider black slaves as allies. A comprehensive understanding of race and race relations—historical and contemporary—requires an awareness of the class origins of racism and slavery.[46]

Racism continues to serve this function. If we can imagine a different scenario, according to which the presence of Africans in the United States is accounted for only in economic terms—to lessen the scarcity of labor—without couching this scenario in an ideology of racial inferiority, then once slavery was abolished, and blacks moved out of the plantation economy of the US South, they would only have to leave behind the shackles of servitude to be truly free and equal. But the racialization of that experience has ensured that genuine freedom and equality will remain elusive as long as blacks have to carry the burdens that racism fostered.

The Chinese were the largest group of Asians who started coming to the United States, even before the Civil War. They came voluntarily to work in contract labor and low-wage jobs in the California mines, in the construction of the railroads of the Central Pacific, and in the four key industries in San Francisco—boots and shoes, woolens, cigars and tobacco, and sewing. Many Chinese became tenant farmers, transforming the nature of farming in California. But when the US economy went into a depression in the 1870s, "labor leaders, newspapers, [and] politicians accused the Chinese for driving down wages and taking jobs from whites."[47] Chinese were described in racial terms as being morally inferior—very much like the Native Americans and the blacks.

Resentment from white workers led to anti-Chinese riots and violence, and eventually led to the Chinese Exclusion Act of 1882, which officially prohibited Chinese immigration. Faced with such hostility, the Chinese abandoned the mines, factories, and farms and sought out different ways to make a living, branching out to restaurants, stores, and laundries.[48] As the number of Chinese diminished due to the exclusionary legislation, the Japanese were recruited to fill their spots in the low-wage work of mines, farms, and construction. By the 1920s, they were the largest group of Asians in the United States. They had originally been recruited to labor in the sugarcane plantations in Hawaii, where they worked alongside other immigrants from Asia and made up 40 percent of the population.

In the mainland, the Japanese were a racial minority and faced the contempt of the white workers. Much of the hostility was directed at their success as farmers and the competition their economic competence presented. World War II accorded a great opportunity to eradicate that "threat." The anti-Japanese propaganda and the campaign to put them into concentration camps, on the charge that they were spies and conspirators, were led by the farming lobbies of California. Succumbing to this pressure, on February 19, 1942, President Franklin Roosevelt authorized the internment of 110,000 Japanese and Japanese Americans with Executive Order 9066. Both individual and commercial land and property belonging to the Japanese were pilfered and vandalized, and sold off at rock-bottom prices.

> The dollar loss suffered by Japanese-Americans is unknown. After the war, Congress permitted victims to seek compensation from the government, but failure to produce any documentary records demanded by the government was punishable by a $10,000 fine and five years imprisonment. Victims who had already lost thousands of dollars and several years of liberty to the federal government did not rush to take advantage of the offer. Those who did make claims often received compensation far below actual loss.[49]

It was not until 1987 that Japanese Americans received a formal apology. Those who had been interned, or their heirs, each received $20,000 in compensation.

Southern, Eastern, and Central European immigrants came to fill the ranks of the wage laborers in the fast-developing factory and construction jobs of industrial capitalism. Many came from Italy; many others were Jews from Russia and Poland. Between 1880 and 1927, 23 million European immigrants came to work in the US factories. All equally poor, they inhabited the grimy urban neighborhoods of New York, Boston, and Philadelphia. Not only were they the poorer cousins of the Europeans who had preceded them, but they were also considered racially inferior. They were entering the United States at a time when the Russian Revolution of 1917 was making the United States, the bastion of capitalism, uneasy, and the presence of immigrants from Eastern Europe, especially the Jews, made for much perturbation.

The strong nativist, anti-immigrant movement of this period was spawned by all these currents. Racism, the "red scare," and anti-Semitism proved to be a powerful mix as an unsteady economy, a growing labor movement, competition from immigrants, and the downward pressure on wages all made the economic fate of the native-born white worker progressively more unsteady. Nativist groups, which had their roots in groups such as the Supreme Order of the Star Spangled Banner, known as "know-nothings" for the secret oaths that members took, experienced a resurgence in the first two decades of the twentieth century. If the parent group was anti-Catholic, in their reincarnation the new nativists were vehemently anti-red, anti-radical. Socialists, anarchists, and unionists were the new targets, as were Italians and Jews. These nativists became influential enough to persuade

Congress to pass the Immigration Act of 1924. Known as the National Origins Act, it restricted immigration by imposing quotas on how many immigrants could enter the United States from each country. The restrictions were not lifted until the Immigration Act of 1965.

The case of the Mexicans and by extension other Latin Americans is somewhat different, since this single land mass known as the Americas is their place of origin, even though the title "America" has been usurped by the North for its own exclusive designation. No oceans have to be navigated for those here to move throughout this huge, diverse, and rich continent. For centuries, people did just that; like the currents of the air and the water, they traversed this land naturally, without the need to heed political borders.

In the American Southwest, it was the European American frontiersmen who were the immigrants—illegal immigrants to the Mexican territories that would become the California and Texas of today. At first they were welcomed by the Mexican government, given land, and persuaded to become Catholics. But the land and resources started attracting thousands of European American settlers, who came to own and transform it with their "enterprise," which they believed the Mexicans lacked. There was land into which the plantation economy and slavery could be expanded; there were rich troves of raw materials that would feed the factories in New England—cattle hide for the Irish laborers to manufacture boots and shoes; sperm oil from the whales off the coast of California to provide crucial fuel and lubricants; harbors for whaling ships to dock.

Ronald Takaki's evocative and poignant description of the transformation of the Southwest, as Americans crossed over into Mexico by the hundreds with impunity, conveys a powerful premonition of the balance of power that would determine the fate of these territories for almost 175 years, right up to the present moment. In *A Different Mirror,* Takaki tells the story of the Mexicans who lived in California on the eve of the Mexican War in 1846.[50] Spanish colonization of the region had begun in 1769 with the gradual founding of twenty-one mission churches along the California coastline. Some of the settlers came from Spain and others were *mestizos*—born of Native American and Spanish blood. The entire region, along with much of the Southwest, had become part of Mexico when it gained independence in 1821.

It was a society stratified by "color." The *rancheros*—the descendants of the Spanish—were white. They were the landed gentry who formed the upper crust of society. Some, like Don Mariano Vallejo, owned vast tracts of land. For these prosperous rancheros, Takaki says, wealth was not something to be accumulated, but something to support a lifestyle of genteel refinement. These rancheros spoke fluent Castilian, danced the waltz, lived in graceful homes with mahogany furniture and a piano in the parlor, and took repose in beds with embroidered linen. They liked their pastoral, aristocratic lifestyle.

Below them was the laboring class—the mestizos and the Native Americans. They were stratified by color, with the lowest being the darkest in color. The laborers worked inside and outside the ranch and the hacienda. The system was patriarchal, and as Dona Francisca Vallejo explained, the servants were treated as family members, and the *patrons* often became godparents to the children of their servants.

At the beginning, the foreigners from the United States were welcomed and treated with gracious hospitality. Takaki relates the stories that these Americans told of the kindness and hospitality of the native Californians. The Mexican government even offered land grants to encourage these Americans to convert to Catholicism and become naturalized Mexican citizens. Many Americans took the offer.

By the 1840s, however, more and more Americans were arriving, driven by dreams of wealth and landownership. They coveted what the Mexicans had, calling them "idle and thriftless" and chastising them for not putting to proper use the natural resources, forests, and grazing land. The new arrivals were determined to transform this land through their industry.

Takaki tells the story of General Mariano Vallejo and his wife Dona Francisca Vallejo, and how their world was turned upside down on the morning of June 6, 1846, when a ragtag band of thirty armed Americans stormed into their home in Sonoma, California. These were frontiersmen who rode the wave of US expansionism "celebrated as manifest destiny." In striking contrast to his US captors, Vallejo was educated and cultured. His house sported a vast library. A gentleman always, he even offered these men wine before his capture. Vallejo's captors were part of the several hundred Americans whose influx into his bucolic world would start the conquest of the Southwest.

The war came in earnest in 1846. Henry David Thoreau was jailed for refusing to pay taxes that funded a war he believed was unjust. Joshua Giddings and other abolitionists in the North derided the war as an effort to extend slavery to the West. Abraham Lincoln questioned the motives of the war. Regardless, the war waged on until the signing in 1848 of the Treaty of Guadalupe Hidalgo.

Mexico ceded the present-day states of California, New Mexico, and Nevada, and parts of Colorado, Arizona, and Utah, to the United States. Along with Texas, already lost in 1845, Mexico lost half of its territory. The new border was set at the Rio Grande, farther south than the original border on the Rio Nueces. As the border moved southward, thousands of Mexican who lived between the two borders became foreigners in their own land.

But it was not just their land, but also their labor—in mining, railroad construction, ranching, and farming—that would become essential to the growth and development of US capitalism. In the ensuing years, the fields and factories of "El Norte"—the North—would continue to pull Mexicans, and later Central and South Americans, to the border and then beyond.

The US-Mexico border is the only place in the world where first world and third world actually physically meet. Remarking upon this reality, Gloria Anzaldua says that "the US-Mexican border *es una herida abierta* (is an open wound) where the third world grates against the first and bleeds, hemorrhages, the lifeblood of two worlds merging to form a third country, a border culture."[51] Ever since the Treaty of Guadalupe Hidalgo, this "third country" has been a source of militarization, environmental destruction, and violence.

Immigrant Labor

Until the 1920s, the US-Mexico border was comparatively unfortified—individuals from both sides would come and go to work day jobs, shop, or visit relatives without hindrance. But that would soon change, and the welcome mat for the Mexican would be laid out and rolled back in step with the ebb and flow of the labor needs of the US economy. For example, in the 1930s, during the height of the Great Depression, more than half a million Mexicans were deported from the United States, simply to be invited back after passage of the Emergency Farm Labor Agreement between the United States and Mexico, better known as the "bracero" program, in 1942. Between then and 1964, it brought 4.6 million Mexican nationals into the United States to labor as farmworkers.

Initially the idea was to fill the gap left by Americans going off to fight in World War II. But at the end of the war, as the US economy enjoyed unprecedented growth, Mexican farm laborers became a mainstay for US agriculture and provided for much of its bounty. But even as the Mexican "guest workers" were toiling in the farms, over a million were being forcefully deported under Operation Wetback of 1954, which targeted the illegal *mojados,* or "wetbacks." Such inconsistencies and contradictions are characteristic of immigration policy in the United States, most significantly in regard to its southern neighbors.

In 2011, for example, as the debate surrounding comprehensive immigration reform became more and more contentious, many of the same politicians "who want every employer in the country to use E-Verify, the federal hiring database, and fire the workers it flags as unauthorized," were "sponsoring a bill to flood the agricultural sector with up to half a million visas for guest workers." The *New York Times* reminded these politicians that "there's one group that badly needs and deserves visas that no one seems to want to go to bat for. They are the 11 million undocumented immigrants who are already living here and helping make things work."[52]

Migrations of documented or undocumented immigrants are "preeminently migrations of labor." It is noteworthy that when the US Border Patrol was first created in 1925, it was part of the Department of Labor. Therefore, when we recognize that the primary function of immigration laws is to control and subordinate labor, "the incoherence, inconsistencies and contradictions in their tactics, strategies and compromises" make perfect sense.[53] It is in this context of immigration laws and their role in controlling the mobility of labor that the function of the state to facilitate the operation of the global capitalist economy becomes evident. Immigration laws have become arenas where "the protracted and more or less concealed civil war" between capital and labor, as described by Karl Marx, is being continuously fought.[54]

On the one hand, political and legal structures that create these laws constrain the mobility of labor. Therefore, migrations of undocumented labor and the constant threat of its deportability have become complementary realities that "impose conditions of enforced and protracted vulnerability" among migrant workers, says William Robinson. He notes that Latino immigrants have added massive numbers to the lower rungs of the US work force:

> Employers do not want to do away with Latino immigrants. To the contrary, they want to sustain a vast exploitable labour pool that exists under precarious conditions, that does not enjoy the civil, political and labour rights of citizens and that is disposable through deportation. It is the condition of deportability that they wish to create or preserve, since that condition assures the ability to super-exploit with impunity and to dispose of this labour without consequences should it become unruly or unnecessary.[55]

On the other hand, efforts to regulate the mobility of labor are matched with the increased legal and economic freedom granted to capital. Capital has always had the capacity to be more mobile than labor. However, since 1994, trade treaties such as the North American Free Trade Agreement have made borders even more permeable for capital and goods. In the new global economy, therefore, capital and goods can move freely across borders and nestle wherever they can maximize their return. Consequently, "in an apparent contradiction, capital and goods move freely across national borders in the new global economy but labour cannot and its movement is subject to heightened state controls."[56]

The intention of state controls is not to prevent transnational movement of labor, but to control it. If labor were completely free to go wherever it could, this would put an equalizing pressure on wages across national borders. Controlling the movement of labor maintains the wage differentials that the capitalist can take advantage of to maximize profits. And thus, eliminating these wage differentials would cancel the advantages that accrue to capital; this would also strengthen the power of labor in relation to capital.[57] Increased mobility of capital and the parallel efforts to diminish the mobility of labor illustrate "labor and capital as mutually constituting poles of a single, albeit contradictory, social relation"[58]—a social relation that is integral to the system of global capitalism.

The upsurge of transnational migration worldwide is the direct result of forces generated by an increasingly globalized capitalist system, led primarily by corporations headquartered in the United States. Even according to the conservative estimates of the United Nations, close to 232 million individuals constituted the worldwide cohort of immigrant labor as of 2013. In the United States, there were an estimated 30 million immigrants as of 2005, of whom 20 million were from Latin America, and of whom 12 million who were considered "undocumented." An estimated 78 percent of the undocumented came from Latin America—and 57 percent from Mexico alone. Asians made up 13 percent of this group, 6 percent were from Europe and Canada, and about 3 percent were from Africa and elsewhere.[59] Although most of the undocumented workers in the United States come from Latin America, in the national consciousness and in the debates about immigration it is the social construction of all Latino immigrants as "illegals" that looms menacingly, stereotyping an entire population.

The most recent upsurge in Latino immigration to the United States has come on the heels of the implementation of NAFTA, which went into effect in January 1994. Under NAFTA, all tariff and nontariff barriers to trade and investment between the United States and Mexico were eliminated. As a result of the elimination of trade barriers in agriculture, federally subsidized surplus corn and other agricultural products from the United States flooded the Mexican markets. The Mexican farmer and the Mexican government did not have the power to stop the flood or to broker a comparable deal that would provide an equally profitable market for Mexican farm products, such as tomatoes and broccoli, in the United States.

In the end, Mexican farmers lost their share of the market, lost their lands, and started to make their way northward in search of other ways to make a living. Often their first stop is on the border, where hundreds of maquiladoras—the assembly plants of multinational corporations—dot the landscape. But the wages they are paid are inadequate to provide for the basic needs of themselves and their families, especially since the cost of living in border towns is prohibitive, often 30 percent higher than in parts of Mexico farther south of the border. And as the transnational corporations move more and more of their factories overseas, such as to China and Bangladesh, Mexican workers have even fewer options left.

So they cross the desert and swim the rivers, "pay the coyote" to escape detection by all the scanners along the increasingly militarized US-Mexico border. Once in this unfamiliar land, they try to find a way to secure livelihoods and send money back home to their families—living each day in fear of being caught and deported back to a place of even greater economic insecurity, where rampant drug wars, gun trafficking, gang fighting, police brutality, and police corruption all compound the urgency many Mexicans feel to flee northward. Many of those who cross the border today once had middle-class lives and middle-class jobs but fell victim to the random violence engulfing their neighborhoods in the border towns.

Global Contexts of Immigration

Latin Americans have fled from violence before. Thousands fled from the civil wars that engulfed the Central American countries—Nicaragua, El Salvador, Guatemala, and Honduras—in the 1980s. In the second half of the twentieth century, in the shadow of the Cold War, these countries and others in Latin America experienced horrific violence that accompanied US efforts to rid the "neighborhood" of communists. In order to fully understand the Latin American experience with global capitalism today, along with the continuous flow of Latino immigrants to the United States, we must consider the historical context.

In her book *The Declassified Eisenhower: A Divided Legacy of Peace and Political Warfare,* Blanche Wiesen Cook documents the route that US foreign policy, in the guise of fighting communism, took for the express purpose of making the world a friendly place for US capital. "Named a moral crusade against communist tyranny, America's commitment to lead a free world was a life and death contest for access and control of the earth's resources."[60]

The Cold War really began in October 1917, when Vladimir Ilyich Lenin declared that the revolution led by workers and peasants had ended class privilege and that Russia would no longer be available for capitalist investment. In one stroke, one-sixth of the world's land mass became out of reach to global capital.

The rise of the Nazi menace distracted the United States for the duration of World War II. But soon after, beginning in the early 1950s, the Cold War engaged all of America's energies, both domestic and international. What had happened in the Soviet Union could not be allowed to happen anywhere else, and everything necessary would have to be done to stop the specter of communism and its appropriation of what "rightfully" belonged to the "free world."

US foreign economic policy, by the middle of President Dwight Eisenhower's first administration, sought to "transform the United States' corporate system into a world system."[61] And toward that end, no stone would be left unturned. No country would be off-limits. It would be a worldwide crusade to counter any threat from any party or individual who was directly or indirectly sympathetic to communism. To this end, there was interference with the elections in Italy, Germany, and France; and underground resistance, covert operations, counterinsurgency tactics, and guerrilla operations in Vietnam, Laos, the Democratic Republic of Congo, Iran, Guatemala, and Cuba. To "strengthen the orientation to the U.S. . . . all covert operations were to be planned and executed so that US Government responsibility in them is not evident."[62]

The expectation integral to these tactics was that they would usher in the "American Century," signifying the worldwide victory of the American way of life, ensuring a global marketplace for US capital, and delivering the death knell to communism, everywhere. And as Francis Fukuyama reveled, after the fall of the Soviet Union, this would mean the "end of history" itself.

To save the world from communism and shepherd in the American Century, the United States would have to encourage private investment of US capital in foreign countries, including the underdeveloped countries of the world. In a prescient assertion, Clarence Randall, Eisenhower's special consultant on foreign economic policy, in promoting "outward flow of American private investment capital," said: "Private American Capital must do it because we want to and it must be because we will make more money than by investment in the United States."[63] In fact, anyone who urged that investments remain in the United States was dismissed as "creating a receptivity to communist blandishments"; US nationalism became a chief enemy of "our foreign economic policy" and economic nationalists had to be replaced by "more appropriate internationalists."[64]

Nationalism was considered a hotbed for communism. That is why Mohammad Mosaddegh of Iran and Jacobo Árbenz Guzmán of Guatemala, democratically elected leaders of their countries, had to be forcibly removed in 1953 and 1954, respectively, when each claimed that the natural resources of their country—oil in the case of Iran and land in the case of Guatemala—belonged to their nation and were therefore to be developed not for the gain of foreign multinationals but for the well-being of their people.

Árbenz vehemently denied that his ideas for land reform, universal education, and universal health care for his people showed communistic tendencies. But the very fact that these leaders, and others who would come later, would put the interests of their peoples and nations above the interests of the multinational corporations—such as British Petroleum, Shell, Mobil, United Fruit Company, Getty Oil, Anaconda Copper, and Kennecott Copper—made them dangerous to the interests of US capital.

Removing them from power was the only option, said their opponents. It is hard to know how many died, were tortured, or were "disappeared" in the violence that engulfed Latin America in the second half of the twentieth century. What is certain is that these countries have yet to recover from the downward spiral of their communities that US policy caused. As Blanche Cook writes: "For the people in Guatemala, Eisenhower's 1954 legacy has been an endless battle against terror and death. Although the United States has used Eisenhower's Guatemalan model over and over again, for thirty years there have been no final victories."[65] Other than the victories that were secured for capital, for multinational corporations—US and European.

Karl Marx maintained that, contrary to liberal theories "that describe the transition to capitalism as a spontaneous and relatively peaceful process, this historical shift was intricately tied up with relations of force and social struggle. Rather than occurring naturally, Marx argued, 'capital comes dripping from head to toe, from every pore, with blood and dirt.'"[66] In considering the tactics discussed here, it would seem that "the reproduction and extension of capitalism continues to involve relations of violence, coercion and constraint."[67]

The massive numbers of immigrants who have come to the United States are economic refugees seeking escape from the consequences of decades of neoliberalism that have led to capitalist globalization, structural adjustment policies, free trade treaties, and **privatization**. They also have come seeking asylum from the violence that political crises and criminal violence have spawned.

William Robinson writes that these economic and political crises have "imploded thousands of communities in Latin America and unleashed a wave of migration, from rural to urban areas and to other countries, that can only be analogous to the mass uprooting and migration that generally takes place in the wake of war."[68]

Stalled Immigration Reform

As the numbers of immigrants to the United States skyrocketed, so did the hostility, with new waves of nativism and xenophobia permeating a large segment of the national consciousness. Threatened by economic restructuring, deindustrialization, outsourcing, downsizing, and the accompanying uncertainties brought on by terrorism, it was easy for much of the nation to scapegoat the undocumented, and so everyone else who looked like they might be undocumented got caught in that net.

Not only were the undocumented blamed for driving down wages, but they were also derided for helping themselves to benefits that they did not pay for and therefore did not deserve. Therefore, the anti-immigrant lobby argued, the immigrants were draining the economy. The Social Security Administration, however, has credited the contributions of immigrants, as much as $7 billion a year, for keeping Social Security solvent.

Immigrants contribute much more to the US economy than they receive in return in areas such as health care and social services.[69] They have very little to do with setting the wages they receive. It is the capitalist labor market that determines wages and "actively seeks to minimize labor costs (regardless of where the labor comes from) in order to increase profitability."[70] It is most often the migrant workers who get cheated out of their legitimate share.

There are countless instances of migrant workers not receiving wages for their work and receiving no compensation when they become injured or even die from working in dangerous conditions with lethal equipment and substances. The Southern Poverty Law Center published an exhaustive report in 2009 that documents the abuse, exploitation, discrimination, and harassment of Latino workers, including thousands "who flocked to New Orleans to help restore the city after Hurricane Katrina."[71] The report confirms the fact that "the lack of their legal status makes them easy prey for unscrupulous employers and puts them at constant risk from law enforcement. But even legal residents and US citizens of Latino descent say that racial profiling, bigotry and myriad other forms of discrimination and injustice are staples of their daily lives. The assumption is that every Latino possibly is undocumented."[72]

It is the vulnerability of Latino immigrants that makes them so targetable. Before the 1960s, this status was held by blacks. They occupied the lowest rungs of the US caste system. But the civil rights victories, the Black Pride movement, and the role of blacks in the labor movement radicalized their status, making them undesirable to employers, some of whom were still uncomfortable with the idea of desegregation and racial equality.

William Robinson writes: "Starting in the 1980s, employers began to push out Black workers and massively recruit Latino immigrants, a move that coincided with deindustrialization and restructuring. Blacks moved from super-exploited to marginalized—subject to unemployment, cuts in social services, mass incarceration and heightened state repression—while Latino immigrant labour has become the new super-exploited sector."[73]

It is in their experiences as the incarcerated—in prisons and detention centers—that the lives of the "former super-exploited" and the "new super-exploited" converge. As of the fall of 2013, according to a policy report by the National Immigration Forum, almost 31,800 immigrants are being held at approximately 260 Immigrations and Customs Enforcement (ICE) detention centers around the country, at a cost of over $5 million per day.[74] Most are awaiting deportation.

Although a comprehensive bill on immigration reform has stalled in the House of Representatives since summer 2013, when it was passed by the Senate, this did not stop the House from approving a budget of $5.4 billion for ICE operations for fiscal year 2014. Immigration detention has

MAKING CONNECTIONS
Immigration Reform Is Common Sense

Javier Martinez is an intelligent and charismatic young man. He recently graduated from Brookdale Community College in Lincroft, New Jersey. He wants to become a lawyer. He is a "dreamer"—a member of the generation of young people who were born of undocumented parents but Americans in every sense.

President Barack Obama aptly recognized them as "Americans in their hearts, in their minds, in every single way but one: paper" when he announced the Deferred Action for Childhood Arrivals policy. Along with other measures, the policy offers temporary protection from deportation to the young who have not committed a felony or significant misdemeanor and are receiving an education. By August 15, 2013, which marked the one-year anniversary of the enactment of this policy, 430,000 young people had received deferred action. Many more would have registered if they could have afforded the $465 needed to secure the application and the approximately $600 required to cover the legal expenses.

When this policy is combined with comprehensive immigration reform, the United States will be on its way to recognizing the value of the 11 million undocumented immigrants who for too long have been forced to live in the shadows. Providing a path to citizenship is the "commonsense" thing to do when one considers the economic benefits of such an initiative.

According to research by Robert Lynch and Patrick Oakford of the Center for American Progress, providing earned citizenship for undocumented immigrant workers would increase their wages and by 2022 raise US gross domestic product by $568 billion and increase total income for all Americans by $321 billion. The increased income would generate $75 billion in additional state and federal tax revenue from currently undocumented immigrants, and add about 820,000 jobs to the US economy.[1] In the summer of 2013, the Senate passed a bipartisan immigration bill to provide such earned citizenship. But the bill has stalled in the House of Representatives.

In the meantime, the lives of the undocumented continue to be as perilous as ever. Deportations have continued ceaselessly even as the country is engaged in negotiations over immigration reform. It is estimated that between 2009 and 2014, the United States will deport nearly 2 million individuals. By deporting as many as possible before the reforms are enacted, it seems as if the administration is ensuring that there will be fewer immigrants to deal with when the time comes to recognize their citizenship.

Note: 1. Lynch and Oakford, "National and State by State Economic Benefits of Immigration Reform."

grown dramatically over the past decade, with the number of detention beds nearly doubling, from 18,000 in 2004 to 34,000 in 2013.[75]

The total number of immigrants who pass through ICE detention per year rose from 204,459 in 2001 to a record-breaking 429,247 individuals in 2011.[76] This expansion of immigration detention has created a profitable market for private prison corporations and local governments. Just like private prisons, which hold a bulk of the black incarcerated population, and are primarily interested in seeing those numbers rise, similarly when private prisons such as the Corrections Corporation of America branch out into the immigrant detention business, the question that automatically comes up concerns how changes in the nation's immigration policy will affect their business.

The GEO Group is another corporation whose business is prisons and immigrant detention centers. In its 2011 annual report, the company warns of "adverse effects" from immigration reform potentially reducing demand for its services. Lee Fang of *The Nation* reports: "In recognition of the profits at stake, the prison companies have invested in key legislators leading the reform process."[77]

There is also a conflict of interest when the politicians in charge of immigration reform are also supported by the prison industry through campaign contributions. But these lobbying efforts are nothing new. "CCA and other large private prison companies have forged ties with political insiders by spending huge sums on lobbying firms, campaign contributions and grants to friendly think tanks. An analysis by the Associated Press last year found that the three major private prison corporations—CCA, the GEO Group, the industry's largest two companies, along with a smaller company, the Utah-based Management and Training Corporation—spent roughly $45 million over the past decade to influence state and federal government."[78] According to the Center for Responsive Politics:[79]

- The CCA spent $17.4 million in lobbying expenditures between 2003 and 2012.
- In the same period, the CCA contributed $1.9 million to the campaigns of state legislators.
- In 2011, the 91,000 beds in CCA detention facilities generated a revenue of $1.7 billion.
- In 2011, Damon Hininger, the CEO of CCA, earned $3.7 million in executive compensation.
- The GEO Group spent $2.5 million in lobbying expenditures between 2003 and 2012.
- In the same period, it contributed $2.9 million to the campaigns of state legislators.
- In 2011, the 65,716 beds in its detention facilities generated a revenue of $1.6 billion.
- In 2011, George Zoley, the CEO of the GEO Group, earned $5.7 million in executive compensation.

Given the profit-making built around undocumented immigrants in the United States, from exploiting their labor in the economy, to exploiting their **carcerality** in private detention centers, there is nothing just matter-of-fact about the "illegal" status of undocumented immigrants. Nicholas DeGenova writes in reference to this: "The category 'illegal alien' is a profoundly useful and profitable one that effectively serves to create and sustain a legally vulnerable—and hence, relatively tractable and thus 'cheap'—reserve of labor. That proposition is quite old; indeed, it is so well established and well-documented as to be irrefutable. There may be no smoking gun, but there is nonetheless a lot of smoke in the air."[80]

MAKING CONNECTIONS
La Unidad Hace la Fuerza: **In Unity Is Strength**

Emiliano Ruiz and Fernando Aguilar live in Freehold, New Jersey. Both are immigrants from Mexico and have been in the United States for many years. In that period, they have become recognized and respectable members of the immigrant community. Both are board members of Casa Freehold, an immigrant advocacy and support group. Ruiz also serves as the vice president. They are both born leaders.

Yet the seeming normality of their lives is just an illusion. In New Jersey, they risk being caught every time they get behind the wheel of a car. They cannot apply for a driver's license due to their undocumented status. But it is impossible not to drive—people have to go to work, children have to be taken to doctors, groceries have to be bought. Simple daily activities that the rest of us think nothing about take on an entirely different reality in the lives of the undocumented.

In 2011, Fernando was on his way to Washington state to get a driver's license. Washington, like a few other states, allows the undocumented to receive a driver's license. The undocumented, not surprisingly, flock to these states. He was traveling with a friend. While they were driving through North Dakota, their car was stopped for no discernible reason. Fernando was in the passenger seat and was asked to show identification, in clear violation of the constitutional protection against unlawful search and seizure for all individuals who reside in the United States. When he was unable to produce such a document, he was immediately arrested and scheduled for deportation proceedings.

Similarly, in the spring of 2013, Emiliano was caught driving without a license in Freehold itself. "Secure communities" is a provision that gives the local police the authority to match fingerprints and determine undocumented status for every arrest they make. So his traffic violation got Emiliano caught in the deportation web. He was apprehended immediately. He would "do time" in the Monmouth County jail for six weekends, and any decision on his final status would be postponed until the end of the six weeks.

August 16–19, 2013, was Emiliano's final weekend behind bars. To the utter dismay of family and friends awaiting his release, ICE detained him and proceeded immediately with the deportation process.

(continues)

La Unidad Hace la Fuerza: In Unity Is Strength

The news spread by word of mouth and Facebook. The larger Casa Free-hold family mobilized into action, calling ICE and protesting in front of the detention center. Their efforts proved successful. To the relief of all of Emiliano's supporters and friends, he was released and his case deportation was terminated. As Emiliano's lawyer, John Leschak, wrote: "In unity, is strength. *La unidad hace la fuerza!*"

This was an incredible story of victory—but only because of the immigrant support group Casa Freehold and its savvy director, Rita Dentino, who was able to negotiate terms with the local law enforcement agents and ICE representatives, not to mention its many advocates and volunteers.

This turned out well for Fernando too. His friend, a US citizen, paid his immigration bond, and he remains free for now.

For families and immigrant communities who live in the shadows, facing the constant threat of having their lives destroyed through the specter of deportation, knowing that there are individuals and groups who tirelessly advocate for them makes their life in the shadows just a little more bearable. It makes them realize that, despite the inhumanity in so many aspects of their lives, there are those who recognize the true value in who they are—in the common human essence that they share with everyone else regardless of political boundaries and bureaucratic protocol.

Conclusion

The land and resources that enabled the system of US capitalism to grow and flourish were appropriated forcefully from the indigenous population. Although this is a known fact, another fact—that Native Americans, a third of them out of sight in reservations, are absent from so much of the public discourse—necessitates a retelling of some of the circumstances that created their destitution.

When we speak of inequality and the processes that engendered it, the experience of Native Americans is pertinent. Their experience of deprivation and inequality is unique, because the United States, unlike all the other groups who have made the country home, was their home first. And their history since the 1500s has been one of gradual loss of everything they once had. No group has a monopoly on suffering, but the torment of the indigenous of this land is particularly egregious.

January 1, 1994, marked the day that NAFTA went into effect and also the day that the Zapatista national liberation movement started in Mexico's Chiapas state. The Zapatistas organized to defend the rights of the peasants, workers, and indigenous from what they correctly perceived to be an onslaught from global capitalism. NAFTA, which accelerated globalization in the Americas, produced an **immiserization** in Latin America, bringing massive waves of immigrants to the United States. The downward pressures on wages that the presence of immigrants creates, compared to the presence of native-born workers, make for an environment rife with nativist tensions.

Immigrants from Latin America have borne the brunt of the recent anti-immigrant crusades in the United States. Attitudes toward Latinos have ebbed and flowed according to the vicissitudes of the economy. Tossed about on contradictory currents, these immigrants, many of them undocumented, have suffered, as have their communities, their advocates, and even the politicians who are entrusted with the responsibility of passing comprehensive immigration reform.

A rash of racist attacks against them across the country—barely noticed by the mass media—and anti-immigrant legislation in many states, alongside daily experiences of slavelike wages or wage thefts, have brought into stark relief the continued oppression that immigrants, particularly the undocumented, face. Globalization has intensified the contradictions in the economy, exacerbating the already existing structures of inequality and oppression. Worldwide, people have been tossed around as the forces of globalization push them out of their traditional livelihoods, or make it difficult for them to make a living on low wages at multinational factories and maquiladoras, leaving them no other choice but to try their luck at immigration.

Notes

1. Kristof, "Poverty's Poster Child," p. A29.
2. US Census Bureau, "American Community Survey." Unless otherwise noted, this is the source for all statistics cited in these introductory paragraphs.
3. US Census Bureau, "The American Indian and Alaska Native Population."
4. Levene, *Genocide in the Age of the Nation State*, p. 9.
5. Stannard, *American Holocaust*, p. x.
6. Ibid.
7. Quoted in ibid., pp. 126–127.
8. Quoted in ibid., p. 129.
9. Quoted in ibid., p. 134.
10. Quoted in Brown, *Bury My Heart at Wounded Knee*, p. 388. See also Decker, *The Utes Must Go*.
11. Takaki, *A Different Mirror*, p. 44.
12. Ibid.
13. Ibid., p. 39.
14. Ibid., p. 40 (emphasis in original).
15. Quoted in Maybury-Lewis, *Indigenous People, Ethnic Groups, and the State*, p. 3.
16. Quoted in Takaki, *A Different Mirror*, p. 88.
17. Rockman, "Liberty Is Land and Slaves," p. 8.
18. North, *The Economic Growth of the United States*, pp. 68–70.

19. Ibid., p. 190.
20. Limerick, *The Legacy of Conquest,* p. 55.
21. Harmon, O'Neill, and Rosier, "Interwoven Economic Histories," p. 699.
22. Ibid., p. 700.
23. Ibid., p. 708.
24. Schaap, "The Growth of the Native American Gaming Industry," p. 367.
25. Quoted in Takaki, *A Different Mirror,* p. 48.
26. Rosier, "'They Are Ancestral Homelands,'" p. 1305.
27. Takaki, *A Different Mirror,* p. 238.
28. Ibid., p. 239.
29. Harmon, O'Neill, and Rosier, "Interwoven Economic Histories," p. 712.
30. Ibid., p. 707.
31. Ibid., p. 715.
32. Ibid.
33. Ibid., p. 717.
34. Tillett, "Reality Consumed by Realty," p. 153.
35. Manning, "Unleashing the Spirit."
36. *New York Times,* "The Sequester Hits the Reservation," p. A26.
37. *New York Times,* "Abandoned in Indian Country," p. A22.
38. Schaap, "The Growth of the Native American Gaming Industry," pp. 368–369.
39. Ibid., p. 379.
40. Dao, "In California, Indian Tribes with Casinos Eject Thousands," p. A20.
41. Ferry, "I Know I Am, but What Are You?"
42. Takaki, *A Different Mirror,* p. 50.
43. Franklin, "Ethnicity in American Life," p. 14.
44. Ibid., p. 67.
45. Ibid., p. 68.
46. Takaki, *A Different Mirror,* pp. 54–68.
47. Feagin and Booher-Feagin, *Racial and Ethnic Relations,* p. 291.
48. Ibid., pp. 191–222.
49. Miller, "Confiscations from Japanese-Americans During World War II."
50. Takaki, *A Different Mirror,* pp. 166–178.
51. Segura and Zavella, *Women and Migration in the U.S.-Mexico Borderlands,* p. 4.
52. *New York Times,* "So Much for the Nativists," p. A30.
53. DeGenova, "Migrant 'Illegality' and Deportability in Everyday Life," p. 422.
54. Ibid., p. 425.
55. Robinson, "'Aqui Estamos y No Nos Vamos!'" p. 84.
56. Ibid., p. 83.
57. Ibid.
58. DeGenova, "Migrant 'Illegality' and Deportability in Everyday Life," p. 423.
59. Lin, "Undocumented Workers in the US," p. 4871.
60. Cook, *The Declassified Eisenhower,* p. 183.
61. Ibid., p. 307.
62. Ibid., p. 183.
63. Ibid., p. 312.
64. Ibid., p. 314.
65. Ibid., p. 292.
66. Quoted in LeBaron and Roberts, "Toward a Feminist Political Economy of Capitalism and Carcerality," p. 19.

67. Ibid.
68. Robinson, "'Aqui Estamos y No Nos Vamos!'" p. 85.
69. Ibid., p. 88.
70. Lin, "Undocumented Workers in the US," p. 4871.
71. Southern Poverty Law Center, *Under Siege,* p. 7.
72. Ibid., p. 5.
73. Robinson, "'Aqui Estamos y No Nos Vamos!'" p. 87.
74. National Immigration Forum, "The Math of Immigration Detention."
75. Ibid.
76. Ibid.
77. Fang, "How Private Prisons Game the Immigration System."
78. Ibid.
79. Cited in Lee, "By the Numbers."
80. DeGenova, "Migrant 'Illegality' and Deportability in Everyday Life," pp. 439–440.

Part 3

Is Change Possible?

12

Advocating for Workers

THE OBJECTIVE OF THIS CHAPTER IS TO EXPLORE THE WAYS IN WHICH attempts to reduce inequality are thwarted. Historically, labor unions played a critical role in promoting efforts for change in capitalist societies, by championing movements that advocated for social justice. In both Europe and the United States, fundamental social reforms were realized through the union movement. Unions spoke up for and sided with the poor and the middle class. They provided a countervailing power to the hegemony of the "power elite." Strong unions were responsible for ending many of the most egregious workplace violations and also for urging the creation of programs that today make up the social safety net.

Since the early 1970s, however, the United States has seen a gradual eclipse of the union movement and a consequent undermining of its role in effecting social change. This decline has occurred as the membership in unions has dwindled as a result of changes in the structure of the economy, employment, and the workplace. At the same time, a deliberate and persistent endeavor by anti-union forces in business and government, fed by a conservative, neoliberal ideology, has chipped away at the legal guarantees of the 1935 National Labor Relations Act, which gave workers the right to unionize and exercise collective bargaining to correct the power imbalances in the workplace.

The declining clout of the unions has left large segments of working people, in both the private sector and the public sector, powerless to deal with the continuous threats of joblessness, reshuffling and curtailing of their work schedules and work hours, and cuts in wages and benefits. Consequently, the gulf between them and the affluent has grown steadily and invariably. This chapter considers the reasons why the union movement is faltering and how this will impact the future economic well-being of the United States, and also considers, more broadly, the kind of society and the kind of democracy that this steady eclipse of the union movement portends.

The Golden Age of Unions

In order to judge how much the unions have weakened, it is important to remind ourselves of the "golden age of unions," between 1947 and 1973, when union density was at its peak and 35 percent of the working class belonged to unions.[1] Real wages rose 75 percent from the preceding period, before World War II, and workers' share of gross domestic product, the aggregate total of all goods and services produced in the country, rose to 53 percent.

Similarly, between 1947 and 1972, worker productivity grew by 102 percent and the median household income rose by an identical 102 percent.[2] These, of course, were also the years when the economic landscape was verdant, flush from the stimulus of World War II and a strong economy. But the New Deal economic and social policies had also transformed society. The National Labor Relations Act of 1935 guaranteed workers the right to form unions. Collective bargaining was "embedded in the nation's fabric."[3] But the labor movement in the United States has a history of ebbing and flowing.

Even though workers and their collective movements were a particularly powerful presence all through the early 1900s, and even though Congress periodically enacted pro-labor legislation, unions were largely considered "illegal conspiracies" until the 1930s.[4] In 1933, Congress, during the presidency of Franklin Roosevelt, enacted the National Industrial Recovery Act, which for the first time gave workers the right to join and form unions, stating that "employees shall have the right to organize and bargain collectively through representatives of their own choosing, and shall be free from interference, restraint, or coercion of employers."[5] But the Supreme Court promptly struck down the pro-labor legislation, declaring it unconstitutional.

It was not until 1935 that Congress finally passed and President Roosevelt signed the National Labor Relations Act. Craig Becker and Judith Scott, writing for *The Nation,* recall somewhat wistfully the rationale that Congress set forth in the Act:

> The inequality of bargaining power between employees who do not possess full freedom of association . . . and employers who are organized in the corporate or other forms of ownership association . . . tends to aggravate recurrent business depressions, by depressing wage rates and the purchasing power of wage earners in industry. In other words, Congress recognized that economic crisis was linked to disparities in wealth, which, in turn, were inseparable from imbalances of power in the workplace.[6]

The National Labor Relations Act, therefore, gave workers the right to join unions on the premise that "the U.S. needs workers to be able to bargain for higher wages to increase national purchasing power and prosperity."[7] In

1937, the Supreme Court affirmed the law as constitutional, as enabling workers "to deal on an equality with their employers" and creating democracy in the workplace, where workers now had the "fundamental right" to "self-organization and to select representatives of their own choosing for collective bargaining . . . without restraint or coercion from the employer."[8]

It will be worthwhile to take one more detour into labor history to remind ourselves of a tradition of worker progressivism in the United States, all but forgotten today, that improved the lives of Americans in fundamental ways.

The American Roots of May Day

Eighteen workers and trade unionists died in 1886 in the first week of May in Chicago and Milwaukee as they tried to implement a resolution, passed jointly by the Federation of Organized Trades and Labor Unions (renamed the American Federation of Labor in 1886) and the Knights of Labor, declaring that "eight hours shall constitute a legal day's work from and after May 1, 1886," and recommending that "labor organizations throughout this district . . . so direct their laws as to conform to this resolution."[9]

This resolution was a radical call that went against the usual routine of most factory workers in the early years of the industrial revolution in the United States. Employers expected their workers—children as well as adults—to work from sunup to sundown in deplorable working conditions, six days a week, with very little time, if any, for rest and recreation. Workers felt like slaves, having no time they could call their own.

A call for a general strike in Chicago on May 1 went out to all the labor groups, with the resolve that workers would continue to strike unless employers agreed to an eight-hour workday. The eight-hour-workday movement came at a time when workers, farmers, and labor unions were rebelling against the growing power of monopolies and were energized by the vision of a different kind of society, cooperative rather than capitalistic, popularized by the Knights of Labor.

According to historian James Green: "What happened on May 1st 1886 was more than a general strike; it was a populist movement when working people believed they could destroy plutocracy, redeem democracy and then create a cooperative commonwealth."[10] On May 3, the police shot to death six striking workers at McCormick Reaper Works in Chicago. On May 4, when workers held a peaceful meeting at a Chicago square called the Haymarket to protest the killings, the police moved in again. A bomb went off. To this day, no one knows who the perpetrator was. The police opened fire, killing seven or eight civilians and wounding many more. On May 5, as thousands of Milwaukee workers were marching peacefully on the huge Bay View Rolling Mills to support the nationwide effort to bring about the eight-hour day, Governor Jeremiah Rusk brought in the state militia, who fired into the crowd of peaceful demonstrators, killing seven. In the course of those few fateful days in May 1886, lives were sacrificed so generations of Americans would enjoy a "more humane workplace and a more just society."[11]

Eight anarchists—Adolph Fischer, Albert Parsons, August Spies, George Engel, Louis Lingg, Michael Schwab, Oscar Neebe, and Samuel Fielden—were arrested and convicted for the Haymarket bombing, even though witnesses testified that the three who could even be determined to be present at Haymarket were in full view of the assembled and could not have set off the bomb. But a jury comprised of business leaders convicted the eight on murder charges.

On November 11, 1887, after many failed appeals, Parsons, Spies, Engel, and Fischer were hanged to death. Louis Lingg, in his final protest, took his own life the night before. Spies, before he died, shouted out his famous last words: "The time will come when our silence will be more powerful than the voices you throttle today." The remaining organizers— Fielden, Neebe, and Schwab—were pardoned six years later by Governor John Peter Altgeld, a leading figure in the Progressive movement who publicly denounced the travesty of justice that had led to the hanging of innocents.[12]

During his tenure as governor, Altgeld refused to call in federal troops to break the Pullman Rail strikes led by Eugene Debs. The pardon was a defining moment in the governor's political career, and upon his death his gravestone was engraved with the edict that he had died decrying the unfairness of the trial.

The labor movement suffered irreparable damages at the end of that bloody May of 1886. The Knights of Labor fell to pieces. The American Federation of Labor evolved into a much more conservative organization. Union leaders were hounded, their homes and newspapers raided by the police in what can be considered the first "red scare."

It took another forty-two years, with the passage of the Fair Labor Standards Act of 1938, to finally establish the eight-hour workday and the forty-hour workweek as a matter of federal law. Generations of Americans have enjoyed the fruits of that movement and have benefited from the sacrifices of those who gave their lives—yet know nothing of it. The weekend—so much a part of what we cherish—did not just happen; people gave their lives fighting for it.

In 1889, Raymond Lavigne, a French trade unionist, proposed to the newly formed Second International that in the following year, 1890, May 1 be celebrated as the International Workers' Day, to honor the martyrs of the labor movement in the United States.[13] It was meant to be a onetime event. But May Day continues to be celebrated all over the world as International

Workers' Day—except in the United States, which had provided the initial inspiration.

Today, more and more, and especially for the poor and the middle class, the forty-hour workweek is in jeopardy again. In order to keep their families afloat on jobs, often part-time, that pay minimum wage, men and women in the United States regularly work many more hours a week than the forty. According to the International Labor Organization, Americans work hundreds of hours more than their cohorts in other advanced industrial countries—almost 500 hours more than French workers, for example. This has occurred even as the productivity of US workers has increased exponentially, as the Bureau of Labor Statistics reports.

Therefore, even as US workers work harder, their economic well-being has declined precipitously. They are not the ones who are benefiting from the increased hours of work or their increased productivity. Could it be that history might repeat itself, that we might end up fighting the same battles again? As the saying goes, those who fail to learn from history are doomed to repeat it.

The impotence of trade unions today does not diminish by any measure their historical victories, such as the eight-hour workday and forty-hour workweek, which transformed the nation in so many positive ways. As Marick J. Masters and John T. Delaney, authors of "Organized Labor's Political Scorecard," write:

> Many of the laws governing the work place—taken for granted by employees today—were advanced, advocated, and obtained with union support. For example, over the past century, unions have supported federal, state and local government legislation regulating minimum wages, working hours, overtime, unemployment insurance, pension and old age support, disability and injury protection (e.g., workers compensation laws), safety and health, and equal employment opportunity.[14]

Similarly, "important legislation that built a better society came about because of the strong political support of labor. Unions backed civil rights legislation, Social Security, Medicare, environmental laws, wage and hour laws, the ban on child labor, and much more."[15]

Unions and Race: A Checkered Past

When it comes to race and unions, however, a look back at history shows a more checkered past. Unions have been on both sides of the issue of race.[16] They have discriminated against blacks as well as advocated for them. African Americans often had to fight to join unions.

According to historians and social scientists who have studied this past, there are three attributes that stand out as factors that determined the degree of exclusion that unions practiced. First, the more stratified an industry, the more exclusionary the union was. In skilled trades, construction, and railroads, for example, job categories were arranged from highest to lowest in terms of wages and status. In all of these industries, blacks were concentrated in the lowest ranks and were excluded from segregated unions. Second, the more unions tried to accommodate capital and managers of capital—the owners and top management—the more racist and segregationist they were. In times of economic uncertainty, unions often tried to adopt more conciliatory positions in tandem with the racist ideas of management, which led to racial segregation and exclusion. And third, the more radical a union was, the more committed it was to interracial solidarity. Let us consider the experience of African Americans in some of the major unions in the United States in terms of these attributes.

At its inception in 1891, the American Federation of Labor (AFL) was committed to racial equality. Samuel Gompers, the charismatic first president of the AFL, even believed that racial exclusion harmed the solidarity of the labor movement. This progressive mind-set became embattled when the economic depression of the late 1890s created a climate of uncertainty that threatened the AFL, and also became a spawning ground for racial animosity.

Employers wanted to hire the cheapest labor and de-legitimize the unions as much as possible. So they hired blacks at wages far below those paid to white workers. And black strikebreakers were called in to replace striking white workers. In some cases, altercations with employers turned racially hostile. In East Saint Louis in 1917, when blacks were used as scabs to defeat a strike at the Aluminum Ore Company, where the workers belonged to a union affiliated with the AFL, the violence turned into a race riot.

Gompers emerged from this crisis an avowed racist, advocating the exclusion of blacks from the AFL and letting black workers form their own segregated unions. By 1899, the AFL began accepting local unions that barred blacks from membership. Afraid of competition and the resulting downward pressure on wages, the AFL also steadfastly opposed the inclusion of Mexican, Chinese, and Japanese workers into its ranks. The AFL had succumbed to the race-baiting tactics of capital.

Labor historians also agree that the economic crisis at the turn of the twentieth century also made the AFL more accommodating in relation to capital and management as a way to preserve its unions and the higher-paying jobs of white workers in the craft unions as opposed to the industrial ones, where low-paid blacks had a bigger presence. And this meant adopting the same racist attitudes of the authorities. In 1905, W. E. B. Du Bois, along with many other progressive leaders of the time, chastised the AFL unions for "proscribing and boycotting and oppressing thousands of their fellow toilers" in their Niagara's Declaration of Principles.[17]

The United Mine Workers of America (UMW), which came from the coal-producing regions of southern Appalachia in 1890, represented an industry where there was little stratification. Workers toiled in the same appalling conditions in the mines regardless of whether they were white or black. They faced the same dangers and health risks. Black workers were even elected to leadership positions.

The history of the UMW shows repeated attempts by mine-owners to break up the unions by using any tactic that was effective, and integrated unions were often their scapegoat. There are instances in which racist citizen committees would join hands with mine-owners to intimidate the workers. The repeated defeats that UMW experienced in the 1920s, as its members tried to renew their contracts, had much to do with the distractions that race provided. But the UMW never cowered under the racism that the owners used to break the union. The fact that both white and black workers labored under the same conditions and shared similar dangers played a big role in keeping them united.

The Knights of Labor was organized in 1869 as a federation of unions representing garment workers, longshoremen, and bricklayers. Though some locals excluded blacks, the national leadership was committed to interracial solidarity. They welcomed and organized black workers at a time when the United States was deeply racist. What stands out in the history of the Knights of Labor is the repeated intimidation and violence they faced in Southern states where they tried to organize among white and black workers. White organizers were assassinated and black ones lynched in Florida, Georgia, and New Orleans.

At a Knights convention in Richmond, Virginia, in 1886 when a black delegate was refused by a hotel, the other sixty delegates, who were white, declined to stay there too. They stayed instead with black families, worshipped in black churches, and continuously advocated for racial integration. But the Knights could not fight the anti-union climate that came with the economic crisis of the 1890s. Neither could they combat the intense repression that followed them after the May 1886 Haymarket riots. Several Knights leaders were assaulted, arrested, gunned down, or lynched in several cities, especially in the South. All of these factors led to the gradual demise of this forward-thinking union.

Similarly, the International Workers of the World (IWW), the most radical of all unions, was fundamentally committed to interracial solidarity. It was founded in 1905 by individuals who had left the AFL over its abandonment of black workers. They were inspired by a distinctly socialist vision and wanted to unite all workers across racial, ethnic, and gender lines. But the IWW could not stand up to the combined assault against it, primarily by the government's law-enforcement agents. The entire leadership, notably founder Eugene Debs, were arrested and imprisoned at a time when World War I had created a climate of suspicion and volatility.

The Congress of Industrial Organizations (CIO), made up of industrial unions, "aggressively recruited black members and became an important force for desegregation and anti-discrimination before many other segments of American society."[18] CIO unions were also more supportive of "redistributive public policies, including civil rights and the welfare state."[19] By 1945, half a million African American workers were members of CIO unions. But even into the 1960s, when African Americans made up about 25 percent of all US union members, some trade unions continued to oppose their inclusion. Noteworthy among these were unions in the construction trades and garment trades, which represented industries that were occupationally segregated.

But black unionized workers, led by A. Philip Randolph, the legendary African American union leader, were the most pro-union of all workers, especially because union membership had made them equals in the workplace, even before barriers fell in the rest of society. The confidence that they gained from a democratic workplace empowered them to form the backbone of the civil rights movement.

To appreciate the peril society faces as unions steadily disappear, it is valuable to review the role unions have played as some of the most important agents for organizing movements seeking fundamental social justice and civil rights. For instance, they were at the forefront of movements advocating for the right of women to vote. The women's suffrage movement in the United States found strong support from unions such as the Women's Trade Union League (WTUL), which had played a major role in the eight-hour-workday movement. The WTUL, representing a partnership between working-class women and middle-class reformers, participated in massive strikes at the turn of the twentieth century, demanding a living wage and an end to sweatshops. It gave strong support for women's participation in unions, strikes, and picket lines. The WTUL advocated for women's right to vote and supported women's role in politics to achieve gains for working-class women.

The formidable International Ladies Garment Workers Union (ILGWU), with its massive 1909 strike demanding humane working conditions, set a precedent for the power of collective action that was later emulated by other unions. It is instructive to recall, however, that the ILGWU would face allegations of discrimination in the early 1960s, when the New York State Commission for Human Rights found that the union had restricted black and Puerto Rican workers to low-paying jobs.

It is interesting that most of the reporting on the past discriminatory practices of unions can be found in the works of the individuals and policy groups who are among the most fervent opponents of unions and collective bargaining today, such as the Cato Institute, a conservative think tank.[20]

Unions and Civil, Immigrant, and Voter Rights Movements

Ever since the 1940s, civil rights unionism has been a powerful ideal for black workers. In the 1960s, this unionism provided foot soldiers for the civil rights movement that galvanized the nation. Even as they faced discrimination from their white coworkers, they did not lose faith that "if you got a union, a union will stop all of this [job discrimination]."[21]

Max Krochmal, in his recounting of the "working class vision of the civil rights movement," has described numerous instances in which union membership and collective action won black workers the dignity that inspired them to demand equality in civic spheres. In 1951, black garbage collectors, "workers at the bottom of the Jim Crow occupational hierarchy, organized a strike to demand both a higher wage and a degree of dignity on their jobs—and won."[22]

A decade before Martin Luther King Jr. and Bull Connor drew national attention to Birmingham, "300 black workers performing the least desirable of tasks had demanded and won a little respect from the Jim Crow town." When unions "brought better wages, parents got interested in education and began to send their kids to college. Many of the high school and college students arrested for demonstrating against segregation in Birmingham streets were sons and daughters of these union members."[23]

Fred Shuttlesworth, a famous leader of the civil rights movement, came from the working class and presided over a congregation that was distinctly working class.[24] Battles for desegregation, for women's rights, and for economic justice went hand in hand. In recent years, unions have given support for marriage equality and the rights of gays and lesbians. Undeniably, unions are a socially progressive force and fundamental for the preservation of all rights—both human and economic.

Unions get out the vote; they give voice to those who are often invisible in society. In the United States today, where more and more immigrants are made vulnerable by the country's love-hate attitude toward them—valued for the cheap labor they provide but derided for seeking recognition—unions offer a forum where they can find dignity.

In New Jersey, unions such as the Service Employees Industrial Union (SEIU) and New Labor (in Lakewood and New Brunswick, respectively) have stood in solidarity with immigrant workers, supporting them on issues of wage theft, employer harassment and intimidation, illegal seizures, and deportation and the resulting breakup of families. These worker organizations also provide the immigrants opportunities to learn English and acquire computer skills and organizational capabilities. In this way, unions have provided a training ground where immigrants learn important lessons about democratic and civic participation in their adopted country.

On May Day of 2006, immigrants called for a general strike—"a day without immigrants"—to draw attention to the struggles that they encountered in their daily lives despite their critical role in the life and economy of the United States. They had chosen May Day because of its significance, because in their countries of origin they celebrated this day as International Workers' Day and thus felt this was an opportunity to restore the day to its real origins and reclaim it on behalf of all US workers.

The importance of voter participation in a democracy is widely appreciated. The legitimacy of democratic institutions is gauged by how many participate and how well their positions are represented. Since democratic societies are also capitalist and class-based societies, it is important to understand that the power that capital wields can be countered only by a

---

MAKING CONNECTIONS
Unions and Immigrants

In Lakewood and New Brunswick, New Jersey, New Labor is an immigrant support group that has advocated for the rights of the day laborers unwaveringly. In 2000, the group came together through the joint efforts of a visionary union leader, the late Rich Cunningham, and his associates Carmen Martino and Lou Kimmel.

New Labor has spoken up against numerous violations that immigrant day laborers encounter in the course of their work lives. These include wage theft, violations of the Occupational Safety and Hazard Act (OSHA), harassment, false accusations against domestic workers, and physical assault and intimidation of workers generally, but especially of those considered the "ringleaders."

New Labor has also been instrumental in organizing Latino construction workers to "[embrace] workplace safety and health as a fundamental human right, and [who have become] leaders by collaborating with university-based health and safety researchers [and facilitating] classes for more than a thousand of their peers, [providing] safety demonstrations on street corners and parking lots to hundreds of day laborers seeking construction work, and [testifying] before OSHA during April 2014 public hearings, held in Washington, D.C."[1] New Labor was instrumental in researching and authoring a groundbreaking story on the hidden world of abuses and exploitation that transpire in the warehouses and in the transportation for giant retailers such as Wal-Mart, JCPenney, and others.

The organization provides a space where immigrants and their families can find community and support. In its dilapidated but friendly office space, New Labor offers English-as-a-second-language classes, holds local Occupy meetings, and advocates for affordable housing. New Labor also offers a proving ground for rallies to condemn wage theft and the humiliation, harassment, and abuse of domestic workers, and to advocate for immigration reform. Social gatherings, such as summer picnics, Thanksgiving dinners, and Christmas festivities, give the immigrant day-laborer community a time to relax and seek relief from the often oppressive reality of their lives.

Note: 1. Hernandez et al., *Bending Toward Justice*, p. 5.

working class that has strength in numbers. Therefore, workers' representation in the democratic dialogue can be ensured only when they are organized into unions. Political parties are opportunistic; workers have better hope of being heard when they are unionized. Thus, the role of unions in capitalist democracies is doubly vital. And therefore, when unions become weak, they weaken democracy in turn.

Unions in the United States, journalist Harold Meyerson writes, are the most "potent mobilizers of the Democratic vote—getting minorities to the polls and persuading members of the white working class to vote Democratic. For political reasons [such as this] Republicans are determined to deunionize workers even more."[25] But despite these celebratory moments in the history of labor in the United States—both past and more recent—the unions face a very different reality today. As Richard B. Freeman and James L. Medoff observe: "Measured by ability to obtain special interest legislation favorable to unions over the opposition of business groups, unions [today] are far less a powerhouse."[26]

What Unions Mean for Paychecks and Politics

Union membership leads to higher wages. For example, in 2012, according to the Bureau of Labor Statistics, among full-time wage and salary workers, union members had median weekly earnings of $943, while for nonunion members the median weekly earnings were $742.[27] The difference in earnings between union and nonunion workers is a reflection of the power of collective bargaining agreements. Many people attribute the steadily rising inequality in the United States since the 1970s to the faltering role of unions.

In their 1984 book *What Do Unions Do?* Richard Freeman and James Medoff wrote famously but simply: "Everyone 'knows' that unions raise wages." They argued that the more workers a union is able to organize, the higher the wage differential between union and nonunion members. Freeman and Medoff showed through their statistical analysis that in the 1970s the union differential was 20 to 30 percent (wages of union workers were 20 to 30 percent higher than wages of nonunion workers).[28] The difference in wages between the United States and other OECD countries can be explained by what is termed "union-pay leveling effects"—whereby unions compress wage distribution.[29]

Since 2008, as inequality has increased in the United States, there has been a renewal of interest among social analysts in exploring the relationship between unions and inequality. As David Card, Thomas Lemieux, and W. Craig Riddell write: "The fact that two of the countries with the largest declines in unionization—the United States and the United Kingdom—also experienced the biggest increases in wage inequality raises the question of whether these two phenomena are linked. If so, how much of the growth in earnings inequality can be attributed to the fall in union coverage?"[30] In their own analysis, Card, Lemieux, and Riddell were able to infer the effect of unions on overall wage inequality by comparing the structure of wages for workers covered by union contracts to the structure of noncontracted wages. They found that in both the United States and the United Kingdom a significant part of the inequality (70 percent) could be attributed to the effects unions have on wages or what they refer to as "union wage compression effects." They were led to conclude that the "steady erosion of the equalizing effect of unions explains a significant fraction of the growth of inequality in the US and UK."[31]

Sociologists Bruce Western and Jake Rosenfeld maintain that "the decline of organized labor in the United States coincided with a large increase in wage inequality. From 1973 to 2007, union membership in the private sector declined from 34 to 8 percent for men and from 16 to 6 percent for women. During this time, wage inequality in the private sector increased by over 40 percent."[32] They further maintain that "unions also contribute to a moral economy that institutionalizes norms for fair pay, even for non-union workers." Thus, in the 1970s, when one in three men belonged to unions, the union workers were "prominent voices for equity, not just for members, but for all workers. Union decline marks an erosion of the moral economy and its underlying distributional norms."[33]

Western and Rosenfeld's research shows that if union density rates had remained constant at 1973 levels, income inequality, for example, for men in both union and nonunion sectors, would be much lower today. They reason that "deunionization" is responsible for a third of the rise in wage inequality.[34] When unions are weak, they become ineffective in helping to "shape the allocation of wages not just for their members, but across the labor market."[35] The diminishing power of the labor unions signifies that they are no longer politically effective in sheltering their members from the "encroachment" of the vicissitudes of the marketplace in equalizing economic rewards.

As Frank Levy and Peter Temin write:

> In the quarter century between 1980 and 2005, business sector productivity increased by 71 percent. Over the same quarter century, median weekly earnings of full-time workers rose from $613 to $705, a gain of only 14 percent. Median weekly compensation—earnings plus estimated fringe benefits—rose from $736 to $876, a gain of 19 percent. Since productivity growth expands total income, slow income growth for the average worker implies faster income growth elsewhere in the distribution. In the U.S. case, growth occurred at the very top. . . . [T]he share of gross personal income claimed by the top 1 percent of tax filing units—about 1.4 million returns—rose from

8.2 percent in 1980 to 17.4 percent in 2005. Among tax returns that report positive wage and salary income, the share of wages and salaries claimed by the top 1 percent rose from 6.4 percent in 1980 to 11.6 percent in 2005.[36]

And as the income gap between the middle and the top widens, the United States stands out among developed countries as having the highest percentage of low-wage workers, those who make less than two-thirds of the nation's median annual income, which was $50,054 in 2011. Fully 25 percent of all American workers make no more than $17,576 a year.[37]

Harold Meyerson adds: "Surely the fact that the great majority of American employers no longer have to sit down and hammer out collective bargaining contracts with their workers has contributed to the increase in profits at wages' expense. And many of those employers want to keep it that way."[38]

Kim Moody, a noted labor analyst, writes in significant detail about other ways in which labor's collective bargaining power has been undermined in the United States. Following the end of World War II, labor was able to negotiate a system that originated in the Treaty of Detroit, in which competition among firms was reduced and worker incomes were raised by industrywide bargaining. Instead of negotiating contracts with each firm, unions settled on contracts with the larger industries—such as automobile manufacturing, meatpacking, steel, and road haulage—encompassing the individual firms. But beginning in the 1980s, individual firms started breaking away from existing industrywide contracts, "in order to make their own deals or skip unionization altogether, by moving to the South, for example."[39]

In every industry, fragmentation of collective bargaining had devastating effects. When master agreements were dismantled in the airline industry, for example, average wages for airline mechanics fell by about 40 percent from 1979 to 1989. Flight attendants lost almost half their monthly salary in the same period. Similar decreases happened in trucking and road haulage, as the National Master Freight Agreement covered fewer members. Similarly, the breakup of AT&T in 1984 ended the national master agreement of the Communications Workers of America. Communication workers now dealt with the regional telecommunication companies with fewer workers and less clout.[40]

There is wide consensus among a range of social scientists and analysts that the relative well-being of workers depends to a large extent on the success of unions in demanding initiatives that build a fair, just, and egalitarian society. There is also agreement that as unionization rates and the equalizing effect that unions have on the dispersion of wages have declined, the general well-being of the entire society has correspondingly deteriorated. Sociologists, labor studies' scholars, and political scientists are all in agreement with Card, Lemieux, and Riddell's conclusion that, "by linking the decline in unionism to the dramatic increase in inequality since the 1970s, our research strongly confirms that the ongoing decline in private sector unionism indeed has socially undesirable consequences."[41] Even the US Census Bureau confirms the fact that unions put upward pressure on wages. In 2012, union members made almost $10,000 more than their nonunion counterparts—average union pay was $49,036, compared to average non-union pay of $38,584.[42]

Emmanuel Saez summarizes the primary parameters of the argument that we have discussed so far:

> The labor market has been creating much more inequality during the years 1975–2005, with the very top earners capturing a large fraction of macroeconomic productivity gains. A number of factors may help explain this increase in inequality, not only underlying technological changes but also the retreat of institutions developed during the New Deal and World War II—such as progressive tax policies, powerful unions, corporate provision of health and retirement benefits, and changing social norms regarding pay inequality. We need to decide as a society whether this increase in income inequality is efficient and acceptable and, if not, what mix of institutional reforms should be developed to counter it.[43]

Unions have other consequences for the general welfare and well-being of society. Take the case of vacation days and holidays, as shown in Figure 12.1. The United States is unique among the advanced industrial countries of the world in that it does not guarantee its workers paid vacations. Not one day. In Europe, employers are legally bound to give their workers twenty to thirty days of paid leave annually. In the absence of such standards in the United States, one in four Americans has no paid vacation and no paid holidays.

Whatever vacation time is available is distributed unequally. Low-wage workers and part-time workers are far less likely to enjoy paid vacation time. The United States is also the only country among advanced industrial nations that does not have paid family leave. In Europe, it is mandatory for parents to take leave after the birth of a newborn. There is no such mandate in the United States.

Consequently, Americans work much more than their counterparts in the developed world. But because productivity per worker has continuously increased since the 1950s, it would seem logical that Americans should have to work fewer hours to attain the same desired standard of living. Yet increases in productivity have not translated into higher wages or better and more secure lives.

What sets apart the countries in Europe from the United States? Strong unions. All the other countries shown in Figure 12.1 have unions that are able to engage in collective bargaining with management to ensure that

Figure 12.1 Paid Holidays and Vacation in OECD Countries, 2013

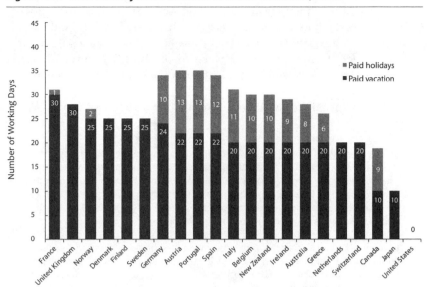

Source: Ray, Sanes, and Schmitt, "No-Vacation Nation Revisited."

employment agreements are fair and just. In each of these other countries, representatives of national unions bargain with employers' associations to determine wages in each industry and region of the economy. These wage agreements are then extended, under government scrutiny, to the nonunionized sectors.[44] In these other countries, employers, labor, and government work together.

Unions have also been key in securing days workers can take off to fulfill their functions as citizens and union members. It is also worth noting that many of the European countries provide paid leave for workers to vote (such as Greece), for performing civic duties (such as Spain), and for community work as well as union work to extend "international solidarity abroad" (such as France). In Sweden, employers are mandated to provide workers with paid leave to fulfill union duties.[45] In the United States, on the other hand, there is at most a grudging tolerance for unions, primarily because most Americans are unsure about the role of labor unions in promoting democracy.

As Bill Fletcher, a noted labor and racial justice activist, writes: "This is no exaggeration. As the percentage of workers represented by unions declines, and the right advances its anti-union propaganda, huge chunks of the population have no, or very distorted knowledge of unions. When people do not understand the issue or when they feel that it does not concern them, it is that much harder to win."[46] And Andy Stern, a senior fellow at Columbia University's Richman Center for Business, Law, and Public Policy, writes: "Many middle class Americans have mixed views on unions, and some feel strongly negative. Much of the hostility toward labor is driven by the relentless antiunion drumbeat of the right wing as well as corporate America."[47]

Labor historian Joshua Freeman recalls the years after World War II when

> unions were strong [and] they used their workplace strength to win political influence and used their political influence to win government benefits and protection for workers. . . . Business loathed the position labor had achieved. [They considered] the increased political activism of unions . . . as a threat to their firms' profitability and their personal liberty. Many business leaders and trade associations also came to believe in the necessity of a long term effort to win public opinion to their side. Companies began mounting large scale education and advertising campaigns, aimed at school children, the general public, and their own workers, which stressed the virtues of capitalism. [They] sought to change public attitudes by equating freedom with the free market and labeling any attempt to interfere with the market, by unions or government, as a step toward tyranny.[48]

In Chapter 13, we will revisit this lack of awareness regarding unions, and also the lack of political consciousness that underlies the indifference to civic engagement that is rampant in the United States today. With the 99 percent asleep at the wheel, the country is increasingly being driven by the interests of the 1 percent.

Organized labor's role is not just limited to collective bargaining in the determination of wages. Ideally, strong unions should be able to intervene in corporate and government decisionmaking processes and successfully block policies that can negatively impact workers and eventually all of society. Labor unions are ultimately political entities that, as Jacob Hacker and Paul Pierson explain, "offer an organizational counterweight to the power of those at the top. In the United States, and elsewhere, unions are the main political players pushing leaders to address middle-class economic concerns and resisting policy changes that promote inequality."[49] This political function that unions perform is the primary means of countering the power of money in politics, which has enabled those at the top to shape policy outcomes with complete indifference to the will of the people—outcomes that are often at extreme odds with what most voters would want.

Martin Gilens shows a strong correlation between public preferences and the positions unions take on a large number of policy areas. The unions are clearly on the public's side, particularly regarding the poor and the middle class. Unions oppose policies that correlate with increases in economic inequality and insecurity, such as free trade, cuts in capital gains and corporate income taxes, efforts to privatize Social Security or reduce Medicaid and Medicare benefits, and other initiatives that weaken the social safety net. And they support policies that could help reduce economic inequality, such as increases in the minimum wage, the right of all workers to earn a living wage, and also the right to strike for groups such as firefighters, police officers, and college teachers.[50]

Given that unions champion many of the same policies as do the general public, it would appear that they are the "most promising interest group bases for strengthening the policy influence of America's poor and middle class."[51] But Gilens, Hacker, and Pierson, in trying to temper any optimism, remind us that because of the routine opposition unions face from other interest groups that usually have an upper hand both in Congress and in the workplace, the success rate of unions in advancing policies that support the poor and the middle class is fairly limited.

This argument is echoed by Masters and Delaney, authors of "Organized Labor's Political Scorecard," in which they report statistics on labor's legislative record based between 1996 and 2002. The results were generally disappointing, as labor won only 35 percent of key legislative roll calls during that period. Further, labor lost a majority of the votes on bills pertaining to trade, the minimum wage, fiscal policy, welfare, education, and the budget. Masters and Delaney attribute labor's failure to "Republican control of Congress and the more conservative, aggressively partisan brand of politics practiced in Washington today. In general, fiscal, tax and budget policies are predictably more pro-business when the GOP runs Congress."[52]

But this is not to say that the unions have fared any better with the Democrats. The North American Free Trade Agreement, the most far-reaching of US trade treaties and which has devoured millions of well-paying union jobs, was conceived and enacted into law during the presidency of Bill Clinton, an earnest Democrat. A poll taken a few weeks before the signing of the treaty in 1994 showed that a majority of Americans opposed NAFTA, as did the unions. But the Clinton administration, with enormous assistance from corporations in the United States, denounced the opposition—primarily organized labor—as being "anti-growth, obstructionist and dangerously out of step with global realities."[53] According to Michael Dreiling, it has been estimated that businesses spent $30–50 million lobbying for NAFTA.[54]

The stifling of unions highlights the power of corporations in the United States and signals "that the third man—government—[is] leaving the ring," as economists Frank Levy and Peter Temin have remarked.[55] As government has essentially relinquished its responsibility for the welfare of the common man and woman, and as unions have gradually been eviscerated, the fate and prospects of "the commons" now reside more and more precariously on the decisions of corporate entities, which the government is more than willing to accommodate.

As Hacker and Pierson note: "The near extinction of private sector unions has had a much broader and less appreciated effect on the distribution of American economic rewards. It has created a political and economic vacuum that has proven deadly to those seeking to redress winner-take-all inequality and friendly to those seeking to promote and consolidate it."[56]

Labor in Today's Anti-Union Environment

In terms of its numerical strength, where does labor stand today? Let us look at some facts from the US Bureau of Labor Statistics.[57]

- The overall union membership rate in 2012 was 11.3 percent—6.6 percent in the private sector and 35.9 percent in the public sector.
- In 2012, 14.4 million wage and salary workers belonged to unions.
- In 1983, the union membership rate was a modest 20.1 percent and there were 17.7 million union workers.
- By contrast, in the early 1950s, one out of three Americans belonged to unions. In the 1940s, when US manufacturing grew rapidly, so did union membership. By 1945, 36 percent of the work force was unionized.[58]
- Even in states where unions have been strong historically, the membership rate has fallen. In 2011, New York had a union membership rate of 24 percent. By 2012, that number had fallen to 23.2 percent. In states where unions have traditionally been weak, today they are even weaker. In North Carolina, in 2011 the union membership rate was 3.2 percent; in 2012 it was 2.9 percent.
- In 2012, public-sector workers had a union membership rate of 35.9 percent, which was five times higher than the union membership rate of 6.6 percent in the private sector. The most-unionized public-sector employees are teachers, police officers, and firefighters. This fact is important to keep in mind in view of the increasing backlash that public-sector unions, especially teachers' unions, have faced in recent years, such as the successful initiative in Wisconsin to ban collective bargaining in the public sector altogether.

What Explains the Decline in Union Membership?

The reason that there are fewer union members in the United States today is not because workers do not want to be part of unions. Rather, membership has declined due to radical changes in the structure of the US economy and in the structure of work itself, as well as due to the increasing barriers that workers face when they do want to unionize. Surveys show that many workers would choose to be represented by unions if they had a choice.

As Andy Stern notes, a 2007 poll found that a majority of nonunion workers in the United States—53 percent—indicated they would vote to have a union in their place of work if they were given that choice. If even half of these workers actually formed unions, it would double the size of the labor movement in the United States. The support for unions has grown steadily, especially since the uncertainties associated with work and the economy have escalated.[59]

The National Labor Relations Act of 1935 gave workers the right to form unions in their places of work. It also made provisions for elections to be held to determine the feasibility of forming such unions. Elections were to be held without interference and intimidation from employers. The National Labor Relations Board was specifically formed to supervise this process, to ensure that these worker rights were being respected by employers.

One of the most grievous reasons behind the falling numbers in union membership has been the protracted assault on workers' collective bargaining rights—which are guaranteed by the National Labor Relations Act—by businesses, corporations, and their conservative, anti-union supporters in Washington and state capitals. The backlash against unions and the deliberate tactics to neutralize them are the primary reasons why there are only 14.4 million union members in the United States as of 2012. If the 53 percent of respondents to the aforementioned poll who expressed the desire to be part of a union did in reality have that opportunity, there would be 60 million union members.

Let us first consider how this backlash against unions materializes. We will then return to reviewing the changes in the structure of the economy and work—due to globalization, mechanization, corporate restructuring, and financialization—that have led to a smaller pool of workers from which the unions can draw members.

Ideological Underpinnings of the Backlash

If a "Detroit Consensus" arising from the Treaty of Detroit dominated the post–World War II political and economic mood, in which the union leaders were considered the "new men of power," an expression made famous by C. Wright Mills in his book by the same name, then a "Washington Consensus" was the defining mood of the decades that followed the presidency of Ronald Reagan in the 1980s. According to Frank Levy and Peter Temin, the institutional norms that were embedded in these ideologies strongly shaped the income distribution of each period.

The Treaty of Detroit, which came at a time dominated by unions, provided a negotiating framework in the context of progressive taxes and high minimum wages, all integral to the government commitment to "lift all boats." Levy and Temin confirm that the "golden age" of economic growth in the post–World War II period was most definitely the result of economic expansion, but that it was the institutions and norms that had been erected by the New Deal that ensured that the fruits would be distributed fairly.[60]

The Washington Consensus has prevailed under a very different set of institutional norms, in which deregulation and privatization are critical. Neoliberalism, which underpins the Washington Consensus, considers government's role in the economy as intrusive. Market forces are regarded as the primary arbiter of economic activity and economic outcome. The government's job is to be a passive onlooker at most. From this perspective, the government's rationale for enacting the National Labor Relations Act of 1935 is surmised as being invasive and obstructionist. It is this ideology that ultimately informs the backlash that unions face today.

The sheer muscle of this ideology became clear with the defeat of one of the most closely watched National Labor Relations Board elections in recent times, that of February 14, 2014, at the German-owned Volkswagen plant in Chattanooga, Tennessee, a traditionally anti-union region. The 1,550 workers voted on whether to join the United Automobile Workers (UAW), which would create the first employee work councils in the United States. Work councils are critical in providing worker input at the enterprise level and promoting cooperation and flexibility between workers and employers. In stark contrast to positions that US employers have taken in union elections, Volkswagen, well-honed in the matter of unions and employee work councils, did not oppose the union drive; in fact, in some ways it offered quiet support to the union.[61]

Steven Greenhouse, reporting for the *New York Times* in February 2014, wrote: "Volkswagen did not oppose the UAW partly because its officials were eager to create a German-style works council, a committee of managers and blue-collar and white-collar workers who develop factory policies, on issues like work schedules and vacations. Volkswagen, which has unions and works councils at virtually all of its 105 other plants worldwide, views such councils as crucial for improving morale and cooperation and increasing productivity."[62]

By the fall of 2013, a majority of the plant's workers had signed on to support the UAW. Even so, the initiative failed by a mere eighty-seven votes. Republican politicians—including Tennessee's governor, a US senator, and various leaders of the state legislature—along with other fervently anti-union conservative groups, carried on an unprecedented campaign of intimidation to pressure the workers to defeat the membership vote.

According to the Greenhouse article, "Volkswagen officials had urged 'third parties' to remain neutral and stay out of the unionization battle."[63] With total disregard for that request, right-wing activists helped to form organizations, such as the Workplace Fairness Institute, Worker Freedom

Institute, and Center for Worker Freedom,[64] that successfully persuaded the workers that voting for the union would make Volkswagen less competitive and hurt their standard of living. The right-wing activists suggested that the UAW had hurt Detroit's automakers and was responsible for the city's downfall. The Center for Worker Freedom put up billboards in Chattanooga warning that the city might become the next Detroit if the workers voted for the union.[65] At least 626 workers heeded the message.

The Backlash Against Unions in the United States

By all accounts, when Ronald Reagan broke the 1981 strike of the Professional Air Traffic Controllers Organization (PATCO) soon after assuming the presidency, he sealed the fate of labor unions irrevocably. His action gave corporations in the United States the confidence to adopt a much more aggressive posture in the workplace, certain that they were simply following suit to a precedent set by the highest leader of the land.

Reagan also filled positions on the National Labor Relations Board, the supposed watchdog for enforcing the National Labor Relations Act, with individuals who favored management. This highlighted the inherent weakness of the act to withstand or challenge vigorous anti-union activities.[66]

In the 1980s, businesses became confident that "they enjoyed, not only the opportunity to defeat organizing campaigns, but to get rid of the union threat once and for all. One consultant wrote in the *Wall Street Journal* that the 'current [Reagan] government and business climate presents a unique opportunity for companies . . . to develop and implement long term plans for conducting business in a union-free environment.' The 'critical test,' he insisted was whether management had the intellectual discipline and foresight to capitalize on this rare moment in our history."[67]

The "Union Avoidance" Industry

It is this environment that gave birth to the extensive and sophisticated "union avoidance" industry, which according to John Logan "has developed into a multimillion-dollar concern that profited from promoting adversarial labour-management relations. Several studies have demonstrated that employers who recruit the services of union avoidance experts are more likely to defeat organizing campaigns than those who do not. Several union avoidance firms operate internationally, but only in the US do employers, policy makers and (to a lesser extent) the general public consider the activities of union avoidance experts a legitimate part of mainstream industrial relations."[68]

The Burke Group is the largest union avoidance agency in the United States. Its consultants—including lawyers and psychologists—are paid

MAKING CONNECTIONS
PATCO and the Future of Unions

When President Ronald Reagan fired the striking workers of the Professional Air Traffic Controllers Organization in 1981, he dealt a death blow to the heart of labor unions in the United States and undermined the rights of all workers. He also de-legitimized the power of the strike, which unions had until then always been able to use as a tool to pressure management.

Just before becoming president, candidate Reagan had written to Robert Poli, director of PATCO, pledging the support of his administration for air traffic controllers if he should win the presidency. But when he became president, he broke his pledge. In August 1981, when PATCO members went on strike, Reagan gave them forty-eight hours to get back to work or forfeit their jobs. About 2,000 heeded his warning and returned to work, but 11,435 workers did not and were immediately fired.

In 1962, President John F. Kennedy signed Executive Order 10988, giving federal employees the right to bargain collectively. But it denied them the right to strike. In 1968, PATCO was formed as a federal employee union, with the Federal Aviation Association as its immediate employer.

As air travel became more and more popular and the work load of air traffic controllers increased and became more stressful, they demanded an increase in salary, a five-day, thirty-two-hour workweek, and the provision to retire after twenty years of service. The total package would cost $770 million. The federal government regarded this package as outrageous and nonnegotiable, even though 95 percent of PATCO employees had voted for it. When the government dug in its heels, PATCO made the decision to strike, believing that the government would give in. But instead they were fired en masse.

Reagan, in defending his action, said that PATCO members were federal employees and had taken the solemn pledge at the time of their employment that they wouldn't participate in any strike activity against the government. Because they knew what they did was illegal, claimed Reagan, he had no alternative but to fire them.

The Federal Aviation Administration had to immediately hire and train an entirely new pool of air traffic controllers. According to Joseph McCartin, who has written extensively about the PATCO incident, it took several years and billions of dollars for the aviation system to recover.[1] The government had spent much more than the $770 million that the striking workers had asked for.

It is important to keep in mind that Reagan, in denying PATCO the right to strike, did not deny the right of PATCO to exist. Even when he fired its members, he defended their right to organize and to bargain collectively. He even mentioned his own days as a union organizer in the Screen Actors Guild.

But none of that mattered. What employers in the private sector took away from the PATCO incident was how Reagan had dealt with the strikers. What he did stood out loud and clear. He had drawn a line in the sand.

Many private employers have followed Reagan's tactics in dealing with their workers. Phelps Dodge, International Paper, and many other employers have replaced their striking workers instead of negotiating with the unions. In the spring of 2011, Governor Scott Walker of Wisconsin went a step further than Reagan had and stripped public employees of collective bargaining rights altogether, denying public unions their very right to exist.

Note: 1. Lehmann, "Winging It."

$180–250 per hour plus expenses. One leading psychologist, Charles Hughes, has even written a union avoidance manual, *Making Unions Unnecessary.* The Burke Group's clients include Blue Shield, Coca Cola, DuPont, General Electric, Heinz, Honeywell, K-Mart, Lockheed Martin, Mars Inc., MGM Grand, NBC, and the University of California at Los Angeles, to name a few.[69]

Kate Bronfenbrenner, director of labor education research at the Cornell School of Industrial and Labor Relations, has conducted a series of comprehensive surveys of how employers' union avoidance tactics have changed in sophistication, aggressiveness, and intensity over time. These surveys have consistently shown that an "overwhelming majority of U.S workers believe that they would be better off if they had a union in their work place, but they also feel that they would be taking a great risk if they tried to organize one. For these workers, the right to organize and bargain collectively—free from coercion, intimidation and retaliation—is at best a promise infinitely deferred."[70] And the underfunded and disempowered National Labor Relations Board is becoming increasingly powerless to implement the National Labor Relations Act guarantee of the right of workers to organize without fear of threats and intimidation.

The data that Bronfenbrenner has gathered show a chilling pattern:

> The overwhelming majority of employers—either under the direction of an outside management consultant or their own in-house counsel—are running aggressive campaigns of threats, interrogation, surveillance, harassment, coercion, and retaliation [and] . . . the overwhelming majority of US employers are willing to use a broad arsenal of legal and illegal tactics to interfere with the right of workers to organize, and . . . they do so with near impunity. The data show that:
>
> - 57 percent of employers threaten to shut down all or part of their facilities;
> - One-third of employers fire workers for union activity;
> - 47 percent threaten to cut wages or benefits;
> - 28 percent attempt to infiltrate the organizing committee;
> - 14 percent use surveillance;
> - 22 percent use bribes and special favors;
> - 89 percent of employers require their workers to attend "captive-audience" meetings during work hours;
> - 77 percent had supervisors regularly talk to workers one-on-one about the union campaign, with a focus on threats of plant closings, wage and benefit cuts, and job loss; and
> - More than 60 percent use one-on-one meetings to interrogate and harass workers about their support for the union.[71]

In her conclusion, Bronfenbrenner makes these following observations: "And although most of these actions are illegal (under the National Labor Relations Act of 1935), the penalties are minimal or at best weak; employers regularly violate the law with impunity; patterns of employer behavior have become so deeply engrained that we as a society have begun to accept illegal behavior as the norm; and for a long time now many workers have become resigned to the fact that no branch of government [is] going to listen to their pleas that the system [is] not just broken, but it [is] operating in direct violation of the law."[72]

Bronfenbrenner cites labor historian Nelson Lichtenstein, whose study on how Wal-Mart fights unions showed that, between 1998 and 2003, unions filed 288 unfair labor practices suits against this retail giant. These included charges of improper firings, threats to employees if they joined a union, improper surveillance, and illegal interrogation.[73]

With more than 2.1 million employees who make an average of $8 an hour and who often have to depend on food stamps and Medicaid to get by, Wal-Mart, more than any other company, sets the standards for wages and how workers are treated across the retail industry. And even though Wal-Mart employs just 1 percent of the US work force, this "retail behemoth" promotes a business model—one that deploys "ever more creative and ruthless tactics to suppress the right to organize, while driving down wages and benefits in the retail industry and beyond"—that is widely and eagerly "mimicked across industries."[74]

MAKING CONNECTIONS

Political Consequences of Union Advocacy

In Ocean County, New Jersey, more than a fifth of the population (21.5 percent in 2012) is age sixty-five or older. It is not just happenstance, therefore, that the highest spikes in jobs have been in the area of nursing home workers and home health aides. Like more than 30 million such jobs all around the country, at $10–12 an hour, these jobs don't pay enough to lift a family of four above the federal poverty line. And contract renewals, in three-year cycles, are often held up in contentious negotiations.

The Service Employees Industrial Union (SEIU) has been steadfast in organizing the nursing home workers and advocating for them, especially when contracts have to be renegotiated. But in a climate rife with anti-union sentiment, belonging to a union can be perilous—as Melissa Martinez found out the hard way.

Melissa, thirty years old, has three children: Anthony, age twelve; Ethan, age seven; and Emma, just two months old. Both Melissa and her husband, David, work in nursing homes in Lakewood, New Jersey. Prior to being fired, she worked 37.5 hours a week, earning $10.61 an hour. She liked her work hours—6:30 A.M. to 2:30 P.M.—which allowed her time to be with her children.

She did her job mostly in the kitchen, pulling and pushing heavy loads and carts. "No one bothered me," she says. "I was invisible." But in the fall of 2012, when she became a shop stewardess for the SEIU at the nursing home, she was no longer invisible.

(continues)

Political Consequences of Union Advocacy

In her new position, she was responsible for looking out for the welfare of her coworkers. She complained that the heat in the kitchen was unbearable. With no ventilation, the temperature would often reach 120 degrees in the summer months. There were days when the workers were feeling faint or seeing double because of the heat. The management not only turned a blind eye, but also began treating her differently— and often verbally abusing her.

In the fall of 2012, Melissa got pregnant. But the heavy lifting, the pushing and pulling, did not let up. She was expected to work just as before and was given no reprieve. In December 2012 she was accused of "stealing" two six-ounce cans of soda and was fired from her job. The SEIU stepped in to advocate on her behalf. Her case was withdrawn and she was reinstated. But the harassment did not stop, and she felt she was under constant scrutiny.

Every three months, all nursing home workers where Melissa works are expected to attend an in-service workshop for half an hour. In early March of 2013, Melissa signed up for one such workshop. But she got held up in the kitchen; she wanted to leave it clean—afraid that she would be reprimanded if she did not. The cleaning took longer than she had anticipated, as her advanced pregnancy was slowing her down. She missed the in-service workshop, but thought nothing of it since she felt getting her work done was her primary responsibility. Her employers thought otherwise, and—for the second time in four months—she was fired from her job and charged with "abandonment of duty." This time the SEIU has been powerless to do much other than file appeals.

In the meantime, her family is making do on David's income, which is smaller than Melissa's was and has no benefits. Melissa says that not many of her coworkers are as fortunate as she is to have a working spouse. So her coworkers keep their mouths shut and stay away from unions, because if they lose their jobs, they will have no one to depend on and will also risk losing their children to the state.

David has been fighting for full-time hours but is constantly passed over, and is afraid his job might be in jeopardy. Melissa and he are five months behind on their rent. Although they are receiving food stamps and assistance with paying their utility bills, and are covered by New Jersey's family health care program, Melissa has begun to suffer from depression and anxiety over the uncertainty of her family's future.

The Fallacy of Right-to-Work Laws

A pervasive anti-union atmosphere can also be seen in the increasing number of states considering the option of supporting right-to-work laws, which some states, mainly in the South, already do. For example, in December 2012, in Michigan, a Republican-controlled legislature and a Republican governor passed a law that turned "that historic union stronghold into the country's newest (24th) anti-union 'right to work' state."[75]

Though supporters of right-to-work initiatives maintain that these initiatives help workers who are unemployed, the right to work is not about guaranteeing workers a job. What it does do is to make it illegal for unions to ask members to pay union dues, even when members benefit from the union's terms of contract, since unions are obligated by law to represent all workers in a unionized facility fairly and equally.[76] By making it harder for unions to sustain themselves financially, right-to-work laws undermine their ability to bargain and deprive them of the ability to fully represent their members.

For states that support the right to work, the main objective is to draw companies and businesses with the promise of lower wages. According to Gordon Lafer, "the impact of [right-to-work] laws is to lower average income by about $1500 a year and to decrease the odds of getting health insurance or a pension through your job—for both union and nonunion workers. But while [the right to work] succeeds in cutting wages, it fails to boost job growth."[77] Lafer quotes Dr. Martin Luther King Jr., who in the 1960s warned against "the false slogans such as 'right to work' [whose] purpose is to destroy labor unions and the freedom of collective bargaining by which unions have improved wages and working conditions of everyone."[78]

Even Human Rights Watch, which monitors abuses of human rights around the world, commented on the "legal loopholes and a culture of impunity which tilt the playing field steeply against workers' freedom of association in the United States in violation of international human rights standards."[79] This was reported in September 2000. One wonders what Human Rights Watch would say about the United States today.

Assault on Public-Sector Unions

Having almost neutralized the private-sector unions in the United States, the anti-unionists are now focusing on the more powerful public sector, where strong contracts negotiated by public employee unions, such as the American Federation of State, County and Municipal Employees and the American Federation of Teachers, have provided workers with good wages and benefits.

The success of these public employee unions, relative to the beleaguered private-sector unions, has drawn the ire of the anti-union lobby. Having impeded the private-sector union and its ability to bargain for better wages and benefits, the conservative assault on public-sector unions focuses on their gains as being ill-deserved and fiscally unwise. Instead of asking how the public-sector workers were able to win such strong contracts, most Americans have bought into the propaganda, relentlessly aired by the anti-unionists and their media allies, condemning the public-sector employees as being selfish and greedy at a time of government fiscal uncertainty.

Teachers' unions have been the target of the most unremitting assault. Anti-unionists frame their assault on such public-sector unions in the context of the budgetary deficits so many state governments are facing. State governments would prefer to balance their budgets by cutting their workers' salaries and benefits, along with a host of other social spending. The strong contracts of the strong public-sector unions are seen increasingly as the primary obstacle to realizing these budget-cutting aims.

The other alternative would be to undo the drastic cuts in corporate taxes, fallen from an average of 9.7 percent in 1980 to 6.7 percent in 2009.[80] According to Citizens for Tax Justice, in 2011 the average statutory state corporate tax rate was about 6.2 percent. Between 2008 and 2010, 265 companies that fully disclosed their state and local tax payments had paid only 3 percent of their US profits in taxes. Some states, Citizens for Tax Justice reports, are even considering doing away with the corporate income tax altogether.[81]

Could it be that state budgets are in such dire straits because the richest corporations have not paid their share of state taxes? In states facing budget deficits, revenues from corporate taxes declined by $2.5 billion in 2010. In Wisconsin, two-thirds of corporations pay no taxes, and the share of state revenue from corporate taxes from those that do pay has fallen by half since 1981.[82] But these facts never make their way into the public consciousness, which drowns them out.

In February 2011, the *New York Times* reported on the events in Wisconsin: "Mr. Walker [the governor] is . . . seeking to definitively curb the power of government unions in his state. He sees public-employee unions as a bane to the taxpayer because they demand—and often win—generous health and pension plans that help push up taxes and drive budget deficits higher."[83] Ironically, Wisconsin was the first state to recognize public-worker unions, in 1959.

The attack had already begun in Indiana in 2004, "where Governor Mitch Daniels repealed collective-bargaining rights for state workers. The consequence was that union membership among state workers fell from 16,408 in 2005 to 1,490 in 2011. No doubt inspired by events in Indiana, right-wing governors in Wisconsin, Ohio, and Michigan pushed legislation that would abolish or severely limit bargaining for public workers."[84]

Why Attack Unions?

The potential power of unions can be appreciated in the tremendous efforts and enormous expenses incurred to undermine them by businesses, corporations, and their anti-union supporters in the media and government, who justifiably recognize that workers who are organized into unions present a formidable force in bargaining for fairness and equity and demanding for workers a fair share of the economic pie.

When workers are unionized, they weaken the ability of businesses to maximize their own returns (in the form of higher profits) by denying workers, who create the wealth in the first place, their proper share. These anti-union tactics are being pursued more aggressively to ensure that "larger and larger pieces of the pie go to shareholders, executives, Wall Street bankers, and others at the top."[85] And these tactics are paying off.

Unions are unable to fight them, especially in a political climate that increasingly sides with big business, and their membership has steadily declined in the private sector, where in 2012 only 11.3 percent of workers were union members. As membership in unions has fallen, so has their ability to bargain for better wages and benefits and to withstand the onslaught from businesses and corporations, the latter emboldened by weak enforcement of collective bargaining laws and a big business–friendly government.

Therefore, it is no coincidence that the concentration of wealth in the upper echelons of society has occurred at a time when workers' voices have become increasingly suppressed by their employers and anti-union politicians.[86] Workers are poorer today even though their level of productivity is at a pinnacle. As a result, unit labor costs have fallen and employers are getting more and more work out of a shrinking and cheaper labor force. The surplus values have risen, guaranteeing high rates of profit.

Since the unions are increasingly under siege, labor has lost the collective power to demand its fair share. And as the power of the unions fades, they are less and less able to pressure employers to raise wages even as worker productivity increases. It is this reality—of stagnant incomes despite rising worker productivity—that has led to rising corporate profits and unprecedented levels of inequality.

Unions in a Changing Economy and Changing Workplace

As discussed throughout this book, the loss of jobs is the defining factor of inequality in the United States today. With fewer individuals in the workplace, unions simply have fewer people to draw from. As discussed in Chapter 5, the processes that have combined to produce this job loss are mechanization, globalization, corporate consolidation, and financial speculation.

In addition is the phenomenon of "lean production" systems, which have changed the structure of work and the workplace and thereby also reduced the numbers of workers from whom unions can draw their members.

Jobs have been lost as mechanization has transformed the workplace. Firms have installed labor-saving devices in every industry to reduce the cost of labor and improve their bottom line. Automation, mechanization, and robotics have made workers redundant. Mechanization also means that there is even less room for unskilled labor in the key industries. Those workers fortunate enough to keep their jobs produce more and more with the aid of the machines and thus reduce the need for more workers.

Machines are preferred because they are considered cheaper and more effi-cient. As a result, there are fewer workers in the industries that formed the backbone of the union movement, such as automobiles, steel, coal, and meatpacking.

Similarly globalization, aided by free trade treaties, has enabled corpo-rations to relocate their capital investments to regions around the world where labor is cheap; laws regulating how workers are to be treated and paid or where waste is to be dumped are absent or weak at best; and tax laws are more lax. As globalization has opened up the US market to China, Mexico, Bangladesh, and Brazil, labor's job security has eroded and often vanished.

Workers in the United States face competition from unseen laborers from around the world who are willing to work for a fraction of US wages, weakening the bargaining hand of US workers. So they have lost either their jobs or their pay advantage. As the options to maximize returns for capital have opened up and the corporations have done exceptionally well, the market power of unions has plummeted. But what US workers have experienced is not inevitable.

For German workers, the experience of globalization has been quite different from that of their US counterparts. In Germany, unions are more powerful and German law mandates that workers' representatives sit on corporate boards in equal numbers as management. As a result, German workers have been able to keep their jobs in multinational corporations such as BMW, Daimler, and Siemens even as the corporations have globalized.[87]

In 1946, when United Automobile Workers president Walter Reuther demanded that workers have equal representation along with management on the corporate board of General Motors, he was soundly defeated. Today we see the profound consequences of that defeat. Workers have absolutely no say in how companies—where they have worked sometimes for genera-tions—make decisions that affect their lives in such critical ways.

The US South is a vast region where serious unionization never took root. Today it exists as a low-wage region that lures corporations to relocate from other, unionized regions. Since the 1980s, there has been a substantial move away from the highly unionized Northeast and Midwest into the states of the South. By 2000, the percentage of jobs in manufacturing in South Carolina (with union density of 3.2 percent), Mississippi (6.2 per-cent), North Carolina (6.2 percent), , and Arkansas (7.5 percent), had sur-passed that of unionized states Michigan (21.5 percent) and Illinois (18.0 percent) as well as that of all the states of the upper Midwest and the North-east.[88] Therefore, one reason why unions have been losing numbers is that corporations have moved to regions that either are union-free or support right-to-work laws.

Corporate consolidation means that there are fewer places for people to find work. As we saw in Chapter 5, through mergers, acquisitions, leveraged buyouts, and simply driving out the weaker players, the corporate players of the global market constantly narrow the field of competition and concentrate economic power and decisionmaking in the hands of fewer and fewer monopoly corporations. The process of consolidation sheds thousands of middle-class and blue-collar jobs but adds millions of dollars to a corporation's profit margin, widening the income divide between workers and employers. As corporate consolidation swallows up even more jobs, unions face dwindling numbers from which to draw members. For example, as the "big three"—General Motors, Ford, and Chrysler—and their suppliers outsourced, consolidated, and shrank, the membership of the UAW, a giant among US unions, plunged from a high of 1.5 million in 1970 to 355,000 in 2010, with only half the members coming from its traditional core industries.[89]

Global financial speculation, which encompasses economic activity that yields quick returns for those with the finance capital to participate, yields nothing in terms of real jobs or real wealth. Trillions of dollars change hands at the touch of computer keyboards each day, adding no jobs but robbing the global economy of capital that, if invested in the production of goods and services, could sustain individuals and their families. Again, another reason why there are fewer people in unions is because the jobs men and women could have had that would have enabled them to become members of unions are just no longer present.

Even more important has been the rapid introduction and adoption of "lean production" systems. Marketed as the "workplace of the future," this form of reengineering of work and the workplace has made union organizing difficult, if not impossible. Practices such as telecommuting and Internet conferencing, which are attractive because of the flexibility they offer, have also become detrimental to union organizing.

This is especially true in the telecommunications industry, where the once-powerful Communications Workers of America now has to divide its organizational capacity among the seven regional telecom companies that resulted from the breakup of AT&T and the abandonment of the industry practice of following systems of "master agreements." As a result, the union has become fragmented and its bargaining capability much reduced.

No corporation has mastered the concept of leanness as well as the retail giant Wal-Mart, which has replaced General Motors as the largest private employer in the United States. What Wal-Mart does, the rest of the retail industries emulate; therefore, the consequences of restructuring of work at Wal-Mart bode trouble for workers and their unions everywhere. Wal-Mart dominates the retail industry and has the power to dictate the terms of business to all of its suppliers and transporters. Wal-Mart prides itself for the low cost of the products it sells. But it pays its workers so little that they have no other choice but to shop at Wal-Mart.

One way Wal-Mart, its suppliers, and many other companies keep their prices low is by hiring their workers not as employees but as temporary or independent contractors. As a result, the workers exist in an amorphous, ill-defined space where they are in fact employees yet are not defined as such. Of course, companies do this to release themselves from any obligation to provide benefits, which is lamentable to begin with.

But this makes the task of unions even more arduous. Hypothetically, let us assume that the workers at Wal-Mart wanted to hold an election to determine whether they wanted to be unionized—a prerogative that the National Labor Relations Act grants them. How will they reach out to workers who are not employees of Wal-Mart, even though they are? As workers are restructured in ways that they are not counted as employees, it becomes very difficult if not impossible for unions to gauge how many employees there are. Therefore, the critical mass number, the number needed to hold an election to vote to unionize, may never materialize. According to labor journalist Harold Meyerson, "roughly 35 percent of all American workers fall into this contingent-worker category."[90]

How does a union reach out to employees who work part-time, without set schedules? Worker density and worker presence in the workplace, which once facilitated unions' organizing efforts, are historical artifacts today. And one of the reasons why unions are becoming so beleaguered is because they have often failed to adjust to this new reality of work and this new defini-tion of what a workplace is.

Beginning in the 1970s, as a combined result of the structural changes in the US economy and the workplace, unemployment began to increase. By October 2009, the official unemployment rate was 10 percent, with 15.6 million out of work. If we include the 5.6 million who wanted to work but who were considered outside the labor force because they gave up actively looking for work (the US government does not count those who are not actively looking for work), the total would be 21 million. Some 6 million private-sector jobs were lost between May 2007 and October 2009. The fate of the unions in this situation was predictable. In 2009, unions saw a net loss of 834,000 members in the private sector. Collective bargaining lost its effectiveness in stopping job loss, in negotiating better pay, or in challeng-ing the backlash. The outcomes of collective bargaining plummeted follow-ing the loss of union density.[91]

Since the 1970s, therefore, structural changes in the economy and the workplace have steadily reduced the power of the working class to organize and unionize. Deindustrialization, globalization, and mechanization have all led to a deteriorating market for unskilled labor, increasing use of part-time work, telecommuting, use of temporary workers and contractors, and unfixed working schedules, leaving workers struggling to hold on to their livelihoods.

Unions had already experienced massive declines in membership and had lost their power to fight for fair and just contracts for their remaining members. It was against this background that the union avoidance industry, the aggressive union-busting tactics of businesses, the right-to-work laws, and the assault on public unions went into action—almost destroying an institution of profound value to the civic, democratic, and economic health of the nation.

Self-Inflicted Wounds?

According to those who have studied and analyzed unions, labor's weakened authority in the United States today might have much to do with its own timidity and limited vision. It is also the result of labor's inability to accommodate the new realities of the economy and workplace and seize new opportunities. Could labor have also become too complacent as numbers grew and the standard of living of most workers rose? George Meany, a former president of the American Federation of Labor and Congress of Industrial Organizations (AFL-CIO), is reported to have said in 1979: "Frankly, I used to worry about . . . the size of the membership. But quite a few years ago, I just stopped worrying about it."[92]

Content with salary, benefit, and cost-of-living increases, labor lost sight of the bigger picture: the question of strategic control of capital itself. If addressed, this issue would have ensured for workers a voice in decisions about the most fundamental areas of their work lives—not just regarding salaries and benefits, but also in decisions regarding the structuring and restructructing of jobs as globalization and technology changed the structural contours of capitalism.

A narrow **economism** never expanded into a broader class analysis of the real power dynamics in capitalist society. Economism, as Italian sociologist and political philosopher Antonio Gramsci admonished, separates economics from the system in which it is embedded. A focus solely on economics without challenging the political system in which inequalities are embedded has led inequality itself to become a reified entity hiding the system and the players whose decisions deliberately spawn it. The fact that the power of unions went into a freefall at the most critical juncture is exactly because of their inability or unwillingness to see the larger systemic picture and challenge it.

It has even been argued that labor, labor unions, and their leaders, having bought into the ideology and logic of capitalism, have never been able to consider or offer an independent vision or a different political agenda.[93] In Chapter 13, we will return to this topic as we frame the possibilities for creating "alternative social futures of just and egalitarian societies."[94]

Labor historians point to the conciliatory strategies union leaders willingly negotiated with employers, often to the dismay of rank-and-file members, that progressively weakened labor's hand. In 1946, Walter Reuther, leader of the United Automobile Workers, backed down from the demand that labor have coequal representation on GM's corporate board, which would have given workers some control over major corporate decisions. Instead, Reuther settled for concessions such as higher salaries, more vacation time, and cost-of-living increases, essentially sealing labor's fate.

Over and over, labor has surrendered, compromised, and retreated in the face of employer attacks and threats. In 1979, under the leadership of Doug Fraser, the UAW agreed to wage cuts and changes in working conditions and work rules in negotiations with Chrysler Corporation, almost without a fight. In one instance after another, as unions have faced systematic assaults, threats of job cuts, outsourcing, changes in work rules, and wage and benefit cuts, they have taken a conciliatory stance, all but abandoning their most powerful weapon: the right to strike.

Strike activity has plummeted exponentially throughout the United States. Historically, strikes were the only leverage that unions had to counter the power of capital. The movements in the 1930s and 1960s were successful because they disrupted the civil order through massive rallies, marches, nonviolent civil disobedience, strikes, and dissent. But since the 1970s, timid unions and timid workers, fearful of job loss, have foregone the timeworn methods of grassroots organizing, resistance, and strikes to demand that their rights be honored.

In Madison, Wisconsin, in the spring of 2011, even as the town was overflowing with rank-and-file unionists, students, and community activists from around the country—enough people-power to shut the town down—union leaders were willing to compromise with an intransigent governor instead of standing firm on their legally guaranteed collective bargaining rights. Labor lost in Wisconsin in 2011, and in Indiana and in Michigan in 2012, leading some unionists to "recognize that the labor relations laws at both the federal and local levels are mostly rigged against them."[95] But in the face of this deeply disturbing reality, as Stanley Aronowitz bemoans, "the official labor movement . . . until now has shown a remarkable capacity for retreat alone."[96]

As threats to their power grew and an anti-union attitude gained currency around the country, unions fought with each other instead of uniting and gathering strength. Petty infighting and corruption damaged and compromised their ability to reclaim and protect their own integrity. Unions became a nonentity exactly at the time when the working class, facing challenges of historic proportions, needed them the most. The notorious squabbles between the AFL-CIO, the SEIU, and several other major unions diminished labor's ability to confront the economic crisis that was imperiling the working class and the United States as a whole.

MAKING CONNECTIONS
Social Justice Unionism

Carol Gay is the president of the Industrial Union Council of New Jersey. She has been an ardent unionist since 1972, when she became an organizer for the Communications Workers of America, one of the largest unions in the country. During this time, she has recognized the power that lies in building partnerships that include workers from every social realm. She attributes the past victories of the unions to "people sticking together" regardless of rank and title. In public-sector bargaining, when white-collar workers, such as librarians, doctors, teachers, and other professionals in state institutions, stood together with blue-collar workers, such as janitors and custodians, and when people from other walks of life joined the picket lines, the power of the unions to galvanize the community was palpable.

The 1970s was also a time when New Jersey was bustling with economic activity. There were plenty of well-paying jobs in manufacturing in cities such as Edison, Elizabeth, Linden, and Trenton. General Motors and Ford had auto parts manufacturing. There were textile, refrigeration, and air-conditioning plants, as well as oil refineries. The workers were represented by powerful unions like the United Automobile Workers; the United Electrical, Radio, and Machine Workers of America; and the Amalgamated Clothing and Textile Workers Union. By the end of the 1970s, though, the economic currents had changed course and factories started closing their doors. The first to leave were the textile plants, then the auto plants, followed by the rest. As recently as January 2013, the Hess Corporation announced that it would be closing its last refinery in Port Reading, New Jersey, where it had operated for fifty-five years. Almost 200 people lost their jobs immediately, but countless others will lose their jobs in the coming months as Hess also closes 1,350 retail gas stations in New Jersey and seventeen other states of the East Coast.

Carol bemoaned the consequences for unions of the downward spiral of good manufacturing jobs. Unions such as the United Electrical, Radio, and Machine Workers of America, which had survived the "red"-baiting of the McCarthy years, buckled under the strain of the economic onslaught. In the face of imminent unemployment, they saw their main function as negotiating good severance packages for their members or engaging in concessionary bargaining as a last attempt to keep the plants open and salvage jobs.

Unions themselves had many problems. Prior to the slump, decades of good economic times had also made the union leaders complacent. They preached to the choir instead of reaching out to others. Elitism and top-down management infected many unions, leaving the rank and file feeling invisible and voiceless. Infighting and "union-raiding" weakened the labor movement from within.

(continues)

Social Justice Unionism

Today, the only way unions can redeem themselves is to broaden their economic platform to include a broader, focused social justice unionism—that is, to relinquish the narrow agenda of economism and embrace a more visionary and progressive platform with the following goals:

- Decrease economic insecurity and the urgency for creating jobs through government programs.
- Raise the minimum wage; defend, expand, and improve Social Security, Medicare, and Medicaid; defend civil rights; and stop voter suppression.
- Improve public education and oppose attempts to privatize it.
- End all detention/deportation, and defend immigrant rights by calling for immediate legalization of the 11 million undocumented immigrants in the United States.
- Establish a single-payer health-care system that recognizes health care as a right, not a commodity to be bought and sold for profit.
- Repeal all free trade agreements that encourage well-paying jobs from the United States to relocate to countries where workers are exploited and forced to labor under oppressive conditions.
- End all unjust wars and occupations.
- Preserve and protect the environment so it can sustain future generations.

Such goals, as envisioned by newly formed groups such as the Labor Fight Back Network, could provide the foundation on which to build a genuine and sustainable social movement that is more concerned with the struggles of the average American than with economism or a narrow electoral politics that primarily seeks to get Democrats elected.

Unions have also been unable to take advantage of new opportunities to expand their membership, instead hanging on to outmoded practices and beliefs. They doggedly continue to represent themselves primarily as being blue-collar when the majority of workers in the new economy are service workers—temporary workers, part-time workers, telecommuters, and freelancers. Their language is archaic and incomprehensible to the young and immigrants.[97]

Latino immigrants are a vital part of this new economy. They have the capability to infuse the labor movement with new energy, new tactics, new ideas and visions, much like immigrants from Eastern Europe did in the early twentieth century. Immigrants come from countries with rich histories of collective movements and struggles. They understand—almost intuitively—that their individual fates are inseparable from those of the collective, an awareness in which they are comparatively more advanced than their native-born counterparts in the United States.[98]

Kate Bronfenbrenner of Cornell University, who well understands the perils that unions face, urges them to "put organizing first." The unions need to spend their resources to bring in those who have remained on the margins of the movement. Emphasizing the notorious infighting between the unions and the miserly amounts (4 percent of their budgets) devoted to organizing, she warns how inopportune their attitude is at a time when the country needs a "strong, united labor movement to take on the corporate right—now more than ever."[99]

Labor's strength lies first and foremost in its numbers and its potential for building a united front. Toward realizing this end, the labor movement needs to embrace the mission of seeking agreement on a basic agenda of social and economic justice for all, and should be forthright about spreading that message out in every manner possible. But that message needs to be modernized and contemporized. Labor needs to build coalitions with citizens' groups, civil rights advocates, advocates for the poor and for affordable housing, church and other activists in the sanctuary movement, immigrant rights activists, environmentalists, LGBT activists, campus organizers, progressives, and socialists, with the most important and primary objective being one of consolidation and empowerment.

The impunity with which the guarantees of the National Labor Relations Act are regularly violated, especially because the penalties for breaking the law are so trivial, has led Richard Kahlenberg and Moshe Marvit of the Century Foundation, a renowned liberal think tank, to consider the option of extending "the Civil Rights Act, which now bars discrimination based on race, sex, religion and national origin, to ban discrimination against individuals who are trying to form a union. Protecting workers who are trying to form a union under the Civil Rights Act would take the issue out of the obscure confines of labor-law reform."[100]

Noted labor historian Nelson Lichtenstein, in his article "Why American Unions Need Intellectuals," recalls one of the many perceptive observations of sociologist C. Wright Mills in the latter's 1948 book *The New Men of Power.* Mills wrote: "To have an American labor movement capable of carrying out the program of the left, making allies among the middle class and moving upstream against the main drift, there must be a rank and file of vigorous workers, a brace of labor intellectuals, and a set of politically alert labor leaders. There must be the power and the intellect."[101]

Student activists and labor activists seem to be a natural fit. Student-initiated mobilizations focusing on frustrations stemming from exorbitant tuitions along with wider campaigns against sweatshops, globalization, militarization, and genetically modified food, while also promoting environmental protection and advocating for the homeless and immigrants, have showcased what had been missing in the larger union movement: the awareness that all these various strands in the collective movement address ills that stem from the same global capitalist system.

The 1999 protests in Seattle that forced the World Trade Organization to cancel its meetings are a prime example of this campus-union alliance and provide a model for uniting all the different segments of society who are on the receiving end of the global capitalist system's ruinous policies. Additionally, in an excellent example of campus-union alliance, researcher Kate Bronfenbrenner was commissioned by unions to conduct an empirical study of how employers thwart attempts by employees to unionize.[102]

Conclusion

Labor cannot win on its own. It needs to find common cause. It should choose allies by using an astute class analysis, and should be mindful of historian Arthur Schlesinger's counsel that "class conflict is essential if freedom is to be preserved because it is the only barrier to class domination."[103]

The visionaries of today, those seeking change, need to be like the Sankofa bird, as often evoked by African and African American historians: a mythical creature that flew forward while looking backward to learn lessons from the past. Historian Peter Rachleff recalls how "in the spring of 1886, organized by the Knights of Labor, a bi-racial coalition of working men and women created a Workingmen's Reform Party and swept to control of the city government [of Richmond, Virginia]. Yes, biracial, with African Americans and whites organized separately but linked together in one campaign, with a shared set of goals. And, yes, men and women in a political campaign, even though women did not have the right to vote."[104]

The coalition between academicians and trade unionists, between blacks and whites, was able to do this because it chose issues that resonated with all groups it wanted to reach. And "it moved from workplace to politics and from politics to the workplace, and it never neglected social arenas and activities. . . . It encouraged workers to organize in their own milieus, but it also fought for the rights of all workers to be treated decently."[105] Study the past, Rachleff urges, because you care about the future.

Harold Meyerson asks rhetorically: "Will anyone notice if unions cease to be? Perhaps not. But they will notice the consequences."[106] Without a strong union movement, the middle class and the poor will continue to lose their economic foothold. Wealth will continue to flow upward, concentrating overwhelmingly in the hands of a few whose domination over government will grow, canceling out all other voices. Without the countervailing power of unions, democracy itself will be weakened. As Columbia University historian Eric Foner has notably said, without a strong labor movement "there is no real hope for progressive social change in this country."[107]

Notes

1. Greenhouse, "Union Membership in the U.S. Fell to a 70 Year Low."

2. Meyerson, "If Labor Dies, What's Next?" p. 21.

3. Becker and Scott, "Isolating America's Workers," p. 27.

4. Stern, "Unions and Civic Engagement," p. 128.

5. A transcript of the National Industrial Recovery Act of 1933, http://our documents.gov/doc.php?flash=true&doc=66&page=transcript (accessed May 1, 2013).

6. Becker and Scott, "Isolating America's Workers," p. 27.

7. Meyerson, "If Labor Dies, What's Next?" p. 20.

8. Becker and Scott, "Isolating America's Workers," p. 27.

9. Chase, "The Brief Origins of May Day."

10. Quoted in Remes, "May Day's Radical History."

11. Kaye, "Remembering the 1886 Wis. Tragedy."

12. Chase, "The Brief Origins of May Day."

13. The Second International was an international coalition of socialist and labor parties formed in Paris on July 14, 1889.

14. Masters and Delaney, "Organized Labor's Political Scorecard," p. 385.

15. Stern, "Unions and Civic Engagement," p. 121.

16. Much of the information here draws from the work of Carter A. Wilson. In his book *Racism: From Slavery to Capitalism,* Carter does a detailed analysis of the intersection between race and the history of unionism in the United States. His work in turn draws from the historical analysis of Philip Foner (*Organized Labor and the Black Worker*); Herbert Northrup (*Organized Labor and the Negro*); Michael Reich (*Racial Inequality: A Political and Economic Analysis*); and Thomas Brooks (*Toil and Trouble: A History of American Labor*).

17. Arnesen, *Encyclopedia of U.S. Labor and Working-Class History,* p. 389.

18. Ibid., p. 132.

19. Western and Rosenfeld, "Unions, Norms, and the Rise in U.S. Wage Inequality," p. 533.

20. Moreno, "Unions and Discrimination."

21. Krochmal, "An Unmistakably Working Class Vision," p. 935.

22. Ibid., p. 928.

23. Ibid., p. 941.

24. Ibid.

25. Quoted in Stern, "Unions and Civic Engagement," p. 127.

26. Freeman and Medoff, *What Do Unions Do?* p. 206.

27. Bureau of Labor Statistics, "Union Membership News Release."

28. Freeman and Medoff, *What Do Unions Do?* p. 46.

29. Dreher and Gaston, "Has Globalisation Really Had No Effect on Unions?" p. 165.

30. Card, Lemieux, and Riddell, "Unions and Wage Inequality," p. 519.

31. Ibid., pp. 554–555.

32. Western and Rosenfeld, "Unions, Norms, and the Rise in U.S. Wage Inequality," p. 513.

33. Ibid., p. 514.

34. Ibid., p. 528.

35. Ibid., p. 533.

36. Levy and Temin, "Inequality and Institutions in the 20th Century," pp. 2–3.

37. DeNavas-Walt, Proctor, and Smith, "Income, Poverty, and Health Insurance

Coverage in the United States: 2011," p. 5; see also Meyerson, "If Labor Dies, What's Next?" p. 22.

38. Meyerson, "Corporate America's Chokehold on Wages."
39. Moody, "Contextualising Organized Labour in Expansion and Crisis," p. 8.
40. Ibid., pp. 9–10.
41. Card, Lemieux, and Riddell, "Unions and Wage Inequality," p. 556.
42. Breslow, "Two American Families."
43. Saez, "Striking It Richer," p. 4.
44. Hout and Lucas, "Narrowing the Income Gap Between the Rich and the Poor," pp. 623–624.
45. Ray, Sanes, and Schmitt, "No-Vacation Nation Revisited," p. 6.
46. Fletcher, "For Labor, What's After Michigan?" p. 24.
47. Stern, "Unions and Civic Engagement," p. 129.
48. Freeman, *American Empire,* pp. 40–42.
49. Hacker and Pierson, *Winner-Take-All Politics,* p. 57.
50. Gilens, *Affluence and Influence,* p. 157.
51. Ibid., p. 158.
52. Masters and Delaney, "Organized Labor's Political Scorecard," p. 383.
53. Ibid., p. 384.
54. Dreiling, "Class Embeddedness of Corporate Political Action," p. 24.
55. Levy and Temin, "Inequality and Institutions in the 20th Century," p. 34.
56. Hacker and Pierson, *Winner-Take-All Politics,* p. 57.
57. Bureau of Labor Statistics, "Union Membership News Release."
58. Meyerson, "If Labor Dies, What's Next?" pp. 19, 21.
59. Stern, "Unions and Civic Engagement," p. 125.
60. Levy and Temin, "Inequality and Institutions in the 20th Century."
61. Greenhouse, "VW Vote Is Defeat for Labor in the South," p. B1.
62. Ibid., p. B2.
63. Ibid.
64. Logan, "Why Are GOP Politicians and Anti-Union Groups Interfering?"
65. Greenhouse, "VW Vote Is Defeat for Labor in the South."
66. Levy and Temin, "Inequality and Institutions in the 20th Century," p. 58.
67. Logan, "The Union Avoidance Industry in the United States," p. 654.
68. Ibid., pp. 651–652.
69. Ibid., p. 655.
70. Bronfenbrenner, "No Holds Barred," p. 4.
71. Ibid., p. 25.
72. Ibid.
73. Ibid., p. 4.
74. Eidelson, "Walmart Workers Walk Out," p. 11; Featherstone, "Rollback Wages," p. 11.
75. Eidelson, "Walmart Workers Walk Out," p. 15.
76. Fletcher, "For Labor, What's After Michigan?" p. 22.
77. Lafer and Allegretto, "Does 'Right to Work' Create Jobs? Answers from Oklahoma."
78. Quoted in Lafer, "Right to Work—for Less," p. 26.
79. Greenhouse, "The Big Squeeze," p. 335.
80. Moody, "Contextualising Organized Labour in Expansion and Crisis," p. 22.
81. Citizens for Tax Justice, "Corporate Tax Dodging in the Fifty States."
82. Nichols, "The Spirit of Wisconsin," p. 16.

83. Davey and Sulzberger, "Dueling Protests in a Capital," p. A14.

84. Moody, "Contextualising Organized Labour in Expansion and Crisis," p. 22.

85. Stern, "Unions and Civic Engagement," p. 123.

86. Ibid., p. 125.

87. Meyerson, "If Labor Dies, What's Next?" p. 23.

88. Moody, "Contextualising Organized Labour in Expansion and Crisis."

89. Ibid., p. 9.

90. Meyerson, "If Labor Dies, What's Next?" p. 24.

91. Moody, "Contextualising Organized Labour in Expansion and Crisis," p. 20.

92. Quoted in Meyerson, "If Labor Dies, What's Next?" p. 26.

93. Albo, Gindin, and Panitch, *In and Out of Crisis,* p. 10.

94. Feagin, "Social Justice and Sociology," p. 1.

95. Aronowitz, "Reflections on the Madison Uprising," p. 219.

96. Ibid., p. 222.

97. Meyerson, "If Labor Dies, What's Next?" p. 20.

98. Milkman, "Immigrant Workers, Precarious Work, and the US Labor Movement."

99. Bronfenbrenner, "Put Organizing First," p. 11.

100. Kahlenberg and Marvit, "Make Organizing a Civil Right," p. 12.

101. Quoted in Lichtenstein, "Why American Unions Need Intellectuals," p. 72.

102. Ibid., p. 71.

103. Quoted in Meyerson, "If Labor Dies, What's Next?" p. 25.

104. Rachleff, "Labor History for the Future," p. 34.

105. Ibid., pp. 34, 36.

106. Meyerson, "If Labor Dies, What's Next?" p. 20.

107. Quoted in Kahlenberg and Marvit, "Make Organizing a Civil Right," p. 12.

13

Seeking Alternative Social Futures

THE TITLE OF THIS CHAPTER IS INSPIRED BY SOCIOLOGIST JOE FEAGIN'S presidential address to the American Sociological Association in August 2000, in which he urged sociologists to "engage in the study of alternative social futures, including those of more just and egalitarian societies," if they were to truly fulfill their vocation as sociologists. Such an endeavor, Feagin stressed, would enable sociologists to "rediscover their roots in a sociology committed to social justice."[1]

In this book, I have tried to answer the questions that have accompanied the ever-widening chasm between the very rich and everyone else in American society, which some have likened to a new gilded age. Since my primary objective has been to inquire into the structures that generate, reinforce, and thus perpetuate inequality, my main argument originates from the premise that in a capitalist society, inequality is created as part of the natural functioning of the system.

The need to accumulate more and more capital through ever-increasing profits has set in motion actions and decisions that have led to a massive transfer of societal wealth, as the lion's share has surged upstream into the hands of the richest. The increasing concentration of wealth in the hands of the richest 1 percent is attributed to their gains from capital investments, which in turn creates the conditions for **patrimonial capitalism**, whereby wealth is increasingly inherited and not earned. Income becomes secondary to gains from capital investments in this equation of inequality.

In the eyes of many social observers, the United States is beginning to look more and more like a developing country. It is a difficult fact to swallow that some of the major cities in the United States have levels of inequality rivaling those of cities in the developing world.[2] On all the indices that usually determine well-being, the United States is at the bottom end of the list.

If health is the ultimate wealth and an undeniable gauge of the real well-being of a people, then consider the fact that, compared with ten other Western, industrialized nations, the United States has failed to improve from its last spot between 2004 and 2014 in the effectiveness of its health-care delivery system. At the same time, the United States also has the distinction of spending far more than the rest at $8,508 per capita. Norway, with the second most expensive system, spends $5,669. All the other countries—Australia, Canada, France, Germany, the Netherlands, New Zealand, Norway, Sweden and the United Kingdom—spend significantly less but deliver better care.[3]

As the income gap between the top earners and the rest continues to widen, the United States stands out among developed countries as having the highest percentage of low-wage workers (those who make less than two-thirds of the nation's median wage of $50,054 as of 2011). Fully 25 percent of all Americans make no more than $17,576 a year.[4] Even as the productivity of US workers has grown, they are less and less able to claim their fair share of that productivity. With an ever-increasing share of income going to capital rather than labor, the wealth of the top 1 percent matches the combined wealth of the bottom 95 percent.[5] And with that wealth has come the ability to wield power to stack political decisionmaking further in their favor—to continue the conversion of US democracy to a winner-take-all system.

Is There Room for Social Justice in Capitalism?

Some have observed that it is impossible for capitalism to be anything but cutthroat. If it is to remain duty-bound in fulfilling its singular drive to maximize profit for the sole purpose of capital accumulation, there is little room for economic justice for the masses. As Michael Parenti writes, "Marxists condemn the capitalist system, not because it has failed to provide economic justice but because it cannot."[6]

However, numerous instances in the United States and Europe have shown that it is possible to curb the excesses of capitalism. It might not be possible to change the system fundamentally, but it is possible to rein it in. An ideal system would combine the creative and productive capabilities of capitalism with institutional and normative structures that would ensure the fruits of such a system are enjoyed by all, and would also protect individuals and families against the risks that can come from the cyclical fluctuations of the economy. In the United States, President Roosevelt's New Deal and President Johnson's Great Society programs successfully created such provisions.

New Deal programs such as Social Security (which provided for old-age pensions, unemployment insurance, and the program Aid to Dependent Children), the Fair Labor Standards Act (which banned child labor and set a minimum wage), the National Labor Relations Act (which allowed workers to unionize and engage in collective bargaining with their employers), the Works Progress Administration (which provided work for 8 million unemployed workers between 1935 and 1943), and the Servicemen's Readjustment Act (which provided government aid to returning World War II veterans to cover the costs of medical expenses, higher education, and homes to help them readjust into civilian life) were credited with initiating a period of unparalleled prosperity in the decades following World War II.

The New Deal programs offered the framework within which the more expansive Great Society programs took root. The Great Society brought into its fold groups, such as African Americans, who had previously been left out, not in terms of the spirit of the initiatives but in matters of implementation. The Great Society established programs to eliminate poverty (food stamps, the National School Lunch Act, and many others), to guarantee health care for the elderly and the poor (Medicaid and Medicare), and to ensure that the children of the poor would have a chance to start school on an equal footing with children from more privileged families (Head Start). The program Aid to Dependent Children was expanded to include mothers and families and was renamed Aid to Families with Dependent Children. The Great Society empowered the federal government to ensure the well-being of all segments of society and fulfill, to a certain extent, its role as the "true custodian of the rights and freedoms of all Americans."[7] Social Security, Aid to Families with Dependent Children, Medicare, and food stamps, which have become so much a part of the American fabric, were the result of decisions made at the highest levels of government to create institutions and norms that would support a safety net below which no American would be allowed to fall.

Beginning in the decade after the Great Society programs went into effect, and continuing until the mid-1970s, rates of inequality seemed to level off somewhat. Even in the poorest communities, poverty rates fell quite steadily. Much of this positive turn has been attributed to the fact that the economy was humming along happily and a rising economic tide was lifting all boats. But historians and social scientists agree that much of the parity in economic well-being was a result of the institutional and normative changes that the New Deal and Great Society programs had put in place.

The changes did not happen on their own, or in a vacuum, but in an environment in which strong unions were able to collectively bargain for workers' fair share. These were changes that strong trade unions wrested from the government and employers. The political apparatus of the Democratic Party similarly had its finger on the collective pulse of the nation's citizens and intervened on their behalf.

Much has changed since then. The rising inequalities in the United States are surely due in part to structural changes in the economy—globalization, mechanization, and the corresponding losses in workers' economic potential—but are also the result of weak labor unions that were unable to question or stop the most egregious changes that were eviscerating working-class communities.

The European Alternative

In comparing the United States with European countries on various indices of economic and social well-being, it is apparent that the latter have drawn up a social compact that is qualitatively different and better able to deliver the good life to more of society. These are the countries of the European Union (EU), which are deeply committed to the principles of a capitalist economic system. The primary objective behind the formation of the EU, now comprising twenty-eight member states, was to consolidate the market power of its members to compete in a global market dominated by the United States and China.

Today, the EU has indeed become the largest and wealthiest trading alliance and makes no apologies for its unabashed commitment to capitalism. It has more Fortune 500 companies than any other peer country. It accounts for nearly 75 percent of all foreign investment in the United States.[8] It is also ruthless in its pursuit of the lowest costs when it comes to fattening its bottom line.

Of the multinational corporations blamed for running sweatshops in the collapsed building that claimed the lives of over a thousand Bangladeshi workers in April 2013, those from the EU were as much to blame as Wal-Mart and JCPenney. When it comes to maximizing profits, the Europeans are as impenitent as are Americans. Their steadfastness in pursuing the holy grail of profit is as unwavering as that of their US counterparts. European capitalism and US capitalism have the same foundation—profit maximization and capital accumulation.

This point merits repetition, since the Europeans, because of their comprehensive social welfare system, are constantly derided in the US media for being closet socialists. But this accusation couldn't be further from the truth. Europeans themselves will admit that their idea of social welfare finds inspiration more in religion than in socialism. As Dutch writer Geert Mak explains, the Dutch social welfare system "developed not after Karl

Marx, but after Martin Luther and Francis of Assisi."[9] But that has not silenced the critics on this side of the Atlantic.

Though European and American ways are rooted in the same philosophical and Judeo-Christian tenets, Europe and the United States have taken different paths in the evolution of their civil societies. This is most apparent in the different interpretations of the social compact, which undergirds the ideas regarding the role of the state in civil society.

The theory of the social compact is based on the political philosophies of Thomas Hobbes, John Locke, and Jean Jacques Rousseau. It embodies the idea that as members of civil society, individuals willingly give up some of their freedom and their sovereignty to the state. In return, they expect that the state will ensure the well-being of the collective and of the commons and establish a common good. For example, individuals give up some of their income by paying taxes so that the state has revenue to secure the common good.

What that common good entails can be defined expansively or narrowly. In Europe, the collective compact that undergirds the civil infrastructure includes a comprehensive system of social welfare programs, an extensive system of mass public transportation, and a sincere eye toward meeting the world's increasing environmental challenges by devising ways to create an ecologically sustainable future.

Steven Hill, author of *Europe's Promise: Why the European Way Is the Best Hope in an Insecure Age,* has described the social welfare programs of capitalist Europe as "striking a new, twenty-first century balance between individual property rights and the common good, between liberty and equality, and between government regulation and the free market."[10] Much of the discussion here on the European social welfare system is based on information gleaned from Hill's book.

Hill renames Europe's social welfare system as the "social workfare" support system, to emphasize the philosophical differences that undergird the divergent approaches to welfare in the United States as compared to Europe. In the United States, the attitude toward welfare is one of scorn and disdain. Conversely, the primary intent of the European system is to ensure the health and well-being of all workers, whose labor is recognized as being the most critical component to the functioning of the capitalist economic system. Hill writes that this workfare support system "is part of the overall capitalist matrix in which Europe's powerful economic engine produces the wealth needed to underwrite its comprehensive workfare supports, which in turn maintain a healthy and productive workforce that keeps the economy humming, like a well-tuned Swiss clock."[11]

Recognizing also that the capitalist business cycle is naturally given to ups and downs, the European system of benefits is meant to support the worker in times of economic downturns. In the United States, however, "Europe's workfare system has been grossly mischaracterized by Americans in thrall to a fundamentalist free market ideology" as being one of socialistic handouts.[12] The American public blindly parrots this narrative, with little understanding of its implications for their own lives.

Borrowing from Alberto Alesina and Edward Glaeser, we can describe this difference in the following way. In the United States, the collective politics of redistribution that welfare embodies is part of a **dominant ideology** that portrays iconic welfare programs such as food stamps, Temporary Aid to Needy Families, and Head Start as being "vertical" in nature, meaning that benefits flow from the majority at the top to a minority at the bottom. This system is seen as distributing wealth from a hardworking majority to a minority who are behaviorally, culturally, racially, and ethnically different from the rest, and who are generally regarded as being undeserving of such help.[13]

In contrast, "Europe's workforce support program is for everybody— middle class, rich, poor; its application is universal," writes Hill. The objective is to "maintain a healthy and productive workforce."[14] As a result, Europe's middle class is set on a "more solid and secure footing; and there are fewer poor people." The Europeans, writes Hill, "have constructed their system so as to support families better and to minimize the personal risk for individuals in an age of globalized capitalism that has brought increasing economic security."[15]

Sociologists Ho-Fung Hung and Jaime Kucinskas make a similar argument in their study: when governments have a redistributive mechanism in place, such as a generous welfare program, the most vulnerable populations are better equipped to defend themselves from the insecurities of an increasingly globalized economy.[16]

Europe's work force support system, Hill argues, is the very embodiment of the quintessential belief among Americans in rights to life, liberty, and the pursuit of happiness. He also posits that the programs that fall under Europe's work force support system make real what is merely rhetoric in the United States—the family values often talked about by US conservatives and leaders of the Republican Party. For Europeans, family values are more than just talk. Europeans have put in place concrete programs to make these values a reality:[17]

• *Paid parental leave.* European countries offer paid leave from work to both mothers and fathers following childbirth or to care for a sick child. Along with Lesotho, Liberia, Papua New Guinea, and Swaziland, the United States is one of only five countries out of a total of 173 that does not guarantee some form of paid maternity leave.[18]

• *Child care.* When parents return to work after having taken care of a newborn for up to two years, the child goes to a professional state-run or state-certified day-care provider. Parents pay for this service on a sliding scale. The typical rate is about $130 a month per child, which includes lunches. From age three, children are entitled to enrollment in the free public school system. There is almost 100 percent participation in child care, early education, and pre-primary education and preschool programs. A US parent typically pays $500 monthly for unstandardized, private, and often mediocre day care.[19]

• *Kiddie stipend.* For some context on this provision, consider the experiences of Russell Shorto depicted in a May 2009 article he wrote for the *New York Times Magazine* while living in the Netherlands. Shorto, father of two daughters, recounts his utter surprise at discovering two payments in his bank account of about $410 each from the Social Insurance Bank of the Netherlands, designated simply as "accommodation [for] schoolbooks."

This was in addition to four quarterly payments of $665 for a child benefit allowance, or *kinderbijslag,* that the Dutch government pays because, as its website rationalizes, "babies are expensive and the Dutch government provides for child benefit to help you with the costs of bringing up your child." Any parent living in the Netherlands receives these quarterly payments until their children are eighteen years old.[20] Kiddie stipends are for everybody, regardless of income. Some have compared this provision to the earned income tax credit in the United States, but the EITC is merely a refundable tax credit for poor families, not a cash payment. Middle-class families receive nothing from it.[21]

• *Balancing work and leisure.* Russell Shorto was in for another surprise when in late May 2009 another deposit of $4,265, labeled as *vakantiegeld,* or vacation money, arrived in his bank account. Virtually everyone in the country receives this before the summer holiday season. This amount constitutes 8 percent of one's salary, which the employer is required to provide to all employees along with a minimum of four weeks of vacation, during which employees continue to receive their regular salary.

For those who are unemployed, the government pays the *vakantiegeld* under the reasoning that, "if you can't go on vacation, you'll get depressed and despondent and you'll *never* get a job,"[22] which bolsters Hill's point that such programs are ultimately meant to keep workers mentally healthy. The United States is the only advanced country in the world where vacation time is not guaranteed. Europeans call the United States the "no-vacation nation." Consequently, Americans work the equivalent of nearly two months longer per year than European workers to maintain a comparable standard of living, but a diminished quality of life.

• *Sick leave.* European countries, along with 160 nations around the world, have mandatory paid sick leave, with 127 providing a week or more annually. The United States has no such national law mandating paid sick leave.

• *Health care.* European countries provide affordable, quality health care for all, including universal dental care, until age nineteen. Russell Shorto reports that while living in the United States, he paid about $1,400 a month for a policy that did not cover dental care, on top of which he had to take care of endless co-pays, deductibles, and exemptions from coverage. A similar policy in the Netherlands cost him $390 a month, and with no co-pays, deductibles, or exemptions. It also included dental coverage and paid 90 percent of the expenses for his daughter's braces.[23]

Such anecdotal accounts fill reports on Europe's health care system, a signature part of its social welfare infrastructure. And no report ever ends without the ubiquitous reference to the "general practitioner" (or primary-care physician, as known in the United States), who still makes house calls.

• *Retirement and pensions.* In both the United States and Europe, retirement pensions are funded by payroll deductions from both the workers and their employers at comparable rates, with about 8 percent of salary paid by each. However, Europeans can expect to draw retirement pensions that average 70–80 percent of their working salary, compared to only 40 percent in the United States.

The difference can be explained by the government's contributions, which in Germany make up about 85 percent of an individual's overall retirement income, as compared to only 45 percent in the United States. Consequently, workers in the United States need to save substantial amounts of money to supplement their future pensions and ensure a secure retirement. Given that most Americans not only have a negative savings rate but also are likely to carry heavy personal debts, many face an insecure future.

• *Elder care.* The elderly in Europe have the option of staying at state-backed nursing homes or assisted-living facilities, or receiving cash benefits from the government to stay home or in communities of peers with the assistance of hired caregivers, who are regarded as regular municipal employees, drawing salaries and benefits. Overall, European governments spend 25 percent more on the seniors than does the United States.

• *Education.* In most European countries, college and university education is free or almost free. In the United Kingdom, where students pay on a sliding scale, tuition is based on income, with a maximum tuition of $4,000 per year. In Germany, some state universities have started charging a maximum tuition of $630 per year. Compare this to the average tuition in the United States, where, in 2010–2011, four-year private colleges and universities charged an annual average student tuition of $32,617 ($43,289 for 2012–2013), while two-year private institutions charged an average of $23,871. Four-year public institutions charged an annual tuition of $15,918 ($22,261 for 2012–2013), while two-year public institutions charged $8,085.[24]

Between 1982 and 2007, college tuition and fees rose a whopping 439 percent and have since risen between 4 and 10 percent annually.[25] At the time of graduation, US students can expect to carry debts of $100,000.[26] Unlike US students, their European counterparts are not saddled with debts that mortgage their futures.

• *Affordable housing.* Decent and affordable housing is also part of the workfare support system. In fact, adequate affordable housing is considered a right. Though government owns some of the affordable housing, most of it is provided by private, nonprofit housing associations. Hill emphasizes that the system is not-for-profit; it pays for itself. Qualified people get apartments for below-market rates. Almost one-third of the apartments are considered "social housing," which does not carry the stigma attached in the United States to "public housing."

In Europe, social housing is simply a good, inexpensive place to live. And the apartment buildings house people with different income levels, not just the poor. There are few abject slums in the cities of Europe, because government-owned or private, nonprofit homes and apartment buildings of the social housing sector can be found in every neighborhood. The availability of more than adequate social housing also helps to hold down rents and mortgages in the private, for-profit sector.

• *Support for the poor and unemployed.* The fact that social welfare programs in Europe support every individual, regardless of economic status, likely explains why Europe has fewer poor people compared to the United States. The European workfare support begins at birth, continues for the entire life cycle of individuals, and is not dependent on a person's employment status. Unlike in the United States, in Europe universal coverage prevents loss of health care and other social welfare support.

There are also fewer poor people in Europe because of higher minimum wages, which typically are 53 percent of the average wage, compared to only 31 percent in the United States. Since the US minimum wage is not corrected for inflation, it has continued to decrease in real value since its high of 56 percent of the average wage in 1956. Almost a quarter of Americans are low-wage earners, compared to 6 percent of Swedes and 16 percent of Germans, for example.

The unemployed in the United States receive unemployment insurance for a period of six months, at a rate of 50 percent of their last salary. The unemployed lose their employer-covered health insurance and, unless poor enough, cannot qualify for Medicaid. When their unemployment insurance runs out, people are left to fend for themselves.

In Europe, on the other hand, unemployed workers receive a monthly payment of 70–90 percent of their last salary for up to four years. And they never lose any of their other benefits, which they continue to receive for the simple fact that they are members of the society.

The poor and unemployed in Europe, therefore, never lose their dignity. In the United States, the poor and unemployed face a different attitude, as responsibility for their status is primarily attributed to individual shortcomings rather than to cyclical economic forces. The social welfare system in Europe is indeed a true safety net, protecting the individual's well-being and dignity. In the United States, the poor and unemployed lose the services that are part of employment packages, just when they need them the most.

Europe's social welfare system also includes **subsidies** for home heating bills during the winter season, as well as subsidies for transportation, together with an extensive mass transit network that eliminates the need for automobiles.

Having borrowed extensively from Steven Hill's account of what he refers to as the European workfare system, let us conclude this section with his words: "A comprehensive catalog of the full range of workfare supports would take too long to list. They are the sea in which Europeans swim, suffused throughout the system in which health care, pensions, vacations, and the like are not called 'benefits' but instead are considered to be basic universal rights."[27]

How Do the Europeans Pay for All These Programs?

All of Europe's social welfare programs are primarily paid for by the government, but are also subsidized by employers. It is a private-public partnership that makes this happen. Europeans pay into it through their taxes. As opposed to the 35 percent maximum tax rate for salaries and wages in the United States, Europeans on average are taxed at a higher rate, such as 52 percent in the Netherlands. Critics of the social welfare system in Europe typically cite this tax differential. But considering how comprehensive the social welfare system in Europe is, the 17 percent differential in tax rates compared to the United States may seem less excessive.

Steven Hill notes that the tax rate in the Netherlands includes social security, which in the United States is an additional 6.2 percent. And in the United States, we must also consider state and local taxes and much higher property taxes compared to the Netherlands. Altogether, in the United States this amounts to a tax rate of close to 52 percent as in the Netherlands.[28]

Hill adds that, "in return for their taxes, Europeans receive a whole host of benefits and services for which Americans must pay out of their pocket with their discretionary income by using fees, premiums, deductibles, and tuition, *in addition* to their taxes." US presidents from Ronald Reagan to George W. Bush declared that the United States lets families keep their own money and lets them handle their health-care costs, retirement, child care, and university education. But this deregulated, laissez-faire system leaves people to decide on their own what many Europeans receive as standard fare for the taxes they pay.[29]

But this would be a hard sell in the United States, where the public has been conditioned to think of taxes as inherently bad and an imposition that supports big government to do as it pleases to curb people's freedoms. Absent from the diatribe against taxes is the simple fact that taxes are our dues for being members of society, just as one pays fees to belong to a health club or a country club or a homeowners' association, and thus enjoy its many privileges. Similarly, taxes are paid so as members of society we can enjoy the benefits of membership.

Without taxes, how can a society pay for all the amenities that members enjoy, such as roads, schools, firefighters, policemen, social security, and national security? In Europe, this list also includes health care, child care, child subsidies, elder care, vacation stipends, paid family leave, sick leave, unemployment insurance, and affordable housing.

The "Impending Threat" to the European Welfare State

As globalization has intensified immigration to Europe, from a trickle to a deluge, warnings have been raised about the future viability of the social welfare state in a Europe that is vastly different today compared to its colonial past. On the one hand, immigrants have been a boon to nations experiencing steep declines in their populations due to low birthrates.

But on the other hand, immigrants, who typically have higher birthrates compared to the native-born, are changing the social and cultural geography in radical ways. This has led to resentment among the native-born. Social scientists urge caution, such as Dutch sociologist Wim Van Oorschot, who warns that "when immigrants reach the point where they form the largest part of welfare users in European countries, and immigrants as a group are subjected to negative images—conditions which apply to both African Americans and Hispanic people in America—the societal legitimacy of welfare arrangements as a whole may diminish quickly."[30]

Similarly, observing the rise of an anti-immigrant politics in Europe, Alberto Alesina and Edward Glaeser wonder whether the future of the European welfare state is an American one: "As Europe has become more diverse, Europeans have increasingly been susceptible to exactly the same form of racist, anti-welfare demagoguery that worked so well in the United States. We shall see whether the generous European welfare state can really survive in a heterogeneous society."[31]

Let us consider this threat in historical terms, lest we go astray in framing the European model as the best alternative for US capitalism if the latter is to save itself. The European social welfare model has certainly succeeded in offering a way of life "enfolded in civilization,"[32] but we must be fully aware of the colonial antecedents of European wealth and capital, in the conquest of which the modus operandi was anything but civilized. Forgetting this context would compromise our ability to grasp the threats to the European welfare system posed by the immigrants who have appeared on European soil from those distant former colonies. It is important to remind ourselves of the poignant message that these immigrants want others to understand: "We are here, because you were there."[33]

The wealth of European colonial empires was built on the conquest of the wealth and resources of Asian, African, Caribbean, and Latin American peoples. All historical accounts indicate that at the end of the colonial experience, colonies were much poorer than they were at the moment of first contact with the colonial powers. As a result, when the time came after decolonization to draw up plans for their own economic development, fewer resources remained for the former colonies to draw from. Economic globalization and the internal dynamics of the former colonies did little to change this fact. Facing few economic opportunities at home and also the increasing social turmoil and violence that often ride on the back of people's dashed hopes, many in the former colonies found that migrating in search of livelihoods and better prospects became their only option—a journey that often brought them to the same Europe that their wealth had enriched.

Europeans carried their own crosses when the two world wars descended on them. If the colonial experience failed to open Europe's eyes to the capacity of its own cruelty and inhumanity, the two wars brought that message home loud and clear. The concentration camps, more than anything, raised questions about Europe's claim to civilization and reason.

The single-minded initiative to draw up a comprehensive social welfare infrastructure was, in many ways, a deliberate attempt to wash away those transgressions. If the genocide was the ultimate consequence of singling out people for elimination, the social welfare programs would do the opposite. They would go out of their way to embrace all people, all residents of a country, for unquestioned inclusion. For almost two decades after the end of World War II, the social welfare programs made it possible for Europeans to attain the proverbial heaven on earth.

As the pressures from globalization, the **debt crisis**, and structural adjustment policies intensified, derailing whatever hopes for development their countries had, citizens from the former colonies started showing up at the doors of their former colonial masters. And in the climate of heightened postwar humanitarian awareness, they were not turned back. So more and more came, drawn by the generous provisions of the social welfare programs.

And unlike in the United States, where racial and ethnic diversity has been an integral though sometimes contested reality, in Europe the immigrants were coming to nations that until the very recent past had been largely homogeneous. Thus, the arrival of the immigrants dramatically changed the social landscape. Naturally, there was resentment—a very normal, human reaction when the familiar world becomes unfamiliar. We may contest this reaction, but we cannot deny its fundamental human logic. People like to keep things the way they are, and simple.

But economic, political, and global factors always make the simple complex. It was true when colonization burst into the third world, and it is true today as the colonized seek to claim their share—not necessarily deliberately or consciously, but because they have been forced by historical and economic circumstances. But their presence in growing numbers strains the fiscal budgets and threatens the programs. It is therefore not surprising that a far-right neofascism is taking hold in many European countries. Supporters of this movement want the immigrants out, but unlike the right and the far right in the United States, they typically do not advocate antiwelfare policies; rather, showing a kind of **welfare chauvinism**, they question who should receive it.[34]

Most European social scientists have no worries that the European social compact is in danger of dissolution or that a far-right victory is imminent. Instead, they believe that a strong tradition of progressive, left-wing politics, along with a powerful union movement, will be able to "insulate welfare systems against the impact of greater diversity among citizens." The preceding quote comes from Peter Taylor Gooby, a social policy analyst who is internationally noted for his pioneering work on "new social risks." He writes quite unequivocally that "once left [wing] politics is taken into account, the impact of diversity on social spending falls dramatically. When a left wing influence is established and has influenced political institutions, as is the case in Europe but not in the US, different patterns of development set in."[35]

Similarly, Dutch sociologist Wim Van Oorschot, whose research involves analysis of European social welfare policy, agrees that "the degree to which a country can afford to treat immigrants as an equally deserving category" will depend on the role of left-wing politics in that country.[36] And, indeed, left-wing and progressive politics have a strong following among the men and women of Europe—the true guardians of the social welfare compact. As Steven Hill writes, Europeans are certain that they must preserve, at all costs, the "most egalitarian and democratic societies that the modern world has ever seen, all the while producing robust capitalist economies with competitive businesses and a productive workforce."[37]

Social Capitalism and Economic Democracy

The European social welfare system is rooted in a philosophy shared across the political spectrum—that the commitment to ensure the health and well-being of workers and their families is not just a governmental responsibility.[38] A comprehensive system of collaboration among government, for-profit and non-profit institutions, employers, and workers bears the responsibility to bring this philosophy to fruition. The recognition of the coequal voice of the average worker in the corporate decisionmaking apparatus is probably the most radical aspect of this perspective. It leads to the unprecedented extension of democratic principles to the workplace. It is in these principles of "economic democracy" and "social capitalism" that the entire European social welfare/workfare system is intricately rooted.

In the 1880s, the German monarchy was facing a growing challenge from the Social Democratic Party. Followers of two socialist leaders—Karl Marx and Ferdinand Lassalle—had joined forces and presented a sure threat. There was talk of revolution. German leader Otto von Bismarck promptly outlawed the party and, "convinced that repression was insufficient," as Paul Starr writes, "sought a welfare monarchy to assure workers' loyalty,"[39] but also to calm the growing influence of their trade unions. It was an early attempt to "stabilize the political order by integrating the workers into an expanded welfare system. The proponents of social insurance also expected that it would increase industrial productivity by diminishing class antagonism and create a healthier labor force."[40]

After the ravages of the two world wars, German politicians and policy-makers expanded on the seed that Bismarck had planted and offered Europe the ambitious ideals of economic democracy and social capitalism rooted in the belief "that a free market should also serve broader social goals."[41] They looked for macroeconomic structures that might facilitate that objective. One such macroeconomic structure was known as "codetermination." It created a framework in which elected worker representatives sat on supervisory boards along with stockholder representatives and corporate directors. In every workplace, elected worker representatives sat in on works councils, allowing for critical worker input at the level of the factory floor.

Such measures, formally established as federal law in Germany through the Codetermination Act of 1976, "launched the most democratic corporate governance structure the world had ever seen."[42] Other European countries were quick to adopt this model of economic democracy as the foundation on which to build their social capitalisms—systems that allow businesses to be both competitive (make money) and socially responsible (care for one's fellow human beings, one's workers, and the environment).

Codetermination ensures that half of the supervisory board members of the largest corporations in Germany—Siemens, BMW, Daimler, and many others—are elected by workers. Imagine such a scenario in the United States, perhaps for Wal-Mart or Nike. From the American point of view, such a practice is inconceivable—yet European companies do it as a matter of course. The works councils have the responsibility to meet with management to discuss and provide input on an array of matters that affect the workers, such as daily work schedules, the length of the workweek, work organization, scheduling of holidays, wages, job training, and decisions regarding the introduction of new technologies, mergers, and layoffs.

Consider the situation in the United States, where unions are banned outright from the workplace of many companies, such as Wal-Mart, thus giving management a monopoly over decisionmaking, with no input whatsoever from the workers. As we saw in Chapter 12, a recent effort at the German-owned Volkswagen plant in Chattanooga, Tennessee, to organize workers under the auspices of the United Automobile Workers union and to also establish works councils, was defeated by a narrow margin when outside anti-unionists pressured the workers to vote against the initiative, even though the Volkswagen management were themselves in favor of such a move.

At a time when workers in US corporations are facing layoffs and plant closings, German companies are benefiting, as they have for decades, from almost "unparalleled labor harmony, job security and broad sharing of company profits."[43] Codetermination has given German workers a say in their places of work, something US workers can hardly imagine.

The voice of labor, of the worker, is indelibly imprinted on the social compact of Europe. It is a recognition that European workers have claimed through decades of collective movements, as the rich history of labor in Europe exemplifies. In addition, astute politicians, policymakers, and corporate leaders have recognized that the robustness of the economies of Europe depends to a large extent on the health and well-being of workers, which in turn is contingent on the key role that workers play in claiming their fair share in the workplace.

Democracy in the workplace and the philosophy that undergirds it are crucial cornerstones of social democracy and the social welfare system—a natural extension from the individual to the collective of honoring the dignity of the worker by including all members of society, irrespective of race, ethnicity, class, or gender, in the system. Economic and political democracy go hand in hand—one cannot be realized without the other.

In addition to benefiting from codetermination, workers in Europe also form strong labor unions. European workers find it much easier to unionize compared to their US counterparts, and as a result, a much higher percentage of European than American workers are unionized. In Sweden, 78 percent of workers are unionized; and in Belgium the rate is 55 percent.[44] In the United States, the unionization rate has fallen to an all-time low, 11.3 percent as of 2011.

US companies that try to expand to Europe face a very different work culture—one that embraces the idea of the right of workers to be heard.

When GM announced in 2000 that it was going to close a plant in the United Kingdom, the works councils for GM-Europe mobilized 40,000 workers in five countries to participate in rallies at many GM sites. GM changed its plans and agreed to discuss all future moves with the works councils. In recounting this case, Steven Hill writes that "GM did not change Europe; Europe changed GM."[45]

Similarly, when McDonald's in Denmark refused to abide by the collectively bargained wage agreements, unionized workers protested until the company relented. The agreement was not just about a $20 per hour living wage but five weeks' paid vacation, paid parental leave, overtime pay, and schedules, which are set a month in advance. McDonald's still made profit after the agreements.

In the face of economic downturns, economic insecurity, and a widening gulf between the rich and the poor, why is the United States not looking to Europe for alternatives? Are not the strong safety net, expansive social welfare, and social democracy of Europe exactly what the United States needs the most?

Nobel Prize–winning economist Paul Krugman, writing for the *New York Times* in June 2013 on the rising inequality in the United States, thinks so. "So what is the answer?" he asks.

> The only way we could have anything resembling a middle-class society—a society in which ordinary citizens have a reasonable assurance of maintaining a decent life as long as they work hard and play by the rules—would be by having a strong safety net, one that guarantees not just health care but a minimum income too. And with an ever rising share of income going to capital rather than labor, that safety net would have to be paid for to an important extent via taxes on profits and/or investment income. I can hear conservatives shouting already about the evils of "redistribution." But what, exactly, would they propose instead?[46]

How can anyone argue that the United States has no need for the generous provisions so integral to the social welfare programs in Europe? As more and more people fall off the economic ladder, what better way to support them? If Americans and Europeans are similar in so many ways, why are they so far apart when it comes to such a fundamentally important matter of securing a social compact that ensures the well-being of all members of society?

Is it not common sense that a country cannot call itself fair and just if it cannot guarantee the basic means to live with dignity to all its citizens? What exactly does democracy mean when citizens have been systematically stripped of their ability to be heard in the halls of power, when political will bends only in the direction of wealth and affluence? What forces have steered the United States onto such a different trajectory compared to the European social welfare model?

What Makes Change So Hard?

The answer lies in the growing political trend in the United States whereby the very structures and institutions of society are increasingly bent to the benefit of the few at the expense of the many. This has been accomplished with very little opposition, as large numbers of people "willingly accept and sometimes even actively endorse" proposals that are "clearly to their disadvantage."[47]

This phenomenon forms the basis for Thomas Frank's 2004 book *What's the Matter with Kansas?* in which he makes the case that a "great backlash" against the changes that the rebellious sixties ushered in has dominated the US political scene since the 1980s. The main assertion of this movement is that "culture outweighs economics as a matter of public concern—that [cultural] values matter most."[48]

Conservatives have successfully rallied the masses using this platform of traditional values, which rejects abortion rights, gay rights, the teaching of evolution, gun control, taxes, and big government—or whatever needs defending or opposing in the ongoing battle to maintain the conservative interpretation of tradition, family, and the American way of life. The beauty of this line of argument is that these cultural issues, which are almost never black-or-white, will therefore never cease to be divisive. There will always be disagreements over these issues. They can always be revived, differently incarnated, to provide easy fodder during every election cycle. However, once conservatives are elected to office, they typically drop their focus on these cultural issues and immediately turn their attention to an economic regimen of stopping increases to the minimum wage, blocking extensions of unemployment benefits, rolling back workplace standards, endorsing financial deregulation, supporting privatization of schools, busting unions, cutting corporate taxes, and then sequestering budgets so that Head Start, food stamps, education, and Medicare can be further slashed.

Frank says that "the leaders may talk Christ, but they walk corporate."[49] Ronald Reagan, who made himself the champion of family values and under whose presidency the culture wars were ushered in, was really just interested in repealing the New Deal and deregulating capitalism to the ultimate extent possible. Since that time, the welfare state has been impaired, the tax burdens for the wealthy and for corporations have been dramatically reduced, and privatization and deregulation have increased, all of which, as Frank writes, have facilitated "the country's return to a nineteenth century pattern of wealth distribution. It is a working class movement that has done incalculable, historic harm to working class people."[50] Yet, according to Frank, it is the working-class movement itself that is responsible.

The birth of the culture wars, with eager conservatives as midwives, has successfully returned conservative politicians to power and strengthened movements such as that of the Tea Party. Egged on by a willing media, the culture wars have also turned public discourse almost entirely away from the economics and politics of inequality. Instead, the most passionate debates are about abortion, gay rights, gun control, and the like. In September 2011, the Occupy movement made a valiant attempt to put economic inequality at the center of public consciousness. It still has a strong and defiant presence in some circles, but has been largely ignored and sidelined by mainstream media.

If seeking a fair and just future involves a battle over ideas, then it is quite clear who is winning. Those with the biggest purses have the loudest voices, and because of these loud voices, the United States will not become like Europe anytime soon. Most Americans, and probably also their leaders—even progressive ones—are basically unaware of the degree of sophistication of the European system.[51] The little that is known is easily dismissed and ridiculed in rhetoric about "socialists" and "freeloaders," especially because the European system is subsidized by a tax rate that is unthinkable, unacceptable, and seemingly un-American to the core. In the current political climate in the United States, this remains the dominant mind-set, virtually unchallenged. Any change will require a dramatic shift in this entire dynamic.

MAKING CONNECTIONS
The Affordable Care Act

In the United States, few things lead to more contentious debate than health care. Unlike in Europe, where an ethics of common good and common sense informs health-care policies, in the United States health care is considered a commodity that is bought and sold for profit; consequently, the ruthless ethos of the marketplace trumps all other concerns.

Just like with any commodity, whether or not people are able to avail themselves of medical care depends on their ability to pay. In Europe, all individuals have health care for life, regardless of employment status. By contrast, most Americans depend on their employers for coverage, for which they still have to pay premiums and deductibles.

However, employment-based health care leaves out minimum-wage workers whose employers do not offer health coverage, people who have lost their jobs or only work part-time, and individuals who are self-employed, like my friend Stasy. Until passage of the Affordable Care Act (also known as Obamacare) in 2010, people in these categories had to buy their own health insurance, at unaffordable prices, from among the thousands of insurance companies in the market.

As discussed in Chapter 3, Obamacare has begun to reduce the number of uninsured people in the United States. When the first sign-up period ended on March 31, 2014, nationwide, more than 8 million people had enrolled in the private plans offered in the Affordable Care's health insurance marketplace. Another 4.8 million had signed up to the expanded Medicaid program.

(continues)

The Affordable Care Act

I am still trying to convince Stasy, who pays close to $600 a month for private insurance, to check out Obamacare. But she has misgivings about it, even though, as of May 2014, 161,775 of her fellow New Jerseyans have signed up for private health insurance and 98,240 have enrolled in New Jersey Family Care, part of the expanded Medicaid program.

Much of Stasy's hesitation comes as a result of the right-wing propaganda that has surrounded Affordable Care. Any talk of reining in the ever-increasing cost of health care or exploring ways to make its delivery more humane and egalitarian is quickly dismissed by the right wing as socialistic and anathema to the system of free enterprise and market competition. Most Americans buy into this propaganda, often to their own disadvantage, without having any idea what it really entails.

The Tea Party grassroots movement, which was born right after President Barack Obama took office, has made defeating Obamacare its holy grail, with the ultimate objective of making government so small that it can be "drowned in the bath tub."[1] Harvard political sociologists Theda Skocpol and Vanessa Williamson, in their book *The Tea Party and the Remaking of Republican Conservatism,* identify the rank and file who make up this grassroots movement as being primarily white, middle-class, married couples aged forty-five and older—many of whom are retired and beneficiaries of Social Security and Medicare, which bear the unmistakable fingerprints of big government.

Yet they seem unaware that they are biting the hand that feeds them. They are given "visibility and viability" by the all-encompassing right-wing media, which, according to Skocpol, they listen to for eight to ten hours a day. And they have support from ultra-right billionaires such as the Koch brothers.

Since the 2010 elections, when Tea Party candidates swept into Congress, they have also dominated the political scene in many states. Their main objective is to dismantle not only any attempts at health-care reform, but also any attempts at redistributing the economic pie.

Note: 1. Bauerlein and Jeffery, "The Job Killers."

Hegemony, Dominant Ideologies, and Apathy

Control over a society's means of material production gives the capitalist ruling class the ability to control the means of mental production. This notion remains as true today as it was in the 1840s, when Karl Marx and Friedrich Engels first expressed it in their book *The German Ideology.* As they wrote: "The ideas of the ruling class are in every epoch the ruling ideas: i.e., the class, which is the ruling material force in society, is at the same time its ruling intellectual force."[52]

Through their control of the means of mental production, the ruling class produces ideas and regulates the production and distribution of the ideas of their age. Those ideas and the ideologies they produce have the power to make the material circumstances "appear upside down as in a *camera obscura.*"[53]

The main thrust of this argument has not weakened over the centuries, even through myriad interpretations. What Thomas Frank discusses in his book *What's the Matter with Kansas?* is this upside-down world of ideas, where people under the thrall of a dominant ideology endorsed by the corporate ruling class willingly accept and enthusiastically promote an agenda that continues their disadvantage and powerlessness—and, by the same token, reject ideas that would benefit them.

Antonio Gramsci, the Italian political theorist, proposed the concept of hegemony in building on this position of Marx and Engels. But contrary to Marx and Engels, Gramsci locates society's power struggles in the realm of ideas instead of the material means of production. Through control of a society's ideas, the capitalist ruling class controls society's means of production.

The elites are able to manipulate the ideological battle lines in such a way that the masses in society, even those whom the elites oppress, do not question the legitimacy of the structural and institutional arrangements that are the sources of elite power. Gramsci introduced the concept of hegemony to describe the power of the capitalist ruling class to control the content of these ideological, cultural, moral, and normative structures.

The all-encompassing power of the elites is seen in their ability to impose their interpretations on every medium through which cultural messages reach the people—the mass media, political parties, churches, schools and universities, civic and voluntary associations, and even trade unions. Everywhere people turn, they are inundated with the same messages, which they internalize, often unconsciously. As a result, an omnipresent ideology convinces citizens to unquestioningly support positions that reinforce the interests and power of society's elites. The rich and the poor, as well as the powerful and the powerless, internalize this ideology, and it keeps everyone in their place.[54] Thus, according to Gramsci's position, anyone who seeks social change must first win the ideological battle and overcome the dominance of the elites.

Counter-hegemony offers an alternative vision of society in which first the hearts and minds of the people must be won over before they can support genuine, material social change. Once the fog lifts from people's minds and they are cured of their **false consciousness**, they will be more amenable to considering alternatives.

Ken Johnson, in a July 2013 report in the *New York Times,* writes: "Gramsci thought that the overthrow of capitalist hegemony should come not by violent revolution but through the rise of 'counter-hegemonies'—alternative cultures developed by disenfranchised groups. Through self-education, self-organization and the creation of its own institutions, a proletarian culture might someday become powerful enough to displace the bourgeois culture of modern, industrial society."[55]

Mass Media in the United States

Unlike the material and institutional structures of capitalism—low wages, sweatshop-like workplaces, long hours of work, physical drudgery, food insecurity, and powerlessness—that lead to tangible oppression, ideological and cultural hegemony does not produce such visible signs of coercion and domination. In fact, it does just the opposite.

The culture industry, through such media as television, movies, and the Internet, is the primary vehicle for disseminating ideas to the public. This creation of mass culture is a "pleasant" method of control. German American philosopher Herbert Marcuse saw technology not as a neutral entity but as facilitating capitalist domination over the people. The prime example is television, which entertains, amuses, and creates diversions. It does so pleasantly even as it compromises people's ability to think critically and independently.

It creates a **one-dimensional society** in which a "cognitively incurious" public often accepts unquestioningly the ideas that the elites disseminate through their control over the culture industry. Having lost their independent perspectives and judgments, people think like they have been conditioned to think—mindlessly, not mindfully—without even being aware of their indoctrination and, as West Virginia senator Robert Byrd said, basically "sleepwalking through history."[56]

The power of the elites is seen most significantly in the way the news media function. In a democracy, the news media play an important and critical role in educating the citizenry. A politically judicious, clear-eyed public is the bedrock of a government of the people, by the people, and for the people. It is the function of independent, unbiased news media to provide men and women with information and analysis about the most critical issues of the day, so they are equipped to play their role as stewards and guardians of the common good. The news media are the watchdogs of the people.

But more and more, according to analysts, the news media have become lapdogs for the elites, whose ideas and priorities form the main content, analysis, and interpretation of news. Democracy has been "deterred" as the media turn more and more to the function of "manufacturing consent" among the masses in accordance with the goals and priorities of the ruling elite. Edward Herman and Noam Chomsky have developed a "propaganda model" to describe the performance of the mass media of the United States.

It is based on their observations, garnered through many years of study, that the media, under the cloak of the First Amendment, "serve to mobilize support for the special interests that dominate the state and private activity. In a world of concentrated wealth and major conflicts of class interest, to fulfill this role requires systematic propaganda."[57] Their analysis is based on tracing "how money and power are able to filter out the news fit to print, marginalize dissent, and allow the government and dominant private interests to get their messages across to the public."[58] This is accomplished by applying what Herman and Chomsky refer to as a set of news filters.

The first filter is the "size, concentrated ownership, and profit orientation of the dominant mass-media firms." The media giants who control the dissemination of the news are large, profit-seeking corporations, owned and controlled by wealthy people and closely interlocked and sharing common interests with other major corporations, banks, and the government. They have the power to squelch alternative media just by their sheer size and connections.[59]

The second filter is "advertising [which is] the primary income source of the mass media." The advertisers' choices influence the prosperity and survival of the media. The media therefore are cautious in what they choose to air. Corporate advertisers will be unlikely to sponsor programs that might engage in serious discussion and criticism of their corporate activities, such as the oppressive conditions in their factories in Bangladesh or China, their decisions to divest from North America to ensure higher profits by doing business elsewhere, their tax dodging, and their oil spills, fracking, and other environmentally destructive actions.

The media learn over time to self-censor and not air anything that will present their sponsors in a bad light. Advertisers similarly will not support programs that will interfere with the viewers' "buying mood." The primary objective is to entertain and present the news in a superficial way without covering anything disturbing or of serious complexity that might sully consumers' desire to go shopping.[60]

The symbiotic relationship between the mass media and powerful corporate interests is also apparent in the third filter, which highlights the sources from which the media get their news. Because profit-minded news corporations want to get their news in the most cost-efficient way, they look to government and corporate bureaucracies, "where significant news happens, important rumors leak out and where regular press conferences are held"[61]—none of which might be places where the "real" stories that reflect the rhythms of people's everyday lives and struggles materialize.

People get attention only when something sensational and dramatic happens that has the power to attract a large audience and raise the Nielsen ratings for a network, which translates into millions of dollars' worth of advertising revenue. But other than drama, the substance of serious routine news that the media provide comes from government and corporate sources such as the Pentagon, the State Department, and the "corporate collective"—

the US Chamber of Commerce. As Herman and Chomsky write, "non-routine sources must struggle for access."[62]

These filters and others narrow the range of news that the media present and that people watch, hear, and read. Since the media, controlled by big corporations, are primarily in the business of making money, they choose those paths that will maximize their profits. Providing news to enable the functioning of a healthy democracy is not their objective. Therefore, they do not educate citizens to enable them to question the oppressive structures of society; rather, they encourage people to uncritically accept the premises of their lives and be passive agents in their own dehumanization.

Next to making profits, the deliberate goal of the media is "propaganda," which, by minimizing the opportunities for public scrutiny of the actions of the corporate and ruling classes, functions instead to "manufacture consent" in society for the very economic and political structures, institutions, and practices that lead citizens to be silenced in the most critical areas of their lives. As a result, people are denied the basic information and analysis that they need in order to understand the circumstances of their lives, to hold their leaders accountable, and to fully exercise the rights that the Constitution gives them.

Falsehoods and Misperceptions

The absence of media that truly educate means that the public are often misinformed and ignorant of the major circumstances of their lives. When individuals receive their news from talk shows that are preponderantly conservative, the information they receive is frequently even more "inadequate, misleading, or patently inaccurate" and often contains undertones warning about the dangers of a liberal media, such as National Public Radio and PBS.[63]

The Program on International Policy Attitudes and Knowledge Networks conducted polls in 2003 to survey the American public's perceptions regarding the Iraq War, Iraq's involvement in the attacks September 11, 2001, its connections to al-Qaeda, and weapons of mass destruction.[64] The polls showed widespread misperceptions among the American public, a majority of whom believed that Iraq was involved in the 9/11 attacks, that the hijackers were Iraqis, that Iraq had close ties with al-Qaeda, and that weapons of mass destruction had not only been found in Iraq but also used during the Iraq War.

On the basis of these falsehoods, the American public overwhelmingly supported the war, contrary to world public opinion, which overwhelmingly opposed military intervention. The investigators were further interested to see if "the extent of Americans' misperceptions [varied] significantly depending on the source of their news." They concluded that Americans who received most of their news from *Fox News* were more likely to have misperceptions. Those who received their news from National Public Radio and PBS were less likely to have misperceptions. The frequency of misperceptions was 80 percent among the listeners and viewers of *Fox News* and 23 percent among listeners and viewers of National Public Radio and PBS.[65]

Since those who receive their news from National Public Radio and PBS are more likely to be exposed to news that gives them relatively accurate information and that is often followed by analysis, the rationale for the attack against these "liberal media" becomes clear. However, since both National Public Radio and PBS are heavily bankrolled by corporations, their ability for liberal indiscretions is severely limited, since they cannot survive financially without corporate support.

The more people are fed falsehoods by the media, the less they are able to challenge the material and institutional arrangements that imprison them in structures that spawn increasing economic insecurity, inequality, powerlessness, and hopelessness. The dominant ideology assures them that this is the best of all possible worlds, that if they just keep working hard and face their problems stoically and without complaint, they too will one day join the ranks of the privileged in this land of opportunities.

And because they hope to someday join the privileged, they do not want to encumber the elite with unnecessary taxes and regulations. Thus, in the absence of a counter-hegemony that challenges and subverts the ideological and cultural precepts of the dominant ideology, people are paralyzed into willingly accepting and actively promoting an agenda that continues their own disadvantage.

Television: Discouraging Civic Participation and Promoting Anti-Intellectualism

In this supposed citadel of democracy that is the United States, there is little democratic dialogue and civic participation. Many studies have confirmed this trend. In his groundbreaking sociological study *Bowling Alone: The Collapse and Revival of American Community,* Robert Putnam writes about the unraveling of the fabric of American community life with the decline in civic engagement and social capital.

He describes social capital as social networks with "associated norms of reciprocity," whether that means belonging to bowling leagues or voluntary associations, or joining community-based groups based around religion, philanthropy, or the like. In each of these areas, "beginning in the 1960s and 1970s and accelerating in the 1980s and 1990s . . . the fabric of American community life began to unravel."[66]

Putnam points to a slew of suspects as having contributed to the decline. He writes about the "pressures of time and money, including the special pressures on two-career families" as well as "suburbanization, commuting and sprawl as having a dampening effect on community life," each of which he says "spells the end of authentic civic life."[67]

What stands out among Putnam's findings is the significant generational divide between who participates and who does not. The middle-aged and elderly participate much more than the young. It is with the baby boomers, the first generation to be exposed to television in a significant way, where the precipitous decline in participation begins. All forms of civic engagement continue to plummet with each successive generation.

Putnam writes: "The more exposed a generation was to television in their formative years, the lower was its civic engagement during adulthood." Television "news and entertainment changed virtually all features of American life." The more time people spent on their family-room couch, the less they spent with neighbors, friends, and relatives, and the less they spent on key aspects of citizenship, such as volunteering or becoming politically engaged. In his research, Putnam consequently saw that "dependence on television for entertainment is not merely a significant predictor of civic disengagement, it is the single most consistent predictor."[68] Putnam also notes that each successive generation is also more materialist than its predecessors.

Juliet Schor's research draws a clear connection between television watching and the "new consumerism," which she defines as an upscaling of lifestyle norms, the pervasiveness of conspicuous status goods and of competition for acquiring them, and the disconnect between consumer desires and income. When incomes cannot sustain these lifestyles, individuals and households rack up formidable sums of debt, which, according to the Federal Reserve, stood at $13.3 trillion for the United States as a whole in 2014. In 2011, 56 percent of consumers carried an unpaid balance on a credit card, with an average credit card debt per household of $15,799.[69] Schor's research also confirms Putnam's finding that as people spend less time with neighbors and friends and more time on the couch, television becomes more important as a source of information, not just about consumer goods but also about community and politics.

John Taylor Gatto, in his book *Dumbing Us Down,* contends that if schools are an important training ground for democracy, then the fact that the United States "ranks at the bottom of nineteen industrial nations in reading, writing and arithmetic"[70] does not bode well for the health, well-being, and future of the American republic. US public schooling, Gatto fears, produces, as philosopher Bertrand Russell remarked in the mid-1940s, somewhat imperiously, "a recognizably American student: anti-intellectual, superstitious, lacking self-confidence, having less of 'inner freedom' than his or her counterpart in any other nation . . . with a thin mass character, holding excellence and aesthetics equally in contempt."[71]

Henry Giroux, in his book *Stealing Innocence,* argues that much of this can be attributed to the fact that it is proponents of a market ideology who have shaped the content and culture of public education in the United States, where public education is not viewed in terms of its civic function but "rather primarily as a training ground for educating students to define themselves as consumers rather than multifaceted social actors. Such curricula have little to do with critical learning and a great deal with producing debased narratives of citizenship, suggesting to students that the only roles open to them are defined through the ethos of consumerism."[72]

This "new consumerism" is also profoundly alienating. Consumerism diminishes people's sense of belonging to their communities; virtual ties become more important. Depression and suicide rates skyrocket. Putnam remarks on how "it is hard to believe that the generational decline in social connectedness and the concomitant generational increase in suicide, depression, and malaise are unrelated."[73]

The creation of a media-generated consumer culture causes growing alienation, depression, apathy, and social malaise, leading to a growing disconnect between individuals and their "real" social realities. When television, instead of newspapers, civic associations, labor unions, or advocacy groups, becomes the principal source of information, viewers have no power to contest what they are being told.

A public that is less knowledgeable about history and politics is that much more vulnerable to believing fundamentally false information that bolsters the hands of the power elite. Holed up in front of television, computer screens, and other ubiquitous electronic devices, many Americans today are more connected in the virtual sphere than they are in the real spheres of civic engagement and collective consciousness. But connection is imperative if real social change, toward alternative futures that are just and egalitarian, is to happen.

The battle to win the hearts and minds of Americans now has so far been dominated by individuals who have a real stake in keeping things the way they are. They are the ones who have rejected the European way as being fundamentally un-American and based on ideas associated with **socialism** inimical to the neoliberal political and social philosophies that undergird the present form of monopoly capitalism and its corresponding corporatism in the United States.

They also argue that the European welfare state is based on a system of exorbitant taxation that can never be allowed in the United States. The American public has been conditioned to believe that nothing is more detrimental to their interest than taxes. To convince the public to relinquish its rightful claim to a social compact that ensures a better life just so the wealthiest can keep their tax money and spend it as they wish requires a sophisticated form of propaganda, which US corporate capitalism has honed almost to perfection.

But none of this discourages Nobel Prize–winning economist Joseph Stiglitz, who is certain that the legacy of the economic crisis and its fallout in the worsening economic prospects of many Americans will lead to a "battle over ideas—over what kind of economic system is likely to deliver the greatest benefit to the most people. . . . [A]mong the big losers will be the support for American style capitalism."[74] If the hegemony of the dominant ideology is based on falsehoods, misperceptions, and mythologies, a counter-hegemony will have to be birthed and grown to counter it—both in the realm of political and economic ideologies and also in the structures, institutions, and norms that those ideologies inspire.

Let us now turn to imagining how such a counter-hegemony might materialize and fulfill the commitment that Joe Feagin entrusts to his fellow sociologists: to lay the path for realizing alternative futures of just and egalitarian societies.

Old Ideas, New Directions

No other country has the storehouse of materials and resources to build an alternative future of a just and egalitarian society as does the United States. Right from its very inception, the United States has always held that promise—the same promise that draws people from the rest of the world to its shores. Since the 1970s, however, the promise of America, which was always elusive for blacks, Native Americans, and the poor of all colors, has become a pipe dream for the proverbial 99 percent. The economic downturn has pulled the rug out from under the communities of the middle class as well as the poor.

It is within this context, and in view of the discussion throughout this book, that I offer the following suggestions. The present economic slump and the widening economic inequality that has accompanied it are the results of structural changes in the economy, deindustrialization, globalization, mechanization, financialization, and stagnant wages and salaries—all of which have happened with the blessings of the elected representatives of the people.

The changes have not occurred without purpose, though. As we have seen, the reification of political and economic entities hides the real players from public scrutiny. The changes that have wrecked people's lives and communities have been the result of deliberate changes in economic policy, which corporate leaders demand and the elected representatives of the people willingly and obligingly deliver. The only option left to bring about change, short of a revolution, is to enliven the electoral system and give democracy itself a second chance by embracing to the fullest the rights guaranteed to the people of the United States by the institutions that form the bulwark of the republic.

The Declaration of Independence

No other document summarizes the concept of the social compact between a people and their government as does the Declaration of Independence. It is worthwhile to revisit its profound message. It is the enduring sentiment of this message that I wish to highlight, not the contradictions that can be found in the overall political thought of its author and others who endorsed it at the historical moment it was written.

> We hold these truths to be self-evident, that all men are created equal, that they are endowed by their Creator with certain unalienable Rights, that among these are Life, Liberty and the pursuit of Happiness.—That to secure these rights, Governments are instituted among Men, deriving their just powers from the consent of the governed,—That whenever any Form of Government becomes destructive of these ends, it is the Right of the People to alter or to abolish it, and to institute new Government, laying its foundation on such principles and organizing its powers in such form, as to them shall seem most likely to effect their Safety and Happiness. Prudence, indeed, will dictate that Governments long established should not be changed for light and transient causes; and accordingly all experience hath shewn, that mankind are more disposed to suffer, while evils are sufferable, than to right themselves by abolishing the forms to which they are accustomed. But when a long train of abuses and usurpations, pursuing invariably the same Object evinces a design to reduce them under absolute Despotism, it is their right, it is their duty, to throw off such Government, and to provide new Guards for their future security.

The essence of the profound and enduring message of the Declaration of Independence is this:

- All people are created equal.
- All people are endowed with certain unalienable rights—to life, liberty, and the pursuit of happiness.
- Governments are instituted to secure these rights.
- Government derives its just powers from the consent of the governed.
- People are not inclined to abolish what they have become accustomed to. They will tend to wait, and to suffer, as long as they can.
- But when government fails to fulfill its commitment, it is the right and duty of the people to alter it, or abolish it and institute a new government that will better ensure their safety and happiness.

　　The social contract between the government and its people is a two-way street. The people agree to follow the rules and regulations that government institutes if the government does its part to take care of them. In turn, it is the right and the duty of the people to stay vigilant. But all the evidence seems to indicate that the American people have been asleep at the wheel as corporate elites and their henchmen in government have taken the country for a ride.

　　The unprecedented inequality that we see in the United States today did not happen overnight; it took decades of deliberate intervention from the government to stack the rules of the economy in a way that facilitated this transfer of wealth. The Declaration of Independence urges the people to take back the reins of the country when necessary, and to change the rules of the game so everyone benefits—a framework that President Roosevelt unambiguously delineated in his Second Bill of Rights.

FDR's Bill of Economic Rights

Even as World War II waged on, President Franklin Delano Roosevelt began to delineate the vision he held for the nation to which surviving veterans would be returning at its end, still a year and a half away, with the surrender of Germany in May 1945 and then Japan in August 1945. While delivering his State of the Union address on January 11, 1944, President Roosevelt observed that the political rights guaranteed by the US Constitution and the Bill of Rights had proved to be inadequate "to assure us equality in the pursuit of happiness."

　　As the economy changed and people became subject to the uncertainties of an industrial capitalist system, it was time to establish a Second Bill of Rights—a bill of economic rights—that would protect citizens and enable them to secure livelihoods, which would in turn allow them to realize their political rights completely. In this, he was inspired by the wisdom of Thomas Paine, who believed that an individual cannot be free to pursue political rights in the absence of economic security and independence.

　　Here is the text of that State of the Union address in which President Roosevelt introduced his philosophy behind the bill of economic rights and what he believed it should encompass:

> We have come to a clear realization of the fact that true individual freedom cannot exist without economic security and independence. "Necessitous men are not free men." People who are hungry and out of a job are the stuff of which dictatorships are made. In our day these economic truths have become accepted as self-evident. We have accepted, so to speak, a second Bill of Rights under which a new basis of security and prosperity can be established for all—regardless of station, race, or creed. Among these are:
>
> • The right to a useful and remunerative job in the industries or shops or farms or mines of the nation.

- The right to earn enough to provide adequate food and clothing and recreation.
- The right of every farmer to raise and sell his products at a return which will give him and his family a decent living.
- The right of every businessman, large and small, to trade in an atmosphere of freedom from unfair competition and domination by monopolies at home or abroad.
- The right of every family to a decent home.
- The right to adequate medical care and the opportunity to achieve and enjoy good health.
- The right to adequate protection from the economic fears of old age, sickness, accident, and unemployment.
- The right to a good education.

All of these rights spell security. And after this war is won we must be prepared to move forward, in the implementation of these rights, to new goals of human happiness and well-being.

Americas' own rightful place in the world depends in large part upon how fully these and similar rights have been carried into practice for all our citizens.

For unless there is security here at home there cannot be lasting peace in the world.

Using FDR's bill of economic rights as the blueprint, an agenda for a comprehensive system of social welfare/workfare can be tailored to include the following:

- All workers have the right to earn their living in a job freely entered.
- All workers have the right to a living wage and salary that enables them and their family to have a decent standard of living.
- All workers have the right to reasonable daily and weekly working hours.
- All workers have the right to paid vacations, sick leave, and family leave.
- All workers have the right to unionize and bargain collectively (as guaranteed by the National Labor Relations Act of 1935).
- All businesses, large and small, have the right to conduct business in an atmosphere free of monopolies and unfair competition.
- Every family has the right to receive financial assistance in times of economic insecurity to meet its basic needs.
- Every family has the right to decent and affordable housing.
- Every individual has the right to quality and affordable medical care.
- Every individual has the right to be protected from the economic insecurities of old age, sickness, injury, and unemployment.
- Every family has the right to free or subsidized child care and elder care.

- Every child has the right to a free primary and secondary public education.
- Every individual has the right to affordable higher education or vocational training.
- Every individual has the right to live in an environment free of pollutants.

The European Social Charter, the treaty undergirding the social welfare programs of the twenty-four European countries that have signed it since its adoption in 1961, was inspired by the framework and provisions of FDR's bill of economic rights. The overarching and comprehensive terms of the FDR bill gave the Europeans a model to emulate. Only in its country of origin was this bill committed to the waste bin of history.

It has made occasional appearances, such as in Martin Luther King Jr. and the Southern Christian Leadership Conference's Poor People's Movement; in filmmaker Michael Moore's rediscovery of the video of FDR's Second Bill of Rights speech and its inclusion in his movie *Capitalism: A Love Story;* and in the websites of advocacy and activist groups, whose messages of change never make it to the mainstream media. But any social movement that aspires to change the prevailing systems of economic and political inequality has a model to follow in FDR's bill of economic rights.

Building a Just and Equal Future

Jacob Hacker and Nate Loewentheil's 2012 policy manual, "Prosperity Economics: Building an Economy for All," is a good place to start if an alternative future is to be constructed. It offers a comprehensive agenda by focusing on what the authors refer to as the three pillars on which economic reform and prosperity can be built.

They begin by addressing the most persistent attribute of the present economic inequality and insecurity: unemployment. With 23 million people unemployed or underemployed in the United States, including those who have dropped out of the job market entirely, a chronic state of joblessness has led to "growing insecurity and inequality; stagnant wages and contracting social mobility."[75] This, they assert, has been engendered by a policy in Washington whose "answer is to get government out of the way, [give] businesses free rein and let the market work out everything on its own."[76]

The "austerity economics" that has come in the wake of this policy has resulted in tax cuts for the wealthy, budget cuts in government programs that benefit everyone, slashing of rules that protect the work force and protect the environment, and budget cuts to the primary sources of economic security—Medicare, Medicaid, and Social Security.

The assumptions on which "austerity economics" is based are fundamentally wrong. Economic prosperity cannot flow downward in the present system of winners and losers. Real prosperity is generated by everyone participating in the economy—workers as well as employers, small entrepreneurs as well as corporate giants, and unions as well as visionary managers.

Drawing from the lessons of history, and building on current theories and research in economics, Hacker and Loewentheil offer an approach that they call "prosperity economics," with three pillars to undergird it: (1) growth to jump-start the economy and ensure that it is able to provide people with good jobs and rising wages for decades to come; (2) security for workers, their families, public finances, and the environment; and (3) a democracy that works and is based on accountability instead of being held hostage by money or political procedures that allow the wealthiest and most partisan to dictate policies.

Hacker and Loewentheil's policy manual is an imposing document whose provisions cannot be fully discussed here. Hacker, who coauthored with Paul Pierson the book *Winner Take-All Politics,* has a keen eye. He is familiar with the intricacies of how the US political economy works, how democracy has become weighed down by the power of big money, and how, in the present state of overwhelming monopoly control, a vibrant, innovative capitalism and dynamic market competition are becoming increasingly beleaguered and are losing their ability to provide every member of society what he or she absolutely needs. The policies he and Loewentheil offer focus on the following criteria:

• *Reining in the power of big money and facilitating redistribution of its profits*. End the George W. Bush tax cuts for high earners, create new tax brackets for the highest earners, treat capital and labor income equally, eliminate preferential treatment of capital gains and dividends, reduce incentives for tax avoidance and off-shoring, reduce defense spending, weed out tax subsidies for established businesses (such as oil, gas, and agribusinesses), check corporate executive pay, and reverse the Citizens United decision, which made it possible for corporations and the highest earners to give unprecedented amounts of money for election campaigns.

• *Supporting workers and their families*. Achieve full employment, drive manufacturing growth, foster innovations in education, invest in infrastructure and building communities, expand support for housing, raise the minimum wage, expand job-training programs, create pathways out of low-wage work, maintain expansions of the earned income tax credit, adopt legislation guaranteeing a fair process for workers to choose union representation and have the power to bargain collectively, implement stronger penalties for violations of labor laws, develop a more comprehensive legal regime to support collective bargaining, mandate paid family and sick leave, and expand opportunities for affordable child care.

• *Promoting inclusivity.* Create a path to citizenship for undocumented immigrants, manage future immigration flows based on principles of family reunification and economic demand, and hold employers responsible for labor and immigration law.

• *Securing health, retirement, and support for the unemployed.* Secure health care by adding a public option to the Affordable Care Act, strengthening Medicare, and increasing federal financing of Medicaid; secure retirement by replacing the 401(k) system with a simple, universal, and mandatory public-private plan (with responsibility being shared by employers and the workers in which both are required to set aside a certain sum for an account distinct from Social Security that will be available upon retirement); and secure support for the unemployed by strengthening unemployment insurance and continuing federal unemployment benefits.

• *Securing the environment.* Put a price on carbon and other greenhouse gases; shift transportation, housing, and development patterns; and drive energy innovation and efficiency by augmenting investments in clean energy.

• *Securing democracy.* Eliminate disenfranchisement efforts and create a national voting holiday, which "would help create time and space for citizens to think seriously about their votes and boost voter turnout, creating a more engaged citizen body and holding elected officials more accountable for their performances."[77]

The blueprint is here. Elected leaders who are looking for a plan have one at the ready. It was even published before the November 2012 presidential election. We have yet to see, though, if it has made any inroads into the consciousness of our leaders in a way that informs the positions and policies they introduce. But if history is any judge, even a well-meaning manifesto as visionary as this will not go very far unless the next needed thing happens.

How Will Change Come?

No change can happen until a critical majority of Americans recognize that it is in their interest for the United States to move in a new direction. For large segments of the American public, life has become difficult and arduous in unprecedented ways due to the policies of the past three decades, since the 1980s. Economic security, hope, and dignity must be restored to all communities, to peoples of all colors and creeds.

The critical majority will have to encompass every segment of society and every region in the country if it is to succeed. Grassroots advocacy groups in every state, every city, and every region will have to be mobilized to reach out, educate, and organize. Unions, immigrant rights groups,

LGBT groups, Occupy groups, people with leftist and progressive political persuasions, the academic community—all must form a coalition to plan the next steps if the economic rights sketched out by President Roosevelt are to be upheld at every level of government.

People power must subvert the power of money. As the union movement has demonstrated, there is real strength in numbers. Elected officials must become accountable to their constituencies and not to big money. If needed, a third political party to represent the interests of working Americans, rather than corporate interests, will need to be established. All this is easier said than done. But what alternative is there other than working to establish a system that has the potential to speak for all people?

Recognizing the urgent need for change and the historical role that unions have played in instigating change, AFL-CIO president Richard Trumka sent out a rallying call in September 2013 to "all of our progressive partners," urging "that none of us can do it alone. If we're going to change the political and economic environment, it's going to take us all working together."[78]

He therefore invited into the ranks of the unions millions of nonunion workers, even if their own workplaces were not organized. He welcomed advocacy groups who had worked to protect the environment or worked for immigrant rights, civil rights, women's rights, gay and lesbian rights—even faith-based organizations—to become either formal partners or affiliates of the AFL-CIO.

The unions have also set up committees of academics, college students, youth workers, Web experts, and pollsters to propose ways to reinvent labor. The Service Employees Industrial Union has organized strikes of fast food workers to create a nationwide movement to raise the minimum wage. The unions are also looking to organize adjunct professors at colleges and universities, who are often paid exploitatively low salaries and consequently must work at multiple colleges just to make a living, but accruing no benefits.

Through all these efforts, unions are trying to fortify their collective strength as a political counterweight to the corporations and conservative billionaires, and their minions in government. Building such a broad coalition is imperative to advancing a worker-friendly political and economic agenda that raises the minimum wage, advocates for a living wage, increases taxes on the wealthiest Americans, fortifies the social safety net, protects undocumented workers, protects jobs for all workers, protects the rights of workers to unionize, cleans up safety hazards at workplaces, and bridges the widening chasm between the top 1 percent and the bottom 99 percent.

Any movement for change has to begin locally and then build up to encompass the entire country. Like-minded individuals and groups will have to bring to the table political and organizing experiences, and a vision for a fair and just United States that will go beyond particular political campaigns and specific issues. Veteran labor organizers, such as SEIU's Neal Gorfinkle, have faith that grassroots mobilization can transform even local election campaigns into movements for change.

The electoral system must be put to the test. People need to vote, attend town hall meetings, and talk to each other and those running for office. If the leaders know their constituents, they will be less likely to betray them. The constituents should occupy the lobbies of Congress and not relinquish that space to only the corporations and their lobbyists. People need to become educated about the issues and vote from positions of real awareness. Reciprocity, dialogue, awareness, mindfulness, and fairness are important elements if the electoral system is to fulfill its true potential of ensuring the well-being of everyone. The movement cannot be about just sitting around and having polite, impassioned, and righteous discussions. There is a need for collective action, such as rallies, demonstrations, strikes, and civil disobedience, if the people are to be heard.

On Saturday, August 24, 2013, as 250,000 people from every walk of life gathered in Washington, D.C., to celebrate the fiftieth anniversary of the March on Washington—the day made iconic with Martin Luther King Jr.'s "I Have a Dream" speech—the signs of such a movement seemed in place. People were demanding an "economy for all," jobs that pay living wages, racial justice and protection of voting rights, the building of schools rather than prisons, immigration reform, the right of people to love whomever they choose, protection of the environment, and an end to all wars.

The march gave evidence of the broad coalitions of people who are impatient for change and willing to reach across the aisle and join hands with anyone dedicated to move the country down a different path to realize alternative futures of just and egalitarian societies. Change will not happen any other way.

We must take to heart the warning by Frederick Douglass that "power concedes nothing without a demand. It never did and it never will." Martin Luther King Jr. showed the country the power of nonviolent civil disobedience. It is time to hone those skills again and revive the country's remarkable history of public dissent. And in this democracy of ours, it is possible to make change peacefully when citizens become politically aware, shake off their apathy, and seriously hold their elected officials accountable to do the right thing. If people across the country get organized, real change can happen. And that would indeed be revolutionary.

Barbara Ehrenreich writes with assurance in her book *Nickel and Dimed* that, when this day does come, "the sky will not fall, and we will all be better off for it in the end."[79]

Notes

1. Feagin, "Social Justice and Sociology," p. 1.
2. For example, for the period 2005–2009, Atlanta had a Gini index of 0.571, New Orleans 0.546, Washington, D.C. 0.540, and Miami 0.540. See Weinberg, "U.S. Neighborhood Income Inequality."
3. Bernstein, "Once Again, U.S. Has Most Expensive, Least Effective Health Care System in Survey."
4. DeNavas-Walt, Proctor, and Smith, "Income, Poverty, and Health Insurance Coverage in the United States: 2011," p. 5; see also Meyerson, "If Labor Dies, What's Next?" p. 22.
5. Domhoff, "Wealth, Income, and Power."
6. Parenti, *Land of Idols,* p. 73.
7. An allusion to the famous words of Massachusetts senator Charles Sumner.
8. Hill, *Europe's Promise,* p. 2.
9. Quoted in Shorto, "How I Learned to Love the European Welfare State," p. 45.
10. Hill, *Europe's Promise,* p. 11.
11. Ibid., p. 21.
12. Ibid.
13. Alesina and Glaeser, *Fighting Poverty in the US and Europe.*
14. Hill, *Europe's Promise,* pp. 20–21.
15. Ibid., p. 21.
16. Hung and Kucinskas, "Globalization and Global Inequality."
17. Ibid., pp. 75–92.
18. Ibid.
19. Ibid.
20. Shorto, "How I Learned to Love the European Welfare State," p. 44.
21. Hill, *Europe's Promise,* pp. 75–90.
22. Shorto, "How I Learned to Love the European Welfare State," p. 44 (emphasis in original).
23. Ibid., p. 46.
24. National Center for Education Statistics, "Tuition Facts of Colleges and Universities"; College Board Advocacy and Policy Center, "Trends in College Pricing."
25. Bernstein, "The Hidden Costs of Higher Education," p. A19.
26. Rampell, "It Takes a B.A. to Find a Job As a File Clerk," p. A1.
27. Hill, *Europe's Promise,* p. 90.
28. Ibid., pp. 93–94.
29. Ibid., p. 23.
30. Oorschot, "Solidarity Towards Immigrants in European Welfare States," p. 4.
31. Alesina and Glaeser, *Fighting Poverty in the US and Europe,* p. 181.
32. Shorto, "How I Learned to Love the European Welfare State," p. 44.
33. Mohanty, "On Being South Asian in North America," p. 270.
34. Oorschot, "Solidarity Towards Immigrants in European Welfare States," pp. 3–14.
35. Gooby, "Is the Future American?" p. 671.
36. Oorschot, "Solidarity Towards Immigrants in European Welfare States," p. 7.
37. Hill, *Europe's Promise,* p. 20.

38. Ibid., p. 75.
39. Starr, "The Mirage of Reform," p. 409.
40. Ibid.
41. Hill, *Europe's Promise,* p. 53.
42. Ibid., p. 54.
43. Ibid., p. 57.
44. Ibid., p. 59.
45. Ibid., p. 64.
46. Krugman, "Sympathy for the Luddites," p. A27.
47. Kollmeyer, "Explaining Consensual Domination," p. 1.
48. Ibid., p. 6.
49. Ibid.
50. Ibid.
51. Hill, *Europe's Promise,* pp. 64–65.
52. Quoted in Erich Fromm, *Marx's Concept of Man,* p. 212.
53. Ibid., p. 197.
54. Johnson, "A Summer Place in the South Bronx," p. C19.
55. Ibid.
56. Chaddock "Robert Byrd."
57. Herman and Chomsky, *Manufacturing Consent,* pp. xi, 1.
58. Ibid., p. 2.
59. Ibid., p. 3.
60. Ibid., pp. 14–18.
61. Ibid., pp. 18–19.
62. Ibid., p. 22.
63. Kull et al., "Misperceptions, the Media, and the Iraq War."
64. Ibid.
65. Ibid.
66. Putnam, *Bowling Alone,* p. 184.
67. Ibid., p. 210.
68. Ibid., p. 231.
69. Schor, *The Overspent American,* pp. 3–12.
70. Gatto, *Dumbing Us Down,* p. 20.
71. Quoted in ibid., p. 70.
72. Giroux, *Stealing Innocence,* pp. 95–96.
73. Putnam, *Bowling Alone,* p. 265.
74. Quoted in Hill, *Europe's Promise,* p. ix.
75. Hacker and Loewentheil, "Prosperity Economics," p. 1.
76. Ibid.
77. Ibid., p. 55.
78. Quoted in Greenhouse, "The Ecumenical Union," p. B1.
79. Ehrenreich, *Nickel and Dimed,* p. 221.

Glossary

Absolute poverty and **relative poverty** refer to the two dimensions sociologists often associate with poverty. Absolute poverty is absolute deprivation, which is when people don't have what they absolutely need to survive. Relative poverty occurs when people do not have what is customary in the society where they live—that is, when they don't have what they are culturally expected to have. Thus, a person is therefore in poverty relative to those who are not. If owning a car is customary and someone doesn't have one, then that person is relatively poor compared to those who own cars.

Accumulation by dispossession is David Harvey's concept to describe the process in which capital is accumulated not through real economic growth, in which real, tangible wealth is created, but through dispossession, in which public goods (e.g., public schools) are taken away and repossessed by private, corporate entities (e.g., charter schools), thus expanding their purses. In this case no new wealth is generated but is redistributed from public to private hands.

Accumulation of capital is the primary force that propels a capitalist economic system. The entire endeavor of capitalism is fueled by its infinite desire to accumulate more and more capital, in turn to generate more and more capital. Capital that is continuously invested and reinvested, and generates more and more profit, leads to increasing levels of capital accumulation, which is the fundamental motive of the system.

Affirmative action policies are **race- and gender-based preferential policies** that encourage employers and institutions of higher learning to take deliberate steps to recruit women and people of color. Affirmative action policies are meant to be temporary arrangements, to be phased out when structural changes correct the inequalities in education and in the economy. But in the absence of those changes, affirmative action has become a permanent fixture, often leading to animosity and conflict. There has been an overestimation of benefits that has often led to bitter resentment. Many legal challenges have occurred from a sense among whites of having been wronged when they have been unable to secure places at universities and medical schools, which they felt had undeservedly gone to less-qualified candidates solely because of their minority status.

Alienation is a concept usually attributed to the writings of the young Karl Marx. It falls under the general idea that capitalism engenders not just material but spiritual oppression as well. Alienation refers to the separation that humans feel from their "species being," that is, the humanity integral to their own self and that which they share with the rest of the human species. This alienation is experienced in people's work and work lives when work becomes a means to an end instead of being an end in itself, as it was meant to be. Marx argued that it is in work/labor that humans objectify their inherent creativity. Work humanizes when it connects naturally to the objects it creates and the people with whom it creates connections. But this natural relationship is distorted under capitalism when work simply becomes a way to make a living and people have to compete to get it. These are the circumstances in which work becomes oppressive and alienating.

Anomie is the term Emile Durkheim used to identify a state of normlessness. This occurs when individuals seem to have lost their bearings in society along with a sense of belonging and solidarity with others. Durkheim theorized that this would happen when societies experience rapid change. Today, this sense of alienation is exacerbated as the structures that once held individuals and communities together rapidly fall apart.

Bacon's Rebellion refers to the rebellion in 1675–1676 that was instigated when Nathaniel Bacon organized a militia by arming both white indentured servants and black slaves. He initially targeted the Native Americans in Virginia. But when the governor of Virginia, William Berkeley, declared Bacon a rebel and charged him with treason, Bacon stormed into Jamestown and burned the city to the ground. Bacon and the rebels were soon defeated, but not before demonstrating the power of class that can be realized when the white poor and the black poor join forces. Bacon's Rebellion demonstrated to the colonial aristocracy the power of racial separation to thwart class solidarity.

Biased pluralism is a variation of the pluralist tradition arguing that interest-group conflict and the policies that are generated by this conflict represent the wishes of corporations, businesses, and professional associations as opposed to representing the needs of the public.

Birth lottery is the idea that no one has any control over where they are born. Yet the capriciousness of birth determines so much of people's lives as well as their "life chances" to overcome that fate.

Bourgeoisie is a French term originally signifying "middle class." It was applied by Karl Marx and Frederick Engels to signify those who own the means of production. The bourgeoisie is therefore the capitalist class, the "haves" who own capital.

Capital is money that is continuously invested and reinvested, whether in corporations or in speculative ventures, to make a profit. Money that continuously circulates in trying to augment its worth is capital in its truest form.

Capitalism is an economic system in which the means of production are privately owned and the primary objective of economic activity is the maximization and private appropriation of profit.

Carcerality is the notion that capitalist societies are increasingly using carcels—prisons and immigration detention centers—to manage the deepening tensions, insecurities, and contradictions that are characteristic of contemporary capitalism.

Causal relationship is one in which changes in one variable cause changes in another variable. For example, outsourcing of jobs causes unemployment.

Class warfare is the fundamental conflict between the capitalist class, or the bourgeoisie, and the working class, or the proletariat. It is the conflict between cap-

ital and labor, which Karl Marx considered as being the defining and fundamental characteristic of all class societies, shaping all other conflicts.

Classlessness is the absence of an unfair economic divide among classes in a society. A society can be considered classless when it is equitable—that is, fair and
just in the distribution of society's resources—so that each individual receives
what is necessary to live and flourish.

Collective social movement is organized political action aiming to alter how power
is distributed in society. Such a movement occurs when political leaders, and
the institutions and structures they represent, are seen as being unjust and
therefore lose legitimacy in the eyes of large segments of society. Collective
social movements can be nonviolent or violent, short-lived or prolonged. They
occur when conventional ways of political participation are not available or are
seen as inadequate to realize the objectives of the movement.

Commodity is anything—goods or services—that can be bought and sold for a profit.

Commons are the common wealth of societies and communities. They are the common inheritance of such life-giving things as water, air, land, natural resources,
and the environment at large. The commons also include the institutions and
social structures on which each person's welfare depends, such as schools, public transportation, public safety, health care, child care, senior care, green
spaces, and roads, bridges, and tunnels. Cultural resources that enrich people's
lives aesthetically also make up the commons, such as music, dance, story-
telling, art, and museums. Integral to the concept of the commons is that such
resources should not be regarded as commodities.

Communism, according to Karl Marx and Frederick Engels, is the ultimate stage in
the evolution of human societies—when class struggle ends, and along with it
all conflicts between the exploiters and the exploited, between the rulers and
the oppressed. All of a society's wealth—the means of production and the
goods and services that production creates—are commonly held and commonly
managed. As class conflict ends, the state becomes superfluous and withers
away. As the need for weapons ends, all of a society's wealth becomes devoted
solely to enhancing the well-being of its people.

Conflict and consensus inform two of the most important theoretical perspectives in
sociology. The conflict position argues that conflict is ubiquitous—it is present
in every realm of society. It is in the constant back and forth between conflicting positions and conflicting groups that social life is experienced.

Consensus position argues that it is possible to construct society through consensus.
According to this position, culture is the glue that holds society together, and
people follow the dictates of culture because it enables them to adapt, survive,
and evolve.

Conservatism emphasizes stability and order in society. Conservatives believe in
the sanctity of private property and the primacy of the marketplace. They stress
the importance of tradition, religion, strict moral codes, and rule of law for
controlling people's behavior. They believe that individuals shape their own
fortunes and misfortunes, irrespective of social forces. And although conservatives advocate for small government in some areas of society, they strongly
support government intervention to protect markets, protect private property,
and ensure free competition and free enterprise.

Conspicuous consumption and **conspicuous leisure** are concepts developed by
Thorstein Veblen to illustrate the ostentatiously wasteful ways of society. People buy and display things they don't really need, and waste time unproduc-
tively in pursuit of leisure.

Core and periphery are concepts attributed to American sociologist Immanuel Wallerstein. In his theory on modern world systems, which he sees as dominated by the capitalist economic system, Wallerstein designates the core as being the areas of the world economy that are the principal owners of capital, and the periphery as the areas that are exploited by the core for natural resources and cheap labor.

Corporate capitalism is capitalism dominated by corporations, as opposed to the system envisioned by Adam Smith, wherein the capitalist marketplace comprises numerous "sellers." The dominance of corporations is felt not only in economic affairs, but also in the political sphere, where their financial power is seen as influencing government decisions for their own advantage, and often bypassing the democratic process.

Correlational relationship between two variables implies that change in one coincides with a change in the other. But correlation does not necessarily mean that the change in the first variable has caused the change in the other. For example, it has been reported that during the Super Bowl the number of domestic violence cases goes up. This is a correlation and does not imply that one causes the other. It can generate interesting discussions on how the portrayal of male roles and masculinity somehow encourages violent behaviors, but does not show a direct correlation between football and domestic abuse, per se.

Counter-hegemony offers an alternative vision of society in which first the hearts and minds of the people must be won over before they will support social change. A counter-hegemony arises to counter, oppose, and eventually dismantle the dominant ideology that rules in both direct and subtle ways. The most pernicious aspect of a hegemony is that it is able to sway the public through systematic nurturing of a "false consciousness" or a distorted logic of why the system functions as it does, and in so doing wins the consent of the people. A successful hegemonic thinking makes people partners in their own oppression. A counter-hegemony's biggest challenge is to work toward freeing people's minds of this false consciousness.

Culture of poverty was a concept created by anthropologist Oscar Lewis. He proposed that poverty, which is initially imposed by the structural forces in society, engenders a set of behaviors and attitudes that impede efforts to overcome poverty. In his studies of poverty and the poor, he isolated at least seventy traits that become characteristic of a way of life that is handed down from one generation to the other. He considered this way of life the "culture of poverty." Traits such as fatalism, helplessness, dependency, inferiority, and powerlessness defeat all efforts to overcome poverty. He found that the culture of poverty was an endemic feature of capitalist and colonial societies. The culture of poverty does not exist among the poor in preliterate/primitive societies, in lower castes in India, Jews in Eastern Europe, and socialist societies, such as Cuba.

Debt crisis refers to the crisis that has been created as debt repayments have become due, primarily for third world countries, at a time when their economies are flagging and public revenue has dwindled. These debts were incurred when the countries borrowed money for their development projects, which seldom came to fruition. Consequently, many of these countries have put in place structural adjustment policies—slashing government budgets in education, health, public utilities, and the like—which disproportionately harm the poor.

Deindustrialization is the structural change that occurs in an economy when the primary areas of economic activity—in employment and production—no longer take place in manufacturing but rather in the service sector, whether in low-skilled, low-paid sectors such as fast food or in high-paid sectors such as financial services.

Descriptive category is one that gives each human being their unique identity—such as race, phenotype (facial configuration), gender, sexual orientation, nationality, or language. These are the characteristics that make for the diversity of the human family, but that take on more than just a descriptive character due to the meanings attributed to them.

Dialectical is the philosophical notion that everything carries within itself its own contradiction. Therefore, a thesis has its antithesis, the resolution of which generates a new thesis, which in turn has its own anti-thesis, and so on. Karl Marx applied this notion to argue that capitalism too carries within itself its own contradiction, which manifests in class conflict, which in turn must ultimately lead to the destruction of capitalism.

Dominant ideology is most often the ideology of the dominant group in society. According to Karl Marx, the ideas of the ruling class form the basis of the dominant ideology in every society.

Don't Ask, Don't Tell is a policy that banned openly gay men, lesbians, and bisexuals from serving in the US military. It was in effect for seventeen years, from its inception in 1994 under President Bill Clinton until President Barack Obama repealed it in 2011. Don't ask, don't tell was a policy that allowed the military to avoid the accusation of being discriminatory toward homosexual men and women by denying them the right to serve outrightly. Instead, it encouraged a practice in which gay military men and women would be allowed to serve as long as they kept their sexuality hidden and did not disclose their homosexuality. It enforced a mandatory and oppressive invisibility on homosexual servicemen and women and bisexuals.

Durable inequality is sociologist Charles Tilly's concept to describe the phenomenon of enduring inequality in society. He identifies four processes that promote the longevity of inequality: exploitation, opportunity hoarding, emulation, and adaptation.

Economic base and **superstructure** refer to the mode of production and the entire array of political, cultural, legal, and all other social attributes that the mode of production creates. It is the idea that the character of a society depends on its economic system.

Economic elite domination is a theoretical tradition in the study of US politics arguing that US policymaking is dominated by individuals who have sizable economic resources, such as income and wealth, and who may also be owners of businesses and corporations.

Economies of scale are the cost advantages that occur when a product or service is produced on a large scale. The larger the scale in which a product or service is produced, the smaller its per-unit cost of production.

Economism is the tendency, especially in the trade union movement, to reduce all activism solely toward augmenting the economic aspects of unionization—such as wages and benefits. Those who counter this tendency support the idea that unions must also organize to attain representation in decisionmaking in their places of work and, more broadly, to secure political power on a national scale.

End of history is an idea attributed to German philosopher G. W. F. Hegel and his intellectual progeny Karl Marx. For both Hegel and Marx, social evolution was not open-ended. It came to an end when the level of social evolution that was considered optimal was attained. For Marx, that would have been communism. The present dialogue on the end of history originated in the writings of Francis Fukuyama, who reconceptualized the idea of an end of history to argue that with the defeat of the Soviet Union, it was the system of capitalism that actually attained worldwide victory to become the unparalleled, unquestioned, and universally preferred economic system of choice. He maintained that the fall of the Berlin Wall marked the end of the ideological warfare that dominated the Cold War, and therefore marked the end of intellectual, geopolitical, military squabbling between two ideologies—capitalism and socialism—and the two nations that, more than any others, had embodied the two ideologies, the United States and the Soviet Union.

Externalization is the phenomenon of producers keeping prices of commodities low, in order to lure consumers, by not factoring the real costs of production into prices. The cost is externalized by paying workers very low wages, by not offering benefits such as health care, and by considering natural resources to be free of cost and the environment dispensable.

False consciousness is a false and distorted interpretation of social reality, deliberately created by the dominant ideology in society, such that the oppressed are unable to recognize the real, class-based roots of their oppression.

Fractal inequality refers to the inequality at the top of the income distribution. One of the unique features of inequality in the United States today is the vast and growing gap in income within the top 1 percent. In determining fractal inequality the question we need to ask is what "fraction" of total income that goes to the top 1 percent goes to the top 0.1 percent? What "fraction" of the total income that goes to the top 0.1 percent goes to the top 0.01 percent? This analysis shows that even within the top percentile, there are those whose riches far outpace those of others who also belong to that topmost stratum.

Fetishism of commodities is a concept developed by Karl Marx to signify the central role played by commodities in the capitalist system. The buying and selling of commodities provides the fuel that keeps the capitalist system churning. In order to encourage people to buy more and more, to buy what they don't need, commodities must become more than what they really are. A shoe, or a car, or a handbag must become a "fetish" desired for qualities that are enigmatic and mysterious, beyond its ability to fulfill a need.

First-wave women's movement was a seventy-five-year struggle for women's suffrage. In the United States, it succeeded in 1920 when the Constitution was amended with the Nineteenth Amendment, which gave women the right to vote.

Gender socialization is the process in which individuals learn the roles and expectations that are associated with the gender they belong to. Gender is the cultural edifice that determines masculinities and femininities—the behaviors, statuses, roles, expectations, and responsibilities that are assigned to individuals on the basis of their sex.

Gentrification occurs when established urban communities draw middle-class and affluent individuals at the expense of the usually poor and minority individuals who have always lived there, but who can no longer keep up with rising property values and property taxes. Gentrification displaces the poor and minorities when richer neighbors move in.

Gilded Age refers to the last decade of the nineteenth century and the first decade of the twentieth, a time of great, ostentatious wealth and vast economic inequality. A term attributed to Mark Twain, it has become symbolic of a time of lavish wealth for the few and grinding poverty for the many.

Gini index, also known as the Gini coefficient, is the most common measure of income inequality. It ranks the amount of inequality on a scale of 0 to 1. An index of 0 indicates perfect equality, with everyone having an equal share of the national income and each quintile having a 20 percent share of that income. An index of 1 indicates perfect inequality, with one person having all the income and the rest having none.

Globalization is a process that has transformed the world into a single marketplace in which all buying and selling, all producing and consuming, take place on a global scale. Multinational corporations are the primary agents of globalization. Aided by free trade treaties, which lower barriers to trade between countries, multinational corporations have made national borders superfluous as they continuously expand their operations to incorporate more and more areas of the world in order to accelerate the process of capital accumulation.

Gradational determination of class is a relatively straightforward way of placing individuals into classes—upper class, middle class, and lower class—in terms of how much income and wealth they have. The most important attribute of class in this determination is therefore the variable ownership of income and wealth.

Haves and have-nots is the distinction based on ownership or lack of ownership of society's means of production or capital.

Hegemony is Italian political theorist Antonio Gramsci's concept to describe the power the capitalist ruling class has to control the content of the ideological, cultural, moral, and normative structures of society. This all-encompassing power is seen in the ability of the capitalist class to impose its interpretations on every medium through which cultural messages reach the people—the mass media, political parties, churches, schools and universities, civic and voluntary associations, and even trade unions.

Heterosexism is the attitude that considers the sexual attraction between men and women to be the normal and superior expression of sexuality, and any other orientation to be abnormal and problematic. It assumes a compulsory heterosexuality and is the root of homophobic and discriminatory attitudes toward homosexuals.

Ideology is the compendium of ideas, doctrines, worldviews, beliefs, and mythologies that together represent the aspirations, objectives, and visions of a group and a society.

Immiserization is a concept that as capitalism advances, inequality widens, increasing the polarization between rich and poor, thereby increasing the degree of poverty and its accompanying "misery" for large segments of the population. The concept also captures the existential or lived reality of poverty and economic inequality in human terms. Poverty and economic inequality mean inequality not only in terms of money, but also in the conditions of people's lives, such as unsanitary housing, ill health, hunger, pain, lack of education, and dangerous workplaces.

Income and wealth are two attributes that are used to determine economic equality or inequality. Income is what people are paid on a regular basis for the work they do—wages, salaries, and tips; it is also what they earn from the properties they own—rent, interest, and dividends.

Income-based measure of social mobility gauges differences in income between adult children and their parents—in the same occupations—to determine if the economic situation of children has improved or deteriorated relative to that of their parents. It focuses on a more limited version of social mobility, since the assumption is that children have remained in the same occupations as their parents without moving to entirely different ones—such as the daughter of a housecleaner becoming a lawyer.

Institutional discrimination occurs in two ways: first, when consequences of historical discrimination combine with current structures of economic and institutional exclusion to create stubborn patterns of oppression and disadvantage; and second, when rules that are built into institutions without intent to discriminate, end up discriminating.

Institutionalization occurs when social practices become formalized and established through rules and laws to give them legitimacy. For example, the denial of opportunities for women to pursue their own careers became formalized and established when the US Supreme Court, in *Bradwell v. Illinois* (1873), decided that a woman's rightful and natural place was in the home. Institutionalization also occurs when informal structures become formalized through incorporation in handbooks, constitutions, and charters.

Interactionist theories in sociology are primarily interested in studying patterns of interaction between individuals. Called symbolic interactionism, this theoretical perspective studies how individuals use and interpret symbols in the process of their interaction.

Interest groups are made up of individuals who share similar ideas on issues (guns, abortion, environment, minimum wage, school prayer, etc.) and who attempt to influence public policy to reflect and bolster their preferences. Interest groups are also referred to as pressure groups, lobbies, advocacy groups, and special interests.

Intergenerational social mobility is the movement of individuals up and down the socioeconomic ladder comparative to the position of their parents. Whether an individual becomes richer or poorer than their parents—based on their ability to move from one occupational category to another—illustrates the degree of openness or closedness in a society's social stratification system.

Interlocking directorate refers to the practice of a handful of individuals occupying positions on the boards of multiple corporate entities. It points to the inordinate concentration of power in the hands of a few people who can control decisions that minimize competition among corporations and allow them to coordinate their activites to maximize profit. The corporations act as a unified group, magnifying its power to influence political decisionmaking. Workers, consumers, and members of the general public are affected by these decisions but cannot counter their power.

Invisible hand refers to how the forces of the marketplace—supply and demand—determine every aspect of the economy imperceptibly. Adam Smith put much faith in the invisible hand, which he argued would deliver maximum good to the maximum number, but only under conditions of perfect competition.

Iron cage is the concept coined by German sociologist Max Weber to describe the phenomenon in modern society of rational structures producing irrational consequences such as impersonality, alienation, and inhumanity.

Jim Crow was a style of dance of slaves in the US South and became the moniker for the period of legal discrimination that formally ensued with *Plessy v. Ferguson* in 1896, in which the Supreme Court decided that separate facilities for blacks delivered equal-quality services compared to facilities for whites. It justified racial segregation and made racial discrimination de jure, or legal. In 1954, in *Brown v. Board of Education,* the Supreme Court decided that "separate was not equal" and started the process of dismantling the edifice of racial segregation and legalized racial discrimination. The passage of the Civil Rights

Act of 1964 finally ended the legal practice of racial discrimination, though it has continued in de facto form—as a fact of experience.

Labor theory of value, first proposed by Adam Smith, became a cornerstone in the economics of Karl Marx. Integral to this concept is the position that all value is created by labor. It is labor that gives a commodity or service its final form, the form that enables it to earn value. No matter how many machines and how much raw material a capitalist might accumulate, value cannot be created or earned until labor assembles a commodity or provides a service.

Laissez-faire is the belief that government should not interfere in the marketplace. The economy should be self-directing and free of government intervention, and the best government is one that governs the least.

Liberal political thought today is different from classical liberalism, which in emphasizing the sanctity of private property, the primacy of the market, and the benefits of small government, is indistinguishable from modern-day conservativism and neoliberalism. Liberals today are those who support the expansion and equal distribution of opportunity, and support each individual's right to free expression regardless of color, gender, sexual orientation, and class. They recognize that the government has a responsibility to ensure economic and social progress for all segments of society, and advocate for government intervention in the economy to eliminate poverty, unemployment, and discrimination. They want to reform the capitalist system, not replace it.

Life chances is a term attributed to German sociologist Max Weber. It refers to the chances an individual has to attain a quality of life that the economic and cultural goods of their society offer but the realization of which, in unequal class societies, ultimately depends on the degree of access the individual has to critical resources such as food, shelter, education, employment, and health care.

Luddites were early-nineteenth-century English textile workers who protested against the growing use of machines in tasks that were formerly performed by skilled labor. They expressed their frustration at the imminent loss of their livelihoods by smashing the machines.

Majoritarian electoral democracy is the political theory that considers government decisions as reflecting the collective will of the citizens. Participation in democratic elections empowers people to influence public policy such that government becomes "of the people, by the people, and for the people."

Majoritarian pluralism, also known as pluralist/populist democracy, is a political theory arguing that power is located in plural spheres, not just in the hands of one class or entity. Public policy becomes the arena for conflict between interest groups, and the positions of different interest groups are taken into consideration when decisions are made. According to this theory, all interest groups wield equal influence, which therefore leads to decisionmaking that is inherently democratic, pluralist, and majoritarian.

Market price is the price that is determined by supply and demand. It is the price at which things are sold. Adam Smith distinguishes market price from natural price.

Marxism is the body of economic and political thought that originated in the works of Karl Marx and Friedrich Engels. Their method of analysis was dialectical and therefore focused on the internal contradictions that every society carries within itself, which ultimately become the fundamental force of conflict and historical change. It is in class struggle that these contradictions find expression, and therefore Marx and Engels considered all history to be the history of class struggle.

Means of production are the raw materials, machines, tools, and technology that labor employs or puts to use in the production of goods and services.

Mechanization refers to the use of machines, instead of human labor, in the production of commodities.

Median household income divides the income distribution into two equal parts, with half falling below the median and the other half rising above.

Misogyny is the attitude of entrenched hatred and prejudice against women.

Model minority is a stereotype that is often associated with Asian Americans. It exaggerates certain characteristics and ignores others. It emphasizes Asian American success as an example of a group that has overcome discrimination on their own. They are held up as a "model" for groups that are seen as slackers. Although there is ample evidence of Asian American attainment in education and material success, it does not compensate for the continuing disadvantage of many others. The model minority image becomes a convenient way to deny the assistance that many Asian Americans need and overlooks the institutional discrimination many face.

Monopoly occurs when a handful of sellers control the market and are able to exert undue control over prices, wages, and quality of products being bought and sold. It is the opposite of perfect competition, a state that Adam Smith believed was fundamental if the invisible hand was to operate fairly.

Nativism is the ideology that the only true Americans are the native-born. Not Native Americans, but those white Anglo-Saxon Protestants who were born in the United States. Nativism as an anti-immigrant ideology became popular in the late 1800s and early 1900s, during the massive wave of immigration to the United States from Southern, Eastern, and Central Europe. Nativists were also called know-nothings, for the secret oaths they took in their organizations, whose existence they denied.

Natural price is the price that reflects the actual cost of producing a commodity. The market price can be either more or less than the natural price.

Necessary labor time is the amount of time workers need to work to earn their wage. The idea being that, during the time they work in excess of the necessary labor time, they are not working to earn their own pay but to create surplus value, which creates profit for the capitalist.

Neoliberalism emphasizes a marketplace that is free of government intervention. Neoliberals believe that government should intervene only to facilitate the freeing of the market, and this by continuously minimizing its own role through deregulation and privatization.

Occupy Wall Street movement started on September 17, 2011, in New York City. This collective, nonhierarchical movement focused primar-ily on the societal divide between the richest 1 percent and the other 99 percent. It attributed the Great Recession of 2008 to the greed and corruption of the major banks and multinational corporations, to their corrosive hold on the democratic process, and to their close partnership with the government. The movement advocated a nonviolent, worldwide revolution against the financial elite as the only solution to the ills of the unfair global economy.

Official poverty measure is the threshold that determines who is poor and therefore eligible for benefits under the government's social safety net. It was developed in 1963–1964 by Mollie Orshnasky, in conjunction with President Lyndon Johnson's war on poverty. Orshnasky calculated the measure by taking the price of a nutritionally minimum market basket of food, for one year, and then multiplying that price by three, given that, on average, Americans spend one-third of their income on food. The number yielded the official poverty measure. Families who make less than this threshold annually are considered to be living below the poverty line.

Oligarchy is the form of government where real decisionmaking power is vested in the hands of a few individuals or groups. Increasingly, numbers of social scientists think that the United States is headed toward becoming an oligarchy.

One-dimensional society, according to German social scientist Herbert Marcuse, is one in which individuals have lost the ability to think critically and negatively about society.

Opportunity hoarding occurs when people in the top ranks of society monopolize the tools necessary for social mobility, such as education and professional opportunities, instead of sharing them. This is done by influencing the policies that shape the institutional frameworks of higher education and labor markets in favor of the affluent and powerful.

Othering is a social practice whereby individuals who are seen as being different from the social norm are considered not just different, but also deficient and therefore subject to exclusion and discrimination.

Patriarchy literally means "rule of the father," with the power of the father, and by extension the power of men, expanded to all realms of society. It is a system in which men are considered the primary authority figures and is therefore contingent upon the subordination of women.

Patrimonial capitalism is Thomas Piketty's concept of the United States as a society wherein the concentration of wealth in the hands of fewer and fewer individuals is leading to a future in which inheritance will determine economic advantage and disadvantage, especially as the rich wield ever-greater power over politics.

Peculiar institution was a euphemism for the term *slavery* in the US South, which was considered inappropriate and indecorous. Thus the practice of owning human beings as property was referred to as "peculiar."

Political economy is the concept that highlights the role of government and government decisions in the economy. It illustrates how politics affects economics and vice versa, and how they together determine the most fundamental issues in society.

Postracial is the evolutionary characteristic of a society seen as having successfully moved beyond the stage where race is considered a significant identifier of status. This is a society where race no longer matters, where the color of a person's skin no longer matters, and where, in Martin Luther King Jr.'s words, a person is judged by the "content of their character." The United States is not yet a postracial society.

Postracist is the attribute of a society that does not judge individuals on the basis of racist ideas. Such a society takes race into consideration only to correct past oppression.

Power elite is the term coined by sociologist C. Wright Mills to identify the entity within which the power to dominate American society resides. He argued that the power elite comprises the individuals who occupy the dominant positions in the political, economic, and military domains. Together, these individuals form an "interlocking directorate" with sufficient power to control political decisionmaking in the United States. Mills argued that critical decisions that affected all Americans, as well as those in other countries, were being made by a handful of individuals who represented giant corporations, the federal government (primarily the executive branch), and senior military officers.

Primitive capital accumulation refers to the historical processes that created the preconditions for the development of the capitalist mode of production. Capital was created through exploitation of labor, appropriation of resources, and colonial plunder. For example, the enclosure movement in Great Britain, through legislative acts supported by the landed gentry, led to the appropriation of land that belonged to the commons, thus dispossessing the peasantry. The appropriated land was used to create capital through commercial agriculture for the nascent capitalist enterprise, with the landless peasants becoming the reserve army of labor for the newly developing factories, thus giving birth to the material basis on which capitalism grew.

Privatization is the process in which public goods, public wealth, and public property find their way into the hands of private entities, for example when a public school becomes a private charter school. Privatization is a consequence of deliberate decisionmaking when a government decides to transfer a public service into private hands. This is usually done in the name of efficiency to deliver water, electricity, and mail in a more economic way. When government budgets are tight and savings revenue is paramount, privatization of service delivery has often become the answer. Many argue that privatization is a convenient way for public wealth to be channeled into private pockets and functions for private gain.

Proletariat is a term coined by Karl Marx and Frederich Engels to identify those who do not own the means of production. The proletariat are the "have-nots." They are the workers, who, in order to make a living, depend on the means of production, that is the capital controlled by the bourgeoisie.

Protestant ethic is a set of norms that emphasized hard work, frugality, deferred gratification, punctuality, and the like. Max Weber believed that the "spirit" that these norms inculcated in the Protestant business leaders of Western Europe enabled them to accumulate capital and expand the capitalist system.

Quintiles refer to class categories as the highest, fourth, middle, second, and the lowest fifths. In determining quintiles, the entire population of the United States is divided into five equal segments of 20 percent each along a gradational sequence, from the lowest (or poorest) fifth of earners to the highest (or richest) fifth. In a perfectly egalitarian society, each quintile would receive 20 percent of the nation's wealth. How much more or less than a 20 percent quintile receives shows the degree of inequality in a country.

Racialization is the process by which people, cultural practices, and institutions are given a racial character, such as when the native tribes of Africa and North America are characterized as "blacks" and "Indians," as juxtaposed against the dominant and "superior" group, who are racialized as "whites."

Racism is an ideology based on the notion that the racial attributes of an individual determine the individual's worth as a human being.

Rank-based measure of social mobility considers children's chances of climbing from lower to higher rungs on a society's socioeconomic ladder, acquiring greater wealth and status in the process. A housecleaner's daughter becoming a lawyer is an example of rank-based social mobility.

Rationalization, a concept central to German sociologist Max Weber's theory of social action, refers to the various rationalities that are intrinsic to determining the actions of individuals, institutions, and organizations. Even though all social action is driven by rationalities, Weber was particularly interested in the overarching rationalizations that typified the actions of bureaucracies and capitalism.

Reconstruction (1863–1877) refers to the period in US history immediately following the Civil War. This was a time when the newly emancipated slaves tried to fulfill the true promise of freedom by claiming their rights as citizens. The Fifteenth Amendment gave black men the right to vote, with which they elected more than a hundred blacks to public office during the fourteen years of Reconstruction. This was the first experiment with interracial democracy in the United States, at a time of genuine progress for the former slaves. It ended with the Compromise of 1877, as a result of which federal troops were withdrawn from the former Confederate states and thus the Republican state governments lost their protection and ability to keep the white Redeemers and Ku Klux Klan at bay.

Reified entity evokes the idea of reification, which sociologists describe as the phenomenon in which social structures that are created by people are seen as functioning without human agency. It is when the social system, economy, mass media, education system, and commodities become reified entities seen as having materialized on their own, that is, as having a life of their own independent of the human actors who created them.

Relational determination of class emphasizes the fact that class is more than just a category that someone occupies; it also embodies a relationship between the proverbial haves and have-nots in terms of ownership (or lack of ownership) of the means of production or capital, which ultimately structures and reproduces inequality.

Reproductive work entails the work that is performed predominantly by women within the family to maintain and nurture the current and future generations of workers. Because this labor is unpaid, it is not considered true "work."

Reserve army of labor comprises all the unemployed and underemployed in society who are seeking work. The presence of people who are willing, even desperate, to work drives down wages and lowers the cost of production for capitalists, increasing their profit margin.

Restrictive covenants are contractual agreements that prohibit the purchasing or renting of property by a particular group of people. Asian Americans, Jews, and particularly African Americans have been kept out of certain neighborhoods as a result of these covenants. Use of restrictive covenants became common after 1926, when the US Supreme Court validated the practice in *Corrigan v. Buckley*. In 1948 the Court changed its position, but by then racial discrimination in housing had become an entrenched practice.

Revenue is value that is earned when a commodity or service is sold.

Ruling class in a capitalist society is composed of the upper class, the class who own the means of production. They either occupy positions of power themselves or, as G. William Domhoff points out, have disproportionate power in controlling institutions and key decisionmaking groups.

Second-wave women's movement combined with the civil rights movement and the antiwar movement to fundamentally change the status and role of women in the Western world. The second wave grew out of the disaffections of white middle-class women, as captured profoundly in Betty Friedan's book *The Feminine Mystique,* which inspired the movement and also encouraged the development of a distinctly feminist worldview.

Sexism is an ideology based on the notion that the gender of an individual determines the individual's worth as a human being.

Sexual objectification occurs when women are regarded as property, such as when women's bodies are bought and sold as a commodity, as in prostitution or pornography, or when women's bodies, and men's bodies too, are used in advertising to sell products.

Shares approach measures inequality by considering how much of the national income is received by households or families.

Small government is the idea of minimizing the role of the government, especially in the economy. Proponents of small government believe that the market should be the main arbiter of all economic activities and that government should not interfere. They also advocate reducing both taxes and government revenue, especially by eliminating regulatory activities and social welfare programs.

Social capital comprises those forces in society that promote an individual's sense of belonging through social solidarity and social reciprocity. Important components of social capital are the mutually understood social values, norms, moral obligations, and trust that undergird social networks and relationships among individuals, their families, and groups.

Social compact, also referred to as the social contract, is the notion in political philosophy, most associated with Jean Jacques Rousseau, that individuals, as members of society, voluntarily relinquish some of their freedom and agree to follow the rules and laws of society, but with the understanding that society will in turn reciprocate and take care of them and ensure their well-being.

Social construction is integral to the concept of the social construction of reality, which is the distinctly sociological notion that the world around us is full of meanings and that we interact with each other in terms of those meanings. Meanings are not intrinsic to people and objects, but are socially constructed by those in power who have an interest in constructing those meanings in particular ways. The social constructions and meanings filter down to every realm of society, affecting how people view their social reality.

Social facts is a term coined by French sociologist Emile Durkheim. Social facts are things that exist in society—such as values, norms, social structures, institutions, customs, and languages—that are external to the individual but exert control over the individual.

Social inequality is the unequal distribution of income, wealth, opportunities, social status, prestige, and power, that is, the resources people need in order to survive, thrive, and reach their full potential as human beings.

Social justice unionism advocates for a wider social justice emphasis for twenty-first-century unionism by moving away from a narrow focus on purely economic matters such as wages and benefits. It recognizes that economics is only a part of the overall experience of class oppression. Social justice unionism envisions building sociopolitical alliances to strengthen the political power of the working class.

Social mobility refers to the movement of individuals from one social class to the other. Sociologists measure social mobility by comparing the social class of children in relation to that of their parents. Also called intergenerational mobility.

Social relations of production are the relations that individuals enter into with each other for the sake of producing goods and services in society. In capitalism, this involves the relation between the capitalist, who owns the means of production, and the worker hired to work with the means of production to produce value-bearing goods and services. For Marxists, this is where the inherent contradiction of capitalism is lodged—the private ownership of the means of production and the private expropriation of profit, versus the public or social nature of production.

Social stratification is how different dimensions or sources of inequality—economic, political, social—combine to form complex structures of inequality of entire categories of people who have different degrees of access to vital resources, such as jobs and education, and rewards, such as good health and general well-being.

Socialism is an economic system in which the means of production are socially owned and society is guided by the principle of cooperation instead of competition. This is a society in which wealth is distributed according to the principle of "to each according to their need."

Socioeconomic status is an individual's position in the societal hierarchy, as determined by a combination of variables such as income, wealth, education, occupation, and place of residence.

Structural adjustment policies are economic policies, inspired by neoliberal ideas and promoted by the International Monetary Fund and the World Bank, delineating conditions that must be met by developing countries if they are to receive loans from the World Bank. The policies include cutting social programs to reducing government spending and control, privatizing public-sector services, opening the country to foreign multinational corporations, and promoting market competition. By all measures, countries that have implemented such policies have experienced deterioration in the general well-being of their people.

Structural functionalism is a theoretical perspective in sociology that sees society as a system made up of related parts integrated by value consensus, system interdependence, and integration.

Subsidy can be considered the opposite of taxes. In the latter, the government takes from the people; in the former, the government gives monetary support to help people and businesses cut costs, achieve specific objectives, or realize profits. For example, when a corn farmer is encouraged to harvest a crop with the assurance that the government will pay a subsidy to make up for any loss the farmer may incur when he/she sells the corn cheap; or when an entrepreneur is given a subsidy for expenses incurred to get a business off the ground. A subsidy is a monetary transfer from the government to the public for realizing a particular objective that is deemed worthy of support.

Supplemental poverty measure expands the official poverty measure by adding the value of noncash benefits (such as nutrition assistance, subsidized housing, and home energy assistance) and subtracting necessary expenses for critical goods and services (such as income taxes, Social Security payroll taxes, child care, child-support payments to another household, other work-related expenses, and medical out-of-pocket costs) from the value of cash income.

Supply and **demand** are the two most fundamental concepts in economics. Supply is how much of a product is actually brought to the market to be sold. Demand is how much of a product consumers are willing to buy at a particular price. The intersection of the two determines the market price.

Surplus value is the value or revenue that workers produce over and above the value they need to produce to earn their own wage. This idea is integral to the labor theory of value, which argues that all value inherent in a commodity or service is ultimately created by the laborer.

Third-wave women's movement, a distinctly postmodern movement, is the analysis of women's agency in a host of issues, including race, class, sexuality, imperialism, postcolonialism, globalization, immigration, and the environment.

Third world comprises countries, primarily in the Southern Hemisphere, that were colonized by the European powers. These are countries that gained independence by the second half of the twentieth century. In their quest for economic development, they have adopted the neoliberal policies of the Washington Consensus and have opened their doors to foreign investment, mainly as a home for factories of multinational corporations.

Top 1 percent, top 0.1 percent, and **top 0.01 percent** are measures for determining the degree of inequality in a society through comparison. The top 1 percent compares with the bottom 99 percent; the top 0.1 percent with the bottom 99.9 percent; and the top 0.01 percent with the bottom 99.99 percent. These percentiles are also evoked to demonstrate the degree of inequality within the top 1 percent category itself, as the top 0.1 percent are increasingly pulling away from the top 0.9 percent, and the top 0.01 percent are increasingly pulling away from the top 0.09 percent.

Transfer payments, also called transfer income, identifies assistance payments made by government to its citizens in the form of food stamps, social security, rental assistance, medical care, and the like, as a way to redistribute income and moderate gross inequalities.

Transnational financial speculation comprises speculation on the future prices of currencies, food, petroleum, and real estate on a transnational basis. Any commodity that is subject to price changes due to a host of factors, such as weather, wars, political climate, disease, and disasters, can be speculated on. Given the enormous amounts of money involved in such activities, with billions of dollars changing hands each day, even a slight change in price can yield a huge gain. Speculators opt for this form of economic activity because the return is immediate and national boundaries are completely permeable, allowing for speculation to take on a global form. Much of the globalization of economic activity relates to transnational financial speculation.

Truly disadvantaged is sociologist William Julius Wilson's term for those who are mired in super-concentrated poverty in the inner cities of the United States. These are areas from which the black middle-class moved out when the Civil Rights Act of 1964 pulled down barriers to housing discrimination, leaving behind the poorest of the poor.

Underclass, a term used primarily by sociologist William Julius Wilson, underscores the changes that have taken place in the lives of the black poor in the United States since the 1970s. The term suggests that the poor who live in the inner cities today are "collectively different" from the poor who lived there in earlier years. Wilson characterized them as the most disadvantaged segments of the black urban community, those who are completely disengaged from the mainstream economy, lacking education, skills, and training. They are individuals who are involved in street crime and experience long-term poverty and welfare dependency. The term *lower class,* Wilson contended, did not capture these additional dimensions in the lives of the inner-city poor. But most liberals eschew the term *underclass,* maintaining that it puts undue attention on behaviors rather than structures. Wilson defended his position by arguing that structures, culture, and behaviors are interrelated; to ignore this dynamic would be a failure to capture the most important social transformations in the recent history of the United States.

Washington Consensus is a set of policies, based on neoliberal ideas, that the US government and the international financial institutions—the International Monetary Fund and the World Bank—offer as a prescription that countries should adopt to increase their economic growth. These policies include reducing the role of the state in the economy, deregulation, fiscal discipline on the part of the government, privatizing state enterprises (such as in water and utilities), tax reform (mainly by cutting tax rates), and trade liberalization (such as increasing foreign investment by removing trade barriers).

Wealth and income are two attributes that are used to determine economic equality or inequality. Wealth is net worth—fixed, marketable assets minus debts. Real estate, stocks, bonds, jewelry, valuable artwork, household goods, automobiles all add up to a person's or family's net worth after debts such as home mortgages and credit cards have been subtracted.

Welfare chauvinism is the belief among some segments of the population in European countries that the services of their generous welfare programs should be restricted to the native-born population. This idea is gaining popularity as European countries observe the changes to their once homogeneous populations due to immigration from their former colonies. In national elections since the mid-2000s, far-right parties with strident anti-immigration rhetoric have done remarkably well in the United Kingdom, France, Austria, Denmark, and Sweden.

Bibliography

Ackard, P. 1992. "Corporate Mobilization and Political Power: The Transformation of U.S. Economic Policy in the 1970s." *American Sociological Review* 57:597–615.

AFL-CIO. 2014a. "Executive Paywatch." http://www.aflcio.org/Corporate-Watch /CEO-Pay-and-the-99 (accessed March 3, 2014).

———. 2014b. "Executive Paywatch 100 Highest-Paid CEOs." http://www.aflcio .org/Corporate-Watch/CEO-Pay-and-the-99/100-Highest-Paid-CEOs (accessed March 3, 2014).

Ahearn, R. 2012. "Globalization, Worker Insecurity, and Policy Approaches." Congressional Research Service, February 27. http://www.fas.org/sgp/crs/misc/RL34091 .pdf (accessed September 9, 2012).

Albo, G., S. Gindin, and L. Panitch. 2010. *In and Out of Crisis: The Global Financial Meltdown and Left Alternatives*. Oakland: Spectre.

Alderman, L., and S. Greenhouse. 2014. "Serving Up Fries, for a Living Wage." *New York Times*, October 28: B1, B8.

Alesina, A., and E. Glaeser. 2004. *Fighting Poverty in the US and Europe: A World of Difference*. New York: Oxford University Press.

Alexander, M. 2010. *The New Jim Crow: Mass Incarceration in the Age of Colorblindness*. New York: New Press.

Alfred, M. V., and D. Chlup. 2009. "Neoliberalism, Illiteracy, and Poverty: Framing the Rise in Black Women's Incarceration." *Western Journal of Black Studies* 33:240–249.

American Civil Liberties Union. n.d. *Title IX: Gender Equity in Education*. http://www .aclu.org/title-ix-gender-equity-education (accessed February 26, 2013).

An, C. 2011. "What We Know About Housing First." National Alliance to End Homelessness, August 4. http://blog.endhomelessness.org/tag/housing-first (accessed December 4, 2012).

Anderson, S., A. P. Halter, and B. M. Gryzlak. 2004. "Difficulties After Leaving TANF: Inner-City Women Talk About Reasons for Returning to Welfare." *Social Work* 49:185–194.

Anyon, J. 1997. *Ghetto Schooling: A Political Economy of Urban Educational Reform*. New York: Teacher's College Press.

———. 2005. *Radical Possibilities: Public Policy, Urban Education, and a New Social Movement*. New York: Routledge.

Appelbaum, B., and R. Gebeloff. 2012. "Even Critics of Safety Net Increasingly Depend on It." *New York Times,* February 12: A1.

Apuzzo, M. 2014. "Uncovered Papers Show Past Government Efforts to Drive Gays from Work." *New York Times,* May 21: A13, A19.

Arnesen, E. 2007. *Encyclopedia of U.S. Labor and Working Class History.* Vol. 1. New York: Taylor and Francis.

Aronowitz, S. 2012. "Reflections on the Madison Uprising." *South Atlantic Quarterly* 111:214–222.

Associated Press. 2012. "Labor Productivity Rises 1.6%." *New York Times,* August 9: B9.

Aviv, R. 2014. "Wrong Answer." *The New Yorker,* July 21: 54–65.

Badger, Emily. 2014. "The Meteoric, Costly, and Unprecedented Rise of Incarceration in America." *Washington Post,* April 30. http://www.washingtonpost.com /blogs/wonkblog/wp/2014/04/30/the-meteoric-costly-and-unprecedented-rise-of -incarceration-in-america/ (accessed October 28, 2014).

Bai, M. 2012. "How Did Political Money Get This Loud?" *New York Times Sunday Magazine,* July 22: MM14.

Bajaj, V. 2012. "Fatal Fire in Bangladesh Highlights the Dangers Facing Garment Workers." *New York Times,* November 26: A4.

Bakija, J., A. Cole, and B. T. Heim. 2010. "Jobs and Income Growth of Top Earners and the Causes of Changing Income Inequality: Evidence from U.S. Tax Return Data." Working paper. Williamstown, Mass.: Williams College.

Barber, B. 1995. *Jihad vs. McWorld: Terrorism's Challenge to Democracy.* New York: Ballantine.

Baron, H. 1992. "The Demand for Black Labor: Historical Notes on the Political Economy of Racism." In *A Turbulent Voyage,* by F. Hayes, 511–543. San Diego: Collegiate Press.

Bartels, L. 2008. *Unequal Democracy: The Political Economy of the New Gilded Age.* New York: Russell Sage.

Bartlett, D. L., and J. B. Steele. 1992. *America: What Went Wrong?* Kansas City: McMeel.

Bauerlein, M., and C. Jeffery. 2011. "The Job Killers." *Mother Jones,* November/ December. http://www.motherjones.com/politics/2011/10/republicans-job-creation -kill (accessed November 2, 2014).

Beard, C. A. 2012 [1913]. *An Economic Interpretation of the Constitution of the United States.* New York: Simon & Schuster.

Becker, C., and J. Scott. 2012. "Isolating America's Workers." *The Nation,* October 8: 27–29.

Beckert, S., and S. Rockman. 2011. "Partners in Iniquity." *New York Times Opinionater,* April 2. http://opinionator.blogs.nytimes.com/2011/04/02/partners-in-iniquity /?_php=true&_type=blogs&_r=0 (accessed May 2, 2014).

———. 2011. *Slavery's Capitalism: A New History of American Economic Development.* Philadelphia: University of Pennsylvania Press.

———. 2014. "How Slavery Led to Modern Capitalism." *Bloomberg View,* February 24. http://www.huffingtonpost.com/2014/02/24/slavery_n_4847105.html (accessed May 5, 2014).

Bell, D. 1976. *The Coming of Post-Industrial Society.* New York: Basic.

Bernstein, J., and J. Schmitt. 2000. "The Impact of the Minimum Wage." Economic Policy Institute. http://www.epi.org/publication/briefingpapers_min_wage_bp/ (accessed October 25, 2014).

Bernstein, L. 2014. "Once Again, U.S. Has Most Expensive, Least Effective Health-

Care System in Survey." *Washington Post*, June 16. http://www.washington post.com/news/to-your-health/wp/2014/06/16/once-again-u-s-has-most-expensive -least-effective-health-care-system-in-survey/ (accessed October 30, 2014).

Bernstein, N. S. 2011. "The Hidden Costs of Higher Education." *New York Times*, August 22: A19.

Bonilla-Silva, E. 2006. *Racism Without Racists: Color Blind Racism and the Persistence of Racial Inequality in the United States*. 2nd ed. Lanham: Rowan and Littlefield.

Bowles, S., and H. Gintis. 2001. "Schooling in Capitalist America Revisited." November 8. http://www.umass.edu/preferen/gintis/soced.pdf (accessed March 29, 2013).

———. 2003. "Schooling in Capitalist America Twenty-five Years Later." *Sociological Forum* 18:343–348.

Bravve, E., M. Bolton, L. Couch, and S. Crowley. 2012. "Out of Reach, 2012: America's Forgotten Housing Crisis." National Low Income Housing Coalition, March. http://nlihc.org/sites/default/files/oor/2012-OOR.pdf (accessed April 25, 2012).

Bread for the World Institute. 2012. "Fact Sheet: Hunger and Poverty Hurt African-American Women and Children." February. http://www.bread.org/what-we-do /resources/fact-sheets/african-american-2012.pdf (accessed March 17, 2013).

Breslow, J. M. 2013. "Two American Families: The State of America's Middle Class in Eight Charts." *PBS Frontline*, July 9. http://www.pbs.org/wgbh/pages/frontline /business-economy-financial-crisis/two-american-families/the-state-of-americas -middle-class-in-eight-charts (accessed July 14, 2013).

Bricker, J., A. B. Kennickell, K. B. Moore, and J. Sabelhaus. 2012. "Changes in the US Family Finances from 2007 to 2010: Evidence from the Survey of Consumer Finances." US Federal Reserve. http://www.federalreserve.gov/pubs/bulletin/2012 /PDF/scf12.pdf (accessed December 15, 2012).

Brodkin, K. 2004. "How Jews Became White Folks—and What That Says About Race in America." In *Race, Class, and Gender in the United States*, by P. Rothenberg, 38–53. New York: Worth.

Bronfenbrenner, K. 2009. "No Holds Barred: The Intensification of Employer Opposition to Organizing." Briefing paper. Washington, D.C.: Economic Policy Institute. http:// www.epi.org/publication/bp235/ (accessed July 14, 2013).

———. 2013. "Put Organizing First." *The Nation*, March 4: 11.

Brooks, T. 1971. *Toil and Trouble: A History of American Labor*. New York: Dell.

Brown, D. 1970. *Bury My Heart at Wounded Knee*. New York: Holt, Rinehart, and Winston.

Bruenig, M. 2013. "The Racial Wealth Gap." *The American Prospect*, November 6. http://www.prospect.org/article/racial-wealth-gap (accessed October 27, 2014).

Burdick-Will, J. 2011. "Converging Evidence for Neighborhood Effects on Children's Test Scores." In *Whither Opportunity? Rising Inequality, Schools, and Children's Life Chances*, by G. J. Duncan and R. J. Murnane, 255–276. New York: Russell Sage.

Bureau of Labor Statistics, 2012. "Occupational Employment Statistics." May 2012. http://www.bls.gov/oes/2012/may/featured_data.htm (accessed October 24, 2014).

———. 2012. "The Recession of 2007–2009." The BLS Spotlight on Statistics, February. http://www.bls.gov/spotlight/2012/recession/pdf/recession_bls_spotlight.pdf (accessed October 24, 2014).

———. 2013. "Occupational Employment and Wages." May 2013. http://www.bls .gov/oes/current/oes434171.htm (accessed October 20, 2014).

———. 2013. "Union Membership News Release." January 23. http://www.bls.gov /news.release/archives/union2_01232012.htm. (accessed October 29, 2014).

———. 2014. "Employment Situation Summary." http://www.bls.gov/news.release /empsit.nr0.htm (accessed October 24, 2014).

Burkhauser, R. V., and J. Larrimore. 2011. "How Changes in Employment, Earnings, and Public Transfers Make the First Two Years of the Great Recession (2007–2009) Different from Previous Recessions & Why It Matters for Longer Term Trends." US2010 Project, April. http://www.s4.brown.edu/us2010/Data/Report/report3.pdf (accessed May 24, 2012).

Callis, R. R., and M. Kresin. 2012. "Social, Economic, and Housing Statistics Division." January 31. https://www.census.gov/housing/hvs/files/qtr411/q411press.pdf (accessed April 3, 2012).

Cancian, M., and D. P. Meyer. 2000. "Work After Welfare: Women's Work Effort, Occupation, and Economic Well-Being." *Social Work Research* 24:69–86.

Card, D., T. Lemieux, and W. C. Riddell. 2004. "Unions and Wage Inequality." *Journal of Labor Research* 25:519–562.

Cassidy, J. 2014. "Forces of Divergence: Is Surging Inequality Endemic to Capitalism?" *The New Yorker,* March 31: 69–73.

Center for American Progress. 2014. "A New Force for America's Families." January 12. http://www.americanprogress.org/issues/race/report/2014/01/12/81907/a-new-force-for-americas-families-2 (accessed August 25, 2014).

Centers for Disease Control and Prevention (CDC). 2003. *Health Disparities Experienced by American Indians and Alaska Natives.* August 1. http://www.cdc.gov/mmwr/PDF/wk/mm5230.pdf (accessed March 1, 2012).

———. 2011. "CDC Health Disparities and Inequalities Report." http://www.cdc.gov/minorityhealth/CHDIReport.html (accessed May 1, 2012).

Chaddock, G. R. 2010. "Robert Byrd: A Zeal for Preserving the Senate's Power and Civility." *Christian Science Monitor*, June 28. http://www.csmonitor.com/USA/Politics/2010/0628/Robert-Byrd-a-zeal-for-preserving-the-Senates-power-and-civility (accessed November 2, 2014).

Chase, E. 1933. "The Brief Origins of May Day." Industrial Workers of the World. http://www.iww.org/en/history/library/misc/origins_of_mayday (accessed May 2, 2013).

Chemaly, S. 2014. "Women Don't Fear Power, Power Fears Women." *Ms. Magazine Blog,* May 16. http://www.msmagazine.com/blog/2014/05/16/women-don't-fear-power-power-fears-women (accessed May 24, 2014).

Chetty, R., N. Hendren, P. Kline, E. Saez, and N. Turner. 2014. "Is the United States Still a Land of Opportunity? Recent Trends in Intergenerational Mobility." Working paper. Cambridge, Mass.: National Bureau of Economic Research.

Chicago Tribune. 2014. "Chicago Shooting Victims." http://crime.chicagotribune.com/chicago/shootings (accessed October 25, 2014).

Chu, J. 2011. "American Made?" *MIT News*, September 16. http://newsoffice.mit.edu/2011/manufacturing-event-pie-0916. (accessed May 15, 2013).

Citizens for Tax Justice and Institute on Taxation and Economic Policy. 2011. "Corporate Tax Dodging in the Fifty States, 2008–2010." November. http://www.ctj.org/corporatetaxdodgers50states/CorporateTaxDodgers50StatesReport.pdf (accessed June 8, 2013).

Citizens for Tax Justice. 2012. "Buffett Rule Bill Before the Senate Is a Small Step Towards Tax Fairness." April 10. http://ctj.org/ctjreports/2012/04/buffett_rule_bill_before_the_senate_is_a_small_step_towards_tax_fairness.php (accessed January 17, 2013).

———. 2012. "Who Pays Taxes in America?" April 4. http://www.ctj.org/pdf/taxday2012.pdf (accessed October 25, 2014).

Clark, K. 2014. "Hungry for Savings." April 3. http://www.marketplace.org/topics

/wealth-poverty/secret-life-food-stamp/anti-hunger-movements-strange-bed fellows (accessed April 10, 2014).

Clawson, R., and R. Trice. 2000. "Poverty As We Know It: Media Portrayals of the Poor." *Public Opinion Quarterly* (Spring):53–64.

Clifford, S. 2013. "Textile Plants Humming, but Not with Workers." *New York Times,* September 20: A1, A22.

Coates, T. 2014. "The Case for Reparations." *The Atlantic,* June: 54–71.

Colbert, S. 2013. "McDonald's Budget for Minimum Wage." July 22. http://video cafe.crooksandliars.com/heather/colbert-mcdonalds-budget-minimum-wage -empl (accessed July 24, 2013).

Coleman, J. S., E. Q. Campbell, C. J. Hobson, J. McPartland, A. M. Mood, F. D. Weinfeld, and R. L. York. 1966. *Equality of Educational Opportunity.* Washington, D.C.: US Department of Health, Education, and Welfare, Office of Education.

College Board Advocacy and Policy Center. 2013. "Trends in College Pricing." http:// trends.collegeboard.org/college-pricing (accessed January 17, 2014).

Collins, J. L., and V. Mayer. 2010. *Both Hands Tied: Welfare Reform and the Race to the Bottom in the Low-Wage Labor Market.* Chicago: University of Chicago Press.

Collins, P. H. 1989. "Toward a New Vision: Race, Class, and Gender as Categories of Analysis and Connection." Keynote address, "Integrating Race and Gender into the College Curriculum." May 24. Memphis: Center for Research on Women.

Common Cause. n.d. "The American Legislative Executive Council (ALEC)." http:// www.commoncause.org/site/pp.asp?c=dkLNK1MQIwG&b=7743229 (accessed January 17, 2014).

Condron, D. J. 2009. "Social Class, School and Non-School Environments, and Black and White Inequalities in Learning." *American Sociological Review* 74:683–708.

Congressional Budget Office. 2011. "Trends in the Distribution of Household Income Between 1979 and 2007."

Conniff, R. 2002. "The Right Welfare Reform." *The Nation,* July 22: 5–6.

Cook, B. W. 1981. *The Declassified Eisenhower: The Divided Legacy of Peace and Political Warfare.* New York: Doubleday.

Counts, G. S. 1932. "Dare the Schools Build a New Social Order?" New York: John Day. http://www.freewebs.com/fmei75/pdf/dare%20the%20school.pdf (accessed October 6, 2013).

Crawford, S. P. 2011. "The New Digital Divide." *New York Times Sunday Review,* December 3: 1.

Cremin, L. A. 1957. *The Republic and the School: Horace Mann on the Education of Free Men.* New York: Columbia University, Teacher's College Press.

Cuban, L., and D. Shipps. 2000. *Reconstructing the Public Good in Education.* Stanford: Stanford University Press.

Dahl, R. A. 1961. *Who Governs?* New Haven, Conn.: Yale University Press.

Dao, J. 2011. "In California, Indian Tribes with Casinos Eject Thousands of Members." *New York Times,* December 13: A20.

DasGupta, K. 2005. "A Checkered Legacy: Consequences of Affirmative Action Policies Around the World." *H-Net Reviews in the Humanities and Social Sciences,* July. http://www.h-net.org/reviews/showpdf.php?id=10729 (accessed November 10, 2013).

Davey, M. 2014. "Detroit Urged to Tear Down 40,000 Buildings." *New York Times,* May 28: A1.

Davey, M., and A. G. Sulzberger. 2011. "Dueling Protests in a Capital As Nothing Much Gets Done." *New York Times,* February 19: A14.

Davey, M., and M. W. Walsh. 2013. "Billions in Debt: Detroit Tumbles into Insolvencey." *New York Times,* July19: A1.

Davis, K., and W. Moore. 1944. "Some Principles of Stratification." *American Sociological Review* 10:242–249.

Decker, P. 2004. *The Utes Must Go.* Golden, Colo.: Fulcrum.

DeGenova, N. P. 2002. "Migrant 'Illegality' and Deportability in Everyday Life." *Annual Review of Anthropology* 31:419–447.

DeNavas-Walt, C., B. D. Proctor, and J. C. Smith. 2011. "Income, Poverty, and Health Insurance Coverage in the United States: 2010." US Census Bureau, September. https://www.census.gov/prod/2011pubs/p60-239.pdf (accessed January 17, 2012).

———. 2012. "Income, Poverty, and Health Insurance Coverage in the United States: 2011." US Census Bureau, September. https://www.census.gov/prod/2012pubs/p60-243.pdf (accessed February 3, 2013).

Denby, D. 2012. "Good Fights." *The New Yorker,* September 10: 108.

Department of Defense. 2014. "US Casualty Status." http://www.defense.gov/news/casualty.pdf (accessed October 25, 2014).

Desmond, M. 2012. "Eviction and the Reproduction of Urban Poverty." *American Journal of Sociology* 118:88–133.

Dewan, S. 2014. "Evictions Soar in Hot Market: Renters Suffer." *New York Times,* August 29: A1.

Dine, P. M. 2008. *State of the Unions: How Labor Can Strengthen the Middle Class, Improve Our Economy, and Regain Political Influence.* New York: McGraw-Hill.

Dobbs, L. 2004. *Exporting America: Why Corporate Greed Is Shipping American Jobs Overseas.* New York: Warner.

Domhoff, G. W. 2005. "Wealth, Income, and Power." *Who Rules America?* September. http://www2.ucsc.edu/whorulesamerica/power/wealth.html (accessed May 2, 2012).

Dreher, A., and N. Gaston. 2007. "Has Globalisation Really Had No Effect on Unions?" *Kyklos* 60:165–186.

Dreiling, M. 2000. "Class Embeddedness of Corporate Political Action: Leadership in Defense of the NAFTA." *Social Problems* 47:21–48.

Dreiling, M., and D. Darves. 2011. "Corporate Unity in American Trade Policy: A Network Analysis of Corporate-Dyad Political Action." *American Journal of Sociology* 116:1514–1563.

Drum, K. 2013. "Death by a Thousand Cuts: Belt Tightening Wasn't the Cure for an Ailing Economy—It Was the Last Straw." *Mother Jones,* September–October: 64.

Du Bois, W. E. B. 1953. *The Souls of Black Folks.* Greenwich, Conn.: Fawcett.

Duhigg, C., and K. Bradsher. 2012. "How US Lost Out on iPhone Work." *New York Times,* January 22: A1.

Duhigg, C., and D. Kocieniewski. 2012. "How Apple Sidesteps Billions in Taxes." *New York Times,* April 29: A1.

Duncan, G. J., and R. J. Murnane. 2011. *Whither Opportunity? Rising Inequality, Schools, and Children's Life Chances.* New York: Russell Sage.

Egan, T. 2013. "Good Poor, Bad Poor." *New York Times,* December 22: SR11.

Ehrenreich, B. 2001. *Nickel and Dimed: On (Not) Getting By in America.* New York: Henry Holt.

Ehrenreich, B., and A. R. Hochschild. 2012. "Global Women in the New Economy." In *Conformity and Conflict: Readings in Cultural Anthropology,* by J. Spradley and D. W. McCurdy, 316–323. Boston: Pearson.

Eidelson, J. 2013. "Walmart Workers Walk Out." *The Nation,* January 7: 11–15.

Falk, G. 2012. "Temporary Assistance to Needy Families (TANF): Welfare-to-Work Revisited." Congressional Research Service, October 2. https://www.fas.org/sgp/crs/misc/R42768.pdf (accessed January 7, 2013).

————. 2014. "Temporary Assistance to Needy Families (TANF): Eligibility and Benefits Amounts in State TANF Cash Assistance Programs." Congressional Research Service, July 22. http://www.fas.org/sgp/crs/misc/R43634.pdf (accessed October 27, 2014).

————. 2014. "The Temporary Assistance for Needy Families (TANF) Block Grant: Responses to Frequently Asked Questions." Congressional Research Service, September 19. http://www.fas.org/sgp/crs/misc/RL32760.pdf (accessed January 29, 2014).

Fang, L. 2013. "How Private Prisons Game the Immigration System." *The Nation,* February 27. http://www.thenation.com/article/173120/how-private-prisons-game -immigration-system# (accessed July 14, 2013).

Fanon, F. 1963. *The Wretched of the Earth.* New York: Grove.

Feagin, J. 2001. "Social Justice and Sociology: Agendas for the Twentieth Century." *American Sociological Review* 66:1–20.

Feagin, J., and C. Booher-Feagin. 1993. *Racial and Ethnic Relations.* Englewood Cliffs, N.J.: Simon and Schuster.

————. 2003. *Racial and Ethnic Relations.* Upper Saddle River, N.J.: Prentice Hall.

Featherstone, L. 2004. "Rollback Wages: Will Labor Take the Wal-Mart Challenge?" *The Nation,* June 28: 11–17.

Federal Reserve System, Board of Governors. 2014. "Federal Reserve Statistical Release: Z.1 Financial Accounts of the United States, Second Quarter." http://www .federalreserve.gov/releases/z1/current/z1.pdf (accessed December 2, 2014).

Feldman, J. N. 2012. "Letters—Sunday Dialogue: How Corporations Behave." *New York Times,* September 2: SR2.

Ferry, D. 2013. "I Know I Am, but What Are You?" *This American Life,* March 29. http://www.thisamericanlife.org/radio-archives/episode/491/tribes (accessed March 29, 2013).

Finch, I., and L. Schott. 2013. "The Value of TANF Cash Benefits Continued to Erode in 2012." Center on Budget and Policy Priorities. March 28. www.cbpp.org /files/3-28-13tanf.pdf (accessed October 27, 2014).

Fischer, W. 2011. "House Bill's Deep Cut in Public Housing Would Raise Future Federal Costs and Harm Vulnerable Low Income Families." Center on Budget and Policy Priorities. http://www.cbpp.org/cms/index.cfm?fa=view&id=3583 (accessed April 25, 2012).

Fletcher, B. 2013. "For Labor, What's After Michigan?" *The Progressive,* March: 22–24.

Foner, E. 1988. *Reconstruction: America's Unfinished Revolution, 1863–1877.* New York: Harper and Row.

Foner, P. S. 1981. *Organized Labor and the Black Worker 1619–1981.* New York: International Publishers.

Fox, M. 2013. "Jean Anyon Dies at 72, Author of Ghetto Schooling." *New York Times,* September 30: A22.

Frank, T. 2004. *What's the Matter with Kansas? How Conservatives Won the Heart of America.* New York: Metropolitan.

Franklin, J. H. 1993. "Ethnicity in American Life: The Historical Perspective." In *Experiencing Race, Class, and Gender in the United States,* by V. Cyrus, 14–20. Mountain View, Calif.: Mayfield Publishing.

Franklin, N. 2012. "Former Cops Agree: Legalization Is the Path to Controlling Drugs." *US News and World Report,* July 9. http://www.usnews.com/debate-club/is-it-time-to-scale-back-the-war-on-drugs (accessed April 5, 2013).

Freedman, D. S. 2011. "Obesity—United States, 1988–2008." Centers for Disease Control and Prevention, *Morbidity and Mortality Weekly Report,* January 14. http://www.cdc.gov/mmwr/pdf/other/su6001.pdf (accessed April 28, 2012).

Freeman, J. 2012. *American Empire, 1945–2000.* New York: Penguin.

Freeman, R. B., and J. L Medoff. 1984. *What Do Unions Do?* New York: Basic.

Friedan, Betty. 1963. *The Feminine Mystique.* New York: Norton.

Friedman, T. 2005. *The World Is Flat.* New York: Farrar, Straus, and Giroux.

Fromm, E. 1961. *Marx's Concept of Man.* New York: Frederick Unger.

Frosh, D. 2014. "Nestled Among Toxic Waste, a Navajo Village Faces Losing Its Land Forever." *New York Times,* February 20: A10.

Fukuyama, F. 1989. "The End of History." *The National Interest* (Summer):3–18.

Gabriel, T. 2014. "50 Years Later, Hardship Hits Back." *New York Times,* April 21: A1.

Galeano, E. 1997. *Open Veins of Latin America.* New York: Monthly Review Press.

Gates, H. L. n.d. "Why Was Cotton 'King'?" http://pbs.org/wnet/african-americans -many-rivers-to-cross/history/why-was-cotton-king (accessed May 1, 2014).

Gatto, J. T. 2005. *Dumbing Us Down: The Hidden Curriculum of Compulsory Schooling.* Gabriola Islands, Canada: New Society.

Germany, K. B. n.d. "War on Poverty." http://faculty.virginia.edu/sixties/readings/War %20on%20Poverty%20entry%20Poverty%20Encyclopedia.pdf (accessed February 7, 2012).

Gilens, M. 2012. *Affluence and Influence: Economic Inequality and Political Power in America.* New York: Russell Sage.

Gilens, M., and B. Page. 2014. "Testing Theories of American Politics: Elites, Interest Groups, and Average Citizens." *Perspectives on Politics* 2:564–581. http://journals .cambridge.org/download.php?file=%2FPPS%2FPPS12_03%2FS153759271400 1595a.pdf&code=09b463afaa6fc93e83c2e95bce65491e (accessed October 25, 2014).

Gilson, D., and C. Perot. 2011. "It's the Inequality, Stupid." *Mother Jones,* March– April. http://www.motherjones.com/politics/2011/02/income-inequality-in-america -chart-graph (accessed October 24, 2014).

Gilson, D., and M. Severns. 2013. "How Big Debt on Campus Is Threatening Higher Ed." *Mother Jones,* September–October. http://www.motherjones.com/politics /2013/09/college-student-loans-debt-tuition-charts (accessed October 3, 2013).

Gimenez, M. E. 2005. "Capitalism and the Oppression of Women: Marx Revisited." *Science and Society* 69:11–32.

Giridharadas, A. 2014. "The Immigrant Advantage." *New York Times,* May 25: SR1–SR5.

Giroux, H. E. 2000. *Stealing Innocence: Corporate Culture's War on Children.* New York: Palgrave.

Glaeser, E. L. 2011. "Rethinking the Federal Bias Toward Homeownership." *Cityscape: A Journal of Policy Development and Research* 13:5–37.

Goldstein, F. 2008. "Why Bosses Need Wal-Mart." In *Globalization: The Transformation of Social Worlds,* by D. S. Eitzen and M. B. Zinn, 92–96. Belmont, Calif.: Wadsworth.

Goldstein, J. 2014. "Nora Ephron and Why Women Take Jill Abramson's Firing Personally." *Think Progress,* May 16. http://thinkprogress.org/culture/2014/05/16 /3438585/jill-abramson-and-nora-ephron-its-personal (accessed May 24, 2014).

Gomstyn, A. 2010. "Walmart CEO Pay: More in an Hour Than Workers Get All Year?" *ABC News,* July 2. http://abcnews.go.com/Business/walmart-ceo-pay-hour-workers -year/story?id=11067470 (accessed July 14, 2012).

Gooby, P. T. 2005. "Is the Future American? Or, Can Left Politics Preserve European Welfare States from Eroding Through Growing Diversity?" *Journal of Social Policy* 34:661–672.

Greenhouse, S. 2008. *The Big Squeeze: Tough Times for the American Worker.* New York: Alfred A. Knopf.

———. 2011. "Union Membership in the U.S. Fell to a 70 Year Low Last Year." *New York Times,* January 21: Business Day.

————. 2012. "In Standoff, Latest Sign of Unions Under Siege." *New York Times,* September 11: A1, A14.

————. 2013. "The Ecumenical Union." *New York Times,* September 7: B1.

————. 2014. "VW Vote Is Defeat for Labor in the South." *New York Times,* February 15: B1–B2.

————. 2014. "The Walls Close In." *New York Times*, March 17: B1.

Hacker, J., and N. Loewentheil. 2012. "Prosperity Economics: Building an Economy for All." Creative Commons. http://www.prosperityforamerica.org/wp-content /uploads/2012/09/prosperity-for-all.pdf (accessed February 26, 2013).

Hacker, J. S., and P. Pierson. 2010. *Winner-Take-All Politics: How Washington Made the Rich Richer—and Turned Its Back on the Middle Class.* New York: Simon and Schuster.

Hansen, W. W. 1996. *A Frantz Fanon Study Guide.* New York: Grove.

Hardt, M., and A. Negri. 2009. *Commonwealth.* Cambridge: Belknap.

Harmon, A., C. O'Neill, and P. C. Rosier. 2011. "Interwoven Economic Histories: American Indians in a Capitalist America." *Journal of American History* 98:698–722.

Harrington, M. 1962. *The Other America: Poverty in the United States.* New York: Macmillan.

Harvey, D. 2010. *Enigma of Capital—and the Crises of Capitalism.* Oxford: Oxford University Press.

Hedges, C. 2010. "City of Ruins." *The Nation,* November 22. http://www.thenation .com/article/155801/city-ruins#axzz2ZWElO85o (accessed October 20, 2012).

Heilbroner, R. L. 1999. "Commanding Heights: Adam Smith and the Origin of Capitalism." http://www.pbs.org/wgbh/commandingheights/shared/pdf/ess_adam smithorigin.pdf (accessed September 9, 2012).

Herbert, C. E., and W. C. Apgar. 2010. "Report to Congress on the Root Causes of the Foreclosure Crisis." US Department of Housing and Urban Development, January. http://www.huduser.org/publications/pdf/foreclosure_09.pdf (accessed April 17, 2012).

Herman, E. S., and N. Chomsky. 1988. *Manufacturing Consent: The Political Economy of the Mass Media.* New York: Pantheon.

Hernandez, G., L. Kimmel, B. Marshall, C. Martino, M. Ochsner, and M. S. Pabellón. 2014. *Bending Toward Justice: How Latino Immigrants Became Community and Safety Leaders.* New Brunswick, N.J.: Center for Construction Research and Training.

Herrnstein, R., and C. A. Murray. 1994. *The Bell Curve: Intelligence and Class Structure in American Life.* New York: Free Press.

Hill, S. 2010. *Europe's Promise: Why the European Way Is the Best Hope in an Insecure Age.* Berkeley: University of California Press.

Hochschild, A. 1998. *King Leopold's Ghost: A Story of Greed, Terror, and Heroism in Colonial Africa.* New York: Houghton Mifflin.

Hooks, B. 2000. *Where We Stand: Class Matters.* New York: Routledge.

Hout, M., and S. R. Lucas. 2004. "Narrowing the Income Gap Between the Rich and the Poor." In *Race, Class, and Gender in the United States,* by P. Rothenberg, 620–625. New York: Worth.

Hughes, D., H. D. Dean, J. H. Mermin, and K. A. Featon. 2011. "HIV Infection, US 2005 and 2008." Centers for Disease Control and Prevention. http://www.cdc .gov/hiv/risk/racialethnic/aa/facts/index.html (accessed April 28, 2012).

Hung, H., and J. Kucinskas. 2011. "Globalization and Global Inequality: Assessing the Impact of the Rise of China and India, 1980–2005." *American Journal of Sociology* 116:1478–1513.

Hungerford, T. 1. 2012. "Taxes and the Economy." Congressional Research Service, December 12. http://fas.org/sgp/crs/misc/R42729.pdf (accessed October 31, 2014).

Hunt, E. K. 2003. *Property and Prophets: The Evolution of Economic Institutions and Ideologies.* New York: Sharp.

Hursh, D. 2007. "Exacerbating Inequality: The Failed Promise of the No Child Left Behind Act." *Race, Ethnicity, and Education* 10:295–308.

Igra, A. 2006. "Marriage as Welfare." *Women's History Review* 15:601–610.

Ingraham, C. 2014. "Our Infant Mortality Rate Is a National Embarrassment." *Washington Post,* September 29. www.washingtonpost.com/blogs/wonkblog/wp/2014/09/29/our-infant-mortality-rate-is-a-national-embarrassment/ (accessed December 29, 2014).

Inskeep, S. 2010. "Former 'No Child Left Behind' Advocate Turns Critic." March 2. http://www.npr.org/templates/story/story.php?storyId=124209100 (accessed October 31, 2014).

James, C. L. R. 1992. "The Atlantic Slave Trade and Slavery." In *A Turbulent Voyage,* by F. Hayes, 213–236. San Diego: Collegiate.

Jeter, J. 2013. "Worse Than Apartheid: Black in Obama's America." *Black Agenda Report,* October 29. http://www.blackagendareport.com/content/worse_apartheid_black_obama%E2%80%99s_america (accessed May 2, 2014).

Johnson, K. 2013. "A Summer Place in the South Bronx." *New York Times,* July 25: C19.

Johnson, L. B. 1965. "To Fulfill These Rights." Lyndon B. Johnson Library, June 4. http://www.lbjlib.utexas.edu/johnson/archives.hom/speeches.hom/650604.asp (accessed February 3, 2013).

Johnston, D. C. 1999. "The Gap Between Rich and Poor Found Substantially Higher." *New York Times,* September 5: A14.

Justice Policy Institute. 2011. "Gaming the System: How the Political Strategies of the Private Prison Companies Promote Ineffective Incarceration Policies." October. http://www.justicepolicy.org/uploads/justicepolicy/documents/gaming_the_system_executive_summary.pdf (accessed September 11, 2013).

Kahlenberg, R. 1996. *The Remedy: Class, Race, and Affirmative Action.* New York: Basic.

Kahlenberg, R., and M. Z. Marvit. 2013. "Make Organizing a Civil Right." *The Nation,* March 4: 12.

Kaufman, A. C. 2014. "Pope Francis: 'Inequality Is the Root of Social Evil.'" *Huffington Post.* http://www.huffingtonpost.com/2014/04/28/pope-francis-tweet-inequality_n_5227563.html (accessed October 20, 2014).

Kaye, H. J. 2011. "Remembering the 1886 Wis. Tragedy, Where 7 Workers Were Killed." May 2. http://www.aflcio.org/Blog/In-The-States/Remembering-the-1886-Wis.-Tragedy-Where-7-Workers-Were-Killed (accessed May 1, 2013).

Keenan, N. L., and K. A. Rosendorf. 2011. "Prevalence of Hypertension and Controlled Hypertension." Centers for Disease Control and Prevention, January 14. http://www.cdc.gov/mmwr/pdf/other/su6001.pdf (accessed April 26, 2012).

Keenan, N. L., and K. M. Shaw. 2011. "Coronary Heart Disease and Stroke Deaths." Centers for Disease Control and Prevention, January 14. http://www.cdc.gov/mmwr/pdf/other/su6001.pdf (accessed April 26, 2012).

Keynes, J. M. 1930. "Economic Possibilities for Our Grandchildren." In *Essays in Persuasion,* by John Maynard Keynes, 358–373. New York: Norton. http://www.econ.yale.edu/smith/econ116a/keynes1.pdf (accessed October 24, 2014).

Kirvo, L. J., R. D. Peterson, and D. C. Kuhl. 2009. "Segregation, Racial Structure, and Neighborhood Violent Crime." *American Journal of Sociology* 114:1765–1802.

Kitwana, B. 2002. *The Hip Hop Generation: Young Blacks and the Crisis in African American Culture.* New York: Basic Civitas.

Klass, P. 2013. "Poverty's Lasting Ills." *New York Times,* May 14: D4.

Klein, E. 2012. "11 Facts About the Affordable Care Act." *Washington Post,* June 24. http://www.washingtonpost.com/blogs/wonkblog/wp/2012/06/24/11-facts-about -the-affordable-care-act (accessed November 10, 2013).

Knapp, P. 1994. *One World, Many Worlds: Contemporary Sociological Theory.* New York: HarperCollins.

Knapp, P., and A. J. Spector. 2011. *Crisis and Change Today.* Lanham: Rowman and Littlefield.

Kochhar, R., R. Fry, and P. Taylor. 2011. "Wealth Gap Rises to Record Highs Between Whites, Blacks, Hispanics." *Pew Research Social and Demographic Trends,* July 26. www.pewsocialtrends.org/2011/07/26/wealth-gaps-rise-to-record-highs-between -whites-blacks-hispanics/ (accessed October 27, 2014).

Kollmeyer, C. 2005. "Explaining Consensual Domination: Moving Beyond the Concept of Hegemony." eScholarship, Global and International Studies, University of California. https://escholarship.org/uc/item/0rj9f4dm#page-1 (accessed November 23, 2014).

———. 2009. "Explaining Deindustrialization: How Affluence, Productivity, Growth, and Globalization Diminish Manufacturing Employment." *American Journal of Sociology* 114:1644–1674.

Korten, D. C. 1996. "The Mythic Victory of Market Capitalism." In *The Case Against the Global Economy,* by J. Mander and E. Goldsmith, 183–191. San Francisco: Sierra Club.

Kozol, J. 1991. *Savage Inequalities: Children in America's Schools.* New York: Harper Perennial.

———. 2001. *When Corporations Rule the World.* Bloomfield, Conn.: Kumarian.

Kristof, N. 2012. "Poverty's Poster Child." *New York Times,* May 9: A29.

———. 2014. "It's Now the Canadian Dream." *New York Times,* May 15: A29.

———. 2014. "When Whites Just Don't Get It." *New York Times,* August 31: SR11.

Krochmal, M. 2010. "An Unmistakably Working Class Vision: Birmingham's Foot Soldiers and Their Civil Rights Movement." *Journal of Southern History* 76:923–960.

Kroll, A. 2014. "Meet the New Kochs: The DeVos Clan's Plan to Defund the Left." *Mother Jones,* January–February: 18–25.

Krugman, P. 2011. "The Social Contract." *New York Times,* September 23: A35.

———. 2013a. "Free to Be Hungry." *New York Times,* September 23: A23.

———. 2013b. "Sympathy for the Luddites." *New York Times,* June 14: A27.

———. 2014a. "Now That's Rich." *New York Times,* May 9: A27.

———. 2014b. "Three Expensive Milliseconds." *New York Times,* April 14: A23.

Kull, S., C. Ramsay, E. Lewis, and P. Warf. 2003. "Misperceptions, the Media, and the Iraq War." *Political Science Quarterly* 118:569–598. http://www.uky.edu/AS /PoliSci/Peffley/pdf/475%20PIPA%20MisperceptionsofIraqWar_10_02_03.pdf (accessed October 30, 2014).

Labaree, D. E. 2000. "No Exit: Public Education as an Inescapably Public Good." In *Reconstructing the Common Good in Education: Coping with Intractable American Dilemmas,* by L. Cuban and D. Shipps, 110–129. Stanford: Stanford University Press.

Lafer, G., and S. Allegretto. 2011. "Does 'Right to Work' Create Jobs? Answers from Oklahoma." Briefing paper. Washington, D.C.: Economic Policy Institute. http:// www.epi.org/publication/bp300/ (accessed June 8, 2013).

————. 2012. "Right to Work—for Less." *The Nation,* February 6: 24–26.

Lawrence, K. 1976. "Karl Marx on American Slavery." Sojourner Truth. http://www
.sojournertruth.net/marxslavery.pdf (accessed October 6, 2012).

Leach, J. 2013. "Citizen's United: Robbing America of Its Democratic Idealism."
Daedalus: The Journal of the American Academy of Arts and Sciences 2:95–
101.

LeBaron, G., and A. Roberts. 2010. "Towards a Feminist Political Economy of Capitalism and Carcerality." *Signs: Journal of Women in Culture and Society* 36:
19–44.

Lee, S. 2012. "By the Numbers: The Growing For-Profit Detention Industry." *Mother
Jones,* June 21. http://www.motherjones.com/politics/2012/06/prison-profit
-industry-corporation-money-jail (accessed July 14, 2013).

Lehmann, C. 2012. "Winging It." *The Nation,* April 9: 33–48.

Leonard, A. 2010. *The Story of Stuff.* New York: Free Press.

Leonhardt, D. 2008. "Washington's Invisible Hand." *New York Times,* September 28:
MM32.

————. 2012. "Globalization and the Income Slowdown." *New York Times Economix
Blog,* August 21. http://economix.blogs.nytimes.com/2012/08/21/globalization
-and-the-income-slowdown (accessed November 10, 2012).

Levene, M. 2005. *Genocide and the Age of the Nation State: The Rise of the West and
the Coming of the Genocide.* New York: I. B. Tairus.

Levine, L. 2012. "The U.S. Income Distribution and Mobility: Trends and International
Comparisons." Congressional Research Service, November 29. https://www.fas
.org/sgp/crs/misc/R42400.pdf (accessed February 3, 2013).

Levine, M. V. 2010. "Race and Male Employment in the Wake of the Great Recession."
Working paper. Milwaukee: Center for Economic Development, University of
Wisconsin.

Levy, F., and P. Temin. 2007. "Inequality and Institutions in the 20th Century." Working
paper. Cambridge: Industrial Performance Center, Massachusetts Institute of
Technology.

Lewis, O. 1966. "The Culture of Poverty." *American* 215:19–25. http://lchc.ucsd
.edu/MCA/Mail/xmcamail.2010_11.dir/pdfKPNFlustp6.pdf (accessed October
20, 2014).

Lichtblau, E. 2011. "Economic Downturn Took a Detour at Capitol Hill." *New York
Times,* December 27: A1.

Lichtenstein, N. 2010. "Why American Unions Need Intellectuals." *Dissent* (Spring):
69–73.

Limerick, P. N. 1987. *The Legacy of Conquest: The Unbroken Past of the American
West.* New York: Norton.

Lin, S. G. 2006. "Undocumented Workers in the U.S." *Economic and Political Weekly*
41:4867–4872.

Lindhorst, T., and R. J. Mancoske. 2006. "The Social and Economic Impact of Sanctions and Time Limits on Recipients of Temporary Assistance to Needy Families."
Journal of Sociology and Social Welfare 33:93–114.

Lipman, P. 2002. "Making the Global City, Making Inequality: The Political Economy
and Cultural Politics of Chicago School Policy." *American Educational Research
Journal* 39:379–419.

————. 2004. *High Stakes Education: Inequality, Globalization, and Urban School
Reform.* New York: Routledge.

————. 2011. *The New Political Economy of Urban Education: Neoliberalism, Race,
and the Right to the City.* New York: Routledge.

Logan, J. 2006. "The Union Avoidance Industry in the United States." *British Journal of Industrial Relations* 44:651–675.

———. 2014. "Why Are GOP Politicians and Anti-Union Groups Interfering with the UAW Vote?" *Truthout,* February 14. http://truth-out.org/opinion/item/21856-why-are-gop-politicians-and-anti-union-groups-interfering-with-the-vw-vote (accessed February 26, 2014).

Lohr, S. 2011. "More Jobs Predicted for Machines, Not People." *New York Times,* October 24: B3.

Lowrey, A. 2013a. "Income Flat in Recovery, but Not for the 1%." *New York Times,* February 16: B1.

———. 2013b. "Top 10% Took Home Half of U.S. Income in 2012." *New York Times,* September 11: B4.

———. 2014a. "Cities Advance Their Fight Against Rising Inequality." *New York Times,* April 7: A1–A3.

———. 2014b. "Even Among the Richest of the Rich, Fortunes Diverge." *New York Times,* February 11: F2.

Luscombe, B. 2013. "Confidence Women." *Time,* March 18: 36–40.

Lynch, R. L., and P. Oakford. 2013. "National and State by State Economic Benefits of Immigration Reform." Center for American Progress, May 17. http://www.american progress.org/wp-content/uploads/2013/05/EconomicsOfLegalization-2.pdf (accessed June 8, 2013).

MacDorman, M. F., and T. J. Mathews. 2011. "Infant Deaths: United States, 2000–2007." Centers for Disease Control and Prevention, January 14. http://www.cdc .gov/mmwr/preview/mmwrhtml/su6001a9.htm?s_cid=su6001a9_w (accessed April 28, 2012).

MacDorman, M. F., T. J. Mathews, A. D. Mohangoo, and J. Zeitlin. 2014. "International Comparisons of Infant Mortality and Related Factors: United States and Europe, 2010." *National Vital Statistics Report,* September 24:1–7.

Magdoff, F., and J. B. Foster. 2013. "Class War and Labor's Declining Share." *Monthly Review* 65:1–11.

Mandel, E. 1990. Introduction to *Capital: A Critique of Political Economy,* vol. 1, by K. Marx, 11–86. London: Penguin.

Mani, A., S. Mullainathan, E. Shafir, and J. Zhao. 2013. "Poverty Impedes Cognitive Function." *Science* 341:976–980.

Manik, J. A., and J. Yardley. 2013. "Building Collapse in Bangladesh Kills Scores of Garment Workers." *New York Times,* April 25: A1.

Manning, J. 2001. "Unleashing the Spirit: The Reagan Administration's Indian Policy." Eighties Club. http://eightiesclub.tripod.com/id54.htm (accessed March 14, 2013).

Marable, M. 2000. *How Capitalism Underdeveloped Black America.* Cambridge, Mass.: South End Press.

———. 2011. *Malcolm X: A Life of Reinvention.* New York: Penguin.

Markham, E. 2011. "The Real Value of the Minimum Wage." July 22. http://www .raisetheminimumwage.com/media-center/entry/the-real-value-of-the-minimum -wage (accessed September 9, 2012).

Marx, K. 1990. *Capital: A Critique of Political Economy.* Vol. 1. London: Penguin.

Marx, K., and F. Engels. 1998. *The Communist Manifesto.* New York: Verso.

Massey, D. S. 2009. "Globalization and Inequality: Explaining American Exceptionalism." *European Sociological Review* (August): 9–23. http://www.esr.oxfordjournals .org/content/25/1/9.short (accessed July 14, 2012).

Masters, M. J., and J. T. Delaney. 2005. "Organized Labor's Political Scorecard." *Journal of Labor Research* 26:365–392.

Maybury-Lewis, D. 2002. *Indigenous People, Ethnic Groups, and the State.* Boston: Allyn and Bacon.

McClelland, M. 2013. "Schizophrenic Killer: My Cousin." *Mother Jones,* May–June: 21.

McCrate, E. 1996. "Samuel Bowles and Herbert Gintis." In *American Economists of the Late Twentieth Century,* by W. J. Samuels, 1–10. Cheltenham: Elgar.

McIntyre, R. S., M. Gardner, R. J. Wilkins, and R. Phillips. 2011. "Corporate Taxpayers & Corporate Tax Dodgers." Citizens for Tax Justice, November. http://www .ctj.org/corporatetaxdodgers/CorporateTaxDodgersReport.pdf (accessed January 17, 2013).

McQuaid, J. 2000. "Unwelcome Neighbors: Civil Rights and the Environment." *Times-Picayune,* May 21: special report.

Meyerson, H. 2011. "Corporate America's Chokehold on Wages." *Washington Post,* July 19. http://www.washingtonpost.com/opinions/corporate-americas-choke hold-on-wages/2011/07/19/gIQAL2ieOI_story.html (accessed October 29, 2014).

———. 2012. "If Labor Dies, What's Next?" *The American Prospect* (September/ October):19–29.

Milkman, R. 2011. "Immigrant Workers, Precarious Work, and the US Labor Movement." *Globalizations* 8:361–372.

Miller, C. C. 2014. "Pay Gap Is Because of Gender, Not Jobs." *New York Times,* April 24: B3.

———. 2014. "Where Are the Gay Chief Executives?" *New York Times,* May 18: SR4.

Miller, R. L. 2001. "Confiscations from Japanese-Americans During World War II." Forfeiture Endangers American Rights, November 6. http://www.fear.org /RMillerJ-A.html (accessed August 15, 2012).

Mills, C. W. 1948. *The New Men of Power: America's Labor Leaders.* New York: Harcourt Brace.

Mills, C. W. 1956. *The Power Elite.* New York: Oxford University Press.

Mink, G. 1988. *Welfare's End.* Ithaca: Cornell University Press.

Mishel, L., and N. Sabadish. 2012. "CEO Pay and the Top 1%: How Executive Compensation and Financial Sector Pay Have Fueled Income Inequality." Economic Policy Institute, May 2. http://www.epi.org/publication/ib331-ceo-pay-top-1 -percent (accessed July 14, 2012).

Misra, A. 2007. "Who Were the Sepoys of 1857?" *Indian Express,* May 8. http:// archive.indianexpress.com/news/who-were-the-sepoys-of-1857/30394 (accessed May 20, 2014).

Mitchell, T. 2000. "Turning Points: Reconstruction and the Growth of National Influence in Education." In *Reconstructing the Common Good in Education,* by L. Cuban and D. Shipps, 32–50. Stanford: Stanford University Press.

Mohanty, C. T. 1998. "On Being South Asian in North America." In *Race, Class, and Gender in the United States: An Integrated Study,* by P. S. Rothenberg, 270–276. New York: St. Martin's.

Moller, S., A. S. Alderson, and F. Nielsen. 2009. "Changing Patterns of Income Inequality in U.S. Counties, 1970–2000." *American Journal of Sociology* 114:1037–1049.

Moody, Kim. 2012. "Contextualising Organised Labour in Expansion and Crisis: The Case of the US." *Historical Materialism* 20:3–30.

Moonsinghe, R., J. Zhu, and B. I. Truman. 2011. "Health Insurance Coverage: United States, 2004 and 2008." Centers for Disease Control and Prevention, January 14. http://www.cdc.gov/mmwr/preview/mmwrhtml/su6001a6.htm?s_cid=su6001a6_w (accessed May 10, 2012).

Moreno, P. 2010. "Unions and Discrimination." *Cato Journal* 30:67–85.

Moretti, E. 2012. *The New Geography of Jobs.* New York: Houghton Mifflin Harcourt.

Morgenson, G., and J. Rosner. 2011. *Reckless Endangerment: How Outsized Ambition, Greed, and Corruption Created the Worst Financial Crisis of Our Time.* New York: Henry Holt.

Motoko, R. 2012. "Segregation Prominent in Schools, Study Finds." *New York Times,* September 12: A16.

Murray, C. 2012. *Coming Apart: The State of White America, 1960–2010.* New York: Crown.

Nasar, S. 1992. "Even Among the Well-Off, the Richest Get Richer." *New York Times,* March 5: A1.

Nation Action. 2013. "Tell CEO Mike Duke: Walmart Workers Deserve a Raise." *The Nation,* June 6. http://www.thenation.com/blog/174698/tell-ceo-mike-duke-walmart -workers-deserve-raise#axzz2WihhxxGq (accessed July 14, 2013).

National Academy of Public Administration. 2003. "Addressing Community Concerns: How Environmental Justice Relates to Land Use and Zoning." July. http:// www.epa.gov/compliance/ej/.../napa_land_use_zoning_63003.pdf (accessed April 22, 2012).

National Alliance to End Homelessness. 2012a. "Rapid Re-Housing: Successfully Ending Family Homelessness." May 21. http://www.endhomelessness.org/library /entry/rapid-re-housing-successfully-ending-family-homelessness (accessed November 10, 2012).

———. 2012b. "The State of Homelessness in America, 2012." http://www.end homelessness.org/library/entry/the-state-of-homelessness-in-america-2012 (accessed July 14, 2012).

National Association for the Advancement of Colored People (NAACP). 2008. "Criminal Justice Fact Sheet." http://www.naacp.org/pages/criminal-justice-fact-sheet (accessed March 1, 2013).

National Center for Education Statistics. 2010–2011. "Tuition Facts of Colleges and Universities." http://nces.ed.gov/fastfacts/display.asp?id=76 (accessed December 15, 2013).

National Coalition for the Homeless. 2009. "Mental Illness and Homelessness." July. http://www.nationalhomeless.org/factsheets/Mental_Illness.html (accessed May 2, 2012).

National Immigration Forum. 2013. "The Math of Immigration Detention: Runaway Costs for Immigration Detention Do Not Add Up to Sensible Policies." August. http://www.immigrationforum.org/images/uploads/mathofimmigrationdetention .pdf (accessed September 11, 2013).

National Public Radio. 2013. "Quality vs. Quantity: Evaluating the Jobs Report." *All Things Considered,* August 2. http://www.npr.org/templates/story/story.php? storyId=208351255 (accessed August 4, 2013).

National Women's Law Center. 2013. "National Snapshot: Poverty Among Women and Families, 2012." http://www.nwlc.org/sites/default/files/pdfs/povertysnapshot 2012.pdf (accessed October 27, 2014).

Navarro, M. 2013. "In New York, Having a Job, or 2, Doesn't Mean Having a Home." *New York Times,* September 17: A1.

Nelson, C. A., and M. Sheridan. 2011. "Lessons from Neuroscience Research for Understanding Causal Links Between Family and Neighborhood Characteristics and Educational Outcomes." In *Whither Opportunity? Rising Inequality, Schools, and Children's Life Chances,* by G. J. Duncan and R. J. Murnane, 27–46. New York: Russell Sage.

Neuman, W. 2014. "For Miners, Increasing Risk on a Mountain at the Heart of Bolivia's Identity." *New York Times,* September 14: A9.

New American Foundation. 2013. "Federal Education Budget Project: Background and

Analysis." June 30. http://febp.newamerica.net/background-analysis/school
finance (accessed February 3, 2014).

New York Times. 2011. "So Much for the Nativists." Editorial, October 27: A30.

———. 2012. "Shuttering Bad Charter Schools." Editorial, February 21: A24.

———. 2013a. "Abandoned in Indian Country; Sequester Cuts Bring Misery to the
Reservations, but Congress Offers No Response." Editorial, July 24: A22.

———. 2013b. "The Sequester Hits the Reservation." Editorial, March 21: A26.

Newman, N. 2002. *Net Loss: Internet Prophets, Private Profits, and the Costs to Community.* University Park: Pennsylvania State University Press.

Nichols, J. 2011. "The Spirit of Wisconsin: How Scott Walker's Union Busting Spurred
a Popular Uprising." *The Nation,* February 19: 13–16.

Nixon, R. 2013. "Anti-Hunger Advocates Put Pressure on Lawmakers over Food
Stamps Bill." *New York Times,* September 18: A19.

Norris, T., P. L. Vines, and E. M. Hoeffel. 2012. "The American Indian and Alaska Native Population, 2010." January. http://www.census.gov/prod/cen2010/briefs
/c2010br-10.pdf (accessed September 11, 2012).

North, D. C. 1966. *The Economic Growth of the United States, 1790–1860.* New York:
Norton.

Northrup, H. R. 1944. *Organized Labor and the Negro.* New York: Harper and Brothers.

Omi, M., and H. Winant. 2004. "Racial Formation." In *Race, Class, and Gender in the
United States,* by Paula Rothenberg, 12–21. New York: Worth.

Oorschot, W. V. 2008. "Solidarity Towards Immigrants in European Welfare States."
International Journal of Social Welfare 17:3–14.

Organization for Economic Cooperation and Development (OECD). 2008. "Growing
Unequal? Income Distribution and Poverty in OECD Countries." October.
https://www.mzv.sk/App/wcm/media.nsf/vw_ByID/ID_CBD2FABFAB495B52C
1257648003959F2_SK/$File/Growing%20Unequal.pdf (accessed July 14, 2013).

Pager, D., B. Western, and B. Bonikowski. 2009. "Discrimination in a Low-Wage Market: A Field Experiment." *American Sociological Review* 74:777–799.

Parenti, M. 1994. *Land of Idols: Political Mythology in America.* New York: St. Martin's.

Parry, Marc. 2012. "The Neighborhood Effect." *Chronicle of Higher Education,* November 5. http://chronicle.com/article/The-Neighborhood-Effect/135492 (accessed
March 15, 2013).

Pattillo-McCoy, M. 1999. *Black Picket Fences: Privilege and Peril Among the Black
Middle Class.* Chicago: University of Chicago Press.

Pazzanese, C. 2014. "Punitive Damages." *Harvard Gazette,* May 13. http://news
.harvard.edu/gazette/story/2014/05/punitive-damages (accessed May 24, 2014).

Pear, R. 2013. "Doctors Who Profit from Radiation Prescribe It More Often, Study
Finds." *New York Times,* August 19: A12.

Pearce, D. 1978. "Feminization of Poverty: Women, Work and Welfare." *The Urban
and Social Change Review* 11:28–36. http://socialworkers.org/feminization
ofpoverty/presentations/pearce/Pearce_The%20Feminization%20of%20Poverty
_1978%20original%20article.pdf (accessed October 27, 2014).

Pena, M. 2013. "Trabajadores de Restaurantes Ganan Menos y Gastan Mas en Guarderias." *Reporte Hispano,* July 12–18: 2.

Penny, L. 2013. "What's the Point of Smashing the Glass Ceiling for a Few Women,
When So Many Live in Poverty?" *New Statesman,* January 25: 18.

Perlstein, D. 2000. "'There Is No Escape from the Ogre of Indoctrination': George
Counts and the Civic Dilemmas of Democratic Educators." In *Reconstructing the
Common Good in Education,* by L. Cuban and D. Shipps, 51–67. Stanford: Stanford University Press.

Peters, J. W. 2013. "No Pay? Little Sacrifice for Many in Congress." *New York Times,* January 30: A13.

Pew Center on the States. 2011. "State of Recidivism: The Revolving Door of America's Prisons." April. https://www.michigan.gov/documents/corrections/Pew _Report_State_of_Recidivism_350337_7.pdf (accessed October 28, 2014).

Phillips, K. 1990. *The Politics of Rich and Poor: Wealth and the American Electorate in the Reagan Aftermath.* New York: Random House.

———. 2002. *Wealth and Democracy: A Political History of the American Rich.* New York: Broadway.

Phillips, M. 2011. "Parenting, Time Use, and Disparities in Academic Outcomes." In *Whither Opportunity? Rising Inequality, Schools, and Children's Life Chances,* by G. J. Duncan and R. J. Murnane, 208–211. New York: Russell Sage.

Philpott, T. 2013. "McDonald's to Employees: Get a (Second) Job." *Mother Jones,* July 26. http://www.motherjones.com/tom-philpott/2013/07/mcdonalds-budget-mcwrap (accessed September 11, 2013).

Piketty, T., and E. Saez. 2004. "Income Inequality in the United States, 1913–2002." http://elsa.berkeley.edu/~saez/piketty-saezOUP04US.pdf (accessed January 17, 2012).

Pollitt, K. 2011. "The Poor: Still Here, Still Poor." *The Nation,* September 26: 10.

Porter, E. 2014. "In the U.S., Punishment Comes Before the Crimes." *New York Times,* April 30: B1.

Povich, D., B. Roberts, and M. Mather. 2013. "Low-Income Working Mothers and State Policy: Investigating for a Better Economic Future." Washington, D.C.: Working Poor Families Project.

Putnam, R. D. 2000. *Bowling Alone: The Collapse and Revival of American Community.* New York: Simon and Schuster.

Rachleff, P. 2012. "Labor History for the Future." *Social Policy* (Fall):34–36.

Rampell, C. 2012. "Majority of Jobs Added in the Recovery Pay Low Wages, Study Finds." *New York Times,* August 31: B1.

———. 2013. "It Takes a B.A. to Find a Job As a File Clerk." *New York Times,* February 20: A1.

Rattner, S. 2012. "The Rich Get Even Richer." *New York Times,* March 25: A27.

———. 2014. "The Myth of Industrial Rebound," *New York Times,* January 25. http://www.nytimes.com/2014/01/26/opinion/sunday/rattner-the-myth-of -industrial-rebound.html?module=Search&mabReward=relbias%3As (accessed October 24, 2014).

Ravitch, D. 2010. *The Death and Life of the Great American School System: How Testing and Choice Are Undermining Education.* New York: Basic.

———. 2012. "Schools We Can Envy." *New York Review of Books,* March 8: 25.

Ray, R., M. Sanes, and J. Schmitt. 2013. "No-Vacation Nation Revisited." Center for Economic and Policy Research, May. http://www.cepr.net/documents/publications /no-vacation-update-2013-05.pdf (accessed July 21, 2013).

Rayfield, Jillian. 2013. "Santorum: Term 'Middle Class' Is 'Marxism Talk.'" *Salon,* August 16. http://www.salon.com/2013/08/16/santorum_term_middle_class_is _marxism_talk (accessed May 26, 2014).

Raymond, J., W. Wheeler, and M. J. Brown. 2011. "Inadequate and Unhealthy Housing, 2007 and 2009." Centers for Disease Control and Prevention, January 14. http://www.cdc.gov/mmwr/preview/mmwrhtml/su6001a4.htm (accessed April 26, 2012).

Reardon, S. F. 2011. "The Widening Academic Achievement Gap Between the Rich and the Poor: New Evidence and Possible Explanations." In *Whither Opportu-*

nity? Rising Inequality, Schools, and Children's Life Chances, by G. J. Duncan and R. J. Murnane, 91–115. New York: Russell Sage.

Reardon, S. F., and K. Bischoff. 2011a. "Growth in the Residential Segregation of Families by Income, 1970–2009." US2010 Project, November. http://graphics8 .nytimes.com/packages/pdf/national/RussellSageIncomeSegregationreport.pdf (accessed May 27, 2012).

———. 2011b. "Income Inequality and Income Segregation." *American Journal of Sociology* 116:1092–1153.

Reese, W. J. 2000. "Public Schools and the Elusive Search for the Public Good." In *Reconstructing the Public Good in Education,* by L. Cuban and D. Shipps, 13–31. Stanford: Stanford University Press.

———. 2005. *America's Public Schools: From the Common School to "No Child Left Behind."* Baltimore: Johns Hopkins University Press.

Reeves, R. 2013. "The Glass Floor Problem." *New York Times,* September 9. http://opinionator.blogs.nytimes.com/2013/09/29/the_glass_floor_problem (accessed February 3, 2014).

Reich, M. 1981. *Racial Inequality: The Political Economic Analysis.* Princeton, N.J.: Princeton University Press.

Remes, J. 2012. "May Day's Radical History." *Salon,* April 30. http://www.salon .com/2012/04/30/may_days_radical_history (accessed May 2, 2013).

Rifkin, J. 1996. "New Technology and the End of Jobs." In *The Case Against the Global Economy,* by J. Mander and E. Goldsmith, 108–121. San Francisco: Sierra Club.

Ritzer, G., and D. J. Goodman. 2004. *Sociological Theory.* Boston: McGraw-Hill.

Roberts, S. 2013. "Poverty Rate Up in City, and Income Gap Is Wide, Census Data Show." *New York Times,* September 19: A24.

Robertson, I. 1987. *Sociology.* New York: Worth Publishers.

Robinson, W. I. 2006. "'Aqui Estamos y No Nos Vamos!' Global Capital and Immigrant Rights." *Race and Class* 48:77–91.

Rockman, S. 2005. "Liberty Is Land and Slaves: The Great Contradiction." *Organization of American Historians (OAH) Magazine of History* (May):8–11.

———. 2012. "The Future of Civil War Era Studies." *Journal of the Civil War Era,* February. http://journalofthecivilwarera.com/wp-content/uploads/2012/2/Final -Rockman.pdf (accessed April 15, 2014).

Rodda, D. T., and J. Goodman. 2005. "Recent House Price Trends and Homeownership Affordability." US Department of Housing and Urban Development, May. http:// www.huduser.org/Publications/pdf/RecentHousePrice_P1.pdf (accessed April 5, 2012).

Roediger, D. 1999. *The Wages of Whiteness.* London: Verso.

Rose, S. 2013. "The Social Inequality of Public Transport." March 25. http://suite 101.com/article/the-social-inequality-of-public-transit-a229957 (accessed March 29, 2013).

Rosenthal, E. 2013. "The $2.7 Trillion Medical Bill." *New York Times,* June 2: A1.

Rosier, P. C. 2006. "'They Are Ancestral Homelands': Race, Place, and Politics in Cold War Native America, 1945–1961." *Journal of American History* (March):1300–1326.

Rugh, J. S., and D. S. Massey. 2010. "Racial Segregation and the American Foreclosure Crisis." *American Sociological Review* 75:629–651.

Russakoff, D. 2014. "Schooled." *The New Yorker,* May 19: 58–73.

Saez, E. 2009. "Striking It Richer: The Evolution of Top Incomes in the United States." August 5. http://elsa.berkeley.edu/~saez/saez-UStopincomes-2007.pdf (accessed July 14, 2012).

————. 2013. "Striking It Richer: The Evolution of Top Incomes in the United States (Updated with 2012 Preliminary Estimates)." September 3. http://eml.berkeley.edu/~saez/saez-UStopincomes-2012.pdf (accessed February 7, 2014).

Saez, E., and T. Piketty. 2013. "Why the 1% Should Pay Tax at 80%." *The Guardian,* October 24. http://www.theguardian.com/commentisfree/2013/oct/24/1percent-pay-tax-rate-80percent (accessed October 25, 2014).

Samuelson, Paul. 1976. *Economics.* New York: McGraw-Hill.

Sanati, C. 2009. "10 Years Later, Looking at Repeal of Glass-Steagall." *New York Times,* November 12. http://dealbook.nytimes.com/2009/11/12/10-years-later-looking-at-repeal-of-glass-steagall (accessed November 10, 2012).

Schaap, J. I. 2010. "The Growth of the Native American Gaming Industry: What Has the Past Provided and What Does the Future Hold?" *American Indian Quarterly* 34:365–389.

Schmidt, W. E. 1984. "Trial May Focus on Race Genetics." *New York Times*, September 6. http://www.nytimes.com/1984/09/06/us/trial-may-focus-on-race-genetics.html (accessed October 23, 2014).

Schor, J. B. 1991. *The Overworked American.* New York: Basic.

————. 1998. *The Overspent American: Why We Want What We Don't Need.* New York: Harper Perennial.

Scott, R. E. 2011. "US-Mexico Trade and Job Displacement After NAFTA." Economic Policy Institute, May 23. http://www.epi.org/publication/heading_south_u-s-mexico_trade_and_job_displacement_after_nafta1 (accessed July 14, 2012).

Seccombe, K., D. James, and K. Walters. 1998. "'They Think You Ain't Much of Nothing': The Social Construction of the Welfare Mother." *Journal of Marriage and Family* 60:849–865.

Segal, D. 2012. "Apple's Retail Army, Long on Loyalty but Short on Pay." *New York Times,* June 24: A1.

Segura, D. A., and P. Zavella. 2007. *Women and Migration: In the U.S.-Mexico Borderlands.* Durham: Duke University Press.

Sen, A. 2000. *Development and Freedom.* New York: Knopf.

Sengupta, R. 2010. "Alt-A: The Forgotten Segment of the Mortgage Market." *Federal Reserve Bank of St. Loius Review* (January/February):55–72. http://research.stlouisfed.org/publications/review/10/01/Sengupta.pdf (accessed October 22, 2014).

The Sentencing Project, 2012. "Trends In U.S. Corrections." http://sentencingproject.org/doc/publications/inc_Trends_in_Corrections_Fact_sheet.pdf (accessed October 28, 2014).

Sharkey, P. 2013. *Stuck in Place: Urban Neighborhoods and the End of Progress Towards Racial Equality.* Chicago: University of Chicago Press.

Shear, M. D. 2013. "Torches and Pitchforks for I.R.S. but Cheers for Apple." *New York Times,* May 23: B1.

Shelby, T. 2014. "It's the Economy: A Historian Argues That America's Supposed Racial Problems Are in Fact Caused by Economic Exploitation." *New York Times Review of Books,* February 16: 19.

Shepard, D. S., E. Setren, and D. Cooper. 2011. "Hunger in America: Suffering We All Pay For." Center for American Progress, October 5. http://www.americanprogress.org/issues/poverty/report/2011/10/05/10504/hunger-in-america (accessed May 15, 2012).

Sherman, A., D. Trisi, and M. Broaddus. 2013. "Census Data Show Poverty and Inequality Remained High in 2012 and Median Income Was Stagnant, but Fewer Americans Were Uninsured." Center on Budget and Policy Priorities, September 20. http://www.cbpp.org/files/9-20-13pov.pdf (accessed October 16, 2014).

Short, K. 2011. "The Research: Supplemental Poverty Measure: 2010." US Census Bureau, November. http://www.census.gov/prod/2011pubs/p60-241.pdf (accessed May 15, 2012).

Shorto, R. 2009. "How I Learned to Love the European Welfare State." *New York Times Magazine,* May 3: 42–47.

Silver-Greenberg, J., and N. D. Schwartz. 2012. "Citigroup's Chief Rebuffed on Pay by Shareholders." *New York Times,* April 18: A1.

Singer, P. 2002. *One World: The Ethics of Globalization.* New Haven: Yale University Press.

Skocpol, T., and V. Williamson. 2012. *The Tea Party and the Remaking of Republican Conservatism.* New York: Oxford University Press.

Smith, A. 1937. *An Inquiry into the Nature and Causes of the Wealth of Nations.* New York: Random.

Smith, M. 2013. "The Retirement Gamble." PBS *Frontline,* April. http://www.pbs .org/wgbh/pages/frontline/retirement-gamble (accessed May 2, 2013).

Smith, R. J. 2006. "Family Caps in Welfare Reform: Their Coercive Effects and Damaging Consequences." *Harvard Journal of Law and Gender* 29:151–200.

Sorkin, A. R. 2012. "Suggestions for an Apple Shopping List." *New York Times,* July 21: B1.

Southern Poverty Law Center. 2009. *Under Siege: Life for Low-Income Latinos in the South.* Montgomery, Ala.

Spence, M., and S. Hlatshwayo. 2011. "The Evolving Structure of the American Economy and the Employment Challenge." Working paper. New York: Council on Foreign Relations.

Stampp, K. 1969. *The Peculiar Institution: Slavery in the Ante-Bellum South.* New York: Knopf.

Stannard, D. 1992. *American Holocaust: Columbus and the Conquest of the New World.* New York: Oxford University Press.

Starr, P. 1991. "The Mirage of Reform." In *Crisis in American Institutions,* by J. Skolnick and E. Currie, 405–425. New York: HarperCollins.

Stern, A. 2013. "Unions and Civic Engagement: How the Assault on Labor Endangers Civil Society." *Daedalus: The Journal of the American Academy of Arts and Sciences* 2:119–138.

Stevenson, A. 2014. "Hedge Fund Moguls' Pay Has 1% Looking Up." *New York Times,* May 6: B1–B2.

Stiglitz, J. E. 2006. *Making Globalization Work.* New York: Norton.

Stille, A. 2011. "The Paradox of the New Elite." *New York Times Sunday Review,* October 23: 1.

Story, L. 2012. "United States of Subsidies." *New York Times,* December 2–4: series.

Stroud, M. 2013. "Philadelphia Schools Closing While a New $400 Million Prison Is Under Construction: Could It Be Worse Than It Sounds?" *Forbes,* June 17. http://www.forbes.com/sites/mattstroud/2013/06/17/philadelphia-schools-closing -while-new-400-million-prison-under-construction/2 (accessed September 11, 2013).

Sweeney, M. M. 2011. "Family Structure Instability and Adolescent Educational Outcome: A Focus on Families with Stepfathers." In *Whither Opportunity? Rising Inequality, Schools, and Children's Life Chances,* by G. J. Duncan and R. J. Murnane, 229–252. New York: Russell Sage.

Tabb, W. K. 2001. *The Amoral Elephant: Globalization and the Struggle for Social Justice in the Twenty-First Century.* New York: Monthly Review Press.

Takaki, R. 1993. *A Different Mirror: A History of Multicultural America.* Boston: Little, Brown.

Tandon, A., C. J. L. Murray, J. A. Lauer, and D. B. Evans. 2000. "Measuring Overall Health System Performance for 191 Countries." World Health Organization. http://www.who.int/healthinfo/paper30.pdf (accessed November 10, 2013).

Tavernise, S. 2012. "Poor Dropping Further Behind Rich in School." *New York Times,* February 10: A1.

———. 2012. "Survey Finds Rising Tension Between Rich and Poor." *New York Times,* January 11: A15.

Terkel, S. 2004. "C. P. Ellis." In *Race, Class, and Gender in the United States,* by P. S. Rothenberg, 423–433. New York: Worth.

Thomas, A. R. 1998. "Ronald Reagan and the Commitment of the Mentally Ill: Capital, Interest Groups, and the Eclipse of Social Policy." *Electronic Journal of Sociology.* http://www.sociology.org/content/vol003.004/thomas.html (accessed April 20, 2012).

Tillett, R. 2005. "Reality Consumed by Realty: The Ecological Costs of 'Development' in Leslie Marmon Silko's *Almanac of the Dead.*" *European Journal of American Culture* 24:153–169.

Tilly, C. 1998. *Durable Inequality.* Berkeley: University of California Press.

Turner, A. 2012. "Is Modern Finance a Productive Economic Activity?" *The Globalist,* August 3. http://www.theglobalist.com/StoryId.aspx?StoryId=9705 (accessed October 6, 2012).

Tyson, L. D. 2012. "Why Manufacturing Still Matters." *New York Times,* February 10. http://economix.blogs.nytimes.com/2012/02/10/why-manufacturing-still-matters/?module=Search&mabReward=relbias%3As (accessed October 24, 2014).

US Bureau of Labor Statistics. 2012. "Increasing Labor Productivity: A Mixed Blessing?" November 8. http://www.triplepundit.com/2012/01/increasing-labor-productivity-mixed-blessing (accessed December 15, 2012).

———. 2013a. "Household Data Annual Averages: Median Weekly Earnings of Full Time Wage and Salary Workers by Detailed Occupation and Sex." http://www.bls.gov/cps/cpsaat39.pdf (accessed May 1, 2013).

———. 2013b. "Usual Weekly Earnings of Wage and Salary Workers, Fourth Quarter 2012." January 18. http://www.bls.gov/news.release/archives/wkyeng_01182013.pdf (accessed May 15, 2014).

US Census Bureau. 2010. "American Indian and Alaska Native." http://www.census.gov/aian/census_2010 (accessed January 30, 2012).

———. 2011. "American Community Survey." https://www.census.gov/newsroom/releases/archives/news_conferences/20121203_acs5yr.html (accessed July 14, 2012).

———. 2011. "Areas with Concentrated Poverty: 2006–2010." December. http://www.census.gov/prod/2011pubs/acsbr10-17.pdf (accessed March 29, 2013).

———. 2012. "The American Indian and Alaska Native Population: 2010." http://www.census.gov/prod/cen2010/briefs/c2010br-10.pdf (accessed January 17, 2014).

———. 2012. "Current Population Report." http://www.census.gov/prod/2012pubs/p60-243.pdf (accessed October 16, 2014).

———. 2012. "Household Income: 2012." http://www.census.gov/prod/2013pubs/acsbr12-02.pdf (accessed October 26, 2014).

———. 2012. "Table 118.8. Credit Cards—Holders, Numbers, Spending, and Debt, 2000 and 2009, and Projections 2012," Statistical Abstracts of the United States. https://www.census.gov/compendia/statab/2012/tables/12s1188.pdf.

———. 2013. "Income, Poverty, and Health Insurance Coverage in the United States: 2012." September 13. http://www.census.gov/newsroom/releases/archives/income wealth/cb13-165.html (accessed October 6, 2013).

US Department of Education. 2002. *Public Law 107-110.* January 8. http://www2
.ed.gov/policy/elsec/leg/esea02/107-110.pdf (accessed January 15, 2013).
———. 2005. "Introduction: No Child Left Behind." January 19. http://www2.ed.gov
/nclb/overview/intro/index.html (accessed February 14, 2013).
US Department of Health and Human Services. 2011. "Overview of the Uninsured in
the United States: A Summary of the 2011 Current Population Survey." September. http://aspe.hhs.gov/health/reports/2011/cpshealthins2011/ib.shtml (accessed
May 6, 2012).
US Department of Housing and Urban Development (HUD). n.d. "Subprime Lending."
http://portal.hud.gov/hudportal/HUD?src=/program_offices/fair_housing_equal
_opp/lending/subprime (accessed May 27, 2014).
———. 2012. "An Overview of the HUD Budget: How HUD Funding Furthers Our
Mission." http://portal.hud.gov/hudportal/documents/huddoc?id=2012Budget
Overview032011.pdf (accessed April 21, 2012).
———. 2013. "Fiscal Year 2013 Programme and Budget Initiatives: Preventing and
Ending Homelessness." http://portal.hud.gov/hudportal/documents/huddoc?id
=FY13BudFSPrvntEndHmlsns.pdf (accessed October 6, 2013).
US Department of Labor. n.d. "Hiring: Affirmative Action." http://www.dol.gov
/dol/topic/hiring/affirmativeact.htm (accessed February 14, 2013).
———. 2011. "Women in the Labor Force." December. http://www.bls.gov/cps/wlf
-databook-2011.pdf (accessed February 26, 2013).
Vehs, K. D. 2013. "The Poor's Poor Mental Power." *Science* 341:969–970.
Venkatesh, S. 2008. *Gang Leader for a Day: A Rogue Sociologist Takes to the Streets.*
New York: Penguin.
Vornovytskyy, M., A. Gottschalck, and A. Smith. 2011. "Household Debt in the U.S.:
2000–2011." http://www.census.gov/people/wealth/files/Debt%20Highlights%
202011.pdf (accessed September 11, 2014).
Wacquant, L. 2010. *Urban Outcasts: A Comparative Study of Advanced Marginality.*
Cambridge: Polity.
Weber, M. 1958. *The Protestant Ethic and the Spirit of Capitalism.* New York:
Scribner's.
Weinberg, D. 2011. "U.S. Neighborhood Income Inequality in the 2005–2009 Period."
US Census Bureau, October. http://www.census.gov/prod/2011pubs/acs-16.pdf
(accessed November 11, 2013).
Western, B., and J. Rosenfeld. 2011. "Unions, Norms, and the Rise in the U.S. Wage
Inequality." *American Sociological Review* 76:513–537.
White House Council on Women and Girls. 2012. "Keeping America's Women Moving
Forward: The Key to an Economy Built to Last." www.whitehouse.gov/sites
/default/files/email-files/womens_report_final_for_print.pdf (accessed October
27, 2014).
Wilder, C. S. 2013. *Ebony and Ivy: Race, Slavery, and the Troubled Histories of Amer-
ica's Universities.* New York: Bloomsbury.
Wilkerson, I. 2010. *The Warmth of Other Suns: The Epic Story of America's Great Mi-
gration.* New York: Vintage.
Wilkins, R. 1990. "Throwaway People." PBS *Frontline,* February. http://www.pbs.org
/wgbh/pages/frontline/programs/info/805.html (accessed October 25, 2014).
Wilson, C. 1996. *Racism: From Slavery to Capitalism.* Thousand Oaks, Calif.: Sage.
Wilson, W. J. 1987. *The Truly Disadvantaged: The Inner City, the Underclass, and
Public Policy.* Chicago: University of Chicago Press.
———. 2009. *More Than Just Race: Being Poor and Black in the Inner City.* New
York: Norton.

Wolcott, B. 2014. "2014 Job Creation Faster in States that Raised the Minimum Wage."
    Center for Economic and Policy Research. http://www.cepr.net/index.php/blogs
    /cepr-blog/2014-job-creation-in-states-that-raised-the-minimum-wage (accessed
    October 25, 2014).
Wood, E. M. 1999. *The Origin of Capitalism.* New York: Monthly Review Press.
Yglesias, M. 2013. "Bad Decisions Don't Make You Poor; Being Poor Makes for Bad
    Decisions." *Slate,* September 3. http://www.slate.com/articles/business/money
    box/2013/09/poverty_and_cognitive_impairment_study_shows_money_troubles
    _make_decision.html (accessed February 3, 2014).
Zornick, G. 2013. "The GOP's No Good: Very Bad Food Stamps Cuts." *The Nation,*
    September 20. http://www.thenation.com/blog/176289/gops-no-good-very-bad
    -food-stamp-cuts# (accessed October 6, 2013).

Index

About the Book

DOES EVERYONE IN THE UNITED STATES HAVE AN EQUAL CHANCE TO succeed? What explains the enduring power of racism and sexism? How does our sociopolitical system generate inequality? These are just a few of the questions explored in this accessible introduction to the complex problem of social stratification.

Kasturi DasGupta clearly explains the social and economic mechanisms that serve to preserve and even deepen social stratification in the United States. Enriched with case studies and examples throughout, her text is carefully designed both to engage students and to help them see past cultural myths to grasp the underpinnings and consequences of social inequality.

Kasturi DasGupta is professor of sociology at Georgian Court University.